John Bu

John Buchan
A Biography

———

JANET ADAM SMITH

Oxford   New York
OXFORD UNIVERSITY PRESS
1985

Oxford University Press, Walton Street, Oxford OX2 6DP

London New York Toronto
Delhi Bombay Calcutta Madras Karachi
Kuala Lumpur Singapore Hong Kong Tokyo
Nairobi Dar es Salaam Cape Town
Melbourne Auckland

and associated companies in
Beirut Berlin Ibadan Mexico City Nicosia

Oxford is a trade mark of Oxford University Press

First published 1965 by Rupert Hart-Davis
First issued, with a new Preface, as
an Oxford University Press paperback 1985

British Library Cataloguing in Publication Data

Smith, Janet Adam
John Buchan: a biography.—(Oxford paperbacks)
1. Buchan, John, 1875–1940—Biography
2. Authors, Scottish—20th century—
Biography   3. Statesmen—Great Britain—Biography
I. Title
823'.912   PR6003.U13Z/
ISBN 0–19–281866–X

Library of Congress Cataloging in Publication Data

Smith, Janet Adam
John Buchan: a biography.
(Oxford paperbacks)
Reprint. Originally published: London: R. Hart-
Davis, 1965. With new pref.
Bibliography : p.
Includes index.
1. Buchan, John, 1875–1940—Biography.   2. Authors,
Scottish—20th century—Biography.   3. Statesmen—
Great Britain—Biography.   I. Title.
PR6003.U13Z78   1985   828'.91209   84–19066
ISBN 0–19–281866–X (pbk.)

Printed in Great Britain by
Richard Clay (The Chaucer Press) Ltd
Bungay, Suffolk

CONTENTS

PREFACE TO THE
OXFORD PAPERBACKS EDITION

When Oxford University Press offered to include my *John Buchan* in their Oxford Paperbacks series, I read the book again to see whether it would bear republication without substantial alteration. I decided that the 1965 text could stand up now, and I have no great regrets that major changes were not possible (though minor errors and misprints could be—and have been—corrected). Had I been able to draw on the material that has appeared since 1965, I would have filled in the background here, adjusted a view there (for instance, of Milner in South Africa, after reading Thomas Pakenham's *Boer War*); but I would not have strikingly altered my original portrait of Buchan nor my assessment of his works.

Books on Buchan published since 1965 include two family impressions: Alice Fairfax-Lucy's *A Scrap Screen* (1979) and William Buchan's *John Buchan—a Memoir* (1982). David Daniell has offered a critique of Buchan's writings—with welcome attention to the earlier and lesser-known—in *The Interpreter's House* (1975), and he has edited two volumes of Buchan short stories, previously out of print. I contributed *John Buchan and his World* to Thames and Hudson's series of short illustrated biographies in 1979.

Much concerning Buchan has come to light in the papers of two of his publishers—Blackwoods (now in the National Library of Scotland), and Nelsons (now in the Library of the University of Edinburgh). After Susan Tweedsmuir's death in 1977, the loft of her house at Burford yielded some items which she had not known about when she originally gave me a free run of all the material in her keeping. These are now in the National Library of Scotland. They include some notebooks kept by Buchan in his university days; some more of those lists of 'Things to be Done' (see page 75), which show how carefully he planned his course in life and in letters; and a volume of correspondence from, among others,

Asquith, Curzon, Gosse, Rider Haggard, Hardy, Haldane and Rosebery. The only letter in the volume I should dearly have liked to include is that from Lord Milner of 12 August 1901 inviting Buchan to join his staff in South Africa: but I had been able to publish it in my *John Buchan and his World*.

As the reception of my biography in 1965 (and of the later books on the subject) has shown, Buchan remains something of a puzzle. 'A curiously elusive character' was one response; another noted his 'mysterious pre-eminence'; even his son William found him 'a mysterious man'. He bothers critics, many of whom are uneasy at the variety of his achievement yet irritated that the achievement was not greater. Could he not have put his gifts as a story-teller to better use? Why did he bother to go into Parliament? Or to be Governor-General of Canada? This last question had certainly puzzled me. When I embarked on the biography I assumed that the Governor-Generalship was an ornamental post, a consolation prize for not having been made a Cabinet Minister. But my reading of Buchan's Canadian papers and my discussions with Canadians, made me realise that this was the job which, more than any other he held, allowed him to make full use of his diverse talents.

I don't pretend to have unravelled all the puzzles and complexities of his character and career: the biographer is not the final arbiter on the Day of Judgment, from whom no secrets are hid. But I hope to have provided the evidence on which others can make their judgments.

It was Alastair Buchan who invited me to write his father's life, and who read my typescript with the rigour of a historian rather than the piety of a son. Alastair had crowned a remarkable career—*Observer* correspondent in Washington, co-founder and first Director of the Institute for Strategic Studies, Commandant of the Royal College of Defence—by his appointment to the chair of International Relations at Oxford, when he died suddenly in 1976, at the age of fifty-seven. I sat with his mother in Burford on the afternoon of his funeral at Brill: her courage and dignity on that day of grief have stayed bright in my mind. She died not long after, in her ninety-fifth year. To her memory, and to Alastair's, I dedicate this new appearance of *John Buchan*.

JANET ADAM SMITH

INTRODUCTION

To write the life of a man who had written so well about himself as John Buchan in *Memory Hold-the-Door* seemed at first a daunting enterprise. But Buchan was at pains to make clear in his preface that it was 'not a book of reminiscences in the ordinary sense, for my purpose has been to record only a few selected experiences.' To a friend he wrote that it was 'not an ordinary autobiography, or any attempt to tell the unimportant story of my life; but rather an attempt to pick out certain high lights and expound the impressions made upon me at different stages.'

He wrote *Memory Hold-the-Door* in the last years of his life, in Canada, where he had few of his personal papers. His book then is a work of memory; mine aims to be a work of reconstruction. I have tried to build up his life from letters and documents and other people's memories, and to show it as it happened at the time, and not as it appeared in retrospect. In this I have had the great advantage of a free run of the letters which he wrote to his family and friends, which show him living through experiences that, in memory, took on a different aspect; as an example, the rawness and liveliness of the young Buchan's first impressions of Oxford contrast with the Augustan calm with which he later recalled his Oxford days. I have always preferred to use contemporary evidence, and I have quoted from *Memory Hold-the-Door* only when I could not find what I wanted from any other source.

Buchan set himself certain limits in *Memory Hold-the-Door*. His portraits there are all of the dead; so they include Ramsay Mac-Donald but not Stanley Baldwin, T. E. Lawrence but not Franklin D. Roosevelt. There is a chapter on the United States but, since he could not write frankly about Canada while he was Governor-General, nothing about the Dominion where his last four fruitful years were spent. He quotes nothing from his own letters or his early writing; he says very little about his books or their popular success. I have tried to fill in these gaps, and to supply the background to his experiences: to show, for example, what was involved in being one of Milner's Kindergarten or Governor-General of Canada.

I could not have embarked upon this biography, or worked on it for six years, without the help which was given me at every stage and in every way by John Buchan's family. To them go my first and deep-felt thanks; to his children—the second Lord Tweedsmuir, the Hon. Mrs Brian Fairfax-Lucy, the Hon. William Buchan and the Hon. Alastair Buchan—and above all to his wife, Susan Lady Tweedsmuir. She turned over all her papers to me, she opened freely to me her remarkable memory, she was ready to talk and to answer my questions at any time. The view of John Buchan which I present is my own; at many points his family's would be different. It has always been easy to discuss such divergences. I have found the writing of his biography a continuously interesting business; I know that I have been lucky, not only in my subject, but in his family. I am grateful too for their forbearance when the project took much longer than I had hoped; it strikes me as ironical that the life of this most efficient of writers, who moved easily into top gear the minute he sat down to work, should be written by one who is in comparison a grinding slowcoach.

Next I must thank Queen's University, Kingston, Ontario, who for some years have been the owners of Buchan's library, and of the bulk of his papers. Dr H. P. Gundy and the staff of the Douglas Library of that University have given me every help, both when I worked there in 1961 and 1964, and when I have corresponded with them about papers already in their keeping. They too have waited very patiently, for the papers which I have been using in this country.

John Buchan had such a variety of experiences, and practised such a number of professions, that no biographer could hope to be conversant with them all. I am immensely grateful to all those who have expanded my education, from South Africa to the Arctic. Their names, and those of all who have shared their memories with me, or whose brains I have picked, appear in the Notes and References; but I must mention here three without whom I could not have attempted to write on Buchan in Canada: Sir Shuldham

Redfern, who was Private Secretary during his Governor-Generalship, Professor George Glazebrook of the University of Toronto, and Professor F. W. Gibson of Queen's University, Kingston.

My thanks are due to Her Majesty the Queen for permission to quote from Buchan's letters as Governor-General to King George V, King Edward VIII and King George VI and from one written by King George VI to Buchan; and to all those others who have given me permission to quote from copyright material. Their names will be found in the appropriate places in the Notes and References.

JANET ADAM SMITH

May 1965

CHRONOLOGY

CHAPTER ONE

SON OF THE MANSE

1875–92

'I was born a Scotsman, and a bare one. Therefore I was born to fight my way in the world.'

Sir Walter Scott

Though on his mother's side he was kin to Stewarts of Appin, and on his father's there might have been a far-back connection with the ancient House of Auchmacoy in Aberdeenshire, the family into which John Buchan was born in 1875 was now firmly planted in the Borders. His father's father was a lawyer in Peebles—in Scots a Writer—and it was this John Buchan who put up the brass plate on the door of Bank House at the west end of the Peebles High Street on which can still just be traced 'Mr Buchan, Writer'. He was also Manager of the Peebles branch of the Commercial Bank of Scotland (the rôles of lawyer and banker were often combined in country places) and acted as legal and financial adviser to the flock-masters of Tweeddale. Among his clients was John Masterton of Broughton Green, twelve miles up the Tweed; and in 1874 the eldest son of the Peebles lawyer married the elder daughter of the Broughton sheep-farmer. This second John Buchan, born in 1847, a graduate of Edinburgh University, had recently been ordained to the ministry of the Free Church of Scotland, and during the winter of 1873–4 he was in charge of the Free Church at Broughton in the absence of the regular minister. It was the year when the American evangelists Moody and Sankey visited Scotland—'the Moody revival came like a cyclone across the Border;' the young minister introduced their hymns to Broughton, and held evangelical meetings night after night in the little church, to which people walked and drove from miles around. Helen Masterton was only sixteen when they met, famous in the neighbourhood for her long yellow hair; she and the young minister became engaged in the summer of 1874, when he had been called to the Knox Church, Perth, and were

married in December. There was a family legend that she put up
her hair for the first time on her wedding day. She often wore it
down after that, not liking the feel of the pins; and, as she later told
her children, 'there was many a time when I could have left your
father and run away home.' On 26 August 1875 (a week after her
eighteenth birthday) at the manse at 20 York Place, Perth, she bore
a son: another John Buchan.

From this ancestry John Buchan inherited toughness of body and
independence of mind. A minister of a Church which had seceded
from the Established Church of Scotland on the question of lay
patronage took his stand on his calling and on his character, and
not on any position in a social hierarchy. Nor was a Border farmer
part of such a nicely graded rural society as his counterpart in
southern England. In this countryside of farms and tweed-mills,
where there were few great houses to cast a feudal shadow, the man
with John Masterton's eye for sheep stood square on his own skill
and had no need to defer to anyone.

In 1876 Mr Buchan was called to the Free Church at Pathhead in
Fife, a small town between Kirkcaldy and Dysart on the Firth of
Forth; there he stayed for twelve years, and there four more children were born—Anna in 1877, William in 1880, Walter in 1883,
and Violet in 1888. There, at the age of five, the young John Buchan
had his first serious adventure. He fell out of a carriage and the
back wheel went over his head and fractured his skull. The obvious
result was the scar on the left of his forehead which to the end of his
life enhanced the lean Red-Indian character of his face. A more
important, though secondary, effect was the striking change in his
general health made by the year he had to spend in bed after the
accident. Before it he had been, as he tells us, 'a miserable headachy
little boy;' after it he was tough and hardy, and never had a serious
illness till 1911. He does not tell us what he did during the year in
bed, but it may not be fanciful to guess that inactivity and solitude
developed his inward eye and ear, encouraged his faculty for picture-
making and story-telling, and nourished his imagination, as Walter
Scott's had been nourished when he had to nurse his lameness on
a Border farm. We know for certain how much Buchan owed to
his father. John Buchan senior had grown up in a place with everything to fire a boyish imagination: woods, river, hills, the old castle
of Neidpath just upstream from Peebles, their names linked with
legend and ballad. Merlindale and Altarstone spoke of an old
magic, and Beltane Eve still kept its place in the Peebles calendar

—a Beltane Queen was, and still is, crowned every midsummer. From *his* mother he had learnt to love books, and especially poetry; like her he was an outstanding story-teller, particularly of fairy-stories. Grimm, Hans Andersen, George Macdonald, were his familiars, and the *Red Etin of Ireland* was a tale he told his children with particular zest. (John was never much frightened by anything in these; but *Alice in Wonderland* scared him, for he hated the idea of going down a rabbit-hole, and Alice's loss of identity haunted him like a nightmare.) Mr Buchan had a great repertoire too of Scots and plantation songs, which he sang or played on the penny whistle, and he was a splendid reciter of the ballads of his own Border country.

The Pathhead Free Church manse was a grey stone house set by a railway, a linoleum factory, a coal-pit, a bleaching-works and a rope-walk; but from the house and its big garden there were long prospects. From their nursery on winter evenings the Buchan children watched the beam from the lighthouse on Inchkeith, on clear days they could see across the twenty miles of Firth the roofs and spires of Edinburgh rising to the hump of the Castle, the scarp of the Pentlands and, away to the east, the Lammermoors. Just along the shore was Ravenscraig Castle, from which Scott's lovely Rosabelle had tempted the stormy Firth; Sir Patrick Spens sailed from this coast. In the harbour at Dysart the Buchan children were once taken aboard a Norwegian ship and given coffee in gaily painted bowls; another time it was a Dutch schooner, 'painted green, with a cage of singing birds and a pot of tulips in the cabin.' Behind the railway were woods; and from the woodlands ran two burns in deep-carved 'dens,' through the smelly bleach-works and rope-walk down to the beach. At this point the shore was dirty with drains and the debris of the works, but farther on it was clean and, over an easily climbed wall, there was the demesne of Dysart House, a place of sandy creeks and seaweed backed by a great forest of rhododendrons. As soon as young John Buchan had re-learnt to walk after his year abed, he had there his natural playgrounds.

Years after, in the first chapter of *Prester John*, he lived again these ploys of wood and sea-shore: the fishing and apple-stealing, the games of pirates and Jacobites, the tracking and ambushes, the lan-terns and sentry-go, the driftwood fires and the cache of treasure at the back of a cave. Occasionally there were fights, with his Kirk-caldy school-friends against the lads at the bleach-works or the sons of the local gentry (mostly manufacturers from Dunfermline or

Kirkcaldy), fair game for the village boys' insults: 'Wha called ye
partan-face, my bonny man?' One memorable night John's gang
set forty tar-barrels alight and rolled them down into a disused
quarry. As a family the Buchans were easily 'dared' to actions that
ran the risk of considerable bodily hurt or adult disapproval and
punishment. But in general the adventures were created by lively
imagination out of the properties that lay to hand.

After a few months at a dame school (from which he was expelled
for upsetting a broth-pot on to the kitchen fire) John went to the
Pathhead Board School, then to the Burgh School of Kirkcaldy,
then to the High School. He walked to Kirkcaldy every day, three
miles each way; there were no compulsory games, but a contemporary remembered 'running paper-chases in Johnnie Marshall's
Loan.' At home there was the firm discipline of a well-run household—Mrs Buchan was a notable housekeeper—and of a firmly-held
belief. There was a diet of family worship—prayers every morning
(with Mr Buchan's arm round the youngest, so that he would not
run round and make the others laugh), and also on Sunday evening,
after the two church services and the Sunday School. Looking back
in later life, John and Anna Buchan could remember impatience with
long sermons and with the drawn-out solemnities of the services of
preparation for the spring and autumn Communions (John bored
a hole in the manse pew through which he could pass papers and
sweets to a friend in the pew in front). But neither could remember
any gloom, any repressions coming from the doctrine they were
taught, or the practices expected of them. Not for the Buchans the
Calvinist nightmares of hell that oppressed Robert Louis Stevenson's childhood: the Devil appeared to John as he did to Burns—
half-humorous, half-earthy, a Hallowe'en bogy, a scarecrow, a
figure of fun ('a fair Satan-face' was a favourite word of Mrs
Buchan's when the children pulled faces in distaste at something
they had been told to do). The Calvinism that Mr Buchan transmitted was a sense of a life lived under the eye of Almighty God in
a world ruled by unalterable law: a sense which stayed with John to
the end of his life. It did not teach them to despise the world—the
earth is the Lord's and the fulness thereof—but it taught them to
set the world in perspective, and to accept the existence of a mystery
beyond it.

Nor did religious practices damp down imagination or high
spirits. After the Sabbath evening hymns the Buchan children
wound up with a chant which demanded 'Where is now the Prophet

Daniel?' (three times) and triumphantly answered, 'Safe in the Promised Land.' The great point about this hymn, Anna Buchan remembered, 'was that any favourite hero could be added at will. Of Sir William Wallace we sang, "He went up from an English scaffold" and always insisted on adding Prince Charles Edward's name, defiantly assuring ourselves that the Prince who had come among his people seeking an earthly crown had attained to a heavenly one, and was safe in the Promised Land.' Bible characters, entirely familiar from the daily readings, and the even more familiar figures from *The Pilgrim's Progress*, populated wood and shore alongside the heroes of ballad and Scots history. The children's fine mixed diet of books and stories seems to have been singularly free of the 'improving' moral tales so dear to Victorian parents, and so hotly denounced in their day by Charles Lamb and Coleridge for their priggishness and their narrowing of imagination. Even the round of church activities had its imaginative reward. Special collections in church, strange objects at missionary bazaars— toothbrushes made from tropical wood, grass mats of brilliant dyes—brought far places like Calabar or Nyasaland within the Pathhead child's experience; and once a black minister came to preach.

To the Pathhead days belongs John Buchan's first published work: a New Year's Hymn for 1887, composed 'By a Scholar' for the Free Church Sabbath School, whose members lustily sang:

> To Thee, our God and Friend,
>   We raise our hymn today,
> O, guard and guide us from above
>   Along life's troubled way,

while many of their elders were working off a Hogmanay hang-over.

Yet the freedom of the Buchan children in Fife was only a shadow of the freedom that they enjoyed during the two months they spent every summer with their Masterton grandparents at Broughton Green. The journey was a cheerful ritual: to Edinburgh by the Forth Bridge, and lunch in a shop; tea at Peebles with the Buchan uncle and aunts in Bank House; the branch line up Tweed, the hope of seeing a heron at the meeting of Tweed and Biggar Water, the arrival at the flowery station of Broughton. The Mastertons' farm was at the north end of the village, which straggles for about a mile along the Edinburgh–Carlisle road—now a main highway, but in the eighteen-eighties an unmetalled country road, used only by an occasional gig, waggonette or farm-cart. The white-washed house opened straight on to the road, which separated it from the farm buildings. Three unmarried sons worked the farm—John, James and Ebenezer (Eben was only six years older than his nephew John Buchan); a daughter Agnes ('Antaggie' to the young Buchans) helped her mother with the house and acted as a buffer between Mrs Masterton and her high-spirited grandchildren. The house had its wet-day delights: a playroom called Jenny Berry, a garret known as Frizzel's End (the children decided Frizzel was a highwayman), with bound volumes of *Blackwood's*, *Punch* and *Good Works*. Within living memory Broughton Green had been an inn, and the rooms had numbers painted on the doors. Across the road were the pleasures of byre and stackyard; behind the house was a biggish garden with plenty of gooseberry and currant bushes. But the real playground lay beyond farm and garden, on the green steep hills that encircle Broughton glen.

Here, as in Fife, were pleasure-grounds at hand—the old beech-tree, the trout-pool in the burn, the ruined kirk, the deserted quarry. Here too were the far prospects, the higher hills across the Tweed which stretched fold on fold to the English border, the upper glen of the river where it turns south and the road rises to the heights of Tweedsmuir, then so remote that the *Scotsman* arrived a day late and the carrier's cart from Peebles bearing provisions for the scattered community called only once a week. The prospects were not for the imagination only. John Buchan developed into a hardy walker and ranged the hills in search of new burns to fish, until the ranging became an end in itself, and with his catch in his pockets he would drop down again to Broughton for tea—new-baked scones, and apple-and-rowanberry jelly—having charted yet another corner of his world, Scrape, or Broad Law, or set eyes on yet another new landmark, as once from Dollar Law he saw a far-off gleam of silver, St Mary's Loch. He traced the burns to their sources, and could have drawn a map of the upper Tweed with all its tributaries accurately plotted. He was always to see a new country in terms of its rivers. In this country the ballads and stories the children heard from their father came to life. The peat-hags between Tweed and Clyde had sheltered Covenanters, the road south had been trodden by Prince Charlie's army—one of their great-uncles had talked as a little boy to an old woman who as a child had seen them pass—up the glen at Broughton Place was the home of the Prince's secretary, the renegade Murray. There were still oral traditions of Scott and Hogg, and of the reivers and raids that had been so near in time to them. There were other experiences too. Often as he pushed up into the hills in search of the unfished headwaters of burns, John Buchan would find himself in a green 'hope' enclosed by a shoulder of hill. If sheep were grazing, all was well; but if he were the only creature, a wave of fear would sweep over him, and send him rushing down-hill till he came in sight of a herd's cottage. 'Silent and aware' were the words which he found later to express this presence which so awed him.

Above all it was a countryside to which the children felt they belonged in a way they did not belong to Fife. At Peebles, in the house where their grandfather had put up his plate, their father's brother Willie—sharing the house with his sisters, Jean and Kate—was carrying on the firm of John Buchan, Writer; he was also Town Clerk. There were Masterton relatives all over the countryside; and the young Buchans quartered the hills with the shepherds, attended clippings or sheep-sales, and accompanied their grandfather in the pony trap on his visits to outlying farms, not as town children come for two months' holiday, but as natives forced away from Tweed-dale for ten.

Children are often unconscious of natural beauty at the time. The banks of Tweed between Peebles and Broughton, Neidpath Castle, the house of Barns, the woods of Stobo and Dawyck, Merlin's Grave; the clean, upthrusting line of the hills that border Manor-water; the gentler green hills to the north of Tweed—to the Buchans all these were simply 'home', but it meant that how-ever far they went in space and time from these Tweeddale holidays they kept in their inward eye pictures of great beauty—both homely and wild—on which could be centred feelings of happiness and security, of enterprise and adventure, of sadness and nostalgia.

Like the manse at Pathhead, the home at Broughton Green was a mixture of order and freedom: the order of a well-run farm as well as the order of a well-run, godly household. There were family prayers, and two services on Sunday; but the Bible-reading that closed the Sabbath was remembered as a golden moment when, after the enforced ease, next day's adventures would be planned. The religious restriction felt to be intolerable—and not imposed in their own home—was their grandfather's ban on the reading of any secular book on Saturday and Monday as well as on Sunday:

'Though there's naething in the Bible about it, I hold that the
Lord's Day shall aye get plenty of room to steer in.' Otherwise Mr
Masterton was a mild grandfather who could on occasion flash into
severity, as when he told John, aged twelve, that it was time to stop
leading the others into mischief (he had just intervened between
them and an angry blacksmith whose caged birds they had taken it
upon themselves to free). Mrs Masterton (a distant cousin of Mr
Gladstone) was a formidable grandmother who could soften into
tolerance—'Never daunton youth,' she would say, and was easy
on the children's comings and goings and their missed meals.
'Since ever I was a very little boy I have liked Broughton better
than any other place in the world,' wrote Buchan when his grandmother died in 1901, 'and she was always the chief part of
Broughton.'

Twice in verse John Buchan caught the flavour of those holidays:
in the dedication of *Montrose* to his brother Willie, written more
than twenty years later:

> When we were little, wandering boys,
>   And every hill was blue and high,
> On ballad ways and martial joys
>   We fed our fancies, you and I.
> With Bruce we crouched in bracken shade,
>   With Douglas charged the Paynim foes;
> And oft in moorland noons I played
>   Colkitto to your grave Montrose—

and in lines written while he was at Oxford, for his sister's commonplace book. They began:

> We were two children, you and I,
> Unkempt, unwatched, far-wandering, shy.

Mrs Buchan was affronted by 'unkempt' and said the next word
might just as well have been 'unwashed.'

Important as were these holidays in Tweeddale during the Fife
years, they were even more important after the Buchans moved to
Glasgow in 1888. Mr Buchan had been called to the John Knox
Church, the oldest Free Church in the city, situated in the Gorbals,
then simply a working-class quarter which had not yet earned its
reputation for violence. The church, a nineteenth-century Gothic
building of the plainer kind, and like all the houses in the Gorbals
black with Glasgow soot, stood about a quarter of a mile from the
river and the Broomielaw in a district that had residentially gone

downhill since merchants had ceased to live beside their ware-houses.* Mr Buchan's stipend was now £410 a year (at Perth it had been £187) but there was no manse attached to the church. So the Buchans found themselves a house two miles away, in the suburb of Crosshill on the south side of the river near the Queens Park. After the linoleum-haunted atmosphere of Kirkcaldy the children's first impression of Glasgow was of the purity of its air. Queen Mary Avenue was a broad, quiet road of Victorian villas, some standing singly, some semi-detached, with plenty of trees in the gardens. The Buchans' at No. 34 (Florence Villa) was a plain, square, stone house with a copper beech in front, and at the back a long narrow garden, bounded by an old brick wall, with two big elms and a little grove of ash and lindens where jackdaws and magpies, flycatchers and cuckoos brought their country notes to town. The real country was not so far away as now, and on Saturdays there were expeditions to the woods of Aikenhead and the pleasant country towards Car-munnock and East Kilbride. And naturally the Buchan children in no time dug up romantic associations—they once literally dug up a little cannon-ball, three hundred years old, which they supposed had been fired when Queen Mary lost the Battle of Langside, near by. Over the wall was an old ivy-covered house with crow-stepped gables where had lived Robert Woodrow, the seventeenth-century historian of the Scottish Church, who complained to Cotton Mather that the 'ravening Prelatists' and 'lukewarm professors' of his unhappy Scotland were worse than the wild men and beasts of Mather's New England. Patriotism was strong in the Buchan chil-dren; some half-English cousins who lived at Clapham were regarded with pity if not contempt.

Mr Buchan's last year and a half at Pathhead were, as a fellow-minister put it, 'a season of rich spiritual harvest.' There had been a religious revival—again, as at Broughton, with nightly meetings in the church and a whirl of evangelical activity. It had drained Mr Buchan's nervous energy, but had also exhilarated and encouraged him in his calling. A different work and atmosphere met him at John Knox. After the overflowing congregations of Pathhead, here was a church half-full, for many of the families that used to live in the terrace houses near the river had migrated to the suburbs.

*When the John Knox Church was united with the Gorbals Church in 1943 there was a proviso that the building could be disposed of, if the united congregation should so decide. In 1958 it was up for sale, 'suitable for storage'; a few years later it was burned. It was in any case due for demolition in the general reconstruction of the Gorbals.

Instead of the close-knit community of a little town there was the larger, sprawling and increasingly godless mass of an expanding industrial city. Mr Buchan accepted this challenge, and brought the Gospel outside the church. 'He stood,' a contemporary remembers, 'with bare head at the street corners, often in stormy weather, and warned men to flee from the wrath to come.' At his prayer-meetings inside the church people would come in from the slums and squalor outside and be 'lifted into the seventh heaven, as our minister described, with kindling eye, the house of God's elect:'

> Thy walls are made of jasper stones,
>   Thy bulwarks, diamonds square,
> Thy gates are of right orient pearls,
>   Exceeding rich and rare.
>
> Thy gardens and thy gallant walks
>   Continually are green;
> There grow such sweet and pleasant flowers
>   As nowhere else are seen.

The other world was entirely real to him, and the words chosen to commemorate him on a memorial tablet in the church after his death in 1911 were 'He set his face steadfastly to go to Jerusalem.'

But the task to which the John Knox Church had called him was not to inspire a general evangelical mission, but to rebuild the congregation. So there were innovations in the service—an organist and choir instead of a precentor, hymns as well as psalms—and constant social activities; soirées, sales of work, sewing-classes, talks from missionaries, as well as the regular Bible-classes, prayer-meetings, and classes for young communicants. The young people, a fellow-minister recorded, were 'trained in Scripture knowledge and literary culture' and there was an 'intense intellectual and social life among the members.'

Mr Buchan, whose ardent Calvinism went with a dreamy gentle nature, great sweetness of character, and vagueness about money—he never could remember his salary, and Mrs Buchan had to put the money in his pocket—was not altogether happy in this bustle. 'I was ordained to preach the Gospel,' he would say, 'not to stand on people's doorsteps begging them to open sales of work,' and he did not care for the suburban minister who 'ran a church as he would run a grocery establishment.' His strong points were talking to people and preaching (sermons short by contemporary Presbyterian standards, and delivered without a note), and he had little competitive sense about the size of his congregation. Mrs Buchan was the dynamo that ran the social life of John Knox; and, with her now installed in the house and position she was to occupy for nearly twenty years, it is time to take a look at John Buchan's mother.

She was small, tough, and immensely active. Her roomy house was run more efficiently with one maid than many of her suburban neighbours' with three; she could do anything in the house herself and was a great turner-out of rooms and tidier of drawers, maker of jam and bottler of fruit, and she had a light hand with pastry—'my only talent' she used to say. A word she dinned into her children was 'Do what has to be done *at once*!' and she had nothing but contempt for the slack and slapdash: 'handless,' 'fushionless,' 'like a knotless thread,' were words of bitter reproach, and she could say nothing worse of an acquaintance than that 'she was the sort of woman who would let the fire out when she was sitting in the room.' At spring-cleaning she was in her glory, the smell of beeswax and turpentine was as sweet to her as flowers, and a smoothly running household gave her satisfaction that was, if certainly moral, also almost aesthetic. In her old age she could remember, as the happiest time of her life, the days just after Violet had been born, in the year before the Buchans left Fife.

It was in March she was born. We had finished the spring-cleaning well beforehand, and the Deacons had painted the staircase, and we had saved up for crimson stair and landing carpets, and the house was as fresh as it's possible for a house to be. I lay there with my baby, so utterly contented, listening to your voices as you played in the garden in the spring.

To the end of her days she liked having her children at hand, and kept in touch by daily letters with those who were away from home. She was ambitious for her family, but her ambitions were all within the world she knew. As the bride of a young minister with a gift for preaching she had had daydreams of her husband some day becoming Moderator (in knee-breeches and lace ruffles, with herself in the gallery behind him in the Assembly Hall in a soft grey dress and a hat with feathers—nothing conspicuous, but all of the best). She would dearly have liked one of her sons to be a minister—to have herself a new manse to furnish, and be pointed out as the minister's mother at the induction soirée. A friend who, through her daughters' marriages, had three manses to visit, was considered exceptionally fortunate.

So the greater part of the practical activities of John Knox came

naturally to Mrs Buchan's hand. It was she who ran the Women's
Meetings and the Girls' Bible-class, who organised the sewing-class
and saw that all the work for next winter was cut out and prepared
before the long summer break, who swept all her family and
acquaintances into knitting, baking and carpentering for the annual
sale of work, and collecting for the Sustentation Fund or Zenana
Mission. Religion for her meant prescribed observances and concrete duties, church-going and church activities. 'A good church-
worker' was synonymous with 'a good Christian.'

The young Buchans were bored by a good deal of this church
work, and the part they were expected to play. Anna, even as a girl,
had to do a lot of congregational visiting and collecting, deputise for
her mother at prayer-meetings, and be ready to recite or sing at
church soirées (though she would never oblige with the 'semi-
sacred' songs thought suitable for such occasions). John was pressed
into taking a Sunday-school class of Gorbals boys, whose attention
he held, once the set work for the day was quickly disposed of, by
spinning highly secular stories of his own invention. The number
of church services increased as they grew older. They spent the
whole of the Sabbath at John Knox, with a lunch of sandwiches in
the vestry. As well as morning and afternoon services there were the
young men's meeting, the midday prayer-meeting, the Sabbath-
school, the Bible-class, and perhaps a Mission meeting in the church
hall to wind up the day. John used to calculate that he was piling
up so high a total of attendances that even if he never went to church
again after he was forty, his average would still be higher than
most.

But the children could speak their minds plainly when they were
irked and bored. Conversationally the Buchans were by Victorian
standards remarkably free. There was no parental monopoly of
talk at meals, but a lively interchange; and though Mrs Buchan
would often deplore their pertness and irreverence, as the children
mimicked a neighbouring minister, or made fun of a speaker who
had informed a Bible-class that Jezebel was 'a bad gurrl,' Mr Buchan
was extraordinarily tolerant. One of his own favourite stories was of
the old man at the religious meeting where, bench by bench, people
were confessing their sins. When his turn came, he rose and declared
that he had been deeply interested in all he had heard, and would
have been glad to oblige in the same way. 'But honesty compels me
to admit that my own life for the past three years has been, humanly
speaking, pairfect.' Mr Buchan distrusted excessive piety in the

young, and was thankful that his family were not 'pairfect.' Their
high spirits were certainly not daunted by the move to the city.
There is a story of a John Knox elder, who was also a policeman,
coming to Mr Buchan with his resignation: 'It wouldna' be richt
for an elder to be arresting the minister's deils.' 'Arresting' was no
exaggeration: at Broughton John had been with a gang of poachers
who had been caught burning the waters of Tweed for salmon.
Most of them were hardened offenders, and they were duly tried
and sentenced. John was not brought to trial: the police had no wish
to spare the boy, but did wish to save the Town Clerk of Peebles,
who was also a magistrate, from having to sentence his nephew.*
Mrs Buchan, always apprehensive of public opinion—'What will
the congregation say? What will people in Peebles say?'—was
greatly given to groaning over her son: 'Oh John, John, where'll
you end? There's nothing but the gallows if you're going on the way
you do now.'

But whereas Mrs Buchan always wanted her family to cut a good
figure in the eyes of the neighbours, her husband cared nothing for
other people's opinion, but only for what was right. 'In every small
way he gave in to Mother,' wrote his daughter, 'but if it were a
question of what he believed to be right he was adamant.' 'Trifle
with your earthly master if you will,' he told his congregation, 'but
trifle not with God.' A parish in the Gorbals in the eighteen-eighties
and nineties might have been an utterly depressing experience: the

* 'The salmon-poaching in the close season is the refuge of the vagrant and unsettled part of the community. It is hazardous in the extreme, for the waters are
often swollen high, and men in the pursuit of sport have no care of their lives. The
bailiffs, too, are keen-eyed and always on the watch, so that the game is pursued
under the ban of the law and the hazards of the weather. "Firing the water" as it is
called, consists in flaring torches, made of pine-knots or old barrel-staves dipped in
tar, over the surface of the river, and so attracting the fish. The leister with its
barbed prongs is a deadly weapon in a skilful hand, but in the use of it a novice is
apt to overbalance himself and flounder helplessly in the winter stream. The glare
of light on the faces of the men, the leaping fish, the swirl of the dark water, the
black woods around, the turmoil of the spot in contrast with the deathly quietness
of the hills, the sack with its glittering spoil, the fierce, muffled talk, are in the
highest degree romantic. Then, when the sport is over for the night, and if by a
lucky chance they have escaped unmolested, they will often return to some cottage,
and there with barred door and shuttered windows boil a fish, sup the *broo*, and
finish with deep potations of whisky. But if some bailiff meets them, then Nemesis
has them by the heels, and they make the best of their way to the county jail if they
lack money to pay the fine. If, as sometimes happens, the might of the law be the
weaker, a sharp scrimmage may ensue, some heads may be broken, and the band
will scatter in hot haste to their homes.' John Buchan: 'The Men of the Uplands',
in *Scholar Gipsies* (1896). Buchan used the episode in an unfinished novel, *The
Mountain*.

minister was constantly confronted with evil, misery, squalor and poverty when he visited the tenements; but Mr Buchan could always see the courage (often the courage of merely keeping a family clean in a bug-infested flat with one tap on the tenement stairs), the decency and the goodness that managed to flourish in the most appalling conditions. So he remained eternally hopeful, always seeing things as he hoped they would be, his Sunday-school not as a crowd of dirty little children, but as lives that were going to grow and make all things new, for themselves and for the Gorbals and Glasgow in general. As he pronounced the benediction in John Knox with out-stretched arms, he seemed the vehicle of a power that could trans-form the world. Devoted to his flowers and his penny whistle, to his Border ballads and his Walter Scott, it was the father who con-tributed so much sweetness and gaiety to the family life, to which the mother gave the direction and energy. And, though they never went to the theatre, and indeed had strong views against it, both parents had an innate sense of drama: Mr Buchan could hush a congregation into absolute silence when he preached; Mrs Buchan revelled in the macabre, dearly loved a graveyard, and would retail with immense spirit her encounters when parish-visiting, or the goings-on of her suburban neighbours.

From both came a sense of purpose and responsibility. No child of Mr Buchan could have seen life as anything but a highly serious affair. However light and gay the surface texture, underlying it was a sense that, every day, choices must be made, decisions taken, that were a matter of spiritual life and death. No child of Mrs Buchan could have failed to realise that, with vigour and competence, you could have a cheerful and comfortable home on very little money. From their father the Buchans received a moral lifeline; from their mother a strong practical good sense. It was a good start; for with no money behind them, no influential relatives, no strings to pull, they—like almost every other minister's family in Scotland—had their own way to make.

John Buchan's new school was Hutchesons' Grammar School, founded in 1650 by two Glasgow merchants of the name, in the district just east of the Gorbals called Hutchesontown. It was a decent plain early-nineteenth-century building, set between two noisy streets and overlooked by grimy houses with lines of washing projecting from the windows, but with a hint of elegance under its blackened stone.* The two-mile walk from Queen Mary Avenue

* Hutchesons' moved in 1959 to Crossmyloof.

took the boy daily past factories and warehouses, through cobbled streets greasy with mud and noisy with coal-carts and the keelies' cries, by rough public-houses, tenements where shawled women stood at the close-mouths, and dingy terraces that had known a better day. At Hutchesons' he found the sons of ministers, lawyers, doctors, engineers, shopkeepers, foremen, draughtsmen and clerks. Here he found also, in the top form, a handful of elderly pupils, some in their twenties, many of them Highlanders, who had made a late decision about entering a profession—usually medicine or the Church—and who came to Hutchesons' on special bursaries to work for their entrance to the University. Here was no self-contained community, like a boarding-school set in the country which can so easily become a world to itself, but a component part of a big industrial city, open to the economic and social stresses which played on the streets, shipyards, quays and offices outside: a place where people came for a purpose, to equip them for their work in life.

John's first school experience was of difficulty in understanding the other boys' Glasgow accent, and in making them understand his broad Fife. In general, of his time as a 'Hutchie bug' Buchan himself said little, except that he was unambitious and idle, bored by grammar and mathematics. He did well enough, however, to win a scholarship at the end of his first year, entitling him to free education for the next four years (his fees till then had been a guinea a quarter). Fencing was a regular school subject, and swimming an extra; but there were no organised games, and the boy could use his free time in his own way which, for Buchan, was mostly with books. In his school years he read his way through Gibbon, Scott, Dickens, Thackeray and the major English poets, and knew much of Matthew Arnold's poetry by heart. He also wrote the first canto of a poem on Hell, and to his schooldays may belong the surviving fragment of a manuscript in clear, clerkly writing on exercise-book paper, entitled *The Tale of a Midsummer Night: the Memoirs of Captain John Hepburn of His Majesty's Navy*. (It begins 'I, John Hepburn,' and the last words are 'reached the cutter in safety.')

At fifteen he went on to the classical side at Hutchesons' and under the influence of an outstanding teacher, James Cadell, woke up to an interest in Greek and Latin literature. For Cadell the classics were 'the humanities' in the broadest sense, and he transmitted to his boys a sense of their intrinsic greatness and their continuing significance. In 1892, at the age of sixteen, Buchan came ninth in the bursary competition for Glasgow University, winning a John Clark bursary of £30 a year, as well as one of the ten leaving bursaries awarded by Hutchesons'. So in October of that year, in company with three school-friends, Charles Dick, John Edgar and Joe Menzies, he crossed the Clyde to Gilmorehill.

CHAPTER TWO

GLASGOW STUDENT

1892–95

'Every morning I had to walk four miles to the eight o'clock class through all the varieties of unspeakable weather with which Glasgow, in winter, fortifies her children.'

John Buchan: Address to McGill Students, Montreal, 1936

To move from Hutchesons' to Glasgow University was to pass into an altogether more spacious world. Only twenty years before Buchan became a student in 1892, Glasgow University had withdrawn from its downtown quarters in the old High Street, among the chemical factories, to Gilmorehill, where Gilbert Scott's towers and pinnacles, not yet entirely sooty, looked over Paxton's Kelvingrove Park. To Buchan, when he came up for his Bursary examination on a day of flaming sunset, they seemed to be 'the battlements of a celestial city.' To James Bridie, who came up some years later, the University was 'a hideous building set in a magnificent site.'

It stands at the top of Gilmorehill and looks south over the river, with its tall derricks and its many masts and funnels. On either side of the river are smoking slums and beyond it green hills. The neighbouring hill to the east contains noble terraces, built on the Blythswood estate by the merchant princes of Glasgow. . . . From the top of the tower one can see the Highlands, and, on a clear day, Ben Nevis.*

Hutchesons' was a good local school with a good local reputation; the University drew its professors and its students from far beyond Glasgow, and what they did at Gilmorehill was known far beyond Scotland. In 1892 Kelvin still held the Chair of Natural Philosophy and was the University's Grand Old Man; among the medical professors were men of European reputation. Edward Caird, who later succeeded Jowett at Balliol, held the Chair of Moral Philosophy; A. C. Bradley, of English; George Ramsay, of Latin; and

---

* It is possible to see hills from the tower, but Ben Nevis is Bridie's flight of fancy.

Gilbert Murray had lately, at the age of twenty-three, succeeded
Sir Richard Jebb in the Chair of Greek.*

Though a more spacious world, it was still a strenuous one.
Classes began at eight in the morning and opened with prayer;
during most of the session, which lasted from October to March,
Buchan, in his student's short red gown, had to leave home before
it was light, for his four-mile walk to Gilmorehill—down Eglinton
Street, across the Clyde and along the Broomielaw—and many
students had farther to walk than he. There were 1900 students in
the University, of whom 246 were women, and the classes might
be as large as 200. At the beginning of the session the students paid
their fees (three guineas a class) direct to the professor, who, carrying his strongest walking-stick, took the coin down to the bank
himself. The buildings of the University consisted of lecture-halls
and laboratories; there were no residential hostels, little in the way
of canteens or common-rooms (the Students' Union had been
opened only in 1890), and no playing fields. There was limited
opportunity for the students to sit round and talk, unless they
visited each other in their digs, and no organised games. The
students 'had come to the University to learn, to be taught, and
taught they would be,' said Gilbert Murray, who found them
fresher in mind than his Oxford pupils, if less good at Greek. When
a lecturer was felt to be giving short measure, by being inaudible or
unintelligible, the class would stamp their disapproval with their
boots. There was no summer term because, in those pre-Carnegie
days, only by working half the year could many of the students
afford to be at the University at all. Of Buchan's neighbours in
class in his first year, one went from the lecture-hall to the farm, the
other to a Hebridean fishing-boat; others spent the summer as
pursers on Clyde steamers or gillies on Highland moors.

The year Buchan entered college was the year when the reforms
recommended by the Scottish Universities Commission of 1889
took effect. The chief of these was to make the honours course an
alternative to the general M.A. course, instead of an addition to it;
but in this first year of change the general course had not yet lost
its prestige as the traditional Scottish discipline, with its seven
compulsory subjects: Humanity (Latin), Greek, Mathematics,

* 'Labouchere . . . in *Truth,* had a violent attack on the appointment of Andrew
Bradley to the Chair of English, and continued: "Even this outrageous job is sur-
passed by the appointment of an utterly unknown young man to the Chair held by
Jebb and Lushington."' (Gilbert Murray: *An Unfinished Autobiography,* 1960.)

Logic, Moral Philosophy, Natural Philosophy (the term for Natural Science) and History. In the large classes there was a wide range of ability and 'an enormous volume of eager and generous emulation. The mathematical student contended for a good place in the Latin and Greek class; the classical student for a good place in mathematics and physics; both for distinction in philosophy and literature.'

It was this general M.A. course on which Buchan embarked. He spent a good deal of his first year on Mathematics; in Humanity he came second in class over the whole session. And he did well enough in the ordinary Greek class to pass a preliminary examination which would allow him to do Senior Greek in his second year.

It was in the Greek class this first winter that he came to the attention of Gilbert Murray. At the end of a lecture the seventeen-year-old student came up to ask the twenty-six-year-old professor a question. There was nothing odd in that, but the question itself was highly unexpected. What Buchan wanted to know was what Latin translation of Democritus had been used by Francis Bacon. And the reason he wanted to know was that he was editing Bacon's essays for a London publisher. 'Such a pupil in the Middle Class,' noted Murray, 'was obviously a treasure.'

In his second session Buchan took the senior class in Greek and some private work besides, and enjoyed the full impact of Murray. Whereas the older professors still continued reading their lectures at dictation speed, a practice that had its point when few students could afford the text-books (some members of Professor Veitch's Logic class were able to follow with notes made by their fathers), Murray talked to his students, easy and unselfconscious:

He owed much to a beautiful voice, which he used with instinctive skill, having the orator's gift of rising to an occasion. In all he said he was interesting. His gentle, infectious enthusiasm and his picturesque historical imagination gave a curious excitement to his lectures. His skill in the choice of words delighted his young auditors. He was felt to be original and not entirely academic—great attractions in the eyes of intelligent undergraduates.

But, however informal, his lectures, as a contemporary of Buchan's put it, 'changed the whole outlook of our world.' When he was doing the *Hippolytus* with the class, he would analyse a lyrical passage, then read his own version: this was the genesis of his translations of Greek plays. Murray's influence went far beyond the classroom. He carried over to his Glasgow professorship some of

the habits of his Oxford days, and acted as personal tutor to many
of his pupils, not only the cleverer ones. He and his wife entertained students in their home, a practice not then common in the
University. In those days Murray combined (to quote his own
words) 'an enthusiasm for poetry and Greek scholarship with an
almost equal enthusiasm for radical politics and social reform.' In
the year he came to Glasgow he had written a novel; he now had a
play to his credit (*Carlyon Sahib*); he was a friend of William
Archer and he preached the greatness of Ibsen. Anyone close to him
knew that scholarship, literature and politics did not exist in separate
compartments.

The most stimulating event of Buchan's last session at Glasgow
(1894–5) was the arrival of Henry Jones, who followed Edward
Caird in the Philosophy Chair when Caird succeeded Jowett as
Master of Balliol. Jones was an outstanding teacher; though not so
good a philosopher as Caird, he had the same capacity for kindling
the minds of students, and a great Welsh eloquence. His rhetoric
and flamboyance beat on the defences of the Lowland Scot; the
abler students, who refused to be spellbound, were 'goaded into
a *critical* thinking which by no means spared the dicta of their Professor. The real achievement of Jones as a teacher was that it was
hardly possible for anyone who sat under him to feel that philosophy didn't matter.' In the Moral Philosophy class they read
Kant, Sidgwick, Green's *Prolegomena*, Stephen's *Science of Ethics*,*
and though Buchan could not swallow Jones's particular brand of
Hegelian uplift—'Philosophy was to me always an intellectual
exercise, like mathematics, not the quest for a faith'—he responded
to Jones's enthusiasm and his human warmth. Murray had fired
him to become a scholar; now Jones, 'with his eloquent simplifica-
tion of life, almost persuaded me to be a philosopher.' The admiration was mutual: Jones, handing back one of Buchan's essays, said
he wished he could have written it himself. And when Buchan was
awarded one of the class prizes (equal second) Jones made clear
that it was as much on the strength of his style, judgment and
capacity for thinking, as on the extent of his knowledge.

The three friends from Hutchesons' with whom Buchan had

---

* Buchan's notes taken in Jones's class of 1894–5 show lists of reading and
essay-subjects—*e.g.* 'Contrast the Greek and the Christian moral ideals, as typified
in the conception of measure (golden mean) and of perfection.' They end on
26 March 1895; the next page is headed *Incolae Montium* and begins 'The vale of
the Upper Tweed is distinct from the neighbouring dales of Clyde and Annan'—
a sketch which became 'The Men of the Uplands' in *Scholar Gipsies*.

come to college—Joe Menzies, John Edgar and Charlie Dick*—
were forever crying up the genius of this quiet youth, his exceptional intellect, his polished writing. They implied that a new and
greater Stevenson was about to arrive, and provoked some scepticism in others who had not known him at school, and had never
read a line of his in print. But soon there was solid evidence: an
article in the *Gentleman's Magazine* for August 1893—and not just
in print, but paid for, an altogether more professional appearance
than one in the *Glasgow University Magazine*. Then A. C. Bradley
picked out for high praise Buchan's essay on Carlyle. Further, however loudly Buchan's henchmen insisted on his genius, Buchan
himself remained modest and disarming, not putting himself forward in University activities, nor making any special effort to shine
in class.

In his third year he contributed a few pieces to the *Glasgow
University Magazine*, a Stevensonian sketch, 'On Cademuir Hill,' a
review of Pater's posthumous collection of *Greek Studies*, showing
how much the *Renaissance* and *Marius* had meant to him; and after
Stevenson died in Samoa in December 1894 Buchan wrote an
obituary article. He stressed Stevenson's many-sidedness as a
writer—'one Admirable Crichton in days when narrowness is a
virtue, and a man of many interests and capacities is thought to be
in a fair way to destruction'—but found his primary virtue in his
'gospel of life.'

He is the most romantic figure of these latter days, battling to the end with
disease, tasting life in its true sense, a scholar among dullards, a 'gentleman
among *canaille*,' a gipsy among a race of successful merchants, amongst this
crew of metaphysicians and mountebanks, New Women and New Human-
ists, anatomists and impressionists and Heaven knows what! . . . The gospel
of life, that it is the first duty of man to serve God and his neighbours, to
fight his way through the world, looking upon it as no continuing city, but
at its best a place of pilgrimage, to enjoy the blessings of Heaven with a
thankful heart, to count dishonour worse than death, and to meet the last
enemy without a quiver—this surely is no ignoble creed. In a querulous
age he left us an example of a manly and chivalrous life.

By his third year Buchan had become fairly well known in the
University, and his circle of friends had gone far beyond his school

---

* Dick, Edgar and Buchan had founded, and were the sole members of, the Nameless Club, whose Honorary Presidents were Robert Louis Stevenson, Walter Pater
and Prince Charles Edward. The rules were: 'i. that this Club meets once a year;
ii. that this Club condescends to nothing that is common or unclean; iii. that
membership in this Club is hereditary.'

cronies. They reflected a wide range of temperament and background. There was Dan Scott, who had been a printing apprentice; W. Romane Paterson, who had travelled in Italy and Germany and had 'taken the Carlyle stage in a stride' as a schoolboy; John Roy Tannahill, son of a Paisley exciseman, who translated Verlaine, contributed 'An Agnostic Soliloquy' to the *G.U.M.* and wrote for the *Labour Leader*; Archie Charteris, son of one of the medical professors, who translated (from a German version) one of Turgenev's *Sportsman's Sketches*. There were two public school boys (in the English sense of 'public school')—Donald Cameron from Fettes, son of a famous surgeon, and Jack Monteith from Clifton, son of the minister of Moniaive, and extraordinarily handsome, like Montrose. (The girl-students were bribed to vote for Joe Chamberlain at a Rectorial Election by the promise of a dance with Jack at the next Tory ball.) There was Robert Horne, polished and successful, a minister's son who financed himself through college with bursaries and tutoring.* There was H. N. Brailsford, son of a Methodist minister in Dundee (who sent him to Glasgow in a knickerbocker suit, tam o' shanter and patent collar of his own invention), who used to say 'he had had his Shelley period at the age of five,' and at twelve had written an essay 'Is there a God?' Brailsford had a powerful intellect, a morbid self-consciousness and an obsession with 'What is truth?' which made him forever mull over his own character and his friends', so that they were always scrutinising their actions in relation to 'the highest excellence' and discussing their love-affairs in Hegelian terms. There was Gow, who said 'I feel I have a brilliant future before me if I can only reach it,' and Joe Menzies who was certain that 'I shall never do anything important in the world. I have convictions, but I am too weak and hesitant and indolent to carry them out. I shall stay about here all my life or in some Scotch town and perhaps write a little.' And there was Alexander MacCallum Scott, son of a widow who 'believed that knowledge was the key to power and success,' and, with an income of £150 a year, was grimly determined that the key should be in her son's hands. Alec Scott's own ambition was to write, and among his early exercises were some 'characters' of his college friends. His character of John Buchan is headed 'By Right of Birth':

* When Horne became a member of the Coalition Government in 1919, his mother was heard to remark: 'We always prayed that Robert would become a minister but maybe the Lord mistook our intention.'

He seemed to step into an inheritance. Everything he put his hand to prospered and people accepted him on every hand. He had an air of simple and convincing assurance. He believed in himself, not offensively, but with a quiet reserve. His whole manner inspired trust and confidence and respect. He could depend on himself and others felt that they could depend on him too. His judgment was sane and was therefore listened to. The fact was that he made himself indispensable to people. They knew him for a man who could order and systematise.

Scott also noted down in his commonplace books some of Joe Menzies's talk about Buchan. Menzies, for whom 'romantic feeling' was an important element in 'the highest excellence,' considered that Buchan and Gilbert Murray had this quality: 'I feel that the most excellent men must live in a dream world, and think about the noble things of the past and that this must not hinder their practical ability.' Intellectually Menzies considered Buchan 'as great a man I think as has ever been at Glasgow University. . . He is a real genius and yet he is thoroughly practical. . . . He is not a genius in practical affairs. He is just like Horne in that respect, but he is a genius who is also a practical man in a very high degree.'

All these young men had their own way to make in the world without money or influence; but Buchan seemed, more than any of the others, to have already taken his own measure and mapped his life. His early success with editors made many of his contemporaries suppose that he would make writing his career; but he was firm. Politics was his long-term aim; writing was to be the means to it. His maturity, his air of looking always beyond his University career, greatly impressed his contemporaries; and without achieving University prominence along the usual lines—he never spoke at the Dialectic or Union debates, and took no major part in the Rectorial Election of 1894—Buchan had by 1895 an aura of success.

During these three college years the University and Glasgow were only half Buchan's life. From April to October he was out of the city, with long visits to his grandmother at Broughton and his Uncle Willie at Peebles, shorter visits to college friends, and expeditions on foot or bicycle. There were family holidays—in 1890 in Arran, in 1892 at Rannoch, in 1893 at Broughton (where Mr Buchan took holiday duty at the Free Church) and in 1895 at Kinghorn in Fife.

During his first long vacation he settled down to his University work—set texts, an essay on Tiberius, work for the Lorimer bursary in logic, philosophy and literature, and for the Blackstone in Latin and Greek (he was not successful in either). And he read voraciously. In one letter, written in June 1893, he logs Swinburne's *Poems and Ballads*, *Lorna Doone* ('seventh or eighth time'), Saintsbury's *Essays on French Novelists*, Dumas's *Tulipe Noire*, Maupassant, and some poems of Hugo and Gautier. A month later he is reporting on Andrew Lang's *Lectures on Literature* ('very good'), P. G. Hamerton's *Intellectual Life* ('excellent'), the poems of Robert Bridges ('very good') Henry James's *Madonna of the Future* ('peculiar'), R. L. Stevenson's *Kidnapped* and *Master of Ballantrae* ('fourth or fifth time'), Hugo's *Notre Dame de Paris*, and Ibsen's *Doll's House*, *League of Youth* and *Pillars of Society*. 'I am beginning to like Ibsen more than I did. I understand him better.' Other books he read that summer were Herbert of Cherbury's *Autobiography*, William Morris's *Volsunga Saga*, and a good deal of George Eliot:

I don't like *The Mill on the Floss* nearly so well as *Romola* or *Adam Bede*. The kind of story does not interest me very much. But, of course, if we adopt Sainte-Beuve's canon of criticism, *L'oeuvre—est-il bon ou mauvais en soi-même?*, it is an excellent novel.

In his commonplace book he copied out passages from Gautier, Ruskin, and Villiers de l'Isle Adam. Next summer he was enthusiastic about the Icelandic sagas and Pater ('I consider now that *music* is the finest vehicle of *sensation*').

His French readings were encouraged and often suggested by his Peebles Uncle Willie, a Francophil who kept a good table and a good library (he gave his nephew an Elzevir Tacitus). He bought new books and subscribed to literary magazines, and in Bank House in 1893 Buchan found *Longmans'*, with Andrew Lang's monthly causerie on books, 'At the Sign of the Ship'; the *Speaker*, with Q's weekly article; early Kiplings—*The Story of the Gadsbys*, *Under the Deodars*, and *Barrack-Room Ballads*; the newly published *Catriona* (also giving pleasure that summer to Henry James). A Tweeddale neighbour, John Veitch—Professor of Logic at Glasgow, and close friend of Andrew Lang—put Buchan on to Descartes, an author who became one of his great enthusiasms.

This fine mixed reading was dictated by something more than the intelligent young person's ravenous appetite, equally greedy to gobble up the classics or pounce on the latest novel or book of poetry. Buchan had a purpose—the same that Stevenson speaks of in his essay on his literary beginnings, where he describes how he 'played the sedulous ape' to Hazlitt, Browne, Ruskin, Defoe, Hawthorne, Montaigne and Baudelaire. So too Buchan eyed his authors not just as entertainers or enlighteners, but as models for a young man's style. During this summer of 1893 he not only read but practised assiduously himself—*villanelles* and *rondeaux* in the fashionable Austin Dobson mode; *vers de société* after Praed; essays full of Stevensonian echoes, for Stevenson came very high on the list of authors to whom *he* played the sedulous ape. Then there was the Introduction to his edition of Bacon's essays: 9000 words, and 'simply saturated with quotations from all sorts of writers.' The quotations—mostly from Bacon's contemporaries—are indeed varied, but they are all relevant; there was not much youthful showing-off, only a little youthful condescension ('young Francis, now eighteen years of age,' wrote this editor whose eighteenth birthday was still a month or two ahead), and the business-like summing-up of Bacon's career was based on sound historical reading. Of his prose Buchan wrote, 'There is a dignified stiffness about his style, like some statesman giving audience to meaner men, which has a peculiar charm for us in these days of loose and slipshod writing.' At the end he allowed himself a bit of a flourish: 'a mine of quaint conceits and wise saws, a very orchard of the apples of wisdom.' On publication Buchan's edition received a favourable half-page notice in the *Westminster Review*; and the author cycled from Broughton to Peebles to enjoy the sight of a large pile of the *Essays* in Redpath's bookshop.

How a London publisher—Walter Scott—had come to select a seventeen-year-old Glasgow student for this job I have not been able to discover. (Other editors in the Scott Library were established writers, Richard Garnett, Professor William Knight, Ernest Rhys, T. W. Rolleston.) The initiative may have come from Buchan himself, who would think well of a publisher who had Ibsen (in Archer's translation) on his list. Buchan was certainly by this time submitting work to periodicals, and in August 1893 had his first article published in the *Gentleman's Magazine*. ('The only place where you can see and get the *Gentleman's*,' he advised his friend Charlie Dick, 'is the railway bookstall at the Central Station.')

This 'Angling in Still Waters' is one of the Stevensonian essays: deliberately written, a bit self-conscious, finicky in vocabulary, but still pleasant reading because it is about a subject close to Buchan's experience and affections—a day on the Tweed. It describes the early start, with everyone else asleep in the house with the white

Jacobite roses against the wall and honeysuckle over the porch; the walk on the dusty white road, with lapwings crying over the pastures; the water-meadows bright with ranunculus and globe-flowers; sunlight filtering through Rachan woods on to the velvet turf; the first silvery gleam of Tweed ('what angler ever could resist a certain nervous trepidation at the sight of his stream?'); the awkward casting over the saugh bushes; sounds from the meadow, sheep bleating, dogs barking and shearers yelling, then the deep silence of a hot summer noon. 'Sir James Nasmyth has read my article in the *Gentleman's*,' the author reported, 'and told my uncle that he is going to prosecute me for poaching on his heronry, and produce my essay for evidence.'

So the pleasures of childhood were still secure, but greatly extended in range. Buchan's expeditions as a student took him to country far beyond his boyhood's limits: he fished the Leithen and Manor waters and the headwaters of Clyde, sometimes sharing his supper with the miners who came out from the Lanark or Lothian coalfields for a night's sport. He described such fishermen in a free Scots version of the twenty-first idyll of Theocritus:

> Twae collier lads frae near Lasswade,
> Auld skeely fishers, fand their bed
> Ae simmer's nicht aside the shaw
> Whaur Manor rins by Cademuir Law.

Tweedsmuir, eight miles upstream from Broughton and once an ambitious goal for a day's outing, was now only a first stage in long days that ended in the heart of the hills, beyond Talla Linn, or over the watershed and down by Annan or Ettrick. One June evening of 1893, after a day of rain, Buchan set off from Broughton on his bicycle (solid-tyred; next year he had pneumatics) up the road which is now the Edinburgh–Carlisle highway, but was then overgrown with heather and grass—'I might as well have been riding on the face of the hill'—so that he had to walk and push most of the way to the watershed. It was dark when he started the run downhill to Moffat; his brake refused to work, he fell off, and so did bits of the bicycle, the lamp wouldn't light, rain poured down, he got the machine going with bits of string, and to crown all he found a dead man by the roadside which frightened him horribly.

I did not hold an inquest on the dead man; still less did I inform a policeman, since there wasn't one nearer than six miles, and that one was in bed. What I did was to bolt on as fast as a broken bicycle and a lame leg allowed me.

He reached Moffat and an aunt's house at one in the morning.
After he had slept twelve hours and the blacksmith had tinkered up
the machine, he rode up Moffat Water by the Grey Mare's Tail,
over to the Braes of Yarrow and St Mary's Loch for tea at the
Gordon Arms—'an ashet full of ham and eggs and a pot of mar-
malade beside half a loaf and some other trifles'—then over the pass
of Paddy's Slacks to Traquair and Peebles, supper, and ten miles
up Tweed back to Broughton. 'Be very careful,' Mrs Buchan
begged him, on one of these holidays, 'of your diet and damp.'

On a number of his expeditions he was joined by his friend
Charlie Dick. Cloth-capped and knickerbockered, they walked the
hills and drove-roads of Tweeddale, bicycled south to Beattock and
north to Edinburgh, and explored the lower stretches of the Tweed
and all Scott's places: Ashiestiel, Melrose, the Eildon Hills, Smail-
holm Tower. They wound up one journey by crossing into England
over the bridge at Coldstream, and looking at the battlefield of
Flodden, and the Northumbrian strongholds of Norham, Wark,
Ford and Etal.

Castles, battlefields and scenery were not the only things John
Buchan looked for in these holiday outings. He began to note down
individualities of character and speech:

We have been having magnificent weather here. One old shepherd told me
'that there was nae doot but that the millennium had come, and Auld Nick
was lockit up.' One man saw me reading Browning and told me that 'I
should only read every second line and I wad make as much sense oot o' it.'
Another (and this is one of the best things I ever heard) was talking about
politics with me. 'Ay,' he said, 'there used to be an awfu' lot o' Tories
round aboot here; but oor Makker was merciful to us Liberals and took a
lot o' them to himsel'.' I found afterwards that the speaker's brother had
been one of the Tories which the Almighty had taken to himself. This was
a grand example of forsaking father and brother to follow . . . Mr Gladstone.

This was while he was staying at Broughton Green; and on another
occasion he wrote from there of:

a most interesting tramp staying here just now. He has had the most
astonishing experiences. He was found last winter in a ditch at Hawick
frozen stiff, and was only revived by having a bottle of whisky poured down
his throat. He told me he wished he could be frozen again. He also declared
he had been teetotal since Saturday.

There was the Broughton shoemaker, 'an intelligent man. . . .
His opinion of Sir Walter Scott's novels is that they are "graund
reading, but horrid lees."' And the old woman who declared 'that

her son's socks were no better than Penelope's web (she did not sound the last letter of the virtuous queen's name), for what she mended in the morning was a hole again at night.' One September Buchan went up to Stirling Fair, 'and associated with a lot of Highland drovers from whom I got splendid material for stories.' Ideas were buzzing in his head; 'I intend to keep on writing for the *Gentleman's* and possibly publish a volume of selected essays.' He planned an anthology of poetry about fishing, and wrote an article on 'The Muse of the Angle' which was published in the *Gentleman's Magazine* with quotations from Phineas Fletcher to Thomas Tod Stoddart, a local bard. He thought of following up his edition of Bacon's *Essays* with *The Compleat Angler* and Sidney's *Arcadia* and *Apologie for Poetrie* in the same series, and he had begun to collect notes for a novel of Tweeddale, to be called *John Burnet of Barns*, 'which I intend to write next summer and hope to get accepted by Macmillans.'

In September of 1894 he made his first proper visit to England, staying with an uncle of his father, John Henderson, in Clapham Rise. In the National Gallery he admired the Rossettis, Turners, Constables, Landseers and Hogarths. The Henry VII Chapel impressed him most in the Abbey; the House of Commons he found 'small and bare . . . scarcely so large as half our church.'

On the whole I like London, but it is very different from what I expected. It is so irregularly built that it rather offends one's sense of symmetry; but the old brick gives it a warm colour and a sort of unpicturesque picturesqueness (you know what I mean). The English people seem very polite, especially the policemen and shopmen. In Scotland a shopman serves you as if he was doing you a favour by bothering about it; here it is entirely the other way.

Two family events of this period must be noted. Violet, the baby born just before they left Pathhead, had been taken ill in the spring of 1893 and was carried down to Broughton Green, where she grew steadily weaker, and died at the end of June, aged five. 'I must apologise for not writing to you sooner,' John wrote to Charlie Dick. 'My only excuse is that I hadn't the heart, I was so troubled at my sister's death. I had no idea a death in a family was such a painful thing.' The other event was a meeting in the same summer with a brother of his father's at the Bank House.

My Uncle Tom—the sailor one—is home just now, full of most curious and wonderful stories many of which I have jotted down. He told me among other things that he had lived for six months in Samoa and had often seen Robert Louis. He said that he is a sort of King there, but that he goes about with nothing on him except a blanket, worn toga-wise, and pinned at the shoulder with a Cairngorm brooch. Fancy! Sic a sicht for sair een! A decent honest Scotsman come to that!*

By his third year at the University Buchan had his eye firmly fixed on Oxford. It was not an unusual step for an able student; there were, for Glasgow men, the closed Snell scholarships at Balliol, and one or two of Buchan's acquaintances had gone there. No doubt Gilbert Murray had a hand in the decision; the choice of Brasenose rather than Balliol was due partly to Buchan's enthusiasm for Pater, who was a Fellow of that college, and partly to Richard Lodge, who had come from Brasenose in 1894 to the Chair of History in Glasgow. Murray asked him, as a newcomer from Oxford, 'to give a few words of advice to one of his students who was going up in January to compete for a classical scholarship in a group of Oxford Colleges.' (It was the Brasenose, Exeter and Christ Church group.) Years later, at a Brasenose dinner, Lodge told the story:

[Murray] admitted that the student was not yet a first-class classical scholar, but said that his English work was very promising. I, of course, assented: the student came to see me, and so I had my first interview with John Buchan. I gave him some scraps of advice, and have more than a shrewd suspicion that he paid little attention to them. But, what was more important, I wrote to my late colleagues at Brasenose and urged them not to pay excessive attention to Buchan's Latin Prose or even to his translations, but to read carefully his Essay and General Paper, and, if they were really good, to elect him in spite of possible defects in his other papers.

The examiners seem to have heeded this advice—Buchan's essay struck them as 'just like a bit out of Stevenson'—and awarded him a Junior Hulme scholarship.

In his last weeks at college, with his Oxford scholarship secure,

* The family legend about Tom Buchan is that he went to New South Wales because he had killed a man in Scotland. In 1914 he dyed his hair black and fought right through the war, rising to squadron-sergeant-major in an Australian mounted regiment. On his return to Australia he became religious, and by letter exhorted his nephew John to repentance. When he died, the local minister, who knew little of his past life, wrote to John Buchan to say he was putting up a stone saying 'A true son of the Church,' Buchan suggested altering it to 'A true son of Scotland.'

John Buchan's youngest son Alastair, on a visit to Australia in 1962, heard more about Tom Buchan from a former employer in Brisbane. 'He often spoke of his past being the black sheep more or less. If he was your uncle [great-uncle] I would like you to know that he was with me for quite a long time and was one of Nature's gentlemen, kind and considerate at all times. He eventually gave up drink and was really a remarkable character. He was loyal, trustworthy and what we Australians call a "good bloke."' Tom Buchan died in 1940.

Buchan embarked on a romantic tale, *Sir Quixote of the Moors*, which Fisher Unwin promptly accepted. 'I would do a few sentences in the morning while waiting for breakfast, a few more at the Union, and more at night in the intervals of my College work.' Once classes were over, he went down to Broughton. He allowed himself an occasional day on the hills, and spent one day driving a flock of a hundred ewes from Peebles to Bamflat, near Biggar, for his Masterton uncles. Otherwise it was work for ten hours a day, partly on texts for Oxford—'I do my half book of Homer daily'—partly on his own works: some short stories, the novel *John Burnet*, and more essays.

Macmillan have accepted 'The Drove Road' [for their *Magazine*] and I have already begun negotiations with them about my book of essays. I received a letter yesterday asking for my photograph and a short article on how I write my books. I am going to say that I write them with a J pen, and I am about to get a photograph taken in a sailor hat with little blue ribbons down the back and a spade and a pail in my hand. It will be quite pathetic.

His reading this summer included much Browning, Turgenev's *Smoke* and Kenneth Grahame's *Golden Age* ('which surely is the most beautiful book published for many years').

In August he went down to Sheringham in Norfolk for a few days with the Murrays. They golfed and bathed and in the evenings read *Pendennis*, and *The Master Builder* in Archer's translation. One of the circumstances that made Murray so romantic, so unprofessorial a figure to his students, was his possession of a highborn, high-spirited wife—and the legend that he had danced at Castle Howard till three in the morning before his wedding to Lady Mary. The young men used to discuss her a great deal, and Joe Menzies was probably reflecting the opinion of many Glasgow students when he said: 'I think Lady Mary Murray is the only truly aristocratic woman I have met. Of course you see them in carriages; but she is the only one I have met.' The Murrays had many of the students to stay—George Douglas Brown (later to write *The House with the Green Shutters*) and H. N. Brailsford, to whom Murray gave a revolver when he went off to fight for the Greeks, had been earlier guests. Perhaps in inviting Buchan Lady Mary wanted to give the able young man some tips on the new world he was going to enter; perhaps it was partly the Carlisle enthusiasm for spotting talent; certainly she was most kind to him, and his hero-worship of the Murrays grew quickly into the most affectionate friendship. One of his last acts before leaving Glasgow in October 1895 was to send Gilbert Murray, to whom it was dedicated,* a copy of his first published novel, *Sir Quixote of the Moors*: first-fruits of the gift that was to be his Open Sesame to the world.

The road to Oxford was also the road out of Glasgow. The University had stretched and stimulated him, but his life outside it had become in some ways constricting. The Buchan home was still happy and close-knit (in June 1894 Alastair was born, a year after Violet's death). But, as in most happy families, basic affection did not preclude a certain amount of tension. With his father Buchan may have felt a growing gap between the Calvinism—however gentle—preached at John Knox and the addresses given in the Bute Hall by Principal Caird, for whom 'religion and philosophy are not enemies,' who discussed Erasmus, Galileo, Bacon, Hume in the light of great general principles. The questions raised by Murray about ancient religions, by Jones about the nature of reality, were not to find satisfactory answers in the senior John Buchan's mixture of emotional revivalism and theological rigidity.† His shining serenity and his intellectual unsophistication made him a difficult person for an affectionate but sharp-witted son to argue with. 'My good father has not the proper turn for speculation. He cares too little about logic and sees things in a pictorial way.' Certainly, in spite of his parents' hopes, Buchan had no thought of the Church as a career.

With his mother—only eighteen years older than himself—John Buchan had the closest ties: friends who visited Crosshill, and warmed to the goodness and simplicity of the home, noticed how wrapped up Mrs Buchan was in John, and how to get into favour you had only to appreciate John, or be ready to listen to stories of his boyish escapades. But such an affection can be stifling, especially when the mother's world is so much smaller than the son's. There is a time in all families when the children of spirit develop their own interests and become impatient of those they have inherited from their parents. And when John's new interests—in literature, in politics, in philosophy—were set beside his mother's traditional and limited concerns with the parish and the neighbours, he was bound

---

* 'To Gilbert Murray whatsoever in this book is not worthless is dedicated by his friend.'

† Mr Buchan was a firm opponent of the Higher Criticism and in 1902 was one of the party of ministers and laymen of the United Free Church who indicted George Adam Smith for heresy on the strength of his *Modern Criticism and the Preaching of the Old Testament* (1901). They were not successful.

to want more elbow-room. In later years, in a speech at a Glasgow University Club dinner, he took 'an avenue of respectable villa residences and a well-kept public park' as a symbol of 'unenterprising dullness,'* and when he was in South Africa, and heard that his mother was strongly objecting to his brother William going to India, he wrote angrily to his sister:

Ask her whether she does not think that she keeps her sons far nearer her by letting them go abroad in honourable professions than if she had them married and living in the next street, like so many Tindals. It is not distance that alienates—just the other way.

Mrs Buchan's horizon took in the mission-field as well as the Gorbals, Crosshill and Tweeddale; but it did not take in Oxford. No Buchan or Masterton had been there; it was a place less known, more full of possible dangers, than Livingstonia or Chitambo.

It was easier for Buchan to shape his own life away from home, and natural that he should set his sights on Oxford; but this understandable decision deprived him of a good deal of fun and interest and kept him from appreciating Glasgow to the full. For the decision to go to Oxford meant hard work in his studies, so as to win a scholarship to take him there, and hard work in his writing, so as to finance himself once he had arrived.

Among John and Anna's friends were D.Y. and Katie Cameron, the son and daughter of the minister of the South Park Church. Miss Cameron remembers him as 'just a wee Glasgow student,' but giving an impression of great ambition, thinking much of his future and of making his own way. Often, when the rest of the Camerons and Buchans were off on picnics, he would stay behind to work: 'he seemed to be driving himself on.' And though there was a good deal of falling in and out of love in the Camerons' circle of friends, 'John and Anna didn't have love affairs.' One result of

* Anna Buchan, in her novel *Eliza for Common* (1928), written under the pseudonym O. Douglas, describes her hero's feelings about Glasgow:
    'Warmly clad, healthy children walked beside nurses wheeling perambulators; vans delivered provisions for the week-end; peace and plenty reigned.
    'And Jim's heart failed him. All these villas, smug and prosperous, seemed to lie like a weight on him, holding him down, making certain that he did not escape from Glasgow to that city of dreaming spires, Oxford.
    'It would have been idle to remind him that there was culture in Glasgow, brains of the best, splendid traditions; useless to point out that the suburbs of one city are very like the suburbs of another, that in Oxford, too, on a Saturday afternoon, vans delivered Sunday dinners to roads and roads of villas, nurses wheeled perambulators, and prosperous, busy men took their wives out in serviceable little cars. To Jim, at the moment, Glasgow represented everything in life that was drab and ugly and uninteresting; Oxford lay in rosy mists, a many-towered Camelot.'

this self-imposed discipline of work was that Buchan seems hardly to have noticed the lively things that were happening in Glasgow outside the University. It was the city's heyday as a growing-point of art. Lavery, Pirie, George Henry, D. Y. Cameron, Crawhall and James Guthrie were all painting and exhibiting at the Glasgow Art Club; Alexander Reid the dealer was making Glasgow merchants and shipowners buy Degas, Monet, Pissarro, Sisley, before London had woken up to them; C. R. Mackintosh was building the Glasgow School of Art. The Buchans could have had, through the Camerons, a footing in the circle of Mackintosh, Francis Newbery and the Art School, but John did not seem to have time, and the only effect of the Glasgow art movement on the Buchans was Anna's redecoration of the drawing-room in Queen Mary Avenue, when she replaced dark wallpaper, red rep covers, a gallery of framed photographs and steel engravings of 'The Deacon's Trip' and 'The Murder of Archbishop Sharp' by plain cream wallpaper, printed linen covers, low bookshelves and Arundel prints. But whatever he may have missed in this side of Glasgow's activities, Buchan could take heart, in the shaping of his own life, from the zest and energy of a city whose heavy industries were booming, whose shipyards had built more vessels of the highest class than all other shipbuilding rivers put together. Not less than a Clydeside engineer, Buchan could set out with confidence to make his fortune.

Seventeen years earlier Stevenson had broken away from home and gone abroad to make his own life. He had loved Edinburgh, but had been driven out by east winds and his father's Calvinism, which had made home unbearable with scenes, reproaches and anguished prayings. It was rather the comfort and cosiness of his family life that helped to send Buchan off; it was not a dramatic break, and he did not keep his city in his heart as Stevenson did, an object both of love and of repulsion. Buchan was grateful to Glasgow; he enormously admired and respected Glasgow; but I do not think that he loved it.

CHAPTER THREE

OXFORD UNDERGRADUATE

1895-99

'Every generation, I know, has the same prejudice; but I am convinced that few men have ever had more lovable, more brilliant, more generous, more gallant friends.'

John Buchan: *These for Remembrance*

Oxford in 1895 was a quiet city and a cloistered university. The undergraduate, bicycling along the High and stopping for a horse-drawn tram to pick up or put down its passengers, could see the college buildings without an intervening fringe of cars. After a party half-a-dozen young men could link arms and stroll down the centre of the street—and hear the sound of their own footsteps. There was no industry at Cowley, and the future Lord Nuffield was William R. Morris of the bicycle shop in James Street. Only within the last twenty years had College Fellows been allowed to marry, and North Oxford, largely built to accommodate the new academic families, stopped short of the present Marston Ferry Road. As against today's 8000, there were less than 2000 undergraduates, and in those days before State scholarships and county grants, the great majority were from families who could pay for their sons at public school and university. A scientist was a rarity. The handful of women students lived in chaperoned seclusion. Though Greek was compulsory for entrance, in some colleges nearly half the men might be reading for a pass degree. Oxford was more self-sufficient than now; though the journey to London by train took no longer than it does today, there was far less going up to town. It was politically tranquil. Industrial unrest did not touch it; wars were something that took place on a distant frontier. 'Nothing ever then happened,' wrote a man who came up to Brasenose four years after Buchan, 'that to an Englishman seemed to threaten the main pillars and framework of his ordered society.'

It was overwhelmingly a young man's world. A character in Compton Mackenzie's *Sinister Street* (which Buchan thought a good picture of Oxford in his day, though based on Mackenzie's experiences a few years later) says that 'the great point of Oxford, in fact the whole point of Oxford, is that there are no girls.' Forty years later Buchan wrote to his son, whose Oxford days were being shadowed by the prospect of war, 'I wish you could have had my undergraduate days—spent peacefully in an enclave like a monastery.'

With his head full of Arnold and Pater, and in his waistcoat pocket a gold watch from the John Knox congregation, Buchan arrived in Oxford on 11 October 1895. His first view of it, when he had gone up for his scholarship examination in January, had been unforgettable. Deep in snow, empty of undergraduates, the city had indeed breathed the enchantments of the Middle Ages. Now in the first days of the Michaelmas term he looked on it more critically. There was the disappointment of finding Oxford without Pater. (He had died shortly before Buchan had come up for his scholarship.) After the stimulating lectures of Murray, Bradley and Jones, those he attended 'seemed no better than a valley of dry bones': and the old type of crusted bachelor don struck him as quite out of touch with life. He missed the close connection of city and university. In Glasgow professors had a part to play outside the classroom and the study. A professor had been closely concerned in organising the city's water-supply from Loch Katrine, Henry Jones had founded the Civic Society. Buchan had moved from a place where learning was pursued side by side with, and often in the teeth of, the bustle and drive of a great city earning its living, to a place where learning could be pursued for its own sake, or could simply be one ingredient in a civilised life, full of variety but removed from reality. Compared with his Glasgow contemporaries, the Brasenose undergraduates struck him as 'a curious mixture of overgrown schoolboys and would-be men of the world.' 'On Sunday night I had rather a time,' he told Charlie Dick four days after his arrival:

About half past twelve six drunken gentlemen came into my rooms. They came into my bedroom and with immense politeness wished me goodnight and begged me not to disturb myself, for they would make themselves quite comfortable. They then turned the table upside down and got inside it. Then they wedged a chair across the door. Then they carefully unscrewed the electric light globes and put them inside the fender. Then they upturned the coal-scuttle into one of the presses. Finally they began a search for whisky in my cupboard and found methylated spirits. I waited with intense amusement for developments, but luckily they found out their mistake. Then they left me with profuse protestations of friendship.

And after the Freshmen's Wine one group raided a set of their friends' rooms and 'knocked the furniture to matchwood.' Buchan had himself been covered with peasemeal at a Glasgow Rectorial Election, but the licensed riot of these occasions was the letting-off of high spirits by students for whom life was fundamentally serious; these rather aimless bouts of drunken destructiveness seemed in comparison the work of immature boys who did not know what life was like. Not that Buchan cared any more for the aesthetes; their interests lay in the bizarre and the subordinate, they had 'the conventionality of the unconventional,' and were just as out of touch with life as the hearties. And, boors or aesthetes, they reinforced the suspicion, always near the surface of a Scottish mind, that the southern English are a soft race: they were waited on by servants (Buchan preferred to black his own shoes) and there were no eight-o'clock lectures.

He was certainly quick to sum up his impressions, for only eight days after he had arrived in Brasenose he rushed into print with an article on the leader-page of the *Glasgow Herald* on 'Oxford and her Influence,' in which he generalised with all the facility of a first acquaintance:

The two most distinguishing features of Oxford life now and always appear to be conventionality and comfort. To the stranger, accustomed it may be to hard living and grim work, the atmosphere of the place is one of ease, almost of luxury. Whatever may be the case about the hard thinking, the plain living is not much in evidence . . . As compared, let us say, with the Scots universities, it is materially like the land of Canaan to the Desert of Sin. There are no cheerless walks on sharp winter mornings, no shivering on bare benches in windy class-rooms, no scribbling in dark lecture-halls at rickety desks. Nor is there the pinching, the scraping for an education, the battling against want and ill-health, which make a Scots college such a noble nursery of the heroic. Again, there are not so many gentlemen with designs on the reformation of the world. Things are quieter, easier, more contented. It is like some comfortable, latter-day monastery. The harsh struggle for existence goes on without its knowledge. The world is with it neither late nor soon.

Out of such an environment, he argued, could come no important movement: only revivals, like Tractarianism, 'a resuscitation of the corpse of a past belief.'

When the systems of Mill and Spencer were predominant in England, Oxford knew them not. But as soon as they began to be replaced to some extent by Neo-Hegelianism, then Oxford discovered them and taught them in her schools. Now when the current of popular favour seems to be setting against German philosophy, Oxford has embraced it with open arms.

He ended by asking what then could be the use of Oxford.

Perhaps there is a subtle charm of old art and old memories about her grey walls and green gardens which goes to bind a man's affections to her against his better judgement. It is a place without clearness or breadth of vision ruled by tradition and eccentric fashion. It is correct to admire Dante, but he who praises Milton is a barbarian void of taste; the reason for such a strange preference being in all likelihood that Oxford is capable of admiring moral earnestness and rugged grandeur only when veiled under a cloak of a foreign language and superficial eccentricities of character. The men who are bred in this school must be an exotic race, who, if they make the most of their nurture, will have a hard time of it in the world.

And his peroration must have reassured his Glasgow friends that so far his own judgment had not been insidiously undermined.

Of Oxford as a place of arid study and scholarly labours we have nothing to say; of Oxford as a place of respite, of change, of relief from the battle of life, we can only have the highest praise; but as a nursery for the youth of the land it seems to us to lack all health-giving qualities, all verve and mettle and high spirit. Her most distinguished sons must attain to their distinction by a resolute thwarting of her influence and not by its aid.

Cosmo Lang, the future Archbishop, moving from Glasgow to Balliol a decade earlier, had felt the same disappointment: after the intellectual awakening of Edward Caird's lectures in Glasgow he found that the English public school boys at Balliol 'belonged not only geographically but intellectually to another country.' A little later Gilbert Murray too had felt that the reality of Oxford fell far short of his hopes: 'I had expected so much; new lights on life, new learning, enlightenment and philosophy.'

Brasenose in 1895 was a small college of about a hundred undergraduates, with a reputation for sport, hard drinking, and disorder. (Some time in the eighties an undergraduate had screwed up the Dean in his room, using coffin-screws which, being headless, were almost impossible to extract.) Brasenose men figured, out of all proportion to the numbers of the College, in the University cricket and association Elevens, and in the Rugby Fifteen; but seldom in the First Class lists. A little after Buchan's time a man was ducked on getting a First, for 'breaking the traditions of the college.' The Principal, C. B. Heberden, was an aloof introverted bachelor with a falsetto voice and a passion for music—particularly Greek music—and between him and the run of undergraduates there was little common ground.

Buchan's rooms were at the top of No. 1 staircase, next the Hall, and opposite those of another freshman, B. C. Boulter, who sixty years later remembered their tremendous struggle hauling up the black-and-white reproduction of Gainsborough's 'Mrs Graham' which was Buchan's best possession (one of his early poems was on this portrait, which Mrs Graham's stricken widower had turned to the wall at her death). It reached almost to the ceiling; on the mantelpiece was Gilbert Murray's photograph. Buchan was pleased with his rooms—'the only expensive thing about them is that they are fully lit with three planes of electric light, which is very nice for the eyes.' With the example of Murray to give him confidence (during his four years at Oxford Murray had supported himself entirely on scholarships) Buchan was determined not to cost his parents a penny. So he planned to economise (he took his name off dinner three times a week) and to increase his income by his writing. After a fortnight he reported rather anxiously to Willie:

My college bills for the week came only to 17s. You see I have been so much out at meals. I find that at the end of term we have a payment of 5s. to the porter: this has completely stumped me! So I want you to ask Father to cash the cheque which is sent from the *Herald* for the Oxford article and send it to me. . . . I am going a long walk this afternoon to Cumnor Hall which Scott and Dr Meikle and Matthew Arnold have written about, and I am thinking of writing an article in the *Herald* about it. I must make money.

His programme for work was fourfold. First, reading for Schools (Honour Moderations, to be followed by Greats); second, reading for University prizes (he at once decided to try for the Newdigate Poetry Prize and the Stanhope Historical Essay Prize); third, journalism, for immediate cash needs; fourth, his stories and novels (*John Burnet of Barns* was nearly finished). This fourth part of the programme was by now well organised. He had taken on a literary agent, A. P. Watt from Glasgow; he had three publishers interested in him: Blackwood, Fisher Unwin and John Lane.

Blackwood was making enquiries, through Watt, about *John Burnet*. Fisher Unwin, who had published *Sir Quixote*, came to call on Buchan in Brasenose a few days after term began. ('He was very decent, abused Crockett freely . . . and asked me to write in an extraordinary magazine of his called *Cosmopolis* to be published in French, German and English.)' Lane, to whom Buchan had been introduced by D. Y. Cameron (who had illustrated several books for the firm), had invited him to call on his way to Oxford, and had then offered to publish a book of Buchan's essays, *Scholar Gipsies*, and his anthology of poetry about fishing. Then, three weeks after this meeting in London, Lane came up to Oxford with a proposal. Buchan was bidden to breakfast at the Clarendon Hotel ('splendidly waited') along with John Davidson the poet from Greenock. The upshot was quickly revealed to Charlie Dick in Glasgow:

I will tell you a great secret, which you must not mention to a soul. I am to be exalted to the post of literary adviser to the great firm of Lane *vice* Le Gallienne sacked. That is a joke of course, but he is going to send me manuscripts to read for him, for which I shall be paid. He is very anxious to have *J.B. of B.* (which he will not get). He says he will get it published for me serially in *Scribner's*.

Buchan had always fancied the idea of publishing different books with different firms. In a commonplace book which he kept while at Glasgow University there is a list which shows that he aspired to publish books of essays and criticism with Chatto & Windus, novels with Longmans, poetry with Elkin Mathews and John Lane. So now that he really had become an author, he was determined not to hand himself over bodily to one publisher; not even to such a rising star as Lane. And his self-confidence received a fillip when the *Bookman* chose him for its 'New Writers' column in December. The material had been collected by David Meldrum, Blackwood's literary adviser in London, who had given Buchan dinner at his club on his way to Oxford. The article described *Sir Quixote*, noted Buchan's affinity to Scott and Stevenson, had a word or two about the forthcoming *John Burnet*, and concluded that 'his record is an extraordinary and an interesting one for a writer of twenty years of age.'

But neither his literary concerns, nor his first disillusion, kept Buchan from wholeheartedly plunging into Oxford life. He found the Honour Mods work quite hard, especially the Greek: 'I have risen from the region of the unclassed in my prose,' he reported to Murray, 'to the exalted place of β. I find Demosthenes rather a grind, but the Theocritus is delightful.' His Mods tutor was H. F. Fox, a romantic figure: one of his pupils described him, 'not so much a teacher as one who gave inspiration by permitting sudden glimpses of what the classics were for himself.' He had also played cricket for Somerset. His beautiful wife, who went round with hair flying like a Maenad, may have been startling to Oxford;

she would have been unthinkable in Queen Mary Drive. Buchan
found Fox a thoroughly delightful man. 'He promises me a sure
second and a possible first in Mods, and recommends me strongly
to stand for a Fellowship in Greats.' He golfed with Fox and took
enthusiastically to sculling and canoeing, 'going far up in canoes
and getting into jolly little backwaters among gardens—just like the
Golden Age.' And on foot and by bicycle—often again with Fox—
he began to discover the rural England that lay beyond the base
and brickish skirt of Oxford. There were expeditions to Cumnor
Place and to the Evenlode, and 'twice I have gone down right into
the Berkshire moors, and to Bablockhithe and Didcot and Wantage.'
In the notebook in which he kept a careful note of his expenses there
are several entries of '6d for hire of bicycle from William Morris.'

It did not take him long to revise his first opinion of Brasenose,
and discover that the college did not consist entirely of drunken
rowdies. There were a number of congenial freshmen: John Foster
Carr from Yale, considerably older than most of the others; R. W.
Jeffery, a Yorkshireman from Bradford; and a scholar from Westminster, Taffy Boulter, Buchan's neighbour on No. 1 staircase (his
nickname was not due to any Welshness, but because for a time
they used to call each other by names from du Maurier's *Trilby*,
and Taffy was the one that stuck). Having refused to have anything
to do with the Freshmen's Wine Club, Buchan launched his
counter-attack on the rowdies. 'We have done a very superior
thing here, *i.e.* myself and some of the scholars, with a sprinkling of
commoners,' he reported in mid-November to Charlie Dick. 'We
have founded an IBSEN Society which meets weekly to read and
discuss the dramas of the Master.' But Ibsen was too strong meat,
a vote of censure was passed on the President, and at the end of his
second term Buchan had to tell Murray that:

Our Ibsen Society has, I am afraid, degenerated sadly. First they gave up
Ibsen and went through in succession *Cymbeline*, *The Dolly Dialogues*,
Kenneth Grahame's *Golden Age*, till they came to Rudyard Kipling and
stayed there. Secondly, they have changed their name to 'The Crocodiles'
and adopted a tie of green, grey and white, under a fatuous idea that this
is the colour of a crocodile's back. Finally they seem in danger of turning
into a dining club!

He lunched with the College Jacobite ('who showed me all
sorts of extraordinary and treasonable papers, with "God bless
Queen Mary" on them'), in Torpids he ran on the towpath 'yelling
like a maniac' for the B.N.C. boat, and got on to such good terms

with the rowing men that they used to upset his programme of work by coming round to his rooms for a gossip after their vast training-dinners in Hall.

Though he attended College Chapel regularly, on Sundays he usually went to Mansfield College, to hear Principal Fairbairn or visiting Scots such as Professor Lindsay of the Glasgow Free Church College—'a very sound, kindly discourse'—or 'the Minister of Bowdon, a nice sensible old man, but very long and somewhat dreich.' He also heard Bishop Gore and Canon Scott-Holland preach in the University Church, and one Sunday Taffy Boulter took him out to Dorchester: 'There was some detestable incense in the place which got up my nose and made me cough; otherwise it was very fine.' He showed the usual Scots Presbyterian's reaction to Lent; or maybe he just wished to reassure his mother that in spite of his Anglican sermon-tasting and his white surplice in chapel, he was not falling into popish ways:

This is the first day of Lent, and all the prize idiots here are making a pretence of fasting. . . . I was ill-advised enough to go to chapel, and found a service of nearly twice its proper length.

His social life increased—in his second term he was booked for practically every meal a week ahead—and he kept on devising time-tables of work. In October it was classics from 9 to 1, work in the Bodleian (for the Stanhope Prize) from 3 to 4.30, classics 5 to 7 and 7.30 to 9. In the summer he proposed to get up at six and do all his classical work by one o'clock, reserving his evenings for reading the manuscripts Lane sent him, and for typing *John Burnet of Barns*, and his afternoons for the usual delightful distractions of the Trinity term.

After the Easter vacation in Glasgow and Peeblesshire, he came back to find 'Oxford is looking its best just now. All the trees are out, garden chairs are appearing in the quad. and everyone is in flannels and straw hats.' There was tennis, sailing, rowing—he coxed a boat in the pair races—canoeing and punting.

I have been rowing and sculling on the river nearly every afternoon. It is very pretty for the water-lilies are all out and the banks are simply masses of wild roses. The wild roses here seem to be more scented than the ones in Scotland.

His first English summer is always likely to be a revelation to a Scot. (So is his first English country pub, ministering to sociability, ease, and a sense of the past, where a drab Scottish bar can represent only the temptation of Demon Drink). Hedgerows bulging and bursting with white may, after the wind-bent hawthorns of a Border hillside; verges dense with cow-parsley and convolvulus; cottage gardens with the flowers of 'Thyrsis,' and gardens in North Oxford heavy with lilac and syringa; Evenlode, Cherwell and Windrush winding placidly between pollarded willows—they impress the northerner with a kind of rich, dense, sleepy beauty which can both enchant and oppress. Buchan was enchanted.

Then there was Eights Week:

Oxford is a lovely sight with its greenery and flowers, pretty frocks and pretty faces; speaking generally, the beauty and fashion of England are congregated here just now. When I turned up yesterday on the barge in boating clothes, I was horrified to find it filled with ladies, and opera glasses and parasols.

He reported another occasion when he had felt a trifle underdressed:

I got a curious note on Saturday from a lady (I. Dougall, the authoress of the *Zeit-Geist*), asking me to sign my name in a copy of *Sir Quixote* for the Blenheim bazaar, as there was to be a collection of autographed books by Oxford writers. She asked me to tea yesterday. I went and found that she lived in a very pretty house in the Parks. It was a perfectly tragic affair. I was ushered into a drawing-room full of ladies—and I was in flannels, just come from the river—simply full of ladies. There was Mrs Sidgwick [A. J. Balfour's sister], the Women's Rights person, Lady Mary's friend, and the wife of the President of Corpus, and a lot of others. I had to talk for an hour and a half and pretend to be amused by a tame snake, which wanted to crawl up my sleeve, and of which I was horribly frightened.

It was a splendid summer, but he found the heat trying, and had some trouble with asthma. And it was impossible to fit everything in. As well as Mods work,

I have that ghastly examination in Divinity to get through, which comprises John and Luke in Greek and the Acts. The Chaplain said to me, 'I suppose it will be more or less familiar to you already.' I up and said, 'Alas, I never read a word of the New Testament.' He stared in pious horror. Then I added 'in Greek.'

But the Vice-Principal allowed him to put it off till the following year. All the same he felt overwhelmed by his classical and historical work, and resolved 'to do not a scrap more of desultory literary work, but to devote all my time during the rest of my course here to academic work, and MSS reading.' He wound up the term with his first speech on the paper at the Union, when he seconded the motion (which was lost) 'That motley's the only wear.'

He had made ends meet, but at the price of very hard work on top of his academic load—often he read as many as four manu- scripts a week for Lane. He would reassure his mother that he could 'manage comfortably,' but he economised in the Easter vacation by not going to London as he had planned; he found it quite difficult to raise the money for a machine on which to type *John Burnet*, and did not have himself photographed, which Anna would have liked, because—

in the first place I have not done anything to merit it, not getting the Newdigate and Stanhope. In the second place I am rather poor, having had to pay about £2 for absolutely necessary books, £1 1s. od. for entrance fee to examination in divinity and being compelled to go up to London at the end of the term.

Up to London he went in June, to spend a couple of days with Lane in his flat in Albany. (He had meant to go to his great-uncle Henderson's in Clapham and do his business from there, but the Hendersons had gone away, so he accepted Lane's standing invita- tion—'as I don't want to trespass upon his hospitality, I will only stay Monday and Tuesday night.') He had had two short stories published in the *Yellow Book* that year; he had been reading manuscripts steadily; now he was being taken right into the heart of literary London. Lane's chambers, G1, backed on to his new office in Vigo Street; and the Bodley Head was more like a club than a place of business.

'I had a very gay time in town,' Buchan reported to Taffy Boulter,

but I could not stand it long, and came off after three days. I met all sorts of people, from awful New Women, who drank whisky and soda and smoked cigars, to John Murray, the publisher, who is a sort of incarnation of respectability. I never was in so many theatres and restaurants in my life. I met Mrs Meynell, and lunched with Mrs Henniker (Lord Crewe's sister) and got a card for a reception at Stafford House. I nearly died of exhaustion.

On this visit Buchan met Arnold Bennett whose first novel, *In the Shadow*, he had read for Lane.* Bennett, then aged twenty- nine, noted in his Journal for 23 June 1896:

* It was published in 1898 as *A Man from the North*. In his report Buchan, after praising Bennett's knowledge, insight, style and characterisation, had concluded 'I do not think it is likely to be a striking success.' Bennett recorded later that his profits from the book exceeded the cost of having it typed by one sovereign, with which he bought a new hat. (Reginald Pound: *Arnold Bennett*, 1952, p. 104.)

At John Lane's I met John Buchan, just now principal 'reader' to the Bodley Head. A very young, fair man; charmingly shy; 'varsity' in every tone and gesture. He talks quietly in a feminine, exiguous voice, with the accent of Kensington tempered perhaps by a shadow of a shade of Scotch (or was that my imagination?). Already—he cannot be more than 23—he is a favourite of publishers, who actually seek after him, and has published one book. He told me that his second novel, a long Scotch romance, was just finished, and that he had practically sold the serial rights. . . . A most modest, retiring man, yet obviously sane and shrewd. Well-disposed, too, and anxious to be just; a man to compel respect; one who 'counts.'

Fox had pressed Buchan to come to Germany on a reading party, which included Taffy Boulter and A. P. Oppé of New College. But Buchan was apprehensive of the heat, and went north for a long vacation of hard work and exercise. First he stayed with his uncle at Peebles:

I have only been working very moderately lately—about five hours a day. I have read three books of Horace's Odes, a good deal of history, begun my Newdigate poem, and read a very large number of MSS. Last week Lane sent me ten altogether, which I have finished all but four. . . .

Last week I had some fine days fishing—on Wednesday with the worm in the Laverlaw Burn, on Thursday with the worm on Eddleston Water. But my crowning day was yesterday when the Tennants gave us permission to fish on their private lake at the Glen. We got thirteen fish only, but no one was below $\frac{1}{3}$ lb., and the average was between $\frac{1}{2}$ and $\frac{3}{4}$ lb. I killed nearly all my fish with a new fly, the *Cocky-bendy* as they call it here, peacock hackles with orange dressing. I fished from a boat and had some surprising adventures with wild duck, swans, and big fish. My health is now quite restored, and I am bronzed beyond recognition.

Then he joined the family, first at Innerleithen and later at Gallatown, near Kirkcaldy, where they were on holiday in the Free Church manse. Here John Edgar came to stay; they bathed and golfed, Buchan read manuscripts from Lane and began to write his essay for the 1897 Stanhope Prize (on Raleigh) and finished his 1897 Newdigate poem (on Gibraltar), having failed to win either prize in his first year.

At this precise moment I am feeling mightily morose, owing to my having foolishly embarked on *Robert Elsmere* and *Tom Jones* this afternoon. Somebody downstairs is playing and singing (God help them!!) 'Three Fishers went sailing out into the West' which is not an enlivening ditty. The wind is modestly and unsuccessfully trying to blow down a number of barley sheaves in the field opposite, and a bewildered London express is whistling somewhere down the line. Also I am sitting in a state of raw and bleeding flesh and mangled limbs, having done my best to deserve the name of the Bloody Buchan by diving into a deep channel among rocks which happened to be full of hidden shoals. I came out half-flayed, and blood filled my boots all the way home, so that I felt like one of Stanley Weyman's heroes. I have played bagatelle till I loathe the sight of a cue, and played all my five finger exercises on the piano. Also my hair is completely white with Sir Walter Raleigh, who seems to have ordered his life for the sole reason of perplexing biographers.

Even as I write, I observe from my turret chamber that the Countess of Rosslyn and the beautiful Lady Dudley are driving past from Dysart House in a high dog-cart. I begin to wish I were she, and then, reflecting that her husband has lost all his money on the turf, I am glad I am not. Still a high dog-cart makes up for many inequalities in life. In fact, now that I have been twenty-one years in this Valley of Humiliation, I begin to reflect that life what with over-work, being confined to bed, wind, rain, aristocrats and submerged reefs is played out. But I am consoled by the thought of high dog-carts.

In September he walked in Galloway, 'one of the most enjoyable and adventurous holidays I ever had in my life.' One night he slept in a shepherd's cottage, nine miles from the nearest house and twenty-five from the nearest station; the shepherd had not seen loaf bread since the spring and received his letters a fortnight late. 'Have got much fresh material,' Buchan told Dick; and when Lane suggested a book of short stories, he decided to make it a volume of 'moorland stories,' collecting some already written, and planning five more, 'of which I have the plots sketched.'

During his second year at Oxford Buchan established a firm position in Brasenose, though it was still to the literary rather than the athletic clubs that he belonged. He was a main prop of the college literary society, the Ingoldsby, and became President. The most substantial paper that he read to it was on 'Our Debt to the North,' which involved reading much Celtic and Norse poetry.

He was not a prig—after the Mods exam he and some others celebrated so thoroughly at a dinner in his rooms that they were each fined £1 for breaking windows—but he had a reputation for sobriety. Roger Merriman, a Balliol man from Harvard, remembered how, in the course of celebrating a success in Torpids, the Balliol eight joined the Brasenose eight for drinks and fireworks in the Quad. When a Roman candle was let off inside his trouser-leg, Merriman passed out: 'When I came to, I heard voices shouting for John Buchan. "He's the only sober man in B.N.C.!"' Buchan took Merriman back to Balliol, wangled him past the porter, and put him to bed.

It was in his third or fourth year that Buchan showed himself a force in the College by his action in the Heberden affair. A faction of the rowdies had been making life hell for the Principal, whom they accused of being hostile to sport, and of trying to turn Brasenose into an exclusively intellectual college. Buchan liked Heberden—perhaps he felt that this shy scholarly man with his love of music was carrying on the Pater tradition in the College. There was an anti-Heberden demonstration one Sunday night in Hall, when Buchan spoke up for the Principal, followed by a fight outside during which Buchan told his opponents that they were a lot of schoolboys and drunken boors, whose only form of exercise was being sick in the Quad, and that it was time they grew up.* The baiting stopped, and the chief rowdy was sent down, but Buchan paid for this outburst of anger by a series of sleepless nights.

Certainly the college authorities paid a remarkable compliment to a second-year undergraduate in recommending him to write the volume on Brasenose in the series of Oxford College Histories produced by the London publisher F. E. Robinson. 'It was rather an honour (as all the other volumes are by old and grave Fellows and Principals), so I agreed, but I have only a year and a half to do it in, and it means work.' He kept his deadline, and it was one of the first in the series to be published.†

It is a pleasant history-cum-guidebook, with due attention paid to the College's athletic records, famous men, and local legends, including the story of the President of the Brasenose Hellfire Club (*c.* 1830) who, in the middle of uttering blasphemies, was snatched by the devil, dragged by the hair over the Bodleian, and never seen again. The room whence the blasphemer was snatched had been Bishop Heber's where he had once entertained Sir Walter Scott and, in his third year, it became Buchan's: one of the best in the College. 'We have been having tea and smoking pipes at open windows, watching the sun set behind the Bodleian and the crows beginning to caw in Exeter gardens.'

His continuous effort to keep all sides of his work going at once, his reading for the Stanhope, and his outside literary work, had a

---

* A comment in the *Oxford J.C.R.* (29 November 1898) on 'this discreditable agitation' suggests that undergraduate sympathies in the University generally were against the Brasenose rowdies. The *Isis* also (28 January 1899) referred favourably to Buchan's part in the affair.

† Among the other volumes were *All Souls* by C. G. Grant Robertson, *Balliol* by H. W. C. Davis, *Corpus* by the President, *Jesus* by the Vice-Principal, *New College* by the Rev. Hastings Rashdall and R. S. Rait, *St John's* by W. H. Hutton, *Trinity* by Herbert Blakiston. No other author was less than a Fellow.

good deal to do with Buchan's second class in Mods. He knew himself that he had not yet made good his weaknesses as a classical scholar—'I never felt so like funking an exam as just before Mods,' he wrote four years later to his brother facing the same ordeal—but all the same he was very disappointed. As he wrote to Charlie Dick:

I am very much aggravated about my Mods. It seems that I got 6 αs when 7 would have got me a first; and worse still, in the very subject in which I was supposed to be going to get an α+ —Roman poetry—I got a β —. So you see I had a very near shave.

He set to work for Greats with all the more energy, for (as witness his repeated attempts at University prizes) he hated failure. But he did pull off the Stanhope at his second try, and at Encaenia in 1897 he recited the customary extract from his prize essay on Raleigh to an audience that included, as the first of the Honorary Graduates, Sir Wilfrid Laurier, Prime Minister of Canada.

Buchan had made his place in Brasenose, but it was increasingly outside the college that he made his friends. At University College there were two Scots, Tommy Nelson, the magnificent Rugby footballer who captained Oxford and played for Scotland, and Duncan Grant Warrand. At New College were Stair Gillon from Edinburgh and Harold Baker from Winchester. But it was in Balliol that Buchan found most of his friends: men whom he had known in Glasgow, like John Edgar, as well as men he met there for the first time: Johnnie Jameson from Galloway, Cuthbert Medd from Northumberland, Auberon Herbert and his cousin Aubrey Herbert, and—the last of them to come up, in 1897—Raymond Asquith. With the athletic among them—Johnnie Jameson boxed for the University, Sandy Gillon captained the New College Fifteen, Raymond Asquith captained the Balliol soccer Eleven, and also played for the college Fifteen, Auberon Herbert was a rowing Blue —Buchan was a member of Vincent's, of which Tommy Nelson became President. With the Scots among them he celebrated Burns Night (himself in the chair) and formed the New Caledonian Club: 'We are to dine once a term and wear a very gaudy uniform—a dark green dinner-jacket with Thistle buttons and tartan facings. We hope to get Lord Rosebery down to our dinner on November 30th.' But the link that bound him to the inner circle of his friends—Raymond Asquith, Cuthbert Medd, Harold Baker—was the pleasure of intelligence. They were, intellectually, an élite.

Buchan, Asquith, Baker, Medd, all crowned their Oxford careers with Firsts in Greats; Asquith and Medd won prize fellowships at All Souls, Baker became a Fellow of New College; Buchan won the Stanhope and Newdigate Prizes, Asquith the Ireland and Craven, Baker the Craven and Gaisford. All but Medd became President of the Union.

Some of Buchan's friends at Glasgow, particularly H. N. Brailsford and Joe Menzies, had been sceptical and sophisticated, witty and irreverent; but Asquith, Baker and Medd had a more influential world to be sceptical and irreverent about, the world of politics, London society and country-houses. Though lack of ambition was with them basic good form, they belonged by birth and education to a society where clever young men are helped to find the right jobs more easily than in Scotland. They had gone to Oxford in the natural course of events; Buchan had gone as a result of his own determination and extremely hard work. He could not afford not to be ambitious, not to think of the next step. Even the unworldly Mr Buchan at times viewed life as an affair of effort and competition, as when he once observed 'I wouldn't wonder if Willie gets to the top first.' Like Scott, in a passage which Buchan had copied into his commonplace book as a schoolboy, and often quoted, he could say 'I was born a Scotsman, and a bare one. Therefore I was born to fight my way in the world.' The lessons of poverty—'the first and biggest fact in our history'—were, he once wrote, that nothing comes without effort; that we value most what costs us most; that it hardens the fibre of a man and toughens his character; and that it makes a man take risks.

Yet this staunch and purposeful worker, this careful planner of his life, was enchanted by the ease and grace of his Oxford friends, their combination of intellectual brilliance with apparent lack of ambition, their refusal to take life seriously—and by the air of infinite leisure which hung about them. Thirty years later, in a speech at Winchester, and referring particularly to Raymond Asquith and Harold Baker, he said how struck he had been, coming from 'the hard, bare strenuous life of a Scots university,' by 'their amazing maturity.'

They seemed, while still in their teens, to have covered the whole range of human knowledge. Their urbanity put to shame my angularity. Their humanism confounded my dogmatism. They were certain of only one thing—that all things were uncertain. They were the very opposite of what we used to call 'banausic.' They were interested in the value of things and not the prize.

With this maturity there went, in Raymond Asquith and Cubby Medd, a mordant humour: Medd, 'that sardonic Balliol wit,' whom many considered the most brilliant of the group, was charming to his friends, but often gave to others the impression of being supercilious and ill-mannered. Some years after coming down from Oxford, Buchan wrote to a friend who had reported an adverse opinion on some Balliol men at a ball:

I don't think the description of the Balliol set is fair, though from the point of view of a hostess giving a ball it may be pardoned. Anyhow I differ from it in not being dirty and not being conspicuously blasphemous. 'Woman-hating' is not quite accurate. The true members of the set never troubled themselves sufficiently about the subject to form any opinion. But if the epithet means merely the opposite of 'susceptible' I gladly accept it.

Asquith and Medd were amused that Buchan could be so practical and successful, and yet so romantic. They teased him about his seriousness and Scottishness: 'You would-be outspoken pragmatical, puritanical Scotty you'—goes a letter from Medd. But they also respected him for his greater range of experience. He had shouldered adult responsibilities at an age when they, however precocious intellectually, had not yet had their independence or their judgment put to the test. For some years he had been entirely supporting himself. He had appeared in the *Yellow Book*; he was already in *Who's Who*, along with their fathers—possibly the only person in the 1898 volume whose occupation was 'undergraduate.'* And if they had the entry to country-houses, he had the entry to London publishers. They were tremendously impressed by his books and his journalism. 'He was so quick to do these things,' recalled Harold Baker, 'and then come rioting with us. We thought it wonderful—to do these things so well and at the same time do all the things we did.' He specially remembered Buchan at dinners, and on gay evenings such as the meetings of the Horace Club. This had been founded by the four of them, Asquith, Baker, Medd and Buchan. Its properties were 'an urn and a book'; an Arbiter was

---

* The full entry (which is on the same page as James Bryce, the 6th Duke of Buccleuch and the 13th Earl of Buchan) reads: BUCHAN, John, undergraduate. b. Perth, 26 Aug. 1875, e.s. of Rev. John Buchan and Helen, d. of John Masterton, Broughton Green, Peeblesshire. *Educ.* Glasgow University; Brasenose College, Oxford. Stanhope Historical Essay, 1897. Scholar of Brasenose, 1895; member Middle Temple, 1897. *Publications*: Sir Quixote, 1895; Musa Piscatrix, 1896; Scholar Gipsies, 1896; Sir Walter Raleigh, 1897; John Burnet of Barns, 1898 etc. *Recreations*: golf, cycling, climbing, angling and most field sports. *Address*: Brasenose College, Oxford. *Club*: Devonshire.

elected by lot to be responsible for each meeting when the members*
read their poems, and to draw up the rules—'For comic poems,
Hor. Sat. I, ix should serve as a limit to broadness of the comic
vein.' Arnold Ward of Balliol was the first Arbiter; the second was
John Buchan. The rules he issued ran:

1. The Club will meet at 8 p.m. on Wednesday, June 15, in the President's Garden, at Magdalen College.
2. The rules for the First Meeting will hold good. The Arbiter will
invite all members to read poems, determining the order by lot. Members
are invited to bring contributions of fruit, etc. after Horatian precedent.
3. Rule 6, which refers to the bringing of guests, may, on this occasion,
be interpreted so as to admit ladies.

In his memoir of Raymond Asquith in the privately printed
These for Remembrance Buchan has described some of their other
enterprises: canoeing as far as they could go between a winter's
dawn and dusk; walking to London or Cambridge in twenty-four
hours; riding across country on a compass course, regardless of
back gardens or flooded rivers; sleeping out of doors; scrambling
over Oxford roofs (once the short-sighted Aubrey Herbert fell
through into a bank, and was held up by a manager with a gun),
and never giving a damn for authority, or thinking of the consequences.

Such ploys were gayer and wilder than the golf and bicycle rides
of Buchan's early Oxford days; some of them were a good deal
more expensive. By his third year he could afford the dinners,
tandems, four-in-hands, the subscriptions to Vincent's, the Canning and the New Caledonian Club, and the green dinner-jacket
with tartan facings. The publication by Lane, during his first Long

---

* The members were R. Asquith, H. T. Baker, H. Belloc, John Buchan, F. W.
Bussell, the Rev. A. G. Butler, H. E. Butler, A. D. Godley, the Hon. A. M. Herbert,
St John Lucas, A. C. Medd, L. R. F. Oldershaw, Professor J. S. Phillimore, Pro-
fessor F. York Powell, the President of Magdalen (T. H. Warren), Nowell C. Smith,
Arnold Ward, J. Williams, E. Wright, A. E. Zimmern.

Honorary members were the Hon. Maurice Baring, Laurence Binyon, the Rev.
H. C. Beeching, Professor W. J. Courthope, F. Y. Eccles, J. Meade Falkner, Pro-
fessor W. R. Hardie, Sir Rennell Rodd, Owen Seaman, Frank Taylor, T. Humphry
Ward. B. H. Blackwell was Keeper of the Records, and published a book of mem-
bers' verses, *The Book of the Horace Club 1898–1901*. Among the poems read to the
Club were Belloc's 'The South Country,' and 'Sussex Drinking Song,' five poems
by Buchan ('Ballad of Grey Weather,' 'The Gipsy's Song to the Lady Cassilis,'
'From the Pentlands, Looking North and South,' 'The Last Song of Oisin' and
'The Soldier of Fortune'), a number of Greek epigrams by Raymond Asquith, one
of them on the Dreyfus case, taking Dreyfus's side, and a Madrigal to Queen
Victoria by T. H. Warren.

Vacation, of *Scholar Gipsies*, a collection of his essays, and of *Musa Piscatrix*, his fishing anthology, had extended his reputation.

> *The Times* gave a tremendously good review of *Scholar Gipsies*, and the *Academy* . . . gave me two columns. All the reviews have been extremely favourable, even eulogistic, and Lane tells me that the book is selling very well. Unwin has begun to send me MSS., which will add to the hardships of my lot.

He was asked to review books regularly for the *Academy* ('a fearsome number . . . and I have been spending my evenings in slating them rather savagely'), turned down an offer to review for *Literature*, and was in demand for general articles: 'Two different papers write to me for articles on Lewis Carroll which I am doing my best to supply.' 'The *Academy* wired to me and called for an article on Barry Pain for its Xmas number, and as I had not read that gentleman's works, I had some trouble getting them up.'

In his first year he had scraped by on £150, just over half of which came from his Junior Hulme Scholarship; by his last year his income was over £400, £130 of which came from the Senior Hulme and £100 from John Lane's advance on *John Burnet of Barns*. This was a good deal more than many of his friends enjoyed; none of them (with the possible exception of Harold Baker and Tommy Nelson) came from very wealthy homes.* There was no struggle to keep up, none of that feeling of being debarred from joining fully in university life that could affect many undergraduates, and not only those from grammar schools. A little before Buchan's time Robert Morant (later Permanent Secretary of the Board of Education) found that 'at Oxford, as at Winchester, poverty made it very difficult for him to share in the social life and diversions of the University.' But the price to be paid for Buchan's

---

* Buchan's Oxford friends were mainly from middle-class professional families, though many had a foot in county society. Tommy Nelson's father was a publisher and printer, with an estate in Argyllshire; John Edgar's a minister; Johnnie Jameson's was a Sheriff, with a small property in Galloway; Harold Baker's was a woollen manufacturer, Liberal M.P. for Portsmouth and twice Mayor; Raymond Asquith's a barrister, Liberal M.P. and former Home Secretary, whose second wife was Margot—daughter of Sir Charles Tennant of the Glen who had often given Buchan a day's fishing. Stair Gillon and Cuthbert Medd (a parson's son, connected through the Ridleys with Lady Mary Murray) had been brought up by widowed mothers. The two aristocrats of the group were Aubrey Herbert, the son of Lord Carnarvon, and his cousin Auberon Herbert, who later succeeded an uncle to become Lord Lucas. Auberon Herbert had a highly unconventional upbringing in the New Forest with his pacifist, vegetarian, agnostic, republican father, who had been a champion of Joseph Arch and Charles Bradlaugh.

financial ease was a scrupulous husbanding of his time and work while others were relaxing. Sometimes he felt rather desperate at the constant compulsion to earn:

I am utterly swamped with MSS.—there are twelve just now in my coal-hole mixed up with my coal and faggots. When I want one I light a candle, say my prayers, get the coal-hammer and begin to burrow. I have just finished a review of Frederic Harrison's *William the Silent*.

In this tight-packed programme there was no room for organised games, and not very much for girls. The only evidence that, for Buchan and his friends, there were women studying at Oxford, is a record of an At Home at Somerville, to which he went as the guest of Miss Jane Malloch, a brilliant fellow-student from Glasgow, a great Hegelian, who later married H. N. Brailsford. (Alexander MacCallum Scott, whose view of Buchan was quoted earlier, recorded in his notebook how a fellow-student ranked Miss Malloch first, Gilbert Murray second, Buchan third, in the possession of 'that Romantic feeling' which to his mind was an important constituent of 'the highest excellence.') But during the OUDS production of *Romeo and Juliet* in 1898 Buchan wrote to Charlie Dick that 'I met Juliet at tea yesterday—she is very pretty.' (It was a Miss Lilian Collen who played the part.) And at the end of his third year he was invited to join a party for Commemoration: the other men were Tommy Nelson, Johnnie Jameson and Sandy Gillon. Nearly sixty years later two of the girls, Caroline and Olive Johnston Douglas from Dumfriesshire,* had the liveliest memory of the parties and the fun, and of John Buchan as 'very quiet and a bit shy' among the high-spirited crew. (He thought Car Douglas 'a nice fresh girl, with pretty towzy red hair, and sings like a mavis.') After the New College Ball they had breakfast in Sandy Gillon's rooms—no chaperones were remembered!—then drove off to picnic by the river, and dance reels barefoot on the wet grass. Buchan had another Commem duty to perform: to recite, at Encaenia, a part of his Newdigate Prize Poem—successful at his third attempt with 'The Pilgrim Fathers,' having failed with 'Gibraltar' (1897) and 'Theodoric the Goth in Italy' (1896). 'Commemoration went off very well and I managed to recite my Newdigate better than I expected ever to be able to spout my own nonsense.' Rather high-flown 'nonsense' it was, and more about the spirit of adventure in general than the Pilgrim Fathers of history:

* Now Lady Kinross and Mrs Carruthers.

No faltering shakes their steadfastness whose ways
Lie on the King's Path to the end of days . . .
Though o'er our path the wrack of battle roll,
No wars perplex the sabbath of our soul.
What though the body be a sacrifice
To the fierce sun or the inclement skies,
The lurking wild beast or the savage king,
We are not sad for all their threatening.
Life is not meat nor drink nor raiment fine,
But a man's courage and the fire divine.

In London, too, he was quite at home. He entered his name at the Middle Temple, and started to eat his dinners in March 1897; he was elected to the Devonshire Club; he usually spent a few days in town on his way to and from Oxford, sometimes staying with Lane in Albany, to see publishers and editors, and enjoy himself. 'I had a very gay time in town, what with dining out and meeting people,' he wrote in October 1896, and the following May, 'I had a gay and pleasant time in London and met a great many interesting people. I went to all the Galleries including the Private View of the Royal Academy. You should have seen the frocks! They were wonderful, particularly Mrs George Alexander.' 'On Friday I met Foster Carr, and went to the Rembrandt Gallery with Algy Wyndham and his mother and sister.'

His Oxford friendships extended his range in Scotland, too, socially as well as geographically. Most of the members of the Commem party of 1898 foregathered a few days later at Ardwall in Galloway, the home of Johnnie Jameson's father the Sheriff.* 'I have just had a royal fortnight in Galloway,' he wrote to Gilbert Murray on July 8. They drove, sailed and walked—there was an expedition to the Dungeon of Buchan when they lunched off *pâté de fois gras* and Burgundy—galloped miles on the sands of Fleet, and swam their horses over the estuary.

In his host Buchan discovered a new kind of Scot—or redis-covered an old, for the Sheriff belonged far more to the end of the eighteenth century than to the nineteenth. Like Stevenson's Weir of Hermiston, he was a lawyer laird, with robust religious con-victions, and a power of plain speaking and strong language. He spoke a forceful, antique Scots—'I have a thrawn wame,' he would say of a stomach-ache—and his blasphemy, said Buchan, 'is so

---

* Though his home was in Galloway, he was Sheriff of Perth, till in 1904 he was raised to the Scottish Bench as Lord Ardwall. He was a first cousin of Effie Gray, who married first Ruskin, then Millais.

wonderful and uninterrupted that it almost becomes a sort of rugged piety.' Staying at Ardwall could be quite an ordeal. Jameson blended his own whisky in a great cask, and 'it was no light task to dine with him in his best days.' On one young guest, who had queried the use of foreign missions which were one of Jameson's enthusiasms, he rounded ferociously: 'You have heard the Gospel, you've had your chance, and if you choose to go to Hell, it can't be helped. But the heathen have had no chance, and I'm here to see that they get it.' Buchan was not intimidated, perhaps because on his first encounter with Jameson, dining at the Gridiron at Oxford, he had survived a searching cross-examination on sheep. He found that Jameson's infinite good humour, and his freedom from the pedantries of the elderly, 'destroyed all barriers of age.'

The whitewashed, rather French-looking house of Ardwall was a much less comfortable home than Queen Mary Avenue or Broughton Green; but with the complete liberty to come and go, the families of terriers, Borzois and greyhounds, the children riding bare-legged and bare-back, Jameson roaring out profanities in an accent half east-country, half Border—there was a wild freedom about it quite unlike any other Scottish home he knew, which delighted Buchan.

In Tweeddale he began to be in demand socially. 'I am fearfully bored by people in this neighbourhood whom I scarcely know sending me invitations to meals. The result is that I have lost all my manners and become horribly rude.' When he stayed at Broughton Green he preferred his old fishing and hill-walking and the life of the farm (in that same July of 1898 he was savaged by a prize bull which he and Willie were helping the farm servants to handle). And his spring walking-tour was the high point of Buchan's year, as the spring 'Border raids' had been of the young Walter Scott's: 'almost the happiest recollections of my youth, and I want you to have the same,' Buchan wrote to one of his sons, who was planning a spring holiday forty years later. In 1896 it was through the hills by Loch Skene and the Grey Mare's Tail: in 1897 in Eskdale and Dumfriesshire; and there was a further tour that summer, in Galloway with Taffy Boulter, who had bicycled up from Worcester to Dumfries. Equipped with fishing-rods, half a melon, a flask of cordial, a sketch-book, and the manuscript of a story Buchan was writing they walked from Dalry up the Ken and the Polharrow Burn to the Forest of Buchan: then over the Clints of Millfire and through the bog to the Back Hill of Buss, where the shepherd gave them some tea, lent them a plaid each, and escorted them across the Siller Flow of Buchan.

By this time it was about 5 p.m., and we set our faces to the Wolf's Slock. After a hard climb we got to the top and in about an hour looked down on Loch Enoch. I shall never forget that sight as long as I live. The loch was one sheet of burnished silver with its wonderful milk-white sand, and islands glowing like jewels all athwart it. Sheer above us was Merrick, all swathed in white mist except his top, which was exactly as if a beacon had been lit. Boulter could find nothing to compare it to except the Heavenly City that John saw in Patmos. All the other great lochs of the Dungeon were spread out at our feet—Neldricken, Arron, Valley, Macaterick, Trool etc. We went down to a promontory, had a long swim; then I fished, but had very indifferent sport. About 8.30 we lit a large fire of heather and bog-oak and made supper. Then we rolled ourselves in our plaids, lit our pipes, and lay down before the fire and slept. A horrid dank mist came quite low and shrouded us in. About 1 o'clock I was wakened by a raven, which kept up a dismal croaking on the island opposite. At 2.30 I got up and fished for a little. Then we went for a swim. Did you ever bathe before sunrise? It is a queer effect to be swimming in the blackest water, and see shafts of golden light cleaving ravines in front of you. When dressing we were nearly eaten by midges—they must have been as bad as mosquitoes. Then we set off to Loch Macaterick—6 miles off, where we had better sport. Thence we walked 13 miles to the Back Hill of the Buss, where the shepherd gave us a hearty breakfast. Thence we did the walk of 20 miles home in something like four and a half hours.

In the spring of 1898, with John Edgar, he went up to the Highlands. Starting from Bridge of Orchy, they walked up through the Black Mount to Kingshouse Inn on the moor of Rannoch and, after an unorthodox ascent of Buachille Etive under snow, walked down Glencoe to Ballachulish and Appin, where they followed the tracks of David Balfour and Alan Breck Stewart. (Out of this Buchan wrote an article for the *Academy* on 'The Country of *Kidnapped*'—7 May 1898.)

Buchan very much wanted his family to enter into all his new life and, if possible, share in some of its pleasures. He wrote regularly to his mother and sister—less often to his father, who never wrote a letter if he could help it—of all his doings, his friends, his plans, his work. He invited Mrs Buchan and Anna to visit him at Oxford during his last year; he put them up at the Mitre, showed them all the sights, gave a dinner-party for them in his rooms, took them to the OUDS production of *A Midsummer Night's Dream* (it was Anna's first theatre). Out of his first earnings he had bought his mother a pendant of opals, a rather startling change from Mrs

Buchan's usual accoutrements, the necklace of seeds from Jeru-salem, feather boa, and the watered silk ribbon that held her spectacles. When he sold the serial rights of *John Burnet of Barns* he bought Anna a bicycle, and later gave her a fur: 'I thought I might as well get a good one, for it will wear better, and if you are having the cauld blast that we have it will come in handy.' He was concerned in his family's life—remembered birthdays, asked about the Assembly, hoped his father had had good congregations at the John Knox Church, and attended it regularly himself when he was at home: 'I will make a point of being a Sabbath in Glasgow.' But he did not want his family to assume that he would be com-mitted to Glasgow life, or to cast him in a rôle that was not what he himself had planned, and he was very cross to hear that he had been proposed as a deacon at John Knox. '*I will not have it*,' he wrote to Anna. 'I am away from home compulsorily for more than half the year, and I am always away another quarter, so it is a mere farce proposing such a thing.' He spent little time in the family home, always preferring for the vacation his uncle's house in Peebles, or the farm at Broughton Green, where he could combine work with fishing and walking.

However fond he was of them, he looked at his home and his family with more critical eyes after his absences. Anna, the chief family confidante for his hopes, plans and feelings, and specially sensitive to any change in him, realised that the centre of his life was no longer in Glasgow.* The pride of his parents in his prizes, distinctions and literary success was qualified—in Mrs Buchan's case, at any rate—by doubts about certain aspects of his life in the South. She had a deep-rooted suspicion of the Church of England.† She was always doubtful of the propriety of going outside the sphere you were born in, and would rather her son had been settling to a minister's life in Scotland than hobnobbing with the sons of English Cabinet Ministers in Oxford. To be congratulated on John's doings was no doubt gratifying: but Mrs Buchan would rather the occasion for congratulation had been a sermon, or a

---

* 'Eliza always longed intensely for Jim's coming, but when he came she was conscious of a vague disappointment. She seemed so near him when he was away, and so oddly at a distance when he was actually there. His tales of people she did not know, his descriptions of things, of a dinner here or a dance there, seemed somehow to make a stranger of him.' Anna Buchan (O. Douglas): *Eliza for Common*.

† Lord Haldane records in *An Autobiography* (1929) how his parents thought of sending him, after Edinburgh University, to Balliol, but 'dreaded the supposed influence of the Anglican Church atmosphere of Oxford.' This was in the 1870s.

speech at the Free Church Assembly, than a new novel, or a speech at the Oxford Union. And having been such a splendid manager of the elder John Buchan's modest income, she tended to be critical of what appeared to her the extravagances of the younger. But on this point her son was firm; he would not let his mother criticise or discuss what he did with his money. Gradually there came to be a number of non-discussable subjects between them: those were the terms on which happy relations could be maintained. Buchan continued to be the centre of his family's world; however attached to them he remained, they ceased to be the centre of his.

There was the same natural loosening of ties with his Glasgow contemporaries. He contributed occasionally to the *Glasgow University Magazine*, read papers to the Alexandrian and Philosophical Societies, looked up his friends in the vacations, sent them his books, and sometimes seemed to plan for them as purposefully as for himself and his brothers (the career he had mapped out for Willie was Oxford and the Indian Civil Service; for Walter, the Scottish Bar). He prodded Charlie Dick to publish his sketches, and secured him the job of editing *The Compleat Angler* for the Scott Library, for which he himself had edited Bacon's *Essays*; he gave Brailsford an introduction to John Lane. He wrote freely about his Oxford doings to Charlie Dick and threatened, after Dick became a divinity student in 1898, to come and hear him preach his first sermon at Carsphairn in Galloway.

So beware of airing any heretical opinions, for I am strictly orthodox. When I was young and godless and intended to go in for the Church, I used to resolve that my first sermon would be on Prince Charles from the text in Jeremiah—'Weep ye not for the dead, neither bemoan him: but weep sore for him that goeth away: for he shall return no more, nor see his native country.' I make you a present of the suggestion. By the way, who is the 1st Isaiah? Was the 2nd a sort of Second Mrs Tanqueray or anything of that sort? If you preach about the Blessed Virgin, you'll get shot out of the Unreformed Presbyterian Kirk. So be warned; or better still, leave the U.P.K. and join the Reformed Presbyterians, like J. Edgar and myself.

He did go to Carsphairn, bicycling seventy miles, and took the preacher out to lunch in the hotel after his ordeal. But a year later he was writing, rather sadly, 'I was reminded of you in turning over some old letters the other day, and it seemed to me that we were drifting lamentably out of acquaintance.' Katie Cameron was speaking for a number of Buchan's old acquaintances when she said, 'We thought he had become rather Oxfordy.'

In his fourth year Buchan, and his black collie Dhonuill Dhu, shared rooms with Taffy Boulter and John Edgar at 41 High Street, almost opposite the Schools: 'rather more lordly' than they had been used to, Boulter remembered. (He also remembered Hilaire Belloc shouting from the street below: 'Buchan, have you any beer up there? Very well, I'll come up.') Under the direction of Francis Wylie and of Dr F. W. Bussell (a mildly eccentric scholar who had been Pater's chief Brasenose friend) Buchan had been working very hard at Greats. Philosophy and ancient history were very much more to his taste than the close study of classical texts required in Mods. 'Of course I like the work I am at now and get on much more quickly.' In philosophy he had the advantage of having covered a good deal of the ground in Professor Jones's class at Glasgow; indeed there was talk at one time of doing Greats in four terms, but in the end he took the normal seven. He aimed to do most of the reading in the vacations; he read '360 pages of Plato (Bekker's text) in a fortnight' at Broughton, and ten days later reported 'I have finished Plato and am now labouring in Aristotle's Ethics . . . what hideous Greek the man wrote!' Among the philosophers whose lectures he attended during term were F. H. Bradley and H. H. Joachim, while from A. H. Greenidge he acquired an interest in Greek and Roman Law. At Balliol he heard J. A. Smith on 'Methods and Concepts of Science,' and Edward Caird on 'The Moral Philosophy of Aristotle.' Wylie, a philosophy tutor with a gift for drawing the best out of his pupils, found in Buchan a 'brilliant, and already mature mind.' Buchan attended Dr Bussell's lectures on an obscure period of Byzantine history ('You don't know how brutally ignorant I am,' he replied when it was pointed out that this course was rather out of his main line of work) and Bussell was struck by his particular interest in the survival of pre-Christian cults.

It was difficult to keep scholarship and romance in separate compartments. A notebook titled 'Notes on Philosophy, J. Buchan, Oct. 1898,' begins with notes on Hegel (possibly from lectures by Bradley) and a quotation from William James's *Will to Believe*. A few pages on comes 'The Outgoing of the Tide,' a story later published in *The Watcher by the Threshold*; then a scheme for a work on Philosophical Opportunism ('The Metaphysics of Purpose—The

Relation of Mental Attitude to Productive Energy—Creative Art—Ethics—Religion—Politics'); a fragment of an essay mentioning Huxley and Spencer; and Chapters XIX and XXI of the Jacobite romance he published in 1899, *A Lost Lady of Old Years*.

In January 1899 Buchan attained the double distinction of being chosen as *Isis* Idol No. CXLVII, and elected President of the Union. The *Isis* article (28 January 1899), with a drawing by Taffy Boulter of a Highlander defending, with a knobbly club, a phalanx of whisky bottles, begins with traditional facetiousness, then continues more soberly:

One of the finest things about him is that he has a very good idea of what is worth while and what is not . . . His powers of work are remarkable, and inspire awe in his friends; he confesses to a deep-seated loathing for what is called leisure. . . .

Our Idol is a very good business-man, and publishers world-famous for robbery have wagged their heads over him, owning they have met their match! . . . He has found out something good in everybody. All the same he can be angry when called upon in a right cause. This is established by recent experience.

In politics he is a Tory-Democrat Jacobite . . . He collects etchings. He dislikes dancing, and hates ladies . . .

He does not like to hear about his own books; he refuses to be classed as a literary man. His works have a large circulation in the United States, where the newspapers have portraits of him as a tall, melancholy man with unkempt hair and beard . . .

We know of no one who has had more success, or deserved it better. He is as popular with men as he is with Fortune. We do hate eulogy; but we are helpless.

Six months earlier Buchan had been featured by the short-lived *Oxford J.C.R.* as No. 38 of its Portrait Gallery (14 June 1898): with C. F. Garbett and F. E. Smith, he was one of the very few chosen for other than athletic distinction. He was depicted as Librarian of the Union, with the citation:

An author whose latest work we noticed last week. Attained at a tender age the fame attaching to mention in *Who's Who*. Is fond of climbing many things, Parnassus among others. His poem on the Pilgrim Fathers is invaluable to the student of history, though it is said that the author composed it after reading about the Canterbury pilgrims and Cowley fathers and combining his information. Is an excellent Librarian of the Union. Has been known to catch fish.

Not everyone shared the view of the *Isis* and *J.C.R.* 'In my Oxford days,' wrote a Balliol acquaintance, E. S. P. Haynes, to

Buchan in 1912, 'I had exactly the same prejudice against you
that I have always had against Jowett; not only were you invariably
successful but I thought you were an apostle of success. . . . I am
always "agin the Government" and I most unfairly associated you
with the powers that be.' 'My dear Granny,' answered Buchan,
'I know I was a horrid young prig at Oxford but I really was never
like Jowett.'

Buchan had been a regular speaker at the Union since his first
summer. Speaking on the paper, he had opposed Garbett of Keble
on 'the uselessness of the Concert and the incompetence of Her
Majesty's Government,' Belloc and F. E. Smith also taking part.
With Belloc he had moved in 'a clever and amusing speech'
that 'the popular literature of today is a sign of national degrada-
tion.' With Johnnie Jameson and R. S. Rait he had condemned the
Kailyard school of novelists: 'I ran all the way from dinner and
arrived out of breath. The result was that I was completely at my
ease;' and the *J.C.R.* reported that 'he ended with an extremely
witty application of a good story.' Supported by Raymond Asquith,
he 'regarded with apprehension' the present position of Great
Britain among the powers of Europe, had no confidence in the
policy of H.M. Government in the Far East, and affirmed 'That
this house does not believe in International Morality.' Visitors from
the Cambridge Union took part in this last debate and the *Oxford
J.C.R.* reported that:

The scriptural allusions, usually so typical of Mr Asquith, fell on this
occasion from the Librarian's lips. Mr Buchan concluded with a good
Scotch story, well told. We do not think we have ever heard the Librarian
so good; we certainly have never known him so lively.

Buchan had been elected to the Library Committee in June
1897; to the Librarianship in March 1898, on the proposal of the
President, E. C. Bentley; and in November he was elected President in a three-cornered contest, with 169 votes as against E. Armi-
tage Smith's 99 and H. D. Reilly's 67; Johnnie Jameson was
elected Secretary, and Raymond Asquith Librarian. Buchan's
election brought congratulations from Raymond and Cubby,
written at 2 a.m.:

We are both very drunk: we have both taken our αs at the Quadwranglers
this evening; but that does not prevent us from tendering to you our very
heartiest congratulations on our own behalf and on that of all right-think-
ing men in this University (and the world) upon your election. I wonder if

you are as drunk as we are? We all hope so. We are authorised by the *English CLUB* to communicate to you our sincere admiration of the successful efforts of a struggling and oppressed nationality.

A more pompous note was struck by the President of Magdalen:*

The President's Chair has not seldom held those who have come to notable distinction as public men. I hope and think it not improbable that it will hold next term one of the Literary Statesmen whom your brilliant countryman [Rosebery] so happily described and discussed at Edinburgh some ten days back.

Buchan's plans for his term of office were ambitious—one of his notebooks has a scribbled list of celebrities' names and addresses: J. Chamberlain, Gerald Balfour, John Morley, George Wyndham. But the only distinguished outsider during his term of office was Edmund Gosse, 'deploring the spread of what is called taste.' Other topics discussed during Buchan's presidency were Home Rule, a formal alliance with America, the disestablishment of the Welsh Church, France as a Great Power, 'That the Liberal Party must either renounce its principles or embrace Collectivism' (R. C. K. Ensor and A. D. Lindsay† for, Belloc against), 'That in the opinion of this House the great democratic joke is almost played out,' 'That a university for the people is no impossibility.' There is general agreement that he was an effective President, prompt in the despatch of private business, and had the debates well in control; but opinions differ on his effectiveness as a speaker. Harold Baker always found his speeches impressive, though 'rather hard to make out because of his Scotch voice'; Taffy Boulter also remembered the voice and, though summing him up as 'not a very good speaker—not anything like as fluent as F. E. Smith or Belloc,' emphasised that 'he always had something to say that was solid.' He was a poor party man; often, as in the debates when he was

* Raymond Asquith's Tennysonian parody, 'On a Viscount who died on the Morrow of a Bump Supper,' is also a parody of Warren, who was given to compose in the measure of *In Memoriam*, and who dearly loved a lord. Here is one verse:

> We met, we stood, we faced, we talked,
> While those of baser birth withdrew.
> I told you of an earl I knew,
> You said you thought the wine was corked.

The poem is printed in Buchan's *These For Remembrance*, p. 73.

† 'Buchan was smiling in the chair,' this freshman from Glasgow reported home after a debate: 'The form of wit which seems to appeal to the English mind is to refer to "Gaelic Scots" and wave a hand towards Buchan and Johnnie Jameson who is secretary. Any reference to haggis receives loud and prolonged applause.' I thank Mr T. Lindsay for showing me this letter.

teamed with Raymond Asquith, supporting a Liberal view but for Conservative reasons. Indeed, when he declared himself a Conservative, in the Far East debate, many were surprised.

Buchan's four years at Oxford moved to their expected climax in summer 1899, when he was awarded a First in Greats. His Schools had been enlivened by Raymond Asquith's fooling:

I had a free afternoon, and Raymond and I resolved to be American tourists. We bought wideawake hats, hired an open carriage, and with Baedekers in our hands and our feet on the cushions drove into the country. In some village the name of which I have forgotten, we drew up at an inn, and Raymond addressed the assembled rustics on the virtues of total abstinence. It was the most perfect parody conceivable of a temperance speech, and it completely solemnized his hearers. Then he ordered beer all round.

The result of Schools brought from Raymond characteristic congratulations: 'It was a vast relief to me to see—in so ill-constructed a list—that the examiners had made no blunder about you.'

CHAPTER FOUR

BARRISTER AND JOURNALIST
1899–1901

'The future is before you and you have more than the usual stock of ability and spirit to meet it.'

Cosmo Lang to John Buchan, 3 November 1900

Sir Walter Raleigh used to remind undergraduates that the Oxford Final Schools and the Day of Judgment were two separate examinations. Buchan certainly regarded Greats as a stage on a planned march, and not as journey's end. Two months before his examination he had drawn up a list of *Things to be done in the near future*. On the programme for April and May were his Greats work and 'The Far Islands' (a story later included in *The Watcher by the Threshold*). In June the Greats examination, eating dinners, writing the last book of *The Half-Hearted*; July to October, working for All Souls and on *The Half-Hearted*; then 'read law hard, arrange, if possible, for journalism, write Chancellor's English Essay, work in a solicitor's office' and Bar exams were to take him to June 1900, when he would be called to the Bar.

But for all the careful planning, Buchan did not succeed at All Souls, where he was trying for a prize fellowship in history. These fellowships of a college without undergraduates involve no teaching and run for seven years. They not only confer distinction but are a tremendous help to a young man starting at the Bar. Buchan had been sanguine about the election. He and his friends realised that he probably had not done enough historical reading for the fellowship examination; but there had been an impression that All Souls could pick and choose and not pay too much attention to paper-work. 'I shouldn't spoil a vac for it,' Raymond Asquith had advised; 'I don't suppose you will have any serious competitors.' As a number of All Souls Fellows were known to be anxious to have

Buchan, it was felt to be a foregone conclusion. On the back of a letter from Taffy Boulter he had scribbled the title for a projected book: '*Opportunism—an Essay in the Exposition of an Attitude*. By John Buchan, Barrister-at-Law; Fellow of All Souls College, Oxford.' But this year the electors did go by paper-work, and gave the history fellowship to Dougal Malcolm. 'The worst has happened,' Buchan wrote to his mother; 'I have not got the All Souls. The general opinion in Oxford is that the election is preposterous. I am of course bitterly disappointed, but I will recover. . . . I must cut my coat according to my cloth and take humbler lodgings in town than I intended.' To Gilbert Murray he wrote:

I am rather cross just now, for I have been rejected at All Souls, where everybody thought I was safe. I hate not to do the things I am expected to do.

And to William Blackwood:

As everybody expected me to get it I feel rather ashamed of myself; I shall try and retrieve my credit next year.

He was cheered by 'dozens of letters from dons and undergraduates and from several fellows of All Souls, all declaring that my refusal is a disgrace.' Francis Wylie wrote that 'we are convinced that they will be sorry one day that your distinctions are not part of the All Souls record,' Dr A. G. Butler of Oriel (ex-headmaster of Haileybury), was caustic, sympathetic and sensible:

They have made, I think, not for the first time, a great mistake; and I believe you will live to prove this to them . . . Without however underrating the advantages of such a position, still I think that it is often good for a man to be cut adrift from Oxford. There is little or no career here.

Rejection by All Souls startled, annoyed and wounded Buchan, but it did not scar him as it did Hilaire Belloc in 1895, who, according to his biographer Robert Speaight, regarded it as 'a personal catastrophe. He never forgave All Souls for refusing him. . . . The disappointment became an obsession. . . . The refusal of a Fellowship struck him like the tragic ending of a love-affair. . . . Oxford had brusquely turned away from him.'

Buchan's attitude was that *he* had rejected All Souls. He mentioned the other fellowships he might try for: 'I will not go in for All Souls again for worlds.' And he would make them see what they had missed.

All Souls of course have a perfect right to elect whom they please, but if their aim is to get the best men, I hope to make them in time very sorry for their action.

His friends considered he had taken the reverse well, without grumbles: 'he was always looking ahead.' A week after the blow he had cooled down and was annoyed by 'a vicious attack on the All Souls Election in a paper called the *X*.' 'It is violently in support of me, but I am very sorry about it. I like Malcolm so much, and it is sure to hurt his feelings. He came to see me last night, and was very nice.'

And he was reassuring his mother that even without the £200-a-year Fellowship, penury did not stare him in the face.

I am very well, and you must not take on too seriously. I shan't take nasty lodgings in London—only unfashionable ones, and it will be very good for me to have to lie low and work hard. If I had got a fellowship this year, I should probably have gone hunting and expensive things of that kind which I couldn't really afford. I shall have between £200 and £250 for the next two and a half years, and I should be able to live comfortably enough on that in a quiet way. I wonder if you remember that you owe me £10. Please pay it into my account when you can manage it.

For all his brave words, Buchan did try again for All Souls in 1900, one of his motives certainly being the wish to retrieve his credit; but again he was beaten. Although one of the new Fellows was a particular *bête noire*, Buchan was not, this time, too much cast down. 'I felt annoyed at the time but have forgotten it now,' he wrote to his brother Willie a fortnight after the result; but he wished that he had not exposed himself to such a conspicuous election, 'for it is a painful thing for a man's pride to be rejected by a body whom he in no way respects in favour of at least one man whom he wholeheartedly despises.' The occasion produced an avuncular letter from Cosmo Lang.*

Dear Buchan,
Probably you have already heard the result of our election. I am sincerely sorry that you were not elected, and my sorrow is shared by a very large number of the Fellows, indeed I think I may safely say by all. There was a very striking desire to elect you, and to press every point in your

---

* It was natural that Cosmo Lang should feel avuncular towards Buchan, whose background and career, at a ten-year remove, so closely paralleled his own. Lang too was the son of a Glasgow Manse; had gone from Glasgow University to Oxford (he was at Balliol); had been President of the Union, and had worked, like Buchan, in the chambers of J. A. Hamilton. He too enjoyed active holidays in the wilder parts of Scotland, admired Scott and Stevenson, and had written a romantic novel of the '45, *The Young Clanroy* (published when he was Chaplain of Magdalen).

favour. But to all the good desire in the world a majority felt that the examination placed a limit. And I will tell you frankly how you stood in regard to the examination. I think you would like, and that you ought, to know, though I must ask you to treat anything I may say as confidential. It was very plain that in the special History papers you had not done justice to your abilities. The examiners—who are asked to give a special detailed report—put one or two others in front of you in this respect. It was your general work—the General paper and the essay—that brought you forward and gave you a leading place. Had your specially historical work been up to that level you would have been undoubtedly elected. It only shows that you would have been wise to have read more definitely and systematically for the examination. I am afraid literary and other work and inevitable distractions have been allowed to take up too much of the time that ought to have been given to general historical reading. I did anything that I wisely could do to support your claims, both on personal grounds and on the grounds of the examination. But—though I know with much difficulty and with no little regret—the College as a whole felt that the claims of others on their actual work were far too strong to be passed over. Whitmore, Harrison and several others wished me specially to express to you their great regret that we cannot congratulate you and ourselves on your election.

So there it is. I know it will be a real disappointment to you. It is a very real one to me. But after all the future is before you and you have more than the usual stock of ability and spirit to meet it, and more than usual encouragement in the successes over a wide field you have already achieved.

I hope that we may meet again and not infrequently: perhaps at some General Assembly of the True Kirk! Meanwhile I hope that this disappointment will only momentarily affect that 'alertness and freshness of spirit' which you rightly describe as the best endowment of man.

Yours sincerely

C. G. LANG

But this second reverse was not the blow to Buchan that it would have been to Lang, who had been elected to All Souls after a first failure. Buchan had a tougher, more resilient temperament and had many more irons in the fire. The chief practical result of the failure was simply this loss of £200 a year; it did not deflect him from his long-laid plans. Apart from a moment of restlessness in his third year when various acquaintances were going far afield—'Crowfoot to Phrygia, Pennell to Thibet'—and when he proposed to take Greats as quickly as possible, then 'travel in East Asia Minor . . . doing some historical work, and writing letters to the *Chronicle* on the political aspect of the country,' he had been determined, since early 1897, to go to the Bar.

So in January 1900 he was installed at 4 Brick Court in the Temple, which he shared with a contemporary from Balliol, R. D.

Denman, and was working with a firm of solicitors in Bedford Row. He had asked the father of his Oxford friend E. S. P. Haynes to take him for a fee in the office of Hunter & Haynes where many Bar students learnt the routine of a solicitor's work; but Mr Haynes told him that as he would be practising in Common Law he would do better in the office of Mr Rawle, then President of the Law Society, who had a large agency practice. Buchan took quickly to the office work, and was soon presiding over creditors' meetings to the manner born. A letter to Charlie Dick on January 27 gives his first impressions of living in London. (The South African War had started the previous October.)

I have been leading a curious life lately, very busy and keen on my law, very gay, and at the same time tormented with proposals to go to the front, which unhappily fall in with my desires. These last I have now finally conquered, and I can now watch my friends go off without special bitterness. [Johnnie Jameson had joined the Imperial Yeomanry, Auberon Herbert had gone out as *The Times* correspondent.] My solicitors' work is peculiar. It is an enormous office, and as they do not take pupils except in exceptional cases, they show me a great deal of work. I find that I am picking up the odds and ends of procedure with great facility. I am going to devil for a specialist in commercial law, so after my office work is done I am going for two months into a bank. Then I shall be called about Jan. 1901. I am acquiring an enormous craze for law. Nothing has ever impressed me more with a sense of profound intellectual force than the decisions and pleadings of some of our great lawyers. My practical work is very curious. I go and inspect documents, I wrangle with other solicitors on the taxing of costs at Somerset House, and I watch cases in court for our clients. One day last week I was told to take a young girl, a sister of the respondent in a Society divorce case, down to the Court to get her deposition. She was very young, very pretty and very smartly dressed, and she was very nervous. She was perpetually clutching my arm, and then she began to cry, and—well, I never was so miserable in my life. I got furious at the thought that a young girl should be made to go through this mire. I am afraid that I am rather too sentimental ever to do well in the divorce court.

I have been dining out a great deal, at some charming houses. One I must tell you about. I went to dine with Lady Arthur Russell (the Duke of Bedford's sister-in-law) in South Audley Street. It is a wonderful old 18th century house, with beautiful family pictures. Then a party of us—three Russells, Herbert Lowther and his sister, and the Home Secretary [Sir Matthew White Ridley] went to the Haymarket to see *She Stoops to Conquer*. We agreed that it was the most charming play we had ever seen. Altogether the whole evening had a sort of 18th century flavour which I found very pleasant. By the by White Ridley told me a piece of news which is not generally known. He said that Methuen had been recalled, but that the news would be kept secret to break it more easily. If only some newspaper person got a hold of this! He also said that the Cabinet had had a private wire from Buller, saying that his present operations were merely a forlorn hope and that Ladysmith must fall. I hope it isn't true.

I find that my office work—which is only 10–5—gives me a good deal of time for other things. An article I had in the *Spectator* last week on 'Russia's Imperial Ideal' has excited a certain amount of comment. *Blackwood* want me to do an article on Lord Mansfield, so I am working at that. But my really serious books—my study of Disraeli and my study of Calvinism—recede into the dim future. I think it is perfectly true what people say—that London is the best place in the world for *busyness*, but the worst place for laborious and sustained intellectual work. I find that one is always keen, but it is a keenness which issues only in little things.

Later in the year he went to the chambers of J. A. Hamilton (afterwards Lord Sumner) as his last pupil; when Hamilton took silk early in 1901 Buchan went to Sidney Rowlatt's chambers. Rowlatt, Counsel to the Inland Revenue and one of the juniors to the Attorney-General (Sir Robert Finlay), gave Buchan the chance of devilling a Parliamentary Bill for him. In Rowlatt Buchan found an enthusiast as well as a teacher, and his own enthusiasm increased; he acquired 'a fair degree of legal scholarship,' read the lives of lawyers, and started to expand his work on Mansfield into a book. But he underestimated the amount of work needed for the Bar Finals and was ploughed the first time he sat them. In June 1901 he was called to the Bar of the Middle Temple.

He was running his legal work in double harness with the *Spectator*, which, when Buchan started writing for it, was the liveliest political weekly of the day; the *Economist*, which had been so forceful under Bagehot, was in the doldrums. The *Spectator* itself had been in decline when in 1859 it was bought by Meredith Townsend, a former editor of the *Friend of India*, who had to come home on account of his health. For nearly forty years Townsend had edited the *Spectator* in partnership with R. H. Hutton (Bagehot's lifelong friend); and after Hutton's death Townsend sold the paper in 1898 to St Loe Strachey, though he continued to write for it. Buchan was given an introduction to the new owner-editor by Dr A. G. Butler of Oriel, and soon Strachey was using him often and variously:

I am busy reviewing a book on Tactics for the *Spectator* and also a magnificent book, Colonel Durand's *Making of a Frontier*—all about Cashmire. Last night, when I was settling down to law, a message arrived from the *Spectator* asking me for an article on a special subject, so I had to sit down and write it straight off. This is journalism at last!

The *Spectator's* tone of independent Conservatism suited Buchan

well, and he found the office in Wellington Street far more congenial than the solicitor's in Bedford Row. In an article in the
centenary number of the *Spectator* (3 November 1928) he evoked
its atmosphere:

You entered by a narrow door and ascended a kind of turret staircase.
On each floor there was a single room, where you felt that anything might
happen. On the first floor St Loe Strachey sat, surrounded by new books,
writing articles on foolscap paper in his large illegible hand, breaking off to
stride about the floor and think aloud for the benefit of the visitor, overflowing with gossip and quotations, so full of notions that it seemed as if
no weekly journal could contain one-half of them. He was obviously
D'Artagnan, in his generosity and resourcefulness and zest for life.

In the room above, Meredith Townsend lurked and took snuff. He was
an old man when I first knew him, and had long left the East behind; but
its flavour still clung to him. He was clearly a holy man, a *guru* of some sort,
with his old-fashioned courtesy of speech, and his gift of delivering gnomic
judgments which annihilated space and time. . . . He was sometimes profound, and sometimes fantastic, but he was always impressive. One leader
of his began, 'Recent events have shown us that God not only reigns but
governs.' . . .

On the next floor—there may have been others, but I never penetrated
to them—Charles Graves had his dwelling and I my modest chair. It was
our business to see to the base mechanical details of editing, to correct
proofs, and, above all, to keep the great men below us straight. For
Townsend had sometimes a noble disregard of current news, and Strachey
rarely got a classical quotation quite right. Charles Graves and I were supposed to represent the critical and unsympathetic outer world.

Strachey asked Buchan to deputise for him while he went on
holiday in August 1900; Buchan had another hard bout in December, when Strachey was in Egypt; and at the end of January 1901
he had to see the paper through while the editor attended the
Queen's funeral. He was in charge of the paper for much of the
summer of 1901: 'I took over the *Spectator* yesterday and wrote
cheques for three hours. I am sure I paid away over £1000. It is
odd signing cheques for large sums.' In 1900 and 1901 he wrote
leading articles on the Russian Imperial Ideal, German Foreign
Policy, Strikes and the Poor Law, Municipal Trading, the Coal
Industry, the Politics of Roman Catholicism, Church Union in
Scotland,* Ritualism and Prosecution, Secondary Education and
the School Boards, various parliamentary subjects, Canada (also a

* The union of the Free Church and United Presbyterian churches to form the
United Free Church; one of its effects was to alter the Rev. John Buchan's church
from the 'John Knox Free Church' to the 'John Knox and Tradeston United Free
Church.'

long letter on 'Lord Durham and Canada'), and a number on South Africa: on the hospitals, the refugee camps, and on Chamberlain's plans for future administration.

Here are some samples of his journalism. On 'The Kinship of the English and American Bars' (4 August 1900):

If, then, we have in the United States a Bar essentially like our own, professing a law the same in origin as ours and closely related in substance, and at the same time exerting a great influence upon every domain of politics, we have a common interest more strong than any sudden gust of racial sentiment or half-hearted diplomatic alliance.

On 'German Experiments in Protection' (9 February 1901):

The industrial competition of Germany has long been a source of uneasiness to English manufacturers, and has penetrated even to the academic speculations of Lord Rosebery. Stated simply, it amounts to this. Germany, by demanding a high level of intelligence in her workmen, by being the first European State to appropriate and utilise labour-saving appliances on a large scale, and by organising her industries on an economic basis, is rapidly placing herself in the position of being able to outsell the English merchant, and take the place which he once occupied in foreign markets. Nor has this industrial revival been a mere private enterprise. It has received the imprimatur of Government, and has taken its place with militarism as one of the pocket-appellations for German policy.

On 'Our Duty to the Fleet' (23 February 1901):

When our apprehensions are seriously aroused, we vote money and make efforts to clean out some office, and when we have worked some salutary changes we awaken to the fact that meantime we have let things get into a pretty mess in half-a-dozen other concerns. It is all a consequence of the pernicious system of reform by panic. Rouse the public mind, reduce it to a condition of abject fear, and then reform will follow, but of the sort which robs Peter to pay Paul. Spasmodic innovations are very little better than lethargy, and they may work more lasting damage. True reform is a quickening of the public conscience, an awakening of the public intelligence, and the increase of activity flows from a quickened sense of responsibility which affects all departments.

On 'Mr Carnegie's Gift to the Scottish Universities' (25 May 1901):

Like all Scotsmen, more especially self-made Scotsmen, he [Mr Carnegie] is proud of that ancient tradition of the Scottish Colleges which made all men equal in the pursuit of learning. . . . He would undermine privilege by abolishing its fortresses, and though University education has been less of an affair of privilege in Scotland than in almost any other European country yet as things stand today there is a certain amount of class distinction in the possession of a degree. The mere fact that a poor boy may attain the same end by industry does not detract from this general character. But by freeing education the last trace of privilege would depart. The University would become what it was created to be, a corporation of workers without thought of class or fortune.

On 'Canada' (6 July 1901):

He must be a dull man indeed whose spirit is not fired by the considera-tion of the oldest, most populous, and most mature of our Colonies. To ourselves Canada has always seemed something apart from the others, with more of the old European culture, more long-descended, more Northern, and so in some ways more akin to ourselves. The stock of her population was drawn from our best. The hardy, thrifty settler who went out to clear the forest is a universe away from the treasure-hunter and the speculator. In her French population she has a curious, interesting and difficult class, who so far have been made to live harmoniously within her borders. Bands of Scottish emigrants, from the '45 to the present day, have gone west to Manitoba and Assiniboia, and founded new Badenochs and Lochabers in a country which has much of the character of their own . . . Canada is essentially a country of the larger air, where men can still face the old primeval forces of Nature and be braced into vigour, and withal so beauti-ful that it can readily inspire that romantic patriotism which is one of the most priceless assets of a people.

On top of the law, and the *Spectator*, there was social life. He was a frequent diner-out: for the evenings when he was not being entertained, he had three clubs to choose from, the Piccadilly, the Devonshire, the Cocoa Tree. Among those who entertained him were the Gathorne-Hardys, the Johnston-Douglases from Gal-loway, the Stracheys ('in their new ducal mansion'), Lady Arthur Russell, Canon Ainger of the Temple, Lady Helen Munro-Fer-guson, Andrew Lang ('I took down a rather nice Scottish girl, a Lady Cecily Baillie-Hamilton who lives near Dunbar'). Sometimes the party went on to the play: in 1900 and 1901 he saw *The Rivals* at the Haymarket, *Cyrano de Bergerac* at Wyndham's ('where a great lyrical play is travestied in the ugliest prose. But I liked Wyndham, his Cyrano is intelligible, which is more than I found Coquelin's'), *The Notorious Mrs Ebbsmith* ('an outstanding per-formance with Mrs Pat performing among a crowd of 20th rate people') and Tree's revival of *Twelfth Night*.

There was also an evening, early in 1900, at the Patriotic Display at the Alhambra, where pictures of the opposing commanders in South Africa, Cronje and Roberts, were displayed: 'I was glad to see that Cronje's portrait got nearly as much cheering as Bobs's.' Occasionally, in the season, the evening ended at a ball. To Anna,

reading the following letter in Queen Mary Avenue, as to the heroine of her *Eliza for Common*, it must indeed have appeared that her
brother had an 'aptitude for social life.'

I dined with Lady Arthur on Wednesday—Paul Phipps, Miss Florence
Wolseley (an heiress, begorrah!) the Lindleys, and Lady Mary Morrison.
Then we went to Lady Sligo's dance, which was very crowded. The
Duchess of Northumberland had the most amazing diamonds I have ever
seen. Then I went on to Lady Tweedmouth's which was horribly packed.
I danced once with Lady Grizel Cochrane, and then I got away early.

There were Saturday-to-Monday visits to the Murrays, now
living at Farnham ('I have told Gamage to send Rosalind the game
of "ping-pong," but on thinking about it I am not sure whether it
is for children or for grown-ups'); to Oxford, and to Panshanger in
Hertfordshire, the home of Bron Herbert's uncle, Lord Cowper,
who regularly entertained week-end parties of thirty to forty people.
There at Whitsun 1901 Buchan's fellow-guests included 'Arthur
Balfour, several of the Cecils and Lady Curzon.' ('His first visit to
a really great country-house, and that is always impressive' was
Buchan's comment when one of his sons stayed at Welbeck over
thirty years later.) At Easter 1900 he had ten days with Aubrey
Herbert at Pixton on Exmoor, 'after Northumberland the cream of
England.'

We climbed the hills, fished, slept out one night on the heather, and galloped horses over the downs. On Friday I rode to the last meet of the Dart-
moor Hunt—15 miles to hack, then a wild run on your hunter, then 15
weary miles back. I did pretty well, save that I smashed my bowler, going
over a stone wall.

And in September, before joining his family at Altarstone (a farm
on the Tweed between Stobo and Broughton), he had a round of
shooting visits 'in Yorkshire, the Borders, and the West Highlands.
I had some delightful days yachting among the Inner Hebrides' (probably with the Gathorne-Hardys, who had a house on Colonsay).
In December 1900 he moved from Brick Court to rooms at
3 Temple Gardens—'they are really very jolly, being very large and
looking over the river and the Gardens'—and was better able to
entertain his friends and hospitable elders in return. Lady Mary
Murray and Canon Ainger came up the 144 steps to tea, and 'yesterday morning Cubby Medd turned up for breakfast, having come
from Alnwick Castle where he seems to have had a pretty poor
time, being made to hunt when he was afraid and taken to balls
which he hated.'

This extended social life led to a suggestion for one book, which he turned down without much regret. This was a request by the Duchess of Argyll, to write the eighth Duke's life, 'but I wanted a free hand and we couldn't agree,' he told Anna.

After my interview on Thursday I was very much struck with her bitterness towards the rest of the family. Now it seems to me that it would be most dangerous for me to become a party to any 'Indiscretions of the Duchess,' to quote Anthony Hope. So I asked that I should have full control and the last word in all political and literary questions, and that in private affairs, if we disagreed, the question should be referred to Lord Rosebery and Lord Peel whose decision should be final. I don't know if she will agree.

As at Oxford, in spite of his initial fears he managed to make ends meet, and he had enough money over to send good presents home—theological essays for his father, a gold bracelet for his mother—in exchange for the toffee, cakes and shortbread which they sent him in London. He also paid part of the rent of Altarstone.

His main earnings came from the *Spectator*, but he was also contributing regularly to *Blackwood's*. He was much impressed by Blackwood's London representative and chief literary adviser; 'there is an extraordinarily fine whinstone gravity and common sense about Meldrum.'* For *Blackwood's* he wrote studies of several eighteenth-century characters—Prince Charles Edward, Lady Louisa Stuart, Mr Secretary Murray, and the eleventh Earl of Buchan, 'A Comic Chesterfield.' ('I should prefer the article to have only my initials' he wrote to William Blackwood: 'If I put my name it might look as if I claimed kinship—which Heaven forbid!') His essay on Lord Mansfield—all that survives of his project for a great book on the Lord Chief Justice—struck William Blackwood as rather dull, but Buchan found a home for it in the *Atlantic Monthly*. In *Blackwood's* too appeared the five stories that made up the collection *The Watcher by the Threshold* (1902).

With Buchan well established in London, half barrister, half literary man, perhaps this is the moment to take stock of his writing to this date. His literary interests and appetites were very much what one would expect of a young man of his time, whether at Glasgow, or Oxford, or London. There was the voracious reading in English classics, the excursions into French literature, the eager sampling of contemporaries. Within this wide field there was an

* During these years David Meldrum was the sympathetic middleman between Conrad and Blackwood.

inner circle of special books: Scott's novels, *The Pilgrim's Progress*,
The Compleat Angler. The two moderns to whom he particularly
warmed (both died during his Glasgow University years) were
Stevenson and Pater. Pater he admired above all for his style. What
he owed to Stevenson he described at a dinner of the Stevenson
Club in Edinburgh in 1929, when he tried 'to make the younger
people of today realise what Stevenson meant to those who were
young during the last decade of last century—especially to Scotsmen and Scottish University students.' He pointed out how
Stevenson's experience had been the same as theirs:

And then he had taught himself to write miraculously, and for those of us
who were dabbling clumsily in literature, his expertness, even his 'pre-
ciousness,' were salutary models, for they meant hard and conscientious
labour. . . . As a guide and a friend to the young Scotsmen of the Nineties,
Stevenson filled the bill completely; he was at once Scottish and cos-
mopolitan, artist and man of action, scholar and gipsy.

A signed article which Buchan wrote for the *Glasgow Herald*
shortly after going up to Oxford displays literary tastes and pre-
conceptions which were not strikingly to change during his life. It
is called 'Nonconformity in Literature' (2 November 1895).
Buchan begins by observing that in a time when there are no great
writers, and no burning issues, it is natural that writers should go
after strange gods and experiment; that this spirit of experiment is
in itself excellent, but the theory behind it can be dangerous, for
it assumes that the experimental is all-important. As an outstanding
example he takes the cult of decadence, making clear that he is not
decrying the so-called 'decadent writers,' but their admirers who
'set them on a preposterous pinnacle and compare them advan-
tageously with the great masters of the past.' Then, after a side-
blow at admirers of Kipling, he moves in to his main attack.

But apart from such avowedly objectionable stuff, the pride of noncom-
formity reigns in places where one would little expect it. Idylls of humble
country life have lately grown upon us thick and fast; charming pieces of
literature many of them; nigh perfect in their narrow sphere. We read and
admire them as a pleasing relaxation from greater books, and set them on
our shelves not far distant from Galt and Miss Edgeworth. But some gentlemen of the press, whose interest it is to puff such books, do not let the matter rest here. These unpretentious and delightful volumes are gravely set
above work with which they are scarcely even comparable. We are told that
the 'deep, serious heart of the country' is to be found in them; that the
clatter of hen-wives and clash of a country street are things of paramount
importance. . . . These men in a hatred of morbidity fly to what seems to us
the opposite extreme and enter the land of vapidity and prosiness. . . .

Mr Crockett hates the sickly and the grimy with a perfect hatred. He is all for the wind and the sunshine, hills and heather, lilac and adventure, kisses and fresh-churned butter. And these are all excellent things; far be it from us to deny it. He is clamorous over their beauties; he is all for the great common things of the world—faith and love, heroism and patience. But it seems to us that in this also there is a danger; mere talking about fine things does not make fine literature, and Mr Crockett at his worst is only a boisterous talker. No man, however high his spirits and rich the life within him, can hope to be a great writer save by the restraint, the pains, the hard and bitter drudgery of his art.

The writers he was gunning for were the Kailyard School—S. R. Crockett, 'Ian Maclaren' (John Watson), the early J. M. Barrie of *A Window in Thrums*—whose virtues were often rammed down the throats of the Presbyterian young (Crockett and John Watson were Free Kirk Ministers). Chief among the critics who puffed them was Robertson Nicoll of the *British Weekly*, favourite reading in Scottish manses. Buchan's stings drew blood. Robertson Nicoll retorted in the *British Weekly* that Mr Crockett had more strength in his little finger than Mr Buchan in his whole body. Buchan answered this editorial sharply; then, he told Charlie Dick.

I got a letter from the editor in which he practically apologises and offers as recompense to print anything I like to send him in the *B.W.* and pay me well for it. I have also received a letter from the *Bookman* asking for personal details to furnish up a New Writer article.

Robertson Nicoll was editor both of the *British Weekly* and the monthly *Bookman*, so the article on Buchan in the latter may have been in the nature of an amend. But Nicoll always remained rather cool towards Buchan.

Buchan came back to his attack at Oxford when, supported by his Scottish friends Rait and Jameson, he proposed a motion at the Union condemning 'the Kailyard School of Novelists,' and it was left to an Englishman, R. C. K. Ensor, to support them. The only use of the Kailyarders, Buchan commented much later, was to provoke George Douglas Brown's counterblast in *The House with the Green Shutters* (1901). In their parochialism and their smugness they reflected a side of Scottish life, particularly kirk-and-manse life, from which Buchan had begun to break away before he left Glasgow. If Scottish literary culture meant the Kailyarders, then (like John Davidson before him) he preferred London and the *Yellow Book*. There was no literary counterpart to the Glasgow school of painting. For the young painters of the day it was natural to stay in Scotland; not for the young writers.

Like Stevenson's, Buchan's early works were poems and essays. Only a few of the poems were published: a handful in the *Glasgow University Magazine*, a couple in his book of stories *Grey Weather*. They are the accomplished verses of a young man with a good ear, romantic feelings, and a head full of the poetry of other men— Keats, Arnold, Morris, Bridges, the Greek Anthology, the Ballads: not the work of a man wrestling to make a new thing, to say something that could not be said in any other way. As he quoted later of Neil Munro, 'his poetry loiters in the past.' The subjects are for the most part conventionally 'poetic'—'Spring and Death,' 'An Old Flower-garden,' 'An Evening by the Sea'—and the forms range from ode to triolet and sonnet.

So, too, the essays are full of echoes: several of those in *Scholar Gipsies* (1896)—'Sentimental Travelling,' 'Milestones,' 'Gentlemen of Leisure'—would fit neatly into those little volumes of essays on which unfortunate schoolchildren used to be urged to model their style, which began with Bacon and Addison, were stuffed with Lamb and Hazlitt, and to which Stevenson would be a daring addition.* Yet under the smooth surface of careful, 'literary' writing, of deliberate archaism ('the very sweet o' the year'), of graceful allusion and neatly mortised quotation, is a hard core of observation and experience.

In this *genre* the theme of the Open Road is conventional enough, and Buchan could handle it conventionally:

And the man's voice took a new tone. His eyes lit up, and looking over the darkening valley, he spoke to his comrade many things, and sang in his ear ever so sweetly the 'Song of the Open Road.'

But after this wayfarer has sung in his high-flown way of the early flush of spring, the clear starlit nights, the old romance of the wayside, and so on, he laughs at his own rhetoric and starts speaking broadly, 'as if to point a contrast,' ' "I'll hae to be movin' if I'm to

---

* Charlie Dick reviewed *Scholar Gipsies* for the *Glasgow University Magazine*: and there was a story current in the University that the editor, J. J. Bell, had blue-pencilled a passage in which Buchan's loyal friend said that in mastery of English style this book was only excelled 'by Shakespeare and the better parts of the Bible.' Buchan himself soon began to feel apologetic about his essays; the preface to *Scholar Gipsies*, dated 1896 when he was not quite twenty-one, pleads for indulgence, for 'they were all written in youth.' More measured praise was given by the *Oxford J.C.R.* (2 February 1897), which noted the influence of Borrow, Jefferies and Stevenson, the intimate knowledge of country life—'Mr Buchan is no mere fireside Arcadian'—and concluded: 'The performance is admirable, but the promise is still greater, and we look for great things from a man who, while so young, has achieved so much.'

win to Jock Rorison's the nicht."' And indeed the tramps, gipsies, and shepherds of the essays are never purely literary; they are also people Buchan had walked beside and talked with, however stiltedly he might write about them. Here he is on his essayist's high horse:

So, too, on this Drove Road, we are all like these Frenchmen, we cannot rest till we see for ourselves what lies over yon ridge or round yonder clump of trees. So we go on and ever on, heedless of meals and the passing of Time. Which is a fact alike in Tweedside topography and the conduct of life. For is not half our action prompted by a restless desire to scan the horizon and look over hill-tops?

Earlier, however, he has given good plain accounts of real drovers whom he had met at Stirling Fair and on the road, and of the old drove-roads along which he had walked or bicycled. And there are often quick changes from self-conscious description to the quoted words of a real character. 'As if to make amends for the dearth of colour in the daytime, the evenings are extraordinarily splendid,' sets the polite, 'literary' tone for 'Night on the Heather': but along comes the shepherd of the Redswirehead to give it a breath of life: '"It's an auld bitch fox that gave me sair work i' the lambin'-time."'

In his stories, too, Buchan was Stevensonian; and his view of what constituted a 'romance' came largely from Stevenson's 'A Gossip on Romance' (in *Memories and Portraits*).* The following passages may be judged to have had a particular influence on him:

Drama is the poetry of conduct, romance the poetry of circumstance . . . There is a vast deal in life and letters both which is not immoral, but simply non-moral; which either does not regard the human will at all, or deals with it in obvious and healthy relations; where the interest turns, not upon what a man shall choose to do, but on how he manages to do it; not on the passionate slips and hesitations of the conscience, but on the problems of the body and the practical intelligence, in clean, open-air adventure, the shock of arms or the diplomacy of life . . .

One thing in life calls for another; there is a fitness in events and places. The sight of a pleasant arbour puts it in our mind to sit there. One place suggests work, another idleness, a third early rising and long rambles in the dew. The effect of night, of any flowing water, of lighted cities, of the peep of day, of ships, of the open ocean, calls up in the mind an army of anonymous desires and pleasures. Something, we feel, should happen;

* One of Buchan's early essays (in the *Bookworm*, 1894) was 'A Gossip on Books and Places.' The passage 'The effect of night . . . in quest of it' is the epigraph to Buchan's short story, 'Sing a Song of Sixpence' (in *The Runagates Club*, 1928).

we know not what, yet we proceed in quest of it. . . . Some places speak distinctly. Certain dank gardens cry aloud for a murder; certain old houses demand to be haunted; certain coasts are set apart for shipwreck. Other spots again seem to abide their destiny, suggestive and impenetrable, 'miching mallecho.' The inn at Burford Bridge, with its arbours and green garden and silent, eddying river—though it is known already as the place where Keats wrote some of his *Endymion* and Nelson parted from his Emma —still seems to wait the coming of the appropriate legend . . .

It is one thing to write about the inn at Burford, or to describe scenery with the word-painters; it is quite another to seize on the heart of the suggestion and make a country famous with a legend . . .

True romantic art, again, makes a romance of all things. It reaches into the highest abstraction of the ideal; it does not refuse the most pedestrian realism. *Robinson Crusoe* is as realistic as it is romantic; both qualities are pushed to an extreme, and neither suffers.

Buchan's first novel, *Sir Quixote of the Moors* (1895)*, applied the Stevenson formula to 'the green swelling moors which cradle the Nith and the Annan, the Clyde and the Tweed.' In a contribution to the Fisher Unwin compilation, *Good Reading about Many Books* (1895) Buchan wrote:

The place has a strong individual character, unlike anything that I know of —an impression of greyness and bleakness not unmixed with a certain valiant strength. For long I had been trying to write some story which should embody to my own mind the character of the landscape, as I conceived it. The human counterpart which was most in keeping seemed to me to be that type of man whose life is guided by the conception of honour. At present I am not concerned by the defence of the conception—one, I believe, of doubtful worth, not very wise, somewhat unthinking, and a little cruel, but with a spice of honesty and truth. So I set about writing a tale which should be a study of temptation and victory set against the grim background of the moor. . . . It is in the first intention an effort to show what would be the course of a certain type of character in certain difficult circumstances, and in the second, an attempt, honest, if indifferently successful, to trace the influence of scene and weather on the action and nature of man.

It is a first-person narrative (with some echoes from *Kidnapped* and *Catriona*) of a French gentleman from Touraine who falls in

* Buchan's title was simply *Sir Quixote*, and he was annoyed when he found his publisher, Fisher Unwin, had tacked on *of the Moors*. This was done to bring the book into line with the fashion in titles set by S. R. Crockett whose *Mad Sir Uchtred of the Hills* had just been issued by the same publishers. The American edition provided a further annoyance to the author, by making the hero turn back at the end to the girl he was so nobly leaving, thus ruining the whole conception of the story. Edward Garnett was literary adviser to Fisher Unwin when *Sir Quixote* was accepted.

with various Covenanters as he rides from Galloway to Leith. The construction is rather clumsy ('Now here I must tell what I omitted to tell in a former place') and the writing rather precious. In answer to some criticism from Gilbert Murray, Buchan admitted that 'one of the worst faults of the book, I think, is the tendency to mere sentence-making. I think this is due partly to the excessive admiration which I have felt for some years for Stevenson, partly to the way the book was written. It was built up sentence by sentence at intervals during the last three weeks of the college session. . . . This I think partly accounts for the absence of the "swing of narrative and the increasing progress of drama."' Where Buchan was strong was in rendering the sensations of the traveller: his change of mood from exhilaration when he escapes, to misery when he is cold, and despair when he is lost, and his reactions to cold and wet.

I tried to swallow some of the rain-soaked bread in my pouch, but my mouth was as dry as a skin. I dismounted to drink at a stream, but the water could hardly trickle down my throat so much did it ache.

As Henry James said of Stevenson, Buchan had 'in a high degree . . . what may be called the imagination of physical states,' and he had more experience than Stevenson to help his imagination. He knew very well what it was to be hungry, tired, wet and lost on those moorlands, and here was his attempt 'to trace the influence of scene and weather on the action and nature of man.'

A reviewer in the *Glasgow University Magazine* (whom Buchan took to be Brailsford), while critical of the deficiencies of the 'novel of adventure,' conceded that in Buchan's there was 'a singular compensation' (13 November 1895):

He is not content to talk of the paces of his hero's good steed, to tell of brave blows struck, and fair ladies won, he plunges us before the book is half done in a thorny problem of honour. He does not write a modern novel with a purpose, but yet his interest in conduct is so strong that he must puzzle us with the right and wrong of a situation which could only occur in a bygone century. He reproduces all the hesitation and conflict of a modern Angel Clare or Richard Feverel. He is too healthily modern to be satisfied with mere action, and he cannot save himself from scrutinising motive. In spite of himself, his true interest and strength lies here, for there is nothing in the book so well done as the chapter in which the Sieur de Rohaine 'communes with himself.' It is this anachronism which lifts the romance far above such ingenious trifling as Mr Anthony Hope's *Prisoner of Zenda*.

When four years later Buchan made a collection of his short stories, 'moorland tales of my own people,'* *Grey Weather* was the name he chose. Most of the tales are about shepherds, drovers, and other moorland characters, for whom the weather was not a conversational gambit, but a matter of first importance, for both their comfort and their trade. Two stories in this collection, 'A Journey of Little Profit' and 'At the Article of Death,' appeared in the *Yellow Book* (April 1896 and January 1897): one was of two drovers carousing with the devil—a homely character, passing by the name of Mr Stewart—and the other of a shepherd dying alone in the Border hills while his religion fell from him 'like a rotten garment' and left him with nothing but 'some relic of manliness, the heritage of cleanly and honest doings.' Appearing among work by Baron Corvo, Max Beerbohm, Richard Garnett, Richard Le Gallienne, Henry James and Stephen Phillips, the tales struck a strenuous gusty note. So did another *Yellow Book* story, never reprinted, 'A Captain of Salvation.'† It is a tale of a gentleman come down in the world through vice, but reclaimed through work with the Salvation Army. On a spring day, which reminds him of his former life of pleasure, he is unenthusiastically leading a procession with flags and tambourines into a vicious part of Limehouse when his past rises up to accost him: first, in the person of a street-walker, whom he has little difficulty in staving off ('He looked for one moment at her, and in the utter loathing and repugnance of that look, she fell back'); second, in an old comrade from his wandering past who appeals to the Captain in the name of the days '"when you and I stood behind yon big tree in Kaffraria with twenty yelling devils wanting our blood . . . when we were lost, doing picketing up in the Drakensberg . . . the days at Port Said, when the old Frenchman twanged his banjo and the

---

* Perhaps an echo of 'Stories of Mine Own People,' Kipling's sub-title to *Life's Handicap* (published earlier in the same year as *Grey Weather*).

† January 1896: Buchan's first appearance in the *Yellow Book*, where his fellow-contributors included Gissing, Kenneth Grahame, H. G. Wells, Maurice Baring, Ada Leverson, Walter Raleigh, and many artists of the Glasgow School whose work was reproduced. John Betjeman, in 'The Arrest of Oscar Wilde at the Cadogan Hotel,' makes Wilde address Robert Ross:

> 'So you've brought me the latest *Yellow Book*;
>   And Buchan has got in it now;
> Approval of what is approved of
>   Is as false as a well-kept vow.'

But Wilde was arrested and tried in 1895, before Buchan had appeared in the *Yellow Book*.

girls danced . . . the long nights when we dropped down the Irra-
waddy . . . when we were up-country in Queensland, sugar-farming
in the bush,"' To this call the Captain is responsive; he feels his
resolution waver—so ' "Sing louder, lads," he cried, "we're fighting a good fight." And then his voice broke down, and he stumbled
blindly on, still clutching the flag.'

It is odd to find this story between the Beardsley-decorated
covers of the *Yellow Book*, and it might seem an odd theme for a
young Oxford intellectual with a slightly precious style. But the
Salvation Army was not then so far removed from Oxford; Quiller-
Couch records of his own undergraduate days, a decade earlier than
Buchan's:

We undergraduates held meetings and started missions in dire tracts of
London—in such places as Bethnal Green and Stratford. We gathered to
listen to C. T. Studd and his cricketer missionaries from Cambridge.
Some few, even of the rowdies, left our company to join the Salvation
Army, renouncing all.

And though Buchan may not have known much about Limehouse at that date, he did know about the slums of Glasgow, and
was not inclined to be aesthetically snooty about the Salvation
Army: 'If anything on earth can bring a ray of decency into such a
place, then in God's name let it come, whether it be called sense or
rant by stay-at-home philosophers.' The minister's son of the John
Knox Church was not overlaid by John Lane's young hopeful, any
more than the Shorter Catechist in Stevenson had been overlaid by
the aesthete of the Savile Club.

There was another strong influence in this early work beside the
Stevensonian. *Scholar Gipsies* was published in John Lane's
Arcady Library,* and on the cover a goat-foot Pan piped to three
nymphs. The essays, too, sounded many Arcadian notes—references to Theocritus, to 'people of this Arcady' (*i.e.* the Upper
Tweed), to 'the Piper' ('We can all hear the Piper if we listen, but
some of us stop our ears against him'). The first piece in a projected book of poems was 'The Piper', and the refrain to another
was 'Pan is singing, Pan is playing.' Peter Green, in his biography
of Kenneth Grahame, has described this modish literary paganism
of the nineties and nineteen-hundreds, which showed itself in the
stories of Maurice Hewlett, Arthur Machen, the early E. M.

---

* When republished by Lane in 1927 it was in the Weekend Library: an index
of changing fashion.

Forster, and particularly of Grahame.* Buchan was an early and firm admirer of Grahame's work: he gave Anna *Pagan Papers*, which has a Beardsley drawing of Pan as frontispiece; when *The Golden Age* came out in 1895 Buchan found it 'surely the most beautiful book published for many years': this was well before he and Grahame were fellow-readers for Lane. In his early work there are some clear echoes of Grahame: 'Afternoon' in *Scholar Gipsies*—a boy playing Jacobites who steals into the garden of a big house and meets a girl whom he is sure is a princess—is very much in the vein of the story in *The Golden Age* where children playing Argonauts explore a big garden and meet a girl who they are sure is Medea.

There are, though, considerable differences between Buchan's use of Pan, and the pagan world generally, and that of his *Yellow Book* contemporaries. Pan for them was identified with revolt against convention, respectability, urban life: he was, as Mr Green puts it, 'a convenient symbol into which writers could pour their own anarchic urges.' The cult was at times rather week-endy. Buchan's Pan was not suburban, and the pastoral element in his writing had firmer roots than Grahame's. In his countrysides people worked for a living, and his literary models in this were not all fashionable-contemporary. In the title-essay of *Scholar Gipsies* he quotes the traditional ballad of 'Leader Haughs':

> Pan playing on his aiten reed,
> And shepherds him attending,
> Do here resort their flocks to feed,
> The hills and haughs commending.

Buchan used Pan and the pagan world to give expression to feelings about a landscape, about the changing moods of a man in a landscape (who sees *Natura Benigna* change suddenly to *Natura Maligna*), and about the sensations he associated with certain places. Pagan gods to him stood not so much for anarchy or licence as for something primitive, an element sweet but potentially dangerous.

There was nothing arty or fanciful, however, about Buchan's

---

* The first of E. M. Forster's stories, 'The Story of a Panic' and 'The Road from Colonus' (written in 1902 and 1903) are concerned with Pan, and Rickie Elliott, the hero of Forster's *The Longest Journey* (1907), wrote a book of short stories with the title *Pan's Pipes*.

In the bookplate designed by R. Anning Bell for Buchan's Balliol friend A. C. Gathorne-Hardy, Pan is piping and a scholar listening.

first full-length novel, *John Burnet of Barns* (1898).* Like *Sir Quixote*, this is a first-person story: but the persona through whom Buchan was writing now was no far-off romantic like the Sieur de Rohaine of the earlier novel, but a boy on Tweeddale with a taste for fishing and philosophy and long excursions into the hills. Buchan wrote the story between 1894 and 1896, and a great deal of his own past is in it. John Burnet is not so dissimilar a name to John Buchan (cousins of Buchan's are still farming at Burnetland, near Brough-ton); like nineteenth-century Buchan, seventeenth-century Burnet goes from Tweeddale to Glasgow University, is fascinated by Descartes and the Neoplatonists, and attracted to both the life of action and the life of study. (Buchan makes him a relative of Bishop Burnet the historian, and has him meet Leibnitz at Leyden.) He lives at Barns, in a square stone house which was a familiar sight to Buchan from the road between Peebles and Broughton (it is now a youth hostel). The heroine, from Dawyck further up the river, is Marjory Veitch—the same name as old Professor Veitch, the Tweeddale neighbour who had introduced Buchan to Descartes. The book is full of Buchan's own loyalties and experiences; full, too, of local happenings (the floods, the bowling matches) and of Scot-tish social history. Here and there, indeed, his researches ran away with him, and at one point the action is held up for a recital of old Scottish dishes; largely, it seems, for the author's pleasure in enumerating 'partan pies and rizzard haddies, crappit-heids and scate-rumples, now't feet, kebbucks, scadlips, and skink.'

'Here is the romance,' he wrote in a projected dedicatory letter to Lady Mary Murray,† 'which I have tried to fit to the place. . . . I have cast the story in the most stirring time in its history.' The hero, whose adventures start in 1678, is embroiled in the political and religious troubles of the time; he visits the Low Countries (echoes here of *Catriona*), spends some time with Covenanters in the moors of the Upper Clyde, takes part in a battle between two tribes of gipsies, and saves his inheritance and rescues the heroine from the villain, who is his own cousin. The chapter-headings ('How I Ride to the South.' 'I Fall in with Strange Friends,' 'Of the Fight in the Moss of Biggar') are in the manner of Stevenson—

* Other Lane authors listed on the dust cover of the first edition of *John Burnet* were Max Beerbohm, E. A. Bennett, A. C. Benson, Baron Corvo, John Davidson, Richard Garnett, Lionel Johnson, Richard Le Gallienne, Arthur Machen, Mrs Meynell, M. P. Shiel.

† The book as published was dedicated to the memory of the little sister, Violet Katharine Stuart, who had died at Broughton in the summer of 1893.

and of Stanley Weyman's *Gentleman of France* and Q's *The Splendid
Spur*, devoured at Uncle Willie's house in Peebles—and John
Burnet's servant Nicol Plenderleith, who sings as he fights, has
something of the panache of Alan Breck Stewart. Buchan had learnt
an important lesson from Stevenson: to tell a historical story at a
good pace, and with a minimum of what Stevenson called 'tushery.'
The sense of the past is given by well-chosen detail, and not by
archaic language: his Scots is easy to read. He is again strong in
rendering landscape, weather, physical sensations and sudden
changes of mood, from exhilaration to despair. ('Mr Buchan's
descriptions . . . can be *seen*, and *heard*, and *smelt*.') Two themes,
familiar to readers of Buchan's later work, are heard. First, the
hero, though thrown among fanatics, is a passionate moderate:
'I was never meant for one of them,' he says of the Covenanters 'I ever saw things too clearly, both the evil and the good;
and whereas this quality hinders from swift and resolute action,
it yet leads more plainly to a happy life.' Second, his hatred for the
enemy, his false cousin Gilbert (who has more than a resemblance
to Stevenson's Master of Ballantrae), is tempered by admiration:

His habit of scorn for all which opposed him, and all which was beneath
him, had grown on him with his years and power, and given him that look
as of one born to command, ay, and of one to whom suffering and pain
were less than nothing. As I looked on him I hated him deeply and
fiercely, and yet I admired him more than I could bear to think, and gloried
that he was of our family. For I have rarely seen a nobler figure of a man.

By the time he came to revise the novel for publication, Buchan
had rather lost the zest with which he had embarked on it three
years earlier; once it was published, he admitted to Gilbert Murray
'To tell the truth I am rather ashamed of it, it is so very immature
and boyish. I had no really serious interest in fiction when I wrote
it, and the result is a sort of hotch-potch.' But he had proved that
he could keep action going briskly through 100,000 words. One
of the most appreciative reviews came from the critic ('W.R.') in
Keir Hardie's *Labour Leader* (11 June 1898), who thought it 'a
most remarkable work for so young a man,' and refreshingly free
from 'Kailyarder nonsense.' He particularly admired the duel
between John Burnet and his false cousin: 'a young writer who can
keep his reader positively riveted to the page through a description
extending to about a thousand words of a hand-to-hand fight "may
go far," to use one of the up-to-date expressions which Mr Buchan
puts into the mouth of a Scot of two centuries ago.'

With *A Lost Lady of Old Years* (1899—the title comes from
Browning's 'Waring') he was back at the novel of atmosphere rather
than adventure. The hero Francis Birkenshaw—of good Border
family but apprenticed to a lawyer in Dysart (not far from Pathhead)—encounters romantically in 1745, in her house at Broughton,
the wife of the Jacobite Secretary Murray* and is sent by her on a
mission to Lord Lovat in the North. The subject is the struggle of a
weak man, who comes from a house with traditions of honour,
towards virtue; he finds it in an impossible loyalty. Francis serves
the Jacobites not because he believes in their cause, but to satisfy
a personal ideal of quixotic honour and thus give his life significance: when Mrs Murray asks him for help, 'he felt the ragged
ends of his life gather to a centre,' and when he wins her thanks,
'Francis for a moment sat lord and king in a crazy palace of cloud.'
This achievement gives him the energy to go back to lead a virtuous life in a humdrum sphere; he ends the book as Provost of
Dysart. The novel, which cost Buchan a great deal of trouble to
write—'The *Lost Lady* has now reduced my hair to a silvery white'
—is not nearly such a good story as *John Burnet*: we have to put up
with the vacillations of Mr Francis before we are caught up into
any excitement of action, and Buchan's study of this romantic
temperament is not keen or subtle enough to hold attention
on its own merits. The book takes on momentum with Francis's
ride north to Lovat at Castle Dounie—there are the usual
sharp accounts of physical states, from active well-being to utter
exhaustion, and of quick transitions of mood from high sentiment
to stoic determination. Here and there the construction is a little
awkward: at key-points in the action new characters are introduced for whose appearance the reader has been quite unpre-
pared.

'Buchan is not going to write any more Scotch stories,' Charlie
Dick reported to a Glasgow friend in 1897; 'he is only going to
write psychological studies of cultured people.' That is a pretty
fair description of *The Half-Hearted* (1900), which again the
author soon outgrew ('a stupid book, written during a period of
violent prejudice at Oxford.'). Dedicated to Raymond Asquith,
Harold Baker and Cuthbert Medd, it reflects the mood and talk of

* 'I have lately been reluctantly compelled to the conclusion that Mrs Murray
of Broughton was really a very bad lot, and that her life does not bear inspection.
So I shall have to put a note to my book saying that I have abandoned the historical
conception.' (Letter to C. H. Dick, 4 February 1897.)

Buchan's inner circle of friends. Lewis Haystoun, the hero, clearly owes much to Raymond Asquith:

'He got everything he wanted [says another character of Lewis] but then he got them easily and had a lot of time for other things, whereas most of us had not a moment to spare. He got the best first of his year and the St Chad's Fellowship, but I think he cared far more about winning the 'Varsity Grind . . . I have heard him speak often, and his manner gave one the impression that he was a tremendous swell, you know, and very conceited. People used to think him a sort of universal genius who could do everything. I suppose he was quite the ablest man that has been there for years, but I should think he would succeed ultimately as the man of action.'

Raymond approved the theme: 'I don't think you could have chosen a better subject: half-heartedness is really the most salient feature of the pleasanter sort of modern.'

In the first part of the book the half-hearted Lewis, a young Border laird who has travelled in Central Asia, is contrasted with a bumptious vulgar self-made man. 'I think I understand Lewis,' wrote Buchan to Gilbert Murray,

but Stocks is merely a peg on which to hang some of my private dislikes . . . he was a Roseberyite, I am sure of it. I am glad you think I am getting better at love-making. I hate the stuff. I sit and blush with disgust when I am writing it.

Stocks not only beats Lewis at the polls but, while Lewis stands irresolute, plunges into a deep pool to save the heroine, Alice Wishart (no aristocratic beauty, but the daughter of a great merchant: 'generations of thrift and seriousness had given her a love for the strenuous and the unadorned'). In the second part the scene shifts from the Borders to North Kashmir, where Lewis has been sent on a secret mission to gather news about a suspected Russian agent, and to redeem himself in his own eyes. He is captured by local tribesmen in the agent's pay, and by that implausible convention of the adventure story, whereby the hero is told the enemy's plans because the enemy thinks it is too late for him to thwart them, Lewis learns that Russian hordes are about to swarm through an unknown defile, swoop down on the Punjab and conquer India. He escapes and, having managed to get a message through to alert the British authorities, forces himself on, at the point of exhaustion, to 'the little black rift which was the gate of an empire.' There he dies gloriously if improbably in the neck of the defile, having stopped the enemy with rifle-shot and rolling stones. The Empire is saved.

This was Buchan's first contemporary novel, and it took in more of his non-Scottish experience than any earlier story. True, in the first part he was again writing of Tweeddale, though, with Lady Manorwater's house-party at Glenavelin, it was a rather grander Tweeddale than in the stories of shepherds and tramps in *Grey Weather*. It was the country of Raymond's step-grandfather, Sir Charles Tennant of Glen, rather than of Broughton Green. Hours of talk with Raymond, Cubby and Harold Baker went to the central preoccupation: what sort of action, what course of life, could be possible and bearable for gifted young men who had the world at their feet, but to whom worldly ambition was vulgar? ('The world as I see it just now is a little barren of motives,' wrote Raymond once to Buchan.) How could the truly civilised, sceptical, self-conscious man acquire the power to act which came so easily to more limited intelligences? Where did true happiness lie—in being or doing? To solve such problems satisfactorily for his hero, Buchan takes over the romantic stock-in-trade of A. E. W. Mason and Rider Haggard, where one man, or a small group of men, takes on hopeless odds. The threat his hero faced was not, however, as in these writers, the rising of one African or Asian tribe, dreamed up for the story. It was something very much present in the thoughts of anyone with a concern for foreign policy. At Oxford, at London dinner-tables, the Great Game played by Russia and Britain on the roof of the world was a familiar topic, and Curzon's *Russia in Central Asia* a much discussed book. The Russian threat to India was in the political air, and in the air too (see Kipling) as a literary subject. Buchan may well have read in the *Spectator* (30 September 1899) a long review of Skrine and Denison Ross's *The Heart of Asia*: certainly one of his first articles for the paper was on 'The Russian Imperial Ideal,' and a little later he wrote an enthusiastic review of Colonel Durand's *The Making of a Frontier*: 'The whole diplomatic game which was played among those pathless hills has the excitement of a romance.' By the time he wrote this he had nearly finished the novel, but it is likely that reading Durand helped him with his final revision. His frontier characters, soldiers and administrators (Buchan had not yet mixed much with such persons) are probably drawn after Kipling, and a very long way after; their conversations tend to be either rhetorical ('Keep standing all, and sell yourselves dear. We're all safe for heaven, so keep your minds easy') or, again after Kipling, pseudo-scriptural. But, though for the first time Buchan was tackling a terrain he did not intimately know, the landscape of Northern Kashmir is firmly drawn; he had noted in his review of *The Making of a Frontier* how

many of the landscapes are cunning pieces of art, full of light and colour, and a feeling for the subtleties of place and weather. There is a wonderful little account of a deserted altar among the hills, which is pure poetry—

and Durand may have helped him put those rocks, dry pastures, empty watercourses, dark nullahs, firmly on the map of the reader's imagination. At the last the hero's thoughts turn to home; here Buchan dipped again into his own memories. Lewis, waiting for the first invaders, thinks of wet days on western islands (where Buchan had been in the autumn of 1899), and of a night out by a hill-loch with beaches of milk-white sand (such as Buchan had spent in 1897 with Taffy Boulter by Loch Enoch in Galloway).

Two more points may be made about *The Half-Hearted*. This was the widest range Buchan had yet allowed to his romanticism. There is the sense, not of a lost cause in the past, but of a great action with world-wide effects—'Things look ugly enough in Europe just now, and Asia would naturally be the starting-point' —and the sense of a widely-spread plot.

Word came of native riots in the south, at Lahore and Amritsar, and the line of towns which mark the way to Delhi. In some places extraordinary accidents were reported. Certain officers had gone off on holiday and had not returned, odd and unintelligible commands had come to perplex the minds of others; whole camps were reported sick where sickness was least expected. A little rising of certain obscure rivers had broken up an important highway by destroying all the bridges save the one which carried the railway. The whole north was on the brink of a sudden disorganisation, but the brink had still to be passed. It lay with its masters to avert calamity; and its masters, going about with haggard faces, prayed for daylight and a few hours to prepare.*

Second: in the character of Lewis Haystoun Buchan was not only reflecting his friends' ideas and temperaments, but was working out differences within this close group. As Lewis sets off on his forlorn hope, across wild country, he feels that

At last he had found a man's work. He had never had a chance before. Life had been too easy and sheltered; he had been coddled like a child; he had never really roughed it except for his own pleasure. Now he was out-

---

* Buchan took a less dramatic view of a Russian invasion in his *Spectator* article on 'The Russian Imperial Ideal' (20 January 1900), where he wrote, 'An attack upon India from the North would be the most difficult operation in the world's history, and without absolute naval supremacy she would not hold the country for a week.'

side this backbone of the world with a task before him, and only his wits for his servant. Eton and Oxford, Eton and Oxford—so it had been for generations—an education sufficient to damn a race . . . but now he was in a fair way to taste the world's iron and salt, and he exulted at the prospect.

While he waits for death Lewis sums up his life:

And with it all a great humility fell upon him. His battles were all un-fought. His life had been careless and gay; and the tragic commonplaces of faith and duty had been things of small meaning. He had lived on the confines of a little aristocracy of birth and wealth and talent, and the great melancholy world scourged by the winds of God had seemed to him but a phrase of rhetoric. His creeds and his arguments seemed meaningless now in this solemn hour; the truth had been his no more than his crude opponent's! Had he his days to live over again he would look on the world with different eyes. No man any more should call him a dreamer. It pleased him to think that, half-hearted and sceptical as he had been, a humorist, a laughing philosopher, he was now dying for one of the common catchwords of the crowd. He had returned to the homely paths of the commonplace, and, young, unformed, untried, he was caught up by kind fate to the place of the wise and the heroic.

Asquith and Medd could be taken to stand for 'the easy and sheltered,' the 'careless and gay;' Buchan himself for the values of 'the world's iron and salt,' and for 'the homely paths of the com-monplace.' *The Half-Hearted* may have been a demonstration that both ways have their merits, but that they are better combined; and that too sheltered an upbringing may make a man morally soft, too great a freedom of choice may sap his capacity for action.

The Watcher by the Threshold was not published till 1902, but the five stories in it were all written at Oxford. All except the last, 'Fountainblue,' have a supernatural element in them; all are set in Scotland. (The dedication is to Stair Gillon.) In 'No-Man's-Land' Buchan is in the Galloway of the shepherds and of his walk with Taffy Boulter in the summer of 1897; but as well as shepherds there are Picts, who have survived underground for centuries, and into whose hands the scholar-narrator falls. The hills, moors, shepherd's cottage—peat-fire, box-bed, grocers' almanacs 'and an extraordinary lithograph of the Royal Family in its youth'—are done from the life; the hairy Picts give off an authentic whiff of supernatural horror, there is a splendid scene where a primitive rite is enacted in a cave, and the tension in the hero between his naked terror and his scholarly fascination is excellently done.

'The Far Islands' are off the west coast; at moments of tension Colin Raden sees, beyond the real island that blocks the sea-loch, an island with white sands and a scent of apples, in that western sea where certain of his wandering forebears had vanished. In his visions Colin is always prevented from landing on the island, and manages to leap on to the beach only at the moment when he is dying in a desert battle. Joseph Conrad was indignant about the story (which William Blackwood had brought to his attention*) and held that in idea, feeling and suggestion, it had been 'wrenched alive out of Kipling's late "The Finest Story in the World"' (which appeared in *Many Inventions*, 1893). Buchan, as we know, was influenced by Kipling in some of the local colour of *The Half-Hearted*; later, in *The Moon Endureth* (1912), he was to alternate stories and poems in Kipling's manner. But Conrad's accusation about 'The Far Islands' seems rather to exaggerate the case against Buchan. Kipling's is a story of reincarnation—the bank clerk re-lives his experiences as a Greek galley-slave and as a Viking—whereas Colin Raden is concerned with a sort of hereditary hallu-cination, which derives from the legends of the Hesperides, Avilion, and the blessed isle of St Brandan. The really striking similarity, not mentioned by Conrad, is that women have a fatal effect on the men's psychic experiences. Charlie Mears forgets about the galleys and the long-boats when he falls in love; Colin cannot see his island after he has been in the company of women.

Stevenson was a more evident influence on the stories. 'The Watcher by the Threshold,' which Buchan described as 'my "horrible" story,' was 'an attempt . . . to fit a sort of gruesome comedy to a particular type of Scotch moor.' It is about a case of demoniac possession: a Scots laird living somewhere east of Perth, in the country that was once Manann, 'the holy land of the ancient races,' suddenly develops strange tastes and an obsession with the Emperor Justinian (here Buchan turned to good account his studies in Byzantine history with Dr Bussell). Ladlaw believes that, like Justinian, he is haunted by the devil—'the visible, personal Devil in whom our fathers believed'—and the learned rationalist who tells the story, and the progressive minister who is brought in to help, are shaken out of their scepticism when they feel, hear, and almost see the evil spirit as it finally departs. 'The Outgoing of the Tide'— the only story not set in the present—is another exercise in dia-bolism, in the tradition of Burns's 'Tam o' Shanter,' Scott's 'Wan-dering Willie's Tale,' and Stevenson's 'Thrawn Janet': and, like

* Conrad's *Heart of Darkness* and *Lord Jim* were being serialised in *Blackwood's* at the time when Buchan's first stories appeared in the magazine.

them, it is narrated in Scots ('from the unpublished Remains of the Reverend John Dennistoun, sometime minister of the Gospel in the parish of Caulds, and author of *Satan's Artifices against the Elect*'). Here the devilry is a matter of witchcraft and pagan rites enacted on the coast of Galloway.

There is nothing supernatural in 'Fountainblue' (though Cubby Medd, reading it in the Keep at Bamburgh, with windows looking out on a wild sea, 'felt a little queer'). The landscape of western sea-loch here stands for integrity of imagination and it is in revisiting this place he knew as a boy, and experiencing its storms as well as its beauty, that the successful Maitland sees how hollow is his life in the City and in politics. He renounces it for the hard and danger-ous job of an African governorship, and like Lewis Haystoun in *The Half-Hearted*, he dies bravely on the frontier. There is some-thing of Buchan himself in Maitland: the free independent boyhood (though Maitland is forced by his father's death to work for a while in a bank, one of Buchan's youthful dreads); the hard work to get himself to Oxford; the maturity as an undergraduate (Maitland talks of his college contemporaries as 'little boys'); the wish for public life, success, and the sense of the limitations of such a life; the wish to keep fresh the vision of the places he loved as a boy, and the con-viction that his own imagination and integrity depend on them. In such places people can 'make their peace with their own souls.' Maitland's strength is seen to lie in his capacity to fuse his power to act and his power to dream: he is 'the iron dreamer.' But he is happiest when he ceases to be the exceptional, isolated leader and loses himself in sharing common pleasures with a crowd of friends.

In all the stories, except 'The Outgoing of the Tide,' Oxford (or Oxford and London) and Scotland are contrasted: Oxford standing for comfort as well as knowledge and power; Scotland for some-thing wilder, more primitive, more imaginative and perhaps more virile. Describing how the descendants of Colin the Red, in 'The Far Islands,' had by the nineteenth century become Anglo-Scots, Buchan writes 'Soon the race was of the common over-civilised type, graceful, well-mannered, with abundant good looks, but only once in a generation reverting to the rugged northern strength.' In all the tales there is stress on the thinness of civilisation. The division between 'the warm room and the savage out-doors' is to Maitland no more than 'a line, a thread, a sheet of glass'; the face of Justinian, on the bust which Ladlaw worships, suggests 'the intangible mystery of culture on the verge of savagery.'

The writing in these stories is less mannered than in much of Buchan's early work, and more careful than in *The Half-Hearted*; the characters are seen less romantically than in the novel, and with more insight. The wife of the possessed man in 'The Watcher' displays 'the self-confidence and composure of pain'; in 'Fountainblue' a group of children 'were breathless with excitement, very much in love with each other as common sharers in past joys.' Re-reading his complete works in 1903, Buchan found '*Scholar Gipsies* the best, till you come to *The Watcher*.'

For his stories and essays Buchan had spread himself over four publishers: Fisher Unwin (*Sir Quixote*), Lane (*Scholar Gipsies, John Burnet, Grey Weather, A Lost Lady of Old Years*), Isbister (*The Half-Hearted*), and Blackwood (*The Watcher by the Threshold*). He used a literary agent, his fellow-countryman A. P. Watt (whom he had originally approached about *Sir Quixote* which Watt declined) but at first only for serial-rights, preferring to keep the book-rights in his own hand. (John Lane liked to deal directly with his authors, for whom he was prepared to take a good deal of trouble in securing publication in the United States and in periodicals.) In 1896 Buchan had told his mother that 'I shall keep to Lane, but never for a moment go below ten per cent royalty, which is as much as I could get through Watt.' He received his ten per cent for *Scholar Gipsies* and *Grey Weather*, while for *John Burnet* and *A Lost Lady of Old Years* he received a 15 per cent royalty (rising to 20 per cent after the advance of £100 had been paid off).* Neither of these sold well (whereas *Scholar Gipsies* had quickly gone into a second edition) and this may have decided Buchan to look for another publisher for *The Half-Hearted*; but I have been unable to find any records of the terms he made with Isbister, or of the book's sales.† The novel was serialised throughout 1900 in *Good Words*, a

* The records of the Bodley Head show that in the first year *John Burnet* sold about 600 copies and, up to 1917, about 1150. So Buchan still owed £42 7s. 4d. on his advance and Lane proposed to recoup this on a 1s. edition which he published in 1916, when, now that Buchan was known as the author of *The Thirty-Nine Steps*, it quickly sold in thousands. Buchan queried this arrangement with Lane—thinking Lane's loss should be recouped from *his* profits, not Buchan's—but in the end agreed, for *John Burnet* only. The losses incurred on *A Lost Lady* (which earned only £36 15s. 5d. of its £100 advance—so had sold only about 500 copies—from publication to 1917) which was not being reissued, were not to be set against the author's royalties from the new edition of *John Burnet*.

† The only record now at Sir Isaac Pitman and Sons, who took over Isbister in 1907, is that there were only ten bound copies of *The Half-Hearted* in stock at takeover.

periodical published by Isbister; serial-rights and book-rights may have been part of one deal.

With Blackwood's Buchan had been friendly since he first went up to Oxford—he had dined with David Meldrum in London and with William Blackwood at Gogar Mount outside Edinburgh, and in December 1896 Blackwood had sent him a cheque for £40. This must have been an advance, for Buchan did not publish anything in *Blackwood's Magazine* till January 1899, when 'No-Man's-Land' was the first story. Three of the other four which comprise *The Watcher by the Threshold* also appeared in *Blackwood's*,* so it was natural that Buchan should give Blackwood the book too. He again obtained a 15 per cent royalty (rising, after the first 1000, to 16 per cent) and more than 1500 were sold in the first months after publication, though in the next two years the sales dropped to 17 and nil.

As early as 1898 Buchan wrote to Blackwood that 'I have a man in America who acts for me'; whether through his own exertions, or those of Unwin or Lane, *Sir Quixote* was published in the States by Henry Holt, *Scholar Gipsies* by Macmillan, *John Burnet* by Dodd Mead, *The Half-Hearted* by Houghton Mifflin, *The Watcher by the Threshold* by Doran. His short stories were all published in magazines before they appeared in book form; *John Burnet* and *The Half-Hearted* were serialised in England (in *Chambers's Journal* and *Good Words*) and *A Lost Lady* in America (in *Today*).

At twenty-six Buchan had discovered much about the business of writing. In journalism he could supply a demand with style and professional finish: he could always meet deadlines. In fiction, where he had been trying out a number of modes, he was less sure of himself. The money he had earned for his stories made his life far easier and pleasanter, but there was nothing in his sales so far to encourage him to make writing his sole profession. Perhaps it was this early experience—certainly not disheartening, but as certainly not encouraging to dreams of fame and fortune—that made him decide, as he records, that literature 'should be my hobby, not my profession.'

* 'The Outgoing of the Tide' appeared in the *Atlantic Monthly* only, in January 1902.

CHAPTER FIVE

MILNER'S YOUNG MAN

1901–03

'I would rather go back to Africa than practise again in Peebles.'
Mungo Park, quoted by John Buchan in his foreword to *Leaves from
the Life of a Country Doctor*

'We are all settling down to be responsible members of society,'
wrote Buchan to Charlie Dick in June 1901 on hearing that John
Edgar had found a job and Charlie himself a church. He too seemed
to be nicely settled in law and journalism, but on August 7 he was
summoned to the Colonial Office by Lord Milner, about to return
to South Africa after ten weeks at home for consultations, and
offered a position on his staff.

To young men of Buchan's generation Alfred Milner was the
public servant *par excellence*. Combining a zeal for social reform—
he was one of the founders of Toynbee Hall—with a belief in
Britain's imperial mission, he had held important administrative
posts abroad and at home, as under-secretary of finance in Egypt
(1890–92) and as chairman of the Board of Inland Revenue (1892–
97). In 1897, at the age of forty-three, he had been appointed High
Commissioner for South Africa. To many it appeared that Milner's
intransigence on behalf of the British in South Africa was a contri-
butory factor to the outbreak of war in 1899; but by 1901, with the
end of the fighting in sight, Milner's energies were turned towards
the reorganisation and reconstruction of the two new colonies of
the Transvaal and the Orange Free State, the former Boer republics.
For this work he was anxious to recruit young men with energetic
and unconventional minds. 'I mean to have young men,' he told
Sir Percy Fitzpatrick:

There will be a regular rumpus and a lot of talk about boys and Oxford
and jobs and all that . . . Well, I value brains and character more than

experience. First-class men of experience are not to be got. Nothing one could offer would tempt them to give up what they have . . . No! I shall not be here for very long, but when I go I mean to leave behind me young men with plenty of work in them.

One of those whom Milner invited was L. S. Amery, who, however, could not be released from *The Times*. So Amery suggested Buchan instead. Milner had already heard of him; after reading with approval an article on South Africa in the *Spectator* he had asked Joseph Chamberlain, then Secretary of State for the Colonies, to find out who had written it. And during his weeks at home Milner had plenty of opportunities to hear about the young man. He was seeing a good deal of the Asquiths, he spent a long week-end at Oxford, he visited Bron Herbert's uncle at Panshanger, where Buchan too had been a guest. As for Buchan, he had heard Milner spoken of with admiration and reverence at Oxford, and by Strachey and his friends. (Raymond Asquith, after a dinner-party in 1898, had written of 'Alfred Milner with a mind like a cameo, clear cut, and as quick as lightning.') When the offer came on August 7 Buchan wrote home post-haste, heard from his mother by return, and two days later he wrote again more fully:

My dearest Mother,
Many thanks for your kind and thoughtful letter. I am as distressed as you can be, but I think you have rather misunderstood the terrors of the offer. I am asked to go for two years; I am free to leave whenever I want; I shall probably have to come back to England for Milner once or twice during my term. I am to get £1200 a year, out of which I suppose I could save £600. I have asked the Attorney-General if I come back to the Bar in two years, whether the absence would hurt me. He says it would be all the other way, that it would be a tremendous advertisement, and that having been Milner's Private Secretary would secure me a lot of S. African appeals. Strachey is to give me the refusal of old Townsend's place on the *Spectator* if it falls vacant while I am away, and my old place will always be ready for me when I return. Finally you must remember that it would be going to live in comfort in one of the healthiest places in the world. As the Attorney-General said, it is simply as if I were sent out on a legal mission, like the Venezuelan Arbitration. Also it would be an advertisement for me for the rest of my life.
These are the arguments for it. Everyone—Strachey, the A-G, etc— advise me to take it, and call me names for hesitating. On the other hand there are your feelings. *I am not going if it is to hurt you deeply*. It would only be a temporary absence, I should probably be back once a year, and of course the post annihilates distance.

These are the facts, on which we will have to decide on Monday. Quite seriously, I think it is a great chance, an interposition of Providence, but *you* must be considered.

I am so glad my grandmother is better.

Love to all

your affectionate son

JOHN

Mrs Buchan's fears were assuaged, or over-ridden, and the decision made to go. To Lady Mary Murray Buchan wrote that 'I propose to stay out two years, though of course one may get drawn into administrative work for good. I feel it is a great honour to be associated with a man I admire in so serious and difficult a business.' And he told another correspondent that he wanted to go, 'for I love seeing the world, and I much prefer politics to law.' So instead of reindeer-shooting in Norway with the Gathorne-Hardys, there was a rush up to Glasgow, Peebles and Broughton, and south again with Anna to see him off on the R.M.S. *Briton* on 14 September 1901. Two days before he sailed his friends gave him a farewell dinner— 'Cubby arrived about 6 from Northumberland, and went back by the 11.30 train—very kind of him, surely, to come so far. The dinner was at 7.30 and Cubby, Denman, Amery, Harold Baker, Paul Phipps, Henley and Algy Wyndham turned up—nearly all coming up from the country.'

Whatever Buchan's own doubts—which were mainly on account of his mother's reluctance to see him go so far away—to his friends it seemed a golden opportunity. 'You are really an enviable person,' wrote Raymond Asquith, assuring him that 'arrangements have been made to preserve your position at the Bar and in the Kailyard during your absence.' Cuthbert Medd (who hoped to replace him on the *Spectator*) wrote of his sailing 'with colours flying for the Southern Cross, to see the great Achilles whom you knew and will know much better before you come back.'

As Buchan sailed south in the R.M.S. *Briton*—mixing, in the first class, with rich Transvaalers, colonial statesmen, wives going out to join their officer-husbands, and noting how his fellow-Britons at the Captain's table were 'very unpopular among the other passengers and with cause, for they absolutely ignore them'—how did the whole enterprise strike him? First the prospect satisfied a deep need to travel. He had kept a boy's romantic wish to see the world but this was his first time abroad. In 1898 he had written some lines 'From the Pentlands, Looking North and South' which, in their description of the Firth of Forth and the ships sailing to foreign ports, and of the pastoral uplands to the South, expressed his need for both adventure and security:

> Grant me the rover's path—to see
> The dawn arise, the daylight flee,
> In the far wastes of sand and sun! . . .
> But when the even brings surcease,
> Grant me the happy moorland peace;
> That in my heart's depth ever lie
> That ancient land of heath and sky.

Though he was going from a life of study and writing to a life of action, for which he had no training, he was confident and exhilarated, buoyed up by such good wishes as he received in a letter from his Balliol friend Ramsay Muir:

I would admire your luck, for that post under that MAN is the post in the whole world for a man of your age and training, made for real politics (not Parliamentary rotting) but not trained for them. I say I *would* admire your luck but that I know you to be admirably fitted for your work, and for the splendid things it will lead to. Don't think I am flattering when I say that ever since I knew you I have immensely admired your varied but unostentatious industry, your brilliant but unelated progress, neither unduly depreciating nor unduly appreciating your own or other people's achievements.

Muir went on to say:

I often wondered at what point you would change lines: with your usual good fortune (like most good fortune, mainly an eye for the true opportunity) you seem to have done it at precisely the best junction.

Muir spoke of 'men who have a great new country given into their hands like a lump of clay to be modelled,' and certainly one of the attractions of going to South Africa, for many of Milner's young men, was the apparent freshness and newness of the country.

What were in these young men's heads, too, were liberal ideas about the Boers. The war was creaking to a close, and though Kitchener's peace negotiations with Botha in the spring had broken down, it seemed only a matter of time before the remaining commandos under De Wet, Botha and De la Rey were rounded up; then the rebuilding would start.

'To make the best of the Boers instead of the worst,' the *Spectator* had declared in a leading article written by Buchan, 'The "Edinburgh" on South Africa' (26 January 1901), is the aim which should inspire all our policy. As soon as possible we must substitute civilian for military rule; as soon as possible we must bring the conquered States into line with our Colonial system; all these things are truisms, but they are of the type of truism which lies at the root of statesmanship. . . . We believe that . . . the Dutch and British in South Africa will be fused into one loyal and prosperous people. If we did not believe this, we should regard the war as indeed an unqualified disaster . . . We must make the Colony, not a wilderness where fortune-hunters may find gold, but a civilised and united nation. And to do this we must work alongside the Dutch.

Milner, though appointed by a Conservative Government and working with a Conservative Colonial Secretary, made it his business to keep closely in touch with Liberal opinion at home through a number of correspondents, among them W. T. Stead (even when his anti-war pamphlets were being banned in South Africa), Haldane and the Asquiths. The feelings of liberal-minded men of both parties were expressed in a letter written to Milner on 17 March 1901 by a young Conservative Member of Parliament who crossed the floor to become a Liberal three years later:

My dear Sir Alfred Milner,

At least you must admit I practise discretion in my public utterances: and I hope you may have found time to read my speech in the House on the South African Question—not ill-reported in *The Times* of Feb. 19.

I am certainly not prepared to say anything which may, however feebly, influence public opinion contrary to your having a free hand in the settlement, now I hope not far from its beginning. The task is already hard enough, without being complicated by the well-meant suggestions of anxious friends. But you must regard my letters as stray gleams of light on some accumulations of opinion here in England; for I am not altogether out of touch with popular and political feeling.

We are happier since I wrote last. There is a hopeful feeling that the end of this miserable war—unfortunate and ill-omened in its beginning, inglorious in its course, cruel and hideous in its conclusion—is at last approaching. Your transference to Pretoria is taken—I hope advisedly— as an encouraging sign. I have hated these latter stages with their barbarous features—questionable even according to the bloody precedents of 1870, certainly most horrible. I look forward eagerly to the day when we can take the Boers by the hand and say as Grant did to the Confederates at Appomatox 'Go back and plough your fields.' Personally I am still absolutely determined to strip them of their political independence, but cannot face the idea of their being economically and socially ruined too. They will be our fellow-subjects and as such the fact that they have suffered great calamities by war gives them an additional claim upon us. They must be helped to rebuild their farms; the gold mines must do that. What more fitting function for the wealth of South African soil (better build farms in South Africa than palaces in Park Lane!) Their widows and orphans and crippled soldiers must be our care: and once and for all there must be an end of all those ugly stories of bad faith and military dishonour which ten months' experience in the field has convinced me are mainly founded upon misunderstanding.

I realise—imperfectly perhaps—the amazing difficulty of showing such a spirit in South Africa. Yet it must be our policy to run with the hare and hunt with the hounds. I know we have already quarrelled with the Duteh and must not now quarrel with the British. We must be friends with some one. But although every act of justice or generosity towards the Boers will be regarded by the Loyalists as a personal insult to themselves, you must not shut your eyes to the feeling in this country. The intellect of the nation is piling up on the other side: the strength of the Government cannot be measured by its large majorities. Thousands of votes silenced by the war-like shouts of the crowd these many months will be heard again when peace is restored.

I feel I ought not to write like this to you who have to face so much and struggle against so many difficulties, that you should only hear words of encouragement from those who are earnestly resolved to support you, but I write it because I want exceedingly to hear some public pronouncement from you of a conciliatory character. Surely the Rand is not so mad as not to realise the community of interest they have with the agricultural population. And anything you might be able to say in this direction would disarm enemies and what I daresay are quite as tiresome—officious friends (like me!), and secure you the undisturbed power, which of course is necessary if you are to accomplish anything in the way of reconstruction. Any kindly word that falls from you in Africa will silence a chorus of jangling tongues at home: and win the confidence of a swarm of honest doubters. As for South Africa, my theory (I wonder what you will think of it) is that even if you lose a little, and whatever you lose with the Cape British, you will gain with the Dutch.

Forgive my presumption in pressing my views upon you. If I were singular in feeling these things I would not waste your time by telling them. But you ought to know what some of us are thinking here, and many would understand much less, and so would write much more strongly, than I do. Don't tire yourself by answering this, unless you have something to suggest to me. With all good wishes for you and your burden

Believe me

Yours very sincerely,

WINSTON S. CHURCHILL

But the continent towards which Buchan was sailing was not only the land of warring Boer and Briton, of great powers jostling for influence, territory and market, of Rhodes, King Leopold, Sir Harry Johnston. It was the continent of David Livingstone, of Robert Moffat, of Mary Slessor, and of the Africans to whom they brought Christianity. And the young man on the R.M.S. *Briton* was not only the successful journalist, the promising novelist, the ex-President of the Union—but a son of the Reverend John Buchan, a

member of the John Knox Free Church. Among Buchan's letters
of congratulation was one from an elder of that church, who had
known Buchan since his childhood. After hoping that 'in the midst
of all that may tend to hamper spiritual growth may you receive
grace to withstand it. Nehemiah in the palace could hold converse
with heaven, and there were saints in Caesar's household,' the writer
went on to talk of 'what I hope may be your policy in South Africa.'

I feared for the future of South Africa where there has been so much
corruption, where Christian principles have been stifled by the craze for
gold, and where there is the ever-present opportunity of the white op-
pressing the black. But if I knew that a man like you was helping to hold
the helm, I should have confidence in its future. Rhodes and others are
great men, possessed with large ideas, but they are hardly to be trusted in
their treatment of the blacks and other questions. They see things only
from a utilitarian point of view, and from the angle of their own advantage,
consequently they do not like the missionaries and their impractical
notions. The ignorant sentimentality of Christian people (so they put it) is
a thorn in their flesh, which they would fain be rid of, but which thank God
is still of some power. If these empire-builders require to use the black
races as stepping-stones to further their plans, many people will say they
are justified, but I cannot, and if I can do anything to hinder them I will
do it willingly. It may do for the moment, but it is sure to end in disaster.

I believe however that Lord Milner will do what is right to the dark
race, but he will need some one to help him, some one with the fear of God
before his eyes.

And he closed his letter with 'Remember Lawrence, and remember
Livingstone.'

But it was towards the Boers that the immediate calls upon
Christian feelings were to be directed.

Early in October Buchan landed at Cape Town and, 'as homesick as Davie Balfour,' took train for Johannesburg, a three-day
journey.

Schoeper and Smuts were supposed to be lying about 100 miles up the
line so we went very slowly. It was funny to see the soldiers in the blockhouses along the line turning out to meet the train with fixed bayonets, and
the Kaffir scouts and the watch-fires . . . At Beaufort West there was a
Hussar Tommy, going up to De Aar to have his arm dressed. I took him
into my carriage and gave him meat and drink and dinner at Victoria West.
He was a delightful Irishman, who insisted on showing me his mother's
portrait. He had got the Victoria Cross for riding down the firing line,
saving a wounded man, and then with two bullets in him riding till his
horse was shot to warn his men about an ambush.

Beyond the Orange River 'soldiers began to come in at wayside stations—officers going up to Bloemfontein, so dusty and ragged that only their white teeth and clean nails distinguished them from tramps.' Among them were three he knew, including 'young Haig of Bemersyde.' His first sight of Johannesburg was 'a dusty road, some tin-roofed shanties, with a few large new jerry buildings humped above them: a number of struggling dusty pines and gums, a bit of bare hillside in the distance, and a few attentuated mine chimneys. Everything is new, raw, and fortuitous.' But soon he could write that 'I like the town though it is very new and crude; but in this wonderful air a wooden shanty looks like a Doge's palace.'

Milner's personal staff, when Buchan reported for duty as Political Private Secretary, were Major Lambton (military secretary), Captain Henley and Lord Brooke (military attachés), Osmond Walrond (private secretary), Hugh Wyndham (nicknamed Algy—assistant private secretary), Lord Basil Blackwood (assistant secretary for the Orange River Colony), J. F. Perry (Imperial Secretary—'*i.e.* for Rhodesia and the wilder parts'). Geoffrey Robinson (later Dawson), who had been assistant private secretary to Chamberlain at the Colonial Office, joined them soon after to fill the same post for Milner. Wyndham was an Oxford friend of Buchan's, Basil Blackwood though of an earlier generation knew many of Buchan's Balliol friends, and the three of them decided to take a house, together with Gerard Craig-Sellar, another Balliol man who had been sent by Chamberlain from the Colonial Office. They found, very close to Milner's official residence Sunnyside, a house set among pines and blue grasses 'with a view over 40 miles of veld to a great range of jagged blue mountains [the Magaliesberg] which might be the Coolins.' An old housekeeper of Craig-Sellar's cooked for them, they had an English maid and valet 'and some black boys to attend to the horses' (the only transport) and, as 'the only way of getting fresh milk and eggs,' a cow and some fowls. 'Wyndham and Craig-Sellar are very well-off, Blackwood and I are poor, but we are all simple and economical people, and shall do well together.'

On his return from England Milner, now Governor of the Transvaal and Orange River Colony as well as High Commissioner for South Africa, was faced with a twofold task. First there were the problems of this last stage of the war, when Boer commandos under De Wet, De la Rey and Botha were still slipping between the British blockhouses, harrying Kitchener's troops, and threatening the railways—problems of refugees, repatriation, transport. Almost the most urgent of these was the running of the refugee camps where the wives and families of the Boers who were still fighting had been rounded up; these camps had been taken over from the Army in June 1901. Secondly there were the problems of reconstructing the former Boer republics of the Transvaal and Orange River, where great areas were a wilderness without inhabitants, and almost without cultivation, where most of the mines were still closed down. Boers who surrendered had to be re-settled on their farms where possible; land had to be found for new settlers from Britain and other parts of the Empire; the mines, the necessary basis of economic recovery, had to be restored to full working order, railways repaired and re-equipped; and above all, some kind of civil government had to be organised for the former republics. The young men whom Milner had been recruiting in England in the summer of 1901 were to form the nucleus of the future civil service in the Transvaal and the Orange River Colony. In the meantime they were simply members of Milner's personal staff: 'I am not an official,' wrote Buchan after his first fortnight, 'and I work directly under Milner. My business is to be a sort of Political Private Secretary, to help in dispatches home, and to prepare reports on subjects for his Excy—very much the sort of work an industrious "devil" at the Bar does for his leader.' Chamberlain's idea, in pressing extra secretaries on Milner when he was home in 1901, was to relieve him of detail, and 'leave your mind free for the larger work of settling principles.' In effect Milner delegated to his young men not only details of administration, but considerable responsibility.

Buchan was deeply involved in both aspects of Milner's task: his main work lay, first with the refugee camps, then with Land Settlement. Milner's choice of him for work on the camps may have been influenced by a leading article which Buchan had written in the *Spectator* (22 June 1901), before he had any idea that he was going out to South Africa. There he had explained how the camps had come to be established, and who exactly were the inmates: either women who had remained on their farms when their husbands had joined a commando, or—by far the larger part—'simply the destitute, who either came in voluntarily . . . or who were left on our hands by their far-seeing relatives of the commandos.'* He refuted

* Botha stated on 20 May 1902, shortly before peace was signed, 'One is only too thankful nowadays to know that our wives are under English protection.' (Christian de Wet: *Three Years' War*, 1902.) Mrs Steyn, wife of the President of the Orange Free State, and Mrs Kruger were among those who voluntarily entered the camps.

the charges Lloyd George had directed at the Government, and
quoted Brodrick, the War Minister, on the high rate of mortality
as being largely due to the lack of hygiene among Boer women in
camp conditions. And he added: 'We have to remember that our
charges, while they are the relatives of our enemies, are also the
stock of our future citizens. We have to preserve good temper,
patience and humanity, knowing that every misfortune will be only
too readily interpreted as a crime.' This combination of liberal
feelings towards the Boers with sympathy for the men on the job
in South Africa (as against their critics at home), would appeal to
Milner. He had been shocked by the Army's inefficiency in running
the camps and gave them top priority on his return from England,
as a long series of Blue Books on the question testifies.

In October, when Buchan arrived, there were 118,000 white and
43,000 coloured people in the camps, and the death-rate was at its
peak—344 per thousand. They died from epidemics of measles,
typhoid, whooping-cough, scarlet fever, which themselves were
caused by dirty water (or lack of water), dirty milk, and general lack
of hygiene. Milner reported to Chamberlain in December that

the black spot—the one very black spot—in the picture is the frightful
mortality in the Concentration Camps. I entirely agree with you in thinking that while a hundred explanations may be offered and a hundred
excuses made, they do not really amount to an adequate defence.

To Haldane he owned that 'the camps have taken most of my time
. . . the whole thing has been a sad fiasco.' The day after writing
these words he took Buchan with him to inspect the big camp on
Johannesburg race-course. The coolness and poise of the leader-
writer in London were not so easy to maintain on the spot. 'The
hospital was very clean,' Buchan told Anna, 'but they had no mos-
quito curtains, and the poor children, ill with enteric, were tormented by flies. I have ordered great quantities of curtain from
Cape Town.' And to Lady Mary Murray he wrote, in January 1902:

The Refugee Camps have made my hair grey. When we took them over
they were terrible—partly owing to the preoccupation of the military with
other things, partly to causes inherent in any concentration of people
accustomed to live in the sparsely peopled veld. I shall never forget going
through the hospitals three months ago, when the children were dying like
flies. We have now revolutionised the whole system, and the death rate is
down to something nearly normal now. I have visited most camps, and
have had to decide in emergencies all kinds of complicated questions of
rations, water supply, sanitation and hospital management. I was very
much struck by the heroism of some of the nurses, I got Lord M. to write

his name in their albums, which pleased them. It has been a hideous grind for everybody, but I think we are all better for having gone through it. I say nothing about the original policy of forming camps: it was certainly not wise: but everyone who knows the country admits that it was humane.*

That it was a young bachelor, with not a shred of experience in health administration, who had to decide 'all kinds of complicated questions of rations, water supply, sanitation and hospital management' shows up the fatal inadequacy of the camps policy. The particular horrors which, since the Nazis, have attached themselves to 'concentration camps'† are not to be attached to these South African camps. There was no deliberate policy of cruelty, let alone of extermination: many of the women and children had come in voluntarily, some of them were the families of British loyalists, their rations were the same as the British soldiers'. But the military authorities who set up the camps had not foreseen the likely consequences of herding together people who normally lived in isolated farms and small townships, and had not the resources to run them healthily and hygienically. All was amateur. Infected refugees were sent to hitherto healthy camps; there was no proper isolation or quarantine; sheets from typhoid patients were not disinfected; milk and water were often impure. It was not malevolence, but inefficiency and lack of foresight, that lay behind the camp death-roll that has remained to scar British–South African relations: 20,000 women and children died in the camps during a war in which 3700 Boer soldiers and 5774 British were killed, and 16,168 British died of wounds or illness.

One of Buchan's first jobs had been to 'look after the Ladies' Committee' appointed by the War Office to report on the camps, and headed by Dr Millicent Fawcett. The effect of their recommendations, and above all the arrival of professionals—doctors and nurses from Britain and from the Indian Medical Service—turned the tide, and the epidemics were mastered: by April 1902 the deathrate was reduced to 32 per 1000, which was lower than the rate

---

* In Buchan's novel *The Courts of the Morning* (1929), set in the imaginary South American Republic of Olifa, the Olifa general assumes that his guerrilla opponents 'were based on the villages in the Indian reserve,' so resolves 'to clear that country and bring the women and children into a huge concentration camp.' This move delights the guerrilla leaders, for it relieves them of the duty of feeding the villages, and it strikes them as humane—'He's a humane man, your General Lossberg. The concentrados will be a long sight better off with him than on their own.'

† In the Milner Papers the camps are most often referred to as 'Refugee Camps;' elsewhere, for instance in Ruth Fry's life of Emily Hobhouse (who did so much to rouse British opinion), they are 'concentration camps.'

normal on farms in the veld, and H. W. Nevinson, who had come
out to report the peace negotiations, considered that 'the pitiful
families were now living as decently and healthily as crowds of
women and children can live in long rows of tents upon dust and
withered grass.' In November 1902 Buchan recalled, in the middle
of a press of work on Land Settlement, 'Just this time last year I
was in the throes of the Burgher Camps at their worst. However I
like the present confusion better than the confusion of last year, for
it is not a matter of human life as the other was.'

After the signing of the Peace Treaty of Vereeniging, in May
1902, came the work of repatriating the Boers from the camps.
Farms which had been burnt had to be rebuilt and re-stocked (the
Treaty stipulated that there should be a grant of £3 million for this
purpose). With the Army loath to give up their control of the railways, transport difficulties were tremendous, but by November
Buchan could write that 'Repatriation has taken, I hope, a great
turn for the better,' and within a year of the Treaty a quarter of a
million Boers were back on their farms.

Before he was done with his responsibilities for the camps,
Buchan was deep in the problems of Land Settlement, which, by
comparison, he found 'a fascinating and most hopeful work.' One
of Milner's objectives in the reconstruction of the Transvaal and
Orange River Colony was to increase the British element and to
counterbalance the influence of the mining interests by strengthening the agricultural. So he proposed to introduce British settlers—
not from Great Britain only, but from Canada and Australia.
Strengthening the British element on the land would, too, lessen
'the danger of the race division being accentuated and deepened by
an economic division—a purely Dutch agricultural party opposed
to a purely commercial British one.' And, from his experience in
Egypt, Milner was convinced that by the introduction of irrigation
and of scientific and progressive methods of farming, and improved livestock, the land would be able to support a much larger
population. So money was to be raised to buy land, establish
model farms, carry out experiments in stock-raising and new
varieties of crops; new settlements were to be made from Crown
Lands (formerly State Lands), and suitable settlers picked from the
many applicants, many of whom were discharged soldiers. The
Land Board, cautious and timid in dealing with these applicants,
was to be gingered up.

In January 1902 Milner offered to put Buchan 'at the head of

Land Settlement and give me absolute powers, making me responsible only to the Home Government. At the same time he said that
he found it difficult to spare me and it was only the sense of the
great importance of the work that made him offer it.' Buchan
himself preferred staying with Milner to becoming an official, so a
special Land Settlement Department was set up in Milner's own
office, with Buchan in charge, to act in consultation with the Pro-
visional Board at Pretoria. Buchan's job was to make quick decisions,
cut through red tape, and be available for anything from buying
farms to drafting ordinances: 'I must say I am rather proud of my
Land Act.' This was the Transvaal 'Settlers' Ordinance' of 1902,
based on the experience of settlement schemes in Australia and
New Zealand. Under it holdings were surveyed, valued, gazetted
for application, and publicly allotted after full enquiry by a Central
Board. The Crown Lands Disposal Act, which was mainly Buchan's
work, added considerably to the land for sale.

Here is one of Buchan's accounts of farm-buying (10 February
1902):

Yesterday H.E. asked me to go and see Leewhop, a valuable farm 15 miles
out. I set off early in the morning, and passed the furthest outpost about 9.
They told me to go unarmed, as if I was caught I would be less mis-
handled [De la Rey and De Wet were still at large]. I had no proper directions about the road, but I struck a stream called the Zucskei and followed
it down through awful country. I passed a few lonely farms and rode up
to them, but found them shuttered and not a human being anywhere. It
was a very eerie business, for there were great eagles flapping round, and
in a dingle I found two pariah dogs whom I had to keep off with my hunting
crop. By and by I reached open country with a view for a great distance
and then I found my whereabouts. Alan Breck [his pony] fell into a hole
and flung me, but otherwise I had no mishap. I reached my farm at one
o'clock and ate my lunch in company with a disreputable Irish gentleman
who lived in a blockhouse. I came home by a better way and went up and
had a long talk with H.E. This morning I bought the farm for £11,250.
I am afraid we are going to get into the middle of a Land Boom when prices
will go up to an absurd height. However I will fight a Land Boom or anything else, before I see my scheme fail.

Once the Transvaal Ordinance was passed, Buchan was appointed
to organise the Land Department in Pretoria, and spent the best
part of each week there. (He found the climate trying after the
thousand-feet-higher Johannesburg.) 'I find I have to do everything,' he told his sister, 'for unless I see to it, it is not done, and
my duties are multifarious enough, ranging from financial despatches to the Secretary of State to drafting account forms and

preparing ledger accounts.' A month later he was able to report that 'things are rapidly getting straight, and by Christmas I hope everything will be in apple-pie order. But it is no joke controlling a department with fully 100 officials under you, and at the same time doing ordinary private secretary's work of despatches, etc.' He realised that the pressure might be partly the result of 'being a glutton for work, and doing most things oneself.' He was, in effect, a considerable dispenser of patronage, and found it worrying, 'for if one blesses you, 100 curse you. I am getting pretty fairly unpopular now.' After a few months of it he wrote to Stair Gillon that 'I wish you could see me sitting daily surrounded by every variety of blackguard who wants to make contact with me. I am getting a really first-class judge of rascality.'

In this work Buchan drew a good deal of criticism from people on the spot, mainly for buying land at too high a price, but he also won praise from *The Times History of the War*, which considered the charge of extravagance unjustified, and from a special correspondent of *The Times*, who was writing a series on 'Land Settlement in the New Colonies.' He reported (5 January 1903) that Buchan 'at once brought to bear upon his work, not only an intelligent interest in, and a practical knowledge of matters agricultural, but an aptitude for rapid decision and for taking responsibility.' The writer acknowledged that there had been criticism of Buchan (mainly from disappointed would-be settlers) for not being more of an expert, but considered these other qualities were the ones most needed in the job. Buchan himself, writing about Land Settlement in the *National Review* (April 1902), gave 'a restless vigour and a ready optimism' as the essentials.

The final results, however, were disappointing. Eventually there were only 12,000 British settlers in the Transvaal and Orange River Colony, one-eighth of the figure Milner had hoped for.

'My work is as multifarious as the Army and Navy Stores,' Buchan wrote in September 1902. 'This week I have been sitting on a legal commission, drafting company prospectuses, organising relief camps, founding two new settlements and auditing the accounts of an Irregular Corps. It is a splendid training, but a little too much responsibility is thrown on my shoulders, and I shall be glad when I can turn over a lot of it to departments.' His daily programme in November, when he was down in Pretoria in weather 'like a Turkish bath,' was 'Rise at 5 and ride till 7. Breakfast at

7.30. Office at 8 and straight on till 7. Dinner 7.30. Back to office from 8 to 10. A pretty heavy day, considering how full of responsibility and worry the work is.' During this spell he contracted mumps (one of the Johannesburg papers regretted to learn 'that young Mr Buchan is suffering from one of the maladies incident to extreme youth'), but this seems to have had little effect on his activities.

On Wednesday it became necessary for me to go down and settle up some trouble in our new farm at Standerton. Not being able to get away in time to catch the mail train, I had to travel all night in a goods train in a cattle truck with a draft of utterly intoxicated Seaforth Highlanders, who kept falling over me and murmuring 'Scotland for ever.' I wished that Scotland had been a little less 'for ever' that night. It was very cold and unpleasant and did my mumps no good. The next day I rode 40 miles and enjoyed it immensely in a magnificent breezy upland country. I returned on Friday and had to set out at once to meet a gathering of Boers in Rustenburg who were in trouble about their farms and other matters. I went there yesterday and talked away all day—interesting but wearing work. The old fellows were very nice and very hospitable, and appreciated my broken Dutch immensely.

'I have had a lot of these wild rushes lately,' he wrote his brother Willie. 'It is the only way to keep a big concern going, to look into it yourself. None of my people know when I may not turn up and ask for a reckoning.' But work at such high pressure 'tries the nerves of even so nerveless a person as myself,' and at times he felt that 'this whole show is getting too big for the present staff.' In March 1903 the Land Board was firmly established, with a former Minister of Lands in Western Australia, Dr Adam Jameson, as Commissioner; Buchan was given a farewell dinner ('I was vexed to part with the people, all of whom I had myself appointed, and a nicer lot than which doesn't exist'), and in April was finding life much easier. 'What a simple thing Private Secretary's work is, after the harassing responsibility of a big department.' Henceforth, till he left South Africa in August, he was mainly concerned with the administrative problems of the two new colonies—such as franchise, budgets, military commands—and the Inter-Colonial Council of the Transvaal and Orange River Colony, which met in July and of which he was Secretary. This body (set up by an Order in Council in May) was to be a first step towards federation. It administered the railways and police for both colonies; later, surveys and education were added to its scope.

On top of all the day-to-day work there were the ceremonies,

which Buchan enjoyed more than his chief: the Military Thanksgiving in June 1902 after the signing of the Treaty of Vereeniging,
the swearing-in of Milner as Governor of the Transvaal ('I stood
at the right hand, with a face as long as the Spey, so I am told. On
Friday there is a great levee in Pretoria when I have to put on kilt
and lace and siccan vanities') and the presentation to Milner by
Portuguese envoys of the Grand Cross of the Order of Jesus Christ.
The visit of the Colonial Secretary in January 1903 was more than
a ceremonial occasion; Milner's young men were kept on their toes
to satisfy Chamberlain's questions:

We have had an exciting week with Joe. He arrived a week ago, and last
Tuesday made the first public speech at the banquet at Pretoria. Very good
—the old professional among amateurs. He was very good on Thursday
too in his meeting with the Boer leaders. I dined with him last night and
lunched with him today and talked with him all afternoon. He cross-
examined me closely, but on the whole I found him a kindly old gentleman.
He thanked me for all I had done, which was very nice of him. Mrs Chamberlain is perfectly charming and very pretty.

All the same, he confessed to Stair Gillon, Chamberlain had
somehow disappointed him:

He is as clever as paint, and sees a point a mile off. But he is too dapper
and business-like; he seems to lack vision and daemonic power. I cannot
imagine him leading men as Gladstone led them, or attracting men as Lord
Milner attracts them, or moulding the future as Rhodes attempted. He is
a business-like clever man from Birmingham, a man whom you want to
make General Manager of the British Empire, but whom you know will
remain for ever a General Manager and not a creator.

'Not so big a man as Lord M' was his later impression: and by
this time Buchan was in no doubt that Lord Milner was a very big
man indeed.

Whatever the stresses and pressures, Buchan found his work
immensely satisfying and exhilarating. He had not been strongly
pro-war; had decided in 1899 that it was not his duty to volunteer;
he was very critical of the military; and after his arrival in South
Africa he thought 'we were *just* in the right.' But he had no doubts
whatever of the rightness of the Reconstruction. The job appealed
to his sense of justice, his sense of order, and his sense of achievement: as he rode to inspect a newly settled farm, or a new herd of
cattle, he could see his plans made concrete in the course of a few
months. Here a man's ideas could quickly develop into action; a
man's actions could quickly become effective. There was no gulf

between the life of intellect and the life of action. 'We were all
hopeful,' one of Milner's staff recalled in 1957; 'we were creating
something.' There was a wonderful sense of buoyancy and optimism; all the problems before them were exhilarating challenges.
'The fascination of what's difficult' was one of the greatest fascinations South Africa offered to Milner's young men.

Buchan could put the more heart into his work because, on the
whole, he liked Boers and got on well with them. Admiration for
the fighting Boer was widespread among the military, and many
regarded the last stage of the war as a sporting encounter with a
sporting adversary.*

General Maxwell told me that many soldiers who were captured by the
Boers and released came back convinced pro-Boers. The truth is that while
there are a certain number of new bandits in the field—Germans, Irish
Fenians, Boer ruffians, and English (and Scots, I'm afraid) deserters—who
wreck trains and behave like swine, Botha, De la Rey and De Wet play the
game like gentlemen, and must be treated as such. There are moments
when one almost wishes one could change sides—it must be such a glorious
thing to fight a losing battle for what is after all a noble object. They are
not fighting for Kruger and his gang now, but for the country, and it is the
irony of fate that we must stamp out the resistance.

But beyond this admiration for the Boer fighter, Buchan had a
Scots Presbyterian's sympathy for the Bible-reading burgher, and
a Borderer's liking for the veld farmer. Milner meant to do right by
the Boer, but could not really like him; Buchan could, and where
Milner saw shiftiness and lies, Buchan saw a practised haggling that
reminded him of Tweeddale farmers selling sheep. 'There is
nothing Arcadian about the Boer,' he noted, 'as there is certainly nothing Arcadian about the average peasant!' And if the
Boer farmer's manners were not exactly those of polite society,
neither were Uncle Jim's or Uncle John's at Bamflat. So much
that he experienced in his treks—the Boer clannishness, the hospitality, the bible-thumping, the women in mutches, the old men
telling racy country stories, the Dutch psalms sung to the tunes he
knew—brought Scotland to mind. And, brought up on the Bible
himself, he could understand how the Boer regarded his one epic
action, the Great Trek from the Cape to the Transvaal, as analogous
to the exodus of the Children of Israel from Egypt to the Promised
Land.

* *Blackwood's* ran a series in 1902 'On the Heels of De Wet.' Two of the episodes
were entitled 'To a New Covert' and 'Full Cry.'

For all such scriptural echoes in Boer life, Buchan detested the Boer's 'unlovely kirk'—though there, too, he had no difficulty in finding a Scottish parallel.

These old rascals, the Dutch Reformed Church, give me a great deal of trouble just now. They lie just like the Scots ministers in the seventeenth century—for the pure pleasure of the art, till the atmosphere of their synods is blue with perjury. I have been collecting some of their chief falsehoods into a very pretty dispatch, which I hope somebody will have the strength of mind to publish.*

And whereas the religion professed by the Boers was in its essentials 'the same which a generation or two ago held sway over Galloway peasants and Hebridean fishermen,' the results were very different.

The stern hard-bitten souls who saw the devil in most of the works of God, and lived ever under a great Taskmaster's eye, had no kinship with the easy-going sleek-lipped Boer piety. The Boer religion in practice was a judicious excerpt from the easier forms of Christianity, while its theory was used to buttress his self-sufficiency and mastery over weaker neighbours. . . . In his religion, God made men of two colours, white and black, the former to rule the latter till the end of time.

Buchan's duties with Milner did not involve him directly in the colour question: but his views, as expressed in *The African Colony*, closely reflected his chief's. Milner in 1897 had written that 'the Anglo-Dutch friction is bad enough. But it is child's play compared with the antagonisms of the White and Black.' The Boers' main motive in originally trekking north had been resentment at British interference between them and the Africans; one of Milner's aims now was to bring the position of Africans in the former Boer republics into line with their less repressed position in Cape Colony and Natal; the penalty of flogging under the Transvaal Pass Law, for instance, was abolished in July 1901. Though his declared view was that 'civilisation, not colour, ought to be the test of fitness for civic rights,' Milner regarded the African's political rights as a very long-term affair. ('The white man must rule, because he is elevated by many, many steps above the black man; steps

* In a leading article in the *Spectator* (24 December 1904) on 'Mr Kruger's Funeral' Buchan wrote: 'In religion he stood for a creed of ugly faults and unlovely virtues, a jealous God and a mercantile Paradise—such a creed as Israel might have evolved if it had remained without a leader on some reserve in Egypt.' He noted in *The African Colony* that no predikant had accompanied the emigrants on the Great Trek. 'The Kirk did not see the Scriptural parallel, and to a man preferred the treasure in Egypt to the doubtful fortunes of Israel.'

which it will take the latter centuries to climb.') The ninth clause of the Treaty of Vereeniging expressly stated that the question of non-white franchise was not to be decided before the grant of self-government to the former republics. (Liberal pressure to end the war here resulted in this illiberal denial of Coloured and African rights: the outcome was to postpone the emancipation of Africans indefinitely, and Milner came bitterly to regret his yielding on this point, in order to secure Boer agreement to the Treaty.) Buchan's view of the matter was that

A subject population, to whom legal rights are denied, tends in the long run to degrade the value of human life, and to depreciate the moral currency . . . The denial of social and political rights is almost equally dangerous, since, apart from the risks of perpetual tutelage in a progressive community, there follows necessarily a depreciation of those political truths upon which all free societies are based.

But, he went on,

The essence of social and political equality must be a standard of education and moral and intellectual equipment, which can be roughly attributed to all members of the community concerned. But in this case there can be no such common standard.

The only solution, as he saw it, was 'patiently and skilfully [to] bring to bear upon the black man the solvent and formative influence of civilisation'—and hope for the best. In municipal franchise racial distinctions had no logical place: 'If a black man is a ratepayer he has the citizen's right to vote.'

Africans did not, however, enter Buchan's daily life except as servants or labourers. Among white people he had friends of all kinds. At the centre was the small enclave of the Milner young men,* particularly the three he shared a house with—Wyndham, Blackwood and Craig-Sellar. They dressed for dinner and—till their work became too exacting—sat in the drawing-room afterwards, as

---

* In *With Milner in South Africa* (1951) Lionel Curtis recalled that the name 'Kindergarten' was given in derision to Milner's young men by Sir William Marriott, then practising at the Bar in Johannesburg. It was after Buchan had left South Africa that the Kindergarten began to act as a political group. L. S. Amery, who described himself as 'informally a member,' mentions the following as belonging to the Kindergarten (*My Political Life*, I, 1953, page 177): Buchan, Geoffrey Robinson (Dawson), Patrick Duncan, Lionel Curtis, Lionel Hichens, Fabian Ware, Basil Williams, R. H. Brand and Philip Kerr (Lord Lothian)—Kerr did not come out to South Africa till after Buchan had left. Others who have been mentioned as belonging to it (*e.g.* in J. R. M. Butler's *Lord Lothian*, 1906, page 14*n*) are John Dove, Richard Feetham, Dougal Malcolm, J. F. Perry and Hugh Wyndham. They were all Oxford men.

if they were in England, carrying on something of the old Oxford talk and jokes, even if the world outside inclined to think them rather brash and rather superior. Like Raymond Asquith and Cuthbert Medd, the others teased Buchan for his ever-sanguine disposition and for his enthusiasm. He was never allowed to forget that he had nearly bought for himself a farm where there was no water-supply, between Johannesburg and Pretoria.

Beyond this inner circle were soldiers, settlers, farmers, journalists, agricultural experts and Rand millionaires. Among the soldiers were Julian Byng, Douglas Haig and Lieutenant Ironside, who had been seconded to do Intelligence work in German South-West Africa. Among the millionaires was Sir Lionel Phillips, who had made a fortune in his twenties, lost it and made another, who had been one of the four Uitlanders condemned to death for their part in the Jameson Raid, and was now a partner in Wernher Beit and President of the Chamber of Mines; and there were the partners in Eckstein's whom Buchan met at the Rand Club and Johannesburg dinner-parties, 'young men with several millions each, and their acumen and good sense is remarkable. Very different from the bloated Jew financier of the pro-Boer and Bellocian imagination.' Buchan was particularly impressed by Schumacher, a Harrovian, who in six years had made his million and over—'a genuine financial genius and at the same time he is a man of great culture and has the best private collection of Napoleonic prints and relics that I have seen.' He thought the influence and character of the Johannesburg Jews had been grossly distorted. This was no 'Judasburg,' he wrote in an article on the city for the *National Review* (January 1903):

You will see more Jews in it than in Montreal or Aberdeen, but not more than in Paris; and any smart London restaurant will show as large a Semitic proportion as a Johannesburg club. For a 'Golden City' it is not even conspicuously vulgar. For one fellow in large checks, diamonds, and a pink satin tie, you will meet fifty quietly dressed, well-mannered gentlemen.

In this Buchan was agreeing with Milner, who remarked to H. W. Nevinson, then visiting South Africa, that 'if you go into a crowded room and find two Jews there you come away saying the place was full of Jews.'

'I find that I get on well with the Johannesburgers,' wrote Buchan shortly after his arrival, 'and hear that I am very popular with them. I think a Scotsman is always more adaptable than an Englishman—he is more of a humorist.' Certainly Scots abounded wherever Buchan went—'one hears every variety of accent from Aberdeen to Hawick;' at the first hotel he entered in Johannesburg the cashier called out 'Whae belongs to this dowg,' and the hall-porter answered 'I dinna ken;' his two clerks at the High Commissioner's Office were Scots, and so were many of the settlers applying for land. Restless Oxford friends were among the applicants too: 'I daresay I shall make an awful hash of farming,' wrote one from the Cocoa Tree in St James's, 'but I should think it would be a better job to fail in than a profession over here.' He was not accepted.

It was a man's world, and Buchan was out of the habit of talking to women. When his Land Settlement work took him each week to Pretoria, early in 1903, he stayed several times with General Neville Lyttelton, who had succeeded Kitchener in the South African Command. The Lyttelton daughters, particularly Lucy the eldest (who later married Charles Masterman) struck Buchan, in his present rôle of practical man of affairs, as rather difficult to keep up with. 'Miss Lyttelton will talk about Dante and Ibsen,' wrote this founder of the Brasenose Ibsen Society, 'and it is no good pretending ignorance and asking if they were horses.'

Into this world of millionaires and adventurers erupted his own family. No sooner had Buchan landed in South Africa than he heard of his parents' proposal to go to Port Elizabeth, to replace a local minister for nine months. He did his best to dissuade them: if it were a question of his father's health, let them go to Madeira or Egypt, and he would pay part of the cost. But in spite of his cables, and warnings about the horrors of living under martial law, and prophecies (largely fulfilled) that 'you would spend there the dreariest and most harassed months of your life,' out they came in December 1901. It was understandably nettling to a young man who had crossed seas to seek fame and fortune, who had begged his mother not to worry and fuss, to find her setting out to join him, not to speak of his father and his eight-year-old brother. After their arrival his letters were full of exasperated references to the venture, and he was justifiably irritated when, after he had visited them in Port Elizabeth in May 1902, Mr Buchan indiscreetly passed on some remarks—which he had misinterpreted—about Milner's anti-Dutch feeling. 'I feel relieved that my aged father is "cleared oot o' the country,"' wrote John to Anna: and he always maintained that

'Port Elizabeth was an unhallowed ploy from the start.' There was an awkward moment too when his uncle Eben Masterton, hearing of John's work in setting up and staffing the Land Department, made enquiries about a job. Explanations had to be sent to Peebles: 'You see we found that South African agriculture is so technical and peculiar that we have been compelled only to employ colonials. A good man from home is quite useless for all work like stock inspection and land valuation.'

Buchan's delight in his work in South Africa was compounded of many elements: exhilaration at responsibility, the discovery of new powers in himself of administration and command, and the engagement of his whole energies, physical no less than intellectual. He had written many stories celebrating physical effort and exhaustion; on his Border holidays he had driven himself hard; but now the effort and exhaustion were in the way of his work. Much of the time he was in the saddle—riding between his home and Johannesburg, or over the veld to inspect a property, interview a settler, see a stud-farm or a tank-sinking experiment, often covering forty miles a day. He had ridden in Galloway, on the Ardwall holidays, but his horsemanship was rather like that of Andrew Garvald, the hero of his *Salute to Adventurers*, 'a clumsy, rough-and-ready affair, very different from the effortless grace of your true cavalier,' though 'I can keep my seat on most four-legged beasts.' He had to; the veld was rough going, with

traps for the loose rider. A conical ant-heap with odd perforations, an ant-bear hole three foot down, or, most insidious of all, a meerkat's hole hidden behind a tuft of herbage. A good pony can gallop and yet steer, provided the rider trusts it; but the best will make mistakes, and on occasion roll over like a rabbit. Most men begin with a dreary apprenticeship to the spills; but it is curious how few are hurt, despite the hardness of the ground. One soon learns the art of falling clear and falling softly.

After his two years of London, where he missed the long walks and rides of the Oxford years, it was delightful to have regular gallops on the veld in the early morning, or at sundown, as well as his necessary journeys. And the young writer, ready to see life in literary terms, must often have thought of Stevenson's pleasure in riding through the lines of the warring chiefs in Samoa, as he himself passed the military outposts and rode on into territory open to the commando raiders.

To the physical pleasure of riding was added the pleasure of

riding in this marvellous country, whose climate gave him such a
sense of complete well-being. At his first sight of it from the train
Buchan had fallen in love with South Africa. 'It is splendid swinging
along in the cool veld air, with the sky above the colour of a sloe-
berry, except for a great fiery sea in the west,' he told his brother
Willie, and years after he had left the continent he remembered
above all 'that wonderful mulberry gloaming which only South
Africa can give.' Describing the prospect from a ridge on the veld,
looking towards the spurs of the Magaliesberg, he wrote (in *The
African Colony*):

There is something extraordinarily delicate and remote about the vista;
it might be a mirage, did not the map bear witness to its reality. It is not
unlike a child's conception of the landscape of Bunyan, a road running
straight through a mystical green country, with the hilltops of the Delec-
table Mountains to cheer the pilgrim. And indeed the land is instinct with
romance. The names of the gorges which break the mountain line—
Olifants' Poort, Crocodile Poort, Commando Nek—speak of war and
adventure and the far tropics beyond these pastoral valleys. The little
farms are all 'Rests' and 'Fountains' the true nomenclature of a far-
wandering, home-loving people. The slender rivulet below us is one of the
topmost branches of the great Limpopo, rising in a marsh in the wood
behind, forcing its way through the hills and the bush-veld to the north,
and travelling thence through jungles and fever-swamps to the Portuguese
sea-coast. The road is one of the old highways of exploration; it is not fifty
years since a white man first saw the place. And yet it is as pastoral as
Yarrow or Exmoor; it has the green simplicity of sheep-walks and the
homeliness of a long-settled rustic land. In the afternoon peace there is no
hint of the foreign or the garish; it is as remote as Holland itself from the
unwholesome splendours of the East and South.

As well as his routine journeys, Buchan had four longer treks
(described in *The African Colony*): in August 1902 to the western
frontiers of the Transvaal; in January 1903 north-east to the Wood
Bush; in March to Swaziland; and at the end of July a farewell trek
up to the Rhodesian border. He had hoped to have some big-game
hunting on the Zambesi or the Limpopo, but this turned out to be
too expensive;* he had hoped too that Stair Gillon might join him
in 1903 for an attempt on the Mont aux Sources in the Drakensberg
on the edge of Basutoland. Buchan had his eye on the unclimbed
north-eastern buttress, but Gillon was ploughed in his Bar finals in
Edinburgh, and the plan fell through.

* When Buchan reviewed Theodore Roosevelt's *African Game Trails* in the
Spectator (15 October 1910), Roosevelt wrote appreciatively that 'of course as soon
as I read your review I knew that you were a big game man.'

On the first trek Buchan took a caravan of two Cape-carts, a spring waggon and eight mules, and two riding-horses; a guide of Kaffir descent and an old cook. They trekked by Klerksdorp, Koranna-fontein and Lichtenburg to Zeerust, and back to Pretoria by Rusten-burg: past ruined farms, and farms where life was beginning again, and kopjes and fords where Boer and Briton had so lately fought each other. But it was not all eloquent of war. One morning, after they had outspanned (pitched camp) at Malmani Oog,

We left our drivers to inspan and follow, and set off down the little stream with our guns. There are hours which live for ever in the memory—hours of intense physical exhilaration, the pure wine of health and youth, when the mind has no thoughts save for the loveliness of earth, and the winds of morning stir the blood to a heavenly fervour. No man who has experienced such seasons can be other than an optimist. Dull nights in cities, heartless labours with pen and ink, the squalid worries of business and ambition, all are forgotten, and in the retrospect it is those hours which stand up like shining hill-tops—the type of the pure world before our sad mortality had laid its spell upon it. It is not pleasure—the word is too debased in human parlance; nor happiness, for that is for calm delights. Call it joy, that 'enthusiasm' which is now the perquisite of creeds and factions, but which of old belonged to the fauns and nymphs who followed Pan's piping in the woody hollows of Thessaly. I have known and loved many streams, but the Little Malmani has a high place in my affections. The crystal water flowed out of great reed-beds into a shallow vale, where it wound in pools and cataracts to a broad ford below a ruined mill. Thence it passed again into reed-beds fringed with willows and departed from our ken. There was a bamboo covert opposite full of small singing birds; the cries of snipe and plover rose from the reed-beds, and the fall of water, rarest of South African sounds, tinkled like steel in the cold morning air. We shot nothing for we saw nothing; the glory of the scene was all that mortal eye could hold at once. And then our waggons splashed through the ford, and we had perforce to leave it.

On the treks to the Wood Bush and Swaziland the route lay often on the edge of the high ground, whence Buchan looked eastward over the wild tangle of glens between the Drakensberg or Zoutpans-berg and the Lebombo hills on the Portuguese border. This type of view he found 'of infinite charm, for you stand upon the dividing line between two forms of country and two climates, looking back upon the endless prairies and their fresh winds and forward upon warm glens and the remote malarial tropics.' It was the Wood Bush that gave Buchan his best days in South Africa—days of 'intense ex-hilaration, when one seemed to be a happy part of a friendly universe.' Here is his account to Anna, written in a hotel at Pieters-burg (4 January 1903):

For the last 5 days I have travelled about 1100 miles, partly in trains, partly in waggons, and largely on horseback. I have been over to Wood Bush, an elevated plateau in the Zoutpansberg mountains overlooking the low fever country. I have never been in such an earthly paradise in my life. You mount up tiers of mountain ridge, barren stony places, and then suddenly come on a country like Glenholm. Terrific blue mountains rise to the South but the country is chiefly little wooded knolls, with exquisite green valleys between. The whole place looks like a colossal nobleman's park laid out by some famous landscape gardener. And when you examine it closely you find it richer than anything you can imagine. The woods are virgin forest—full of superb orchids and fern, and monkeys, and wild pig, and tiger-cats and bush-buck. The valleys have full clear streams flowing down them and water-meadows—where in place of meadowsweet and buttercup you have tall blue agapanthus and huge geraniums and great beds of arums and the ferns. The perfume of the place is beyond description. The soil is very rich: the climate misty and invigorating, just like Scotland. I went in the hottest season of the year, and the air was like a Highland June. The place is a plateau with deep precipices falling away on every side. When you get to the edge of my water-meadows you look down 4000 feet to the shimmering blue plains of the fever country. The land belongs almost wholly to the Government and I have an idea of buying a little farm on the edge of the plateau and having it as a kind of African country-house, where you could grow every known flower and fruit. I only wish my old father could have seen the place. He would have realised where the garden of Eden really was situated.

One day I rode down into the fever country—appallingly hot but very interesting. I slept New Year's Night there in the house of a German called Altenroxel where I ate the most wonderful tropical fruits and saw a lot of snakes. Yesterday coming home I was nearly done for. I sent all my party out on different routes and arranged to meet my waggons at a certain place. And I somehow missed my waggons and had to ride straight in here. My horse was dead-beat, the night pitch dark and I had nothing from 6 one morning till 1 the next morning when I got in. I lost my road and was really rather scared for a little. I rode over 70 miles, say the distance from Glasgow to Selkirk, under a blazing sun, without food or drink, and was altogether 14½ hours in the saddle. I had a long good sleep and am perfectly well and fresh today.

. . . This Wood Bush has really fascinated me—a kind of celestial Scotland and I am very keen to have a bit biggin of my ain in it. I wish I could take you to see it. Hardly anybody knows anything about it. To reach it you sail 5000 miles, travel 1500 in a train and then drive 60 on the worst mountain roads in the world. So it's fairly inaccessible to the tripper for Saturday to Monday. Here is the address of the notepaper of my Wood Bush residence.

Station	Pietersburg 63 miles	BUCHANSDORP
Telegrams	,, ,, ,,	WOOD BUSH
Letters	Haenertsburg 12 miles	

To the end of his life Buchan saw the Wood Bush as 'a *temenos*, a place enchanted and consecrate.'

It was this eastern scarp of the berg, midway between the high veld and the fever-flats, that fascinated him, where the heads of the glens running east were rounded green cup-shaped hollows, like the 'hopes' of a Border glen. Compared with the bareness of the high veld,

this garden-ground is wholly human. Natura Benigna was the goddess who presided at its creation, and no roughness enters into the 'warm, green-muffled' slopes, the moist temperate weather, and the limpid waters. . . . It is that most fascinating of all types of scenery, a garden on the edge of a wilderness.

The place had overtones of England; a little lower, and it was a different atmosphere:

The heavy tropical scents which the rain brought out of the ground, the intense silence of the drooping mists and water-laden forests, the clusters of beehive Kaffir huts in the hollows, all made up a world strange and new to the sight and yet familiar to the imagination. This was the old Africa of a boy's dream.

No longer the Africa of the missionary or the imperialist: Rider Haggard's Africa.

On this trek to the Wood Bush, as on those to Swaziland and the Rhodesian border, Buchan had with him R. H. Brand, who had joined Milner's staff late in 1902. Half a century later Lord Brand remembered it clearly—particularly the time when he and Buchan saw a secret Kaffir rite, near a big farm run by Germans at the eastern edge of the Wood Bush, down the Machubi glen: 'Kaffir boys, covered in a contraption of straw,' performing a ritual which was probably a circumcision rite: 'enormously impressive.' Brand too fell in love with the Wood Bush, and it remained in his memory as the most beautiful place he knew. But 'I hardly recognised some of the places when I read about them in *The African Colony*—John had a wonderful imagination.'

'It is horrible to come to an end of anything, and feel that a door has been shut on part of your life,' wrote Buchan shortly before he sailed for home in August 1903.

I have had a very fine time, a great deal of pleasure too, but the chief advantage is that I have come on so much, learned so much, known so much better what I can do and what I can't do. I wouldn't have missed the experience for worlds, and nothing can make me regret that I came out here two years ago.

The gains had been various. His work towards rebuilding South Africa had given him a sense of purpose which he had so far missed at the Bar, and which his closest friends were not finding in their work at home. 'It must be a pleasant sensation doing work which produces an ostensible result,' Raymond Asquith had written.

It is one which those who read the Digest in Oxford rarely feel, I can assure you. Whether anyone else in England feels it I should be puzzled to say: it is certain that no one has a right to.

And Cuthbert Medd thought seriously of coming out to join Buchan, if a job could be found, giving several reasons:

First, the Bar is too selfish and egotistic a profession to satisfy me; I would sooner be working for some great extrapersonal end; secondly, Lord Milner is *the* man of all under whom I would soonest serve, and thirdly, the work which he is guiding is, I think, the finest work now being done in the world.

Medd obtained, through Buchan, Milner's promise to take him on his staff when there was room, but on a holiday in the Adriatic he went down with typhoid, and died in London at the end of 1902. 'It seems such a stupid and senseless thing for a man so brilliant and courageous to die of a thing like fever in a place like London,' wrote Buchan to his sister. 'He was one of my nearest friends, and though I have a great many so-called friends, I haven't very many real ones—Cubby and Raymond, John Edgar and Boulter, Sandy [Gillon] and John Jameson about make up the list.'

Though the purpose of his job might be lofty, Buchan had learnt to work for it in the most down-to-earth ways: 'I have to see that *things get done*, as well as make theories. . . . Academic cobwebs get swept away and one becomes sublimely practical.' From the refugee camps, the repatriation centres, the Land Administration Office, he had learnt that 'sound government . . . means a perpetual effort, a keen sense of reality, a constant facing and adjusting of problems.' Valuable as this experience was, it was experience of a very special kind of administration. Milner had to do things in a hurry, often starting from scratch. He had to put a ruined country somehow on its feet; and do it against the clock. For—especially after 1902—the Conservative Government in Britain was losing ground, and he could not count on such a free hand from the Liberals. Buchan excelled at this extemporising, improvising kind of work: he pushed things through and got things done, and his ability to make quick appreciations and decisions was exactly what Milner wanted in the circumstances of the time. But, as one colleague put it, Buchan 'left carcasses in his way.' Amery, looking back fifty years later, considered that

The Kindergarten often made mistakes. Their ideas about money were sometimes over-generous. Their manner occasionally too cocksure. But by sheer enthusiasm and ability, devotion to duty and passionate loyalty to their chief they achieved a gigantic task.

Perhaps Buchan's biggest gain was to have worked so closely with Milner, to have watched a first-class mind in administrative action, to have been in close touch with a man whom he saw as magnanimous and selfless. He has painted a splendid picture of Milner in *Memory Hold-the-Door*. Here, to set beside it, is an estimate written in 1905 for *The Times* on Milner's final return to England:

South Africa has shown us that we possess a public servant of a very rare and remarkable type, not merely a competent man or a strong man, but a man with tempered, steel-like qualities of will and intellect. Lord Milner's power is high-strung and spiritual in its essence; his resolution is unfaltering, because it is the fruit of profound mental toil and a high devotion to duty . . . He has no care for his reputation, only for the accomplishment of his task. More than once he has risked everything for a principle when a lesser man would have hesitated and hedged. . . . A kindly, cultivated man in the ordinary relationships of life, with ordinary feelings and prejudices, he has the gift of complete mental detachment when face to face with a problem. He can isolate it from all adventitious circumstances, delete the emotional and the irrational, and work out the solution with unswerving logic. . . . He is incapable of deceiving himself, or of becoming a prophet of smooth things. A weaker man would seize on some Boer protestation of loyalty as material for a rosy forecast of racial union. But Lord Milner is no self-deceiver. He faces the facts, however dismal.

Two of Milner's beliefs deeply affected Buchan's outlook. The one was his unshaken faith in the possibilities of the Empire; the other his impatience with the trivialities of domestic politics.

To a young man who now seemed poised for a political or proconsular career, his early literary ambitions rather pushed behind him, the two years had been invaluable. But, though this at the time was less clear, they were also immensely valuable to him as a writer. Buchan came home from South Africa with memories of moments and places where everything seemed possible, where any adventure might begin—and this expectancy is a large part of the appeal of his later stories; and also with experience of government that was invaluable in reading the mind, and appreciating the problems, of the public men whose lives he later studied: Montrose, Cromwell, Augustus.

Out of Buchan's experience in South Africa came three books, and three short stories. He had been only a few months in the country when he began to plan a work to be called '*African Studies* on the same lines as Alfred Lyall's *Asiatic Studies*—containing essays on scenery, sport, people, and politics.' Early in 1903 he told Gilbert Murray:

I am writing a book! I could not help it. I am so much in love with this country, and have so many things to say which I think ought to be said . . . I want to talk about the beauty and the mystery of the landscape, the Union history, the intricacies of the Boer character, and the racial and economic questions ahead. A funny hotch-potch, but I think 'it will have a certain unity.

In the first section of *The African Colony* (1903) Buchan aimed to refute the common view that South Africa

is a country without history, or, if she has a certain barbarous chronicle, it is without significance. The truth is nearly at the opposite pole. South Africa is bound to the chariot-wheels of her past . . . Phoenician, Arab, Portuguese, Dutch, and English—that is her Uitlander cycle.

When he came to the Portuguese, 'who remained adventurers and aliens,' he spoke as the Milner young man, severe on the system whereby the viceroy had to restore his fortunes at the expense of the provincials:

There is more in bad government than hardship for the private citizen. It means the weakening of the intellectual and moral nerve of the race which tolerates it.

Though he had more sympathy with the Boers, he found them 'without that dash of adventure which belongs to all imaginative men,' called the Great Trek 'this Marathon of an unimaginative race,' and summed them up as 'a hodden-grey burgess society.' The second section of the book was a record of Buchan's treks, which have already been described, and the third was a useful summary of the main problems facing the rulers and people of the Transvaal. Here the voice, as the reviewer in *The Times Literary Supplement* remarked (27 November 1903), was that of the Private Secretary to the High Commissioner, and very discreet; there was no discussion of Chamberlain's or Milner's policies. On the native question the same reviewer found Buchan 'very moderate.'

remote alike from Exeter Hall* as from the extreme view that the native should be driven to work by any and every device of direct and indirect compulsion.

The African Colony received respectful notice and sold just over five hundred copies in its first two years.

Buchan's first shot at putting his views on South Africa and the Empire into a freer form was *The Mountain*, begun in 1905, which he intended to be 'a big novel' but never finished. In it a shy young man finds himself in a country-house on the Borders, where men of influence and experience are discussing the morality of politics and imperialism. Perhaps Buchan felt that the discussion was hampered by the novel form; at any rate, in the same year he started *A Lodge in the Wilderness*, a symposium in the style of W. H. Mallock's *New Republic* (1877). It was published anonymously in 1906, though the second edition a year later carried the author's name.

In the introduction which he wrote in 1916 for the cheap edition Buchan spoke of having felt that

certain larger matters, which did not truly belong to party politics, were in danger of being obscured or degraded. In [the writer's] opinion these matters not only involved none of the traditional party antagonisms, but contained in truth the conditions under which alone each party could realise what was enduring in its creed and beneficent in its purpose.

Reflected in the book are years of discussion with friends and colleagues; with Raymond Asquith, who professed to think an Empire vulgar ('The day of the clever cads is at hand. . . . I always felt it would come to this if we once let ourselves in for an Empire,' he wrote in 1901); with Cuthbert Medd, who had written for the *National Review* (February 1903) of the state of the Empire at the end of the Boer War; with Milner and with his fellow-members of the Kindergarten; with Gilbert Murray, who sent Buchan a long letter to South Africa on the difference between the empire-builder with a real sense of *noblesse oblige* and the less reputable kind who makes a statement of ideals, such as 'An Englishman likes fair play,' and then assumes it as a fact.

Buchan allows himself a good deal of fictional play in the setting of the symposium. The company assembles at Musuru, the house which Francis Carey, 'an intelligent millionaire,' has built nine thousand feet up on the East African plateau in a country of shallow

---

* A hall in the Strand used for meetings of religious and philanthropic organisations; associated with liberal and progressive views.

glens and clear streams to the west of the Rift Valley. The house is
in Cape Dutch style, with wide verandahs and cool stone pillars,
set with its gardens, orchards and vineyards in a spacious parkland.
It is the country-house which, in *The African Colony*, Buchan said
he would build in the Wood Bush 'when my ship comes home.' No
wonder that it 'has the airy perfection of a house seen in a dream.'
And like Buchan's dream-house, Musuru combines civilisation with
wildness. There is a library of 62,000 volumes, some Louis Quinze
cabinets, a blue drawing-room with fluted white walls, Sèvres china
and a Watteau shepherdess.

Nor do the characters in the symposium fall below this high
standard. Lord Appin is a former Prime Minister, Lord Launceston
a former Viceroy of India, Mr Wakefield a Canadian statesman,
Mr Loewenstein a Jewish financier; also of the party are a big-game
hunter, a famous explorer, and a far-travelled journalist. Several
married women are there without their husbands, for Mr Carey
thinks a party goes better without couples, but these absent spouses
are equally eminent. Spotting the originals of the characters was
one of the pleasures of the book for its first readers. The closeness
varies, but Carey is undoubtedly Rhodes, though Buchan makes
him more sympathetic than he had found Rhodes at a first meeting
in 1902, when he wrote 'I don't like him, but he is undoubtedly a
great man.' Launceston derives from Milner, Loewenstein from
Alfred Beit, and Lord Appin is a mixture of Rosebery and Balfour.
Lady Warcliff, wife of the G.O.C. India, comes from Lady Lyttelton; Lady Lucy Gardner from Lady Lugard; the artistic Mrs
Deloraine (who sings 'La Princesse Lointaine' to 'a melody of her
own making, very wild and tender') from Pamela Wyndham, sister
of George Wyndham the politician, who married Lord Glenconner.
Hugh Somerville, 'a young man of thirty, who, after some years of
foreign travel, was now endeavouring to make a fortune,' is Buchan
himself; and the Meredithian Lady Flora Brume is a girl he was
seeing much of at the time he wrote the book. The women are, for
1906, emancipated, given to smoking and adventuring—one goes
off to Ruwenzori with the two Chamonix guides who are among the
ideal inhabitants of Buchan's dream-world. All are well-read, well-
informed, articulate and witty. They contribute a great deal to the
discussion, and are listened to seriously by the men. There is a
general atmosphere of good birth, good breeding, easy circumstances, high-mindedness and intelligence; a hint of Hatfield and
more than a whiff of Balliol. It is a governing élite. Some of the

party are Tory, some Liberal—though no Little Englanders are
present—but there is always much common ground between the
debaters. The argument proceeds not so much by statement and
rebuttal as by a continuous dialectic, out of which the debaters
hope that a synthesis will emerge.

The question which engages the company every evening (during
the day they are allowed to read, ride, sketch or hunt lion) is Imperialism. The aim is to 'get our minds clear, not to frame a political
catechism.' They are all agreed on what Imperialism is *not*. 'Why
is it,' asks Mrs Wilbraham, the general's wife,

that many of us . . . grow nervous when the word 'Empire' is mentioned,
and get hot all over?

and Flora Brume starts a competition in writing 'imperial poetry':

You simply get all the names of places you can think of and string them
together, and then put at the end something about the Flag or the Crown
or the Old Land.

Rhetoric about the island race, or the mother country gathering her
children round her knees, or painting the map red, are as much
anathema to this company as the jelly-bellied flag-flappers were to
Kipling's schoolboys. Nor is the Empire to be regarded

as a mere possession, as the vulgar rich regard their bank accounts—a
matter to boast of, and not an added duty.

Carey is insistent that Imperialism can never be satisfactorily
defined:

It is a spirit, an attitude of mind, an unconquerable hope. You can
phrase it in a thousand ways without exhausting its content. It is a sense of
the destiny of England. It is the wider patriotism which conceives our
people as a race and not as a chance community.

The others try their hand at description. 'The impulse to deeds
rather than talk,' says the explorer; 'an enlarged sense of the beauty
and mystery of the world,' says Mrs Deloraine; and the philosophic
ex-premier, 'the realisation of the need of a quantitative basis for
all qualitative development.' The Canadian statesman, who is
always trying to 'bring imperialism out of the clouds' and his
companions down to earth, sees it as

the closer organic connection under one Crown of a number of autonomous
nations of the same blood, who can spare something of their vitality for the
administration of vast tracts inhabited by lower races—a racial aristocracy
considered in their relation to the subject peoples, a democracy in their
relation to each other.

The proconsul insists that imperialism implies 'the realisation of new conditions for all our problems, an enlarged basis, and fuller data,' and a willingness to make new analyses of the facts rather than 'simply to shuffle the old cards at any crisis' as all the political parties tend to do. He approves, for instance, of the proposed link-up between the Labour parties in Britain and the colonies because that is a recognition of the 'enlarged basis' of labour's problems.

The discussion ranges over various questions relevant to imperialism: emigration policy, the movement of labour, the ethics of indentured labour, the special problems of the tropics (here the Lady Lugard character is given her head). On the question of an Imperial Federation, or Council, or Round Table, there is a difference between the proconsul and the Canadian, who puts the case for colonial nationalism; but in the end this is fined down to a question of timing. In the millionaire's dream drawing-room Carey leads a discussion on the economics of Empire, though without reference to tariffs or Imperial preference, and points out some dangers consequent upon the extended spheres that will open to the great capitalists:

Remember that the great fortunes of the future will not be made by old methods . . . The millionaire of the future will be a statesman. He will administer affairs as complex and vast as the politics of a small nation.

How can his power be controlled and himself made responsible?

Down by the lake 3000 feet below Musuru they talk with a Scots missionary who has worked there since the bad days of the Arab slave-dealers, and hear Carey address an assembly of armed Africans:

I will not have these people meet me except as free men, and in this country it is the badge of a free man to carry spear and shield.

Afterwards Carey speaks to the white population of teachers, traders, planters and government officials, of the danger of underrating the status of the black man:

The law must look upon him not as a potential but as an actual citizen, and must give him the dignity of such. He must stand before it as an equal with the white man—not a social equal or a political equal, but a legal equal.

Earlier Carey has talked of 'races for whom autonomy is unthinkable, at any rate for the next century or two.'

Wakefield, the Canadian, gives a warning about English insularity, and reminds the company that the centre of gravity of the Empire

will change according to natural economic laws. If electricity should replace coal as the motive force of the future, a country such as Canada, with her immense water-power, will be far better endowed by nature than England. Or some undreamed-of force may be discovered by science which will make some other colony the predominant industrial partner . . . We must provide for some elasticity in our interests, and this can only be secured by thinking of the Empire not as England plus a number of poor relations, but as one organic whole, whose centre is to be determined by the evidence of time. This is no new doctrine. Adam Smith, who will not be suspected of wild-cat dogmas, preached it as the logical corollary to any policy of colonisation.

The Hegelian synthesis to which the philosopher-statesman leads them ('Does Rosebery read Hegel,' asked Stair Gillon, 'or did you just put a bit of Haldane on to him?') is that

Imperialism, sanely considered, is the best guardian of peace . . . England has completed her great era of expansion. Her work for ages was to find new outlets for the vigour of her sons, and to occupy the waste or derelict places of the earth. Now, the land being won, it is her task to develop the wilds, to unite the scattered settlements, and to bring the whole within the influence of her tradition and faith. This labour we call empire-building, and above all things it is a labour of peace.

The ideal is not Dominion, not even *pax Britannica*, but the spread of civilisation; this is very much in the line of Rosebery's Rectorial address in Glasgow in 1900.

The proconsul (who has been very firm in condemning any use of imperialism for party ends) insists that it makes certain moral demands: 'a quickened civic conscience and a tireless intelligence . . . a wider patriotism.' The younger members of the party are sure that it also demands imagination. Buchan had been convinced of Rhodes's greatness when he saw how many prosaic characters had been forced, because of him, to take long views. And in this symposium even the down-to-earth Mr Wakefield is made to acknowledge that 'the individual with his heart on fire' is needed to inspire men to 'plant civilisation in the wilds and turn savages into orderly citizens.'

The book ends with Lord Appin and Mr Wakefield walking arm-in-arm on the terrace, 'their cigars glowing in the darkness.' Appin plans to visit the colonies, for theorising is not enough, and Wakefield is ready to take a wider view.

Buchan's friends had reservations on minor points (Stair Gillon was 'annoyed with the Waddesworth [*sic*] Manor fittings of the colossal bungalow') but all enjoyed its sanguine, happy tone, 'the freshness of it all, the riotous hopefulness.' The hopefulness is still apparent to the reader today, but he is also struck by some omissions. There is, for instance, only the briefest reference to India, and none at all to the other European colonial powers, nor to the scramble for Africa. 'Truth can only be known to the man on the hill-top,' says Carey, and the *Spectator* reviewer ended his appreciative article (15 December 1906):

There is in the whole book a power of vision which makes one feel as though one looked down from a great height, saw the world laid out, and were entrusted with the sobering, yet fascinating, task of saying how the pieces shall be moved, how the great game of our heritage shall be played.

From our present perspective there seems too much, figuratively as well as geographically, of this view *de haut en bas*, of people secure in their own intelligence and high-mindedness looking on the world from above, and knowing what is best for it.

Africa is the setting for three of Buchan's short stories. The dream house in the African wilderness reappears in 'The Grove of Ashtaroth' (1910), whose hero plans to bring out to it 'the Tintorets from Hill Street.' But in the end he leaves the Tintorets and the Ming pots behind, for his house is built by a grove at the centre of which stands 'a little conical tower', like the one at Zimbabwe; there is no place for the artefacts of other cultures in this sanctuary whose magic seduces him, as the ritual of Ashtaroth seduced Solomon. He is rescued only by the common-sense of the narrator, who himself has felt the sweetness as well as the evil of the haunted place. To save his friend he burns the grove and dynamites the tower, but he is certain that in doing so he has outraged something 'lovely and adorable.' There is a similar desecration in 'The Green Wildebeeste' where, in a native kraal set in a green cup in the Wood Bush, an ignorant young Boer shoots a creature in a wood held sacred. The hero of 'The Kings of Orion' (1906) is the Governor of an African colony where the demand for labour in the mines has unsettled the natives. He appears hopelessly incompetent, but for years in his dreams he has been the conqueror and master of Central Asia. When the crisis comes and the natives are about to rise, his dream takes over, and he rides unarmed among the African warriors with the authority of a king.

'Here we are in Prester John's country,' says Carey, surveying his domain in *A Lodge in the Wilderness*, and the name of this fabulous king served Buchan for the title of his third African book. *Prester John* was written as a boys' story, and came out in the *Captain* from April to September 1910 under the title *The Black General*** before book-publication the same year. It opens in true Stevensonian vein with a mysterious stranger irrupting into the boy-hero's homely world; in *Treasure Island* it is the blind man tapping his way to the Admiral Benbow, in *Prester John* the black minister tracing his magic circle round the fire on the Fife shore. There are other echoes of *Treasure Island*; as Jim Hawkins overhears the plotters on the *Hispaniola* from his apple-barrel, so on the steamer bound for Delagoa Bay David Crawfurd eavesdrops on the minister and his seedy accomplice. As there is admiration as well as enmity between Jim and Long John Silver, so there is between David and the Reverend John Laputa, the reincarnation of Prester John, who is to lead a mighty native rising against the whites.

The second chapter of *Prester John* has the same title, 'Furth! Fortune!', as Buchan later gave to the South African chapter of his memoirs, and when David arrives in the Transvaal he is in John Buchan's country. He goes as storekeeper to Blaauwildebeestefontein, and his description of it parallels Buchan's of the Wood Bush. Most of the action takes place on the eastern edge of the high veld, where the ground falls away to the glens between the berg and the Lebombo hills on the Portuguese border. Machudi's glen, 'a green, cup-shaped hollow' where David hides Prester John's treasure, has already been lyrically described as 'Machubi's glen' in *The African Colony*. When David travels over the berg by night, ponders how best to cross a crocodile-infested river, sees the dawn come up over the veld, his experiences are Buchan's own. In the account of the mustering and march of the Kaffirs, of their rounding-up by soldiers and police, Buchan is drawing on his knowledge of the last stages of the Boer War, when De Wet's and De la Rey's commandos were roaming the veld. And there appears, for the first time in a Buchan story, the motif of the group of men

* The Editor announced it as 'a thrilling story by Mr John Buchan who is well known as the author of a number of romantic works.'

from different backgrounds—Arcoll the Intelligence officer, Wardlaw the schoolmaster, Aitken the hunter, David the storekeeper—coming together in a great enterprise; was this the influence of the Kindergarten?

In David's final scene with Laputa in the treasure-cave on the berg there is something of Rider Haggard—in his commonplace book Buchan had written of the 'savage glory' of *King Solomon's Mines*—but Buchan's own experience of rocks in Highlands and Drakensberg is behind David's climb up beside the waterfall and out of the cave, with his back pressed against one side of the cleft, his knee on the other. David, a minister's son, is a Calvinist and a fatalist, with a strong sense of duty. 'We are in God's hands,' he says when he hears the drums beat at sunset to mark the start of the rising, 'and must wait on His will.'

If anything, I was more cheerful since I heard the drums. It was clearly now beyond the power of me or any man to stop the march of events.

So Buchan's reading and experience blend to produce a tale whose wildest moments have a backing of credible fact. After his ventures into 'psychological studies of cultured people'—*The Half-Hearted*, the unfinished *Mountain*—he is back with the novel of action, and showing a greater pace and ability to create tension, a more assured handling of plot, than in any of his previous experiments. Though David Crawfurd is a sensitive, thinking hero, no self-communings of his are allowed to hold up the narrative; his insights come to him through action and event. For the first time Buchan is showing his true paces as a born story-teller.

It took a further quality, a rare imaginative sympathy, to conceive the figure of John Laputa. From his first appearance on the Kirkcaple shore he is a man of mystery and power. He has 'a hawk nose like an Arab, dark flashing eyes. . . . He was black as my hat, but for the rest he might have sat for a figure of a Crusader,' and his voice is 'the most wonderful thing that ever came out of a human mouth. It was full and rich, and gentle, with the tones of a great organ.' The police officer Arcoll (something of a first draft of Sandy Arbuthnot), who has trailed him from the lower Limpopo to a meeting of the Royal Geographical Society in London and back to the kraals, says of him:

'He is a born leader of men, and as brave as a lion. There is no villainy he would not do if necessary, and yet I should hesitate to call him a blackguard. Ay, you may look surprised at me, you two pragmatical Scotsmen;

but I have, so to speak, lived with the man for months, and there's fineness
and nobility in him. He would be a terrible enemy, but a just one. He has
the heart of a poet and a king, and it is God's curse that he has been born
among the children of Ham.'

Laputa has told his people that he is

'the Umkulunkulu, the incarnated spirit of Prester John. He told them that
he was there to lead the African race to conquest and empire. Ay, and he
told them more: for he has, or says he has, the Great Snake itself, the
necklet of Prester John.'

His password to his forces is 'Immanuel—God with us.'

Laputa is the real hero of the book, and his death its moment of
strongest drama. When David finally confronts him in the cave, he
is mortally wounded; 'to see him going out was like seeing the fall
of a great mountain.' David watches 'the old worn man standing
there among the ashes,' no longer a king, nor a Christian minister:

Death was stripping him to his elements, and the man Laputa stood out
beyond and above the characters he had played, something strange, and
great, and moving, and terrible.

Laputa croons the Latin epitaph of Prester John, cries out Antony's
last words, then with his dying strength strips off his leopard-skin,
twines Prester John's collar of rubies round his neck and plunges
into a chasm of underground waters.

After such a royal ending there can be no vulgar triumph, only
reconciliation. Arcoll and David go unarmed among the warriors,
talk of Laputa's greatness and persuade them to lay down their arms.
The happy ending of a boy's adventure story turns into a blueprint
for a new Africa. The experience has transformed David (like the
hero of Conrad's *Shadow Line*) from a boy to a man; it has also
made him wealthy. With the rest of Prester John's treasure he goes
home to finish his education at Edinburgh University. And with the
money from the diamond pipe which has been discovered through
Laputa's cave, Blaauwildebeestefontein is transformed. There is a
great native college:

no factory for making missionaries and black teachers, but an institution
for giving the Kaffirs the kind of training which fits them to be good
citizens of the state. There you will find every kind of technical workshop,
and the finest experimental farms, where the blacks are taught modern
agriculture . . .

There are playing-fields and baths and reading-rooms and libraries just
as in a school at home. In front of the great hall of the college a statue
stands, the figure of a black man shading his eyes with his hands and

looking far over the plains to the Rooirand. On the pedestal it is lettered 'Prester John,' but the face is the face of Laputa.

Laputa has failed, but out of the respect he inspires, some at least of his white opponents come to appreciate the potentialities of the black African.

Very understandably the references in *Prester John* to 'blacks' and 'niggers' have put off many a reader today, but it would be a pity if these put him off so much that he failed to see with what humanity Buchan has portrayed the African leader. The conflict is not between black and white; it is between civilisation, towards which Laputa could be leading his people, and savagery, to which he is pulling them back. ('He was back four centuries among the Mazimba sweeping down on the Zambesi,' says Arcoll after watching Laputa blood a black cock at full moon.) From Buchan's standpoint at the time he wrote the book, the Zulu wars and Chaka's mighty killings were less than a century away, and faith in white civilisation had not yet suffered the shock of 1914–18. The events of the rising and the resettlement of the Kaffir army have taught David Crawfurd

the meaning of the white man's duty. He has to take all risks, recking nothing of his life or his fortunes, and well content to find his reward in the fulfilment of his task. That is the difference between white and black, the gift of responsibility, the power of being in a little way a king; and so long as we know this and practise it, we will rule not in Africa alone but wherever there are dark men who live only for the day and their own bellies. Moreover, the work made me pitiful and kindly. I learnt much of the untold grievances of the natives, and saw something of their strange twisted reasoning. Before we had got Laputa's army back to their kraals, with food enough to tide them over the spring sowing, Aitken and I had got sounder policy in our heads than you will find in the towns, where men sit in offices and see the world through a mist of papers.

It may be a paternalistic view, but by the lights of 1910 it is not mean.

Professor George Shepperson, joint author of *Independent African* (1958), considers it very likely that in writing of Laputa and his rising, Buchan had in mind Bambata and the revolt which he led in Natal in 1906, 'the last militant stand of the Zulu against the inroads of the European way of life.' He points out the references in the novel to 'Ethiopianism,' the African nationalist and religious movement with its contacts with American Negroes. Citing a passage from *A Lodge in the Wilderness*, he says that Buchan

had obviously thought deeply on the dangers of Africans who had been educated beyond the capacity of the European colonies to assimilate them into their structures.

Professor Shepperson also points out an even more striking parallel, with the Reverend John Chilembwe and the Nyasaland Rising of 1915, five years *after* Buchan published *Prester John*. *Independent African* is a study of Chilembwe, and it opens with a quotation from a missionary magazine of 1917:

Some years ago the well-known writer Mr John Buchan published a romance called *Prester John*, the theme of which was a great native rising in South Africa. The leader of this rising was a native clergyman who had been educated abroad and had returned full of the determination to found a great native empire and to drive the hated white intruders into the sea. The tale of its preliminary success and ultimate failure, those who have read it are not likely to forget. It is not often that fact plagiarises fiction. Those who have enjoyed Mr Buchan's excellent yarn probably never dreamed that there was the slightest chance of anything approaching to it really happening. The idea seemed bizarre and utterly impossible, excellent for the plot of a story, but out of the question as a plot in real life.

They will have been much surprised, then, if they came across any account in the newspapers of the rebellion of John Chilembwe in Nyasaland.

In both risings, fiction and fact, 'it was the native preacher, the Ethiopian—taken popularly to be a synonym for pro-African and anti-European native working through a church organisation—who was at the heart of the affair.' In the story David asks Laputa, 'What in God's name are you doing in this business? You that are educated and have seen the world.' Laputa's answer—'They are my people'—would, in Professor Shepperson's view, stand for Chilembwe too. In his spell in prison Jomo Kenyatta is said to have read *Prester John*.

So, within the framework of a boy's adventure story, and limited by the simplicities and crudities of the *genre*, Buchan had put his imaginative view of Africa and the shape of things to come. And he had created at least two images haunting and powerful as any in Rider Haggard: a naked black man with a necklace of rubies poised kinglike above a chasm of boiling waters, and a boy desperately climbing up the black cleft by the waterfall into the daylight.

At the head of 'The Green Wildebeeste' Buchan placed Sir Thomas Browne's sentence: 'We carry with us the wonders we seek without us; there is all Africa and her prodigies in us.' In *Prester John* and the three short stories Africa provided the physical correlatives for feelings and perceptions deep in Buchan himself.

CHAPTER SIX

INSIDER

1903–07

'He seems to know all sorts of people whose names you see in the papers, and Katie says the mirror above his mantel-piece is stuck full of invitations.'
Anna Buchan: *Eliza for Common*

Buchan's original plan had been to go out to South Africa for a limited time, at most two years, and then come back to the Bar with increased reputation and the chance of some South African appeals. But he had not been long on Milner's staff before he began to consider other ideas. 'The power and influence of the administrative work has got hold of me, and I may go on with it—here or in Egypt.' Milner entered sympathetically into his junior's concerns— he too had been a young man anxious for public service but with no private means—and strongly urged Buchan to give up the Bar, as he had done at the same age, saying to Jowett that 'I had rather be a poor obscure man all my life, doing the work I care for very much, than a well-to-do and possibly distinguished man doing work I scarcely care for at all.' Raymond Asquith, too, discussing his friend's future ('What do you propose to do? Come back to the Bar? or administer the Empire in perpetuity?') had advised administration: 'I am sure it must be the better career of the two— the law is a lean casuistical business.'

Up to May 1903 Buchan was still uncertain:

My future is not quite decided. I have three courses open to me. I can accept the *Spectator*'s offer and go back to the Bar at the same time—with the intention of going into Parliament at the earliest opportunity. Or I may accept an administrative post, probably in Egypt. Something of the sort will probably be offered me, as I have made a sort of mild reputation out here. Or, finally, I may do what Lord Milner urges me to do, and go into a great financial house for the purpose of making a fortune quickly, and then when I am independent go in for administrative work on a large scale.

I have many plans which my wealth could enable me to realise. Not that I
have any love of luxury—out here I have become a sort of Spartan—but
you must have money if you are to do constructive political work.*

To his mother he explained the advantage of going into a financial
house:

You see I am good at finance, and am a trained organiser. I would not
go into any house unless one of the 2 or 3 biggest ones, and then only
high up. But what Lord M. says is self-evident. I have no money. I shall
not make a fortune in journalism and, though I might at the Bar, I would
be too old by the time it was made. I am sure Providence meant me to be
a politician, and to be a free and honest and effective politician, one must
be independent of office. Besides I have my own scheme, which could only
be realised with a fortune. If therefore a good chance (and it would have
to be a very good chance) offered of making a fortune in 10 years (which
is the limit H.E. lays down) don't you think it would be right to take it?
However all this requires 'careful and prayerful consideration' and there
is no need to decide till I come home.

He also wrote to sound his Peebles uncle as to the effect a record of
ten years 'in an American house' (he was probably referring to
Pierpont Morgan) would have on the Scottish voter; Uncle Willie,
marshalling his arguments under eight heads, was cautious and
non-committal. There was a tentative approach from the South
Edinburgh Unionists early in 1904 (the sequel to a lecture Buchan
gave on 'The Future of South Africa') but till the main lines of his
work and income were clear, he would not consider it.

There was one job in Johannesburg, which Buchan had no hesitation in turning down.

I have been offered the editorship of the chief paper here at £3000 a year,
and I think they would have gone as far as £4000. I declined, because
though I might have stayed five years in the job and returned home with a
modest fortune, yet I think if one does a thing purely to make money one
is apt to make a mess of it.

Meanwhile Strachey had been making it clear how much he would
like Buchan to come back to the *Spectator*, assuring him a minimum
income of £250 as a contributor, and renewing his offer of the
reversion of Meredith Townsend's job as political editor at £800
(Townsend was seventy-two, in poor health, and expected to retire
shortly). Strachey too was sympathetic to Buchan's ambitions, and

* In July 1901 Milner's Balliol friend, Clinton Dawkins, now in Morgan's, had
offered Milner the chance of joining the firm in order to make money and so be free
to do the public work he most cared for—championing the causes of National Service
and Imperial Federation. Members of Parliament were not paid a salary till 1911.

predicted that 'Milner will be so determined not to lose you that he will make you a very good offer and that you will accept it and stay.'

But when Buchan did resume work on the *Spectator* and at the Bar in October 1903, it was very much with the idea of filling in time while he waited for a job in Egypt. That had always been one of the obvious possibilities: the work of the administration was in many ways similar to the work in South Africa, and Cromer was the other great proconsul of the day. The chances seemed good: Milner was ready with recommendations and introductions, Cromer thought well of Buchan's *African Colony* and told him so in a twelve-page letter in his own hand. But on the possibility of a job he was more reserved. 'I should be extremely glad to see you employed out here,' he wrote in January 1904, 'but I must, on the other hand, say that I do not see any reasonable probability of a suitable opportunity occurring yet awhile and I certainly cannot advise you to wait on the off-chance.' He advised Buchan to see Sir Eldon Gorst, the Financial Adviser to the Egyptian Government. Buchan had already seen him—'Gorst is in London,' he wrote to his mother in November 1903, 'and I am dining with him next week, so something may happen soon. I fancy he is as keen to leave as I am to go.' Now after receiving Cromer's letter he talked over his prospects with Gorst and Sir Clinton Dawkins, who told him that they were ready to recommend him to Cromer for the post of Under-Secretary for Finance if the present holder were, as they hoped, transferred to the *Caisse de la Dette*. (The Under-Secretary—Milner, Gorst and Dawkins had all held the post— was regarded as next in succession to the Financial Adviser, and *he* was regarded as the most important British official in Egypt.) But Cromer had another candidate for the *Caisse*, so the Under-Secretaryship was not free to offer.*

For two years Buchan kept on hoping something would turn up

* This account, based on Buchan's letters home, and on letters to him from Cromer, Gorst and Clinton Dawkins, does not altogether tally with Buchan's own account on p. 126 of *Memory Hold-the-Door*, written when he was in Canada and away from most of his own records. 'When I returned to England late in 1903 it was in the expectation of going soon to Egypt, where Lord Cromer had selected me for an important financial post; but the home authorities declined to ratify his choice, no doubt rightly, on the ground of my youth and inexperience.' I have found no record in Foreign Office papers nor in the Cromer papers of such a suggestion. The records do show that Cromer was in England in August and September 1903, so he may have spoken about the matter at the Foreign Office; they also show that the Foreign Office were apt to counter his recommendations to a post with a candidate of their own, sometimes to Cromer's annoyance. The real bar was that in the end there was no vacancy.

in Egypt. Some of his friends thought it was lucky for him that it never did. Working for Cromer, as part of an existing and tight-knit administration, hedged about with diplomatic niceties, would have been a different matter from a free-ranging job under Milner. In South Africa he had been given a free hand in a fluid situation; in Egypt he would have had to toe the line and bow to convention without nearly so much play for initiative and individual decision.

After a family reunion at Altarstone near Stobo—John back from Africa, Willie about to sail for India—Buchan went back to his old rooms at 3 Temple Gardens, which he now shared with Harold Baker and Austin Smyth. It was in an unsettled mood that he took up his London work again. In South Africa he had held more power and responsibility than most of his contemporaries, and had earned a great deal more, only to come back to the same routine of devilling for Rowlatt and leader-writing for the *Spectator*. 'After the last two years I cannot help feeling that the law is all rather a pother about trifles.' He prepared Board of Trade and revenue cases for the Attorney-General (Sir Robert Finlay, who assessed his mind as not exact enough for supremacy at the Bar); he was briefed in a peerage case and in a 'heavy electrical case of which I cannot understand even the alphabet,' there were several briefs from the Transvaal Chamber of Mines, and in the spring of 1905 he went to Cape Town on a case. But it was in tax cases that he specialised and in this field his abilities were highly regarded; nearly thirty years later Sir John Simon, as chairman of the enquiry into the R101 disaster, asked Buchan to spend a whole day with him going over the technical evidence, for he remembered and admired Buchan's mastery of intricate detail from his days at the Bar.

Most of Buchan's work was in chambers, and he seldom appeared in court—though he had one embarrassing moment when his outspoken friend Andrew Jameson, newly appointed to the Scottish Bench as Lord Ardwall, accompanied him to hear a case: 'Presently, to the confusion of the ushers, he began to expound to me his view of certain *obiter dicta* from the Bench till I hastily suggested we might finish the conversation outside.'

Buchan saw a good deal of R. B. Haldane, to whom he warmed as the Liberal statesman who had stood most firmly by Milner. The two Scots had much in common: they combined an appetite for hard work and hard physical exercise with a taste for English country-house life, their intellectual interests were in philosophy and religion as much as in law. It was Haldane who suggested that Buchan should write a book on *The Law Relating to the Taxation of Foreign Income*, which in 1905 appeared with a dedication to the Attorney-General and a preface by Haldane ('scholarly and comprehensive treatise'). The aim of this least-known of John Buchan's books was to extract the law on the subject from about 150 cases, and deduce the general principles behind it for the benefit of lawyers, businessmen with investments abroad, and foreigners paying tax on British investments.

Work on the *Spectator*, which he wanted kept quiet ('Don't let people think I am doing anything but the Bar'), went on much as before South Africa: indeed, he found the *Spectator* the only unchanged thing in the world on his return. He wrote a review every week, usually one and sometimes two leading articles, and some front-page notes (in one issue he wrote eleven of these paragraphs) and editorial work when Strachey was away on holiday, and when he was contesting a seat in 1906. In January 1906 Meredith Townsend resigned, and Strachey asked Buchan to become 'Second Assistant Editor' (with Graves) at £800 a year, and to write 'a maximum of a review and two leaders . . . and nine notes per week . . . the magazines when required and such editorial work as may be necessary both in normal and holiday times.' Strachey also asked Buchan to 'leave the Bar.' In accepting Strachey's offer Buchan (who with the change of Government had lost his work for the Attorney-General) agreed, in the sense of giving up his room in the Temple and not going into court, and not holding himself available for practice; but he reserved the right to do legal writing and, in fact, seems to have given a number of opinions.

Buchan noted a change about this time in the paper's tone and appeal:

From 1895 to 1903 the *Spectator* was the chief weekly organ of the educated classes throughout the Empire. There were no violent problems to split the centre party to which it appealed [not the South African War?]. But with the beginning of the Tariff Reform controversy it found its public divided. Strachey was probably the most effective editor in Britain during the earlier period. He had an infallible instinct for knowing what his readers wanted. But he was the last man to sacrifice his convictions to the task of keeping his circulation up. He became a fiery protagonist of Free Trade, and for the rest of his life he was as much fighter as conciliator.

Although Strachey called himself a Whig (he stood as an Independent in 1906) and Buchan was a Tory, they worked with little

political friction. As a former Liberal-Unionist, Strachey agreed
with Buchan over larger questions of imperial policy; as a Conservative Free Trader, Buchan agreed with Strachey on protection, one
of the main issues in the 1906 election. His special subjects for
leading articles were South Africa and Imperial topics generally;
other African questions (such as 'Germany in Africa', 'The Congo
State'); Hungary; France; Tibet (a number of articles on the
Younghusband mission of 1904); United States foreign policy; the
Scottish Church case (in which Haldane was heavily involved). He
wrote occasional articles on a variety of subjects, from 'Science in
National Life' to 'Russia and the Jews.' In his reviews he turned
his hand to books of all kinds: exploration and mountaineering,
biography, finance, history, recent verse. The output would have
been good for a full-time journalist: it was remarkable for a half-
timer. But Buchan, in addition to his excellent memory, had the
lawyer's ability to marshal his thoughts clearly. Thinking did not
begin with pen touching paper; it had already happened, and he
would write his articles and reviews straight down, with little hesitation or alteration. 'I never failed to find it a real intellectual treat
to work with you,' said Strachey when Buchan left the paper. Yet
he missed the scope, the responsibility and the steady rhythm
of administrative work. An administrator has the satisfaction of
knowing that he has brought about some change; a journalist
can only hope that he has moved some man of action towards
it.

Buchan missed too the riding and the outdoor life which had been
part of his job with Milner: 'Any prospect of exclusively indoor
work saddens me,' he had written to Anna before leaving South
Africa, 'I have far too much physical and mental energy to be
cooped up.' But if he could not exercise his body enough in the
course of his London work, he could give it plenty to do in his
holidays; and if his holidays had to be short, he could see that the
exercise was concentrated and intense. It was in the year after his
return to London that he became enthusiastic about mountaineering, as distinct from the hill-walking which he had enjoyed since
childhood. His first serious climb had been an ascent of Buachille
Etive in Glencoe in the course of a walking-tour with John Edgar
in the spring of 1898: the account of their adventure which he wrote
to Taffy Boulter has the high spirits and exaggeration of the novice
('. . . marked in all the guidebooks as inaccessible . . . sheer madness,

for we had no mountaineering tools and we were encumbered
with waterproofs . . . terrible crevasses of snow . . . within an ace
of losing our lives fifty times.'). He had managed to do some
mountain-scrambling in South Africa, on the Drakensberg,
Blaauwberg and Zoutpansberg, and in 1904 he made his first visit
to the Alps. He took Anna to Zermatt in the Whitsun recess. It was
splendid for flowers, though far too early for any big climbs, but he
enjoyed the Riffelhorn, from the glacier, and the Untergabelhorn.
Two years later he and Anna went to Chamonix, but again it had
to be in June; they managed to do the smaller rock-climbs, the
Petits Charmoz, the Aiguille de l'M, and a good deal of guideless
scrambling in the Aiguilles Rouges.* Buchan did not have the
chance to stretch himself on a big snow- and ice-climb, but in any
case he was temperamentally drawn towards rock, enjoying the
combination of physical and mental agility, the quick decisions
demanded by this kind of climbing. 'He is far more cool and
wary than at home in the Law Courts or the City,' he wrote of the
rock-climber in an article in *Blackwood's*, and quoted approvingly
what Gautier said of mountaineers: '*Ils sont la volonté protestant
contre l'obstacle aveugle, et ils plantent sur l'inaccessible le drapeau de
l'intelligence humaine.*' So it was natural that he should have loved
Skye above all, where he had two September holidays, in 1905 and
1906. On the first he climbed with his brother Walter and the guide
John Mackenzie; on the second he had Anna and Willie, who was
not nearly so good a climber as Walter. On these two visits Buchan
led most of the then standard climbs, also a new climb on the north
face of Sgurr-nan-Gillean, from the Bhasteir Corrie—'the most
sensational piece of cliff-climbing I have ever done'—which
Mackenzie wished to call 'Buchan's chimney.' Buchan was a neat
climber and very fast—both on rock and on the approaches. 'John
[Mackenzie] says we are the fastest people on the hills he has ever
seen except the Gurkhas whom Major Bruce brought up here some
years ago;' this was to Sandy Gillon, with whom he planned to
traverse the whole length of the Coolin ridge. In Skye he felt most
keenly the rock-climber's contrasted enjoyments: now concentra-
ting on cracks and chimneys, now surveying the Minch and the
Hebrides. Walter Buchan found his brother 'exhilarating and terri-

---

* In the story 'Space,' written in 1910 and published in *The Moon Endureth*,
Edward Leithen (making, incidentally, his first appearance) refers to new routes
up the Montanvert side of the Charmoz, and to the Mer de Glace face of the
Grépon, which was not climbed in fact till 1911.

fying' on the hills; he felt compelled to follow John in anything he had planned, but was often frightened.

In spite of his slender Alpine experience, Buchan was elected to the Alpine Club in 1906, on the strength of his writings about mountains (in *The African Colony* and in *Blackwood's*) as well as his actual record in Scotland, the Alps and South Africa; he was proposed by Douglas Freshfield and among his 'supporters from personal knowledge' was L. S. Amery.

Buchan was also associated with Amery in The Compatriots ('a disreputable Imperialist dining-club which I belong to,' he explained to Lady Mary Murray; Buchan was rather fond of adding a tang of the rash or wild to some perfectly respectable affair). Another member was F. S. Oliver, who became a close friend. Oliver was eleven years older than Buchan, and his career had followed a comparable course. A Borderer from Roxburghshire, he had gone to school and college in Edinburgh, then to Cambridge—where he knew Austen Chamberlain, Leo Maxse and Charles Whibley—and the Inner Temple. After some years at the Bar he accepted the offer of his Cambridge friend Ernest Debenham to join the management of Debenham & Freebody, which he helped to transform from a small wholesale concern into a leading retail and wholesale business. He was now one of the most successful drapers in London, and the most intellectual. Dry goods in no way limited his horizon; he was a sharp-tongued publicist for certain political ideas, which included national military service and tariff reform. When Buchan first met him he was at work on a life of Alexander Hamilton; this book, subtitled 'An Essay on American Union,' and published in 1906, was widely taken as 'an eloquent sermon on the text of Imperial unity.' In Buchan's view *Alexander Hamilton*

had probably more influence than any other political work of the decade. It became a text-book for all those up and down the Empire who were giving their minds to Imperial reconstruction, and it had a very special and direct influence on the group who conceived and carried through the Union of South Africa.

Fred Oliver was handsome, worldly and sceptical, with a mind both logical and intuitive. In talk and letters he could be rumbustious and fantastical, irreverent and witty—'He's that most loveable of all things, an incompetent Scotsman,' he remarked of a friend—and he drew out a robust, free-speaking streak from the primmer Buchan. Oliver's outspokenness could take a savage turn; about political opponents he was, in private, sometimes nearly as scurrilous as the writers of the *Action Française*.

Violet Markham, a spirited and intelligent young woman whom Buchan met soon after his return from South Africa, was another friend with whom he shared political interests. She was three years older than him, the daughter of a wealthy Derbyshire mine-owner, and granddaughter of Joseph Paxton who built the Crystal Palace. When a legacy in 1901 made her independent, she bought a house of her own in Gower Street, started a settlement in her native Chesterfield, concerned herself with miners' housing, and travelled widely, interesting herself particularly in Imperial affairs.

Though he kept complaining of the press of social life, Buchan dined out a great deal, and spent many of his week-ends in the country. To those who had entertained him in his earlier London years were now added friends from South Africa, the Ecksteins in Park Lane and the Lionel Phillipses in Hampshire. Raymond Asquith used to tease him about his life with the upper classes; no doubt Buchan took a certain pleasure in the spectacle of the son of the John Knox manse going to the Duchess of Wellington's ball (along with the King). But a main reason why Buchan liked his visits to Panshanger, Polesden Lacy, Crabbet Park and other houses, was that in those days the people who lived in them were near the centre of affairs. There he met statesmen, administrators and journalists, Milner and Lugard and Alfred Lyttelton and the future Lord Northcliffe (with whom he spent a Sunday in Surrey 'rushing about a frost-bound country . . . in a magnificent motor-car'), and talked with men and women who were well-informed and prepared to discuss politics seriously. Cuthbert Medd had once warned him, after a week-end in the company of Brodrick and Selborne, that 'if you want to keep up your opinion of your own country, you must sedulously avoid meeting the men who govern it,' but Buchan liked meeting them and feeling at the centre of things as he had in Johannesburg. One such week-end was with Haldane in September 1906 at Cloan, in Perthshire. Haldane, now Secretary for War, was newly back from Germany where he had been studying military organisation, and had talked to the Kaiser and Edward VII at Marienbad; Buchan's fellow-guests were Lord Esher (who had been chairman of the committee set up after the South African war to examine the state of the War Office), Lord French and Sir Ian Hamilton.

I am giddy with trying to understand complex Army 'shop' and with trying to live up to Esher's standard of good manners. Haldane is in tremendous form and very wicked. His accounts of his life with the King at Marienbad and the Kaiser at Potsdam are extraordinarily funny. . . . Yesterday I had a long day's wandering in the hills with him, discussing every subject in heaven and earth, from the meaning of a disputed passage in Hegel to scandals about Royalty. We found a house in the hills called Castle Gloom, and the names of the two burns on either side of it were, we found, Sorrow and Care.

One change Buchan noted in London life from his earlier years: the new emphasis on wealth, the greater ostentatious spending and display. He described one occasion in Park Lane as 'a true millionaire's dinner—fresh strawberries [in April], plovers' eggs, hooky noses and diamonds.' The Edwardian era has been recently described as a period in which 'wealth rather than intellect or noble birth was valued at the Court.' Certainly financiers abounded in Edward VII's social circle; the old guard who did not belong to the King's Marlborough House set thought such persons vulgar and regrettable, and saw their own traditional values in danger of being replaced by money values. So, for different reasons, did the professional middle classes, who deplored money without taste, and money won with a minimum of effort and responsibility.

There is a discussion of these matters in the novel which Buchan was writing in 1905, *The Mountain*, but which he never finished: 'The only thing we care about is success, and we measure that by hard cash,' says Durward, the hard-boiled successful barrister. And he scoffs at the old stuffy society,

who believe we should only dine with our own class and marry our daughters into select families . . . Whatever the caste was founded upon it is going rapidly. We have got another standard today, and at any rate it is a fairly rational one.

This Durward is a new Tory, who thinks

Disraeli did many great things, but the greatest was when he put his foot on the neck of the grandees who used to correspond with him through their solicitors.

There is also an old Tory, who denounces the new men in Africa who 'exploit a land they had no business in' and believes that 'love of money is corrupting us;' and a Buchan-like young man who muses on this Tory's use of words like 'gentleman' and 'honour,' concluding that they 'are very rough working rules of life and not the whole of it.'

As many of the notably rich Edwardians were Jews, this widespread suspicion of conspicuous wealth became, for many people, a suspicion of Jews in general. (Cuthbert Medd, in an article published posthumously in the *National Review*, linked Jews with American millionaires, stockjobbers, Afrikanders—and, strangely, solicitors—as having corrupted the tone of English society.) Buchan, in his letters and talk, often followed this habit of loosely equating 'Jews' and 'vulgar wealth'—as at other times it has been 'Americans'—and he did very much dislike certain Jews he had met in Johannesburg, who had made their money not too scrupulously and then scuttled out of the country. But in *The African Colony* there is a friendly reference to the business acumen of the South African Jew, which Buchan compares with the Aberdonian's. Certainly there was no trace in him of the anti-semitism of Belloc and Chesterton, and in an article in the *Quarterly* he deplored the Liberals' suspicions of the Rand capitalists, because these ministered to 'that *Judenhetze* which is dormant in all northern nations.'

Some critics* have deduced anti-semitism from slighting references to Jews scattered through his novels (*Prester John*, which contains some of them, is dedicated to a Jew, Lionel Phillips). These are usually in the mouths of fictional characters, but the views of Richard Hannay, the mining engineer, who had made his pile in South Africa, are not necessarily Buchan's, any more than Hannay's jargon ('He belonged to my own totem,' 'A sportsman called Nietzsche') reflects Buchan's way of talking. And against his characters' contemptuous references to Portuguese Jews and the like should be set the sympathetic portrait of Lowenstein, the Jewish financier in *A Lodge in the Wilderness*. The speaker is American:

'I like his face,' said Mrs Yorke thoughtfully; 'there is a fire somewhere behind his eyes. But then I differ from most of my countrymen in liking Jews. You can do something with them—stir them up to follow some mad ideal, and they are never vulgar at heart. If we must have magnates, I would rather Jews had the money. It doesn't degrade them and they have the infallible good taste of the East at the back of their heads.'

---

* For instance, Gertrude Himmelfarb in her article 'John Buchan: An Untimely Appreciation' (*Encounter*, September 1960). [David Daniell has pointed out to me that her many errors in writing about Buchan's books cast doubt on the conclusions she draws from them.   J.A.S. 1985]

The Jewishness of the central character of 'The Grove of Ashtaroth' (1910) is stressed, because the narrator thinks that, as a member of this ancient and mysterious race, Lawson is particularly sensitive to supernatural phenomena. Indeed Buchan might be thought to have overdone, in his stories, the 'romance' of the Jew: the narrator of 'The Grove of Ashtaroth' marvels that the descendant of an antique dealer in a back street in Brighton should preserve, subconsciously, a sense of Eastern magic and a taste for Eastern gorgeousness. Disraeli was one of Buchan's political heroes, about whom he had once thought of writing a book.

Thirty years before Hitler people felt little self-consciousness in talking about Jews they disliked, and the Jews whom the upper-class Briton particularly disliked were Jews who were successful, rich and well able to take care of themselves. Buchan certainly at times did talk carelessly, and to our more sensitive ears offensively, about Jews; but when he was giving his mind seriously to 'the Jewish question' (as in a *Spectator* article of 18 November 1905 on 'Russia and the Jews') his attitude was quite different. And when he liked a Jew—as he liked Lionel Phillips, Alfred Beit, Moritz Bonn, Chaim Weizmann—he was not inhibited by any prejudice about race.

Going into politics at home was still one of Buchan's long-term aims; but so long as he continued to hope for something in Egypt he made no effort to find a constituency. His political activities were limited to a few speeches about South Africa, and he did no speaking in the 1906 election, for Strachey was standing as an Independent candidate, and Buchan had to fill in for him at the *Spectator*. But through his friendships he felt involved in all the election excitements:

The new Cabinet strikes me as pretty good. The only mistake was putting Winston—an avowed Little Englander—at the Colonial Office. Haldane is very happy at the War Office and will clean out that stall if any human being can. I have been living in a whirl of political gossip for the last month. I have never been in London before during a change of Ministry, and knowing all the people makes it great fun.

Soon after the election his opinion of Churchill declined further, owing to his attitude in the Milner censure debate in March 1906. One of the chief issues in the election had been Chinese labour in South Africa. Milner, who believed that the economy of South Africa would never recover till the mines were working fully, had in

1904, as a temporary measure, organised the employment of Chinese indentured labourers.* In Britain there was widespread uneasiness about the decision, and the Radicals in the Liberal Party denounced it in and out of Parliament. The treatment of these Chinese coolies became a critical issue; and in December 1905 it was revealed that, contrary to assurances given previously, some coolies had received corporal punishment, and the infliction of it had been authorised by Milner. Milner took complete responsibility for this 'oversight:' he had made a distinction, not so apparent to others, between 'flogging,' which was not authorised, and 'slight corporal punishment, limited in degree to punishment of such a nature as is permitted in schools in England.' In the election 'Chinese Slavery' became a battle-cry for the Liberals, and it was even suggested that the Tories' next step would be to import coolies to work the Welsh slate-quarries. On 21 March—two months after the election, and nearly a year after Milner's final return from South Africa—a Liberal back-bencher moved a resolution of 'high disapproval' of Milner 'in authorising the flogging of Chinese labourers in breach of the law, in violation of treaty obligations, and without the knowledge or sanction of His Majesty's Secretary of State for the Colonies.' An official amendment, which substantially endorsed the motion while refraining from passing censure on individuals, was moved by Churchill as Under-Secretary for the Colonies, in a speech described by one observer as 'ungenerous, patronizing and tactless.'† Not one Liberal Imperialist—Asquith, Haldane, Grey—spoke in the debate. Milner's friends boiled with fury that one mistake of their chief should, for the sake of party advantage, be blown up in such a way as to belittle his whole work of reconstruction, and that a great administrator should be patronised by a brash young man half his age.

Two days after the debate Buchan wrote to Violet Markham who, though a fervent Liberal, was a Milner partisan:

* Professor F. W. Gibson of Queen's University, Kingston, Ontario, suggested to me that in this matter Milner was misled by the Rand magnates. They supported Chinese labour because they did not want labour troubles such as had happened in the Australian mines, but covered up this motive with talk about the supreme importance of the mines to the South African economy. 'Milner swallowed it hook, line and sinker.'

† Edward Marsh, Churchill's Private Secretary, was surprised that a speech which had seemed 'wholly innocent of antagonism or condescension' when rehearsed before him in the office, should have made such an unfavourable impression in the House. (Christopher Hassall: *Edward Marsh*, 1959, p. 121.) Kipling expressed the indignation of Milner's friends in his poem 'The Pro-Consuls.'

I am nearly as angry as you about South Africa. The only remedy now is fire from heaven, but I see no sign of it in this weather.

At the same time I don't think anything very bad is going to happen. It is the insufferable insults to Lord M. which make me furious. I sat through all the debate on Wednesday—you may imagine with what feelings! I would far rather have had the vote of censure passed, than have it burked by the intolerable patronage of Winston. And I am very angry at the talk about getting up a national testimonial to Lord M. I don't mind Halifax's motion in the Lords, but the journalistic enterprise which the *Morning Post* talks of seems to me most undignified. It is far better to leave the heathen to rage unnoticed, and that is what Lord M. wants, I know.

I have been much cheered by the attitude of some of the Labour Party —Ramsay MacDonald especially. I rather agree with Lord M. that they are our natural allies. Fatted souls like Liberals can never be Imperialists.

Buchan was probably the author of a front-page note in the *Spectator* of 24 March which declared that 'The Resolution was vindictive, and the amendment standing in the name of Mr Churchill was cowardly, for it was framed to catch votes by pointing at Lord Milner without naming him'; and he certainly wrote the denunciation in the *Quarterly* for April 1906 ('The Government and South Africa'):

The unseemly and unconstitutional motion of censure on Lord Milner for a minor blunder which he readily admitted, the disingenuous device adopted to evade its consequences, and above all the insolent tone of patronage in which Mr Churchill reflected on the conduct of one of the greatest of living public servants—whose assailants, moreover, he stigmatised, five years ago, as 'rebels, traitors, and pro-Boers'—have already done much to alienate the better class of public opinion from the Government.

In this episode of the vote of censure may lie the clue to Buchan's pronounced coolness towards Churchill. On the face of it one would expect the romantic young Scot, who wanted both to write books and lead a life of action, to be fascinated by this near-contemporary who too had written books and led a life of action far more varied than Buchan's own. Indeed Churchill in 1906, with his far-flung adventures and his early Parliamentary success, had had very much the kind of career with which Buchan was later to endow some of his heroes. But though he admired his books Buchan never warmed to Churchill; he had made cheap jibes at a great man.

One evening in 1905 Buchan was taken by a friend to dine with Mrs Norman Grosvenor in Upper Grosvenor Street; when he paid his duty call at tea-time a few days afterwards, he was entertained by her daughter Susan. He and Susan Grosvenor then met a good deal at dinner-parties and country-houses, particularly at Crabbet Park near Crawley in Sussex, where the Edward Ridleys—connections of Cuthbert Medd—entertained parties of young people. (Buchan stayed there during August 1905, travelling up daily to work on the *Spectator*). The two had many friends in common—Murrays, Asquiths, Humphry Wards, Stracheys, Ecksteins, Wernhers, Beits, Gertrude Bell—and Buchan had known Susan Grosvenor's Lyttelton cousins in Pretoria when their father was Commander-in-Chief.

There were careful manoeuvrings on his part to visit the same houses at the same time ('I hope we shall meet at Rounton'); Buchan even took to dancing a little when he knew Miss Grosvenor would be at a ball ('I hope you will spare a few minutes from your Guardsmen to talk to me'); and when, in October 1905, he and some other young men gave a ladies' dinner-party at the Savoy there was much consultation with her as to guests and arrangements. He dined frequently in Upper Grosvenor Street; she and her mother often came to tea in Temple Gardens. There were jaunts to music halls and to East Ham ('I don't think chaperones are necessary'). He sent her books—French poetry, Plato, A. E. W. Mason's *Running Water* ('about a very jolly girl who climbs like a chamois') —and white heather from Skye. He put her into *A Lodge in the Wilderness* as Lady Flora Brume. After eighteen months' acquaintance Buchan was certain, for the first time in his life, that he wanted to marry.

Susan Grosvenor's father, who died when she was sixteen, was a son of Lord Ebury, a cousin of the Duke of Westminster, and a great-nephew of the Duke of Wellington. He was something of a gentle rebel against his world, and regarded by some of his high Tory and Whig relations as 'a traitor to his class.' He was a Radical in politics, an agnostic in religion, a friend of Charles Booth, William Morris* and Burne-Jones, a member of the London Library, subscriber to the *Yellow Book* and founder (with Walford Davies) of the People's Concerts. His tall and handsome wife, born Caroline Stuart-Wortley, shared his views and his tastes; her mother had been a great friend of Edward Lear; she herself painted, sculpted and published three novels. After Norman Grosvenor's

---

* One of his brothers, Richard Grosvenor, was a member of the party organised by Morris to row from Kelmscott House, Hammersmith, to Kelmscott Manor, Lechlade, in the summer of 1880.

death she lived quietly with her two daughters; there were many rich relations, but she was not well off by their standard, so there was no smart or showy entertaining. Among her friends were William de Morgan, Hugh Lane and Leslie Stephen, who once brought his daughter Virginia to dine. Years later Virginia Woolf wrote to Mrs Grosvenor that 'I think it was the first time I dined out in evening dress and I was very shy. I could still tell you what was talked about. My father I think had a special affection for you.' (In one of the last letters she wrote, in the spring of 1941, Virginia Woolf again recalled that evening.)

Susan Grosvenor had spent a good deal of her childhood at her paternal grandparents' house, Moor Park, in Hertfordshire—a Palladian mansion with grounds laid out by Capability Brown, and full of eighteenth-century chinoiserie. Her grandfather Lord Ebury (in this resembling Mrs Buchan), liked to have his children clustered round him, even when they were married. Mrs Norman Grosvenor found the hierarchical family society at Moor Park rather irksome, with its protocol and precedence and forbidden topics, and greatly preferred the freedom and comparative informality of their own house in London. On her side of the family too there was independence and some nonconformity. One of her sisters had been at the Slade and studied architecture, then had married Lord Lovelace, Byron's grandson, a friend of Henry James and Francis Galton. He was a rather moody recluse, obsessed by Byron; Lady Lovelace was a strong-minded woman who deplored plumbing, adored parrots (a white cockatoo was 'William of Ockham'), and was a warm supporter of the architect C. A. Voysey, whom she engaged to alter their Jacobean house at Ockham in Surrey. Mrs Grosvenor's brother Charles Stuart-Wortley had married, first a cousin of Trollope, then a daughter of Millais, who was also a very able amateur pianist. The Stuart-Wortleys were close friends of W. S. Gilbert and of Elgar, who was a regular visitor at their house in Cheyne Walk. Elgar called Caroline Stuart-Wortley 'Windflower' and she often played for him.

Mrs Grosvenor and her two daughters did a good deal of country-house visiting, encumbered by mountains of luggage, including sketching equipment. Susan did not ride, hunt or play tennis, or like talking about bags of pheasants; and though they enjoyed most of their balls and parties, she and her Lyttelton cousins despised what they called the 'sweetheart brigade' of predatory girls. She was serious in her interests, and a passionate reader (her father had given her an un-Victorian run of his library). She read Dante with a crib, tried to make something of Hegel, went to the Royal Court for Gilbert Murray's version of *The Trojan Women*, and to Covent Garden for Wagner. She painted china for William de Morgan, attended classes at the Polytechnic, worked in Mrs Humphry Ward's settlement in Tavistock Place. With her mother and sister she had studied painting and German in Dresden, art-history and Italian in Florence; on this trip they were accompanied by Mrs Grosvenor's friend Elizabeth Robins, the actress.

Yet for all these activities she was suffering from a sense of aimlessness when she met John Buchan. So was he—still unsettled after the Egyptian appointment, and feeling he had come to rather a dead end at the Bar, in his narrow channel of company law and income-tax law. So when he decided that marriage with Susan Grosvenor was what he wanted most of all, he went up to Edinburgh to talk over a suggestion which had been made by his old Oxford friend Tommy Nelson: that Buchan should join Nelson's as chief literary adviser, working mainly in London. All went well, they agreed on a salary of £1500 a year, and Buchan went back to London to propose. He followed up his proposal with a letter:

I used to think only of my ambitions, but now everything seems foolish and worthless without you. . . . I have not very much to offer except chances. But I think I could make you happy, and one thing I can give you, the most complete devotion and loyalty. You are the only woman I have ever been in love with, and ever shall be in love with.

Susan said yes, but they had to wait eight months to be married, for Nelson's wished Buchan to spend January to June at their works in Edinburgh before he started at their London office. Everyone who knew them both was delighted (Raymond Asquith congratulating Buchan 'on being the occasion of the first interesting paragraph there has been in *The Times* since Pigott ceased to be a contributor'); and among Susan's friends and relatives there was a general feeling that in plunging for this Scot of unknown background but brilliant prospects she was doing well for herself. 'So you aren't going to be a fat Duchess after all,' wrote one. 'I had always looked forward to being given one finger to shake at an omnium gatherum garden-party by your Grace, and now you're going to marry something like a genius instead.' Mrs Grosvenor was tremendously pleased, not only because everyone told her what an able young man he was ('The excellent work that Buchan has done for me and the great help he has given me have shown me

what splendid stuff there is in him,' Strachey wrote to her), but
because she had grown to like him so much herself. He called her
'Gerald,' advised her about literary agents and publishers, gave her
Haldane's Gifford lectures to read on holiday in Bavaria ('I am so
glad she is getting on with *The Pathway to Reality*. She mustn't
mind if she comes to great snags. The book I thought she ought to
read next was Wallace's *Prolegomena to Hegel*, but on second
thoughts I think Plato would be better'). 'I love him dearly,' wrote
Mrs Grosvenor, announcing the news to one of her sisters; 'I don't
think you could help loving him. He is so manly and simple and
so intelligent.'

It was with no such joy that Mrs Buchan received the news in
Glasgow. It reached her at a bad moment. Ever since the ill-starred
South African trip she had been difficult and depressed; her son's
letters were full of exhortations to cheer up, to take a proper holiday, not to worry about money. ('I sent Mother a cheque for £6
for a new dress,' he wrote to Anna; 'you will be sure and see that it
is really spent on that, and not put into that bottomless sink, the
Sustentation Fund.') Affectionate concern was tempered with
exasperation at 'that old obstructionist, my mother,' who needed a
holiday and yet raised endless objections to any suggestions for one.
And he burst out quite fiercely when, having had *her* holiday at
St Abbs Head, organised and largely paid for by him, she then
besought him not to go climbing in Skye. He was particularly
concerned for Anna, who was bearing the brunt of Mrs Buchan's
low spirits and becoming, as she put it, a 'blighted being': part of
the trouble as he saw it was that his mother was

too preoccupied with one thing—that old Kirk of yours—while Nan has
nothing to occupy herself with. I am very sorry for you all but especially
for my old Nan. She is suffering what anyone must suffer who has an
extended horizon and a limited opportunity. It is a complaint common to
most young women nowadays. Had I been a minister in Glasgow and
William a doctor in Strathbungo, and had we all lived together, there
would have been no horizon, and therefore no complaints.

One thing he felt he could do for his sister. 'I am going to open
a banking-account for her, and pay into it £100 yearly,' he wrote
in June 1905. 'That will give her pocket-money for clothes and any
travelling she wants to do. I look to you all to see that she spends it
on herself or at any rate *by herself*.' And he was really cross when his
mother supposed that, on taking a wife, he would stop his sister's allowance, and not pay for a holiday she was to have in India with Willie.

Mrs Buchan had always been apprehensive as well as proud about her son's successes, always suspicious of the world beyond her own small world. And now her son was marrying right out of her sphere, taking to wife a girl of whose class and Church she thought little. So news of the engagement brought Susan Grosvenor a stiff letter from Mrs Buchan—'I think you are to be congratulated,' but no word that her son might be lucky too—and a most friendly one from Anna:

John has been all the world to me since I can remember anything and I don't really think there ever was a kinder or more considerate brother. I used to wonder what I should do when John married but now that John has found the one woman in the world I find I don't grudge him to you in the least.

There was a rather difficult first meeting, when Mrs Buchan and Anna came up to Brown's Hotel for a short visit in January 1907; then in May Susan paid her first visit to the Buchans—not to Glasgow but to Peebles, where Walter had lately succeeded to his Uncle Willie Buchan's Town Clerkship and home in the High Street. Anna kept house for him, and was already finding her life less of a fight than at home in Glasgow. John had to exercise some diplomacy beforehand; Mrs Grosvenor did not want Susan to travel without a maid, Anna was adamant that there was no room in Bank House for such a creature. So Buchan, then working in Edinburgh, travelled to London to escort his fiancée back to Scotland.

For her it was quite an ordeal. She was marrying a man who, though not born in her world, was already at home in it when she met him; but she was also marrying into a family whose world was entirely strange to her. She had paid visits to Scotland, but these had been to Anglicised Scots, who belonged to Mayfair as well as to Highland castle or shooting-lodge. Now she was in a foreign country, where she could barely understand the language; Mrs Buchan, speaking of 'a cow in a frem'd loaning,' or dismissing an incompetent housewife as 'fushionless,' or 'throughhither,' might almost have been talking Greek. She was taken to see Aunt Aggie at Broughton, and Uncles Jim and John Masterton at Bamflat, whose speech was even less understandable than the other Buchans', and there was a tea-party at Bank House for Peebles to inspect Miss Grosvenor. Everywhere were black silk dresses, home-made scones, and talk about ministers and missions. At first Mrs Buchan's and Anna's purposeful bustle in the house made Susan feel incom-

petent and inadequate, but she came to admire a great deal in
their lives: 'There is something very keen and strenuous about
the atmosphere here,' she reported to her mother. 'They all talk
awfully well—so intelligently and keenly and the amount of poetry
quoted is amazing—one feels very alive and invigorated.' She particularly liked Mr Buchan: 'He has the most heavenly good-
tempered way with him—and laughs and is laughed at by his
family all the time. He plays the penny whistle delightfully!'

One aspect of the Buchans' life made a deep impression:

I had known extravagant people who spent money on their own pleasures
and had nothing left to give to others. I had also met many kind and
generous people, but I had never before come in contact with any one
family who economised so much on themselves and gave away money so
unsparingly.

Not long after this visit Buchan came back to London with
relief—'I am simply fed up with this confounded unnatural
separation'—to work at Nelson's office in Paternoster Row. Raymond Asquith was going to be married that summer too, to Katharine Horner, so a bachelor party had to be arranged ('Smyth,
Harold, Raymond and I are arranging a great DRUNK in June.
Horrid, isn't it? Raymond is anxious to drown care in the flowing
bowl'). In the past Buchan had tended to greet the news of his
friends' marriages with a mock concern, as if somehow they were
now lost to male society, tamed, reduced to domesticity, the keen
edge gone. 'I have become thoroughly undomesticated,' he had
written of himself before leaving South Africa. 'Marriage and
settling down, even the Highland shooting-box, which John Edgar
and I used to dream of, seem poor ideas.' Now when he told Susan
Grosvenor that 'I used to think only of my ambitions, but now
everything seems foolish and worthless without you,' he was a
maturer man. On the morning of her wedding Susan received a
letter from Lady Mary Murray, 'assuming the privilege of a friend
of his boyhood . . . to say to our friend's Bride how happy we feel
sure so loyal and strong and imaginative a man will make her.'

They were married on 15 July 1907 at St George's, Hanover
Square, the Grosvenors' parish church. Susan was sent trundling
to her wedding in the Grosvenor family coach, lent by the Duke of
Westminster. Cosmo Lang, then Bishop of Stepney, took the
service; Hugh Wyndham, the best man, remembered with amusement how Mrs Buchan had glowered at Lang's scarlet cassock. She
had a right to disapprove of this renegade son of the manse, for the

Reverend John Buchan had not been allowed to take any part in the marriage service.

For their honeymoon the Buchans went first to Tylney Hall in Hampshire, lent them by Lionel Phillips, and then (without a maid) to Achensee, Cortina and Venice. Buchan longed to make his wife, as he had made his sister, share the pleasures of climbing. She was very ready to try—and had heard much of the Dolomites from her uncle, Lord Lovelace, who had made many pioneer ascents round Cortina. But her enthusiasm did not survive an ascent of Monte Cristallo, which they made with Pierre Blanc, a French guide whose client Charlie Meade, an Oxford acquaintance of Buchan's, had been called away for a few days. She enjoyed the flowers and the views but, embarked on steep rock, discovered she suffered from vertigo. '*Mettez vos pieds dans le vide, madame,*' Pierre Blanc would cry encouragingly; but it was no good. However, 'somehow or other I was pushed up by John and Pierre.'

Otherwise all was delight—'our heavenly honeymoon,' she wrote—and thenceforward Buchan's career was built on the firm base of a blessedly happy marriage.

CHAPTER SEVEN

PUBLISHER AND PARLIAMENTARY CANDIDATE

1907–14

'If we are to have clear and sound thinking the people must take politics
very seriously and be very well informed about them.'
                    John Buchan: Address on 'Literature and Life,' 1910

The young Buchans' first home was at 40 Hyde Park Square, near
the park at Marble Arch, and Buchan worked at Nelson's office in
Paternoster Row. But his work took him north a great deal; indeed
the young couple's first weeks of housekeeping were in Edinburgh,
in the Nelsons' Gothic villa just under the Salisbury Crags, while
Tommy Nelson was on holiday and Buchan on duty at the Parkside
works next door. There they entertained their first guests—Susan's
mother and sister, John's parents—and at week-ends they visited
the Nelsons at Achnacloich on Loch Etive and the Ardwalls in
Galloway. (The judge alarmed Susan by roaring at her, over the
dinner-table as he carved a fowl, 'Do you think I gave Lady
Ardwall too much for this hen?') In following years Buchan went
up to Edinburgh at least once a month, for three or four days, and
every spring for a longer spell, when he and his wife would stay
with the Alec Maitlands in Heriot Row.

Nelson's was a firm which printed and bound its books as
well as publishing them. Tommy Nelson's father had been a man
of drive and imagination. He bought a great stretch of land to
allow for the works' expansion, and built his own house on a part
of it. A fire once broke out at the Parkside works, and before
the firemen had left Mr Nelson was ordering new plant. When
he felt himself growing old he sent for a nephew from Canada,
George Brown, to share the direction with his sons Tommy and
Ian. George Brown imported new machines from America and

Germany, installed an American accounting system, and had the idea of starting a new library of cheap reprints of copyright works. Tommy Nelson wholeheartedly supported Brown's ideas, and made them work. The atmosphere at Parkside was both old-fashioned and go-ahead: old-fashioned in the way that employees, who tended to stay at Parkside all their working days, were regarded as personal friends, whose lives were of interest and concern to their employer (in one hard winter Tommy Nelson bought 150 tons of coal to give the Parkside people the advantage of bulk-buying at lower cost): go-ahead in being the first firm in Edinburgh to have a full-time Welfare Supervisor. Nelson's technical efficiency was generally recognised: in 1906 Lord Cromer sent the new head of the government printing works in Egypt to see over Parkside.

Where this excellent organisation was weak, when Buchan joined it, was in the matter published: new titles were mainly religious books and children's books, but the chief output was in miscella-neous reprints. The list was anything but distinguished: the firm was out of touch with good contemporary writing, and it was John Buchan's function to put this right. He was editor and literary adviser (and, after Nelson's became a limited company in 1915, a director) and his main job in the London office was to make con-tacts with new authors. But Tommy Nelson and George Brown brought him into all the discussions of policy and organisation, saw that he was familiar with questions of machinery, paper supply, and safety in the factory ('I am having a wire rail put round the little fiend of a machine,' he wrote soon after joining the firm), and Buchan often held the fort when the senior partners were on holi-day or abroad on the firm's business. He briefed Nelson's travellers ('very superior people compared with the ordinary bagman'), took the chair at the annual concert, and judged the literary competition ('There is one Platonic dialogue about current questions written by a man in the case-room').

The three men formed a happy and harmonious partnership. For George Brown, by some years the oldest of the three—and a distant cousin of his own as well as first cousin to Nelson—Buchan had great affection and complete trust; for Tommy Nelson he had affection, trust and a sort of hero-worship. 'Tom is the same stolid old jewel,' he told Anna after deciding to join the firm. At Oxford Buchan had been dazzled by the splendid captain of the University XV and Scottish International; he still liked Tommy for being such a good shot, fisherman and rider to hounds, for always looking so handsome and fit; but now at Parkside he was most struck by Tommy's seriousness, his moral solidity and bigness, and found him a 'rare being because he was so superbly normal, so wholly in tune with ordinary humanity.'

With this splendid machine at hand, equipped to produce books plentifully, cheaply, and decently, Buchan set to his work with zest. He chose the titles for the Nelson Sixpenny Classics, for the shilling series of non-fiction still in copyright, and for the famous Sevenpenny Library—formally the 'Nelson Library of Copyright Works'—which, bound in stiff covers, had nothing in the least cheap about their format or their print.* It was a project that suited very well with Buchan's experience—he had profited from Walter Scott's Camelot reprints and Canterbury Poets, 'a godsend to a young man'—and with his democratic feelings. Like Allen Lane twenty-five years later, he believed that the taste for good books was widely spread and constantly increasing. His job with the Sevenpennies was to bring good modern fiction to this new public; when they proved an immediate success—'do you know we are going to sell out the whole of the great enormous edition . . . before publication?'—and had encouraged other series (Collins soon followed with *their* Sevenpennies) Buchan wrote of the changes which all these reprints had made in the bookshops and on the book-buying habits of the public:

The philosophy of the reprint is that people are made to read who did not read before, and to buy who before only read. A demand is created by forcing a particular supply on the world. Books formerly were never sold, except in America and a little in Germany, as any ordinary article of commerce is sold. The old-fashioned bookshop was a kind of club to which bookish people resorted. They were never pressed to buy, books were never forced on their notice, and certain booksellers we remember would have resented such a suggestion as a personal affront. No other retailer sells his commodity like this.

But the reprint, appearing in myriads and covering bookstalls and shop counters with attractive colours, pushed itself from very numbers. Instead of hiding shyly, like most books, on a shelf, it clamoured to be bought. Accordingly, for almost the first time in the history of literature, we find books selling as freely and widely as, say, soap or bootlaces. There is no loss of dignity in the comparison. In a properly constituted community books are as much a necessity to all as tobacco, and are bought and sold in the same way.

* The first of the Sevenpennies, Mrs Humphry Ward's *The Marriage of William Ashe*, was exhibited in 1958 in a display of Scottish printing at the National Library in Edinburgh.

And after the Nelson reprints had sold in millions he drew some conclusions:

The first is that the better the work is the better it sells. We have tried experiments, and occasionally included a book of only trivial interest which has been a great success at a high price. But the comfortably-off people who subscribe to the big circulating libraries are not a good guide to the tastes of the people who are only able to afford a few pence for a book, and want to buy rather than to borrow . . . Books of serious value which have failed with the middle class public have often had an enormous success in these cheap libraries, and trivial books which have delighted that better-off public have been neglected. . . . The new reading public, which has grown up in the last twenty years, and is a thousand times larger than any reading public before in the world's history, is an intelligent public, a serious public, a public which, if I were a great writer, I would far rather write for than for the bored ladies who get a weekly box from the library.

So, although there was plenty of light entertainment among the Sevenpennies—A. E. W. Mason, Hornung's *Raffles*, W. W. Jacobs, Somerville and Ross, *The Riddle of the Sands*, and *Sherlock Holmes* —the list included Mark Twain (*Tom Sawyer* and *Huckleberry Finn*), Henry James (*Roderick Hudson* and *The American*), Arthur Morrison (*A Child of the Jago*), H. G. Wells (*The Country of the Blind* and half-a-dozen others), George Douglas Brown's *House with the Green Shutters*, Gissing (*The Odd Women* and *Born in Exile*), Conrad and Hueffer's *Romance*, and novels by Jack London and Frank Norris.

Other successful series were the shilling non-fiction reprints, the Nelson Library of Notable Books at one-and-sixpence, and the Nelson Library of General Literature at the same price. Among the titles chosen for the various series, many of them recalling Buchan's own early enthusiasms and discoveries, or reflecting his current interests, were Arnold's *Culture and Anarchy* and *Literature and Dogma*, the Goncourts' *Journal*, Conrad's *A Personal Record*, Kenneth Grahame's *Golden Age*, Whymper's *Scrambles among the Alps*, Mummery's *My Climbs in the Alps and Caucasus*, Durand's *Making of a Frontier*, Winston Churchill's *Malakand Field Force*, Belloc's *Path to Rome*, Rosebery's *Napoleon: The Last Phase*, Birrell's *Self-Selected Essays*, Colvin's *Making of Modern Egypt*, F. S. Oliver's *Life of Alexander Hamilton*. Not quite so successful was another series started by Buchan, the two-shilling new novels, even though one of the titles was *Mr Polly* and another E. C. Bentley's *Trent's Last Case*.

Buchan's other special work at Nelson's was editing Encyclopaedias—for a Spanish one he learnt the language at high speed—and editing a weekly paper published by Nelson's, the *Scottish Review*. This had started with the firm's acquisition in 1905 of a paper called the *Christian Leader*, and their aim was to produce a distinctively Scottish weekly, comparable to the sixpenny English weeklies, but at a penny. To begin with, the *Scottish Review and Christian Leader* was strongly tinged with the ecclesiastical character of the parent paper; an issue early in 1907 has an advertisement for pulpit robes on the front cover, reviews of theological literature, an article on 'Festive Scottish Funerals' and a sermon by Dr Alexander Whyte of Free St George's Church. But in April 1907 (three months after Buchan had started at Nelson's) an editorial announced that though 'the present features will remain . . . it will be also a first-class literary weekly, containing reviews, literary articles and literary competitions.' Its aim, so Buchan told Lord Rosebery, was

to deal fully with all interests, literary, political and social, with something Scottish in the point of view. We want to make it the centre of a Scottish school of letters such as Edinburgh had a hundred years ago.

According to his assistant editor, W. Forbes Gray, Buchan wanted to make the *Review* a Scottish *Spectator*:

It was Buchan's view that the paper was too parochial. He wanted a wider, saner, and more tolerant outlook, more articles on literary and social subjects, a good class of serial fiction, and a plentiful supply of book reviews by first-rate writers. Moreover, the Radical politics and ultra-nationalism which had dominated the paper in the past were to be less obtrusive. As indicative of the new spirit, I recall that Buchan's first editorial was entitled, 'Liberalism on the Continent,' while among the book reviews in the same issue appeared a detailed criticism of Dean Inge's lectures on *Personal Idealism and Mysticism* from the pen of a well-known theologian.

Buchan also instituted topical paragraphs under the heading 'News of the World,' columns on universities, art and music, and a page for women; he himself wrote a weekly London Letter, and the ecclesiastical matter was relegated to the back pages.

The new policy was immensely successful in improving the paper's contents and prestige. Among the contributors whom Buchan secured were R. B. Haldane, R. W. Seton-Watson, Andrew Lang, George Saintsbury, Hilaire Belloc, Neil Munro, Katharine Tynan, the Reverend Sabine Baring-Gould, Robert Rait, W. W. Skeat, J. Arthur Thomson. The special features included six pages of articles on the Milton tercentenary in 1908, a symposium on the

future of Scots as a language, and a series of articles on the industries of Glasgow. Buchan himself wrote every week, as well as the
London Letter, an article of about 1200 words, very much in the
style of his *Spectator* leaders, though his range could here be wider:
imperial questions, foreign affairs, home politics, current social
problems. Often he wrote on books and authors, or on some outstanding public person. In the collection rescued from the files by
Mr Forbes Gray under the title *Comments and Characters* there
are articles on 'Mr Winston Churchill as Man of Letters,' on Kelvin, Livingstone, Balfour, Haldane, Cosmo Lang (on his appointment as Archbishop of York).

Yet at a penny it was not a financial success. Buchan's hopes may
have been the same as for his reprints: given the best, a great new
reading public would take it eagerly. But this did not work so well
with journals as with books. Some said the *Scottish Review* was too
intellectual for a penny paper, some that it was too outward-looking
—what did the Scottish reader want to know about the Balkans and
German policy? Others felt that Buchan lacked the popular touch
and had too Anglicised a taste. Buchan had certainly tried to
enlarge his readers' horizons beyond kirk and kailyard. Scottish
affairs were treated seriously (as in the articles on Glasgow's industries and on the proposals for union between the Established and
United Free Churches, or in the symposium on the Scots tongue),
but it was assumed that the intelligent reader would also be concerned with what happened in Parliament, or in Central Europe, or
in Egypt, or the United States. There was to be none of that sealed-
off Scottishness, those stereotyped views of Scottish life and
character, that Buchan had consistently decried in the Kailyarders.
Accused of 'Anglicisation,' Buchan could have retorted that he was
rather continuing the tradition of Jeffrey and the *Edinburgh Review*.

Certainly that cosiness which warms the members of a self-
sufficient community, in which lay the appeal of the Kailyarders,
was not to be found in the *Scottish Review*, where cold blasts from
Russia or Morocco would blow through the editorials, and where
a taste for books implied a taste for Meredith, for Flaubert, for
Ibsen, rather than for J. M. Barrie and S. R. Crockett. So when,
with the last issue of 1908, the *Scottish Review* expired, it was
much lamented by its Scottish university readers—'the most
thinking classes' at which Buchan had aimed—but perhaps not so
much by the original subscribers who had been quite happy round
the parish pulpit.

With his unparochial outlook Buchan was particularly interested and concerned in Nelson's foreign activities. He went to Paris with Tommy Nelson to organise, in association with Bernard Grasset, their series of Nelson's French classics. These were printed and bound at Parkside, and one of the great advantages of '*Les Collections Nelson des meilleurs auteurs français et étrangers*' over native French products was their '*reliure aussi solide qu'élégante.*' Buchan was concerned in similar negotiations with Ullstein in Germany. Magyar and Spanish were other languages in which Nelson printed cheap editions; projects for a Russian series were in hand in 1914.

In London the Buchans led the agreeable life of a young couple with plenty of friends, of kindly and congenial relatives, a growing family of their own, satisfying occupations, and no acute money problems (though in 1910 Buchan warned his wife that 'we must be economical this winter, for Mother's illness is going to be expensive'). Susan attended lectures (including a course given by Professor Hobhouse at the London School of Economics), worked at the Personal Service League, was active on the constitutional side of the women's suffrage movement, and continued to learn Greek, thus provoking her husband to the couplet:

> To patronise the poor, with votes to fuss,
> And leave Greek grammars in the casual bus.

Their daughter Alice was born in 1908—as soon as he heard all was going well Buchan, delighted but sleepless, had to rush off to Oxford to keep an engagement to speak at the Union. He fell asleep the minute the train left Paddington, and woke to see Winston Churchill, his fellow-speaker, reading and making notes. In 1911, a year after they had moved from Hyde Park Square to 13 Bryanston Street, their first son was born. In 1912 they moved again, to 76 Portland Place, one of the eighteenth-century houses at the Regent's Park end, with a blue French wallpaper in the drawing-room found for them by Sir Hugh Lane.

On Sundays they went to the Church of Scotland, St Columba's in Pont Street, of which Buchan became an elder in 1912. Shortly after a keen discussion as to whether the choir should wear purple cassocks or stick to black (Buchan voted for black) he and his wife were asked to dinner by the formidable Lady Frances Balfour, A. J. Balfour's sister-in-law, who was almost as influential as the minister at St Columba's and much more feared.

They dined out a great deal—with the Stracheys to meet Theodore Roosevelt, with the Dougal Malcolms, the Amerys, the St John Hornbys of the Ashendene Press, the F. E. Smiths; 'by all means,' wrote Buchan from Edinburgh, 'let us accept the Tullibardines and Trevelyans.' They lunched at Downing Street with the Asquiths. Milner and Haldane came often to their dinnerparties, and one evening they invited the Philip Snowdens to meet the Robert Cecils and discuss the suffrage campaign, all six of them being keen supporters.

Among the friends they saw most of were two of Susan's Lyttelton cousins and their husbands, the Arthur Grenfells and the Charles Mastermans; Violet Markham, so ardent an Imperialist, so zealous a reformer; the F. S. Olivers, and the Moritz Bonns. Bonn was a brilliant young Jewish economist from Frankfurt, who came to England to be one of the first teachers at the London School of Economics after its foundation in 1903, and married an English wife.

The Buchans' house was always ready to serve as holiday place or staging-post for the Scottish family—though Mrs Buchan, independent as always, often preferred to stay with relations at Clapham. She could be a formidable guest: would show her daughter-in-law how to make the coal go further by banking the fires with damp paper, or would insist on worshipping not at St Columba's (probably tainted for her as being the *Established* Church of Scotland) but at the Regent Square Presbyterian Church, whose minister she preferred. Willie was with them a good deal in 1909, when he had six months' leave from India. Susan was devoted to this brother-in-law who had wholeheartedly welcomed her into the family. He was gay, yellow-haired and handsome, 'one of the finest-looking young men I have ever seen,' and he breathed a larger air than the Buchans in Scotland. He danced and rode and played polo, and after a strenuous tour of duty up-country in Bengal would throw himself with zest into the gaieties of London or Calcutta. He was more unpredictable in temperament than the other Buchans, more critical of other people; and he was the only one of the family who was not a compulsive reader. He had idled till he was sixteen, then had strenuously applied himself to win the scholarships that would take him to the university and so to the Indian Civil Service. He stood up for the oppressed: whether it was a Glasgow professor who became unpopular for his pro-Boer sympathies in the South African war, or the Bengal villager bled white by the money-lender.

Often the Buchans went away at week-ends—to the Lionel Phillipses at Tylney, where they had started their honeymoon; to the Portmans in Berkshire, to the F. S. Olivers at Checkendon near Reading, to the Rayleighs at Terling in Essex—'a big party, Edmond Warre, Tommy Lascelles, Lord and Lady Wolmer, Lady Evelyn Grey and Violet Asquith,' reported Buchan to his mother after a visit there in the summer of 1913. They were frequent guests of Susan's aunt, Lady Lovelace, either at Ashley Combe near Porlock, or at Ockham. After a Whitsun at Ashley Combe Buchan wrote to Hugh Walpole that the week-end would always be memorable, for

I have made a new friend (and I haven't many, though I have a bowing acquaintance with half the world). You and I are going to keep together, old man, or I shall jolly well know why.

Often on these visits they were fellow-guests of Henry James, who was an old friend of the Lovelaces, and whom the strong-minded Lady Lovelace once tried to settle in a small house on the estate. She marched James out to see it, with the Buchans and Hugh Walpole in tow. 'It was not an especially interesting dwelling,' Susan Buchan remembered,

and it was sunk in rather dull fields. Henry James praised it in elaborate sentences, but as we started to walk home he said under his breath to Hugh Walpole, 'I should call it Suicide Cottage.'

James used to chide Buchan for some of his literary tastes (his liking for romances and thrillers?), but persuaded him to read Stevenson again—the idol of Buchan's Scottish youth in whom, after Oxford, he had lost interest. Buchan immensely admired James, the man even more than the books: 'I have never known anyone whose mind more repaid minute exploration, for it was full of constant surprises, and I have rarely known any finer piece of human nature.'

Buchan has given a vivid account in *Memory Hold-the-Door* of a week-end at Ockham in the autumn of 1909, when he and Henry James were asked by Lady Lovelace 'to examine her archives in order to reach some conclusion on the merits of the quarrel between Byron and his wife.' (Lord Lovelace, it will be remembered, was Byron's grandson; the Byron affair had been his obsession, and he had written *Astarte* with the object of vindicating his grandmother.) Buchan's account of this episode was written nearly thirty years later in Canada, relying on his memory alone; the report he wrote with James, which is printed in an appendix,* shows that the papers they examined were not the papers which had descended from Lady Byron to Lord Lovelace, and are generally referred to as the Lovelace Papers, but the Melbourne correspondence (then owned by Lady Dorchester, now by John Murray) of which Lord Lovelace had taken copies. Buchan recalled how they 'waded through masses of ancient indecency. . . . The thing nearly made me sick, but my colleague never turned a hair.' This slip of Buchan's memory gave the impression that the Lovelace Papers were full of obscenity; not only were these *not* the papers James and Buchan examined, but the Melbourne correspondence which they *did* examine was published by Murray in 1922 without expurgation, in *Lord Byron's Correspondence*, and without public outcry.

James, when dining with the Lovelaces in 1895, had already seen various papers concerning Byron's relations with his half-sister Augusta Leigh; both he and Buchan (who had reviewed it in the *Spectator*) had read Lord Lovelace's *Astarte*, which tells the story of this relationship. They may have talked about these Lovelace Papers when they were examining the Melbourne correspondence, and Buchan may have telescoped the two lots of documents in memory. He was certainly, in his wife's opinion, shocked by Lady Melbourne's cold-blooded amorality (she pressed Byron to take a mistress to divert him from Augusta): he was also shocked, when he read *Astarte*, at the idea of love-letters, innocent in themselves, passing between brother and sister. But Buchan was not particularly squeamish: one friend speaks of his 'mildly Rabelaisian turn,' and he enjoyed exchanging cheerful bawdy letters with F. S. Oliver. So the question how he came to remember these letters in terms that suggest obscenity remains a puzzle.

Summer holidays were spent mainly in Peeblesshire—the children, from their earliest days, were the most welcome of guests at Bank House—with short visits to friends in the Highlands. After the honeymoon experience on Monte Cristallo, Buchan had given up serious mountaineering, but his unabated love of the hills found an outlet in deer-stalking. In 1909 he killed one of his first stags just under the top of Bidean nam Bian in Glencoe.

The sport had not the sustained tension of mountaineering; indeed, much of its charm lay in the long spells of idle waiting, one's nose in thyme or

* See page 472.

heather, when the mind was gathered into the mountain peace. The high moments were the start in the freshness of morning, when the dew was on the birches, and one had the first spy from a hillock in the glen; the sunny hours on the tops when cloud shadows patterned the corries; the return in the evening in a flaming sunset with—or without—a lumpish hill pony carrying a stag. Such a day could not be blank even if one never saw a shootable beast, or missed him when seen, for, as Sir Walter Scott said of himself when he watched Tom Purdie at work, 'one's fancy could be running its ain riggs in another world.'

More distant excursions were combined with visits abroad for Nelson's. In the spring of 1910 the Buchans travelled by Orient Express to Constantinople, where they joined Gerard Craig-Sellar on his yacht the *Rannoch*. In Constantinople (which he found 'pure Arabian Nights') Buchan's experiences varied from 'lunching in state with the Sultan's brother and dining at Embassies to chaffering with Kurds for carpets in a sort of underground bazaar.' Then they cruised in the Aegean; and from Athens, 'because I am at present in your country,' Buchan wrote to Gilbert Murray:

We cruised about those bleak islands, Lemnos, Imbros and Samothrace— very like our West Hebrides. After a roughish voyage we got to the Northern Sporades and thence to Thermopylae, where I got myself lost in the hills through trying to discover what the Phocians did on Kallidromos. We went down the Euripus, and stayed in some delightful little islands called Petali. Two days ago we came to Athens, and, in spite of constant rain, it is magnificent. We go on to Corinth, Delphi and Olympia and thence to Corfu and Venice.

I have been re-reading your *Greek Epic*, and am filled with admiration. Years ago when I was in your class at Glasgow, I remember thinking that a wonderful book might be written about the Ionian migration. Your early chapters are the book. I really think that you have written the most original and convincing and imaginative piece of historical reconstruction that I have ever met with.

Buchan's short story 'The Lemnian' (in *The Moon Endureth*), about the islander who finds himself fighting with the Hellenes at Thermopylae, sprang out of his interest in the Ionian migration, and of his impressions on this cruise.

There was a holiday in 1911 with the Moritz Bonns on the Rosensee in the Wettersteingebirge of Bavaria; in June 1912 a fishing holiday with Tommy Nelson in Norway, where they lived in a wooden farmhouse above the Leardal river; and in June 1913 a cruise to the Azores. Holidays for Buchan were not a matter of rest, but of alternative activity, usually physical; but on this cruise he planned to 'amuse myself writing a real shocker—a tribute at the shrine of my master in fiction—E. Phillips Oppenheim—the greatest Jewish writer since Isaiah.' The man who cheerfully announced this to Hugh Walpole had travelled a good way from the Glasgow student so carefully polishing his essays, or the Oxford undergraduate writing 'psychological studies of cultured people.' Then, even if he shied off literature as a profession, he had been very much the literary man; now he was more the man of action, whose field for the moment was publishing, who hoped it would soon be politics, and who did some writing on the side. His wife remembers him advising Hugh Walpole, one week-end when they were the Lovelaces' guests, against settling down to become a whole-time man of letters; urging him to write, but also to enlarge his knowledge of life by working at some other job too. Another time he explained his refusal to accompany Walpole to a Royal Literary Fund dinner with 'I really can't go to these beanfeasts. I love writers individually, but assembled in bulk they affect me with overpowering repugnance, like a gathering of clerics.'

Buchan still kept up his connection with the *Spectator*, reviewing regularly, and occasionally contributing an article; he also wrote for *The Times Literary Supplement*. To judge by the books he reviewed, his intellectual interests were veering from literature to politics and philosophy; in May 1914 he wrote a front-page article for the *Literary Supplement* on 'Mr Balfour and English Thought.' His own books published between his marriage and 1914 made an individual mixture: two works undertaken to liven up Nelson's list of boys' books, the story *Prester John* (1910) and the biography *Sir Walter Raleigh* (1911)—Raleigh had been the subject of his Stanhope prize essay at Oxford; *The Moon Endureth* (1912), a collection of short stories, most of which had first appeared in *Blackwood's*; a memoir of his old friend *Andrew Jameson, Lord Ardwall* (1913); and *The Marquis of Montrose* (1913).

The quality which comes through the stories in *The Moon Endureth* is a sense of possibilities. You go round a familiar corner and the world opens up:

I had last seen him on the quay at Funchal bargaining with some rascally boatman to take him after mythical wild goats in the Desertas. Before that we had met at an embassy ball in Vienna, and still earlier at a hill station in Persia.

You go round a corner of your prosaic friend, and find that in his dreams he is a king. You go round a corner of history, and find that there might have been an entirely different pattern—the right man coming at the right moment could have created a great civilisation in Central Asia. You go round the corner of your mind, and find a new conception, as Holland does in 'Space,' a story which reflects Buchan's interest both in the works of Bergson and Poincaré and in the problems of climbing the Chamonix Aiguilles. The stories convey, too, a sense that submerged in every man are powers and possibilities which may be released by a place ('The Grove of Ashtaroth,' 'The Green Glen'), by an event ('The Kings of Orion,' a tale in which a daydream becomes a source of practical strength), a ballad ('The Rime of True Thomas'), or even a potion, as in 'A Lucid Interval.' This piece of political high spirits, in the key of Kipling's 'Village that Voted the Earth was Flat,' demonstrates the thesis that 'every man has a creed, but in his soul he knows that that creed has another side . . . which it does not suit him to produce.' A special Indian curry, administered at a political dinner-party, elicits, with startling effect, opinions which had been safely tucked out of sight.

In tackling *Montrose*, 'a serious piece of historical work which has given me a lot of trouble,' Buchan was in a measure charting the development of his own interests. As a boy, when—as he wrote of his brother Willie in the dedicatory poem—

> Oft in moorland noons I played
> Colkitto to your grave Montrose,

it was the great captain who had struck his imagination. Now Buchan's concern was as much with the man of philosophical mind and intellectual tastes, whom events had forced into action. Service with Milner, whose ideal of Empire had led him to undertake works of practical reconstruction with railways, farms and irrigation, prepared Buchan for the study of a man whose views on 'Sovereign Power' led him to organise armies and fight campaigns.

In disclaiming his pretensions to be a professional writer Buchan had another calling well in view. During 1910 Tommy Nelson wrote to him:

I would not have the very least objection to your standing at this or any election—on the contrary I should very much like to see you in Parliament. . . . As to the business side of the matter I personally have not the slightest fear of any effect your standing might have on your work. Your value to the business is not calculated by the number of hours you spend at Paternoster Row.

Buchan did not find a seat that he could feel eager to contest in time for either of the 1910 elections, but in April 1911 came an offer from a most suitable constituency, and he was adopted as Unionist* candidate for Peebles and Selkirk. In 1902, when he was in South Africa, he had heard a rumour that Raymond Asquith might be standing for that same constituency as a Liberal (his stepmother's father, Sir Charles Tennant, lived near Innerleithen). 'If he did,' Buchan had commented, 'he would get in, for no honest county could withstand Raymond. Some day Raymond and I will have a titanic fight there.' Now, however, the fight was to be not with Raymond (who was adopted as Liberal candidate for Derby in 1912), but with Donald Maclean, who in December 1910 had defeated the Unionist candidate (Strang Steel) by 201 votes, which, in an electorate of only 4105, was not such a slender majority as it sounds. Maclean, a Radical and a Free Churchman, suited the constituency well; and the elder Mrs Buchan, for one, took a gloomy view of her son's prospects, especially after she had seen the Macleans in church. She 'thought them a very handsome couple and was greatly depressed by it.'

Though Buchan had for some years nursed Parliamentary ambitions, he had still failed to develop much of a partisan spirit. At Oxford he had described himself as only 'a weak-kneed Conservative.' The years with Milner had inclined him to regard party politics as less important than good administration. Now his friends of both parties felt that if he really wanted to go into politics it was high time he declared himself. The Tory L. S. Amery, meeting Susan Buchan at a dinner-party in 1910, kept on telling her that 'John *must* stand for Parliament, and he must belong to one side or the other;' and a few days later the Liberal Charles Masterman, an Under-Secretary in the Asquith administration, was insisting what a brilliant fellow John was, how he ought to be in the House, 'and don't let him be a mugwump, let him join either the Liberals or the Tories, I don't mind which, but one or the other.'

Liberal or Tory? The terms carried different weight and provoked different feelings in Scotland and England. In England, as Raymond Asquith assured Buchan, 'young men have a much better chance on our side. The Privy Council yearns for a promising

* 'Unionists' (in the *O.E.D.* definition) are members 'of a political party which advocated or supported maintenance of the parliamentary union between Great Britain and Ireland, formed by coalition between Conservatives and Liberal Unionists in 1886, and later known indifferently as "Unionist" or "Conservative".' 'Unionist' is the term generally preferred in Scotland.

Liberal of thirty.'* But in Scotland the Liberals were the Grand Old
Party who had only once been in a minority since the Reform Act
of 1832. In 1906, and in both elections of 1910, they won all but
thirteen seats. (On each occasion the figures were Liberal 59,
Unionist 11, Labour 2.) There was a close link between Liberalism
and the Free Church. 'To a Free Churchman, especially,' Buchan
wrote in his memoir of Lord Ardwall, Gladstonian Liberalism

came as natural as Toryism to a Highland laird. There was in it something of the ancient Scots jealousy of England, the rich and, by repute,
conservative neighbour; a wholesome dislike of snobbery; a partiality for
plain folk . . . some suspicion of denationalised lairds with Episcopalian
proclivities; a distrust of exotic cleverness (Mr Disraeli); a traditional love
of oratory, especially when it smacked of the pulpit (Mr Gladstone).

It added up to 'a loyalty rather than a principle.' So to be a Tory
in the circles in which Buchan had grown up was at least a proof of
independence. Here indeed he had the example of his father: in
the face of solidly Radical congregations at Pathhead and in the
Gorbals, the Reverend John Buchan remained a Unionist; he liked
unpopular causes, never minded getting up in the Assembly to air
some unfashionable view, and maintained that minorities had been
right since the days of Noah. But the rest of Buchan's kin, including
the sheep-farming Mastertons, were solidly Liberal, and the
Radical *Edinburgh Evening News* said that Buchan was 'a bleating
sheep, strayed from the fold, with just enough of the party tar-mark
on him to be recognised, and sent kindly home.'

What Buchan could not stand in Liberals—particularly in Scottish Liberals—was not their programme, but their 'self-righteous-
ness, the constant asseveration that you are better and more tender-
hearted than your neighbours, the cultivation of emotions at high
tension.' He thought there was a lot of humbug about those who
denounced the landlord as a prize villain, when a much more dangerous character was the financier 'who plays with money and the
destinies of men as he plays with dominoes', and about the cocoa-
magnates who, holding gambling in holy horror, yet sold their half-
penny papers on their racing news, all 'for Liberalism's sake.' In
the character of Mr Alexander Cargill, the fictitious Home Secretary in a Liberal Government (he appears in 'A Lucid Interval,'

* The contemporary of Buchan and Asquith who came most nearly to realising
this wish was Auberon Herbert, who at Oxford was far less interested in politics
than the others of their group. On succeeding an uncle in 1906 as Lord Lucas, he
became one of the few Liberal peers, held office in Asquith's administration and was
made a Privy Councillor at thirty-six.

and is supposed to be modelled on the then Lord Advocate, Alexander Ure) Buchan has pinned down much that revolted him in Scottish Liberalism:

He had the face of an elderly and pious bookmaker, and a voice in which lurked the indescribable Scotch quality of 'unction.' When he was talking you had only to shut your eyes to imagine yourself in some lowland kirk on a hot Sabbath morning. He had been a distinguished advocate before he left the law for politics, and had swayed juries of his countrymen at his will. The man was extraordinarily efficient on a platform. There were un-plumbed depths of emotion in his eye, a juicy sentiment in his voice, an overpowering tenderness in his manner, which gave to politics the glamour of a revival meeting. He wallowed in obvious pathos, and his hearers, often unwillingly, wallowed with him. I have never listened to any orator at once so offensive and so horribly effective. There was no appeal too base for him, and none too august; by some subtle alchemy he blended the arts of the prophet and the fishwife. He had discovered a new kind of language. Instead of 'the hungry millions,' or 'the toilers,' or any of the numerous synonyms for our masters, he invented the phrase, 'Goad's people.' 'I shall never rest,' so ran his great declaration, 'till Goad's green fields and Goad's clear waters are free to Goad's people.' I remember how on this occasion he pressed my hand with his famous cordiality, looked gravely and earnestly into my face, and then gazed sternly into vacancy. It was a fine picture of genius descending for a moment from its hill-top to show how close it was to poor humanity.

Yet many of the men Buchan liked and admired—Gilbert Murray, R. B. Haldane, Raymond Asquith, Harold Baker, Charles Masterman—were Liberals, his wife's father had been Liberal M.P. for Chester, and he shared many of their views. So the candidate who set out to woo the electors of Peebles and Selkirk offered them rather an odd mixture of beliefs. In 1910 he was for the Government in the crisis with the Lords, and he was in favour of most of the objectives of Lloyd George's 1910 budget—old age pensions, health and unemployment insurance—though critical of much detail in the Insurance Act. He supported women's suffrage, and wrote a pamphlet on the subject for the Conservative and Unionist Women's Franchise Association, sub-titled 'A Logical Outcome of the Conservative Faith.' He was a Free Trader—as a character in *A Lodge in the Wilderness* put it, 'that strange wild fowl, a Tory Free-trader'—when most Conservatives were Tariff Reformers. For Britain alone, he told Amery in 1904, 'Free Trade is infinitely the better policy. Any form of Protection only becomes thinkable when the unit is the Empire.' He was an avowed Imperialist—but so were Liberals like Grey and Haldane (Buchan's chief apprehension on this score was that the Liberals might appoint the wrong man as Viceroy of India, or Governor-General of Canada or South Africa). The one issue on which he came down firmly on the official Unionist side, and against his Liberal friends, was Ulster, a subject which came increasingly to dominate all others between 1911 and 1914.

On his adoption the *Peebles News* reported—under a cross-head 'Is the Candidate a Liberal?'—that

Mr John Buchan is rather advanced in his opinions to please some of the more rabid Tories. Part of his programme is stated to be: Abolition of the hereditary principle of the House of Lords, Free Trade, and a scheme of Small Holdings. How the Unionist Tariff Reformers will act with such a programme remains to be seen. Certain it is that some who attended the meeting are not at all keen on such an advanced programme.

'A Conservative with a move on' was Buchan's own description of himself.

In one respect he had modified an earlier allegiance. Milner he continued immensely to admire, but with Milner's line on a number of issues he was increasingly out of sympathy. In South Africa he too had dreamed of imperial federation, but on his return to Britain he drew away from the idea.

I realised what Sir Wilfrid Laurier, first of all imperial statesmen, realised, that you could not bind a growing Empire with any elaborate constitutional bonds. I realised the strength of Colonial nationalism—that the different Dominions had still to rise to national stature, and that until that day came, it was idle to talk about any machinery of union.

Perhaps his Scottishness enabled him to appreciate Dominion national sentiment better than Milner or Amery; in 1908 he wrote sympathetically in the *Scottish Review* about Canada's wish to make treaties on her own account. He was certainly more sympathetic than they were to minority cultures that were non-British, like the French-Canadian and the Boer. Buchan was never one of the Round Table group and inclined to think them, and particularly Lionel Curtis, too academic.

In British politics Milner stood 'above party' because he despised the party system (which had rejected him when in the General Election of 1885 he stood as a Liberal candidate at Harrow and was badly beaten). Buchan had hitherto sat loose to party allegiances not because he mistrusted the system, but because he did not much care for the black-and-white simplifications and

divisions that party politics call for. Above all, Buchan had none of
Milner's distrust and contempt for the common voter and the mass
electorate. 'He had never much notion of the ordinary Briton' was
his comment on Milner, 'a lack which would have seriously handi-
capped him in domestic politics.' Buchan trusted his fellow-
citizens, and he knew a far wider range of them than Milner ever
did. Indeed, he rather tended to idealise the political sense of the
common voter, whom he saw as a Border shepherd or tweed-mill
worker, a Nelson's compositor or traveller, a reader of the Sevenpenny reprints, or a Lanarkshire coal-miner with a taste for fishing.

On the question of Ulster, although Buchan was in apparent
agreement with Milner's views, he differed sharply from him on
the action to be taken to implement these views. Milner, as Mr
Gollin has demonstrated in his *Proconsul in Politics*, in 1914 had one
foot on the road to treason; Buchan was always a passionate constitutionalist. But, like Milner, he regarded Home Rule for Ireland
as a retrograde step, an act of separation when, as he thought, the
significant currents of the time were all making towards greater
union. 'We are standing,' he told a Unionist audience at Innerleithen on 18 December 1912,

for a principle which is a universal truth in politics—the principle that
union is strength, that the rights and duties of the whole cannot be sacrificed to the selfishness and vanity of the part. That was the principle for
which Abraham Lincoln stood, the cry which echoed on a thousand platforms and a hundred blood-stained fields of the American Civil War.
Gentlemen, it is a principle which cannot die. When the whole forces of
civilisation are moving towards union, are we alone to fall out of line?

Buchan's immediate objection to Asquith's Home Rule Bill was
that it was illogical, contradictory and incompetent, and would
soon produce a crop of further troubles. He was all in favour of 'a
true devolution of local bodies'—which would apply to Scotland no
less than to Ireland—but firmly against the creation of any new
government based on Nationalism. Here again his Scottishness
marked his thinking. For him there could be a strong national sentiment and sense of national identity without any desire for political
separation. He could appreciate the force of Ulster sentiment, since
it was directed towards *maintaining* union; but the very strength of
his own Scottish sentiment, which demanded no political expression, led him greatly to underestimate the political Nationalism of
Ireland outside Ulster.

It is odd that his sensitivity to Dominion nationalism, as with Boers and French Canadians, did not extend to the Irish. But towards Ireland there was a blank in his political sympathies. He had been there once, in 1910, on a visit to Susan's uncle, Sir Neville Lyttelton, then Commander-in-Chief. They had enjoyed their stay in Dublin, had been entertained by Sir Horace Plunkett, had met George Russell ('A.E.'), then editor of the *Irish Homestead*, and bought one of his paintings. (Buchan later tried to persuade Russell to address a meeting in Peeblesshire on the reorganisation of Irish agriculture; Russell explained that he was only bold with a pen.) As a romantic, brought up on fairy-tales, Buchan had a taste for Irish legend. He contributed 'The Last Song of Oisin' to the *Book of the Horace Club*. His early story 'The Far Islands' is on the Celtic theme of the journey to the Islands of the Blest. In a review for the *Spectator* in 1904, entitled 'The Heroic Age of Ireland,' he was warmly appreciative of Lady Gregory's collection of folk-tales with an introduction by W. B. Yeats, *Gods and Fighting Men*. 'It is the folk-lore,' he wrote, 'of a sensitive and imaginative people, in whose everyday life reality could not be kept separate from dreams,' and he spoke of the 'matchless beauty' of the legend of Oisin. But as a practical politician and public man Buchan could not do with the waywardness and whimsy of the Celt, nor with his argumentativeness—he detested the works of Bernard Shaw. Firm in cutting his own losses, he was out of patience with a people who seemed to be forever harping on old wrongs. (He was also irritated by this trait in the Scottish Highlander; in an article on 'The Highland Clearances' in the *Spectator* in 1914 he insisted that whatever injustice had been suffered in the past, to be forever brooding on it, forever lamenting an imagined golden age, prevented the Highlander from doing anything about his present condition.) In his symposium *The Island of Sheep* (1919) he makes an American Irishman say:

'That poor little island is living in a bogus past and trying to screw some pride out of it, while she's forgetting to do anything to be proud of right now. The ordinary Irishman is ashamed of himself and he hasn't the honesty to admit it. No man's any good unless he has something to swagger about, and Ireland hasn't anything except a moth-eaten ragbag of wrongs. That's her confounded antiquarian habit of mind. And the worst of it is that this sentimental grieving isn't sincere. Apart from a few poets, it's only the stock-in-trade of vulgar careerists. It's enough to make a man sick to hear an Irish ward-politician talk about Dark Rosaleen.'

Yet a Frenchman is made to put the other side:

'I think you are too hard . . . These things that you despise are very near the heart of any honest man. The prejudices of a nation are as vital as its principles, and I do not desire to see a completely rational *bourgeois* world. Would you apply your maxim to Europe also?'

And the title of the symposium is proof of the continuing fascination which Buchan found in Celtic legend. 'Do you know,' explains one of the characters,

'that St Brandan came here on his great voyage? It is his Island of Sheep, where he found the lamb for the Paschal sacrifice . . . He sailed . . . out of tempestuous seas and came suddenly to a green isle of peace with sheep feeding among the meadows. And long after him the monks had their cells on the west shore looking out to the sunset.'

Almost the only Irish characters in Buchan's fiction are Dominick Medina, the half-crazed master-villain of *The Three Hostages*, and his mother, the blind spinner with the scent of peat-smoke about her; through them are expressed some of Buchan's ambiguous feelings about Ireland. They nurse ancient hate and madness, they are destroyers; but they are also 'figures of an antique beauty and dignity . . . like a king and queen in exile, decreeing the sea of blood which was to wash them back again.'

If he was not a wholly orthodox Unionist candidate, Buchan was determined to be an efficient one. He had no opinion of the Conservative Central Office, thought they compared badly with the Liberals in encouraging young men of talent—'The Conservative policy seems to be to accept whoever can put up sufficient funds'— and in an article in *Blackwood's* on 'The Elections and After' (January 1911) he concluded, thirty-five years before Lord Woolton, that 'a man who could drive the party machine on the same methods as a successful manufacturer conducts his own business would be cheap at the salary of a Cabinet Minister . . . to reorganize the Central Office . . . on business lines.' Meanwhile he set about nursing his constituency with thoroughness and dash.

In a succession of two- or three-day raids, usually made from his brother's house at Peebles, and dovetailed into his spells at the Parkside works in Edinburgh, he toured the scattered constituency; on summer holidays at Harehope in the Meldon Hills (1911) and Selkirk (1912) he had more time to become established. Between April 1911 and August 1914 he spoke in almost every village of the two counties. People would walk miles to a political meeting, and to repay them entertainment would often be provided after the serious business was over. (Anna Buchan was a tower of strength in organising this part of the evening, and was always ready to recite from *Wee Macgreegor* herself.) So speeches were made in Eddleston, Walkerburn, Innerleithen, Broughton, Skirling, Stobo, Galashiels, Lamancha, Romanno Bridge, Ettrick, West Linton, Yarrow—all faithfully recorded in the local press: cordial votes of thanks were proposed with a few well-chosen words, songs were tastefully rendered, musical accompaniments skilfully executed. (One elderly, rubicund Tory always sang 'The Lum Hat Wantin' a Croon.') And there were all the ancillary activities that are forced on a political candidate: Buchan proposed the 'Immortal Memory' at Burns Night dinners, opened bazaars and bowling-greens, attended Unionist dances and the opening of the Chambers' Institution at Peebles ('music was discoursed by the Silver Band'), lectured on Scottish poetry at Peebles, on Scottish character at Kirkwood and Ettrickbrigend, and made the principal speech at the dinner of the Peeblesshire Society in Edinburgh.

After the massive Liberal victory in 1906 Buchan had written that 'the Tory working-man, who was our real strength, has become Liberal to a man. We shall have to start at the beginning and do the work of Disraeli all over again, and build up a new Tory democracy.' He believed that in a democracy like Britain an M.P. was no longer a representative, but a delegate, 'elected to carry out a definite mandate from the electors.'

In the old days the representative did all the political thinking for his constituents; nowadays the people themselves have to do the thinking . . . If we are to have clear and sound thinking the people must take politics very seriously and be very well informed about them. Democracy in itself, remember, is not a good thing; it is only good if it is well done, if the people who wield the power are serious and capable.

He had no doubts about the seriousness and capability of the farmers, farm-workers, shepherds, shopkeepers and tweed-mill workers of Peebles and Selkirk; and he conceived it to be his job, not to make fighting party speeches, but to put before his audiences, fully and responsibly, the main issues on which they would be asked to vote. 'I am not very fond of tub-thumping,' he told an Innerleithen audience; 'I would much rather argue.' So he gave them substantial, reasoned expositions on national insurance, Home Rule, Land Reform, women's suffrage, tariff reform, House of

Lords reform, foreign affairs, or free-rod fishing on the Tweed.
He spoke rather fast, but clearly; did not go in much for rhetoric
or sentiment; finished his sentences, and was not afraid to expound
technicalities. He enjoyed a good set-to with the Radicals: 'Good
meeting—the Radical contingent . . . were all there—they must have
walked about eight miles each way.' 'Some interruption from
Radicals from the waterworks' (at Tweedsmuir), 'first-rate heck-
ling,' are among his comments. In contrast, when speaking in a
friend's constituency near London—'I don't care for South of
England audiences. They were desperately unintelligent.'

He was aware of the shortcomings of his own side, and knew it
harmed him when he had an unpopular laird in the chair, or the
best-hated farmer of a district sitting on his platform. Less of a
liability was the cheerful supporter from Lamancha, who arrived
drunk and fell off the platform of the Peebles Drill Hall: 'that is the
sort of thing that happens at Unionist shows.' And Buchan's early
brush with the law, when he had been caught with the salmon
poachers, had, he was assured, won him the poaching vote.

Occasionally Buchan would secure a big gun from outside the
district—F. E. Smith, Lord Robert Cecil, Alfred Lyttelton were
among those who spoke for him; A. J. Balfour one of those who
asked to be excused—but in the main his campaign was personal
and local, familiar and friendly, conducted at clippings and markets
as well as from the platforms of drill-halls and institutes. His wife
lost a good deal of her shyness as she went the rounds with him
when they came up for the summer holidays. In 1912, when they
were at Broadmeadows Cottage, above the Yarrow near Selkirk,
they did a good deal of their visiting in a motor-car, 'a large
and clumsy vehicle,' lent them by Susan's cousin Jack Stuart-
Wortley.

Buchan was personally very popular and had the right local
links; many of the men who tramped to hear him had fathers who
had tramped to the Reverend John Buchan's revival meetings in
1873. Most of his Radical hecklers liked him, but they would never
have dreamt of budging from their own party. With Donald
Maclean Buchan was generally on good terms, though there was a
slight brush when in the summer of 1914 Maclean alleged that
some of the Peebles employers had coerced their employees to sign
the pro-Ulster Covenant, and Buchan angrily asked Maclean either
to make his charges specific or to drop them.

One of the advantages of nursing this particular constituency was that it kept Buchan in close touch with his family in Scotland. In the event these frequent visits to Peeblesshire meant that he shouldered a lot of the family troubles. His concern for his mother's health continued; alternately he sympathised and scolded.

What do you mean, ill as you are, by trapesing through snow and slush to that weariful old Church? Is that taking care of yourself as you so solemnly promised? The only comfort is that you seem at last to realise that you cannot have another winter of this sort. You and Father can perfectly well retire and there is not the slightest money difficulty. *And you have jolly well got to.*

This was early in 1909; Willie had already been brought into a plot to make his father retire from John Knox, and to supplement the pension of £120. 'I only hope you will succeed in persuading our parents to give it up,' he wrote to John, 'and that my lynx-eyed old mother won't spot the arrangement before it is complete.' So when he was home on leave that summer and John was with his family at Harehope, the three sons finally worked out the details of their contributions. Mr Buchan had been increasingly feeling the strain of his Gorbals parish, and recently there had been—perhaps as a consequence of the Scottish Church case—many 'ecclesiastical wars and alarms.' As his son put it, 'He came here [the Gorbals] a comparatively young man, full of vigour; he left it an old man with his health sacrificed in the cause of God, and the voice, which some of us remember as so golden, weakened with preaching the message of the Gospel.' But it was quite as much Mrs Buchan whom her son wished to retire from running the John Knox Church, and she was the harder to persuade. However, the children had their way, and a house was bought in Peebles, just across the Tweed from Walter and Anna at the Bank House. Soon after they were installed in the spring of 1910 the parents, with Anna and Walter, started for a holiday in Switzerland, but in London Mr Buchan had a heart attack and was told he must lead a very quiet life. No sooner did he start improving than Mrs Buchan fell back into the worst kind of weakness and depression. It was supposed to be anaemia; often she was delirious, ran a temperature of 106 degrees, and though she was 'absolutely resigned to dying,' she did a good deal to harrow her children's feelings on the way. However, she pulled through the winter, and in the spring Buchan made her come up to London to see Sir Almroth Wright. He identified the trouble as a virus in the blood, treated her with inoculations, and after three months in the

South she went home in much better shape, and was able to enjoy the younger Buchans' visit to Harehope. In October 1911 she had a bad relapse; as she was slowly recovering, her husband suddenly died on November 19.

> I got here at 9.30. I found Mother very wonderful, reading letters of sympathy, and better in health to my eyes than she has been for long. I took my last look of my beloved old Father. He was lying most majestic in death, like a Greek statue. He was conscious up to the end, and quite cheerful . . . Then he suddenly choked and in a second it was all over. It was a most peaceful death.

There had always been a strong protective streak in Buchan's feeling for his father ('Poor old canny man, I wish I could do something to cheer him'), as if a character so unworldly needed special care; and now he felt that after the rough and tumble of the Gorbals he had steered his father into quiet waters only to lose him. Six days later Buchan's first son was born: 'He is very like Father, I think,' he wrote of the baby; 'the same straight nose and gentle temper. . . . We think of calling it John Norman.' A few days later, when condolences and congratulations were pouring in, he wrote that 'This is the strangest fortnight I have ever spent in my life.'

Willie at once put forward his leave, for it looked as if Mrs Buchan in her turn 'might not live beyond the spring or summer.' However, she picked up, and by April 1912 was jaunting off with Anna and Walter by car to Stratford-on-Avon. Willie came home in July, and divided his time between Anna and Walter at the Bank House, and the John Buchans at Broadmeadows Cottage, Selkirk. He was now Registrar of Agricultural Banks in Bengal, and had had an exceptionally strenuous tour of duty, owing to the recent partition of Bengal. Clearly he was not in good health; he kept on having pains in his back which no one could diagnose. John, back in London, insisted on Sir Almroth Wright being sent samples of blood; a pneumococcal infection contracted in India was suspected, the acute pain continued, and Willie died in a Glasgow nursing home on November 11. Anything had seemed possible for Willie: with his firm character, his sweet nature, the high opinion he had won in India by his integrity and humanity, he might indeed have become the great public servant that John had once hoped to be. The link between John and Willie had always been close—'He was always more than my brother—my greatest friend,' Willie had written to Susan on her marriage; and John now, answering a letter of sympathy, called him 'my closest friend.' It was a shattering loss; as Willie had written, after seeing Anna off at the end of her visit to India: 'It's a great mistake for a family to be too affectionate; partings are too upsetting.'

After Willie's funeral at Peebles, Buchan came back to London for a spell in bed himself. Just before becoming engaged he had had a medical examination and reported with pride 'Lungs magnificent, likewise my heart . . . absolutely first-class life.' Indeed, up to that time he had enjoyed remarkably good health on the whole, though he was occasionally troubled by indigestion when working too hard, and in the spring before his marriage he had been far from well (Willie in a letter had referred to his brother's 'slight breakdown'). Up to 1911 there were only sporadic attacks of indigestion, provoking comments such as 'rather a wreck—liver and the weather,' but henceforth they became a serious concern. His full involvement in his mother's illness, his father's death, Willie's illness and death, made for tension and anxiety. Nursing a constituency meant rush, irregular meals—'changed in a hurry, had two poached eggs and rushed off to the Drill Hall'—and uncomfortable journeys:

There were six in the carriage. . . . Most of the people in the train were ships' captains going home for Christmas, jolly fellows who smoked shag tobacco. At Symington I had to cross the railway bridge on all fours as it was so slippery, and I had a long cold wait there. Your hot milk was very comforting. . . . The night was not a good one, slush underfoot and very cold, but there was an attendance of about 150.

He sounded Amery on his chance of being adopted for the vacant seat at Oxford in 1914:

I have worked this place up to such a pitch that I am convinced that if the seat can be won, it can be won as well by somebody else; and I am beginning to find the strain of a big county so far from London so severe on my health and time that I often wonder how long I can go on.

He dieted ('I can eat anything but beef and fruit'), he dosed ('castor oil has worked its old beneficial effects'), he cut out smoking, and, when compelled, he rested. But he could not bear to be inactive, even in bed, and used the time for his books. A good deal of *Montrose* was written in bed at Portland Place after Willie's death in 1912. In 1913, when advised to try a more restful holiday with a cruise to the Azores, he determined to amuse himself, as we have seen, by 'writing a real shocker.'

A. J. Balfour, whose intellect Buchan so much admired, and with whom he had corresponded about Bergson and Poincaré, had a liking for the novels of E. Phillips Oppenheim. This gave Buchan his notion of trying his hand at a similar kind of 'shocker', but with the difference that the characters should be the sort of people in whom a reader like Balfour could be interested. The result was *The Power-House*,* beginning squarely with 'It all started one afternoon early in May when I came out of the House of Commons with Tommy Deloraine.'

The summer of 1914 was for Buchan a time of personal as well as public anxiety. His daughter had to be operated on for mastoid, some of Susan's family were in great financial difficulties as a result of the Canadian Grand Trunk fiasco, and he was deeply involved in trying to settle their affairs. These anxieties had their now customary effects, and in August the family went to Broadstairs so that Alice could convalesce after her operation and Buchan could rest ('I am longing to get your rest started,' his wife had written when he was in Scotland at the end of July, 'and really grapple with your pain'). They took lodgings at St Ronan's, Stone Road; not far away were Susan's cousin Mrs Arthur Grenfell and her children, in a house with steps down to a private beach. There Buchan lay in bed, 'resting,' following the crisis—the declaration of war on Germany, the fortunes of the British Expeditionary Force, the fall of Liège and Namur, the spy scares—trying hard to join the Army, and fighting down exasperation at his forced inactivity at this moment of history by starting a second 'shocker'. On August 26 he was thirty-nine years old.

* Published in *Blackwood's* in December 1913, but not in book form till 1916; so *The Thirty-Nine Steps*, 1915, is often thought of as the first of Buchan's thrillers.

CHAPTER EIGHT

PROPAGANDIST

1914–18

'You think that a wall as solid as the earth separates civilisation from
barbarism. I tell you the division is a thread, a sheet of glass.'
Mr Andrew Lumley in John Buchan's *The Power-House* (1913).

The war brought early adventure to several of Buchan's friends.
Francis Grenfell, a regular soldier of whom he had seen much that
summer, won the first V.C. in the retreat from Mons. Aubrey
Herbert, who had managed to attach himself to the Irish Guards as
interpreter, had been captured by the Germans and escaped before
Buchan was up and about again at Broadstairs. Tommy Nelson
went into training with his Yeomanry regiment, Alastair Buchan
was given a commission in the Cameron Highlanders. For Buchan,
with no hope of being passed fit for active service, there was only
the bleak prospect of work as usual. But on his first visit to Edinburgh it appeared that there was some war-work he could do, which
would fit in well with Nelson's present needs.

Much of the firm's continental business had been cut off, but it
could not afford to have its plant idle. So, partly to perform a public
service, partly to ensure a steady flow of work for its machines,
the firm decided in October to produce 'The Story of the War
told in a readable narrative.' This *Nelson History of the War* was
planned to appear in fortnightly parts (as time went on, the intervals grew longer) of about 50,000 words, written by Buchan. The
first part came out in February 1915, with a preface by Lord Rosebery, and was an immediate success: 'its large sale and the evidence
forthcoming that it met a certain need induced me to consider it as
a duty,' he wrote later; and though the war brought him duties and
responsibilities of quite another kind, to the end he gave the
History first claim on his ever-decreasing leisure. An assistant, Mr
Hilliard Atteridge, helped in analysing reports, verifying references,

and preparing the maps, but the writing was entirely Buchan's. All the profits of the *History*, including author's royalties, went to the families of the Nelson's men who had enlisted, and to war charities.

At the beginning of November 1914 Buchan was sent back to bed by the doctors and finished the tale he had begun at Broadstairs. On 7 December he sent the manuscript of *The Thirty-Nine Steps*, dedicated to 'Thomas Arthur Nelson, Lothian and Border Horse,' to George Blackwood:

> I have amused myself in bed writing a shocker of the style of *The Power-House*, only more so. It has amused me to write, but whether it will amuse you to read is another matter. I send it to you for consideration.

As the author of the *History of the War* Buchan was invited to give a number of lectures on the course of the war—in Peebles, in Edinburgh, in London. Three which he gave at the Bechstein Hall in April 1915—in aid of war charities and presided over by Sir Edward Grey, General Sir Francis Lloyd and Mr Balfour—were very well thought of by the professional soldiers in the audience; they were impressed by this civilian's grasp of strategy, and his ability to make complex movements clear. In May Buchan was given the chance to see the war for himself, when *The Times* invited him to visit the Western Front as its special correspondent for the second Battle of Ypres. 'The first sight of the front,' he wrote in his first article (17 May 1915),

> is in the nature of an anti-climax. . . . One is accustomed to the heavy preoccupation at home, the list of casualties, the strained expectancy of the Press, the immense scars bitten into our national life. Then come the great ports, crowded with transports and cargo-boats, the huge base hospitals, the supply depots, the 1500 clerks in one department. Then fifty miles of country crowded with military traffic, the various headquarters, the railheads, where punctual daily trains deliver their loads of food and ammunition. The whole hinterland is a beehive of military preparations, and leaves an unforgettable impression of sustained effort.
>
> Then come the last narrow roads filled with battalions retiring into reserve or advancing to the trenches, and motor convoys without intermission, and every hamlet full of khaki. And, at the end of it all, those red zig-zags and smoke puffs and muffled undertones of sound. A spectacular battle with flags and charging masses would seem a fitter climax. But as one looks there seems a greater drama in this secret warfare, hidden in the earth and the crooks of hill. There is something desperate in its secrecy, something deadly in its silence.

Though he made clear to his readers the military situation round Ypres, Buchan wanted them to perceive, and feel, and think, as well as to stick flags in maps. War, which the British had not seen at close quarters for a hundred years, was no longer something fought on an Asian frontier or an African desert; it was down the street.

In appearance the country is very like rural England—red-roofed farms and cottages, little straggling villages, and masses of lilac, may, and laburnum everywhere. Only everything is broken. A wayside cottage has been so tattered by shot that it looks like a skeleton autumn leaf, and from its rickety shade emerges a gnome-like private in the Army Service Corps.
Here the whole front has gone and bedrooms with wrecked furniture are open to the light. Here a 42 cm. shell has made a breach in the line with raw edges of masonry on both sides and a yawning cavern below. Go into one of the houses which have suffered least. In one room the carpet is spattered with plaster from the ceiling, but the furniture is unbroken. There is a Boule cabinet with china, red plush chairs, a piano, and a gramophone—the plenishing of the best parlour of a middle-class home. In another room is a sewing machine, from which the owner has fled in the middle of a piece of work. Here is a novel with the reader's place marked. It is like a city which has been visited by an earthquake which caught the inhabitants unawares and drove them shivering to seek a place of refuge (22 May 1915).

In the same article Buchan described the activity far behind the lines, where there were 'more mechanics than in Sheffield, more transport workers than in Newcastle,' and explained the pyramidal structure of the modern army:

Behind are the railways and the mechanical transport, but at the end a man has only his two legs. Behind are the workshops of the Flying Corps and the squadron and flight stations, but at the end of the chain is the solitary aeroplane coasting over the German lines and depending upon the skill and nerve of one man.

There were one or two romantic touches, such as the story of the British private left behind by his unit who restored some sort of order to the shattered town of Ypres (later used in his tale 'The King of Ypres'), but his conclusion was realistic enough:

All the strategy and tactics of the war depend today upon one burning fact. The enemy has got an amazingly powerful machine, and unless we can provide ourselves with a machine of equal power he will nullify the superior fighting quality of our men. That machine consists in a great number of heavy guns and machine-guns, and an apparently unlimited supply of high explosives. Whoever started the story that the Germans were running short of shells did a cruel disservice to the Allies' cause (24 May 1915).

(Letters about the shortage of British shells were appearing in adjacent columns of *The Times*.)

Buchan's letters home from G.H.Q., however, reflect the hopes which could still be held in 1915 about a quick end to the war, and his own high spirits at no longer feeling himself cut off from his active service friends. The Somme and Passchendaele were still in the future.

We are a very merry and friendly party, it is impossible to realise that we are close to death and suffering . . . Sir John French is very optimistic.

The staff of the Brigade are the jolliest fellows you ever met. They seem quite used to the shelling.

I am acquiring an encyclopaedic knowledge of the inside of an army.

He had talks with Haig, French, Plumer, Allenby and Byng (whom he had known in South Africa). David Henderson, another friend from South Africa, was now in command of the R.F.C. ('I think they are the most wonderful fellows out here'). On his drives round the British lines he managed to look up a surprising number of his friends: Anthony Henley, Alec Maitland, Ian Nelson and Francis Grenfell.

At home, by this time, he was having to carry a heavier load of work at Nelson's, and in July he wrote to Gilbert Murray:

I have never been so hustled in my life. Two of my partners and 67% of our male employees are with the Colours. My remaining partner, most of our managers and some more of our men are with the Munitions Department. So I have the whole business on my hands, besides a lot of Foreign Office work . . . I should have been out in France a month ago with the French Staff, but I cannot get away. Still it is a good thing to be very busy at a time like this, when most of one's friends have fallen. It prevents brooding.

In October he was back in France again, this time for the War Office, and in uniform as a Lieutenant in the Intelligence Corps: 'They want me to be a sort of *rapporteur* of the coming movement.' This was the Battle of Loos. 'Went up to Ypres but could not get into it,' he wrote on 24 September,

as it is being pounded with 15-inch shells . . . Late last night hell broke loose along the line . . . Off to try to get as near as possible to the line . . . Just got back from the Front but could see nothing except the terrific bombardment. We are doing splendidly.

But two days later he was writing, 'I fear we have paid a big price for success.'

These visits to the Front were invaluable to his writing of the
History of the War, and to the lectures which he was continually
being invited to give. Requests for his services were stimulated by
the publication, in October 1915, of *The Thirty-Nine Steps*. It had
been serialised in *Blackwood's* that summer, over the initials 'H. de
V.'; now, with its author acknowledged, it was an immediate success
(selling 25,000 copies between October 19 and December 31), and
made the name John Buchan familiar to a far wider public than
had enjoyed *John Burnet of Barns* or *Prester John*. Reports of his
war lectures began to refer to 'the famous novelist and war correspondent.'

During 1916 Buchan was in demand both by the War Office and
the Foreign Office, which asked him to look after a Russian delegation, which he took up to Scapa Flow in February,* and to
lecture on the Russian army. The timely capture of Erzerum by the
Russians gave him a strong talking-point. He visited G.H.Q. in
France in March, June and July, as a Major in the Intelligence
Corps, working under General Charteris. His main function was to
draft communiqués and compile summaries of the fighting for use
by the Press, and by the propaganda department headed by C. F. G.
Masterman. Occasionally he was detailed to take a distinguished
visitor on a tour of the Front: one of these was Lord Bryce, whom
Buchan and C. E. Montague escorted to Albert, Pozières and Wind-
mill Hill. 'I took him,' wrote Buchan some years later,

into the ruins of Contalmaison the day after it had been occupied by British
troops. The place was being shelled with fair regularity by the enemy, and
we ate our luncheon with crumps falling unpleasantly near. I am certain
that [Bryce] had never in all his adventures been mixed up in a battle
before, and the situation might have produced in him a more emotional
temper than it did. For all he said, as he calmly watched the adjacent shell-
bursts, was that, as soon as I thought it safe, he would like to measure the
holes they made.

In June he told his brother Alastair that 'the Foreign Office have
collared me for good now, and are giving me a department'—to
work on intelligence and be directly responsible to Edward Grey.
In August he told John Edgar (on Foreign Office paper):

I am on Haig's staff in France as well as a slave here, so I have my hands

---

* The delegation included Vladimir Nabokov (father of the novelist and lepi-
dopterist) who was one of the founders of the Constitutionalist Democratic Party.
See Vladimir Nabokov: *Speak, Memory* (1951), p. 187.

full. I wish to God I were with you on the hills, but holidays won't come my way till the end of this bloody war . . . I have as usual too much work to do, but I like it and I think I have got the most interesting job on the globe, for I live at the heart of things here and in France.

One of his duties for the Foreign Office and G.H.Q. was to write a short account of the first phase of the Battle of the Somme, mainly for propaganda abroad.

In September Haig asked the Foreign Office to release Buchan till the end of the year, to rejoin the staff at G.H.Q. and prepare the summaries on the continuing battle.

28 September. In the evening I dined with the Commander-in-Chief, who was perfectly charming . . . I had a long talk with Sir Douglas afterwards and, I fear, if the Foreign Office consent, I shall have to undertake the work.

Buchan was one of the few people who managed to keep the conversation going with the taciturn Haig.

29 September. I must say I am enormously attracted by Sir D. Haig now. He seems to have quite changed since I remember him. He is very gentle and wise.

2 October. I had a very busy day yesterday for I went with Gort down the front to see the different divisions in action.

The enthusiasm of his first visit had gone: 'It is a queer thing war, and a damned silly thing,' was a note often struck in his letters now, and after a chance meeting with Tommy Nelson in October, Buchan reported, 'He loathes the war, which indeed is no war for anybody above thirty.' ('It's a bloody and disgusting war,' says Leithen's nephew in *The Dancing Floor*.) He kept on reassuring his wife that he was perfectly safe, 'I lead a life of most inglorious security, and only visit Army, Corps and Division Headquarters,' but it was his indigestion that chiefly worried her: the long jolting drives, the living in billets with meals of unsuitable food at irregular intervals, were for him the worst possible regime. He had mild bouts of pain in the summer—'My inside is not quite the gentleman it should be' —and did his best to diet; but in October a particularly acute attack nearly killed him. When it came on he was in a billet by himself; it took him hours to crawl in agony to the door and make himself heard by a sentry. He spent a few days in bed in a Casualty Clearing Station, refusing to go to a base hospital, or home, when there was so much to do. So, existing mainly on a diet of Benger's and Allenbury's, he went back to his duties, which included taking charge of

A. J. Balfour, of Arthur Henderson and of Lord Northcliffe, on
tours of the Front. In December he wrote to a young officer who
had been wounded and gassed on the Somme, Captain Liddell
Hart:

> In the last two months I have been endeavouring to get the official record
> of the Battle of the Somme correct. As you may imagine, the Army Diaries,
> based on contemporary information, are very inaccurate, and I am going
> through them and correcting and supplementing them from the Brigade
> and Battalion reports. I hope in this way to get the record of a great battle
> complete before the next stage begins.

Buchan put up to Haig the idea of a Historical Department at
G.H.Q. with an officer attached to each Army headquarters, attending all conferences and recording history as it was being made (a
procedure very like that pioneered by the Canadians and Americans
in the Second World War), but before anything came of it he was
recalled to London.

Buchan's digestive trouble was now diagnosed as a duodenal
ulcer ('I don't think Blenkiron's was as troublesome, do you?' he
asked his wife, having given his ailment to the American in *Greenmantle* which was published that autumn). When he came home at
the beginning of 1917 it was decided to perform the operation of
short-circuiting—then comparatively new and hazardous surgery.
This was done, in Buchan's home in Portland Place, by Mr Lockhart-
Mummery at the end of February; it took two hours. 'I like operations,' Buchan told his wife, generalising from this one experience;
'surgeons do something to you that is some use; medicines are no
good.' A long convalescence was prescribed; but within four days
Buchan was working in bed, and by the time he moved to the
Olivers' house at Checkendon to recuperate, he was doing a full
day's work. He did not feel he could relax his effort any more than
his friends in France could; and he had a new job which he was
impatient to get on with.

In December Lloyd George had replaced Asquith as Prime
Minister, and had included Milner in his small War Cabinet whose
members were free of departmental duties. The spearhead of the
attack on Asquith had been the 'Monday Night Cabal,' a group
which met once a week to dine and talk, whose regular members
were Milner, Amery, Carson, Geoffrey Dawson, F. S. Oliver and
Waldorf Astor. 'Thank God Squiff and Co. have gone,' wrote
Violet Markham to Buchan on 19 December 1916.

Manchester School Liberals soaked with the laissez-faire point of view cannot conduct a war reinforced by Tory octogenarians. I have no illusions about Ll.G. but at least he has the will to win and to will the means to that end. McKenna and Runciman could only recollect the fact of war by a mental effort.

Unfair, no doubt, but reflecting the country's feelings. One of Lloyd George's first moves was to pay more attention to propaganda; and Buchan was invited to prepare a memorandum with proposals for a new Department of Information. Buchan's draft, delivered on his return from France at the New Year, was approved, and by a Cabinet Minute of 9 February 1917 the Department was set up to take over and unify all the foreign propaganda activities, till then conducted by different government offices, and to act as a general publicity bureau about the war. Apparently Lloyd George had had doubts about Buchan's ability to direct the new organisation, for on 17 January Milner wrote to him in a letter marked 'Private':

My dear Prime Minister,
    Don't think me too insistent!
    I wish you would not 'turn down' John Buchan, without seeing him yourself.
    If you had a talk with him, and were not favourably impressed, I should have nothing more to say.
    But I am not satisfied to have him rejected on hear-say, and ill-informed hear-say at that.

Yours very sincerely
MILNER

And by the minute of 9 February Buchan was appointed Director. His salary was £1000, and he was to be responsible directly to the Prime Minister. The agencies now gathered together included the War Propaganda Bureau, the Neutral Press Committee (formerly under the Home Office) and the News Department of the Foreign Office. These were reorganised into a Production Section, conducted by Charles Masterman at Wellington House, and responsible for books, pamphlets, photographs, and the records by official war artists; a section under T. L. Gilmour for cables, wireless, press and cinema; and a political intelligence section. They were housed in different buildings, and Buchan made a point—as in his Land Department days in Pretoria—of visiting all the sections every week or so. He was never very good at ticking people off, but he liked keeping them on their toes. He found Masterman a first-class head of a department, and was delighted to be working closely with a man he so liked and admired.

One of Buchan's first problems was to find extra staff, not an easy matter after two years of war. He secured, as personal assistant to himself, Stair Gillon, who had been wounded in Macedonia ('I would ask for nothing better than to be Jock the laird's man to John'); F. S. Oliver worked with him for a few weeks ('I have been so long . . . a senior partner that I find it very difficult to do work with my own hands'). Others whom Buchan recruited were Reginald Farrer the plant-hunter, whom he had known at Oxford, Stephen Gaselee, George Mair, E. S. P. Haynes, Pelham Warner the cricketer, Roderick Jones of Reuter's who came part-time as Cables and Wireless adviser, and Hugh Walpole, who on receiving a cabled request from Buchan left Petrograd on the day the Bolsheviks took over power.

Propaganda was a novel activity for a British Government. To some it was a dirty word: 'surely our deeds will speak for themselves.' To others it seemed to mean anything that might cheer friend and depress foe. Buchan kept firmly to the line already followed by Masterman in his original propaganda section: that it meant the dissemination of true facts wherever they would do good, and not the manufacture of stories which, however flattering to the Allies, however derogatory to the enemy, had no firm basis in fact. In May 1917 the Department came under fire for not using in its propaganda the story, which appeared in *The Times*, that the Germans were boiling down human corpses in a factory; but Masterman and his staff considered the evidence entirely unsatisfactory, and later it was shown that some of the material from which *The Times* had taken the story was faked.

As for propaganda at home, Buchan believed with F. S. Oliver that 'there is always danger in treating a free people like children in humouring them, and coaxing them, and wheedling them with half-truths.' A free, informed and responsible press was an absolute necessity. 'So far as Britain is concerned,' he said in a speech early in 1917, 'the war could not have been fought for one month without its newspapers;' and he would do his best to see that the press was supplied with the news it needed. He felt strongly that only unity of effort could win the war against the German power-machine; that people in Britain, whether politicians or munition-makers, should feel as much in the war as the men in the trenches. One method of bridging the gap was by films and pictures, and among the more remarkable innovations of the Department were the films made on the Western Front, and the paintings by the official war artists. Nobody who saw the Somme or Arras films—where the mud, the corpses, the devastation, the mess, were presented with a bleak honesty—or paintings like Paul Nash's 'Menin Road' and C. R. W. Nevinson's 'Harvest of Battle' could be in any doubt as to the beastliness of modern total war. By the time of the Second World War this freedom of the painter or cameraman to show war honestly was taken for granted, but the breakthrough had been made in the old Department of Information.

The idea of commissioning a record of the war on canvas had been Masterman's; Buchan was enthusiastic and, though not himself interested in contemporary painting, was willing to listen to those who were. When, for instance, Edward Marsh spoke to him of Paul Nash, recently invalided home, he readily visited Nash's exhibition of paintings of the Ypres Salient at the Goupil Gallery in July 1917. Buchan's comment was that 'either they were little more than curious and interesting as having been made under fire, or they were the crude work of a man of genius with a long way to go,' but he paid attention to the views of Marsh, Roger Fry and others, and arranged for Nash to see Masterman. The result was that Nash, on the eve of embarkation to Egypt with a draft, was told that he had been appointed an official war artist on the Western Front. 'I hope to hear from Buchan shortly,' he told his wife, 'would you like to ring him up and worship him over the phone—he deserves it.'

As well as co-ordinating and reorganising existing activities, Buchan had to extend the Department's range. One of the major problems was British information in America. Northcliffe, who headed the British War Mission to Washington in 1917, came back feeling that the British part in the war was being grossly under-represented: the American public had no idea of the extent of the British effort and British losses, and the American press gave the impression the war was being fought mainly by France and Canada. So one of Buchan's first jobs—and in his view the most important—was to organise a supply of British news to American and Canadian papers, to arrange for the showing of the war films, to set up a British Information Bureau in New York, which was run with outstanding success by Geoffrey Butler. Carefully selected lecturers were sent to the United States and warned not to criticise anything American, and not to mention Ireland; and G.H.Q. in France were persuaded to allocate a château where American newspaper editors or congressmen could see something of the British front for them-

selves. One guest from Baltimore reported enthusiastically that he
had met 'Belloc, Abbé Dimnet and other perfectly delightful
people' at the visitors' château. Buchan started an informal Anglo-
American Society in London and secured Gilbert Murray as President; and himself looked after a number of visiting American newspapermen, among them William Allen White of Kansas. General
Ludendorff, after the war, gave as one of the reasons for German
defeat the superiority of British propaganda in America over the
German.

After America's entry into the war Buchan, in an address at the
National Liberal Club, spoke of his hope that the shared experience
would bring

new sympathy and understanding between America and Britain. All
barriers of prejudice will go down before the whirlwind of war, and the
two peoples will stand revealed to each other as sharing common ideals and
common instincts, as well as common traditions. After the destruction of
Prussianism the alliance of America and Britain will be the greatest safeguard for the peaceful ordering of the world.

But he warned his audience that once the war was won, the isolationists in America might have their way:

Therefore it seems to me that America must keep constantly before her
eyes the need of internationalism in the broadest sense. She has started
upon a road from which there is no returning. She must go through with
the business to the end, and the end is not the end of the war. She must
make herself permanently responsible, as one of the world's greatest
powers, for the world's good governance. That is President Wilson's
policy; let us see that we do nothing by parochialism on our own account
to weaken his hands.

Efforts had to be made with other allies. A Press Bureau and
reference library were established in Paris. 'Buchan is going to do
what he can to disseminate in France information to our advantage,'
wrote Lord Bertie the British Ambassador in his diary, adding
'Buchan is attractive.' The British Institute in Florence was taken
over, and its work extended. Mrs Aubrey Waterfield, one of the
founders of the Institute, has described her reception by Buchan
when she came to London to put the case for government help, and
his invitation to dinner in Portland Place three days later, when she
would hear the decision:

I have forgotten where the Buchans' house was, but a vivid memory
remains of the beautiful and stately lady who opened the door and welcomed
me. She led me upstairs to the drawing-room where supper was laid in

front of the fire. No servants disturbed us. Mr Buchan came in and my heart stood still. With his usual directness, he said: 'I know how anxious you are to hear the answer I promised to give you today, and I shall tell you at once that the Government has decided to take over the Institute of Florence until it can support itself. Come to the Foreign Office tomorrow, ask for Mr Gage and he will tell you what has been arranged about the repayment of expenses and for a monthly allowance for the Institute.' He then handed me a letter for the Ambassador and one for Mr Algar Thorold.

With my mind at rest and feeling confident for the future of our work, I enjoyed to the full the evening spent with these two delightful people.

Susan Buchan was at this time working for the V.A.D. and also running a day-nursery in Gospel Oak Grove.

The Department's work in enemy countries—which involved smuggling pamphlets and information through Holland and Switzerland, and sending leaflets by balloon over the enemy lines—brought Buchan into contact with the secret service. He saw much of Sir Reginald Hall of Naval Intelligence ('If I had a big proposition to handle and could have my pick of helpers I'd plump for the Intelligence Department of the British Admiralty,' says Blenkiron in *Greenmantle*). And every two or three months he was at G.H.Q. Haig in his diary recorded on 24 April 1917:

Lt-Col. Buchan (now in charge of Information Office under P.M.) came to dinner. He is anxious that Milner, Ll.G. and I should work in the closest touch possible. I told him that I am trying to work in harmony with Ll.G., but he has such strange ideas on warfare!

Buchan's letters, mostly to his mother, give some idea of the scope and tempo of his work. I have not been able to find out why he had so much to do at Buckingham Palace, but Susan Buchan remembers that King George V showed great interest in the work of the Ministry and Buchan used to tell Lord Stamfordham, the Private Secretary, about it.

16 May 1917. I was working till all hours yesterday. I had to go to the Palace this morning, for I have a shocking amount to do with Royalties these days. Then I had the War Cabinet in the afternoon and a long time with the Prime Minister; and after that correspondents and secret-service agents till all hours.

22 May 1917. The PM has put on me the organising of a big speechifying campaign especially in the industrial districts.

23 May 1917. I had a busy day yesterday, a good deal of it spent at Buckingham Palace. I have had many queer jobs in my life, but this is the queerest.

8 May 1917. Lunched with Milner and some naval officers . . . I dined with the Salisburys to have a talk with Curzon. Meals are almost the only chance I get of talking business at leisure.

2 June 1917. I had a desperate day yesterday, things crowding on each other, and never less than three people waiting to see me the whole day. My life is all fringes and patches now and I never get time to think things out except in bed.

13 June 1917. This job is certainly the toughest I ever took on and there is no kind of end to it and certainly no kind of credit in it. Still if I can do any good to the country it is worth every effort.

19 June 1917. Got home last night at 20 minutes to 12 and I began my day at 6 o'clock. But I am going to make a stand to cut down my work.

8 August 1917. I had a Post Office and Cable Conference all morning, a War Office conference all afternoon, and an American Committee meeting all evening. I am now about to dine with some Swedes at the Savoy.

20 September 1917. I had a very heavy day yesterday, a conference on Shipping in the morning, War Aims in the afternoon, and the whole *corps diplomatique* seemed to want to pay me visits.

Amery, now an Assistant Secretary to the War Cabinet, sent a cheering word on 3 July:

Though it is strictly against orders to divulge the proceedings of the War Cabinet, I don't think it can hurt if I let you know that A.J.B. this morning expressed himself in very flattering terms on the subject of the Weekly Reports of your Intelligence Bureau.

Stretched and exhausted as he was in the summer of 1917, Buchan was thankful for the load of work, for the Battle of Arras had brought the worst of his personal losses. Tommy Nelson was killed in March and Alastair Buchan died of wounds on 9 April.* The death of this brother twenty years younger than himself was not only a terrible blow—'I somehow regarded him less as a brother of mine than as the eldest of the children'—but it laid a fresh burden on him in consoling his mother. In her misery Mrs Buchan insisted on regarding this loss as a judgment on her for her shortcomings; 'I do wish she wasn't such a self-torturer,' wrote Buchan to Anna, and to herself 'I want you to read *David Copperfield* and study the character of Mrs Gummidge, who talked like you sometimes.' 'We always adored you but never knew till now how

* One of the letters of sympathy—'a most charming and gallant young officer . . . simple, conscientious, and much loved by his comrades'—was from Winston Churchill, who commanded the 6th Royal Scots Fusiliers (to which Alastair had transferred from the Cameron Highlanders in 1915) between his resignation from Asquith's Government in 1915 and his joining Lloyd George's in 1917.

utterly precious and indispensable you are,' Mrs Buchan had written after his operation in February; 'Darling John you are just our pride and our comfort.' However hard the strain of his public work, Buchan never shirked the extra strain this emotional dependence of his mother laid on him, and he did his best to send her a letter every day during the months after Alastair's death.

I wish I could do something to comfort you, and I wish I was nearer you and could see you oftener. You poor wee body, you must try and count your mercies, for you still have some, though you have been sorely tried.

Relaxation he could find with his own family (a second boy, William, had been born in January 1916). Susan and the children were spending the summer of 1917 at Bidborough in Kent, and Buchan managed to get down for most week-ends: 'I find their company the best holiday I know,' he told his mother, and described how he was giving the five-year-old Johnnie his first fishing lessons. The snatched week-ends were the time, too, for his own writing. He was determined to keep up the *History of the War*: 'It is a heavy job keeping the thing going but it is such good propaganda that I must try.' And in July he began *Mr Standfast*.

Writing his thrillers—*The Thirty-Nine Steps* in the first autumn of the war, *Greenmantle* in the first half of 1916, *Mr Standfast* between July 1917 and July 1918, some of it during air-raids—was certainly no extra burden, but rather a release. 'It is the most restful and delightful thing in the world to write that kind of stuff,' he told Gilbert Murray, who was enthusiastic about *The Thirty-Nine Steps*. Richard Hannay dashing up to Galloway in search of the Black Stone gang had compensated for John Buchan marooned in bed at Broadstairs and feeling that he was no use to anybody. Now the writing of *Greenmantle* and *Mr Standfast* satisfied other needs too. One—perhaps a minor consideration—was the need for money, for his salary as Director of Information was less than his salary had been from Nelson's, and the expenses of living were rising all the time. (The Buchans had already economised by letting their Portland Place house for the first two years of the war, when Susan and the children were with her mother, or in the country.) The unexpected success of *The Thirty-Nine Steps* suggested a way in which money could be pleasurably earned. It also showed that Buchan was entertaining a public far wider than he originally aimed at. A. J. Balfour, whose liking for Phillips Oppenheim had first started him on his thrillers, was a great admirer of *The Thirty-Nine Steps*, but it was also enjoyed by thousands of plainer readers. Buchan particularly liked hearing of its success with soldiers: friends were constantly reporting how much in demand it was in the trenches, clearing-stations and hospitals.* So one of his motives in embarking on *Greenmantle* was simply to entertain the troops.

Brisk, improbable action played out against a realistic background had been Buchan's particular recipe in *The Power-House* and *The Thirty-Nine Steps*, and very well it served him now. Richard Hannay is at once established in the first chapter of *Greenmantle* as a man who has been through experiences on the Western Front that were common to thousands of Buchan's readers: his references to Loos, to 'that awful stretch between Cassel and Ypres,' struck sympathetic responses. 'The military details you touch on are so correct,' wrote one serving officer, 'in distinction to many other war stories which have been written.' Hannay's subsequent adventures had more basis in fact than might now be supposed. The earlier exploits of Sandy Arbuthnot (making his first appearance in Buchan's pages) were very close to Aubrey Herbert's pre-war adventures in Albania and the Levant. The Russians' capture of Erzerum from the Turks, the climax of *Greenmantle*, was firmly based on the real capture of the city early in 1916, after a charge by the Cossacks which Buchan had described in his Nelson *History* as 'one of the most skilfully managed episodes of the war.'† The combination of these incidents from the war of movement on the

---

* *The Thirty-Nine Steps* played its part in the Second World War too. When the *City of Benares* was torpedoed in 1940, full of children being evacuated to America, Miss Cornish, in charge of a boatload of boys who were eight days on the Atlantic, kept them interested in a story which she described as 'mostly *The Thirty-Nine Steps*.' This incident was reported to Lady Tweedsmuir by Lady Lenanton (Carola Oman).

† The original of Sandy Arbuthnot was certainly Aubrey Herbert and not, as many readers have assumed, T. E. Lawrence, whom Buchan did not meet till 1920, though he had heard about him before the war from D. G. Hogarth. (So he says in *Memory Hold-the-Door*, page 212, but in a broadcast in Canada in 1936 he speaks of having seen Lawrence in 1915 and in 1918.) There are all the same two connections between Lawrence and *Greenmantle*. First: Lawrence when employed on Intelligence in Cairo had (though Buchan is not likely to have known this) 'a long-range hand in the "capture" of Erzerum by the Russian Caucasian Army after a curiously half-hearted defence' (B. H. Liddell Hart: '*T. E. Lawrence*' *in Arabia and After*, 1934). Second: when this Allied success at Erzerum encouraged a similar attempt to bribe the Turks to call off the siege of Kut, Lawrence was sent on a secret mission to Mesopotamia with Aubrey Herbert—the supposed original of Sandy Arbuthnot and the real one. How they were led blindfold through the Turkish lines to negotiate with Khalil Pasha was described by Aubrey Herbert in *Mons, Anzac and Kut* (1919.)

Eastern Front with a tale of cyphers, conspiracies and a dedicated band of secret agents, was to result in a mixture which was the antithesis of anything experienced by the soldier on the Western Front. 'It was the end of an old army, and an older, and freer mode of war,' Buchan wrote later of the British Expeditionary Force of 1914, 'for now a huge, cumbrous mechanism had cast a blight of paralysis on human endeavour. The fronts had been stricken by their vastness into stagnation.' But here, in *Greenmantle*, was war as many fighting men felt somehow it ought to be: an affair of dash and personal heroism, of fast movement and great spaces (here indeed was the cavalry charge for which many a regular soldier was still hankering); of situations where a handful of men could alter the course of a battle. It was war without the mud, the lice, the boredom, the anonymity, the unimaginative strategy and mass casualties of the frontal assault; it was war (perhaps Buchan's indulgence to himself) without a single committee.

Again, there was instant appreciation from servicemen. 'I'm off with Blenkiron, Sandy and Hannay,' wrote Captain William Fisher, commanding the battleship *St Vincent*, 'to discover meaning of Kasredin, Cancer, v.I.' And a year after publication Buchan received an appreciation from an unexpected source. He told his mother (27 October 1917):

I saw a letter from the Grand Duchess Olga saying that she and her sisters and Papa had been greatly cheered and comforted in their exile by *Greenmantle*. It is an odd fate for me to cheer the prison of the Tsar.

No doubt what did most in *Greenmantle* to cheer and comfort the Tsar in his confinement at Tobolsk was not the exploits of Blenkiron, Sandy and Hannay, but the triumph of the Grand Duke Nicholas's army, when for the last time the Russians had scored a swift and complete success. But by the time the Tsar read *Greenmantle* Erzerum was back in Turkish hands.

Buchan's own problems in the autumn of 1917 were a good deal less colourful than Hannay's. There were administrative bothers in the Department; the Foreign Office was often slippery and obstinate; the Service Departments seemed to hate giving information more than they hated the Germans. There was a continual struggle for the release of war news—a struggle familiar to anyone who has worked in a Ministry of Information. Throughout the year a campaign had been conducted against the Department, and

against Buchan personally, by the *Daily Chronicle* under its editor
Robert Donald. 'Propaganda,' said the author of an unpublished
White Paper, who may well have been Buchan, 'is a work which is
peculiarly liable to miscellaneous criticism, since most men are apt
to consider themselves as born propagandists and are only too
willing to point out where the official department fails.' There were
charges of inefficiency, of extravagance (the story of a journalists'
trip to Ireland, when too many cigars were thought to have been
smoked at public expense, continued to plague Buchan till the end
of the war), of waste of paper, of shortage of news. There were complaints about the few newspapermen employed in the Department,
and about the use of films, the cinema being still generally regarded
as a crude and vulgar medium. Robert Donald did not like Masterman—possibly for his rejection of 'atrocity' stories which the press
had published—and attacked Buchan for keeping him on. And unfortunately for Buchan and the Department, Donald had the ear of
Lloyd George, and persuaded him to agree to an advisory committee of editors with ill-defined powers which was a continual
headache ('an idiotic business which the PM forced on me owing
to his fear of the press'). At the same time, one of Buchan's major
troubles was the difficulty *he* had in getting access to the Prime
Minister, to whom he was directly responsible. 'No decision from
PM yet' is a recurring note. In September 1917 he felt this state
of affairs could not go on, and asked Milner, as a member of the
War Cabinet, to suggest that the Department should be put under
'someone to whom I can have access.' A few days later Sir Edward
Carson was appointed to supervise policy on behalf of the War
Cabinet which he had just entered, Buchan remaining executive
head.

At first Buchan was delighted: 'I have now got a chap who will
defend me through thick and thin. I am going to give the War
Cabinet a weekly report.' But by the end of October he was not so
sure. 'It looks as if I was going to have another big row with the
PM on the question of journalistic interference with my department.'
(Donald was again on the warpath and, apparently with Lloyd
George's agreement, attempting to carry out an unofficial inquiry
himself. Buchan never got over his bitterness at this, to him,
underhand intrigue.) 'I don't know if Carson will support me, for
it is not very easy for him to grasp the precise impossibility of the
PM's proposals.'

A letter from Buchan to the American Ambassador, Walter

Page, written on 6 December 1917, reveals some of his difficulties:

My dear Ambassador,

I am in despair about this business of the Attorney-General. I cannot get an answer out of the War Cabinet, and Sir Edward Carson cannot get one either. I have told Sir F. E. Smith that he must try and get a decision from the Prime Minister himself.

Would it be possible to send an interim answer to Judge Hughes, saying that owing to the situation here it is not quite certain whether the Attorney-General will be able to get to America, and adding that we will cable as soon as anything is settled?

I am exceedingly sorry for the trouble I am giving you.

Yours very sincerely
JOHN BUCHAN

If the indecision of the Prime Minister gave trouble, so did the decision of the President. A month later Page and Buchan were exchanging letters about the cancellation of a long-planned visit to Britain by a group of hand-picked, high-ranking American citizens; ex-President Taft was to be one of the number, and this President Wilson would not sanction, saying that Taft's presence would give the whole proceeding an official character.

When another of Buchan's British-American plans went agley, it was the Ambassador's doing. In December 1917 Buchan had the idea of inviting Page to the dinner of the Burns Club of London the following month. The Club secretary followed up with an eloquent appeal:

It is appropriate that the representatives of the Allies should be asked to assist in the celebration of the birthday of Robert Burns, for it was he who first in the history of the world gave lyrical expression to the desire for that universal brotherhood which the alliance of four-fifths of the world, against military oppression, is helping to consummate.

The Council trust that you will allow us to add your name to the Roll of Honorary Members of the Club, the first of whom was the Italian patriot Garibaldi.

Mr Page was delighted to be numbered with Garibaldi; then Buchan broke the news that he was to respond to the toast of the Allies 'with a reference to Burns.' Page was horrified: 'it is not quite clear to my mind how a man can work in a speech about the Allies on a Robert Burns background.' Buchan pleaded. Page stood firm, and played a clever card:

When you pick up a volume of Burns you would not naturally think of the Japanese Ambassador, I grant; yet he is an Ally and he is a very sensible man, and he spoke to me a day or two ago in quite a pleased way at the invitation of the Burns Club that he had received.

The Japanese Ambassador was willing, but alas, when 25 January came and Buchan proposed 'The Immortal Memory', there was not an Ambassador in sight; the Italian Prime Minister Orlando had suddenly come to London, and all the Diplomatic Corps had been summoned to eat their dinner in Downing Street.

It soon became clear that Carson was not really interested in propaganda, nor even in the war as a whole; his concern was with Ireland, and he was personally hostile to Lloyd George for his support of the pre-war Home Rule Bill. So Buchan was back in the wretched position of having to act and yet not being able to defend his actions publicly; of being criticised without commanding any channel by which the criticisms could be countered. Stair Gillon, his personal assistant, was indignant at Buchan's subordination to 'a battered old political war-horse like Carson who knew as much about propaganda as I did about Croce's philosophy . . . I was not happy because it was evident that John was being schemed against by the L.G. entourage.' He considered that only Buchan's buoyant nature had carried him through 'these ill-requited days in 1917.' Reginald Farrer too thought that Buchan had had 'a very raw deal from the politicians.'

The only solution that Buchan could see was to make the Department a Ministry, with a Minister who could defend it in Parliament. 'The Department can only be worked under a chief who has authority with the War Cabinet, and by a director who has the confidence of that chief,' he wrote to Northcliffe on 23 January 1918. And, after Carson's resignation from the War Cabinet that same month, to devote himself to the Irish problem, this change was made. In February a Ministry of Information was constituted to take over most of the work of the Department (though propaganda in enemy countries was now made a separate agency under Northcliffe). Beaverbrook was appointed Minister, and Buchan became Director of Intelligence.

Beaverbrook soon showed himself to be an active and vigorous chief. Concerned about propaganda as Carson never had been, carrying an authority that had never been granted to Buchan, he made things hum. He never shilly-shallied, fought for his Ministry in the Cabinet, and stood firmly by his subordinates. Buchan had no need to revise his first rosy views.

I am very busy, but finding my work much more satisfying. Beaverbrook has an astonishingly candid mind and is so willing to learn.

On the whole I am having a much easier time than last year, for I have far more assistance now.

Buchan's personal assistants were Harold Baker and an Edinburgh KC, Hugh Macmillan. It was a young Ministry: Beaverbrook and Roderick Jones, his chief executive, were under forty, Harold Baker, Buchan, Masterman, Macmillan, only a year or two older.

Beaverbrook handsomely acknowledged that he was only building on an organisation created by Masterman and Buchan, which had achieved wonders in face of its severely limited powers, and of the indifference and contempt with which it was regarded by established Ministries. He found Buchan a splendidly hard worker, clear-minded, intelligent, quick and safe, who would never make blunders, or go out after a wild idea like Masterman (whom Beaverbrook considered the most brilliant man in the Ministry); but he thought Buchan had not enough drive during the Ministry's many controversies with the Foreign Office.

Free of many of the administrative chores which he found such a burden, Buchan was able to give his energies to the work he enjoyed and did particularly well: writing articles and summaries ('never be abstract when you can be concrete' was his advice to Hugh Macmillan), escorting important visitors to the Front, lecturing twice a week on the war to foreign correspondents in London. He was not closely involved in Beaverbrook's drive to 'repopularise the war' at home, which was specially directed at South Wales and Clydeside, where that other product of Hutchesons' and Glasgow University, James Maxton, was in jail for calling a general strike against the war. Nor was he over-apprehensive about civilian morale: 'I do not see any reason why *The Trojan Women* should not be produced at Birmingham,' he reassured Gilbert Murray early in 1918; 'the audience who will attend the Repertory Theatre is not likely to be driven into pacifist fury by Euripides.' But he played a major part in Beaverbrook's campaign to bring home to Americans Britain's share in the war: organising British lecturers for the States (one of these was George Adam Smith, Principal of Aberdeen University), American newspapermen to London and the Western Front. These included Lowell Thomas, who came over with a photographer in search of a dramatic story; when he could not find what he wanted on the Western Front he appealed to Buchan, who arranged for transport to Allenby's headquarters in the Middle East, where he thought drama might be found—and Lowell Thomas found T. E. Lawrence.

Buchan was asked to go to America himself, as a sort of roving ambassador to speak all over the country, but felt that his health would not stand it.

'All the attacks I had last year are nothing to what Beaverbrook is getting now,' reported Buchan in August 1918. Beaverbrook's view was that 'the wrestle you had with the Department of Information was only transferred to me on a larger scale in the Ministry.' Beaverbrook had a fresh crop of troubles of his own: plenty of enemies, personal and political, gunning for him in his new appointment, particularly on the score of a newspaper proprietor being a member of the Government, which Lloyd George's enemies saw as a move to ensure support for himself from the *Daily Express*. The Ministry's critics staged a debate in the House of Commons in August, when Leif Jones (a Liberal of the kind Buchan most disliked) led the attack. Alec MacCallum Scott spoke up for the Ministry from the Liberal back-benches, Stanley Baldwin defended it on behalf of the Government, and finally Tim Healy, an old friend of Beaverbrook's, skilfully sidetracked the debate into a slanging-match between Irish members. Buchan's work in the old Department came in for some kind words, and he took the whole affair quite jauntily. What did cause him a good deal of irritation was that Mrs Buchan, reading the Parliamentary reports in Peebles, somehow got it into her head that certain criticisms made by the Public Accounts Committee (those Irish cigars again!) meant that her son was being accused of sharp practice. 'However did you get so wrong? There was never the slightest charge against me personally.' Indeed, Buchan suffered financially for his work in propaganda, and was made to pay £101 out of his own pocket because he had spent that sum without proper Treasury sanction.* (Sir Roderick Jones, Beaverbrook's chief executive, had a similar demand for £250, as late as 1921. He did not pay.)

Though by this time the war was being won on the Western Front, everyone working at home was suffering from exhaustion and frayed nerves. 'Everybody is edgy and inclined to be difficult,' 'Nearly everybody I have to deal with officially is cantankerous,' were two of Buchan's comments; and F. S. Oliver told his brother in Canada:

* Lord Beaverbrook, recalling this episode in conversation with me, remembered with zest how as Minister for Aircraft Production in 1940 he had spent a quarter of a million without Treasury authorisation. The Buchan case was mentioned at a meeting of auditors-general from Commonwealth countries in 1954 as 'the classic test-case of personal responsibility—and the last.'

There is a disease at present which is even more prevalent than the Spanish influenza, viz, torantism. You can look it up in the dictionary. It springs from overwrought nerves, and even the sanest people . . . are apt to be swept away by gusts of temper, and the most preposterous mutual suspicions.

There were no longer air-raids to disturb sleep, but rations were low and everyone was hungry. (At the 1918 Burns Dinner already mentioned, polenta had to be substituted for haggis. But Mrs Buchan managed to find a haggis in Peebles for the Scots in the Ministry on St Andrew's Night.) In October Beaverbrook resigned on doctor's orders, no one was appointed to replace him, and half the office were down with influenza. The end of the fighting brought a numb relief, but little exhilaration. Arnold Bennett, whom Beaverbrook had brought in to direct British propaganda in France, described Armistice Day in his diary:

Maroons went off at 11, and excited the populace. A large portion of the Ministry staff got very excited. Buchan came in to shake hands. Girls very excited. I had to calm them . . . Raining now. An excellent thing to damp hysteria and Bolshevism.

Buchan did not feel as aloof from the celebrating crowds as Bennett; he just felt dog-tired—'I never realised how tired I was till the war stopped'—and his personal celebration was to go straight home and sleep.

Though the fighting had stopped, there were jobs still to be done. Buchan had to organise a visit by Marshal Foch; he had to wind up the Ministry. Two days after the Armistice the Cabinet directed him to close down all the departments that could be closed, and transfer the Ministry's remaining functions elsewhere. Buchan went to work promptly—too promptly for Arnold Bennett, who noted in his diary for 15 November that

Buchan, the liquidator, came down to see me, and was very explanatory and apologetic. The behaviour of the Cabinet to me was of course scandalous. But they have treated many others similarly, so I was not surprised.

In his natural pique at this termination of his services—which he had given free—Bennett accused Buchan of having 'gone behind my back.' But the soreness did not last, and the two were soon back on friendly terms. By Christmas Buchan was able to report to the Cabinet that certain propaganda sections had been passed on to the Foreign Office, the Art and Photography sections (which were making a profit) to the Imperial War Museum, and the rest closed down. This was the first of the war Ministries to be wound up.

Buchan would have liked to see his war-work officially recognised; he felt that the work he had done at G.H.Q. and in the Ministry had rated a K.C.B. or K.C.M.G., but though Beaverbrook submitted his name, the suggestion was turned down (there were too many Foreign Office people in the running for the K.C.M.G., Balfour told him) and Buchan felt that he was worth more than the plain knighthoods which were being distributed wholesale. So he ended the war undecorated, but the 'Colonel' which he had acquired in the Intelligence Corps stuck to him, and to many people he was Colonel Buchan years after the war was over.

Buchan was always to be deeply concerned about the fate of the men who had fought and suffered in the war. But at this moment of victory he also showed concern for another group, who had suffered in a different way: the conscientious objectors. With Gilbert Murray, Lord Parmoor and the Master of the Temple, he drew up an appeal to the Prime Minister to release the 1500 conscientious objectors still in prison,

700 of whom have served terms of two years or more, whereas two years is the maximum punishment allowed for ordinary criminals either under our civil or military code. As a result of recent inquiries, it was found that a majority of these men are sincerely convinced that they have acted under the demands of their conscience and in accordance with deep moral or religious convictions.
We urge that men in prison under these conditions should not be kept there during the period of national rejoicing, and that our country should not show itself slow at such a time to carry through an act of just mercy.

After the war, when he was writing the second volume of the *History of the Great War*, he was still of the opinion that:

The genuine conscientious objector was, in many cases, denied even his legal rights, and a number of sincere and honourable, if abnormal, beings were subjected to a persecution which could be justified on no conceivable grounds of law, ethics, or public policy.

In September Buchan had decided to withdraw as Parliamentary candidate for Selkirk and Peebles: 'I feel an intense disinclination to have anything to do with politics just now.' So in December he was delighted not to be involved in 'this silly Election.' He refused all requests to speak for friends who were standing (these included Violet Markham, who was celebrating the Representation of the People Act by contesting Chesterfield as a Liberal) and was quite content to see Donald Maclean retain Peebles on the Coalition ticket. Early in 1919 he and Maclean were made freemen of Peebles: 'They give their freedom very rarely and think highly of it,' Buchan had told Lord Rosebery when he was offered the same honour in 1912. But his present distaste for party politics did not mean a withdrawal from public issues. Like so many others, he felt all the suffering would be pointless unless it led to a better international order, and he told Gilbert Murray that he would do any work, in speaking or in writing, for the League of Nations.

All the enthusiasm that I have always had for my own brand of Imperialism I feel now attaches to this creed, and any political work I do in the future will be done in its service.

The four years of war had immensely enlarged Buchan's experience. He had seen war at close quarters, if mainly from a general's viewpoint; he had met a great variety of people, from Middle West newspapermen to secret service agents. He had organised and run a new department of government, in much less favourable circumstances than he had organised the Land Department in the Transvaal. He had worked with Haig at G.H.Q., he had visited the Grand Fleet with Beatty, he had worked and fought with Lloyd George (his exasperation at the time gave way to a long-term appreciation of Lloyd George's imaginative sweep and his vitality in the worst hours of the war—'a gift so rare and inexplicable that it may rightly be called genius'). He had often met King George; he had seen much of members of the War Cabinet—Milner, Balfour, Smuts, Carson, Bonar Law—and of top-ranking soldiers—Byng, Ian Hamilton, William Robertson. He had been very friendly with the American Ambassador, he had talked with Venizelos and Kerensky; in 1916 he had had Protopopov to dinner in Portland Place—a delegate from the Russian Duma who became an ally of the Empress and Rasputin and was shot by the Bolsheviks. Like F. S. Oliver—who had been active in unseating Asquith, had helped Keyes with his Zeebrugge despatch and had been asked by Haig to help reorganise G.H.Q.—Buchan had become very much the insider in government and the high command. In 1916 he had been elected to the Athenaeum and in 1918 to The Club, the dining-club originally founded by Dr Johnson, whose members now included the Archbishop of Canterbury, Lord Hugh Cecil, Lord Stamfordham, Lord Haldane, Henry Newbolt, H. A. L. Fisher, Rudyard Kipling and Bishop Gore.

Far beyond any gains stretched his personal losses. Towards the end of the war Buchan wrote some lines in which a Border soldier daydreams of the quiet life he will lead once the fighting is over. He will play bowls, cultivate his garden, 'crack wi' Davie and mix a rummer,' and with Davie he will go fishing:

> Davie will lauch like a wean at a fair
> And nip my airm to mak certain shüre
> That we're back frae yon place o' dule and dreid,
> To oor ain kind warld—
>
> *But Davie's deid!*
> *Nae mair gude nor ill can betide him.*
> *We happit him doun by Beaumont toun,*
> *And the half o' my hert's in the mools aside him.*

Half Buchan's closest friends were dead. Raymond Asquith was killed on the Somme in September 1916; Bron Herbert over the enemy lines in 1916 (he had learnt to fly at the age of thirty-nine, in spite of a leg lost in the South African war); Tommy Nelson and his brother Alastair at Arras in spring 1917; Basil Blackwood in a raid near Ypres in July 1917. When, later, Buchan wrote a privately printed memoir of them he prefaced it with Gabriel Harvey's lines:

> Ah, that Sir Humfry Gilbert should be dead:
> Ah, that Sir Philip Sidney should be dead:
> Ah, that Sir William Sackeuill should be dead:
> Ah, that Sir Richard Grenvuile should be dead:
> Ah, that braue Walter Deuoreux should be dead:
> Ah, that the Flowre of Knighthood should be dead.
> Which, maugre deadlyest Deathes, and stonyest Stones,
> That coouer worthiest worth, shall neuer dy.

As he came out of the long tunnel in 1918, Buchan put it more bleakly: 'There are far more dead than living now.'

CHAPTER NINE

COUNTRY GENTLEMAN

1919–27

'As I came out of the Home Wood on to the lower lawns and saw the old stone gables that the monks had built, I felt that I was anchored at last in the pleasantest kind of harbour.'
            Richard Hannay in John Buchan's *The Three Hostages* (1924)

In September 1917 Buchan took his wife on a four-day holiday to the Cotswolds: country known to him from his Oxford days, but to her entirely new. They stayed at the fishing inn at Fossebridge, walked down the Coln valley to Bibury, drove by Stow-on-the-Wold and Bourton-on-the-Water to Burford, 'a wonderful old town on the Windrush which I once went to see when I was at Oxford.' Enchanted and deeply refreshed, they decided that they must live somewhere in this region after the war. The western Cotswolds were out of the question, as Buchan would need to be within daily reach of London; the best place would be close to Oxford and its good train service. So a year later, when Susan was recovering from the birth of her fourth child (Alastair Francis, named after his uncle and Francis Grenfell), Buchan went down to Oxford with Hugh Macmillan to prospect for houses in the Bampton and Charlbury area. (One which they looked at is the subject of Buchan's story 'Fullcircle.') House-hunting went on through the winter of 1918–19, and in the spring Buchan heard from Captain Hutchinson, Treasurer of Christ Church, that the college was buying the village of Elsfield but would consider selling the manor-house and eighteen acres round it. The Buchans bought it.

Elsfield—a village of twenty-five cottages and six larger houses, a school and a church—stands on the ridge between Chilterns and Cotswolds, four miles north-east of Oxford: not sheep country, as the Cotswolds mainly were in 1919, but wooded, with fields originally cleared from the Forest of Stow. At the northern edge the ridge

drops down to the marshy saucer of Otmoor. Buchan had first seen
the village as an undergraduate, looking up from Woodeaton on an
early summer morning: the sight had been one of his golden Oxford
memories. Now in 1919 Elsfield was still self-contained, free from
the pull of the city. There were no buses, goods came out by the
Beckley carrier, the farmers drove their pony-traps along unmetalled roads. The Manor was a tall stone house, opening straight
on to the village street; from the other side it commanded a splendid
outlook. Six fields away a line of willows marked the course of the
Cher, and beyond the valley stretched the plain about Eynsham and
Witney, rising to the western Cotswolds. On a clear day you could
see as far as the bump of Cleeve Hill above Cheltenham, forty miles
away. It could be a dramatic view, with storms chasing each other
across the landscape, mist advancing from the valley and creeping
up the ridge; and it was a greener view than now, for the fields were
then all pasture. Buchan's first improvement was to cut down a
Wellingtonia planted by a Victorian owner, which blocked half the
prospect.

There had been a dwelling on the site since Domesday Book; the
present buildings were mainly seventeenth century, with some rather
ungainly Victorian additions. The most interesting of the Manor's
previous owners was Francis Wise, parson of Elsfield and Radcliffe's
librarian at Oxford; and of its earlier visitors Samuel Johnson, who
walked up with Thomas Warton from Oxford in the summer of
1754. 'At this place,' Warton informed Boswell:

Mr Wise had fitted up a house and gardens, in a singular manner, but with
great taste. Here was an excellent library, particularly a valuable collection
of books in Northern literature with which Johnson was often very busy.
. . . As we returned to Oxford in the evening, I outwalked Johnson, and
he cried out *Sufflamina*, a Latin word, which came from his mouth with
peculiar grace, and was as much as to say, *Put on your drag-chain.**

Wise had planted a fine stand of elms and beeches, laid out the
grounds with ornamental ponds and groves, a gazebo and a bowling-
green, erected a Roman—or sham-Roman—altar on the lawn, and
designed a gardener's cottage in the style of a medieval chantry.
In his day, according to contemporary prints, there was a view of
Oxford; now it is quite blocked by trees, but much the same view
can be seen within two minutes' walk of the Manor, before the road
dips down towards Marston. The garden which the Buchans found

* There is an engraving of Elsfield—after one of a series commissioned by Wise
—in the 1865 edition of Boswell's *Life of Johnson*, Vol. I, p. 151.

was a pleasant mixture of the formal and the wild, the lawns and
flower-beds dropping down to the Crow Wood. Buchan at once
planted a long yew-hedge at the side of the lawn (it had to be
replanted after the drought of 1921) and a copper-beech.

'It was looking ravishing yesterday, and I fell desperately in love
with it,' Buchan told his mother in May 1919, when the sale was
going through. Alterations to the house were started in August (it
lacked bathrooms and electric light) and, having sold 76 Portland
Place, the Buchans took a furnished house at Headington while
work went forward. 'I am only doing the minimum,' Buchan reassured his mother, whose apprehensions then switched to his religious observances. How would he fare with no Presbyterian church
nearer than Oxford, and that operating only in term-time? Buchan
firmly claimed his right to worship in Elsfield Church, but tried to
make her see that '*None of us are or ever will be Episcopalians.*'

Over Christmas he arranged his books in the library, with its
three tall windows looking west; and early in January 1920 the
move was completed, and he was reporting that 'the mornings here
are wonderful, for the whole place swims in light. I greatly enjoy
driving down. The children are wildly happy.' 'It is a happy house,
and would do you good,' Henry Newbolt told his wife after he had
been one of the Buchans' earliest visitors. 'The real joy of the place
turns on the spirit that you and John create in it, a spirit so wonderful and forthcoming,' wrote Violet Markham after 'a golden week-
end.'

Buchan's daily life now took on a new rhythm. Five mornings a
week he left home soon after eight, was driven to Oxford for the
8.40 train, and was in Nelson's office in Paternoster Row soon after
10; then back by the 6 o'clock train (occasionally the 4.45) in time
to see the children in bed. He rarely spent an evening away from
home. 'I find this going up and down to London extremely pleasant
and untiring,' he reported: he could read and work on the train,
but—contrary to popular belief—he never wrote a line of his stories
on the Great Western Railway.

This daily journey to London seemed a small price to pay for
the deep satisfaction of his new home. Elsfield satisfied him for a
number of reasons. There was a simple wish for 'ease after war,
port after stormy seas,' and for Buchan such ease was always
associated with the country: Broughton against Glasgow, the Wood
Bush against Johannesburg. London had been the right place when
he was establishing himself in a career, when possibilities were

opening out, when the House of Commons was his goal. Now, content to settle to a quiet life as publisher and writer, his political ambitions for the moment laid aside, he found that London tired him rather than stimulated. Also, after four years when hardly a bite could be taken without business being talked, he was not going to be vulnerable to casual sociabilities, telephone calls, and people dropping in. So much of his old life had gone, with so many of his friends, and he wanted to rebuild on a new pattern. Then, like so many other men in 1919—and 1945—he wanted more than anything to be with his family, to see his children growing, to give them the kind of country life that he had known in the long holidays at Broughton. Johnnie was inclined to be delicate, and was never on top of his form in London; the wartime summers in Kent had given the three elder children a great taste for the country, and for them Elsfield was a paradise. Taking Johnnie to fish in Glyme or Windrush, teaching him (very soon learning from him) the birds to be seen in Stow Wood or on Otmoor, going off with him and Alice to walk in Wychwood Forest and picnic by an ice-cold spring, Buchan enjoyed that keenest pleasure of a parent in seeing his children respond to his own childhood's delights. And, though this was her first home out of London, Susan responded to the new life as warmly as Alice and the boys.

'Elsfield is curiously like Broughton Green,' Buchan wrote just after he had moved in; and he told Anna that 'it has the same smells that Broughton used to have.' Both houses were solidly planted in their village, opening straight on to the road; yet on the farther side of each was a certain wildness, and a long prospect. Over the centuries they had both played their part in local history. The manor fields had been named in deeds and cartularies for nine hundred years, and its yard had been a gun-park for the Parliamentary army during the siege of Oxford. The fields and woods had been one of Gerard of the *Herbal*'s chief hunting-grounds for wild flowers. There had been famous struggles between the men of Otmoor and the soldiers sent to force the enclosures in the early nineteenth century. As Broughton Green had its highwayman to delight the children, the legendary hero of 'Frizzel's End,' so Elsfield had another: Haynes, who had held up the Oxford coach by Stow Wood and had been hanged by the Beckley road-end. The grandson of the murdered coachman still lived in the district. That balance in Buchan between the future and the past—between the eager planning for himself and others, the zest in new work and experience,

and his feeling for the settled, the traditional, the known—had by
the end of the war been tilted towards the past. In this part of
Oxfordshire, where memories were as long as in the Borders, in
this house with its tradition of scholarship and hospitality, he could
put down his roots.

Like many Scots, Buchan had always appreciated the Englishness
of England, greatly preferring the softer, greener South to the
Lakes or the Pennines, which, till he knows better, often strike the
Scot as a second-rate version of the hills and moors of his own
country. Part of Buchan's devotion to *The Compleat Angler* and
The Pilgrim's Progress was that in the one he found 'a transcript of
old English country life,' and in the other 'an idyll of an older
English world.' Now knowledge of this older England came to him
through his daily contacts and activities. He read a great deal of
local history. He talked endlessly about the countryside with Amos
Webb, the Elsfield man who was his chauffeur and became his close
friend, and with his gardener Tom Basson, who had been born in
1840 and remembered *his* elders talking about the village in the
eighteenth century. He took long Saturday walks by himself round
Otmoor, or the wider circuit by Brill, Arncote and Woodeaton; and
shorter walks with the children. These were always planned, and
always different. There might be a landing in the Mill Meadow on
the Cherwell, a plunge into the jungles of Noke Wood, a search for
the Roman causeway on Otmoor; and the trophies with which the
party returned might be the sight of a golden oriole, the finding of
a badger's earth, the news of a bit of Roman pottery turned up by a
ploughman near Woodeaton.

Buchan kept an old hunter called (like his Transvaal pony) Alan
Breck, for his early-morning rides at the week-end. He did not
hunt, though he was once praised by the Master of the South
Oxfordshire hounds for preserving foxes in his wood, but his real
motive had been less to serve the hunt than to keep down the rabbits
which threatened the self-seeded ashes and little oaks. If the Christ
Church beagles came out Elsfield way, he and the children would
join in; but in general his activities were hardly more on a 'county'
level than they had been at Broughton. In his first burst of hospitable enthusiasm he had taken very seriously the four hundred
acres of shooting he had leased next to the Manor, and the limited
number of birds did not deter him from inviting Lord Edward
Gleichen, a wartime friend who was a crack shot, for a day's sport.
Lord Edward turned up, so Johnnie Buchan remembered,

with a loader carrying his second gun and hung round with bags containing hundreds of spare cartridges. The total pheasant population of the shoot was about forty, in that particular year. But such was my father's enthusiasm that our visitor plainly enjoyed his day, and was as excited as we were about the only three pheasants that came over him.

Buchan soon came to prefer going out by himself after hares or woodcock to joining in an organised shoot with county neighbours; after a few years he gave up even that rough shooting, and turned over the four hundred acres to a syndicate of farmers. His best pleasures were still the long day's fishing, alone or with Johnnie or Amos Webb, and the long day's tramp.

Scott built Abbotsford and was the Laird; Stevenson built Vailima and played the Chief. Does the romantic Scottish novelist long for landed grandeur? Certainly it was the success of his thrillers that enabled Buchan to buy Elsfield, but he had no wish to extend his property or his house, and no ambition to play the squire. He liked joining in certain village activities, like the rook-shooting; he read the lessons in church; he would talk to the village club on politics if they invited him, as he would talk to an undergraduate club; but he had no wish to run the village just because he lived in the Manor, and certainly expected no particular deference. He never served on the parish council. Before the war he had owned to an ambition for 'a smallish estate, somewhere about the head of Megget'; now the tall and roomy Elsfield, in his accounts to friends, was 'the *little* country-house,' 'our little manor-house.' In his copy of Quiller-Couch's *Studies in Literature*—a favourite book—Buchan marked a passage on Horace's villa, 'a small country-house, frugal but with good wine in the cellar, and silver, well-rubbed, on the table,' and pencilled on the same page Stevenson's lines:

> A bin of wine, a spice of wit,
> A house with lawns enclosing it,
> A living river by the door,
> A nightingale in the sycamore!

Buchan loved his garden, his view, his library—strong on history, on philosophy and adventure, and with a splendid seventeenth-century collection—he liked keeping a good table and a good cellar, and enjoyed entertaining his friends. But he had not the slightest wish to make a splash, to cut a dash in county society. There had been a Roman villa in nearby Beckley; Elsfield was Buchan's Roman villa, not his Abbotsford.

There in his manor he could entertain his family and friends. Every April the Peebles Buchans would appear punctually, with the catkins and aconites in the Crow Wood. 'It is all very like a book,' wrote Anna on her first visit, after gathering primroses to decorate the church for Easter. 'He does take such an interest in this place and makes such a fuss if the children disarrange anything in the library.' Mrs Grosvenor would arrive with sketching materials and a majestic pile of luggage, equipped for the contingency of a hot day in March, or a frosty one in May. The F. S. Olivers were within reach at Checkendon, and the Gilbert Murrays on Boars Hill. W. P. Ker, that Glasgow Scot of an older generation, would walk up from All Souls of a Sunday; the Buchans tried to persuade him to take a house in Beckley. 'Elsfield is nearly as bad as Bank House,' Buchan told his mother after a week-end in May 1921:

Dougie Malcolm, Miss Pember and the late Viceroy of India, Lord Chelmsford, turned up at lunch. Then Col. Lawrence of Arabia arrived, and at tea we had Philip and Lady Ottoline Morrell. . . . Yesterday afternoon we had a perfect drove of people—Sir Harry Birchenough, Lionel Curtis, Bob Brand, Colonel Sandford, V.C. (a hero of Zeebrugge), a South African called Rose Innes and a great many more.

T. E. Lawrence, then a Fellow of All Souls, became a frequent if unpredictable visitor, roaring up on his motor-cycle Boanerges, whose performance immensely impressed the Buchan boys. Robert Graves, whom Lawrence introduced to the Buchans, used to look in after captaining the Islip team against Elsfield. (Graves has a memory of Buchan, really angry for once, inveighing against a strong-minded political hostess: 'The worrst woman in the worrld!')

Elsfield was the right distance from Oxford; Buchan could enjoy a good deal of University life without being more drawn in than he wanted. He went down to hear W. P. Ker lecture as Professor of Poetry. He dined occasionally at high tables and Masters' lodges— with the H. A. L. Fishers at New College, the F. W. Pembers at All Souls, and Father D'Arcy at Campion Hall. He often talked to undergraduate societies, became the Senior Treasurer of the Conservative Association, and from 1924 to 1930 was a Curator of the University Chest. At the Union Centenary Debate in 1924 he was one of the four chief speakers, opposing Gilbert Murray on the motion 'That Civilisation has advanced since this Society first met,' with Philip Guedalla and Ronald Knox speaking third and fourth. (The motion was carried.) A less festive occasion was the breakfast in aid of European Student Relief in 1922, at which he spoke; the fare was bread and cocoa, the purpose being to bring home to comfortable Oxford undergraduates what students in former enemy countries were living on.

Of all his contacts with Oxford, those Buchan most enjoyed were with the undergraduates, whom he met when he addressed their societies, or when his friends' children, bringing their friends with them, walked or bicycled up to Elsfield for Sunday tea. This was perhaps the characteristic Elsfield occasion, and to the Buchans an unpredictable one, for anything from one to thirty might turn up—'the Amalekites' the family called these invaders. There would probably be guests staying at the Manor—Violet Markham, or the Amerys, or the Robert Cecils—who would give the undergraduates a fresher view of the world of politics or government than would be found in the North Oxford drawing-rooms they visited. Not that there was any talking-down by the seniors: in the conversation round the large tea-table, which was often general, everyone was encouraged to talk (as in the Buchan home in Glasgow) and everyone was listened to—at least by the host, if not by his own contemporaries. It was not quite the talk of Oxford; cleverness cut less ice here, speakers had to be ready to back up their views with facts. Talking was connected with doing; if at Elsfield an undergraduate expressed a view about his future career, it would be just as well if he had really thought about it and was not merely airing a stray notion that sounded good, for Buchan would be sizing up his hopes and chances: 'I might write to X about it,' or 'Wouldn't it be a good thing for you to talk to Y?' And in due course a letter would come from X, an appointment be made with Y. Seniors often make offers of help; few back up their offers so promptly and practically as John Buchan did. To the young and unimportant he was endlessly generous with his time and interest.

Among the undergraduates who came regularly to Elsfield in those early years were Tommy Nelson's sons, Evelyn Baring, John Strachey, David Maxwell Fyfe, Roger Makins, Frank Pakenham, Mary Somerville, Alan Lennox-Boyd and A. L. Rowse, who discovered that Buchan's

sympathies and indeed affections were readily extended in every direction politically. In fact, I believe it was a special recommendation with him that one was on the other side. I remember well the particular affection and regard in which he held, and always spoke of, Maxton, then much in the public eye as leader of the I.L.P. and a notable figure in Parliament. With one young neophyte of the Left, ardent, impatient, fanatical, touchy, he was patience and courtesy itself.

I myself first met John Buchan on one such Sunday afternoon, brought to Elsfield by my Somerville contemporary Mary Trevelyan, who was his god-daughter, so that I could invite him to talk to the College Literary Society. I was a bit apprehensive of visiting the Manor. In my Aberdeen childhood we used to condemn as 'English' any stuffiness of manner, any undue deference to 'good form,' any lack of interest outside a restricted social circle, any sense of people being measured and judged by accent or schooling, which we associated with the South, and which made us cross and uncomfortable. And I had found much of this 'Englishness' in the few country-houses I had visited. But there was no trace of it in this most English-looking manor-house. At once I felt at ease, and was delighted with the splendid tea, the free and lively talk (I remember Hugh Macmillan there, then Lord Advocate in the first Labour Government) and, above all, John Buchan's warmth. He asked me friendly questions—perhaps about Scotland, or politics, or the English School at Oxford, I cannot now recall, but the important thing was that the conversation was about me, not him, and that my answers really seemed to matter. And he agreed at once to address the Somerville Literary Society on 'The Old and New in Literature'—though not to dine in Hall.

The one flaw in this agreeable new life of Buchan's was, once again, his health. Hopes that the short-circuit operation would put him permanently right soon faded: he continued to have attacks of pain every three or four months. 'I must cure this beastly auto-intoxication which is making me a misery to myself and to other folk,' he wrote in 1920, and again 'I am determined to get rid of the beastly thing, which cripples my work and (if I weren't a very cheerful person) would poison my life.' He consulted specialists; in 1921 he had a spell in Sir Berkeley Moynihan's clinic in Leeds; he visited Dr Marten in Freiburg in the Black Forest (and got an idea for a story, 'The Loathly Opposite'). Dr Marten's speciality was to trace the psychic disorder behind the physical ailment; on Buchan his verdict was: 'Never in my experience have I met anybody less frustrated or less crippled by inhibitions. He is free from neuroses. His trouble must be wholly of physical origin.' Buchan cut out smoking; he dieted: 'I am determined to diet for evermore, if necessary, to extirpate the viper.' The regime he adopted depended on milk and eggs—I have a memory of a delicious dinner at Elsfield much appreciated by hungry undergraduate guests while our host ate one poached egg. He took very little alcohol—one glass of sherry, one nip of whisky. The one thing he would not do was to rest for any length of time. He had in the end to face the fact that a constant carefulness about his food, a constant slight discomfort and, every few months, a crippling bout of pain, were the conditions upon which his life had to be lived. He faced it stoically, absolutely determined that these conditions should not stop his working nor spoil his holidays. 'I hope your hateful malady is abating,' wrote Newbolt in 1923. 'Happily your courage is one of the fixed points of the compass in the life of those who know you.' But on his wife this looming shadow of ill-health imposed a constant strain: she knew he ought to take life easy, and she knew he never would.

Though not on the scale of Abbotsford or Vailima, Elsfield—with the gardener, chauffeur, handyman which the new life demanded, as well as the indoor servants—had to be paid for. Taking it on had been something of a gamble, and Buchan set to make its financial basis firm, and to send his three boys to the Dragon School and Eton, by working if not at the pitch of 1914–18, at least extremely hard. He went back to Nelson's early in 1919, and again visited Edinburgh every month. The firm had had its wartime difficulties; shortage of paper and poorness of quality ('All the butter paper seems to have gone to books'), shortage of skilled workers, the loss of foreign markets, costly and precarious transport. But the war had made more people read books—in trenches and hospitals, in camps and blacked-out houses. 'I had lunch with George Brown yesterday,' Buchan had written in May 1918, 'and talked our business, which in spite of troubles is wonderfully good.' But however well the firm had weathered the war, it could never be the same place for Buchan without Tommy Nelson. He, Buchan and George Brown had worked together with a great appreciation of each other's enthusiasms and strengths. Now Brown and Buchan found it less easy to work with Ian Nelson, who was less inclined than his brother to give his partners their head. The series of reprint copyright novels—the old Sevenpennies—at which both had worked with such zest was not resumed after the war. Then Tommy's death, and his widow's remarriage in 1919 to the painter Paul Maze, had brought practical difficulties, for his share of the capital was held on trust for his children, and could not be used for the firm's business. There was no general agreement on how

Nelson's should expand. The situation was difficult, and when George Brown resigned in 1921 Buchan felt it keenly.

In London, however, he had recruited a most congenial colleague, Henry Newbolt, whom he had come to know well when Newbolt was Cable Controller at the Ministry of Information. As a full director of Nelson's since it had become a company in 1915, Buchan was more concerned with the administrative side of the business than before the war, particularly with paper supplies ('Went out to a paper mill at Penicuik to see a new process'), and Newbolt was a great help on the literary and educational side. The two collaborated on a series of selections from nineteenth-century poets—Morris, Browning, Arnold, Rossetti—with Newbolt editing and Buchan writing the introductions. Newbolt had been chairman of the departmental committee set up by H. A. L. Fisher, then President of the Board of Education, to report on 'The Teaching of English in England.' The Report, which came out in 1921, caused a great stir in schools and training colleges, and Buchan and Newbolt decided to follow it up with a series of books which would carry out the committee's main recommendations. This series on 'The Teaching of English,' about which Fisher was enthusiastic, was followed by another on 'The Teaching of History;' Buchan, as general editor, secured R. S. Rait, David Douglas, A. S. Turberville, G. G. Coulton, R. B. Mowat and other specialists to write the separate volumes. He himself wrote for Nelson's two collections of adventures: *A Book of Escapes and Hurried Journeys* in 1922, and in 1923 *The Last Secrets*, in which he described the goals still remaining for explorers, from the Gorges of the Brahmaputra to the summit of Mount Everest. Buchan worked hard for Nelson's, he gave the firm many of his own books to publish, but he could not put his whole heart into it as he had done in Tommy's day. And when it was once suggested, not that he wasn't doing his work admirably, but that he should be spending more time in the office, he was moved to one of his rare outbursts of rage.

In 1919 Buchan had been invited by Sir Roderick Jones, another friend from the Ministry and now Chairman of Reuter's, to become a director; and early in 1923, when Jones had completed a major reorganisation of the Agency, and was planning to go round the world, he invited Buchan to become Deputy Chairman of Reuter's and to take a more active part in the administration. Before leaving England Jones left instructions with his executor that if he should

not return, Buchan was to take his place as Managing Director—
'Instal John at once by all legal means at your disposal'—for he was
convinced that Buchan would faithfully carry out his plans for
extending and consolidating Reuter's independence. 'I have taken
the Deputy-Chairmanship,' Buchan told his mother, 'but have
arranged that for the present it will make no difference to my connection with Nelson's.' Now he divided his working day between
Paternoster Row—where he would begin to dictate the minute he
arrived in the office—and the Reuter building on the Victoria
Embankment. Jones particularly valued Buchan's capacity, trained
by his years at the Bar, for summarising a mass of complex facts and
presenting them in a clear and simple form for consideration and
decision—and the speed at which he did it.

The programme of writing which Buchan set himself was heavy
and varied. First he had to revise the *History of the War*. Each of the
twenty-four parts had been written soon after the events it chron-
icled; inevitably there were mistakes of fact, something of the
inconsequence of real life, abrupt changes of tone and mood. Now
it must be given shape and perspective. It was a long and grinding
chore—'The correcting of proofs of my History is a big job and
occupies me every night after dinner'—and he was relieved when
the four volumes were finished in the summer of 1921.

They had a mixed reception. From Sir Ian Hamilton came 'admiration which amounts to astonishment at the grip and power you
have manifested;' Field-Marshal Sir William Robertson considered
it 'a wonderful compression, without being in any way a mere
précis' and commended Buchan for avoiding 'the air of superiority
too often assumed by the historian, whose task after the event is
always so much easier than that of the statesman or the soldier who
had to deal with the problems at the time.' But the reviewer in the
Army Quarterly was critical; the original twenty-four-part history
had given an interesting and clear account of the military operations, he said, but in the revision far too many inaccuracies had been
allowed to stand, and he commented on Buchan's 'weakness for
historical parallels.' Captain Liddell Hart, who had thought the
original issues 'a tour-de-force, much better than Hilaire Belloc,'
found the book 'just not good enough,' for Buchan had not made
enough use of the new knowledge available by 1921.

Beaverbrook, though 'sure that it represents the truth roughly,
and therefore I have no quarrel with it,' was critical of Buchan's

handling of the relations between Lloyd George and Asquith in
1915–16; but St Loe Strachey considered that 'there has been
nothing approaching' Buchan's handling of Lloyd George 'for
justice, good sense and knowledge.' The strongest attack came some
years later from Lloyd George himself. In Volume I of his *War
Memoirs* (1933) he made a slighting reference to Buchan's treatment
of the Salonika episode, but the main attack was in Volume III (1934).

Mr Buchan, in his *History of the War*, lapsing into his fictional mood,
gives a fanciful picture of my meeting General Nivelle at the Gare du
Nord on my way back from the Rome Conference in January [1917], of
his seizing the opportunity afforded by the *dix minutes d'arrêt* at the station
to unfold to me his great strategical plan, and he proceeds to tell how, having heard it for the first time, I instantly caught fire. When a brilliant
novelist assumes the unaccustomed rôle of a historian it is inevitable that
he should now and again forget that he is no longer writing fiction, but that
he is engaged on a literary enterprise where narration is limited in its scope
by the rigid bounds of fact . . . The real explanation is that Mr Buchan
found it so much less trouble to repeat War Office gossip than to read
War Office documents.

These comments of Lloyd George were, in Liddell Hart's view,
'needlessly sharp,'* and he admired Buchan's fairness to his critic
in *The King's Grace* (1935). This chronicle of the events of King
George V's reign gave Buchan the chance to revise some of his
views of the war in the light of later publications.

There were other war-debts to discharge. In 1919 he wrote, and
printed at his own expense at the Chiswick Press, *These for Remembrance*, a volume of sketches of his friends who had been killed:
Tommy Nelson, Auberon Herbert, Basil Blackwood, Raymond
Asquith, his brother Willie's friend Cecil Rawling, his wife's cousin
Jack Stuart-Wortley.† Turning over old letters for this purpose was
'like opening graves.' The following year he wrote a short memoir of
Francis and Riversdale Grenfell (1920). He undertook the *History of
the South African Forces in France* (1920) at Smuts's request, and—
because it was Alastair's and the Peeblesshire regiment—wrote *The
History of the Royal Scots Fusiliers* (1925).

* 'You're spoiling your case,' he told Lloyd George after reading the text at
Sir Maurice Hankey's request; 'you should be content with a plain contradiction;
don't rub J.B's nose in the mud.' But 'I'm a pagan, I love fighting' was Lloyd
George's reply.
† Many passages from *These For Remembrance* were incorporated into *Memory
Hold-the-Door*.

In 1920 Buchan was asked by Lady Minto to help her write the life of her husband, who had been successively Governor-General of Canada (1898–1904) and Viceroy of India (1905–10: for a short time Willie Buchan had been on his staff). Soon he was writing the book himself, but *Lord Minto* (1924) bears the marks of its origin as a family memoir. Buchan depended almost entirely upon Minto's own notes and correspondence, and although this did not affect the liveliness of his portrait of the man, it did limit his understanding of Minto's public rôle. When, for instance, it came to the vice-royalty, he unquestioningly took over Minto's view of Indian nationalists, referring to them as 'anarchists' or 'agitators,' as if they were no more than disturbers of the peace. Again, in describing the controversy over the Canadian militia in 1899, Buchan accepted Minto's favourable estimate of the British General Hutton, and his criticism of the Minister of Militia, Sir Frederick Borden. When the latter's cousin, Sir Robert Borden, protested, Buchan was frank in his regrets about

a matter which I fear I tackled very perfunctorily in my book on Minto. Since that book was published I have come to the conclusion that I have been unjust and captious in many details, and from what you write it is quite clear that I was unfair to Sir Frederick Borden . . . I had no know-ledge of the Canadian background to correct my views.

The Canadian Prime Minister Mackenzie King was critical of the way Buchan implied that 'Laurier was kept in the path of political rectitude' by Minto, for in his view it was all the other way round. In a generally favourable review O. D. Skelton (who was Laurier's biographer) said that, though Buchan had tried to be 'fair and sympathetic' to the Canadian position, there were too many 'patronising references to the "opportunism" of Canadian politics,' which came strangely 'from the citizen of a country which has run the gamut from Disraeli to Lloyd George.'

Yet through the writing of the book Buchan greatly increased his knowledge of Canada. He gained understanding of the strength and touchiness of a young democracy, of the development of Canadian nationalism, of the special character of French-Canadian loyalty (he quotes approvingly Minto's remark that 'pig-headed British assertiveness is much more to be feared than French sym-pathies'). He learned to admire Laurier, and to understand the significance of names like Borden, J. W. Dafoe, Mackenzie King. He saw the prairies and the Yukon through Minto's appreciative eyes; vicariously he enjoyed canoeing and fishing in 'the wonderful

Canadian rivers.' Canada was now to him much more than a powerful partner in the Empire; it was a country where another man
brought up on the Borders had found great satisfaction in his work,
great zest in his amusements.

Two Scottish projects particularly engaged Buchan: collecting
pieces for the anthology of poems in Scots which appeared in 1924
as *The Northern Muse*, and making a thorough revision of his
Montrose.

On its appearance in 1913 *The Marquis of Montrose* had some
rough handling. As Stair Gillon later put it, Buchan's

zeal for his idolized 'discovery' . . . led him to commit so many elementary
blunders, all of which invariably told in favour of Montrose and against
Argyll and the Estates, tinged with a certain 'acerbity' and an air of
omniscience, that he was severely taken to task.

Gillon particularly had in mind D. Hay Fleming, who reviewed it in
a five-column article in the *British Weekly*,* Buchan's old antagonist from Kailyard days. First, in the opening paragraph, came the
indictment:

No doubt his book is very interesting—some readers may even find it
fascinating—but otherwise it is a poor and perfunctory performance, biased
and inaccurate, unfair and untrustworthy. In the compass of this review
little more can be done than to indicate its faults and give a few examples.

With relish Mr Fleming buckled to his fault-finding, accusing
Buchan of being careless about some authorities and ignorant of
others, inaccurate in his quotations, vague in his references, rash in
his judgments and emotionally biased. He concluded his prosecution:

There is more need than ever of a straightforward, critical and unvarnished
life of Montrose; but such a life can only be written by one whose heart is
purged of prejudice, and who will take pains to discover the truth, and to
state it impartially. Men of Mr Buchan's gifts and temperament should
eschew historical writing and devote themselves to avowed fiction.

W. L. Mathieson was altogether kinder in the *Scottish Historical
Review*:†

* The only other items on the page are an eight-line verse 'Sunday Afternoon'—
'God be with you in the springtime, When the violets unfold'—and a Prayer
beginning 'O Lord, Thou hast set wondrous things before us.'

† The *Review*, though a quarterly, was much prompter with its notice (October
1913) than the *British Weekly*, whose notice appeared on 12 February 1914.

Mr Buchan has the gift of a singularly vivid, incisive and picturesque style. The general reader has never had so good an opportunity of making himself acquainted with the character and exploits of Montrose; and even those who have seriously studied his campaigns will do well to study them again as here luminously and accurately set forth.

But Mathieson too judged that Buchan had been altogether too summary with the Covenanting part of Montrose's career, and noted 'an asperity of tone and an unguardedness of statement which suggests the brilliant litterateur rather than the cautious historian.' In setting out to revise and correct these faults, Buchan was determined to prove himself a serious writer of history.

The 1928 *Montrose* goes far beyond the correcting of error. It is conceived on a larger scale than the 1913 version; there is a new introductory chapter on the early seventeenth century, the description of the Reformed Kirk in Scotland has been greatly expanded, and Buchan, with a much wider reading in the pamphlets of the period, enters more thoroughly into Covenanting politics. Argyll is no longer the crude foil to the heroic Montrose. Earlier generalisations—'physically he was a coward'—are modified or retracted; slighting phrases—'the eternal fisher in troubled waters, the creature of a medieval twilight'—are removed. The cocksure note has been silenced, and the summing-up is careful:

His troubles came primarily from a divided soul—a clear, practical intellect pulling against an obscurantist creed, the Highland chief at variance with the Presbyterian statesman, a brain, medieval for all its powers, fumbling with the half-understood problems of a new world.

Conversely, the darkest stain on Montrose's record, the sack of Aberdeen in 1644, is more rigorously examined, and Montrose comes out no better than before. Though Montrose's campaigns bulked larger in the earlier version, the accounts of them are now fuller, and they have been set more firmly in their context; there is a new section on the methods of war in the mid-seventeenth century, the weapons, the tactics, the constitution of the regular armies and the special character of the Highland soldier. In *Montrose* Buchan is adding to knowledge, but he is always keeping the general reader in mind.

'I am sending you my *Montrose*,' Buchan wrote to Stair Gillon, 'because (1) it is a guide to the topography of nearly all Scotland and (2) it contains most of my philosophy of life.' He did not really choose Montrose as the subject of his *magnum opus*; Montrose had long since captured him.

He had everything to make him Buchan's hero, as he had been Scott's. He was the marvellous young man who, starting with 'two followers, four sorry horses, little money and no baggage,' in six months had Scotland at his feet. He was the Lowlander who became a hero in Highland song and legend. Everything about him stirred the imagination: his looks, his youth, his poetry, his audacity, his astonishing winter march through the hills, his friendship with Elizabeth of Bohemia, his feyness towards the end when he had himself painted in coal-black armour and devised strange battle-standards for his troops, his demeanour as captive and victim, when he went to his death as a bridegroom and the crowds brought to mock him were silent as he passed.

So Buchan was captivated; but, far beyond this fascination for a romantic of a romantic hero, he was driven to try to understand Montrose. Out of the struggle of Kirk and State, Kirk and people, came much of the Scotland he knew. The seventeenth century (to which Buchan had been drawn as early as *John Burnet of Barns*) was the critical period, and Montrose was at the heart of its tensions, debating in himself the issues of the day. In tracing his course, Buchan was tracing something of the past of every Scot, untangling the threads that had gone to make the fabric of the society into which he was born. Much the same impulse is behind Stevenson's writing of the Scottish past, behind Edwin Muir in his 'Scotland, 1941':

> We were a tribe, a family, a people.
> Wallace and Bruce guard now a painted field,
> And all may read the folio of our fable,
> Peruse the sword, the sceptre and the shield,
> A simple sky roofed in that rustic day,
> The busy corn-fields and the haunted holms,
> The green road winding up the ferny brae.
> But Knox and Melville clapped their preaching palms
> And bundled all the harvesters away,
> Hoodicrow Peden in the blighted corn
> Hacked with his rusty beak the starving haulms.
> Out of that desolation we were born.

Montrose was a true son of the Kirk, yet free of its unlovely aspects, the fanaticism, philistinism, and pride. ('It is greatly creditable to you as a true Scot,' Bishop Hensley Henson told Buchan, 'to exhibit so frankly the repulsive features of the early Presbyterians,' and the comment of that latter-day Scottish Cavalier R. B. Cunninghame Graham was 'What a terrible land to live in Scotland must have been under the Geneva discipline!')

If the 'inspired moderate' Montrose, and all that he stood for, had triumphed in the seventeenth century, the Scotland Buchan was born into might have been a different and more gracious country— perhaps a country from which so many young men of sensibility and intelligence would not have had to go away, as Stevenson and Buchan and Edwin Muir went away. Montrose failed, and the Kirk of the arrogant fanatics won the day; but he remained a pole for the Scot who could not accept what these, so quick 'to crush the poet with an iron text,' had done to Scotland.

So, to Buchan, Montrose stood for an ideal of Scotland and also for an ideal of man. He had done the things which Buchan would like to have done, and had day-dreamed of doing; he had fought battles, set out on forlorn hopes, frequented courts, marched over mountains. He had the courage which Buchan most admired: the courage of intelligence, 'to ask questions and insist upon an answer,' the courage of 'reason and moderation, patience, gentleness and understanding.' He had brought to the solution of his country's problems 'the full powers of a sane and a balanced mind and . . . having reached his conclusion, rushed to its defence with the fire and spirit of a crusader.' He had the 'moderation which is in itself a fire, where enthusiasm burns as fiercely for the whole truth as it commonly does for half-truths, where toleration becomes not a policy but an act of religion.' He had 'that single-hearted gift for deeds which usually belongs to the man whose vigour is not impaired by thought.' In him there was no division between dream and action. ('That rarest of mortals, the iron dreamer' is the description of an early Buchan hero, Maitland in 'Fountainblue.') In an age when

> The best lack all conviction, while the worst
> Are full of passionate intensity—

Buchan's Montrose, the Presbyterian Cavalier, was a shining symbol of a life lived with intelligence, conviction, force and grace— and with an assurance of a world beyond. I say 'Buchan's Montrose' because it is arguable that Buchan (as Keith Feiling suggests in his introduction to the World's Classics edition) is in this book creator as well as historian. He has brought his Montrose to life by his study of books and manuscripts, by his experience of cold and wet and Highland hills, by his thinking about politics, by his interest in the art of war, and by feelings and loyalties about Scotland and the Kirk which ran deep in himself.

Montrose was at once recognised to be indeed Buchan's *magnum opus*, the book into which he had put more of his talents and capacities than any other: and it has since been recognised as the standard work on the subject, affecting the view of all later writers. From all the appreciations which it inspired I select that of T. E. Lawrence, who wrote from Waziristan on 26 December 1928:

For the last weeks I have been reading, inch by inch, your *Montrose*: keeping it in the Wireless Cabin, which lies between our barracks and our offices, and from which I have to collect 'in' signals several times a day. I used to take ten minutes off each time, for *Montrose*, which came as a revelation to me.

I had not suspected, from my desultory reading of the Civil War, that such a man then existed. The *style* of his last words on the gallows! and these profound memoranda on political science. I've tried to think back for other military commanders who could write like that, and I'm bothered if I can think of one: Xenophon was only a Walter Long kind of a sportsman, beside him, and J. Caesar too abstract. Your man stands out, head and shoulders.

He has been unlucky in waiting three hundred years for a real biographer: but he must be warmly happy, now, if anything of his personality can still feel. You unwrap him so skilfully, without ever getting, yourself, in our way. The long careful setting of the scene—first-rate history, incidenttally, and tingling with life, as if you'd seen it—and on top of that the swift and beautifully balanced course of action. Oh, it's a very fine thing . . .

There is great labour behind the book, which yet reads easily, for your digestion has been able to cope with all the stony facts. Your small characters (often only a word long) brighten the whole thing. Incidentally, you have been honest to see the fineness of Cromwell, under the homespun . . .

Too long, this letter. But I couldn't help telling you of the rare pleasure your book has given me. Its dignity, its exceeding gracefulness, its care for exactness, and the punctilio of your manners, fit its subject and period like a glove. You've put a very great man on a pedestal. I like it streets better than anything else of yours.

'A great man on a pedestal.' Montrose had always been a hero to Scots who accepted the anti-Covenanting tradition; Buchan, by his fairness and devotion, broke down the prejudices of many steeped in the Covenanting tradition, and made him a hero whom Scots of both sides could respect.

The stories were the most fruitful source of Buchan's literary income, and perhaps the most agreeably earned. With *The Path of the King* in 1921 began that annual series of Buchans which are discussed in the following chapter. They usually came out in the summer, so that a reader could pack them in his holiday bag, and they made possible a splendid series of summer holidays for the Buchan family.

Buchan was determined that his children should, like himself, belong to both Elsfield and Tweeddale. So in 1919 he rented Gala Lodge, a villa in Broughton, from his Aunt Aggie Robb; Mrs Buchan, Anna and Walter were at Broughton Green, where John joined them when he wanted quiet to write. In subsequent summers the children stayed with their grandmother and Aunt Anna at Gala Lodge, while the parents went off on other visits. Anna was now, under the pseudonym of O. Douglas, a popular novelist too. After her father's and Willie's deaths she had started to write a chronicle of life in a Glasgow minister's family that was remarkably like the Buchans'; had put it aside in the war, then been encouraged by John to pick it up again in the dark days after Alastair's death. Enthusiastically accepted by Hodder & Stoughton, *The Setons* had scored a great success and had won readers by its faithfully observed scenes of Glasgow life occasionally shot through with a romantic glow. Thus encouraged, Anna had started on a series of tales in which romance was allowed a freer run, though there was always a firm basis in Scottish small-town life, and she became as popular an author as her brother in Scotland and among Scots abroad. She and the children got on famously; and if she freely pillaged their words and acts for use in her stories,* she more than repaid them by giving them the best of holidays. About their grandmother the young Buchans had more complex feelings; they admired her spirit, but her sharp comments on their speech and habits, their school reports and their religious observances, often made them feel as if they were renegade Buchans, who had declined from the high standards of the native branch. They were well aware that in the games of Family Comparisons which she played with her contemporaries, in which their aunt and uncles were court cards and their father trumped everything, they rated only as twos and threes. And she could depress them by her bouts of gloom. She rather enjoyed her rôle as prophet of doom and disaster ('her pessimism,' commented a friend, 'was like the bubbles on a glass of champagne') but it could be wearing to others. 'Wee Alastair said Gran is always very miserable,' Mrs Buchan herself reported, adding 'And he spoke the truth.' But the children adored Broughton, and

* 'Fish would laugh,' a comment made by the small boy in *The Setons* when anybody got above himself, came straight from Johnnie; Fish, in fact and in fiction, being a loofah for the bath.

on the journey North from Elsfield their spirits were almost un-
bearably high. To keep them occupied on the drive, their father
would offer small sums for animals met on the road, in an ascending
scale according to their rarity: a penny for a horse, up to a shilling
for a really unlikely animal like a camel. When, to the children's
ecstasy, they once met a circus near Carlisle, the game was stopped
for ever.

Leaving the children so happily installed, John and Susan Buchan
went further North. Nearly every year they spent a week or so with
Gerard Craig-Sellar at Ardtornish in Morven, which could be
reached only by boat; and another with Ian Nelson at Glenetive,
splendid stalking-country too. In 1922 they were with Alec and
Rosalind Maitland at Letterewe on Loch Maree, and the following
year at Rhiconich and Kinlochbervie in Sutherland. Johnnie too
was becoming a very good fisherman, so in 1926 they took him with
them to Shetland. There they stayed with Charlie Dick, now minister of Unst, the most northerly island; fished for sea-trout and
watched skuas, black-backed gulls and gannets sitting in rows on
the rock of Muckle Flugga, the most northerly lighthouse in Britain.
On the Sunday Buchan gave an address in the church of Uyeasound.

Buchan enjoyed stalking, was a respectable shot with a rifle
and very quick on the hill, able to do twenty miles for several days
at a stretch. Increasingly it was the stalk he enjoyed and not the
kill; he would shoot old or deformed beasts who would perish
anyhow next winter in a snowdrift; if he were stalking a young
royal he would persist until he had him well in his sights—then let
him go. But it was as a fisherman that Buchan excelled: he could
throw a salmon-fly thirty yards and use a large greenheart rod all day.

The rod appeared to do his work for him. The perfect curve of his back
cast seemed to follow forward with the fly drawing out the long, straight
line ahead, independent of his agency. It is the hallmark of all experts that
the instrument appears to do its own work.

So Johnnie describes him; and of his father's zest he gives this
instance. They were at Ardura in Mull, with fishing rights on the
river Lussa:

That kind of small river does not seem to have a normal level. It is either
high or it is low, rising or falling. Fishing the first three inches of the spate
on the rise was a great moment. Every fish caught had sea lice on him, and
had been in the sea perhaps half an hour before. When a spate came, we
dropped everything and rushed to the river.

During our third week at Ardura the worst school report that I have ever had—and that is putting it pretty high—arrived by the somewhat erratic post. It was a terrible indictment of wayward idleness. My father was horrified by it. It was a close thundery day when the post arrived. Then the clouds broke and the whole valley was a smoking deluge of thundery rain. Within fifteen minutes it was reported that the river was rising.

My father was a fisherman first. We grabbed our rods and all four of us tumbled down to the sea pool, where there was only room for two to fish at once with any kind of elbow-room. My father went to the bottom of the pool, and I went to the neck at the top. On the bank between us my brothers watched their two corks gyrating side by side in the rising water. We lost several fish, but when we came back—soaked to the skin—we were carrying a heavy basket up the steep slope to the house. Practically nothing was said about my report after that. It was talked over briefly, but without rancour, as one might discuss an unpleasant happening, reported in the newspapers, in some part of the world where Britain had no responsibilities.

It was on that same holiday in 1927 that Buchan received a letter signed 'Three Labour M.P.s,' announcing that the writers were staying in the neighbourhood and proposed to carry out, on Buchan's ground, the poaching exploits of Leithen and his friends in *John Macnab*. 'We have had no excitement for some time and feel if we can accomplish our plan it will be almost as much fun as winning an election.' Buchan was sadly disappointed that, as he was on the point of leaving, he could not take up the challenge, for he knew that among the Clydeside M.P.s were some very fine fishermen.

The drives to and from Scotland gave the Buchans a chance to see and stay with friends on the way: sometimes they stopped in Northumberland, with the G. M. Trevelyans at Hallington, or Helen Sutherland at Rock; sometimes with the F. S. Olivers at Edgerston on its shelf of hill under Carter Bar. Retired from business, and a partial invalid—for the tuberculosis that had shadowed his life was now taking a firmer hold—happy in his Border home with his books and his sheep, Fred Oliver was writing his three-volume study of politics in the eighteenth century which he called *The Endless Adventure*.

More must be said of two other friendships of these years. Buchan's admiration for Lord Rosebery dated back to his boyhood, his acquaintance with him to his Oxford days (perhaps he had been introduced by his friend Hugh Wyndham, Rosebery's nephew). He had been tremendously impressed by Rosebery's Glasgow Rectorial Address in 1900 on the concept of Empire, and had followed, with some exasperation, his Liberal Imperial campaign.

Rosebery's speech at Chesterfield in December 1901, which Buchan read in South Africa, moved him to dissent:

Though it is a fine piece of oratory, the central position is thoroughly illogical and absurd. I wrote him a long letter on Saturday and told him so.

Rosebery's answer was not convincing, 'but he writes a very kind, pleasant letter.' A few years later Buchan enlisted Rosebery's interest in the *Scottish Review* and in the memorial to Wolfe and Montcalm which he was helping to organise, as Britain's gift to Canada on the tercentenary of Quebec: 'We simply cannot do without your name.' He was fascinated by Rosebery's combination of gifts, and by his romanticism: 'he asks too much from politics, and therefore he can never be a great asset to a party.' And he applauded him as a Scottish patriot, writing (in 1908) that

he is identified as no other man is with the politics of Scotland, regarded as a separate unit in our federated Britain. He knows and loves her traditions; he is jealous of her old ways and customs; he would welcome a distinctively Scottish civilisation, with Edinburgh as its centre.

In the years before the war, when the Buchans were on holiday in the Borders, there had been walks with Rosebery on the Moorfoot Hills near the old house called Rosebery; the dedication of *The Northern Muse* is 'To Lord Rosebery, in memory of the green bounds of Tweeddale and Lothian.' But it was after the war, when Rosebery was old and broken by the death of his son Neil, that Buchan became most intimate with him. He would lunch in Berkeley Square, or go down for an afternoon or evening to The Durdans, and accompany the old man on the long drives with which he tried to fight insomnia. Buchan felt that Rosebery's 'cosseted life' had made him hopelessly wrong about the present and unnecessarily gloomy about the future, but Rosebery appealed strongly to his sense of history. Listening to his talk, Buchan could recreate the world of Gladstone and Bismarck; noting his measured conversation—'he spoke finished prose as compared with the slovenly patois of most of us'—Buchan felt he was with 'some *revenant* from the eighteenth century.' He was intrigued by the duality of Rosebery: 'the polished eighteenth-century grandee who loved the apparatus of life, and the seventeenth-century Scottish Calvinist who saw only its triviality.' He wrung from Rosebery a rather grudging permission to make a collection of his articles and speeches.* Rosebery insisted on the royalties all going to Buchan,

* *Miscellanies, Literary and Historical* (2 vols., 1921).

who used some of the money to restore the little temple at Elsfield,

where Dr Johnson (*teste* Boswell) used to drink tea. It is falling into a sad disrepair, and the pious duty of preserving it shall be performed vicariously by you.

The rest was to go 'to help some of the honest men I am always coming across who have been knocked about by the war and these beastly times.'

Buchan wrote letters to cheer him up, such as this account of a Royal visit to Peebles in the summer of 1923: Buchan had been called in to help with the arrangements when his brother Walter, the Town Clerk, was put out of action by a fall.

It was blisteringly hot, with an Italian sky, and the clean little town looked uncommonly pretty. Owing to their having an annual Beltane festival, they have any amount of bunting, and the place was covered with flags. . . .

Comedy was not wanting. Michael Thorburn of Glenormiston, a local manufacturer, had discovered that he held Glenormiston from the Crown by the grant of a red rose whenever the King visited Tweedside. This he insisted on presenting. Practically every piece of land in Peeblesshire is held on similar tenure, and if other lairds had insisted upon this duty, His Majesty would have progressed through the shire at about a mile an hour and had his car filled with gifts of porridge sticks, hens, ducks, swords and goodness knows what else. The King wandered about dangling the red rose of Glenormiston, very like Prince Bulbo in *The Rose and the Ring*. . . .

I think it was all a tremendous success, and it gave infinite pleasure to Tweedside. Every clachan was *en fête*. If loyalty languishes anywhere in these islands, it is not on the Borders.

Their last drive together was in the spring of 1929. Buchan, back in politics, vigorous and sanguine, was about to start off on a tour of election speeches in Scotland. Rosebery, a political ghost, could see no hope. 'I had never seen Surrey so green and flowery,' Buchan remembered,

but he was unconscious of the spring glories and was sunk in sad and silent meditations. When news of his death came a fortnight later I could not regret that my old friend was free of his bondage.

The other friendship was with T. E. Lawrence, who has already appeared in this biography riding up to Elsfield on his Boanerges. He never gave any warning of his coming, and would just slip in diffidently. Alastair Buchan remembers a Sunday morning when the family came home from church to be told by the butler 'There was a man in Air Force uniform on a motor-cycle who wanted to see you, sir, but he wouldn't state his business, and so I sent him away,' and how absolutely furious his father was.

Buchan admired Lawrence immensely—'You are the only person I have ever known before whom I feel shy'—and loved him because 'there seemed to be reborn in him all the lost friends of my youth.' Rosebery appealed to his sense of history, Lawrence to his sense of adventurous and romantic possibility. Like Buchan's admired Montrose, Lawrence was a man of action who was also articulate and introspective. 'Here was an Odyssey and an Iliad combined completed before the age of thirty,' wrote Buchan in a review of *Revolt in the Desert*.

But the book is not an epic, for there is none of the gusto and swing of epic. The scholar has become a superb man of action, but he remains a scholar —reflective, sensitive, tormenting himself with doubts and subtleties, analysing each emotion with a terrible precision. He stands outside himself and comments like an impartial spectator. It is his psychological profundity which makes his book so great a piece of literature. Lawrence owed his success mainly to the fact that his dream rode him like a passion.

Buchan wrote at some length about Lawrence in *Memory Hold-the-Door*, but said nothing there about the help he was once able to give him. The two met by chance in the street one day in the spring of 1925, and Lawrence, then in the Tank Corps, spoke of his wish to get back into the R.A.F. A few days later he wrote to Buchan:

I don't know by what right I made that appeal to you on Sunday. It happened on the spur of the moment. You see, for seven years it's been my ambition to get into the Air Force, (and for six months in 1922 I realised the ambition), and I can't get the longing for it out of my mind for an hour.

After giving his reasons for wanting to be in the R.A.F., Lawrence ended:

There, it's a shame to bother you with all this rant: but the business is vital to me; and if you can help to straighten it out, the profit to me will far outweigh, in my eyes, any inconvenience to which you put yourself!

Buchan at once wrote to Baldwin, who answered wryly 'Come and see me about that exceedingly difficult friend of yours'—Bernard Shaw too had been at him about Lawrence—but agreed to help, and in due course Lawrence had his wish. 'Back to R.A.F. by Buchan's influence with Baldwin against Hoare's will' was his summary to Captain Liddell Hart, and to Buchan he wrote:

The immediate effect of this news was to put me lazily and smoothly asleep:

and asleep I've been ever since. It's like a sudden port, after a voyage all out of reckoning.

I owe you the very deepest thanks.

Early in 1927 he sent Buchan two copies of the limited edition of *Seven Pillars of Wisdom*—one for himself, one for Baldwin. Lawrence also felt he owed it to Buchan to report progress, so in June 1927 he wrote from Karachi:

It will amuse you to know that my satisfaction with R.A.F. life keeps me contented in this dismal station and country. We spend much of our time playing infantry-games! However it is only for a term of years: and my appetite for England will grow and grow and grow, till, upon return, I'll lie down in the Strand and start eating the pavement in hungry delight. With any luck I'll have three years more to serve, after I get home. They will be great years.

In December 1928 he was at Miranshah Fort, Waziristan:

I wanted you to know that I am making the best use I can of the gift you led Mr Baldwin into giving me in 1925. The R.A.F. still suits me all over, as a home: quaint, that is, for it's probably not everyone's prescription.

Six years later he reported from Bridlington in Yorkshire:

If you meet Mr Baldwin in the near future, will you please tell him that the return to the Air Force secured me by him (on your initiation) has given me the only really contented years of my life? Please say that I've worked (and played) all the time like a trooper.

After specifying some of the achievements of these years, Lawrence goes on:

I tell you all this not to boast of it, but to show that you and Baldwin, in gratifying what may have seemed to you my indulgence, have not harmed the public service. I have done all I could, always; and could have done far more, if they had given me more rope. The Air Force is pretty good, down below. I think it deserves more imaginative handling than it gets.

However this note (meant to be a paean of gratitude to two admirable men) mustn't descend into politics. I owe the two of you more than my twelve years work (and another twelve on top of it, were I young enough) in the sheer satisfaction it has been. You have me very hopelessly in your debt; and thank you both very much for it. . . .

Some day I'm going to ask another favour—that you will read my notes on the making of an airman, about 60,000 words of typescript, that date from 1922. They aren't to be published: but I rather suspect that as writing they are almost good—or at least a sight better than my previous attempts at your art! I would value (and keep very dark) your real opinion.

On the day of his discharge in February 1935 Lawrence sent Buchan a typescript of *The Mint*; and on his way from Bridlington to

Dorset by push-bike he looked in at Elsfield, and impressed Buchan
with his splendid health and calm nerves. *The Mint* also impressed:
Buchan considered it 'an amazing picture of the beginning of a
new service,' reiterated his conviction that Lawrence was a great
natural writer, and suggested that, now he had retired from the
R.A.F., he should tackle a biography. Lawrence was delighted—
'I had banked a good deal on your opinion'—and said he had
once contemplated a biography of Sir Roger Casement, but had
given up the idea as he could not have access to the Casement
diaries. This warm, affectionate letter, wishing Buchan well in *his*
next step, was written from Lawrence's cottage Clouds Hill, on
1 April 1935. A few weeks later Lawrence was dead.

In the autumn of 1924 a new prospect opened when Buchan made
his first visit to America. There was some Reuter business to be
done in New York; he had been invited to give the Commemoration
Address at Milton Academy and, once it was known he was crossing
the Atlantic, further invitations followed. Most of them he rejected:
he did not want to go to America just to work, or to make money;
he tremendously wanted to know the country. When he said he was
'going to America for a holiday,' many of his friends and in-laws
were surprised. At that date there were very few people in British
public life with a serious interest in American history and politics.
Apart from the occasional sensation of a spectacular international
marriage, the English upper classes were on the whole profoundly
uninterested and incurious about the United States, and their anti-
Americanism was reinforced by the failure of the States to join the
League of Nations and by the negotiations over the War Debt. To
go to America for pleasure was to them an unusual idea.

For Buchan, as for so many of his contemporaries, Europe had
become identified with the horrors of the Western Front, and he
had no wish to go to the Continent for his holidays; but he was full
of curiosity about America, for he felt that over the Atlantic lay
some of our future. One of the reasons for his impatience with all
schemes to establish any centralised Imperial organisation was that
this would sharply mark off the countries of the Empire from the
United States. He was convinced, as he said in 1917, that 'the
alliance of America and Britain will be the greatest safeguard for
the peaceful ordering of the world,' and he wanted all the countries
of the Empire to be able to work closely with the United States in
many fields. This, he felt sure, could best be realised if they them-

selves were associated in a loose and flexible arrangement rather than a formal constitution.

Buchan's interest in the United States went back a long way. Perhaps his Newdigate Prize poem on the Pilgrim Fathers should not count, for the subject had been imposed. But as a young man he had responded enthusiastically to Thoreau and Whitman; his political thinking had been greatly influenced by F. S. Oliver's study of Alexander Hamilton. His interest in American history had been the source of several tales. In the short story 'The Company of the Marjolaine' he makes four members of the Philadelphia Convention visit Charles Edward Stuart in his exile in Italy, with the idea of offering him a crown in America. ('We have got rid of a king who misgoverned us, but we have no wish to get rid of kingship.') One look at the elderly toper sends the delegates back to America and a Republic. *Salute to Adventurers*, written just before the war, is about a young Glasgow merchant in the tobacco trade in Virginia. The scenes in the Jamestown manors, in the great forests inland, on the Blue Ridge and among the Carolina keys, are evoked with vividness and accuracy remarkable in a writer who had never crossed the Atlantic. Buchan's interest in the Civil War, which had started with a reading at Oxford of Colonel Henderson's *Stonewall Jackson*, had been fanned by talks with Susan's uncle Sir Reginald Talbot, who as a young soldier had been attached to Sheridan's staff. One of Buchan's long-term ambitions was to write a life of Lee, 'the greatest of the great' as he called him in the dedicatory poem to *Salute to Adventurers*. 'I would rather write that life than do any other piece of literary work I can think of,' he told the American author Gamaliel Bradford, with whom, just before his visit, he was corresponding about books and papers on the subject. In 1916 Buchan had lectured on the parallels between the Civil War and the present struggle, making the point that 'when the full strength of the North was made available and used, victory was assured.' The Civil War was the subject of lectures he gave after the war—to Workers' Educational Association meetings, to historical societies, to the Royal Institution. In his *Spectator* days he had written a number of articles on current American politics, such as 'President Roosevelt and the Senate' and 'The Monroe Doctrine in Practice.'

Whenever an American had appeared in Buchan's fiction—Mrs Yorke in *A Lodge in the Wilderness* (1906), Virginia Dasent in 'The Green Glen' (1912), Scudder in *The Thirty-Nine Steps* (1915),

Blenkiron in *Greenmantle* (1916) and *Mr Standfast* (1918), the banker
Julius Victor in *The Three Hostages* (1924), he or she had been a
sympathetic character; shrewd, sensitive, decent. Lincoln was one
of Buchan's great heroes. In 1917, after America's entry into the
war, he tried to organise a function in Edinburgh on Independence
Day, at the statue of Lincoln in the Calton Burial Ground, the first
of him to be erected in Europe. 'It is a little difficult for Britons to
celebrate the Fourth of July which commemorates our defeat, but
we can all celebrate the memory of Lincoln.' His admiration had
been manifest in the historical fantasy *The Path of the King* (1921),
which sprang from 'the notion that no man knows his ancestry, and
that kingly blood may lie dormant for centuries until the appointed
time.' The incidents begin with a Viking's son lost in a raid on the
coast of Normandy, and end with Lincoln. He is seen, in the epi-
logue, through the eyes of a young English diplomat who watches
Lincoln's funeral procession in Washington in the company of
James Russell Lowell, and is shaken out of his usual urbane detachment.

He found himself regarding the brilliant career which he had planned for
himself with a sudden disfavour. It was only second-rate after all, that
glittering old world of courts and legislatures and embassies. For a moment
he had had a glimpse of the first-rate, and it had shivered his pretty palaces.
He wanted now something which he did not think he would find again.

And when Lowell comments 'There goes the first American,' the
Englishman replies 'I think it is also the last of the Kings.' Later,
in *The Blanket of the Dark*, Buchan linked Daniel Boone with the
royal Bohuns.

For Canada, where he was to land first, Buchan was also well
prepared. He had a Scot's interest in the country that Scots have
had such a hand in shaping. As a disciple of Milner, he had thought
much about Canada's place in the Empire; had introduced a
Canadian statesman into the discussion in *A Lodge in the Wilderness*;
had written on Canadian relations with Britain in the *Spectator* and
the *Scottish Review*. Recently his work on Lord Minto had given
him some knowledge of Canadian politics at the turn of the century. He was very friendly with Lord Byng, the Governor-General
of the time, whom he had known in South Africa and in France.
He had met Mackenzie King the previous autumn at Chats-
worth, when the Duke of Devonshire had entertained the Dominion
Prime Ministers, then meeting in London—'You and John were
out and away the nicest people he had met in England,' Violet

Markham told Susan—and now Mackenzie King had invited the Buchans to stay with him in Ottawa.

They sailed at the end of August in the *Empress of France*, landing at Quebec, and spending a few days at Grand Metis with Robert Reford of the Cunard Line. Then they went on to Ottawa, whence Susan wrote on 14 September:

The Prime Minister, Mackenzie King, met us, and several other ministers. We are staying in a house which Sir Wilfrid Laurier left him— most comfortable. He is extraordinarily kind, and gave a dinner-party for us last night. Today we are motoring down to his country-house.

From Ottawa the Buchans went to Boston, and were taken under the wing of Ferris Greenslet, a wartime friend of Buchan's, and partner in Houghton Mifflin, which had just secured *The Three Hostages* (thereafter nearly all of Buchan's books appeared in America with Houghton Mifflin). He escorted them to Washington, where Buchan had an interview with President Wilson and did homage to his two great American heroes. He considered the Lincoln Memorial 'the most beautiful architectural work I know,' and was charmed by Lee's 'little manor' of Arlington. Then they were joined by the historian Samuel Eliot Morison and with him made a ten-day tour of the battlefields of Virginia.

Ferris Greenslet has described the trip in *Under the Bridge*:

We drove through the fat fields of Maryland to Antietam and Harper's Ferry, and up the valley of the Shenandoah. Equipped with old Confederate battle maps, we followed the marching and counter-marching of Stonewall Jackson's Valley campaign. At Port Republic, we approached a house marked on the map 'Lewis House,' and found old Miss Lewis sitting on the piazza where she had sat, a young girl, on a June day in 1862, and seen Wheat's Tigers of Taylor's Louisiana Brigade burst from the woods back of the house to capture a Massachusetts battery on its front.

To my Brady and Frank Leslie's-own-artist-in-the-field-fed imagination, the Valley Pike and the wood roads that climb through the gaps of the Blue Ridge and the Massanuttens were thronged with thin, bearded men in shabby grey uniforms. But it was John who told us, told even Sam Morison, who had joined us at Washington, the names of the mountains without looking at the map.

From Staunton, we drove to Charlottesville, pausing at 'Mirador' for a glass of Langhorne Madeira; then on to Richmond, and under the expert guidance of Douglas Freeman, covered the terrain of the Seven Days, from the Chickahominy to Malvern Hill. There John decided to leave to Freeman the biography of Lee on the scale of Henderson's *Stonewall Jackson*, that he had long planned to undertake. We visited the great houses along the James, Westover, and Shirley, and turned north again through Fredericksburg to Washington.

(Douglas Freeman, editor of the Richmond *News-Leader* and a great liberal figure in Virginia, published his biography of Lee in 1934.)

Then followed Philadelphia, and an address to the Transatlantic Society, and a few days in New York, with much Reuter business ('our colleagues of Associated Press . . . protected me nobly from interviewers') and a lunch at the Century Club given for Buchan by General Harbord. Then Boston again, this time in Brattle Street as the guest of Roger Merriman, the Balliol friend whom Buchan had once rescued in the Brasenose quad, and who was now head of Eliot House. With the Merrimans the Buchans dined with the President of Harvard, saw their first football game ('a gory scene'), visited Plymouth Rock and Groton (where Buchan startled Dan Merriman by his knowledge of American birds and trees), and dined with 'Miss Amy Lowell the poetess. A wonderful house and an amazing library, but we thought her rather a tiresome egotist.' Then the Greenslets motored the Buchans to New Hampshire, where they stayed in a farmhouse, renewed acquaintance with Mrs Walter Page next door, and climbed Mount Chocorua. 'The view was beyond belief,' wrote Buchan, 'from Vermont to the sea and from Maine to Massachusetts—the whole country like a marvellous Persian carpet of autumn colours. I have never had such a Pisgah sight in my life.' He came back to give his Foundation Address at Milton, which had been the original occasion for his visit.

Two things particularly impressed Buchan in the United States: enthusiasm for education, and a search for quality in every field. He became a sharp critic of English anti-Americanism, and many years later, when his youngest son was making plans for a year at the University of Virginia, Buchan wrote 'I want you to be, like me, a real lover of America.'

In late October the Buchans were back in Canada, for a visit to the Byngs at Government House, and a round of lunches, dinners and speeches in Ottawa, Montreal and Toronto. They met Canada's wartime Prime Minister, Sir Robert Borden, and General Sir Arthur Currie, now Principal of McGill. At Toronto they stayed with the Vincent Masseys—Buchan had particularly wanted to see Hart House, a centre for graduates and undergraduates of the University of Toronto which Massey had founded and named after his grandfather. Among the topics touched on in his speeches were Canada's rôle in the Empire, and the first Labour Government in Britain—he stressed that the Labour Ministers were no Bolsheviks but competent and responsible statesmen ('the miner of today is as capable a legislator as the duke of yesterday'). Although there was some criticism of the delivery of the speeches (his audience often found him hard to hear) the general impression was most favourable. In a leader the *Ottawa Citizen* expressed appreciation of Buchan at the expense of some other British visitors:

Some of our kinsmen from over the water have the unhappy faculty of rubbing us the wrong way. It is not that they criticize Canada and things Canadian, for Canadians as a rule accept criticism without undue irritation. . . . But the attitude that really hurts, that might if there was too much of it completely sour the relations of Canadians and Old Countrymen, is the attitude of unconscious superiority that one finds particularly in a certain type of Englishman. He does not mean to be offensive, he would be shocked if you suggested that he was offensive, and just because that is so he is most irritatingly offensive.

Now a man like John Buchan is the complete antithesis of this type.

The article went on to list the things they liked in Buchan: his curiosity, sincerity and modesty.

So well rooted himself—in the Borders by birth, in Oxfordshire by choice—Buchan had a special feeling for other people's roots, and an interest in the ties that bound them to *their* Broughtons and Elsfields. He was firmly patriotic, but I do not think he ever felt that a man was unlucky *not* to have been born in the British Isles. Certainly he and his wife deeply appreciated 'that special feeling of being fêted that one only has in North America,' and missed it after coming back to the bleaker social atmosphere of Britain.

Soon after his return home Buchan received an enthusiastic letter from Lord Byng reporting 'the inundation of nice things said about you, your visit and your speech at the Canadian Clubs here and elsewhere . . . Dear John, you said the right thing at the right time, in the right way.' The success of his visit to Canada led to a further development. The Buchans' old friend Violet Markham had known Mackenzie King since 1905 when she was staying with the Greys in Government House, and Lord Grey had brought a young man over to her at a party, saying she must meet a future Prime Minister. Now, elated that her three friends had got on so well together, delighted at the good reports of Buchan from Canada, Miss Markham conceived the idea in the autumn of 1925 that Buchan should succeed Byng as Governor-General: he would be such a healthy change from 'the correct and conventional peer usually selected for these posts.' She put it to Mackenzie King, who much liked the idea but pointed out that the nomination of a new Governor-General for the King to appoint lay with the British Government. However, he had asked Baldwin to send him the suggested names for approval, and would certainly like Buchan's to be added to the list. Miss Markham, who made it clear that she was acting as 'an unofficial post-box' for making Mackenzie King's views known to the British Government, then approached the Colonial Secretary, L. S. Amery, in April 1926. Although he had seen a lot of Buchan recently, Amery was entirely taken by surprise at the suggestion. Miss Markham also approached Amery's immediate predecessor at the Colonial Office, the Duke of Devonshire, who thought it a good idea, and told Baldwin so.

Buchan himself responded warily, and made it clear that he would not lift a finger to canvass for such a job. 'John says it is impossible for him to do what M.K. suggests,' Susan told Miss Markham:

> He can only accept the thing if it was *strongly* put to him as a matter of duty without any attempt on his part to get it. He says the point is theological and that you will understand it!

As Mackenzie King continued to press the matter, further reasons for wariness became apparent. In the summer of 1926 Canada faced a constitutional crisis. The previous autumn Mackenzie King's Liberal Party had come second at the polls to the Conservatives under Arthur Meighen. King however did not offer to resign, for he counted on the support of the Progressive and Labour groups to give him a majority in Parliament. The following June, in the knowledge that a Conservative vote of censure would be carried, King asked the Governor-General for a dissolution. Byng refused on the ground that Meighen could carry on in the same Parliament, and when Mackenzie King resigned, invited Meighen to form a Government. This Government Mackenzie King brought down on the technical point (on which Meighen did not receive Progressive support) that none of the new Ministers had taken the oath of office. Meighen then asked for a dissolution, and this time, to Mackenzie King's rage, it was granted.

With Byng at the centre of a constitutional storm, and at loggerheads with his Prime Minister, the Governor-General's job did not appear particularly enviable. Buchan, who heard a good deal of the story direct from Byng, had no wish to embroil himself. So it was without regret that he saw Lord Willingdon succeed to the Governor-Generalship in the autumn of 1926.

CHAPTER TEN

STORY-TELLER

'I suppose I was a natural story-teller, the kind of man who for the sake of his yarns would in prehistoric days have been given a seat by the fire and a special chunk of mammoth.'

John Buchan: *Memory Hold-the-Door*

Every summer from 1922 to 1936 there appeared 'a new Buchan': a story, or group of short stories, of adventure and suspense. They were part of Buchan's financial plan; his budget depended upon so much revenue a year from the new book, and from cheap editions of earlier ones. To produce one a year was a wholly delightful necessity. The tale would be clear in his mind before he put a word on paper; at week-ends or on holidays, whenever he could find a stretch of a few days, he would write it out, with very few corrections, in an unlined manuscript book of foolscap size, noting at the end the date and place of composition. On *The Three Hostages*, for instance, he noted 'Begun (as *Enchanter's Nightmare*) Finchcox, May 1922. Finished Elsfield May 1923'; on *The Island of Sheep* 'Begun Feb. 1934. Written at Elsfield and finished with difficulty in May 1935 after my appointment to Canada.' Then the manuscript would be sent to Mrs Candy, one of the few who could read Buchan's increasingly cryptic handwriting, and the perfectly typed copy would reach Hodder & Stoughton round about 1 December for publication the following summer.

Early in *The Three Hostages* Buchan makes the far-travelled Dr Greenslade give a recipe that fits his own practice:

'I want to write a shocker, so I begin by fixing on one or two facts which have no sort of obvious connexion . . . Let us take three things a long way apart . . . say, an old blind woman spinning in the Western Highlands, a barn in a Norwegian *saeter*, and a little curiosity shop in North London kept by a Jew with a dyed beard. Not much connexion between the three? You invent a connexion—simple enough if you have any imagination, and you weave all three into the yarn. The reader, who knows nothing about the three at the start, is puzzled and intrigued and, if the story is well arranged, finally satisfied. He is pleased with the ingenuity of the solution, for he doesn't realise that the author fixed upon the solution first, and then invented a problem to suit it.'

And in the dedication of *The Thirty-Nine Steps* to Tommy Nelson Buchan said that his aim was to write 'romance where the incidents defy the probabilities, and march just inside the borders of the possible.' 'That's a pretty good formula for the thriller of any kind,' said Raymond Chandler when he read the passage. It served Buchan well for the historical no less than the contemporary stories, and to it he added the ingredients that mark the special Buchan product: an authentically rendered background, romantic yet not preposterous characters, an atmosphere of expectancy, a sense of world-wide conspiracies and of old magics, the mixture laced with a current enthusiasm of his own.* Such shockers—I use Buchan's own name for them—were, he told E. C. Bentley, 'twenty times easier than writing a detective story, like *Trent's Last Case*.'

Buchan wrote his stories with ease and dash because these special ingredients came from his own temperament and experience. Like Jaikie in *Castle Gay*, 'he had the gift of living for the moment where troubles were concerned and not anticipating them, but in pleasant things of letting his fancy fly happily ahead.' He had a perpetual sanguine looking-forward, a faith in possibilities. He had some highly-coloured acquaintances to draw upon, and a varied experience to put to use. I have been continuously interested, in writing his life, to discover facts and incidents which turn up in his stories: to learn that Buchan, like the sinister Mr Lumley of *The Power-House*, collected Wedgwood; that Susan once worked in Gospel Oak, where Buchan placed the blind spinner of *The Three Hostages*; that in 1917, before Richard Hannay met his future wife at Fosse Manor, Buchan and his wife stayed at Fossebridge.

Although it was the war thrillers that gave Buchan his name and his public, it was in his first attempt in the Phillips Oppenheim vein, *The Power-House* (1916), written in the smooth days before the war and published in *Blackwood's* in 1913, that he worked out the formula which was to serve him for twenty years. There had been references to the thinness of civilisation in his early collection of stories, *The Watcher by the Threshold* (1902); to Maitland, in

* Or of his family. Almost the only Buchan enthusiasm not represented is Susan Buchan's for the Women's Institutes. To bring the W.I. into a thriller was left for Buchan's follower, Michael Innes, in *The Secret Vanguard* (1940).

'Fountainblue,' the division 'between the warm room and the savage out-of-doors' is no more than 'a line, a thread, a sheet of glass;' in the title-story the face of Justinian suggests 'the intangible mystery of culture on the verge of savagery.' In *The Power-House* this notion is central.

'You think that a wall as solid as the earth separates civilisation from barbarism. I tell you the division is a thread, a sheet of glass. A touch here, a push there, and you bring back the reign of Saturn.'

So says Mr Lumley whose Power-House is to supply the touching and the pushing. Leithen is made to experience the fragility of this division without moving from his familiar London (Buchan shows himself as much at home in the alleys, mews, and backways of W.1, W.2 and S.W.1 as ever he was on the tracks of Tweeddale). Entrenched in his work at the Bar and in Parliament, Leithen has stranger adventures, and narrower escapes, than Tommy Deloraine who goes off to Bokhara. As he sniffs the summer smell of town— 'a mixture of tar, flowers, dust, and patchouli'—he feels this is 'the homely London I knew so well, and I was somehow an exile from it.' Walking up Piccadilly at the height of the season with friends sitting at club-windows and policemen at hand, but aware of the executives of the Power-House all round him, he is startled by his vulnerability.

Now I saw how thin is the protection of civilisation. An accident and a bogus ambulance—a false charge and a bogus arrest—there were a dozen ways of spiriting me out of this gay, bustling world.

Other motifs appear which also were to serve Buchan well. The villain's disguise is to be 'above suspicion, an honourable and distinguished gentleman, belonging to the best clubs, counting as [his] acquaintances the flower of our society.' And the man who finally beats him has 'a good commonplace intelligence' but also 'a quite irrelevant gift of imagination' and is 'a foursquare being bedded in the concrete of our civilization.'

The formula satisfied. 'Though it is Sunday and I am Professor of Divinity,' wrote a Glasgow reader,

I must tell you I have just finished *The Power-House* having read it through at top speed. You seem to me to have struck a vein such as opened to Gaboriau and Du Boisgobey, which were the favourite reading of Prince Bismarck and me! You make London a city of romance, as they did Paris.

The model for Richard Hannay of *The Thirty-Nine Steps* was Ironside, the soldier whom Buchan had first met in South Africa.

Ironside, six foot four inches high and known as 'Tiny,' could speak fourteen languages including Cape Dutch or *taal*. He had fought through the Boer War, escorted Smuts to the peace conference at Vereeniging, and then done intelligence work in German South-West Africa. (Hannay in *Greenmantle* 'knows all about Damaraland'.) Disguised as a Boer transport-driver and speaking such good *taal* that he was unsuspected by the genuine Boers under him, he had accompanied a German military expedition against the Hereros. Several times—once when a German officer spotted his real name on the collar of his dog—he was on the brink of being discovered, but he bluffed through and was awarded a German military medal before disappearing back to British South Africa. In 1914 he was the first British officer in uniform to land in France, and spent the whole of the war on the Western Front till 1918, when he was sent to command the Allied expedition to Archangel. After the war there was a mission to Hungary and a hand in drawing up its frontiers, the command of mixed Allied troops on the Ismid Peninsula against what might be a Turkish uprising; and of forces in North Persia against a possible Bolshevik invasion, then promotion to Major-General, the youngest in the British Army. Like Hannay, he never worried much about comfort, and like Hannay's ally Blenkiron, when he wanted to think out a problem he would sit and play patience.

There was one significant difference between fact and story. Where real-life Ironside met adventure in the way of his profession, fictional Hannay of *The Thirty-Nine Steps* is the peaceful civilian who is drawn into adventure accidentally. This solid and respectable citizen finds himself hunted by the police, and slowly it is borne in on him that solidity and respectability are no defence against the powers of evil and disorder. He, too, is made aware of the thinness of civilisation; in a twinkling he is beyond the protection of the law. Before the final climax in a Buchan tale there is often a pre-climax, when the hero is no longer playing a lone hand but is once more fighting the enemy with the resources of law and order behind him.

Into the hunt Buchan crammed a mass of his own experience. There are the Galloway walking-tours and the nights in shepherds' cottages, the political meetings in the Masonic Halls of Border towns which gave him 'The Adventure of the Radical Candidate.' In 'The Literary Innkeeper' who wants

'to see life, to travel the world, and write things like Kipling and Conrad. But the most I've done yet is to get some verses printed in *Chambers's Journal*—'

Buchan looks back at himself aged eighteen. When at last Hannay contacts law and order in the person of Sir Walter Bullivant, it is by the waters of the Kennet, where Buchan had stayed with the Gathorne-Hardys. The final unmasking of the enemy is in such a villa, with steps leading down to the beach, as that where Buchan lay in bed in August 1914. Here and there he has taken something from a favourite author. Hannay's scorching hours on the roof of the dovecot after he has blown his way with gelignite out of the house of the bald archaeologist recall Alan Breck and Davie Balfour on the top of the rock in Glencoe while soldiers search the moor beneath.* To E. Phillips Oppenheim he perhaps owed his fine fictional nerve; this blasting feat of Hannay's (but there is logic in it too, for he is a mining engineer), and the impersonation of the First Lord of the Admiralty by a German spy, certainly 'defy the probabilities and march just inside the borders of the possible.' But the special Buchan marks are here: the theme of a far-flung conspiracy—

I got the first hint in an inn on the Achensee in Tyrol. That set me inquiring, and I collected my other clues in a fur shop in the Galician quarter of Buda, in a Strangers' Club in Vienna and in a little bookshop off the Racknitzstrasse in Leipsic. I completed my evidence ten days ago in Paris—

and the sense that the worst of enemies may have something in him to admire:

A white fanatic heat burned in them, and I realized for the first time the terrible thing I had been up against. This man was more than a spy; in his foul way he was a patriot.

In *Greenmantle* Hannay is joined by Sandy Arbuthnot, whose prototype was as startling a man as Ironside. Something has already been said in Chapter Nine about Aubrey Herbert's exploits in the war, but his adventures had started many years earlier when he travelled in Albania, Greece, Turkey and Arabia, making friends everywhere (to quote his friend St John Lucas) 'with the most extraordinary heroes and ruffians, facing danger and discomfort with a zest that never failed, revelling in life.' Many passages in his record of these travels, *Ben Kendim* (1924), read like Franklin P. Scudder on the machinations of the Black Stone. This is of Salonika about 1910:

The coming storm had not yet broken, but already its mutterings were to be heard. The Grand Orient [the chief Masonic Lodge of the Near East]

---

* Lord Attlee pointed out this similarity to me.

was at work. There were links between New York and the bootblacks of Salonika, and again between Salonika and the unruly Albanians. Talaat was studying the literature of the French Revolution; Karasso was engaged in Freemasonry; Enver, in the mountains of Macedonia or in a sailing-boat in the Gulf, was engrossed in tactics.

And here is the opening of a chapter on the Yemen:

One day, early in 1905, I met Leland Buxton in the lobby of the House of Commons, and, in ten minutes' conversation, we decided that we would try to reach Sanaa, the capital of the ancient Arabia Felix and of the modern province of Yemen. . . . We met again in Cairo, in the full glare of Egyptian August. Buxton had just come from fighting the Turks in Macedonia, with Bulgarian bands, and had not more than a few months to dispose of, so we made our plans quickly.

With the real Aubrey Herbert in view—an aristocrat who looked like a tramp, a master of languages, a champion of minority views, a hopelessly short-sighted man who had got himself into the B.E.F. in 1914 by putting on khaki and joining a battalion of the Irish Guards as it swung out of Wellington Barracks, who was invited by the Albanians of America to command the regiment they had raised —Buchan had little need to invent. Sandy is one of the best documented, as well as one of the least probable, of Buchan's creations.*

The two other main characters of *Greenmantle*, Blenkiron and Peter Pienaar, were based on types rather than individuals. Peter Pienaar was the kind of Boer whom Buchan liked; independent, crafty, religious in a simple Bible way, brave, a tremendous hunter, a bit of a rascal as well as a hero. Blenkiron was drawn from the American journalists and businessmen whom Buchan had worked with and liked in the war, and was made sympathetic to the reader by being saddled with Buchan's own duodenal complaint—so realistically that a London surgeon wrote bidding Buchan himself hasten off to the Mayo Brothers' clinic. After their separate adventures these four characters, drawn from such different worlds, come together to fight for a common cause; having played their lone hands and won, they are once more back with their own side.

Remember that for three months we had been with the enemy and had never seen the face of an Ally in arms. We had been cut off from the

---

* Saki's Tom Keriway in *The Unbearable Bassington* (1912) may also have owed something to Aubrey Herbert. Keriway had 'wandered through Hungarian horse-fairs, hunted shy crafty beasts on lonely Balkan hillsides, dropped himself pebble-wise into the stagnant human pool of some Bulgarian monastery, threaded his way through the strange racial mosaic of Salonika,' etc. Saki had been in the Balkans in 1902 and 1903 for the *Morning Post*.

fellowship of a great cause, like a fort surrounded by an army. And now we were delivered, and there fell around us the warm joy of comradeship as well as the exultation of victory.

There is a lot of melodrama in *Greenmantle*, and the language sometimes echoes the heroics of *The Half-Hearted*—'I may be sending you to your death, Hannay—Good God, what a damned task-mistress duty is!'—but with four such characters to drive along the plot Buchan was easily outdistancing his master Phillips Oppenheim. However wild the fantasies, they had some basis in fact: the seer of the blood of the Prophet who was called Greenmantle had something in him of Gordon's Mahdi—the Expected One—and of those other religious leaders who were a constant problem to the administrations in Egypt. The Constantinople scenes combined Buchan's own memory of his visit in 1910, when he had found the city 'pure Arabian Nights,' with an Aubrey Herbertish intrigue. Perhaps the really daring innovation in *Greenmantle* is the introduction of the Kaiser—in 1916—as a sympathetic character: an imaginative man, haunted by the horrors of war, 'a human being who . . . had the power of laying himself alongside other men.' Hilda von Einem was given her due as prophetess of evil—'Mad and bad she might be, but she was also great'—but she after all was fiction; to take the Kaiser out of his stereotype as Britain's Bogey No. 1 was an altogether bolder achievement.*

Three of the four main characters of *Greenmantle*—Sandy Arbuthnot is absent on some desperate mission—reappear in *Mr Standfast* (1919). Blenkiron has been renewed by the short-circuit operation; Peter Pienaar has lost a leg like Buchan's friend Bron Herbert, and like him dies in an air-fight. In the course of the book the 'little confederacy,' as Hannay calls it, has been joined by the airman Archie Roylance, the Scots Fusilier Geordie Hamilton, Andrew Amos from the Clyde shipyards, the pacifist Launcelot Wake, and Mary Lamington, whom Hannay meets at the Cotswold manor of Fosse. The code by which they communicate is built on references to *The Pilgrim's Progress*, which Peter reads while a prisoner of the Germans, and applies to his own situation; here Buchan may have thought of his old friend Ardwall who, in his last illness, rather complacently remarked, 'I think I am like old Mr Honest in *The*

* In 1914 Buchan had written, in Chapter I of *Nelson's History of the War*, 'To future ages the Kaiser will present a curious psychological study. A man of immense energy, highly susceptible to new ideas, emotional to a fault, but essentially bold and confident, the defects of his character are as patent as its merits.'

Pilgrim's Progress, who trysted with one Good Conscience to help him over the River.'

Greenmantle was twice as long as *The Thirty-Nine Steps*, and *Mr Standfast* half as long again, with a wider range of characters and incidents. Buchan was increasing his mastery of suspense, and skirting ever nearer to the borders of the possible. Not merely boxed up in a locked room as in *The Thirty-Nine Steps*, but also gripped by an infernal vice, Hannay extricates himself coolly from the Pink Chalet. When Buchan makes the villain reveal his plans to the man whom he supposes to be at his mercy, he indulges in the hoariest of devices; but the account of the Underground Railway by which the Wild Birds nip across frontiers is in his own particular vein.

In a back street of a little town I would exchange passwords with a nameless figure and be given instructions. At a wayside inn at an appointed hour a voice speaking a thick German would advise that this bridge or that railway crossing had been cleared. At a hamlet among pine woods an unknown man would clamber up beside me and take me past a sentry-post.

The background remains firmly within his experience, except possibly for the garden city of Biggleswick, with its quacks and cranks, for which I can find no parallel in Buchan's life. The narrative moves with assurance to Clydeside and its shipyard agitators—when Hannay visits the old Border Radical Andrew Amos, it is the only description of a Glasgow tenement in Buchan—to the Coolin, to London in an air-raid, to the Alps, to the Western Front. On the way there are some sharp little sketches, of a Highland crofter with his sad tale of evictions, of a bagman travelling in 'wee religious books' for an Edinburgh publisher, of Douglas Haig himself. Buchan's expertise shines in the episodes in Skye—though W. P. Ker told him 'You travel uncommon free back and forth over the Coolin'—and in the crossing of the Col des Hirondelles, the pass from Italy to Switzerland over which Hannay, no Alpinist, is led by Launcelot Wake. It is a most convincing account not only of the terrain and the climbing, but of a novice's sensations during such a climb, with the descent as the more frightening part, and of the kind of tiredness it would produce:

I was still strung up to a mechanical activity, and I ran every inch of the three miles to the Staubthal without consciousness of fatigue. I was twenty minutes too soon for the train, and, as I sat on a bench on the platform, my energy suddenly ebbed away.

The scenes on the Western Front were the work of a man who knew, not only the disposition of brigades and battalions, but the look on the faces of men coming out of the front line 'like ghosts who had been years in muddy graves.' The story ends with the checking of the German offensive in March 1918, when all the members of the 'little confederacy' have their parts to play. Hannay's prototype Ironside *had* played an outstanding part in this action. When the Allied line was broken on the Fifth Army front he was ordered to go up to the gap with the new machine-gun battalions; with three hundred Vickers-guns and a battalion of Lewis-guns he re-established the line and broke up several German attacks. This story of Ironside and his machine-gunners may have given Buchan the nerve to make Hannay and his group of friends save the day.

'From personal knowledge I am in a position to verify practically all the details you have given of our position at the time of the German Advance,' wrote a reader of *Mr Standfast* who had been Town Major of Péronne at the time. But Buchan's tale has authenticity in a more fundamental matter: the experience of fear, the practice of courage. Different kinds of courage are displayed—in the heat of action, in the bearing of pain, in pushing on, like Launcelot Wake on the descent from the Col des Hirondelles, at the limit of endurance. Peter Pienaar tells Hannay that the rarest kind is fortitude—'just to go on enduring when there's no guts or heart left in you.' 'You get right home about courage and fortitude,' wrote a New Zealand soldier, just demobilised, on reading the book in 1919:

I've never before been in such a disgusting cold-sweat funk as I experienced in this war. It finds out the yellow streaks all right or what you call 'soft spots.' It was rotten. The spirit may be there but the flesh takes control and Wake in your book is an illuminating character set alongside Ivery.

Forty years later a French critic made the same point. Writing in *Planète* Jacques Bergier said:

Personnellement, je n'ai réellement compris l'oeuvre de Buchan, que je connaissais pourtant parfaitement, qu'au cours de mes aventures de résistance, et qu'au camp de concentration. Certaines réflexions sur le courage dans *Mr Standfast* ne sont, me semble-t-il, compréhensibles que pour quelqu'un qui a été lui-même aux frontières de la peur et de la résistance physique.

In *Greenmantle* Buchan was unexpectedly sympathetic to the Kaiser: in *Mr Standfast* he was unexpectedly sympathetic to the conscientious objector. Launcelot Wake is perhaps the first of Buchan's characters to be given what I will call the 'root-of-the-matter' treatment. This involves taking a man whose views or values are opposed to those of the hero and his allies (Mr John Raymond

has called such characters the Sheep among the Goats), to make the
reader begin by disliking him, to reveal some facet of him—a taste
or ability shared by his author, perhaps—that will modify the
reader's attitude, then to show him in a situation where he behaves
as well as the hero, and proves that he too has the root of the matter
in him. Launcelot—at Fosse a prig, in Biggleswick a fanatic—comes
into his own on the Coolin, where he shows himself a much better
cragsman than Hannay, and in the hazardous crossing of the Col
des Hirondelles. At the climax on the Western Front, and without
giving up his pacifist and non-combatant principles, he is allowed
a courageous rôle and becomes one of the 'little confederacy.' For
the authenticity of Launcelot too there was praise. A United Free
Kirk minister in Fife thanked Buchan

for the sympathy and understanding with which you have sketched Launcelot Wake. . . . Next to the men who died I honour the real objector and
only feel that the one perfectly abominable thing is that he should grumble
at his own sufferings or in any way comport himself as other than a different
kind of soldier in a fight as grim and wounding; and your Launcelot Wake
seems this sort and is, I fancy, more typical than the mean fellow the
general press has depicted. Even if they have not all been equal to the
occasion of their vision, have not such men been hanging on to something
immensely true and heroic, all the more so that it is unhonoured? Of
course, if they 'can no other' they will be serene as Wake.

And a man who had served in the Friends' Ambulance Unit in
France wrote of the

wonderful description of a meeting at night on the slopes of the Coolin,
and its consequences. I never had either Wake's courage or his fanaticism;
but that scene and its effects made a great impression on me, and may have
saved at least one insignificant fellow from becoming a sanctimonious
poseur.

Wake and Hannay are both mouthpieces for Buchan's post-war de-
testation of war; and the punishment meted out by Hannay, with
Wake's approval, to the master-villain Ivery/Graf von Schwabing,
is to put him into the trenches so that the contriver of war 'will have
understood the hell to which you have condemned honest men.'

The powers of evil which Hannay is called on to destroy in *The
Three Hostages* (1924) are not Germans—there is a characteristic
sketch of the 'good enemy' in Gaudian, an engineer already met in
Greenmantle, who appears providentially in Norway to rescue one
of the hostages from a *saeter*—but the consequences of the war

which the Germans made. *The Three Hostages* plays on widespread
post-war fears and uncertainties, the concern at the shattering of
old regimes, at the fragility of the new. The tale projects such tensions on to a fantastic screen, and resolves them. As in *The Power-
House*, there is stress on the thinness of civilisation; war has let the
forces of destruction and irrationality break through. Wreckers on
the grand scale are at work.

The conspirators' weapon in *The Three Hostages* is power over
people's minds. The bald archaeologist of *The Thirty-Nine Steps*,
Hilda von Einem of *Greenmantle*, had both tried to master Hannay's will, and now the terrible Dominick Medina gives him the full
works. Hannay's strength to resist comes from his very ordinariness
and solidity; he thinks it a great impertinence that anyone should
rob him of his will and consciousness. (Buchan as a child had been
haunted like a nightmare by Alice in Wonderland's loss of identity.)
Common-sense and reason are his weapons against Medina's fanaticism and fascination. This villain is on an altogether grander scale
than the Black Stone gang or Hilda von Einem. Medina is a fallen
angel, the wildly gifted man who has deliberately chosen evil, 'a
god from a lost world.' In his fall Medina inspires pity as well as
hatred.

The energy that moves the fantastic plot comes from this general
concern with post-war unrest, and also again from Buchan's personal experience, particularly his delight in Elsfield, and in his best
holiday places. In the episode of the Norwegian *saeter*, in the climax
on the rocks at Machray—a mixture of Ardtornish, Letterewe and
Kinlochbervie—he was re-living his holiday with Susan and Tommy Nelson on the Leardal in 1912, his stalking days on the deer-
forests of his friends, his climbs in Skye with Anna, Walter and
John Mackenzie.

The enthusiasm which drove along the next book in which
Hannay figures, *The Courts of the Morning* (1929), was military.
Hannay himself disappears after the introduction, and the book is
really Sandy Arbuthnot's. The scene is a South American republic
—for the terrain, Buchan drew a good deal on the Transvaal—and
the machinations to be foiled are those of Castor, the Gobernador,
who has collared the minerals of Olifa (his Gran Seco seems not
unlike Katanga as run by the Union Minière) and wishes to
make mischief for the United States. Castor is another of the
charmer-villains: a mixture of Chaim Weizmann (he is a great
chemist), a Rand magnate, Ivar Kreuger and A. J. Balfour (he

discusses over lunch the works of Balfour, Ossian and Proust). Sandy leads an insurrection to take over the mines and, eventually, the whole country. His first coup is to kidnap Castor and proclaim that *he* is leading the insurrection; and the campaign in which he gets the better of the regular Olifa army—very up-to-date and mechanised, but rigid—is an affair of highly mobile guerrillas, who know the country intimately, and are not tied down to any lines of communication. They put the mines out of action, cut the railways, and live off the enemy's supplies. It is like T. E. Lawrence's desert fighting. (The original title of the book was *Far Arabia*.) 'I hate war, except my own sort,' says Sandy; and another character notes of him that he hated bloodshed, that 'for war he had no use unless it was war on his special plan, an audacious assault upon the enemy's nerves.' When Sandy expounds this new type of war, it sounds very like that described by T. E. Lawrence in 'The Evolution of a Revolt,' an article which he contributed to the *Army Quarterly* of October 1920. ('I should greatly like to see Lawrence's article on Guerrilla Warfare reprinted,' Buchan wrote to Liddell Hart on 1 October 1927, when he was at work on *The Courts of the Morning*.)* And Sandy, that master of disguises, who so distinctly was *not* T. E. Lawrence in the earlier books, has now become very like him. A 'tallish' man in *Greenmantle*, he has shrunk to 'a head shorter' than Castor, which would bring him down to T. E. Lawrence's five foot four inches, and he is saddled with Lawrence's 'finical conscience.' 'Unless he is tied to duties which need every atom of his powers, he will begin to torment himself with questions.'

'I rather fancied the military philosophy in *The Courts of the Morning*,' wrote Buchan to Captain Liddell Hart, 'and I am proud indeed that you approve it.' Liddell Hart approved to the extent of putting it—along with Denys Reitz's *Commando* and C. E. Montague's *Right Off the Map*—on the reading-list appended to his *The Future of Infantry* (1933).

The last Hannay story, *The Island of Sheep* (1936), is Johnnie Buchan's book: dedicated to him, full of his enthusiasm for birds and for wild places, and with a thirteen-year-old boy, Dick Hannay's son, added to the cast. Buchan had not himself shot wildfowl on the Norfolk marshes, where the tale begins, but Johnnie went several winters to Wells, and Johnnie's knowledge of birds was more ex-

---

* Liddell Hart, with the *Army Quarterly* article in mind, was hoping to get Lawrence to write on Guerrilla Warfare for the fourteenth edition of the *Encyclopaedia Britannica*, of which he was Military Editor.

tensive and exact than his father's; with a Border sheep-clipping a little later in the story, Buchan was on his own ground. The Island of Sheep—Buchan had used the same title for the symposium which he and Susan wrote after the war—is a name for the Faeroes, where he and Johnnie spent a fortnight in 1932. The plot involves happenings in a Rhodesian kraal, a Chinese jade tablet with a strange inscription, one of the villains is a left-over from *The Courts of the Morning* (though Sandy has resumed his Aubrey Herbert *persona* after his T. E. Lawrence episode), yet most of the significant moments in the action have to do with wild life. A hunted man recovers his nerve as he watches a wild goose evade a falcon. Peter John Hannay outwits his pursuers when he remembers that pink-foot geese, when disturbed, tend to move *nearer* the intruder. Salvation to the beleaguered garrison on the island comes with the Grind, when all the island boats herd a school of whales into one of the voes, and there is a great slaughter. But if the book is about the sharp eyes and general knowledgability of children, it is also about the middle-aged keeping—or recovering—their zest for life. Hannay feels a bit stuck in his pleasant rut; one of his allies is a man whom he thinks hopelessly sunk in suburban dullness. But both can meet adventure when it comes.

Edward Leithen first made his appearance in 'Space' (1911), a short story in *The Moon Endureth*, where he is shown as rational and imaginative, keen on stalking and climbing; he is then the hero in *The Power-House*, which has already been discussed. His next appearance is in *John Macnab* (1925), a light-hearted tale whose starting-point was an exploit of Captain Brander Dunbar of Pitgaveny in Morayshire, who had once bet in the mess that he could poach a stag in any forest in Scotland, and succeeded in Inverlochy Forest. In Buchan's story there are three poachers, who collectively call themselves John Macnab—the lawyer Leithen, the politician Lamancha (the name comes from a village near Peebles), the banker Palliser-Yeates. Because they are all overworked and bored with life, they decide to poach a salmon and two stags from three adjoining estates, after duly warning the owners. It reflects the sort of pre-holiday feeling that Buchan himself knew very well: the wish of responsible, overworked, middle-aged men to be young, larky and irresponsible. The story runs along happily on his enthusiasm for Highland sport, Highland shooting-lodges and Highland weather, with a little electioneering thrown in, and a Unionist chairman of

the kind who had made Buchan blush in the days when he was a
Parliamentary candidate:

> The Duke of Angus was very old, highly respected, and almost wholly
> witless. He had never been very clever—Disraeli, it was said, had refused
> him the Thistle on the ground that he would eat it.

There are some agreeable New Englanders; and in Fish Benjie,
the ragamuffin who becomes Macnab's ally, Buchan was remembering both a little lad he had seen at Durness during his holiday at
Kinlochbervie, and the impudent urchin Benjie, that 'grinning
blackguard of a piscator,' who pops in and out of the action in
Scott's *Redgauntlet*.

There are no villains, sinister or fascinating, and no world-wide
conspiracies; the risk run by these distinguished poachers is simply
that of being found out and made fools of, and their strength is their
skill as fishermen, stalkers and shots. But at the end the risk is
shown to be no risk; one of the landowners who is poached is Lord
Claybody, a *nouveau riche* of the war, at whom a certain amount of
superior fun has been poked. He has the last word, and makes the
poachers look small, by explaining how even out of self-interest *he*
would never have risked making a laughing-stock out of three such
pillars of the Establishment by exposing 'John Macnab.'

So 'John Macnab' is revealed as really belonging to the world of
landed gentry which he has appeared to be challenging; yet his
activities have raised some questions about that world. Gertrude
Himmelfarb calls the story 'a parable about authority and property.'
'The old life of the Highlands is gone,' says the daughter of a laird,

> 'and people like ourselves must go with it. There's no reason why
> we should continue to exist. We've long ago lost our justification.'
> 'D'you mean to say that fellows like Claybody have more right to be
> here?'
> 'Yes. I think they have, because they're fighters and we're only survivals.
> They will disappear, too, unless they learn their lesson.'

There are some reflections on the healthy fluidity of American
society, as against Britain where people are 'fixed in a class and
members of a hierarchy'; and an affirmation that 'the man who
doesn't give a damn for anybody can do anything he likes in the
world.'

A year later Leithen, in *The Dancing Floor* (1926), was engaged
in a more desperate and exotic enterprise. When the Buchans were
in the Aegean in 1910 on Gerard Craig-Sellar's yacht, they landed

briefly on one of the Petali islands. Susan has described the occasion:

> We walked up a beach, where there sat a circle of peasants round a fire. They paid no attention to us, though in such a remote island the arrival of a yacht and the landing of strangers might well have stirred their curiosity.
>
> Some way back from the shore, standing in what appeared to be walled gardens, stood a long low house with a mellow red roof. It was shuttered and impenetrable. We stared at it hoping that someone might emerge from it who would tell us who lived there, but no one came, and we had to content ourselves with walking along a carefully made road fringed with bushes which dipped and wound round hills and promontories.

In the manner of Stevensonian romance this island house cried out for a tale to fit it; and Buchan's first attempt was the short story 'Basilissa,' which appeared in *Blackwood's* in April 1914 but was never reprinted in England, though it was included in the American edition of *The Watcher by the Threshold* (1918). In it Vernon Milburne dreams every spring in his north-country home of a series of rooms, with the last one, where lurks a nameless Something, coming nearer every year.

> He thought of it as a great snake of masonry, winding up hill and down dale away to the fells or the sea.

When he reaches the end of the series he is on a Greek island, in a room in a great house above the harbour which he realises is the room of his dreams. There is indeed a monster—a satyr-like Greek —and from his clutches Vernon rescues a beautiful girl who sees in him her Perseus. When ten years later Buchan came to expand the tale to novel length, he introduced Leithen, put in several chapters of London and country-house life to balance the exotic element, and made the danger come not merely from black-hearted villains, but from a perversion of old rites (here were echoes of his reading in Gilbert Murray and Jane Harrison, and of his studies under Dr Bussell in the survival of pre-Christian cults). The islanders have been seduced from their Christianity to an older religion, in which are elements of both horror and beauty. At the climax Vernon and Kore Arabin are about to be destroyed as devils. But this First War hero and the 'modern' girl—'a crude Artemis but her feet were on the hills'—face their enemies in the guise of gods, Kore and Kouros, and at this terrible epiphany the islanders rush back to their abandoned church. Leithen, the legal, rational man, demonstrates the power of this old magic; first sceptical, he is bewitched by the sight of the Dancing Floor where the rites of spring are held, for it is a type of landscape that has always haunted him as 'broken hints of a beauty of which I hoped some day to find the archetype:'

an upland meadow . . . cut off like a garden from neighbouring wildernesses, secret and yet offering a wide horizon, a place at once a sanctuary and a watch-tower.

It is a *temenos*, as the Wood Bush was to Buchan, and when he sees the islanders celebrating their spring rites there in the moonlight he experiences 'a mixture of fear, abasement and a crazy desire to worship;' but is saved by his power of reasoning.

Leithen's rationality again plays a part in *The Gap in the Curtain* (1932), a group of related tales on the subject of foreseeing the future (Buchan had been reading J. W. Dunne's *An Experiment with Time* and Drayton Thomas's *Some New Evidence for Human Survival*). Six of the guests at a Whitsun country-house party are instructed by a Scandinavian Professor (who has something in him of both Nansen and Professor Lindemann) to put their minds on the future in the field in which each is concerned—finance, politics, and so on. In the final stage they are to foresee one item in *The Times* of a year hence which will concern them. Leithen, who has been under the Professor's spell as much as the rest of them, nursing his perceptions and repressing his scepticism, breaks loose from him in the final session, but becomes the confidant of the others whose cases he relates. There is an entertaining account of a financier's attempt to corner the supplies of michelite, for his foreknowledge has been of a world merger in that mineral—here Buchan drew profitably on his experience at the Bar of company cases —and some gay political manœuvres which result from a politician's foreknowledge of a new Prime Minister. Two of the tales concern foreknowledge of death: the man who is obsessed by it dies miserably of his fear, the other loses *his* fear when he thinks that the girl whom he loves is going to die, and ceases to think about himself. He goes through the fatal day without a care, and it turns out that the expected announcement, which duly appears in *The Times*, refers to somebody else. In Buchan's final story *Sick Heart River* (1940) it is Leithen's turn for the problem of how to face death; that novel will be discussed in the last chapter.

With Dickson McCunn, the hero of three novels, Buchan is paying a belated tribute to the Glasgow bourgeois, such as had lived in Queens Park and attended the John Knox Free Kirk, and to

whose virtues he had been indifferent when he lived among them
and looked on 'an avenue of respectable villa-residences and a well-
kept public park' as the essence of dullness. Yet Buchan himself
had spent most of his boyhood in a villa near a well-kept public
park, and it had not blunted *his* spirit of adventure; so the retired
provision merchant, who is an elder of the Guthrie Memorial Kirk,
whose wife's idea of bliss is a holiday in a hydropathic, is given the
soul of a romantic. Dickson McCunn, who makes his first appearance
in *Huntingtower* (1922) is a literary character—conceived, as Buchan
explained in the dedication to his fellow-citizen W. P. Ker, on the
lines of that other Glasgow hero, Bailie Nicol Jarvie of *Rob Roy*,
that 'triumphant bourgeois' as Buchan calls him in his life of Scott.
To Richard Hannay adventure is an interruption of his regular life
—orthodox soldiering in the war, in peace his country-gentleman
existence; to hard-worked Leithen adventure is, like climbing mountains, a shot in the arm, a recharging of his batteries; but Dickson
McCunn is always on the quest for Prince Charlie. He reads the
Waverley Novels 'not for their insight into human character or for
their pageantry, but because they gave him material wherewith to
construct fantastic journeys.' His quest for adventure takes him to
Carrick and Galloway (where his steps retrace those of Buchan on
several of his Oxford vacation tours) and he finds it in the shape of
a Russian princess, held in duress with the crown jewels in an old
house by the sea. He finds there too his allies, the Gorbals Die-
Hards. This gang of keelies, with their guerrilla tactics and their
proletarian ditties sung to hymn-tunes—

> Class-conscious we are, and class-conscious wull be
> Till our fit's on the neck o' the Boorjoyzee—

is a fantasy embroidered on the Gorbals boys of the John Knox
Sunday-school whom Buchan had entertained with stories and in
whom his father had been so ready to see possibilities. Dickson
McCunn too sees possibilities in the Gorbals Die-Hards, who have
never 'had a proper chance or been right fed or educated or taken
care of.' 'There's the stuff in you to make Generals and Provosts—
ay, and Prime Ministers,' he tells them—and ends by adopting the
lot. It is a Glasgow fairy-tale.

The story is filled out with a left-wing poet, who is given the
root-of-the-matter treatment (he did well in the war and climbs in
the Alps), and some Russian royalties straight from Phillips Oppenheim, and the climax is a great convergence of all the right-minded

on Huntingtower. For all the exotic touches, the driving force in the story comes from the author's interest in Dickson McCunn and the Die-Hards who, however far removed from the probabilities of Queens Park and the Gorbals, are rendered with zest and affection, as if Buchan would have loved to find such characters in Glasgow. It was a make-believe into which he put his heart. 'To us elders I think,' wrote Lady Betty Balfour from Whittinghame, describing how she had read it aloud to a family audience of varying ages,

> perhaps the chief charm of the book was the revelation of romance and adventure in the frame of the middle-aged, the respectable, the business-like. I believe that I and the Aunts all felt that in McCunn we ourselves had been understood and revealed. To the young ones it was of course rapture the way the real initiative authority and efficiency rested with the Gorbals Die-Hards.

In *Castle Gay* (1930) two of the Die-Hards are on the way up, thanks to McCunn: Dougal is doing well as a journalist on the Craw Press, Jaikie is playing wing three-quarter for Cambridge and Scotland. In Jaikie, the young Scot who has gone South to college, whose friends feel that he is becoming less of a Scotsman, there is something of the young Buchan. (At one point Jaikie 'would have given all he possessed for another stone of weight and another two inches of height.') Again Buchan's Galloway holidays—particularly the walking-tour with Taffy Boulter in July 1897—supply the young men with their hill tramps and shepherds' cottages, but more recent interests come in with the characters of Red Davie, the Clydeside M.P., and the newspaper magnate Thomas Carlyle Craw who, Buchan told Beaverbrook, was 'a cross between Rothermere and Robertson Nicoll.' ('I would send a copy to Rothermere,' answered Beaverbrook, 'if I were not on good terms with his secretaries.') Craw is a type of Scot whom Buchan disliked, and he is sharply sketched:

> He must always be generalising, seeking for principles, philosophising; he loves a formula rather than a fact; he is heavily weighted with unction; rhetoric is in every fibre.

Craw's first journalistic success had been to find 'a niche in a popular religious weekly, where, under the signature of "Simon the Tanner," he commented upon books and movements and personalities,' much as Buchan's old antagonist Robertson Nicoll did in the *British Weekly* under the signature 'Claudius Clear.'

There is another sharp sketch, of a well-born lady whose interest in politics is strictly dynastic, which may have owed something to Susan Buchan's aunts:

> Politics she cared nothing for, except in so far as they affected the families which she had known all her life. When there was a chance of Cousin Georgie Whitehaven's second boy being given a post in the Ministry, she was much excited, but she would have been puzzled to name two other members of that Ministry, and of its policy she knew nothing at all.

The plot is an affair of royalties and republicans in a small central European country called Evallonia, to which Craw has given loud support in his papers, but in whose affairs he has no wish to be actually involved. When violence threatens, Dickson McCunn's common-sense releases the tension. For the last McCunn story *The House of the Four Winds* (1935) the setting has been shifted to Evallonia itself, unfortunately, for Buchan is not at his best in the Anthony Hope terrain of imaginary European states with princes, pretenders and disguises. There is one good moment when Dickson McCunn recommends to the royalists and their candidate for the throne the tactics once successfully pursued on the Glasgow Town Council in the election of a Provost; but in spite of some spirited work with a circus, the adventure is on the feeble side. There is no familiar setting to provide Buchan with sharp little scenes and characters between the moments of melodrama; no over-riding enthusiasm such as the military interest which gave substance to the imaginary republic of Olifa in *The Courts of the Morning*. Ruritania was not Buchan's country.

Sixteen years after *A Lost Lady of Old Years* Buchan came back to the historical novel with *Salute to Adventurers* (1915), though he had kept his hand in with some short stories in *The Moon Endureth* (1912). 'The Lemnian', which Quiller-Couch said 'any man in my generation might be proud to sign,' shows a power of getting inside the physical conditions of a remote time and place. It is about an island seafarer blown by storm upon the mainland of Greece, whose pride and dignity as a man make him choose to face death with the Spartans at Thermopylae, though it is not his quarrel. 'The Riding of Ninemileburn' presents a Border raid with the glamour left out. A poor man is robbed of his cow, without milk his child will die, and so may his wife; the retaliatory raid is successful, but the cow is dead. There is no milk—and no glory.

Written in the early months of 1914, *Salute to Adventurers* was the fruit of Buchan's enthusiasm for American history, and though

it is set in the seventeenth century, it uses the knowledge of Virginia
which he had gained in his Civil War readings. It is dedicated to
Susan's uncle Sir Reginald Talbot, who had been attached to
Sheridan's army as an observer. *Prester John* was written as a boys'
book; *Salute to Adventurers* might be called a grown-up boys' book.
Like *Prester John*, it starts in a homely way in Scotland before the
hero seeks his fortune overseas. Here again is a plain young Scot—
Andrew Garvald, sent out from Glasgow to Jamestown to develop
the tobacco-trade—who is given the chance to discover, and foil, a
native rising. The action sweeps from the manors of the Tidewater
through the frontier settlements of the piedmont and up to the
Blue Ridge, from which Andrew has a clear vision over the Shenandoah:

> An immense green pasture land ran out to the dim horizon. There were
> forests scattered athwart it, and single great trees, and little ridges, too,
> but at the height where we stood it seemed to the eye to be one verdant
> meadow as trim and shapely as the lawn of a garden. A noble river, the
> child of many hill streams, twined through it in shining links. I could see
> dots, which I took to be herds of wild cattle grazing, but no sign of any
> human dweller.

As Andrew nudges a boat into a landlocked harbour in the Carolina
keys, rides through the pathless foothills where

> the open spaces were marshy, where our horses sank to the hocks. The
> woods were one medley of fallen trees, rotting into touchwood, hidden
> boulders, and matted briars,

or jogs along a hill-ridge with the ferny grass and juniper clumps
dripping with wet, everywhere is evidence of a lively geographical,
as well as historical, imagination.

At moments Buchan's is the Virginia of romantic legend. There
are great plantations, fine mansions and high-handed cavaliers,
horse-races and a duel, and a lovely girl who sings Montrose's 'My
dear and only love.' But the hero is firmly not of this aristocratic
world. He is a plain body, and his pride is in being an honest and
enterprising merchant: 'I smacked of travel and enterprise, which
to an honest heart are dearer than brocade.' He has no use for the
gentleman who won't soil his hands with common trade:

> The thing was so childish that it made me angry. It was right for one of
> them to sell his tobacco on his own wharf to a tarry skipper who cheated
> him grossly, but wrong for me to sell kebbucks and linsey-woolsey at an
> even bargain. I gave up the puzzle. Some folks' notions of gentility are
> beyond my wits.

And he is appalled by the provincialism of the great plantation-owners, who are content to confine Virginia to the Tidewater when there is a continent to be discovered.

When the Indian rising threatens it is Garvald the trader who is intelligent about defending Virginia, and not the fine cavaliers. When the tribes are swayed by a fanatic Scots preacher (first met in a hollow of the Pentland Hills) it is Garvald's common-sense, his feeling for the earthy and the homely, that recall Muckle John Gib to his senses, and win the day. Buchan realised who were the real makers of Virginia: not the Tidewater squires but the farmers and traders, the back-country pioneers who pushed back the frontier and worked with their hands. However highly-coloured in its action, his tale is true in this particular; he did not fall for the aristocratic legend.

There is a strong Stevensonian echo in Andrew's friend and hero Ninian Campbell, Red Ringan, 'the best blade in the Five Seas,' who, like Alan Breck, and like Nicol Plenderleith in *John Burnet of Barns*, sings as he fights. Ringan the freebooter and Andrew the merchant make a Highland-Lowland dashing-canny pair like Alan Breck and David Balfour; they even quarrel along the same lines, with Andrew shocked by Ringan's killing of a man, and Ringan contemptuous of Andrew's Whigamore morality. But the true Buchan notes sound clear. At the crisis a group of men from different backgrounds, but 'all men to ride the ford with,' come together: merchant, farmer, freebooter, Indian, even a regenerated cavalier. Events are seen in majestic sweeps: 'The Tidewater thinks it has put the fear of God on the hill tribes.' The hero, who is very canny in assessing any hazard, is exhilarated and gay in a crisis once all is done that man can do: 'My dispositions completed, the thing was in the hands of God.' There is an ambivalent attitude to the Indian enemy, who is seen now with 'all the demoniac, panther-like cruelty of his race,' and now as a noble visionary who rides towards the sunset 'on the path of a king.' There is, above all, a zest for America and its possibilities. Andrew may go back to Scotland in his old age, but—the book ends—' I am very sure that our sons will be Virginians.'

The theme of *The Path of the King* (1921) has already been described in the previous chapter. The words had been in Buchan's mind at least as early as his Newdigate Prize Poem of 1898, on the Pilgrim Fathers. The epigraph quotes 'Counsel for the true-hearted: to follow the Path the King of Errin rides,' and in the poem itself there are repeated references to the King's path. About the same time, in a list of published and projected books, Buchan included 'The Path of the King—to be begun after taking my degree.' The notion that the kingly strain—*i.e.* the heroic, with something almost fey added to it—is more likely to descend through younger sons 'with their fortune to find' is demonstrated in fourteen episodes. Beginning with a Norse hero-king, Buchan traces the line of descent through a Norman knight, the wife of a Flemish burgomaster, a highly-born French girl whose life was changed by a meeting with Joan of Arc, a French lord who sailed with Columbus on his second voyage and became one of the first Protestants, an adventurer from Devon, one of the 1649 regicides, a professional spy (the Titus Oates plot), a secret agent in 1715, a friend of Daniel Boone, and finally Abraham Lincoln. The outward symbol of the kingly strain is a gold ring; even the outcasts of the line, like the spy, are at a critical moment moved to act for once in a heroic way. 'The historical vignettes are each clear-cut, bright,' wrote G. M. Trevelyan, whose favourite Buchan this was,

full of the spirit of each passing age, psychologically interesting, and yet with a moral 'uplift' in them that 'done me a lot of good,' and a unity to the whole book given by the entrancing mystery of heredity. What a grand idea to hang it on to Abe . . . I have often thought and dreamed of this mystery of heredity—and seen history just *like* that, but I never have had the inventive gift and now you have done it for me just as I have often longed to have it done. . . . And it's just rightly *tragic* enough, as life is, but yet very comforting and strengthening that in spite of all it *goes on* and even gets somewhere sometimes and anyway is fun all along if you have courage.

Midwinter (1923), begun at Elsfield in June 1921 and mostly written there during the following winter, is the first-fruit of Buchan's love-affair with his new home, the record of his exploration of it in space and in time. The year after he moved into Elsfield Manor a neighbour, Vernon Watney of Cornbury Park, gave him a copy of his privately printed *Cornbury and the Forest of Wychwood* (1910). In this history of the house and of the forest where Buchan often took Alice and Johnnie for picnics he found facts and associations which touched on many of his own interests. Lord Mansfield, on whom he had once thought of writing a book,*

---

* I have been using, for the chronology of Buchan's life, a stout notebook with marbled covers inscribed 'J. Buchan, 3 Temple Gdns,' and headed on the first page '*Lord Mansfield*, Chapter V. *Chief Justice of the King's Bench.* (1756–1788). Continued.' Otherwise Buchan left it blank.

had stayed at Cornbury in 1746 when Solicitor-General. Lord Cornbury, great-grandson of the great Lord Clarendon, 'was from his earliest days a friend of the lost cause of the Stuarts,' and there was a story of a Charlbury lad bringing bread to Cornbury for Jacobite fugitives after Prince Charles's retreat from Derby. Now to these elements Buchan added the greatest character from Elsfield's story: Dr Johnson, who had walked out from Oxford to have tea with Mr Francis Wise in the summer of 1754. Another—fictitious—visit by Johnson to Elsfield in 1764, with Boswell, is described in the preface to *Midwinter*; from the arbour 'constructed after the fashion of a Roman temple, on the edge of a clear pool,' Johnson stares across the valley and asks the names of the hills. When Wychwood Forest is mentioned he is disturbed, and Boswell remembers the strange gap in his knowledge of Johnson's life in the years 1745 and 1746. (Buchan had also been in correspondence with Sir Charles Russell, who contributed an article on 'Johnson the Jacobite' to the *Fortnightly Review* for February 1922.)

The tale itself takes Johnson to Cornbury in 1745, and takes too, on Jacobite business, a young Highland soldier Alastair Maclean. There is a chase for a runaway heiress, a traitor's plot to be foiled, a winter ride to Derbyshire, a meeting with General Oglethorpe, an escape from death in a pothole in the Peak. It is a brisk exciting tale —J. B. Priestley thought it Buchan's best so far, though he considered Johnson's talk more convincing than his actions—but its spring and life come from Buchan's delight in the Oxfordshire country and in the feeling about the past which they gave him.

For Cornbury and Wychwood he took much from Vernon Watney's book, especially from a letter quoted there from Mrs Delany, 'correspondent of Swift and friend of Miss Burney,' describing life at Cornbury in 1743 and 1746: the new Indian room, the Chinese paper of birds and flowers and flower-hung pagodas, the park with winding walks, mounts covered with all sorts of trees and flowering shrubs, the social routine of the day ending with 'a pool at commerce.' For the country beyond this cultured enclave Buchan drew on his long solitary walks and on his reading in local history. Balancing the high life at Cornbury is the secret earthy life of Midwinter and his men on Otmoor. This character (the name is still common in Oxfordshire) is devised, in a Stevensonian manner, to fit the particular character of Otmoor—not as Buchan saw it now on his walks from Elsfield, drained and fertile, but as it had been two centuries earlier, a green fenland with jungles of blackthorn and elder. The gentle-born Midwinter, who lives like a gipsy but wears silk next the skin, is a mixture of the Scholar-Gipsy and the Scarlet Pimpernel, and calls himself and his followers the Naked Men, for they 'travel light, caring nothing for King or party or Church.' They are half-pagan, and their secret meeting-place is by an old Roman altar on Otmoor. Also called the Spoonbills, they are a country-wide network of vagabonds, charcoal-burners, wood-cutters, who do not fight but can—at the whistle of a tune by a stake with a bunch of broom—hide and protect any man whom they champion. They belong to

an Old England, which has outlived Roman and Saxon and Dane and Norman and will outlast the Hanoverian. It has seen priest turn to presby-ter and presbyter to parson and has only smiled. It is the land of the edge of moorlands and the rims of forests and the twilight before dawn, and strange knowledge still dwells in it.

This is what Midwinter tells Alastair Maclean when he strays on Otmoor; for the Englishness of England is demonstrated through the perception of a Scot. Alastair, and Samuel Johnson, have em-barked on their adventure with romantic hopes of love and glory; the events which they live through strip them of illusions. They too are Naked Men, but, with Midwinter's help, each survives to pursue his calling. Johnson returns to his dictionary, Alastair to his service in the cause which he now knows to be hopeless.

Witch Wood (1927), Buchan's favourite among his novels, was based on the same readings as his *Montrose* (1928), and it illustrates dramatically a passage in the biography where he talks about the Kirk and its ministers:

If they gave manhood and liberty to Scotland, they did much to sap the first and shackle the second. Condemning natural pleasures and affections, they drew a dark pall over the old merry Scottish world, the world of the ballads and the songs, of frolics and mummings and 'blithesome bridals,' and, since human nature will not be denied, drove men and women to sinister and perverted outlets.

Buchan had so read himself into the seventeenth century in Scot-land that he could now discard knowledge; there was no need, as in the early *John Burnet of Barns*, for the accumulation of fact to prove authenticity. His ear was so attuned to the rhythms of con-temporary writing, particularly religious writing, that his dialogue, even at its most theological, seems fresh and unstrained, comparable at moments to Scott's in *Old Mortality*. Montrose himself makes a brief appearance, and through one of his lieutenants, Mark Kerr, his ideas affect the action; it is to Montrose's view of the value and function of the Kirk that the hero is finally converted. He is a young minister fresh from college, a Platonist and a humanist, who comes to a parish where the witch-cult is in full cry. Witchcraft had been the subject of one of Buchan's early stories, 'The Outgoing of the Tide;' now he had a much more extensive reading behind him. Running too in his mind was the theme of the early 'Watcher by the Threshold' and of the previous year's *Dancing Floor*—the survival of pagan rites in a supposedly Christian society.

The kirk to which David Sempill is called at 'Woodilee' is the old kirk at Broughton; by Buchan's day there was nothing left but a ruin in the graveyard where his little sister Violet was buried. So the story is rooted in familiar country—where men are known by the names of their farms, Chasehope, Nether Fennan, Mirehope; where the year is measured by the lambing, the sowing, the harvest, the bringing down of the sheep to the infields. It is also unfamiliar; one of the strengths of the book is Buchan's ability to imagine this country three centuries earlier, when upper Tweeddale was mainly forest:

Everywhere, muffling the lower glen of the Woodilee burn and the immediate vale of the Aller, and climbing far up the hillside, was the gloom of trees. In the Rood glen there was darkness only at the foot, for higher up the woods thinned into scrub of oak and hazel, with the knees of the uplands showing through it. The sight powerfully impressed his fancy. Woodilee was a mere clearing in a forest. This was the *Silva Caledonis* of which old writers spoke, the wood which once covered all the land and in whose glades King Arthur had dwelt.

This wood is a main character in the story. It is the place where in a clearing by an old Roman altar half-naked women and men with animal masks celebrate with obscene dances a travesty of the sacrament. It is also the place where in a flower-strewn glade David finds an enchanting girl. Katrine Yester is one of Buchan's more successful women because there is no attempt at realism: she is more like a character in a ballad, particularised by her green gown, her voice like a bird, her black hair. So the wood, like Leithen's Dancing Floor, becomes a place of attraction and repulsion, good and evil, where David finds both a sense of life's golden possibilities and a realisation of the possible depravity of men.

Behind this picture of life in the parish of Woodilee were all Buchan's readings in seventeenth-century theology, in Covenanting pamphlets, in the diary of a fanatic like Johnson of Warriston, in the records of trials for witchcraft, in the visionary writings of William Guthrie of Fenwick or the luscious outpourings of Samuel Rutherford. He could describe with familiarity a witch-hunt and the activities of the witch-pricker, a trial before the Presbytery, the preaching of a vacancy, the visit of three older ministers to the newly arrived David with their different emphases on their common creed. He could embody in his characters the various strains in the Kirk of the seventeenth century: David, the man with a mission to preach Christ's gospel, is hedged round by colleagues and elders to whom the Word is in the Old Testament, and he has to find his allies in the war against plague and witchcraft outside the ranks of the unco' guid, among the publicans and sinners. Chasehope, a more sinister Holy Willie, is the complete predestinarian. He is an elder of the Kirk, and also the dog-faced piper of the Satanic revels, for, secure in his election to grace,

To him the foulest sin would be no sin—its indulgence would be part of his prerogative, its blotting out an incident in his compact with the Almighty. He could lead the coven in the Wood and wallow in the lusts of the flesh; and his crimes would be but the greater vindication of God's omnipotence.

There is none of the liberating jollity of the witches' revels in 'Tam o' Shanter;' there is rather a sense of people deliberately shutting themselves off from good, and the moral evil is dramatised by the setting in the Black Wood. To it Buchan has imparted something of those feelings of uneasy terror which he had once experienced in a wood in the Bavarian Alps, when

I ran too, some power not myself constraining me. Terror had seized me also, but I did not know what I dreaded.

One of his most appreciative readers was C. S. Lewis. 'For *Witch Wood* specially I am always grateful; all that devilment sprouting up out of a beginning like Galt's *Annals of the Parish*. That's the way to do it.'

Eight years after *Midwinter* Buchan came back to the Cotswolds for *The Blanket of the Dark* (1931), which reflects his mature experience of that countryside as the earlier novel reflected his enthusiastic discovery. Two years before, in a preface to the *Survey of the Thames Valley* prepared by the Council for the Preservation of Rural England (1929), he had presented a series of pictures of the valley: as it was in 400, with the Romans there; in the Middle Ages,

when the traffic moved 'up and down the valley instead of across it;'
early in Henry VIII's reign, when the monasteries were being dis-
solved; in the first years of the Civil War. 'A cameo of classical
beauty' Sir Michael Sadler of University College called this preface:

> Whenever I think of the Thames, or am near it, your picture of it (like
> Jefferies' *After London* and W. Morris's *News from Nowhere* and the Mat
> Arnold stanzas) will come into my mind, and colour my thinking, and give
> me the picture of time—which is really a double thing—chronological for
> some purposes, eternally the same for others.

As in *Midwinter*, Buchan was again dealing in the might-have-
beens of history. The epigraph to *The Blanket of the Dark* is the
question asked by Sir Ranulphe Crewe in 1625:

> Where is Bohun? Where is Mowbray? Where is Mortimer? Nay, which
> is more and most of all, where is Plantagenet? They are intombed in the
> urns and sepulchres of mortality.

Peter Pentecost is a clerk at the great abbey of Oseney, just outside
Oxford: a country boy, brought up in Wychwood, destined for the
Church but attracted by 'the happy bustle of men with purpose
and power.' Then three such men tell him who he really is: a Bohun,
son of the last Duke of Buckingham, sixth in descent from Edward
III, who should by rights be King instead of Henry VIII, the son
of the Tudor upstart. He is half delighted, half repelled, because he
sees clearly that he is simply the tool for more cunning and less
scrupulous men to use. The first step in the rising is to kidnap the
King; from high up a tree in Woodstock, Peter spies him hunting:

> The face was vast and red as a new ham, a sheer mountain of a face, for it
> was as broad as it was long, and the small features seemed to give it a
> profile like an egg. The mouth was comically small, and the voice that came
> from it was modest out of all proportion to the great body. He swept like a
> whirlwind up the glade, one hand pawing the air, screaming like a jay.

Later Peter rescues him from the floodwaters of the Windrush and
holds him prisoner in Minster Lovell, a place and family which
pulled at Buchan's imagination (*The Path of the King* is a fantasy
about the younger sons of the 'tragically fated' Lovels). There Peter
learns that the King, for all his grossness,

> had the greatness of some elemental force. He hated him, for he saw the
> cunning behind the frank smile, the ruthlessness in the small eyes; but he
> could not blind himself to his power. Power of Mammon, power of Anti-
> christ, power of the Devil, maybe, but something born to work mightily in
> the world.

In a time of violent upheaval and change England might need Henry's strength more than the idealism of better men.

Again, as in *Midwinter*, high life is balanced by low. Peter is upheld at every stage by Solomon Darking and his followers, who are in the line of the Naked Men. They are rufflers and rogues and highwaymen, coney-catchers, cozeners and horse-priggers, tinkers, pedlars and minstrels, a great network of vagabonds with their own communications:

> I saw Catti the Welshman yesterday on the Burford Road, and old John Naps was at the Rood Fair on Barton Heath, and there is word of Penny-farthing in the Cocking dingle.

They hold their Parliament of Beggars in Little Greece, a sanctuary among a maze of furze on Kingham Waste, and they represent 'the only part of England that is stable.' Romantic as these brotherhoods may be, they are Buchan's way of showing history from the point of view of the unimportant. They stand for the backworld and underworld of England as Scott's Meg Merrilees and Edie Ochiltree do for Scotland. The movements of history touch them no less than the great and powerful. 'It is a dim land nowadays,' says Pierce the Piper,

> The blanket of the dark lies heavy on it . . . But there is an uneasy stirring.

and that stirring may soon be an upheaval that will shake down crowns and mitres. There is a new world coming to birth . . . though men know it not and crave rather to have an older world restored.

After the failure of his political venture it is the beggars who rescue Peter, and it is among them that he disappears. Bohun is lost to history.

To me *The Blanket of the Dark* is Buchan's most deeply felt novel: characters and actions are devised which fittingly embody his sense of a time of drastic change, and his own deep—I would almost say wild—love of his adopted countryside. The girl in the tale, like Katrine in *Witch Wood*, is a creature of ballad or myth. For Peter this Sabine Beauforest merges into the goddess of the Painted Floor, the Roman pavement which he uncovers in the glades of Woodeaton, and even—in a vision which comes to him when he is exhausted in the snow—with the Queen of Heaven. For Buchan she is the expression of the exhilaration, the quickened sense of life, that came to him as he roamed round Oxfordshire and felt in his bones the past. And felt too how the future could have looked to that past. Simon Rede, who sailed with the Cabots of Bristol, looks westward: 'There is a dark blanket which covers Europe, but beyond it there are open skies and the sun.' There is a hint that though the Bohuns are lost to sight in old England, they have survived in the New World.

In *The Free Fishers* (1934) is another brotherhood of honest men with remarkable powers of communication—'We've our ain canny ways and our ain private lines set.' They are seamen from the Firth of Forth with some landward allies such as the hero, who is a young Professor of Divinity at St Andrews. The period is the Napoleonic Wars, the scene is the coast of Fife, the moors of Northumberland, the fens of East Anglia, the enterprise is the rescue of a young man from a black-hearted fanatic. Framed in the quiet domestic setting of the hero's lodgings at St Andrews are some spirited chasing on the turnpikes and skulking on the moors. The exploits of a Regency whip and the appearance of the Prime Minister, Spencer Perceval, add some colour. It is lively enough, but rather short in suspense, for the Byronic villain is too lightly sketched. Like the heroes of *Witch Wood* and *The Blanket of the Dark*, Antony Lammas has a vision of romantic love which cannot be fulfilled yet gives his life a new brightness, but there are none of the deeper resonances of those other novels about the past.

A Prince of the Captivity (1933) does not fit into any of these groupings of Buchan stories, and I find it an odd mixture. It opens on a melodramatic note which recalls *The Four Feathers* and other A. E. W. Mason tales: the hero Adam Melfort, condemned to two years in prison for forgery and drummed out of his regiment, resolves to dedicate the rest of his life to expiation. Only it was not he, but his wife, who committed the crime for which he chivalrously took the blame. His quest for a cause to spend himself on takes him into the secret service in the 1914 war, to the Greenland ice-cap, to the industrial Midlands and finally to Germany, where after the war he foils those who wish to destroy the statesman who is bringing his country back to health and sanity. (This Loeffler has a good deal of Brüning in him; Buchan's friend Moritz Bonn was Brüning's economic adviser.) The book is full of topics with which Buchan, as a public man in politics, was seriously concerned: the leadership of the political parties, problems of the land, of trade-unions, of relations between the classes ('There's no more contemptible figure than a Labour leader who allows himself to be made a lap-dog by

the enemy.') But he tackles them with his thriller equipment, which
is inadequate. The question how men of good-will can best help to
rebuild civilisation in a world shattered and fatigued by war is presented in terms of political activity in the town of Birkpool, and
this activity takes the familiar Buchan form of the brotherhood of
men from varied backgrounds. As well as Adam Melfort they
number Utlaw the trade-union official (who is given the 'root-of-
the-matter' treatment by being made an enthusiastic angler and 'a
dashed good battalion officer' in the war), an American explorer,
a peer who is 'a mixture of high Tory and rampant Bolshie,' a
well-born parson who preaches like a medieval friar, and a radical
shop-steward from the Clyde. This character illustrates the weakness of Buchan's method in this novel; the shop-steward is the
same Andrew Amos who played a part in *Mr Standfast*. There
his characterisation was sufficient for the part he had to play in a
thriller; here, where the social order is the central point of discussion, it is quite inadequate. Admirably as Buchan's tale-spinning
served to reflect some contemporary tensions—as *The Three
Hostages* reflects fears about post-war anarchy—it was not the
instrument for a straightforward presentation of social questions.
The tale gathers energy only in the last section, with a man-hunt in
the Italian Alps and a final escape in which Adam confounds his
enemies, at the expense of his own life, by bringing down a rockfall
to block their path: an ending like that of *The Half-Hearted*.
Indeed, in theme and tone *A Prince of the Captivity* often recalls
that early novel.

'John Buchan puzzles me,' wrote T. E. Lawrence to Edward
Garnett on 1 August 1933:

Did you read his latest? [*A Prince of the Captivity*] He takes figures of
today and projects their shadows on to clouds, till they grow surhuman
and grotesque: then describes them! Now I ask you—it sounds a filthy
technique, but the books are like athletes racing: so clean-lined, speedy,
breathless. For our age they mean nothing: they are sport, only: but will a
century hence disinter them and proclaim him the great romancer of our
blind and undeserving generation?

The same ambivalent attitude, the same note of exasperation, appears in almost all those who have written critically about Buchan's
novels: Graham Greene, Gertrude Himmelfarb, Hugh MacDiarmid, John Raymond, Philip Toynbee, Richard Usborne. They are
exasperated that a writer who could be so good should often be so

careless, that a spell-binder who has his reader on the hook should seem to subscribe to values which the victim finds repulsive.

High among the irritants which such critics find in Buchan is the upper-class atmosphere: the *Westminster Gazette* spoke of 'the rich vein of self-complacent snobbery.' What irks many is not the fact that Hannay lives a country-gentleman life, that Leithen hunts with the Mivern, that both have manservants (their batmen in the war), as the implication that this is the world that all decent chaps belong to. Buchan's heroes foregather at select dining-clubs where they spin yarns about past adventures, and at country-houses where every guest is distinguished. (In 'Whitsuntide at Flambard,' the opening of *The Gap in the Curtain*, there are a couple of Cabinet Ministers, a city tycoon, a few peers, some handsome young men, a glamorous debutante: it is so rich as to be almost a self-parody, yet the Elsfield visitors' book could show comparable characters, though they would not all have been there the same week-end.) Between the members of this circle is woven a fine network of common allusions and shared experiences—especially of the 1914 war, that enormous landmark for all men of Buchan's generation. Hannay, who enters his first adventure as a raw Rhodesian, who has no 'real pal' in Britain to come forward and vouch for his character, becomes steadily more of an Insider: Leithen, Sandy and Lamancha always have been. This exclusiveness, which some find so irritating, is to many a less sophisticated reader one of Buchan's attractions; such a one finds pleasure in becoming, vicariously, a member of this in-group, whether in a country-house in Oxfordshire, a Greek island, or a camp in the mountains of Olifa. (Perhaps it is easier thus to join one of Buchan's groups, which contain men of widely varying experience, than one of the tight groups in Kipling's stories, whose members usually belong to the same profession or trade.)

Generally Buchan's personal enthusiasms add vigour and interest to his stories, but I would gladly dispense with his enthusiasm for Eton. Again, it is not so much the fact that most of his characters have been there—Sandy, Leithen, Lamancha, Palliser-Yeates—as that he writes as if his readers would recognise and share his Etonian allusions, would know what was meant by 'a half,' or 'a lower boy,' or 'getting one's twenty-two.' Such allusions are particularly thick on the ground in *The Courts of the Morning*, which was begun soon after Johnnie went to the school; one of that story's villains is an Old Etonian who—like Barrie's Captain Hook—has gone wrong, though he is allowed to turn over a new leaf and die rather well.

This aspect of Buchan probably grates on his sophisticated and class-conscious fellow-countrymen more than on other readers, who take it as part of the décor, just another element in the fantasy. From such limited evidence as I have, it does not seem to be a particular irritant to the foreign reader, nor to the young in general.

Strongly criticised too has been Buchan's 'ethic of success.' Graham Greene talks of 'the Scotch admiration of success' in him, and Richard Usborne says:

> Success in Buchan is competitive. It was not enough to have done a good job well. You had to have made a name for yourself by doing it better than anybody else. Heroes and villains, they almost all 'make big names for themselves.'

A striking instance is the New York lunch-party described at the beginning of *Sick Heart River*, not long after Buchan himself had been lunching with the partners of Morgan's. The guests include the president of one of the chief banking-houses in the world, a young man who is 'making a big name for himself in lung surgery,' a top-flight explorer, a pundit from Yale and, as the star, Bronson Jane, noted polo player, household word in international finance, who in the same week had been offered 'the Secretaryship of State, the Presidency of an ancient University and the control of a great industrial corporation.' In an article on Buchan in *Encounter* ('John Buchan: An Untimely Appreciation,' September 1960) Gertrude Himmelfarb points out that:

> these marks of success are not the ends towards which his heroes—or villains—strive. They are the preconditions of their being heroes or villains at all, much as the characters in fairy-tales are always the most beautiful, the most exalted, the most wicked of their kind. They are the starting-points for romance, not the termination.

This is shrewd; but many of these dazzling people, such as all those in the *Sick Heart River* lunch-party, are not heroes or villains but minor characters, only marginally involved in the action. Here the emphasis on success probably comes as much from Buchan's habit of generously exaggerating the achievements of his friends and acquaintances in real life, whom he liked to see as outstanding in whatever they did. 'The most remarkable person,' he would enthusiastically report of someone met at dinner; a week later the paragon might have passed clean out of his mind.

The emphasis on success in Buchan's thrillers, the upper-class point of view, is not apparent in the historical novels. The Virginian society of *Salute to Adventurers* is seen critically from the outside by the Glasgow trader Andrew Garvald; when he joins forces with the nobs it is not *his* views that are modified, but theirs. The aristocratic world of Cornbury Park in *Midwinter* is seen by the poor Highland soldier Alastair Maclean, who feels alien to its artificiality:

> The place was a vast embattled fortress of ease, and how would a messenger fare here who brought a summons to hazard all?

David Sempill of *Witch Wood*, in love with the gentle-born Katrine Yester, firmly turns down a suggestion that he should leave the ministry and become a laird. Peter Pentecost of *The Blanket of the Dark* rides 'the full range of ambitions' in his months as Bohun; but at the sight of a Protestant reformer, the world of courts and castles

> seemed to go small. The noble hall with its carvings and gildings and escutcheons suddenly shrank into a little bare place. Lord Avelard seemed a broken old man with deathlike cheeks, Sir Gabriel a painted lath, the commissary a hollow thing like an empty barrel, Sabine a pretty mask with nothing behind but a heart ticking foolishly. Even Simon looked wooden and lifeless. But this wisp of a man, manacled to his jailer, seemed to give out life as fiercely as a furnace gives out heat. There was such a convincing purpose in him that in his presence all the rest of them with their brave appurtenances dwindled and withered.

After his taste of high life, Anthony Lammas of *The Free Fishers* returns with relish to his professor's existence at St Andrews. At the end of *Salute to Adventurers* Andrew Garvald is on the road to a long and prosperous life, but the heroes of the other historical tales disappear—Alastair Maclean, his cause lost, to Jacobite exile; David Sempill, defeated by the bigots of the Kirk, to foreign wars; Peter Pentecost to the greenwood: 'the splendour of Avelard was not for him, but he had still a share in the wild elemental world.' This contrast between the values of the thrillers and of the historical novels is striking, and it was the second group that Buchan took the more seriously.

Many contemporary readers have winced at the references in the thrillers to Negroes and Jews. Buchan's attitude in these matters has been discussed in Chapters Five and Six. Gertrude Himmelfarb is again perceptive:

> The familiar racist sentiments of Buchan, Kipling, even Conrad, were a reflection of a common attitude. They were descriptive, not prescriptive; not an incitement to novel political action, but an attempt to express

differences of culture and colour in terms that had been unquestioned for generations. Today, when differences of race have attained the status of problems—and tragic problems—writers with the best of motives and finest of sensibilities must often take refuge in evasion and subterfuge. Neutral, scientific words replace the old charged ones, and then, because even the neutral ones—'Negro' in place of 'nigger'—give offence, in testifying to differences that men of goodwill would prefer forgotten, disingenuous euphemisms are invented—'non-white' in place of 'Negro.' It is at this stage that one may find a virtue of sorts in Buchan: the virtue of candour, which has both an aesthetic and an ethical appeal.

She makes a similar point about his references to Jews.

The women in Buchan's thrillers are another irritant; they irritated their author, who, in congratulating his sister Anna on the heroine of *The Setons*, wrote:

In Elizabeth you draw a wonderful picture of a woman (a thing I could about as much do as fly to the moon).

He keeps the sex out of *Prester John*, *The Power-House* and *The Thirty-Nine Steps* (though the makers of the *Thirty-Nine Steps* films not only supplied a heroine, but literally shackled her to Hannay), and the only woman in *Greenmantle* is the evil Hilda von Einem. When heroines are admitted, they are slim boyish creatures who are splendid with horses and braver than their men. Occasionally, like Kore Arabin of *The Dancing Floor*, they are wild and rackety, but saved by an essential innocence. When there is a heroine there is plenty of romantic love, but no love-making; F. S. Oliver told Buchan that 'the chief blemish' of *The Blanket of the Dark* was

that you don't turn Peter and Sabine loose together in the greenwood, for a week of summer days, and without the blessing of the church.

Mrs Buchan's son would never have been so irresponsible.

I do not find his young men any more convincing except for those, like David Crawfurd and Andrew Garvald, whom he took in some measure from himself. Vernon Milburne in *The Dancing Floor*, Mercot in *The Three Hostages*, Ottery in *The Gap in the Curtain*, are stereotypes of clean-limbed upper-class young Englishmen, rather slackly put together. It is only when a character has a load of experience in a profession, or in politics, or travel, that he becomes interesting in his own right, and not as an agent in the plot.

This weakness in characterisation matched a trait in his own character: he had more sympathy with people than understanding or imagination about them. He could give a character credibility by drawing on the fields of which he had direct experience—supplying Hannay with an authentic South African and war background, Leithen with the law and the House of Commons. He could throw out a few well-chosen facts and leave it to the reader to fill out the picture with his own idea of what an Old Etonian explorer or a Border laird would be like. But when he wished to show in sympathetic light a character from a milieu which he did not know at first hand—a trade-union leader in *A Prince of the Captivity*, the left-wing poet in *Huntingtower*—he did not make an imaginative effort to understand him. He just endowed him with one of his own wholesome tastes and gave him the root-of-the-matter treatment which I have already discussed.

When Buchan's invention flags he falls back on repetition (the account of Bronson Jane in *The Gap in the Curtain* reappears almost word for word in *Sick Heart River*) and on clichés of situation and language. He dips freely into his old stock. The Buchan addict may enjoy his author's fondness for certain unusual words, such as 'brume' and 'herbage'; he may be struck at a first reading by certain phrases, 'a man to ride the ford with,' 'mulberry dusk,' 'eyes like a wise child,' but the sixth or seventh repetition will irritate. And Buchan's way of seeing life in broad sweeps and trends leads him into some odd sentences about Youth. 'Youth's infinite choice of roads' may pass, but not 'Youth was dancing and sky-larking.'

Though Buchan may deal in stereotype and cliché for his characters, he delineates his landscapes as individually, as lovingly, as other novelists do their heroines. Sometimes he paints a broad perspective—David Sempill's view over upper Tweeddale in *Witch Wood*, Andrew Garvald's of the Shenandoah valley in *Salute to Adventurers*. In other scenes—a Highland glen at dawn in *John Macnab*, the glades of Stowood in *The Blanket of the Dark*, the ravine leading up to the *saeter* in *The Three Hostages*—sounds and smells count as much as sight, and the reader feels that he is discovering the place for himself, with all his senses alert.

What is it that draws back the exasperated critic, who discusses Buchan with an attention seldom given to his contemporaries, Phillips Oppenheim, A. E. W. Mason and Sapper? What makes Graham Greene name Buchan, with Mauriac, as a major influence on his novels? A principal reason, I am sure, is the real sense of

tension and struggle. Buchan appeals to something far deeper than
Sapper's jingo patriotism; the 'goods' and 'bads' are not to be distinguished by nationality. The enemy is not necessarily the man
fighting on the other side—there are 'good' Germans like Gaudian,
and Dr Christoph in 'The Loathly Opposite.'* He is the man who
deliberately wills evil and he may, like Mr Andrew Lumley or
Dominick Medina, not only be on your side, but entrenched in
your Establishment.

'Your best villains,' Edward Sheldon told Buchan,

were always the ones with a magnificent streak of perverted nobility running neck-to-neck with their villainy. You liked and admired them yourself. Otherwise you never would have given to Laputa his 'Unarm, Eros,
the long day's task is done' and to Mr Medina that strange and terrible
desire to purify himself in light. (You made us feel that, when he died in
the cleft, Sir Richard lost a potentially wonderful friend.) As for Frau von
Einem, it is clear that you were more than a little in love with her. I know
I was. So next time admire the villain all you want to. The more you admire
him, the better the book.

Buchan sloughed off his father's Calvinism theologically, in the
sense of a belief in predestination and of the Saved-Damned alterna-
tives that had inspired his father's preaching in the rain outside the
John Knox Free Kirk. But he never lost a sense of the ever-present
reality of evil, and the possibility of its breaking through into the
most respectable lives. He had the Calvinist faculty of imagining a
visible devil, in the shape of man or beast, or localising it in a place
or a ritual. It is in his early stories ('The Watcher by the Threshold,'
'No Man's Land,' 'The Outgoing of the Tide') that he gives freest
play to this faculty, but it was also behind his presentation of
Medina or von Stumm. In most of his thrillers evil is felt as a more
general quality, as the powers of unreason, disorder, or destruction,
that may crack the thin crust of civilisation and morality. Nor is the
concept something conveniently manufactured for the thrillers; it
was something he felt in his bones. It was, for instance, the subject
of addresses to the General Assembly of the Church of Scotland in
1933, and to the University of Toronto in 1936. 'We were not
aware,' wrote J. M. Keynes in 1938 of himself and his friends before
1914,

* 'The Loathly Opposite' records the sympathy that grows up between a British
intelligence agent and his opposite number whom he finally outwits. A similar
fascination with a man who has worked in the same line on the enemy side can
be found in J. M. Keynes's 'Dr Melchior: A Defeated Enemy' (in *Two Memoirs*,
1949).

that civilisation was a thin and precarious crust erected by the personality and the will of a very few, and only maintained by rules and conventions skilfully put across and guilefully preserved.

In 1913 Buchan had been demonstrating, in *The Power-House*, just how thin the crust was. 'Let us gratefully admit,' wrote Graham Greene in 1941, when London was being bombed,

that, in one way at any rate, Buchan prepared us in his thrillers better than he knew for the death that may come to any of us, as it nearly came to Leithen, by the railings of the Park or the doorway of the mews. For certainly we can all see now 'how thin is the protection of civilisation.'

This prophetic strain in Buchan has been one of his fascinations. Characters, ideas and situations which once seemed hopelessly melodramatic turn out to portend later realities: African leaders as charismatic and compelling as Laputa, dictators as bent on controlling men's minds as Dominick Medina or Castor (whose Conquistadores foreshadow Hitler's SS bodyguard), a French *maquis* as subtle as Sandy's Olifa guerrillas in sapping the morale of the invading army. In his public activities Buchan displayed no outstanding sense of the day-to-day movements of politics, but to the deeper currents that move nations and peoples he was always sensitive. In a review of the French translation of *The Courts of the Morning* Jacques Bergier observes that:

Buchan ne déduit pas Hitler du nombre de chômeurs en Allemagne en 1933. Il nous montre que le véritable pouvoir est celui de l'esprit sur d'autres esprits et qu'une personalité exceptionelle peut changer le destin d'un pays ou même du monde.

Under other circumstances such intuitions might have found expression in a 'higher' artistic form than the thriller, but Buchan had never shown any wish to carve out new channels for what he had to say. One can only speculate as to what he might have achieved if, for instance, he had further explored the possibilities of writing directly for the screen. The film, in the hands of a Hitchcock, can suggest the interpenetration of myth and 'real life' with much more compression and force than the adventure story. But Buchan was content to use this popular form, in which his real imaginative power can be too easily obscured. Some of the dissatisfactions felt by his readers may come from this disparity between the rather old-fashioned tradition in which Buchan wrote —the yarns told in club-room or country-house, the 'grown-up boys' book'—and the intuitions, which seem very much of the twentieth century. Between *The Waste Land* and *The Three Hostages* is the rift between high art and popular entertainment; but there is not such an absolute rift between the visionary perceptions of post-war Europe which underlie both the poem and the thriller.

Struggle in the Buchan thriller is not only with the Enemy but with Nature. Gertrude Himmelfarb says that Buchan's heroes

are periodically beset by fatigue and lassitude, a 'death wish' that is over-come by divesting themselves of their urban identities—success being an urban condition—and donning the shabby, anonymous clothes of the countryman. Only when the perils of nature and of the chase have rough-ened up the smooth patina of success, leaving the body scarred and the mind tormented, can they resume their normal lives and identities.

'Death-wish,' 'tormented'—fiddlesticks! Buchan had to find a pre-text—in a search or a mystery, in overwork and the need for a change—to start up his story, to get his heroes out of their clubs and chambers and into the wild. And he sent them off to climb rocks, stalk stags, cross the Alps, walk thirty miles across country, lie in a fenland marsh at dawn, because these were the things *he* best liked doing on his holidays. Episodes and situations that strike some of his critics as pure torment were to him exhilarating, as climbing and sailing are exhilarating to all those responsible citizens who find in the concentrated effort these activities demand, and the kind of victories they offer, the perfect complement to their working lives. Back in 1906, in *A Lodge in the Wilderness*, Buchan had written that:

There is no satisfaction so intense as victory over some one of the savage forces of nature. Better for the moment than viceroyalties or Garters or millions is the joy of making the first ascent of some hard peak, or sailing a boat home through a tempest, or seeing some wild animal fall before your own courage and skill.

As well as this sense of a continuing struggle—between man and his environment, between good and evil—is the sense of human possibilities, including the possibility of regeneration. Jacques Bergier, who says that he found Buchan characters 'sur les routes de France au temps des parachutages,' considers Buchan 'le type du véritable romancier réaliste' because:

La véritable vie, la véritable action, ce qui fait qu'un homme se révèle et s'affermit, c'est tout de même Buchan et non pas Sartre ou Céline. Car le courage et l'intelligence sont des réalités psychologiques au même titre que la nausée, sinon plus.

In nearly all his stories some character appears as 'new.' Launcelot Wake in *Mr Standfast* is 'a new man' when he turns up in the Coolins; in the same book the German offensive in 1918 makes of the Wodehousian Roylance 'a new Archie'; the Gobernador of *The Courts of the Morning* becomes 'a new man' when made to realise how evil was his former creed; even Mr Thomas Craw, the unctuous newspaper magnate of *Castle Gay*, is 'a new man' when forced to live the simple life on the Galloway moors, and the shoddiness of his values is exposed. Many of the stories end not so much in triumph as in reconciliation. On the final page of *The Courts of the Morning* soldiers of both factions, who have lately been fighting each other, march through Olifa in triumph as the Army of Revolution; at the climax of *The Three Hostages* Medina and Hannay cease to be enemies, the hunter and the hunted, and become fellow-climbers on difficult rock. The heroes are often content with success rather than victory (this was a point which Buchan also made about the Emperor Augustus); the villains are sent to deaths that are striking and symbolic rather than horrifying or ignominious. Ivery of *Mr Standfast* is machine-gunned by fellow-Germans as he rushes towards them across No Man's Land, the crippled Russian of *Huntingtower* is caught between the ebb-tide and the offshore gale on the Galloway coast. There is no vindictiveness, no gratuitous pain.

John Buchan would have thought it absurd that so much close attention should be given to his 'shockers' or 'tushery.' He seldom read any reviews of them; 'if writers mind bad reviews,' he told his wife, 'they shouldn't write books.' To himself he was a serious historian but not (though as a young man he had different views) a serious novelist except in *The Path of the King*, *Midwinter*, *Witch Wood* and *The Blanket of the Dark*. He was a tale-spinner and, like the tellers of fairy-tales, whom he discussed in a paper to the English Association in 1931, his job was to deal in the reversal of fortune:

weakness winning against might, gentleness and courtesy against brutality, brains as against mere animal strength, the one chance in a hundred succeeding. . . .

The scale must be weighted against the hero . . . His task must be made as difficult as possible, for how otherwise can we get the full drama—how otherwise can ordinary folk be persuaded that life has colour in it and a wide horizon?

Buchan enjoyed writing his tales because in them he could re-live the best of his holidays, could vicariously set off on a hurried journey, explore the mountains west of the Mackenzie River, hold a rocky defile against awful odds. 'His tongue is never in his cheek,' one critic noted. 'He writes of just those adventures which would afford him the keenest personal enjoyment.' He could recall the happiness of being one of a group of friends—at Oxford, in South Africa, in his bachelor years in London; there could be no such group now, too many had been killed. He could let his fancy play on places that stirred his imagination—the rock jutting from a Coolin face, the glades of the Wood Bush, the blank house by the island jetty. He could pleasantly keep his hand in with lore which he had once acquired but no longer needed in his professional life, as when he wrote of company transactions in *The Gap in the Curtain* and an international compensation case in *The Dancing Floor*, or used a medieval Latin phrase from the wizard Michael Scott as a trick to unmask Medina in *The Three Hostages*.

As he wrote the books to make money, he naturally kept on the characters who had won his public's affection; but he found it 'huge fun playing with my puppets, and to me they very soon became very real flesh and blood.' His imaginary world was clearly charted, and there are cross-references between the stories in the different groups. Castle Gay had been on his private map since 1897 ('The Rime of True Thomas'); Glenaicill Forest and Correi na Sidhe, where the drama of *The Three Hostages* comes to a climax, had been charted years earlier in 'Space.' The Radens of 'The Far Islands' reappear in *John Macnab*. Tombs, the left-wing politician of *Mr Standfast*, pops up in *Castle Gay*.

Very firmly Buchan made it clear that in his thrillers he was not competing in any literary class, and he rather liked to emphasise his distance from professional literary men. He would not attend any literary gatherings if he could help it, though he always enjoyed the company of journalists (the profession shows up very well in his tales). To Hugh Walpole he wrote that 'I have never been very much interested in the careers of men of letters. . . . I am an amateur in letters.' The genuine modesty about his own tales, the dissociation from the world of men of letters, perhaps conceal some uncertainty or dissatisfaction; after all, the author of *Scholar Gipsies* and *The Half-Hearted* had nursed serious literary ambitions. Scottish writers of the last two centuries have—unlike Scottish painters—been loath to admit that their profession was enough in

itself. 'A great romantic—an idle child,' said Stevenson of Scott, for
not working hard enough at his art; at the end of *his* life Stevenson
was not satisfied with his own devotion: 'I ought to have been able
to build lighthouses and write *David Balfours* too.' Scott, Stevenson
and Buchan each lived a life of action as well as of writing; with all
three the writing became a major action in their personal drama.
Scott wrote to build Abbotsford and pay his debts; Stevenson to
build Vailima and support his clan of dependents: Buchan to keep
up Elsfield and send his boys to Eton and Oxford. I do not think
that any of the three felt he had prostituted a gift. They believed
that you did pay your way, you did meet your obligations; and the
things they were paying for with their books satisfied a deep
romantic need—to be a laird, a chieftain, an Oxfordshire country
gentleman. Had anyone reminded Buchan the best-seller of the
severe judgment which he passed on the Kailyarders when he was
twenty—

No man, however high his spirits and rich the life within him, can hope
to be a great writer save by the restraint, the pains, the hard and bitter
drudgery of his art—

he would not have felt it applied to himself, for he was not in the
field as 'a great writer.' In his tales he made signals of recognition
to Scott and Stevenson; not for a minute did he think of himself as
being in the same class.

Offhand about any literary merits in his books, Buchan was glad
if they pleased his friends. 'I find, as I grow older,' he told Stair
Gillon in 1932, 'that I write more and more to please myself and
my old friends, and think of nobody else.' It was A. J. Balfour's
liking for Phillips Oppenheim that started him off on *The Power-
House*, and Balfour became a Buchan fan. Baldwin, who had been
one from the day in 1902 when he bought *The Watcher by the
Threshold* at Paddington Station, wrote of *The Courts of the
Morning*:

You are a ruddy miracle! I think your last is really the best and yet all
your stuff is so good.

Other public persons who were enthusiastic readers were Attlee,
Baden-Powell, H. A. L. Fisher, William Temple, Mr Justice
Tomlin (who in a case in 1924, where an inventor from Leith
claimed that the Admiralty had burgled his office and taken his
plans, said, 'This is more a case for John Buchan than this court').

Buchan was delighted to hear that King George V had enjoyed

John Macnab at Balmoral, that Lord Crewe had revelled in *Midwinter*, that the Trevelyans had read *John Macnab* aloud on their family holiday in 1925, and had re-read *The Three Hostages* and *Huntingtower* to each other ten years and more after publication. Some of the appreciation was unexpected. Ezra Pound wrote from Rapallo in 1934 (of *The Three Hostages*) that 'One of yr/novels occasionally drifts into this seaside village, years late, but still full of activity.' A.E., speaking as one of 'that very large class . . . who rejoices in adventures while they themselves are toasting their toes on a fender,' declared:

> I think I could pass an examination in all General Hannay's adventures from *The Forty-Nine* [*sic*] *Steps* on to *The Three Hostages*.

However much Buchan played down his thrillers, he was very glad when literary friends appreciated his historical novels: when Rose Macaulay considered *The Blanket of the Dark* 'so enchanting and beautiful that I often read it for my pleasure,' and Kipling spoke of being 'rested and delighted' by the same story, which he considered a *tour de force*.

There was one person who found no charm in Hannay, Leithen and Dickson McCunn. Mrs Buchan (no great reader) couldn't do with the thrillers at all.

Admirably did the thrillers fulfil one of his main intentions in writing them: they made money.

Buchan's early dealings with publishers were described at the end of Chapter Four. With the exception of *Prester John* (written as a boys' book for Nelson) and *Salute to Adventurers* (Nelson), his fiction from 1902 (*The Watcher by the Threshold*) to 1916 (*The Power-House*) was published by Blackwood. From *Greenmantle* onwards the first publication of his novels was by Hodder & Stoughton—Buchan met Ernest Hodder-Williams in 1916 when the latter was involved in the publication of government propaganda. Of the biographies, *Montrose* (both 1913 and 1928 versions) and *Minto* (1924) were published by Nelson, *Sir Walter Scott* (1932) by Cassell, *Cromwell* (1934) and *Augustus* (1937) by Hodder & Stoughton. His short books on *Julius Caesar* (1932), *The Massacre of Glencoe* (1933) and *Gordon at Khartoum* (1934) were in series published by Peter Davies, who wrote of his dealings with Buchan as having been

without a single exception the pleasantest of my experience—in the sense that everything was arranged with such uncomplicated smoothness, such decency in the full classical sense of the word.

'He was indeed a model author,' writes Mr John Attenborough of Hodder & Stoughton, remembering how, as a young man of twenty-five, he worked with Buchan on *The King's Grace*, the book written at the publisher's special request to celebrate the Jubilee of King George V in 1935. (It is not a piece of 'royal tushery,' but a history of the events of the reign.)

He wrote the book at great speed, and we made great demands upon him as an author, for different versions of it were produced at different prices, including special editions for school authorities, who wanted to give it away to their pupils as a memento of the anniversary. Buchan took the greatest personal interest in the selection and placing of the photographs of the illustrated edition, and corrected all the proofs with the greatest care. At that time he was heavily involved in Parliamentary duties, and Canada was only just ahead of him. But he never kept me waiting for a moment, and he never made any hurried decisions, although he was working at really top pressure.

At Houghton Mifflin, his American publishers from 1924, Buchan was dealing with his friend and fellow-fisherman Ferris Greenslet, to whom he dedicated *The Courts of the Morning* in verses celebrating their spring fishing on rivers of the old world and the new. In his pleasant relations with his publishers Buchan was greatly helped by his agents A. S. Watt and later W. P. Watt. 'I have had from you the utmost friendliness and the straightest of straight dealings,' he wrote on A. S. Watt's retirement.

In 1896 Buchan had told his mother that he would 'never for a moment go below ten per cent royalty.' In fact for several of his earlier books he received a fifteen per cent royalty. For *The Thirty-Nine Steps*, originally published in a shilling edition, Buchan received 12½ per cent from Blackwood; after its success he was able to obtain 30 per cent for *Greenmantle* from Hodder & Stoughton. For *Mr Standfast* the royalty figure dropped to 25 per cent for the first 5000, then 30 per cent to 15,000, thereafter 33⅓ per cent. Buchan never again touched this truly staggering figure. The royalty for *Huntingtower* and *Midwinter* was 20 per cent rising to 25 per cent, for the next three novels 25 per cent rising after 5000 to 30 per cent, from *Witch Wood* onwards he received a flat royalty of 30 per cent.

Up to 1915 Buchan had not sold more than 2000 copies of any of his novels or books of short stories (with the probable exception of *Prester John*; Messrs Nelson have not been able to give me figures for the earlier Buchans which they published). *The Thirty-Nine Steps*—serialised in *Blackwood's* from July to September 1915 and published at a shilling in October—sold 25,000 copies by the end of the year, and 34,000 during 1916.* Suddenly Buchan was a best-seller.

The Power-House, which had first appeared in the December 1913 issue of *Blackwood's*, came out as a book in May 1916, also at a shilling, and had sold 24,000 by the end of the year. The first of the Hodder & Stoughton novels, *Greenmantle*, serialised in *Land and Water* between July and November 1916, was published in November at 6s. and by the following March had sold 34,000. *Mr Standfast*, which was not serialised, was published at 6s. in the autumn of 1918, and sold 19,000 in its first year. There was a drop with *The Path of the King* (1921), which in its first year sold under 10,000; *Huntingtower* (1922) and *Midwinter* (1923) picked up with over 18,000 and over 16,000 respectively. With *The Three Hostages* (serialised in the *Graphic* from April to August 1924, immediately before publication) the graph rises sharply; the sales in the first year were just under 30,000.

Henceforth the annual Buchans follow much the same course. There was usually pre-publication in serial form—*Witch Wood*, under the title *The High Places*, was serialised in Buchan's old antagonist the *British Weekly*. Then would come a first edition of the novel at 7s. 6d., which sold between 20,000 and 30,000; after eighteen months a cheap edition at 3s. 6d., which in two years would sell between 10,000 and 20,000, and then for a few more years at 1000–1500 a year. About a year after the cheap Hodder & Stoughton edition would come publication in the Uniform Edition of Buchan's work published by Nelson at 4s. 6d.; for a few years the sales would be modest but steady, a few hundred a year.

The Runagates Club and *The Gap in the Curtain*, collections of stories, sold least well of the titles. The immediate sales of the historical stories averaged slightly less than the thrillers, but there was no striking difference, and *Witch Wood*, with 28,000 in its first year, sold outstandingly well. *The Dancing Floor* (31,000 in its first year) did best of all the thrillers after *The Thirty-Nine Steps* and *Greenmantle*. All these figures are for British sales only; they take no account of export sales of the British edition, American sales or foreign translations. In the United States *Prester John*, *Mountain Meadow* (the American title for *Sick Heart River*) and *The Thirty-Nine Steps* sold over 20,000 each: *The Three Hostages*, *The Dancing Floor*, *The Courts of the Morning*, *John Macnab*, *Witch Wood*, *The*

---

* All figures for sales are to the nearest thousand.

Man from the Norlands (*The Island of Sheep*) and *Castle Gay* over 10,000 copies each.

So while 'the new Buchan' was making its splash, earlier ones would still be thriving. The success of *The Thirty-Nine Steps* stimulated the publishers of his youthful books to bring back titles which had dropped out of sight. John Lane brought out a shilling edition of *John Burnet of Barns* (1898) in 1916, and *A Lost Lady of Old Years* (1899) in 1919. Nelson did a new *Prester John* (1910) in 1919. Blackwood did a new *The Watcher by the Threshold* (1902) rather surprisingly a few months *before* they published *The Thirty-Nine Steps*, and it quickly sold 6000. Hodder & Stoughton published new editions of *The Half-Hearted* (1900) in 1920, and of *The Moon Endureth* (1912) in 1921.

In 1930 Hodder & Stoughton started publishing groups of related stories in omnibus volumes: *The Four Adventures of Richard Hannay* was followed by *The Adventures of Sir Edward Leithen* (1935) and *The Adventures of Dickson McCunn* (1937), while *A Fivefold Salute to Adventurers* contains the historical stories. Blackwood produced the books originally published by them—*The Watcher by the Threshold, The Moon Endureth, The Thirty-Nine Steps, The Power-House*—in one volume as *Four Tales* in 1936. Since the mid-fifties all Buchan's fiction has appeared in paperback, except for the early *Sir Quixote of the Moors* and *A Lost Lady of Old Years*.

Here are some totals of the combined sales up to 1960 of editions published by Hodder & Stoughton and by Nelson (or, with books where Blackwood was the first publisher, by Blackwood and by Nelson).

The Watcher by the Threshold	63,000
The Thirty-Nine Steps	355,000
Greenmantle	368,000
Mr Standfast	231,000
The Path of the King	75,000
Huntingtower	230,000
Midwinter	112,000
The Three Hostages	216,000
John Macnab	156,000
The Dancing Floor	122,000
Witch Wood	98,000
The Runagates Club	85,000
The Courts of the Morning	96,000
Castle Gay	151,000
The Blanket of the Dark	73,000

The Gap in the Curtain	78,000
A Prince of the Captivity	83,000
The Free Fishers	100,000
The House of the Four Winds	101,000
The Island of Sheep	122,000
Sick Heart River	96,000 (Hodder only, not in Nelson)

On the basis of these figures—limited as they are, and taking no account of American sales or paperback editions—we can say that the Hannay books are easily top of the list (average sale of 258,000, or 231,000 if we count *The Courts of the Morning* as a Hannay book), followed by the Dickson McCunns (average 161,000) and the Leithens (125,000). Admittedly Hannay had started earlier in book form than the other two heroes, and had a longer run in print, but his greater popularity is borne out by the current sales of paperbacks and the continued demand for the omnibus volume of his adventures. The historical tales come last, with an average of 92,000. Collections of short stories were not so popular as full-length tales, and *The Blanket of the Dark*, one of Buchan's best novels in his own view and in mine, sold least well of any.

In 1952 Pan Books published *Greenmantle* in paperback and since then have added a further eight titles. In 1956 Penguin Books put out ten Buchans together and some years later added two more. Their edition of *The Thirty-Nine Steps* was limited to a single printing of 60,000 copies. The sales figures, which are given below (those for Pan books are up to September 1965 and for Penguin to June 1964), demonstrate the continuing popularity of Buchan with a new generation of readers, and again emphasise the supremacy of the Hannay stories.

	Pan	Penguin	Total
John Burnet of Barns	30,000		30,000
Prester John	110,000	110,000	220,000
The Thirty-Nine Steps	610,000	60,000	670,000
Salute to Adventurers	35,000		35,000
The Power-House	40,000		40,000
Greenmantle	200,000	130,000	330,000
Mr Standfast	30,000	68,000	98,000
Huntingtower		104,000	104,000
The Three Hostages		175,000	175,000
John Macnab		53,000	53,000
Castle Gay		53,000	53,000
The Blanket of the Dark		32,000	32,000
A Prince of the Captivity	35,000		35,000
The Free Fishers		21,000	21,000

The House of the Four Winds		84,000	84,000
The Island of Sheep	40,000	81,000	121,000

In the United States *Mountain Meadow* (*Sick Heart River*) sold just over, and *The Thirty-Nine Steps* just under, 300,000 when they appeared in paperback; *The Three Hostages* and *The House of the Four Winds* sold over 200,000 each, and *Greenmantle* over 100,000.

Outstanding among even these successes has been *The Thirty-Nine Steps*. In English it has sold about a million and a half, and there have been translations into Persian, Arabic, Czech, Swedish, Spanish, French, German, Dutch, Danish, and no doubt more by the time these words appear.

Although Buchan's biographies are discussed in other chapters, this seems a convenient place for recording how they prospered. Unfortunately there are no records of the early sales of his *Montrose*, either in the 1913 or the 1928 versions, though in later, cheaper editions published by Hodder & Stoughton 23,000 were sold; since it appeared as an Oxford World's Classic in 1957 it has sold approximately 4500. In their first year of publication *Sir Walter Scott* (Cassell, 1932) sold 19,000, and in a 2s. edition by Hodder & Stoughton 15,000, between 1938 and 1940; *Oliver Cromwell* (Hodder & Stoughton, 1934) sold 11,000; *Augustus* (Hodder & Stoughton, 1937) 5000. (These figures, again, are for sales in Britain only.) Up to 1960 *Sir Walter Scott* sold 47,000 (there was a new edition in 1961); *Oliver Cromwell* sold 28,000; and *Augustus* (which went into a cheap edition in 1942) 36,000.

Buchan's literary earnings from all sources approximated, from 1919 to 1921, to £4000–£5000 a year; in 1922, £6000; 1923, £8000 (including £3000 for the American rights of the *History of the War*); from 1924 to 1929 the figure was between £7000 and £8000; from 1930 to 1935, between £8000 and £9500, except for £7000 in 1933. In 1936, the last year of his life that he published a new thriller, he earned £7000, as he did in 1937; then there was a decline to £3000 and £1500 in 1938 and 1939.

Whatever large sums he might confidently expect to receive from his novels, the advance which he took on royalties remained steady over many years. The huge success of *Greenmantle* (1916) for which he had an advance of £200, made £750 a reasonable advance on *Mr Standfast*; thereafter he took £750 on each novel up to *The Free Fishers* in 1934 (£950) and *The House of the Four Winds*, for which he took £1250 in 1935, a year of heavy expense in moving to Canada. The figure returned to £750 the next year for *The Island of Sheep*. Larger advances were received for his biographies: £2000 each for *Cromwell* and *Augustus* and for his own autobiography £3000. These are figures for British advances only.

These were substantial rewards, and he worked hard for them. From 1919 onwards there was always a serious work of history or biography on hand; a story simmering away; a steady flow of articles and reviews, some of them, like his front-page contributions to the *Literary Supplement*, requiring considerable reading, and often an editorial work, such as *The Northern Muse*, or the collection of Rosebery's speeches and writings; and he always made the indexes for his scholarly works. In 1922, for instance, he worked on the proofs of Volumes 3 and 4 of the *History of the War*, finished *Huntingtower*, began *Midwinter*, and went on with his researches on Montrose. In 1929 he finished *Castle Gay*, began *The Blanket of the Dark*, and started work on *Sir Walter Scott*. In 1932 he wrote *Julius Caesar*, finished *A Prince of the Captivity*, began *The Free Fishers* and started work on *Cromwell*. He was also writing the Atticus column in the *Sunday Times*; till April, a fortnightly article for the *Graphic* and, from January to March, the Notebook in *The Spectator*. In 1934 he wrote *Gordon at Khartoum*, finished *The House of the Four Winds* and *Cromwell*, began *The Island of Sheep* and *The King's Grace*.

'Like the expert chess-player,' said an editorial in the *Scotsman*,

he would play many hands simultaneously, moving from subject to subject, as the chess-master moves from board to board, without losing grip or slackening attention.

And the writer went on to talk of Buchan's 'power of concentration, combined with unceasing industry.'

It would have been an impressive record for a full-time man of letters.

CHAPTER ELEVEN

MEMBER OF PARLIAMENT
1927–35

'Every man has a creed, but in his soul he knows that that creed has
another side.'
> John Buchan: 'A Lucid Interval' (1910)

'Politics have always been my chief interest.'
> John Buchan to Stanley Baldwin, 4 October 1932

After the war Buchan had twice been asked to stand for Parliament:
in 1920 again for Peeblesshire, in 1922 for Central Glasgow in
succession to Bonar Law. He had no hesitation in saying no; his
health just could not stand ordinary constituency work. But when,
in March 1927, he was invited by the Unionist Association of the
Scottish Universities to contest the seat made vacant by the death
of Sir Henry Craik, he at once accepted.* Here was the ideal Parliamentary constituency: no expenses, no preliminary campaigning,
only an election address; no polling-day frenzy, for the voting was
by post; voters so scattered that there could be no week-end meetings, no socials, no sales-of-work; above all, no need to be a rigid
party man. The member would be expected to concern himself with
education; otherwise he would be free in Parliament to specialise in
the questions he himself chose.

Polling was at the end of April; on the 29th Buchan heard that
he had beaten his Labour opponent, Hugh Guthrie, by 16,903
votes to 2378, with handsome majorities in all four Universities.
'My majority proves that this talk of the democratic Scottish Universities being honeycombed by Socialism is all nonsense,' he
replied to one friend offering congratulations, but he was realistic
about one reason for his overwhelming victory. In response to the

* Until 1948 there were twelve Members of Parliament representing the Universities and elected by the graduates: Oxford and Cambridge had two each, London
one, the other English Universities together had two, the Scottish Universities
three, the Universities of Wales and Northern Ireland one each.

congratulations of his Glasgow University contemporary, Alec MacCallum Scott, now a member of the Independent Labour Party, he wrote: 'I think a great many people must have voted for me as they would have voted for Harry Lauder!'*

'Thank God we have got rid of much of that silly old party stuff,' Buchan had written during the war; and the views which he now brought with him to Westminster were not rabidly partisan. Many of them had been aired in *The Island of Sheep* (not to be confused with the novel of the same title published in 1936), a symposium in the style of *A Lodge in the Wilderness* which he had written with his wife in 1919, when they were in lodgings in Oxford while Elsfield was being put in order. A number of characters—landowner, Labour M.P., journalist, captain of industry, parish minister (whose only fear is 'a prosecution for heresy in the Courts of my Church') —meet in a shooting-lodge on a Scottish island to discuss the post-war world. (Buchan himself had joined in such discussions during the war, at meetings of the New Days Committee with Philip Kerr, Albert Mansbridge, George Drummond, S. L. Bensusan and others.) Peace has been bought with millions of lives; what is to be made of it? The tone is hopeful, there is ridicule of those who 'prophesy darkly about the People, as if they were some new kind of influenza;' scorn for those whose only political emotion is hate. There is recognition that the working class will take an ever larger share in politics, and confidence in their ability to handle affairs. The summing-up is given to the minister:

Politics are a collection of views, most of them contradictory, and nearly all of them true. Statesmanship means admitting the contradictions and paying due respect to the half-truths and trying to harmonise them. The fool seizes on a half-truth, and exaggerates it and pretends it is the whole truth and the only truth.

This echoes a passage in a story of 1909, 'A Lucid Interval,' where certain politicians are given a drug which elicits views and opinions which had hitherto remained dormant:

Every man has a creed, but in his soul he knows that that creed has another side, possibly not less logical, which it does not suit him to produce. Our most honest convictions are not the children of pure reason, but of temperament, environment, necessity, and interest. Most of us take sides in life and forget the one we reject.

* Harry Lauder was at the time playing Dickson McCunn in the film of *Huntingtower* which was being made that spring.

In many of Buchan's writings in the Twenties there is understanding and sympathy with the side he had rejected. When during the
national railway strike in 1921 Lloyd George was calling the Unions
unpatriotic and the Labour Party Bolshevik, Buchan attacked him
for his 'tendency to see things in crude antagonisms.' Buchan made
the point—an elementary one, but it may well have needed making
for the readers he was addressing in the *Oxford Fortnightly Review*
—that membership of a Union was the workers' only security,

without which they are economic waifs unable to bargain on a fair basis.
That is why they struggle so desperately against any infringement of their
Union rules, since they regard such as a weakening of the safeguards
essential to their very existence. I do not think full justice has been done to
the patriotism of the ordinary man during the war in allowing drastic
alterations of these rules as a war measure; it involved putting himself in
the hands of his country, a sacrifice of hardly-bought security, of which
most people have no idea.

And in an article in *English Life*, in the summer of 1926, he explained why the Unions should feel so strongly about the Government's intention, as a consequence of the General Strike, to bring
in a new Trades Disputes Act.

Like so many of his generation, Buchan felt the Great War was
the great divide: 'Everywhere in the world was heard the sound of
things breaking' was his description of the mood of 1919, and ten
years later he wrote that 'Peace is seen to be a slow and difficult
construction.' The public figures whom he most suspected were
those who seemed to be still concerned with breaking, like the
Bolsheviks in Russia, or A. J. Cook, the miners' leader throughout
the 1926 strike. Those whom he most respected were concerned
with rebuilding—statesmen like Stresemann and Briand, trade
unionists like Robert Smillie and Frank Hodges. Contrasting de
Valera with Cosgrave, he wrote that 'the nations since the war have
had two kinds of leaders; the rhapsodists who inflame and embolden,
and the plain, homely realists who try to heal.' Buchan was a League
of Nations man, a Locarno man; he considered the Imperial Conference of 1926, with its new doctrine of the Commonwealth as an
alliance of independent sovereign states, as the most important
event in the history of Empire.

He was always insistent that 'the problem in all politics is how to
give to actual human beings the chance of a worthy life.'

It is four-square human beings whom we have to deal with, not whimsies
such as the 'political' man or the 'economic' man, and it is human beings
with a long descent behind them, and with history in their bones.

This is from an article in the *Spectator* on 'Conservatism and Progress,' and among his other observations are:

There is a perpetual duty for the intellect to examine the bequest of tradition and to get rid of whatever has outlived its usefulness.

The two great problems of today in the widest sense are, I take it, the business of reaching a true democracy, where everyone shall be given a chance not only of a livelihood, but of a worthy life, and the business of building up some kind of world-wide regime which shall ensure peace and co-operation between the nations.

Such seem to be the merits of the attitude of mind which we may call conservative, traditional, or, as I should prefer, historical. Let me add that it has very little to do with current party divisions. I have known members of my own party who had no trace of it, and members of the Labour Party who were inclined to carry it almost too far.

So Buchan's Toryism (he disliked the word 'Conservatism' with its suggestion of the duty of preserving always, at any cost) was not a harking-back to a pre-1914 world, a longing to recreate a vanished social order. It was, rather, a sanguine and romantic looking-forward—perhaps too sanguine and romantic to be practical and effective. 'We are adventurers again,' he said in Glasgow in 1924; 'we are looking at wide and misty horizons.' A few years later he told an audience of schoolboys that 'it is an uncomfortable time for elderly people who are settled in their ways. It is a horrible time for dogmatic and stupid people. It is a disquieting time for timid people. But it is a magnificent time in which to be young.'

'His opinions,' wrote an observer of Buchan in the year after he entered Parliament,

are those of the enlightened country gentleman, the part which he plays so gracefully in his Oxfordshire home. He is robust, sensible, and just a little feudal in his outlook. Yet I fancy that the Young Conservatives, if they are wise, will find in him an ally, for no man is more conscious than he of the futility of mere reaction, or less likely to wield a spade for the entrenchment of vested interests.

But it was not the country-gentleman side of him that determined Buchan's political hopefulness, his willingness to look forward, to see changes, to trust younger people. These came rather from the whole pattern of his career. People with inherited land and capital usually find the thought of change frightening, for their treasure may be snatched from them. Buchan, with only the capital of his brains, energy and character, knew that whatever pattern society assumed, there would always be a place for a man of his abilities.

He was not afraid of socialism in itself. 'I believe profoundly,' he wrote to J. B. Priestley in 1937,

in the progressive socialisation of the State, but the vital thing must always be the preservation of the spiritual integrity of the individual.

Nor was he alarmed by the new functions of the State. It had, he told an audience in 1936,

greatly enlarged its area of duty. We realise that it is not a remote and impersonal thing; but the collective powers of the community organised to help any part which is in distress.

He was not out of sympathy with those who worked for a more egalitarian society. But—with 'the sound of things breaking' in his ears—he had a deep fear of chaos and disorder, and it seemed to him that many of those whose aspirations he shared too easily discounted the possible consequences, in disorder and misery, of too rapid and drastic change. In his Election Address of 1927 he underlined the unpredictability of 'the vast constitutional and social revolution' proposed by the Socialists. Revolution in itself did not frighten him; the chaos which he felt inseparable from too rapid a revolution did.

With this outlook and temperament Buchan was happy to enter the House of Commons when the Prime Minister, and leader of Buchan's party, was Stanley Baldwin—the man to whom Harold Laski said, 'It is tradition rather than fundamentals that has put you among the forces of the right.' To many people today Baldwin is the man who appeared to do nothing when a tenth of the population was out of work, the neglecter of our defences, the man whose lips were sealed. But in the mid-twenties Baldwin stood for progressive Conservatism, for decency in public life, and above all for industrial peace. He was straightforwardly patriotic: in 1919 he had given £120,000, a fifth of his fortune, to the Government towards cancellation of War Loan, in the hope that his example would be widely followed; it was not. He believed deeply in national unity; party conflict was necessary and honourable, but within a framework of acceptance of Parliament and the constitution, and for him it was more important that Labour should learn how to govern than that the Conservatives should always win. He was passionate in his determination to avoid social war at home ('The Conservatives can't talk of class-war,' he said once; 'they started it') and his most eloquent speech in Parliament, in 1925, ended with a plea for industrial understanding: 'Give peace in our time, O Lord.'* He was sensitive to the moral challenge underlying Socialism and refused to treat the Labour Party as enemies. For another passionate belief of Baldwin's was in the essential sanity and reasonableness of the English and, therefore, in their fitness for democracy, which 'means nothing if it does not mean the realisation by the individual of his responsibility.' But people in a democracy would need to be educated in the issues which they would be called upon to face; this was a point Baldwin constantly stressed. His policy beyond Britain, whether towards the Empire or foreign countries, was based on the same convictions. It was always conciliation, discussion, the effort to extend the areas of goodwill and co-operation, never threats or sabre-rattling. India, for instance, must never become another Ireland.

Such general views were sympathetic to Buchan, for reconciliation, between Briton and Boer, was the first political lesson he had learnt under Milner. So was Baldwin's attitude to their party. 'My party,' Baldwin would say, 'what is my party? Diamond Jubilee die-hards and Tory Democrats pulling me two ways at once;' but it was the latter whom he favoured every time, at the expense of those who urged him not to extend the franchise, not to give pensions to widows, but to take a firm line in Egypt and India, and stand no nonsense about democratic institutions. And when Baldwin (in 1924) castigated the party for choosing candidates with money ('If you must have a candidate who can water his constituency with £1000 a year you are going to have a choice of about half per cent of the population, and if you are going to fight a party that has the choice of the whole population, you will never beat them in this world, and, more than that, you will never deserve to beat them') he was expressing what Buchan had felt so strongly in the pre-war days when he was a Parliamentary candidate in Peeblesshire. Privilege, both men were certain, did the Tory Party no good.

The only kind of Party in which either Baldwin or Buchan could

* Soon after the outbreak of war in 1939 David Kirkwood, one of the Clydeside M.P.s who had been deported from the area in 1916, wrote to Baldwin that Britain had gone into this war united, with the Unions spontaneously agreeing to the dilution of labour and to overtime, because of the changed atmosphere largely brought about by this speech, which 'made flesh the feelings of us all, that the antagonism, the bitterness, the class rivalry were unworthy, and that understanding and amity were possible.' (G. M. Young: *Stanley Baldwin*, 1952, p. 95.)

be easy was one which could attract young people of intelligence, energy and idealism; and Baldwin made it his business to give such young people a lead. In May 1925 he went down to Oxford to address the undergraduate Conservative Association at the suggestion of Buchan, then its Senior Treasurer. He spoke to his undergraduate audience of Milner, who had died three days before, and of Arnold Toynbee, whose 'unselfish devotion to social service' had so affected Milner as a young man. He spoke of General Booth's *Darkest England*, of Charles Booth's investigation of poverty, of the need for social reorganisation. He spoke of widows' pensions and cheap electricity, of the new forms of public ownership. He preached 'a modern Conservative creed:'

the creed preached by Disraeli eighty years ago—your first object, whatever you do, is to render social service of some kind. Try to give back to the less fortunate people of this country and of the world something that you owe the less fortunate world for the happiness and for the privileges that have been showered upon all of you.

In temperament there might seem to be a gulf between Buchan, with his apparently inexhaustible resource of nervous energy and his ability to get all his jobs done, and Baldwin, who never read half his Parliamentary papers, whose moments of action and decision were succeeded by periods of lethargy and nervelessness. But they shared some important traits and tastes. They were both sanguine about people, not disparagers; which may not have been a political asset, for, as a colleague observed, 'One of the troubles about being a nice man like Buchan or Baldwin, always prepared to make the best of people, is that you're not sufficiently aware of the facts of life.' Yet both of them also distrusted the flashy and the showy in politics or anywhere else. They were wary of Birkenhead offering his 'glittering prizes' to the young,* and of Churchill champing for battle with the trade-unions or on India—'our two banditti' Baldwin called them. This wariness could indeed co-exist with admiration and liking: Buchan was very fond of Birkenhead, though he continued to think of Churchill as 'mischievous.' Buchan and Baldwin would dine soberly at The Club, with the salt of the earth like Archbishop Davidson and G. M. Trevelyan (and sometimes Buchan would report 'rather a dull dinner'). One cannot but suspect that spirits were higher, talk was livelier, and drink flowed more freely

* In a much criticised passage of his Rectorial address at Glasgow University in 1923: 'The world continues to offer glittering prizes to those who have stout hearts and sharp swords.'

at the dinners of The Other Club, which Churchill and Birkenhead had founded 'as a rival body of political bounders' in opposition to the staid Club, which, they judged, would never want them as members.

Baldwin, brushing up his classics, liked to think of himself as sustaining the tradition of scholar-statesmen, a type which—witness his admiration for Rosebery—made a strong appeal to Buchan. Both loved Walter Scott, and Buchan's centenary biography of Scott is dedicated to Baldwin and G. M. Trevelyan, the two Englishmen whom he most admired. And they had a common taste for F. S. Oliver and his works.*

If Baldwin was a leader to suit Buchan, Buchan was a most useful recruit to Baldwin in his general aim of polishing up the image of the Tory party. He wanted it to show intelligent, forward-looking men with visions of social reform. He did not want it to show hard-faced men who looked as if they had done well out of the war, stupid country squires, retired colonels calling for a whiff of grape-shot, or old fogeys seeing Britain go to the dogs from the windows of their clubs. There were plenty of those in the Party and the House, but it was the others who were to be found and cherished. Here Buchan, with his links with Universities, his interest in young people, his capacity for getting on with them, could be invaluable.

The House in which Buchan took his seat on 3 May 1927 was overwhelmingly Conservative—413 to 151 Labour and 40 Liberals. Yet despite this steamroller majority, and the Prime Minister's gospel of social reform so eloquently preached at Oxford, the Government had quite lost its zeal. The reforming impetus which had produced widows' pensions, the Equal Franchise Act and the Central Electricity Board did not outlast the General Strike of 1926; and since the Strike Baldwin had relapsed into one of his periods of inertia. The chief measure in this session was the Trades Disputes Bill, a concession to the right wing of the party, though Baldwin would himself have been happy to let bygones be bygones. 'The

---

* Baldwin quoted Oliver on Walpole in the famous speech in 1934 when he said that the defence of England was no longer on the chalk cliffs of Dover, but on the Rhine. L. S. Amery, though, considered that Oliver's *Endless Adventure*—'in which, taking Walpole not only as his starting-point, but in fact as his model, he developed a most ingenious and plausible case for inaction and the absence of a policy, and for just keeping in office, as the supreme quality of statesmanship'—had a disastrous effect 'upon a mind already temperamentally disposed towards a Walpole policy of inertia: the mind of Stanley Baldwin.' (*My Political Life*, Vol. I, 1953, p. 271.)

Prime Minister is very tired and has rather lost interest in politics,' Buchan wrote to T. E. Lawrence soon after taking his seat, adding that 'the quality of the debate seems to me atrocious. Winston is the only first-class debater.'

On both sides of the House Buchan found old friends and acquaintances: L. S. Amery, now Secretary of State for the Dominions and anxious for Buchan to join him in an Empire tour (with, as bait, the chance of two days' climbing in the Drakensberg); Robert Cecil, the conscience of the Tories in international affairs; Philip Snowden, whom Buchan had known in pre-war days when they had been associated in the women's suffrage campaign; Ramsay MacDonald, a more recent acquaintance, now Leader of the Opposition. The members whom Buchan saw most were the younger and more liberal-minded Tories: Walter Elliot, Noel Skelton, Robert Boothby, Harold Macmillan (Buchan referred once to there being 'two publishers in Parliament—Captain Macmillan and I'). Buchan's novels ensured him a warm welcome from a number of M.P.s. Ellen Wilkinson described how 'thrilled' she was when she heard he was to be a member; and how (not having been in the House when he took his seat) she had

fixed on a tall dark M.P. whom I hadn't seen before, as being the novelist. The real man was very different—small, Scotch, and not a bit romantic. I didn't meet him until Lady Astor introduced me to Lindbergh whom he was guiding round. Lindbergh was an interesting and charming youth, but I confess that at that moment I was more concerned in taking stock of the Scotchman's rugged, unusual face. Buchan is delightful to meet.

Before long Buchan was able to demonstrate his independence of a strict party line. On July 6 he chose for the occasion of his maiden speech the Labour Party's vote of censure on the Government's proposals for reform of the House of Lords. These, largely the work of Lord Birkenhead and Lord Cave, would have restored certain powers lost by the Lords through the Parliament Act of 1911; coming so soon after the Trades Disputes Act, the measure was bound to appear provocative and reactionary. Ramsay MacDonald moved the vote of censure, and Baldwin defended the proposals rather languidly, as if he did not much care what happened to them. In a neat, witty speech Buchan attacked both MacDonald and his own leader. He did not think the Cave-Birkenhead proposals would make the Lords any more logical or acceptable an institution; he considered the Parliament Act worked perfectly well; he believed that the suggested abolition of the power of the

Monarch to create peers at the request of the Government would not, as its sponsors claimed, be any bulwark against revolution: 'there will be no constitutional revolution in Britain until the great bulk of the British people resolutely desire it, and if that desire is ever present, what statute can bar the way?' As the Liberal *Daily News* summarised it, Buchan demonstrated to the satisfaction of the House 'that the Government are a pack of fools, that the Peers are out of date but exceedingly useful, and that the mission of the Tory Party is to use them.' Lloyd George, in his best form, followed in the same sense, and though the vote of censure was lost, no more was heard of the Government's proposals. 'For some time,' the *Spectator* reported, 'the Cave scheme had been seriously unwell. It wilted and died five minutes after Mr Buchan had risen.'

Congratulations poured in, far beyond those conventionally accorded to a maiden speech. Many compared it with Birkenhead's maiden speech, twenty-five years before. One Parliamentary correspondent thought that 'it was one of those rare occasions when the atmosphere of the House is tense and members are held fast by an oratorical domination.' Buchan described it to his mother the following day:

I never started anything in such poor form. I was feeling very tired and not very well, and it was horrid, hot, muggy weather. To make things more difficult *The Times* announced that I was going to speak, and the whole stage was set as if I had been a Cabinet Minister. I met Neville Chamberlain at lunch and he said that he did not believe that any maiden speech had ever been undertaken under more awful difficulties. Besides, I was going to attack the Government and try to get them to drop this foolish House of Lords scheme, which would split the party, and that is not an easy job for a new Member, especially when the Prime Minister is an intimate friend.

Ramsay MacDonald, who moved the vote of censure, was very bad, but dangerous, and the P.M., who followed, was desperately flat and unimpressive. The arrangement had been that Lloyd George should speak third, and I was to follow him, but Lloyd George sent me a note saying that he intended following me. This, and the fact that Baldwin made an entirely different speech from what I had expected, compelled me to recast very rapidly in my head a great deal of what I meant to say. To crown all, Alice had a tea-party of young ladies at half past four on the Terrace, just when the Prime Minister began to speak, and I had to rush out and start them off while a friend took notes for me of what the P.M. said.

The Socialist Minister who spoke third emptied the House completely, which was lucky for me, as it enabled Members to have their tea. I got up at about half past five with a very empty House, in which interest was absolutely dead. You know I am not often nervous, but my legs knocked together and my mouth was as dry as a stick! There is something about that place which is simply terrifying for a beginner.

I spoke for about five minutes rather labouredly, and then I suddenly realised that the House was full up and packed, with people standing below the gangway (in itself a great compliment). Then I suddenly seemed to get going, and after that I really enjoyed myself. I was cheered to the echo again and again, and when I sat down, after speaking for over twenty minutes, there was so much applause that it was some minutes before Lloyd George could get begun. I am sending you *Hansard* with a full report, and you will see some references to me later in the debate, which I have marked with a blue pencil.

I had a ludicrous amount of congratulations, which I must store up against the day when I shall make a fool of myself!

Baldwin came to me and said that he agreed with every word I said, and he thought my speech had made history, and that he, personally, was very obliged to me. What I did was to kill the House of Lords proposals, and Winston felt it necessary to devote a considerable part of his speech to a eulogy of me. You see, I have 150 Conservatives behind me, the best young men in the party. Baldwin has been put into an awkward fix by Birkenhead and others, and we have got him out of it, for there will be nothing more heard of the scheme.

I was tremendously touched by the Clydeside Labour Members. They came to me in a group, and Maxton said, 'Man, we were terrible nervous when you began, for we thought you weren't going to get away with it, and we were awful happy when you really got started.' I sent you a few cuttings from the morning papers.

Thank goodness it is over, and well over; but I wouldn't like to go through most of yesterday again.

A few weeks later Buchan defended the Act of Union of 1707 against Tom Johnston (the occasion being a new painting in St Stephen's Hall depicting Queen Anne receiving from the Scottish Commissioners their agreement to the Act). In December he gave a Presbyterian's support to the Revised Prayer Book Measure—which drew a swingeing Presbyterian No-Popery riposte from Rosslyn Mitchell, the Labour M.P. for Paisley—on the grounds that the Church of England should have an equal right with the Church of Scotland to enjoy complete spiritual freedom, including the freedom to change its prayer-book.

There were reservations about the delivery of his speeches. Some observers talked of his 'Parliament Hall English . . . that product of attempting to graft English diction on to the burr of Lowland Scots' (this was a Glasgow man, having a crack at Edinburgh as well as at Buchan); another found that his voice accorded more with the atmosphere of the General Assembly than with General Richard Hannay. There were references—often contradictory—to his 'Free Kirk whine,' his 'Oxford accent,' his 'manse intonation,' his 'clipped and mincing tones.' Yet it seemed an auspicious début and the Parliamentary correspondent of the *Nation* considered him, after a year in the House of Commons, 'perhaps the most promising' of the back-bench Tories.

Although he was well liked, and his speeches well thought of, collectively the House was a little chary about Buchan, as it so often seems to be about a new member who arrives with a reputation already made in another field. The professionals, who have made their mark in the House and its committee-rooms, are suspicious of the amateur who comes sailing in on the winds of an extraneous fame. Buchan might yet work his passage, but many other members, though they would come in to hear him speak, were far from sure that he was set for a notable Parliamentary career.

On his side Buchan never outgrew his apprehension at addressing the House.

It was like addressing a gathering of shades, who might at any moment disappear into limbo unless they were clutched by the hair. I felt that nobody wanted to listen to me, that I was only tolerated out of courtesy, and that each of my hearers was longing for me to sit down that he might himself be called. Only on rare occasions did I have an audience with which I felt at ease. On public platforms I was fairly happy, but not in Parliament.

Otherwise he felt very much at home in Westminster and soon, to his wife's rueful amusement, became a Parliamentary addict, spending most of his evenings there and listening to speeches by the hour.

Having been lucky in the ballot, Buchan introduced in March 1928 a Private Member's Bill 'for the licensing of dog-racing courses,' with backing from members of all three parties. Its purpose was to give local authorities the power to veto greyhound-tracks in their area; the reason for it was the mushroom growth of these tracks, and the amount of betting transacted on them. Buchan had no objection to the racing, but did consider that the inhabitants of a district should have the right to decide for themselves if they wanted one of these 'open-air casinos.' The measure was strongly supported by the Churches and by social workers; it was carried on a second reading by a majority of 200, with the approval of the Home Secretary, Joynson-Hicks. Then it ran into trouble in committee; twice there were not enough members to make a quorum, and in July the Prime Minister announced that the Government would not afford facilities for its passage. (There was high feeling, for just as Buchan's bill was being killed, the Government was forcing through a bill legalising the Totalisator on racecourses; this Bill, unlike the greyhound one, would bring in revenue.)

Very soon after his arrival at Westminster Buchan was roped in to liven up the Conservative Party's educational activities, so puny compared with the vigorous and successful efforts of the Labour Party. He was asked to devise a new organisation, and the result was the closing of the Education Department of the Conservative Central Office (of which, in the days of his Peeblesshire candidature, Buchan had been such a sharp critic) and the starting of a new Educational Institute which should be independent of the Central Office, and whose business would be with education, not propaganda. Buchan had many links with the adult education movement, and not long after the war, in an address to the World Association of Adult Education, had praised the Labour Party's broad attitude to political education. They had been successful, he said, because they had not been exclusively political; they had organised classes in literature and the arts as well as in history and economics; a Socialist view of life had been 'disseminated indirectly but insidiously.' Now the Tories were to steal the Whigs' clothes and do the same sort of thing: classes of W.E.A. type in a variety of subjects, but with a Tory slant on world affairs, and a linking-up of classes and students with the courses at the new Bonar Law College at Ashridge. (When a rich man offered to finance a Conservative College, Buchan was charged by J. C. C. Davidson, the party chairman, with finding a suitable building, and eventually recommended Ashridge, a house at which he had stayed in Lord Brownlow's day.) Baldwin was President of the new Institute, Buchan chairman of the executive committee, and among members of the Council were Lady Astor, Walter Elliot and Harold Macmillan.

Buchan's conviction of the need for political education in a democracy went far beyond the need for party advantage. He still believed, as he had when he campaigned in Peeblesshire, that 'if we are to have clear and sound thinking the people must take politics very seriously and be very well informed about them.' I think it is reasonable to assume that the words which he puts into the mouth of the Labour M.P. in *The Island of Sheep* chime with his own views:

'There's only one key to all our problems today, and that is to give the workers the same treasures of knowledge that hitherto have belonged only to the few. Then you will make our democracy safe for the world, for you will have made it an aristocracy . . . Give the worker all the technical training he wants, but don't deny him the humanities, for without them he can never be a citizen . . . Think of what you can make of him. Not culture in the trashy sense, but the wise mind and the keen spirit. He lives close to reality, so you needn't fear that he will become a pedant. You will make your academies better places, for you will let the winds of the world blow through them when you open them to the Many instead of the Few, and you will make a great nation, for the Many will be also the Best.'

Susan Buchan, though sympathetic to his political activities, had no wish to share them, nor could they afford to run a second home in London. She was delighted that a university constituency demanded nothing from its member's wife, and certainly had no ambitions to become a political hostess. A couple of months in the summer was the most she wished to spend in town. So Buchan's life was now lived to a rather different pattern. He spent Monday to Friday in London, staying with Mrs Grosvenor, or with her sister Mrs Firebrace, or at St Stephen's House in Cannon Row. On Friday mornings he travelled back to Oxford in time to attend the meetings of the University Chest before going out to Elsfield for the week-end. In London he worked at Nelson's or Reuter's in the morning, and then went on to Westminster in the afternoon. Hostesses found him a delightful extra man at luncheon and dinner-parties: 'Enid's luncheon was rather amusing,' he wrote:

Margot, Violet Bonham-Carter, Lady Lavery, the Baroness D'Erlanger, Knebworth, Bernsdorff and Abe Bailey. Margot was terribly affectionate. I really enjoyed my talk with Violet, who is one of the most intelligent of human beings.

Often he was a guest of the Londonderrys. Lady Londonderry (whom he had helped with a memoir of her father, Lord Chaplin) was a striking woman, and not only as the wife of a nobleman with great estates in Ireland and County Durham and a house in Park Lane. She had been founder and Director-General of the Women's Legion in the war, and was the first woman to be given the military D.B.E. She lived in state and splendour. Kilted pages stood behind the Marquess and Marchioness as they sat at table; every eve of session she held a reception at Londonderry House and, wearing the Waterloo jewels, received her guests at the top of the double staircase.* Even Violet Markham, who found her far too flamboyant,

* There is an account of such an occasion at 'Anchorage House' in Evelyn Waugh's *Vile Bodies* (1930), and a lusher picture of a Londonderry House reception, 'where the wines were rare and the fittings gorgeous . . . all lit up by jewelled orders looking alive on the coats of costly men,' in Sean O'Casey's *Rose and Crown* (1952).

admitted that on these occasions the glittering creature, 'the product of leisure and wealth,' was a sight to stir the romantic imagination. Alice Buchan, who dined at Londonderry House before her coming-out ball in 1927, will never forget the sound of her knife and fork squeaking on the gold plate. 'You'll have to get accustomed to that,' said her dinner-partner.

Lady Londonderry was a formidable political hostess, issuing quasi-royal commands to promising young Tories to attend her parties.* She liked power, and one of her diversions was to call herself Circe, her friends being the animals whom she had be-witched. This conceit struck some observers as ludicrous: 'a very un-Circe like character,' said one much younger woman; 'a tweedy woman really, with notions about being Lady Bless-ington.' She cultivated writers and painters as well as politi-cians: among her friends were the Laverys and Sean O'Casey, whose turtle-neck sweater struck a bizarre note in Londonderry House.

Buchan enjoyed the splendour, appreciated the liveliness, and was half-amused at, half-disapproving of, 'Circe's antics.'

Speaking at Shrewsbury School in 1928, Buchan declared that there was no more detestable watchword than 'Safety First.' He cannot particularly have relished his party fighting an election with that slogan in May 1929, and posters proclaiming the detestable words below a photograph of pipe-smoking Baldwin, the 'safe' man. However, he campaigned vigorously in Scotland, though he was not called on to do more in his own contest than write an election ad-dress, the keynote of which was 'Advance and Reform.' In spite of a spell in bed in April 'with a young ulcer,' when he was forbidden to do any work, once the election campaign started in May he spoke up and down Scotland, eighteen speeches in ten days, 'and then three days of salmon-fishing till midnight.' One of the speeches was at Peterhead, in support of Robert Boothby, who remembers it as 'good and sensible—almost Radical.' At this election there were four candidates standing for the three Scottish Universities seats; Buchan was again top of the poll in each of the four Universities, as well as in the total: with 9959 votes he was over 3000 ahead of the other Unionist (Sir George Berry) and the Liberal (D. M. Cowan)

---

* Lord Boothby, when I talked to him in 1962, considered that Lady London-derry's political influence had been enormously exaggerated, and that it was not to be compared with that of her contemporary Mrs Ronald Greville.

who were elected with him; Dr Kerr, for Labour, had 2867 votes.*

But over the country as a whole Safety First did the Tories no good; they lost 150 seats, and Labour came into office for the second time with 287 seats, 26 more than the Conservatives alone, but less than Conservatives plus 59 Liberals. Buchan was pleased to see among the new Labour members Philip Noel-Baker and Norman Angell, whose *Great Illusion* he much admired; through Nelson's he had been concerned with some of the foreign editions of the book. Shortly after Ramsay MacDonald had formed his Government Buchan wrote that 'I shall enjoy being in opposition. I lunched with Ramsay Mac on June 4 and rather liked the way he was facing things. He was perfectly sound on one vital matter—America.' (Later in the year MacDonald visited the United States, the first British Prime Minister to do so while in office.)

Soon after this meeting with MacDonald Buchan was ordered to bed again, as a result of his too strenuous campaigning, and told to cancel all engagements till the autumn; he was not much in the House for the rest of 1929. In November he resigned his directorship of Nelson's: he had wanted for some time to slip out of the firm, and now this return of his weakness made it essential to concentrate his activities in one place. So instead of going daily to the office in Paternoster Row, he took an office in St Stephen's House and there installed Mrs Killick, who had been his secretary ever since he joined Nelson's, and had moved with him in the war to the Ministry of Information. Living at St Stephen's, a minute's walk from Westminster, cut down his transport problems and gave him the maximum time for his work. His mornings were now mainly spent upon the journalism which he undertook to make up for the loss of income from Nelson's. Early in 1930 he started to write regularly for the *Graphic*; in 1930 he took on the Atticus column for the *Sunday Times* and kept it up till 1935, and for three months in 1932 he contributed the Notebook column to the *Spectator* under the pseudonym Auspex. The Atticus and Auspex paragraphs, Mrs Killick recalls, were dictated straight on to the typewriter while Buchan walked round the room in St Stephen's.

There were no oratorical fireworks from Buchan in this 1929–31

---

* The election to University seats was conducted on the system of proportional representation. Buchan and Cowan, having received more than the quota necessary to secure election, were declared elected on the first count; a count of the second votes on their surplus papers resulted in the election of Berry.

Parliament, but a speech on unemployment in January 1930 brought praise from the Liberal *Nation*:

Mr Buchan and Mr Boothby followed with two of the best speeches heard from their side in this Parliament. Each of them would have spoken with more appropriateness from the Liberal benches, and each, in attacking the record of this Government, was attacking by implication with even greater force the far more prolonged failure of their own. Mr Buchan was particularly impressive when he warned the House that the ordinary man, if continually disappointed by party leaders, 'might turn to unauthorised practitioners and dangerous remedies', such as Empire Free Trade.

The reply from the Labour Front Bench was by Sir Oswald Mosley, who shortly afterwards resigned from the Government on the grounds of its lack of policy on unemployment.

Scottish affairs and education were the occasion for most of Buchan's other speeches in this Parliament. On education he often went against his party—for example, in voting for the Government's Education Bill of 1930, with its proposal to raise the school-leaving age. And with Robert Boothby and Lady Astor—the only three Conservatives to do so—he voted in support of the Government's recognition of the Soviet Union.

With his party in Opposition, and inclined for some vigorous stock-taking, Buchan was again much in demand by the Conservative Central Office. This time it was Conservatism in the Universities that was causing concern. It had fallen to such a low ebb in Cambridge, for instance, that in 1929 the President of the Union had written to the University Conservative Association complaining of the poor showing the party made in Union debates. So there was to be a drive to encourage and organise University talent; and who better than Buchan to get things going? He had played a big part in the revival of Oxford conservatism after the war; had been Senior Treasurer of the University Association; had encouraged several young men on their political way (Alan Lennox-Boyd, Hugh Molson, David Maxwell Fyfe). So he was now asked to preside over a meeting of Conservative University members, and draw up a plan for a Students' Unionist Federation, on the pattern of the Liberal and Socialist Federations. The idea was to give some practical help to the weaker associations, to encourage debates between the universities—the Toryism of Scottish students would have a good deal to teach Oxford and Cambridge—to send undergraduates to courses at Ashridge, and generally bring them into the main stream of the party. The Federation's first conference was in

Birmingham in January 1931, when Buchan gave the presidential address, as he did at Liverpool and Oxford in the following years.

The fortnightly articles in the *Graphic*, which appeared from 1930 to 1932, give some idea of Buchan's current political interests. He wrote about Britain's relations with America ('It would be a good thing if we gave up all talk about the "likemindedness" of Britain and America, and realised that we are tremendously unlike') and about the slow breaking-down of American isolationism; about the threat to Britain from uncontrolled building; about Britain's air strength and our commercial as well as military needs in an air age; about the prevailing mood of scepticism in politics; about the need for a patriotism of Europe as well as of Empire; about the relations of democracy and the Press. This last article was apropos the Westminster by-election of 1931, when Beaverbrook and Rothermere were noisily backing an Empire Free Trade candidate against Duff Cooper, the official Conservative.

The first of Buchan's articles for the *Graphic* (on 5 April 1930) was on 'Ourselves and the Jews' and reflected his growing interest in Zionism, a cause in which he became wholeheartedly involved. It was Balfour who first kindled his enthusiasm; then he came to know and admire Chaim Weizmann. Nor was it difficult for a historically-minded Scot, who from childhood had sung psalms about remembering Zion, to feel the power of the idea of the Return; nor for a disciple of Milner (himself a convinced pro-Zionist) to respond to the challenge of the reconstruction of a country. If 'Jew' had once —though with many personal exceptions—suggested to Buchan either a seedy adventurer on the Rand or a plushy financier in Park Lane, now it suggested a man of vision and enterprise, a pioneer, a practical idealist. (There is a sympathetic portrait of an ardent Zionist in *A Prince of the Captivity*.) In his *Graphic* article, and in speeches inside and outside the House, Buchan reiterated certain points: the Balfour Declaration of 1917 was 'a categorical promise'; the only limit to the immigration of Jews to Palestine should be the economic capacity of the land; the British Administration had been unconstructive and supine, neither giving the immigrants security, nor allowing them to organise their own defence; the ordinary British official was readier to understand the Arab peasant, 'who does not talk,' than the sharp, argumentative Jewish immigrant from the cities of Europe, for 'he is too vocal, he is always raising problems, he is apt to make the business of administration difficult.'

Buchan was elected Chairman of the Parliamentary Pro-Palestine Committee in 1932 (in succession to Josiah Wedgwood) and was regarded by British Zionists as one of their most useful allies. In the spring of 1934, after Hitler had begun his persecution of the Jews in Germany, Buchan was one of the chief speakers at a mass demonstration in Shoreditch organised by the Jewish National Fund ('Come and welcome champions of the Jewish National Home in Parliament' went the notices). 'When I think of Zionism,' Buchan declared,

I think of it in the first place as a great act of justice. It is reparation for the centuries of cruelty and wrong which have stained the record of nearly every Gentile people. . . . I want to see the 'absorptive' capacity of Palestine interpreted by the British Government, I won't say more generously— we don't want generosity, only justice—but I want to see it interpreted with *facts*.

Buchan's name was written in the Golden Book of the Jewish National Fund of Israel, and when twenty years after his death the Board of Deputies of British Jews (the representative body of the Jewish Community in Britain) gave a dinner in honour of Eliahu Elath, the retiring Israeli Ambassador, and to celebrate the tenth anniversary of the establishment of the State of Israel, Buchan's photograph was in the programme—along with those of Lloyd George, Smuts, Balfour, Amery and Wingate—as a 'Noted Friend of Zionism.' There have been many references to disparagement of Jews in Buchan's novels, but to Jewish organisations in Britain and Palestine Buchan's name is that of a friend.

The M.P.s whose company Buchan enjoyed as much as any, and with whom he often took an evening cup of tea, were the so-called 'Red Clydesiders': James Maxton, David Kirkwood, George Buchanan and Tom Johnston (who, though he did not represent a Clydeside constituency, was closely associated with the group). They had come to Westminster by a very different road from Buchan's: his had been the Oxford Union, Milner's Kindergarten, the Ministry of Information, friendship with Baldwin; theirs the shipyard, the engineering shop, the union meeting, Glasgow Green and Calton Jail (Maxton had been imprisoned for advocating a general strike in 1917, Kirkwood deported from the Clyde in 1916 for promoting a strike among munition workers). But they had all started from the same world. Jimmy Maxton, 'who not only preached the revolution but looked it,' had been at Hutchesons', Maxton and Tom Johnston at Glasgow University, a few years after Buchan.

Maxton was the son of an elder of the Kirk, David Kirkwood was an elder himself, and would thunder his Old Testament denunciations across the House at the Tories ('We shall smite them hip and thigh and pursue them from Dan even unto Beersheba'). Tom Johnston came, like Buchan, of Border stock, and was a devoted fisherman. Geordie Buchanan had spent his life in the Gorbals, which he now represented. Unlike most Tory M.P.s, Buchan could literally understand the Clydesiders. (On one occasion David Kirkwood's defence on a charge of sedition was that the English policeman could not possibly have understood and taken down what he was saying.) Their speeches, racy with quotations from the Bible, old Scots songs and sayings (Baldwin, one of them said, was a fly man who 'doesna sell his hen on a wat day'), may have struck an unaccustomed note in the House of Commons, but they were of the very stuff of talk in the Buchan manse in Queen Mary Avenue or the Masterton farm at Broughton Green.

Buchan warmed to their fierce Scottish patriotism and pride— Bannockburn and William Wallace were far more often on their lips than Marx and the dictatorship of the proletariat—and their equally fervent local patriotism: Kirkwood, engineer and member for Clydebank, put himself in *Who's Who* as 'representing the most important shipbuilding centre of the world.' Buchan found they had a much more imaginative and informed view of the Empire than the English Socialists. Tom Johnston recalls how:

John Buchan and I used to confab in the writing-room of the House of Commons library and I remember particularly his interest in my effort to get the Labour Party swung away from an anti-colonialist attitude to a pro-Empire one.

In England 'Empire-builders' suggested public-school men administering subject races; in Scotland it suggested, literally, builders —men who built bridges, dams, roads and railways, who irrigated the desert, planted tea and cotton. The Clydesiders could sympathise as much as any English Socialist with the nationalist movements in India and elsewhere, but they had a firmer grip of the constructive rôle of Britain in the Empire, because it was Scots like themselves who had done so much of the constructing. The Empire was too big an affair to be left to the Carlton Club.

The Clydesiders refreshed Buchan by taking him back to his roots; and I suspect that they refreshed him too by touching a side of his nature that had been kept rather firmly in check. A great deal has been said and written about the dichotomy in the Scottish character: the opposing strains of the canny and the wild, the thrifty and the reckless, the sober and the passionate. Some of the best characters in Scott and Stevenson are built on this opposition. Bailie Nicol Jarvie and David Balfour are cautious citizens who are given the chance of acting out their reckless impulses, and there is Buchan's own Dickson McCunn, the Glasgow grocer with the heart of an adventurer. In Buchan the canny strain had predominated, but there had once been a deal of the wild. He had chosen a life where convention and good form were rated highly; some freedom and forthrightness had been lost on the way. The men from the Clyde didn't give a damn for good form; they were uninhibited and free. When they interrupted Ministers, when they were suspended by the Speaker, no doubt it shocked the canny John Buchan, the son of Mrs Buchan for whom 'Never make yourself conspicuous' was almost a moral precept; but it struck a deep response from the John Buchan who had poached salmon in the Tweed, whose gang had rolled forty flaming tar-barrels down into a quarry at Pathhead. And the wildness of the Clydesiders was not a personal wildness, a bohemianism—most of them were teetotallers, and went to kirk. It was a purposeful wildness, the expression in action of their social zeal. The gospel they preached was not exactly the Reverend John Buchan's, but their faces too were firmly set towards Jerusalem, only they were bent on starting the building of it here and now.

On their part they looked on Buchan as a good Scot who had done well by his country's history and song,* a decent man who (like Walter Elliot) had got himself into the wrong party. In *Forward*, the Scottish Socialist weekly edited by Tom Johnston, Buchan's politics were spoken of in sorrow rather than in anger, and the paper conceded that he was 'far and away the ablest of the Scottish Tory M.P.s.' When Buchan published his novel of seventeenth-century Scotland, *Witch Wood*, the review which pleased him most, for it showed most understanding, was by one of the Clydeside M.P.s in the *Glasgow Herald*.†

* In 1927 the London Scots Labour Club gave a dinner to William Stewart, the Scottish Secretary of the Independent Labour Party, and presented him with a copy of Buchan's *Northern Muse*.

† I owe this information to Professor Donald MacKinnon, to whose father Buchan had spoken of the review, in Oban, a few days after it appeared. Professor MacKinnon, though quite clear as to the rest of the story, cannot now remember which M.P. it was; nor can the *Glasgow Herald* now discover the author of the review, which appeared on 28 July 1927.

In 1931 the Labour Government was faced with a deteriorating financial situation, industrial depression and mass unemployment at home, and a catastrophic fall in world prices. In August the committee set up under Sir George May to consider national expenditure recommended drastic economies, mainly in the social services; Ramsay MacDonald, failing to secure the agreement of his Cabinet to those economies (which included a cut in unemployment benefit), handed his resignation to King George V, who then invited him to form a coalition Government with the immediate object of restoring British credit abroad. The principal members of this new Ministry were Snowden and J. H. Thomas on the Labour side, the Conservatives Baldwin and Neville Chamberlain, and the Liberals Herbert Samuel and Archibald Sinclair. Snowden, as Chancellor of the Exchequer, introduced a crisis Budget with cuts for the unemployed, the teachers, the police and the services. MacDonald then went to the country in October 1931 demanding a free hand to deal with the crisis.

On doctor's orders Buchan took little part in this campaign. After writing his election address, and speaking at one rally in Stirling, he went off for a brief holiday to Cornwall. There he rather startled A. L. Rowse—an Elsfield undergraduate visitor, now a Fellow of All Souls, and standing as an anti-National-Government Labour candidate for Penryn and Falmouth—by looking in at his committee-room to wish him well. Buchan himself, with D. M. Cowan and Noel Skelton, was returned unopposed for the Scottish Universities: they were the first three members of the new Parliament.*

The result was a landslide: only 52 of the Labour Opposition were elected, against the Government's 552 (made up of 471 Conservatives, 68 Liberals and 13 pro-Government Labour); and this imbalance of parties altered the tone of Parliament in all sorts of ways. 'There is not much life in the House,' Buchan wrote to John Edgar, 'for our majority is too big.' In the two previous years Conservatives—with only thirty fewer seats than Labour—had been alert, on their toes, ready to harass the Government on every possible occasion. Now, with this steamroller majority, Conservative

---

* In a letter to the *Yorkshire Post* commending the candidature of Miss Eleanor Rathbone for the Combined English Universities, the philosopher Samuel Alexander picked out John Buchan and Lord Hugh Cecil as having the 'character and abilities' to justify the existence of University members. Alexander was against University representation on principle, but considered that these two and Miss Rathbone, particularly through their close touch with University life, provided excellent excuses for continuing the anomaly.

members found the day-to-day life of Parliament rather dull. The
Glasgow Herald attributed some credit for this Conservative victory
to the Party's new efforts to educate itself, for which Buchan had
been largely responsible, and pointed out that 61 of the new Conservative members, including 32 who had won seats from Labour,
had attended courses at Ashridge.

Buchan's place in this Parliament was again among the younger
and more forward-looking Conservatives, now augmented by a
number of very young men who had thought they were fighting
hopeless seats and to their surprise found themselves in the
House. He was a member of a group—described by another member
as 'a slightly left-wing Tory group of back-benchers, no more
influential than all these groups were'—who met regularly for dinner and an informal talk from some Minister or expert; the Prime
Minister, Austen Chamberlain and Anthony Eden are three mentioned by Buchan. Colonel Spender-Clay was chairman of the
group, and among the members (who had to resign if they took
office) were Harold Macmillan, Lord Hugh Cecil, W. S. Morrison,
Walter Elliot, Robert Boothby and Lord Balniel (now Lord Crawford).

Often Buchan was called on to put the liberal Tory view in the
House: for instance, when there was criticism of supposed 'left-
wing bias' in the B.B.C. in 1933. In a sharp, effective speech Buchan
claimed that one of the B.B.C.'s first duties was 'the dissemination
of opinions, and especially of controversial opinions,' and declared
that personally he saw no reason why the most heterodox views on
economics or religion should not be broadcast. As for 'left-wing
bias,' given the Conservative temperament that was inevitable,
and not at all to be deplored. Conservatives were apt to be silent, so
assured were they of their convictions; radicals and political non-
conformists were far more likely to be articulate about their views.
'Honest, straightforward, well-regulated controversy is the only
salt which can save the most valuable side of broadcasting from
going rotten, and after all we might surely trust the people.'

A matter to which Buchan, along with other Scottish members,
gave a good deal of thought in this Parliament was Scottish Home
Rule, and he raised it in November 1932 in the debate on the
Address. He began with a spirited recital of Scotland's ills—
declining native population, increase of Irish Catholics, empty
churches, loss of national flavour in education, language and literature, the indignity of tacking 'and Scotland' on to English measures

introduced in Parliament—and went on to appeal: 'We do not want to be like the Jews at the dispersion—a potent force everywhere on the globe, with no Jerusalem.' It was a good rhetorical performance; the Scottish Nationalists almost thought they had gained a convert, and members half-expected him to come out in favour of the full Home Rule programme for an independent legislature. It was something of an anticlimax when Buchan wound up by asking, not for a Scottish Parliament—'such a top-heavy structure would not cure Scottish ills'—but for the transfer of the Scottish Office from Whitehall to a 'dignified building' in Edinburgh (which is more or less what happened in 1939 when most of the Scottish Departments moved from London to St Andrew's House on the Calton Hill—a massive building, if not outstandingly dignified).

For the rest, Buchan's activities in the 1931 Parliament were the usual back-bencher's mixture. He worked hard for his constituents, mainly on educational affairs. He had made himself the spokesman of Scottish teachers, both in schools and universities, and was in close touch with the Educational Institute of Scotland. When teachers' salaries were cut in 1931 as one of the National Government's economy measures, Buchan presided at a meeting of M.P.s to hear the case against the cuts. Through the School Age Council, of which he was chairman, he brought pressure on the Government to raise the school-leaving age to fifteen. (This was finally done in 1936, though the date on which it was to come into effect was given as 1 September 1939.) When the Sunday Cinema Bill came up in 1932, providing that the profits of Sunday shows should be given to charity, Buchan proposed an amendment by which five per cent of the profits should go to finance a National Film Institute, which in due course came to pass; Buchan was one of the Institute's original governors, representing public interests. He served on a Parliamentary Committee of inquiry into Colonial Office appointments, and on a Select Committee on sky-writing. He piloted a Private Member's Bill to prevent the sale abroad of British songbirds, which reached the Statute Book in 1933.

I got my Bird Bill through by a triumphant majority, 214 to 141. It is the first time I have ever been in charge of a Bill, and I think I manœuvred it rather skilfully.*

---

* The Protection of Birds Act 1954, probably the bulkiest Private Member's Bill passed by Parliament, which tore up and replaced every bird protection Act since the days of George III, was introduced into the House of Commons by John Buchan's daughter-in-law and handled in the Lords by his son Johnnie.

It is in letters written at the time, and in the memories of the men he met daily in the House, that we can feel the texture of his political life. Here are some extracts from Buchan's letters:

21 April 1932. I took the chair at a meeting of M.P.s about proposals for a Film Institute, and had great difficulty in explaining things to some very stupid members. Baldwin and I dined together in a corner of St Stephen's Club and discussed many things. He is rather anxious about the P.M.'s health. Sky-writing committee; lunch with Siepmann of B.B.C. I must raise the Palestine question in the House.

14 June 1932. Took the chair for Dr Weizmann at a meeting of the Palestine Committee. I dined quietly at the club and went back for a good many divisions. Today I am lunching with Graves of *The Times* to meet Fitzmaurice of Constantinople. I have another Economy Committee in the afternoon, and I am introducing a deputation of women workers to the Scottish Members.

26 October 1932. Yesterday I had some University professors to lunch, and then had successively Edward Irwin's education meeting, the Ashridge Governors, and a very long meeting of Scottish members on Scottish Home Rule, where I had to speak at length. So of course I missed Lloyd George, who I believe was very amusing. Today I have to lunch with the English Review Club, and then have meetings of the Film Institute people and the British Philosophers, and finish with a long meeting at the House on the Everest flying scheme.

6 July 1933. I lunched with Peter Davies and his partner; had some Australians to tea; and then saw a lot of people about the Bird Protection Bill. I dined at Herbert Samuel's most interesting dinner, with Walter Lippmann, the American, Bob Cecil, and one or two of the delegates [to the World Economic Conference]. We were kept in the House until after midnight. Today I am lunching with Tubby Clayton at Toc. H., and dining with Winston and Smuts, and have a good many other engagements in between.

1 May 1934. The Shoreditch meeting was an astonishing thing—a packed audience, and the most electric one I have ever spoken to. They rose at every point. The whole thing was really very impressive. Joss Wedgwood, Eddie Hartington and I made a funny trio of speakers. Some of the other speeches were in Yiddish.

Then I went to Pratt's with Eddie and ate some devilled kidneys and had a long discussion with Harold Macmillan. Harold had brought his eldest boy, who is just going up to Eton, to Gladstone's house—a very nice-looking little boy.

About the nature of Buchan's interest in politics Lord Davidson, then Chairman of the Conservative Party, remembered the many occasions when Buchan came over to join him and Baldwin in the smoking-room. At once they would be launched into a discussion on education, Commonwealth policy, the future of Anglo-American relations—politics as ideas, not as party manœuvre or electoral strategy. Buchan would throw out an idea, Baldwin would take it up, and perhaps a few days later develop it further in a speech. About Buchan's general friendliness in the House Lord Attlee, then Deputy Leader of the truncated Labour Opposition, remembered 'long chats with John' in the Library: 'a very broad-minded man; a romantic Tory, who thought Toryism better than it was.' And he clearly recalled the occasion, though the context was forgotten, when he and Buchan joined in chanting 'Anti-political, anti-prelatical, true Presbyterian, Church of Scotland.' Altogether 'a most delightful man.'

Why, asked the *Evening Standard* shortly after the 1931 election, was Buchan—and other able Tories like Macmillan, Eden, Duff Cooper, Walter Elliot—not in the reconstructed National Government? Buchan himself seems to have had reason to believe that he might have been offered the Scottish Office, or the Board of Education, but for the Prime Minister's need to give the Liberals a quota of ministries (ironically the Liberal who was President of the Board of Education was Buchan's old opponent in Peeblesshire, Sir Donald Maclean. Another Liberal, Sir Archibald Sinclair, was at the Scottish Office). Violet Markham, sending Susan 'a few lines of love and indignation,' was scandalised: 'All these nonentities stuffed in and John left out.' In the following June this loyal old friend took the matter up privately with Tom Jones, who had recently retired from being Deputy Secretary of the Cabinet, and was much in Baldwin's confidence:

I want a word in your wise ear about John Buchan. I think it a real misfortune in the national interest that he is not in the National Government. I also think he would make an admirable President of the Board of Education. Is there no chance of this being considered? It would be a thousand pities if that appointment is made on the rigid lines of party spoils. John has vision and imagination. He holds a unique place in party life detached from strict party allegiance. . . . He never pushes or clamours and so he seems to get left aside—greatly I think to the public detriment.

Tom Jones saw Baldwin, then Deputy Prime Minister, about Miss Markham's suggestion; his comment was that 'Buchan would be no use in the Cabinet. Ramsay has written me saying he must keep up the numbers of the Samuelites.' But when Sir Herbert Samuel and his Liberals resigned from the Government as a result of the 1932 Ottawa agreement, their places were filled by the Liberals who followed Sir John Simon. Buchan was frankly irritated. To Violet Markham he wrote on 4 October 1932:

What is the good of kow-towing to the Simonites, who are indistinguishable from the ordinary Tories, except that they are more reactionary, and who would not exist for a moment in Parliament except by our permission? I gather that the excessive attention paid to them was not Ramsay's doing, but S.B.'s, who is apt to make a fetish of magnanimity. But my real objection is to their second-rate ability. If the National Government means anything, it should be a pooling of the best talents.

On the same day he made his position clear to Baldwin:

I feel that somehow I have managed to acquire the wrong kind of political atmosphere. Most of my friends seem to think that I am a busy man whose life is completely filled with non-political interests. But that is not the case. I gave up business three years ago in order to devote myself to politics. I do not speak overmuch in the House—there is no need for it—but I do a great deal of speaking up and down the country, especially in Scotland, where I think I have a good deal of influence. Politics have always been my chief interest, and I have had a good deal of administrative experience. I was the equivalent of a Minister with Milner in South Africa, when I was twenty-five; I had a large and difficult Department to manage in the War, and, of course, for nearly a quarter of a century I was one of the directors of a large and successful business. I stood for Parliament before the War, and ever since I have done a good deal of political work both before and since I entered the House —for example on education, and in organising the young men at all the Universities.

Now, I do not want to be thought of as a sort of publicist in the void, like Hugh Cecil, who occasionally makes a speech. I am very well in body now, and, as you know, I can work pretty hard. So I would like to be considered when posts are being filled, for I am no longer as young as I was, and I want to do some useful public work before the Guard comes to take the tickets!

I am not asking for anything, please—I never asked for anything in my life. But I should like my leader to know that I am a free man and really anxious for definite work, so that I may be considered when the occasion arises.

This experience contributed to his assessment of Baldwin, in a letter to Amery of 16 May 1936: the occasion was an article in *John Bull*.

It is wrong to say that S.B. has no capacity for friendship. The truth is almost the opposite! I had a most emotional parting from him last October. What is true is that he intensely dislikes the political game, and he has schooled himself to a kind of hard objectivity about his colleagues in it, and has tried to sink all personal feeling. He is a bad party leader so far as persons are concerned. The personal relationships in a party need careful cultivation, and S.B.'s curious moods of apathy and idleness prevent him from doing this most needful work. Only a perfectly first-class private secretary could have saved him. The result is that he has constantly been, apparently, guilty of harshnesses and disloyalties of which he was completely unconscious.

This failure to become a Minister was less surprising to Buchan's colleagues in the House than to those outside who read his well-turned speeches and admired his all-round abilities. There is no doubt that, though the real die-hards disliked him, he was very popular in the House, especially with the intellectual Tories, but there is also no doubt that he was not a great Parliamentary success. Some of the younger Conservatives, who were prepared to find Buchan a glamorous figure who might do anything, were rather disappointed by his actual performance. The chariness of the House towards a new member with a reputation won in another field has been spoken of earlier. It can be broken down—as it was, a few years later, by A. P. Herbert, another University member, who arrived with a similar disadvantage, but won a Parliamentary reputation by his ability in piloting a major reform, the Divorce Bill, through to the Statute Book. Buchan's success with the Bird Bill was on an altogether different scale, and he had not the temperament for the committee-work of a major Bill—the instinct when to make concessions, when to stand firm—that A. P. Herbert displayed. His training with Milner had been in the direction of action rather than negotiation; at the Ministry of Information, too, he had been more concerned with getting things done than with persuading people to his point of view. He did make a new reputation in Parliament, as an always interesting and polished speaker, but not as an effective politician. Also, however good his speeches, members found too much of the sermon in them—'preaching, not in an unpleasant way but not in the House of Commons way.' In an assembly of professionals he was regarded as a bit of an amateur. In L. S. Amery's view Buchan 'made little mark when he entered Parliament comparatively late in life, for he was not really interested in the subject-matter of politics'; Philip Kerr (Lord Lothian) explained Buchan's failure to fulfil his early promise in the House by 'the almost invariable law . . . that people who enter it in middle life from some other profession never really master its moods.'

'Why does he want to go into Parliament?' T. E. Lawrence asked Mrs Killick when he called in one day at St Stephen's House; 'he is much more of a power behind the throne'—and Lawrence had his own good reasons for saying this. Certainly one of the aspects of Parliament that Buchan most enjoyed was that once again, as in the war, he was at the heart of things. He liked the talk, the gossip, the inside knowledge (all of which was useful to him in the Atticus column of the *Sunday Times*). When Baldwin was at No. 10 Downing Street Buchan was often summoned by a note in the Prime Minister's own hand, or invited to dine quietly at St Stephen's ('I want a chat with you on certain things American. Give me a quarter of an hour on Monday afternoon or evening'). He helped to draft many of Baldwin's speeches, especially those on India, and Baldwin often sought his advice. 'What is your reading,' Baldwin wrote in January 1930, 'of the Beaverbrook-Rothermere game? And under which thimble is the pea, or in other words, Ll.G.?' Baldwin's son, in his memoir, considers that Buchan and Victor Cazalet were closer to his father than ever Ramsay MacDonald was, or Neville Chamberlain.

Not all their confidences were about politics. In 1930 Baldwin was installed as Chancellor of St Andrews University, and Buchan received an Hon. LL.D. on his nomination. (On the same occasion T. E. Lawrence refused—'I naturally concluded it was a student leg-pull, and sent it cheerfully back to the address given, saying that it was no go. How could I be expected to imagine it was serious?') In 1930 both Buchan and Baldwin were concerned with the inception of the Pilgrim Trust. With three others—Hugh Macmillan, Sir Josiah Stamp and Sir James Irvine, Principal of St Andrews—they were chosen by the American financier Edward Harkness (a man of British descent who wanted to give something back to the country) to apply a sum of £2 million towards conserving 'the heritage of Britain.' Baldwin was elected chairman and Buchan wrote the preamble to the Trust Deed. This small group of trustees with their secretary Tom Jones was, Lord Macmillan remembered, 'a singularly happy and congenial body.' They were given the freest of hands as to how they drew on the fund, and how they interpreted 'British heritage;' and they quickly settled the general policy of the Trust which has been followed ever since. Help was to be given to the material objects which make up our heritage—the first Pilgrim Trust grant was to the restoration of Durham Cathedral. But— starting their work at a time of huge unemployment and widespread hardship—the Trustees were firmly of opinion that 'heritage' meant people as well as buildings ('the well-being of the people is a national asset even more important than the preservation of its

material treasures '). So with the aim of 'awakening a sense that life
might still be worth living where all seemed so bleak and hopeless '
they initiated and assisted local activities in the Distressed Areas:
educational centres with classes and libraries, craft industries, clubs
of all kinds, hostels, holiday camps, allotments, community centres,
infant welfare institutions and nursery schools. The Trust financed
an inquiry by the National Council for Social Service into life on
new housing estates at Dagenham and Becontree, and another on
unemployment organised by Archbishop William Temple, which
produced the widely-read report *Men Without Work*.

Buchan was particularly concerned with the grants made by the
Trust to Toynbee Hall; to the Bodleian for the purchase and classi-
fication of the North Papers; to Strathcona House, a centre for the
workers at the Rowett Institute, Aberdeen; and to Oxford House,
Risca, the social and educational settlement in South Wales where
Susan Buchan spent a good deal of time in the early thirties. But,
Tom Jones considered, 'with all his splendid gifts John Buchan
when backing an opposed appeal for a grant could not parry his
tougher fellow-Scots, across the table—Macmillan and James Irvine,
who quickly overpowered him with a stroke or two.'

With Ramsay MacDonald Buchan became almost as close as
with Baldwin. He had first warmed to him for his attitude on the
Milner Chinese Labour debate in 1906, in contrast to that of the
Liberals. In 1924 MacDonald had written to Buchan freely about
the fall of the first Labour Government (this was in a letter of thanks
for *The Northern Muse*—'Our old Scotch songs have for long years
enabled me to make time go with a happy face and a cheerful step ').
Before going into Parliament Buchan consulted MacDonald 'as
to what room there was for anybody like myself in public life.'
After he entered the House they occasionally lunched together, and
talked as much about books and Scotland as about politics. But it
was after the crisis of 1931 that the acquaintance took a new turn.

When MacDonald formed his National Government, Baldwin
became Lord President of the Council—a post with a salary less
than half the Prime Minister's; as some compensation he asked for
No. 11 Downing Street, the official residence of the Chancellor of
the Exchequer. But there was another reason for his request: 'I
could always keep my eye on my Prime Minister.' What Baldwin
was keeping an eye on was not so much the Prime Minister's policy
as his morale. Here was a man who stood practically alone; who had
lost all but a fraction of his own Labour Party; who was barely

tolerated by most of the Conservatives: a lonely figure who needed help. Baldwin regarded it as one of his main jobs to give this help. 'The burden of sustaining the Prime Minister was very heavy,' he said some years later; and again he summoned Buchan to his aid.

Buchan was a willing ally: to him it was clearly a patriotic duty to keep up the P.M.'s spirits. Where Labour people saw a leader who had 'silently, furtively, and without consulting his army . . . gone over to their opponents,' Buchan saw a man of courage and principle who had put national need above party loyalty. 'I think he was one of the bravest men I have ever known,' he wrote on MacDonald's death in 1937. He admired him, in the election that followed the National Government, for sticking to his constituency at Seaham, where the battle would be tough, and not accepting a safe seat in the South. He saw a fellow-Scot in trouble—ostracised by his oldest friends, expelled by the Hampstead Labour Association and the Seaham Labour Party (who called on him to resign his seat). Not long after the election Buchan delivered the principal speech at a birthday dinner given to MacDonald by Scots in London. The 700 diners, Lord Elgin in the chair, the Archbishop of Canterbury (Cosmo Lang) proposing 'Our Native Land,' Will Fyffe entertaining—not to speak of the messages from Dominion Prime Ministers and the Provosts of Lossiemouth, Elgin and Inverness—were all intended to cheer MacDonald and remind him that there were quite a lot of people who thought well of him; the two childhood memories that MacDonald drew upon in his speech of thanks were of unkindness and of kindness—a farm-worker who had boxed his ears on a bitter morning, a girl in the harvest fields who had taken him by the hand and walked home with him through woods where the birds were singing.

Buchan's feeling for MacDonald had in it sympathy, chivalry, a wish to see fair play, and a strong dash of Scottish romanticism:

The whole man was a romance, almost an anachronism. To understand him one had to understand the Scottish Celt, with his ferocious pride, his love of pageantry and poetry, his sentiment about the past, his odd contradictory loyalties . . . His imagination enabled him to understand large grandiose things, the conflict of nations, the strife of continents. Now and then the curtain would be drawn back and something would be revealed of a lonely inward-looking soul.

For MacDonald he had something of the feeling he had for the Gorbals Die-Hards of *Huntingtower* and *Castle Gay*. He liked to think that a barefoot boy from the Gorbals like Wee Jaikie could end up playing Rugby football for Cambridge and Scotland; and he liked to think that MacDonald, with no advantage of birth, money or education, could end up being Prime Minister of Britain: 'His career is one of the romances of modern times and could only have been possible in a true democracy.' It accorded with Buchan's idea of Britain as an open society where talent and energy could rise, a process in which he was always eager to help. But with those whose hopes pointed in a different direction—who put the emphasis not on individual success, but on creating a more egalitarian society —Buchan had less imaginative sympathy.

There were many ways in which Buchan could be of use to MacDonald. He could try to help with his speeches—and here help was certainly needed, for the Prime Minister's habit of rambling round and mixing his metaphors had steadily grown on him since the famous occasion in 1931 when he had announced that the ship (of various economic schemes) had been launched, the pace was not yet satisfactory, they had had to put in petrol, heat up the engines, take off the brakes, and take out parts of the machinery.* 'Ramsay so bad that nobody understood what he was driving at,' is one of Buchan's comments (in November 1932, after a speech on unemployment); with great relief he recorded on another occasion that 'the surprise was the P.M., who wound up with tremendous vigour' on the debate on the Imperial Economic Conference at Ottawa in 1932.

Buchan would also try to help the Prime Minister not to be silly. One of those who had rushed to MacDonald's rescue in 1931 was Lady Londonderry, who quickly constituted herself his guiding star in the Conservative social circles which he increasingly frequented. No less than Buchan, MacDonald was a social romantic, enjoying tradition, old titles, colour and pageantry. Even in his first administration, in 1923, he had insisted on court dress for ceremonial occasions, 'knee-breeches, buckles on the shoes, cocked hat and toy sword and all the rest of it.' So he too enjoyed the panoply of Londonderry House, the hostess at the head of the double staircase, the Waterloo jewels, the kilted pages. Buchan approved when it was a question of lunches and eve-of-session receptions and Gaelic concerts—or even of Lady Londonderry addressing a mass meeting of women at Seaham; but he was far from pleased at MacDonald's being drawn into Lady Londonderry's more eccentric entertain-

* I owe this instance to Lord Boothby, who commented on the speech at the time in the *Spectator* (21 February 1931).

ments, when she assumed the rôle of Circe and among her animal entourage was Ramsay the Ram. News of these antics found its way to the 'Talk of London' column of the *Daily Express*, provoking a wrathful letter from the Prime Minister to Lord Beaverbrook. Buchan felt that MacDonald should never have put himself in such an undignified position, and he did his best to keep him from too close a connection with the volatile Marchioness.*

His chief function with MacDonald was to be friendly, sympathetic, sanguine, and an uphill job it could be with this touchy, humourless, inward-looking man. The regular time for this invigorating process was before breakfast, when Buchan, issuing from St Stephen's at 7.30, would pick up the Prime Minister at Downing Street and walk with him round St James's Park, often going back to breakfast at No. 10. He would fight MacDonald's depression, discuss his current political problems, help him organise his day, give a hand with memoranda or speeches. 'My talk with the P.M. this morning was rather especially interesting,' he wrote on 14 March 1934—had they been discussing Eden's visits to Berlin and Rome, or the proposal to co-ordinate the three services under a Ministry of Defence?—'I really believe I am beginning to do him some good.' 'Another damp walk this morning with the P.M.' is recorded on 21 March 1934. Sometimes there was a note of exasperation: 'The P.M. is a queer bird;' 'I walked with Ramsay this morning and breakfasted and talked with him. His suspiciousness seems to be growing, and I was really very cross with him.' With relief Buchan would announce that MacDonald was retiring to his house in Hampstead for a week, or going off to Lossiemouth, 'so that I am not on duty in the mornings.' While Parliament was sitting in 1934 and during the first months of 1935 there were few mornings off.

MacDonald came to rely upon him—'I am ever so sorry that I shall not see you for such a long time,' 'I have been missing you very much'—and when Buchan went to America in the autumn of 1934, to the opening of the Butler Library of Columbia University, MacDonald 'took a most touching farewell of me and he entrusted me with some very confidential things to say to the President of the U.S.A.' MacDonald even toyed with the idea of giving Buchan some ministerial appointment, though without a department, so

---

* Sean O'Casey in *Rose and Crown* (1952) gives an account of Ramsay MacDonald at Londonderry House. 'MacDonald and [J. H.] Thomas now wandered among them, not as equals but as favoured servants allowed into the drawing-room for a period to admire its stately grandeur.'

that he could act as a sort of personal assistant, and help him re-organise the responsibilities of various Ministers. Lady Londonderry had a finger in this pie; indeed she seems almost to have baked it. 'Circe is living in a whirlwind,' reported Buchan to his wife on 21 February 1934:

> She saw S.B. who was most cordial, but thought that the P.M. would be difficult to ginger up to putting me in the Cabinet straight away. He was rather inclined to suggest that I should be made a Privy Councillor and attached to the P.M. as a sort of first lieutenant till he saw how things went. The P.M. was dining at Londonderry House last night, and Circe meant to speak winged words to him. She complains that he doesn't know his own mind, which is quite true.

Buchan's closeness to MacDonald was not, like his friendship with Baldwin, common knowledge; it came as a surprise, for instance, to Robert Boothby (who also used occasionally to walk round St James's Park with the Prime Minister) and to Lord Attlee. Nor did Buchan give the impression of being keen for office; in fact some thought that his popularity in Parliament came partly from the fact that he was never angling for promotion. (Ellen Wilkinson commented, in 1933, that he had never sought the position his talents and his aristocratic connections might have given him.)

One of the power-behind-the-throne activities in which Buchan engaged concerned Captain Liddell Hart. Buchan had first met him, it may be remembered, during the Battle of the Somme; had much admired his books on Sherman, Scipio and Foch, and had closely followed Liddell Hart's development into a leading thinker and writer on war—the greatest, in the view of some authorities, since Clausewitz. 'If there is an acuter critic or a clearer exponent of military affairs writing today I have not come across him,' Buchan wrote in 1930, in a review of Liddell Hart's *The Real War, 1914–1918*. Liddell Hart (who regarded Buchan as his 'first literary counsellor, guide and friend') was a League of Nations man, and a firm if realistic supporter of disarmament. Buchan felt strongly that he should be in a position directly to influence defence policy. The story of Buchan's plan can be told in some extracts from Captain Liddell Hart's diary:

> 12 November 1931. Lunched with John Buchan at the Athenaeum. . . . Urged me to do a synoptic study of Caesar's generalship. I replied that I had no time and couldn't afford it. Buchan then went on to suggest that the proper place for me was in the Secretariat of the C.I.D. [Committee of Imperial Defence] which is to be reorganised. Buchan was going to take the matter up with Baldwin and MacDonald.

12 April 1932. John Buchan lunched with me at the Rag. Said his heaviest work now was 'holding the P.M.'s hand.' He sees him several times a day, often. The P.M. only trusts those for whom he has a personal affection. Celtic touch has brought Buchan and Ramsay MacDonald together. Baldwin is now equally close with MacDonald.

Buchan told me he had spoken to both of them several times, and was continuing to 'drop the seed,' about reorganising the C.I.D. and appointing 'a first-class man'—specifically suggesting me—as a deputy and future successor to Maurice Hankey.* He asked if I'd heard anything yet. He said Hankey knew more of the machinery than anyone living, and is at present quite irreplaceable. So there is urgent need to prepare a successor.

13 July 1932. Lunched with John Buchan at the Athenaeum. Passed on to him German entreaty (Van Scherpenberg-Schacht) that the P.M. would say something in his speech to the effect that we view the Lausanne agreement as a clean slate, a break with the past, and that the £150 million is something quite different from reparations. Rubbed into B. that Papen is in danger (of being supplanted by Hitler) because Lausanne has brought no political concession. B. promised to pass it on to Ramsay.

Buchan also said that he was urging Ramsay to reorganise the Committee of Imperial Defence and to get me 'in a niche' there where I could 'direct policy' on defence. He wants to arrange a lunch with Ramsay and myself to talk over defence policy in October.

But on 22 November 1932 Buchan had to report to Liddell Hart:

I am afraid there is going to be a good deal of difficulty about the things we talked about. I have been exploring the ground, and I fear there is a certain amount of prejudice against you in War Office circles, and our present governors are terribly at the mercy of official opinion.

During the same week it was officially announced that General Montgomery-Massingberd had been appointed C.I.G.S.—a soldier who was lukewarm about mechanisation and opposed to Liddell Hart's conception of far-ranging independent action by armoured forces. The new C.I.G.S. had fallen out earlier with Liddell Hart over this issue and was strongly against the idea of his being No. 2 to Sir Maurice Hankey, so nothing came of it. And when Buchan suggested that Liddell Hart should receive a knighthood in recognition of his work as a military thinker, the Prime Minister was favourable, but the C.I.G.S. blew up, and again no more was heard of the matter.

So Liddell Hart's mind was not officially at the disposal of the British Army but—through his books—made a powerful impact on

* In 1935 T. E. Lawrence told Liddell Hart that he too had been approached to become successor to Hankey. (*T. E. Lawrence to his Biographers*, 1963, II, p. 230.)

the German Army, and indeed on professional military thinking in general. Later events suggested that Buchan was justified in his backing of Liddell Hart, but in the short run the conservatively minded C.I.G.S. had won.

CHAPTER TWELVE

HISTORIAN AND
HIGH COMMISSIONER

1927–35

'I am one of yourselves, and I have in my bones the tradition of Scottish Presbyterianism.'
John Buchan to the General Assembly of the Church of Scotland, 1933

During these years of public life Elsfield remained the centre of Buchan's private life, and the place where his books were written. When Parliament was sitting he would travel down every Friday morning and have three clear days at home. After a hard week in town he would dip deep into the refreshment of country sights, smells and sounds: 'I grudge every hour spent away from Elsfield,' he wrote in June 1930: 'Susie and I drove back from a little village in the West Cotswolds in the late evening, through miles of sainfoin and white clover. England just now is surely the most beautiful place in the world.' During the Parliamentary recess he could have long stretches in the country, coming up to London only one day a week for business at Reuter's. The regular programme for his Elsfield day would be: up at 7.30 or 8, short family prayers before breakfast at 8.30, then four hours' work in the library. (Buchan once owned that he liked a pipe because it gave him an excuse to stop working every twenty minutes or so.) In the afternoons he walked, by himself or with the children, or did some pruning or hedge-clipping in the garden. One of his domestic arts was flower-arranging, which he did very well—an accomplishment slightly irritating to his wife and daughter; as soon as he got home on Friday he would be out in the garden to pick himself a bunch for his room. After tea there was another couple of hours' writing; he did not work after dinner, or on Sunday. He was methodical, with stated hours for going through the household accounts, and every Saturday morning he pasted up his cuttings-book. Like his mother he was a generous host, with a sharp eye for unnecessary waste: he never saw any reason for making a long-distance call except in the cheap period, and had odd little economies, like making his old cheques into spills for lighting his pipe. He managed all the household's finances, paid the wages, and it was he who decided what kind of a holiday the family could afford. His eldest son remembers him as being rather secretive about money (in the early 1930s he was earning about £8000 a year) and always prudent—he liked to know where money *went*—though always generous. His wife had quite a battle, after his illness in 1929, to make him travel first-class between Oxford and London.

Though Buchan wrote at regular hours, he did not demand complete solitude. Visitors would expect to be barred from the library, but would then find themselves installed there, talking to Susan with children coming in and out, while their host worked away quietly at his desk with enviable concentration. 'Susie and I looked at him with some distaste,' said Anna. 'To us, to whom writing was such a labour, the ease with which he wrote seemed hardly human, and almost insulting.' He was firm about not being interrupted, but he did not need to be alone. Writing his novels and biographies was pleasure rather than work; and though, on family holidays, he would refuse to read newspapers or write articles, he usually put in two to three hours of this pleasant labour every day.

'Everything at home sprang into cheerful new life the moment my father entered the front door,' said one of his children, but they also remembered how the sound of his stick or umbrella being put with a thump into the stand in the hall 'caused a wave of energy to go through the house. Everything was quickly tidied up, and books were put back in their right places. He liked books to be read and immediately replaced on the library shelves.' Buchan enjoyed the company of his children, and liked entering into their lives and interests. When his sons were at school at Oxford he would sometimes go down on Sunday evenings and read to the Dragon boys after prayers or—with the lights out—tell them stories. When they were at Eton he would send them affectionate newsy letters about Elsfield, and the dogs, and fishing in the Mill Meadow, and respond to their news about the half-mile, the trouble over maths, the Rosebery History Prize, the bother with authority ('Sorry you have been quarrelling with your tutor. Do remember that he had a pretty rough time in the war'). With Johnnie he fished, shot and birdwatched; by Alice, always an enthusiastic actress, he was pressed into pageants and plays—acting a prior in 1926 in the Oxfordshire Women's Institute pageant, a crusader in the Masque of Oseney Abbey, which he and Alice wrote for the Oxfordshire Historical Pageant of 1931. For family holidays they took to going to Wales: in 1929 they were at Cwmmeru near Machynlleth, then there were three summers at Ffrwdgrech, a house under the Brecon Beacons where there was fishing in the Usk and pony-riding on the hills, and each member of the family seemed to be writing a book. On one of these Welsh holidays Buchan and Stanley Baldwin visited St David's Cathedral, which was being restored by a grant from the Pilgrim Trust; on another he attended an Eisteddfod in the company of Lloyd George. The one holiday abroad was in 1934 when they tried Annecy—not a great success, for Billy and Alastair, having no head for heights, hated the mild little climbs on which their father enthusiastically led them. In 1932 there was a trip with Johnnie to the Faeroes, and Buchan wrote to his wife from the Governor's House at Thorshavn:

We have been to see the leader of the Nationalists who lives in a wonderful Viking house. We went 30 miles up the coast and humped our kit over 7 miles of hill to a lovely place called Saxen where we had some excellent fishing. I got a sea-trout of 4 lb odd. We came back here for the festival of St Olav when the whole place went daft. We went to church in state. Yesterday the whole family took us a picnic to a lighthouse, where we saw some fowling. Today we start for an island called Samoi where we shall be fishing for several days. A Danish man-of-war is expected from Greenland, and it is willing to take us on a trip to some of the outer skerries. So you see we are filling up our time. It is a wonderful holiday, utterly unlike anything I have done before. We are both very well, and the medicine box is un-opened. The food is unbelieveably good.

Johnnie usually caught more fish, but his father got the biggest ones. On a loch on the island of Sudero Buchan had a vision of a monstrous sea-trout; always conservative in his fishing estimates, he judged this one to be fourteen pounds at least. He cast repeatedly but in vain; the great fish, passing undisturbed on its way, had power to disturb *him* for years to come.

Johnnie was by this time at Brasenose, treating Oxford rather as an extension of Elsfield and often appearing at home—with Roberto Weiss, Christopher Pirie-Gordon or Pat Heathcoat Amory—on his way to exercise his falcons, or to shoot snipe on Otmoor.

Buchan still found time for various activities in Oxford. Until 1930 he remained a Curator of the University Chest. He put in a lot of work for the Oxford Preservation Society—including the writing of a Prologue spoken by Lilian Braithwaite at a charity matinee for the Trust in 1930. (It was printed in the programme which also contained a letter from Evelyn Waugh with suggestions for the judicious destruction of certain buildings in Oxford, including Folly Bridge and Magdalen Bridge, so that 'Oxford could lapse into repose, undisturbed except for the brawling of dons'.) In 1934 Buchan was elected chairman of the senior Conservative Committee, whose main function was to choose two candidates to represent the University in Parliament. For years the Oxford members had been two Conservatives, Lord Hugh Cecil and Sir Charles Oman, but now Oman had announced that he would not be standing again. There was a stormy passage about choosing his successor, for Professor Lindemann, already a controversial figure in Oxford, was anxious for the nomination, and thought he had the backing of a majority on the Committee. A strong opposition mustered. Buchan's choice was L. S. Amery, who would have been glad to retire from the hard work of his Birmingham constituency, but in the end the official candidate was Sir Farquhar Buzzard. Lindemann retaliated by announcing that he would stand as an Independent Conservative. (In the 1935 election the University voters would have neither of them, and returned the Independent Sir Arthur Salter.) Buchan's friends felt that in tactics he was no match for the wily, plot-scarred Lindemann. 'The Prof,' Buchan remarked at the height of the dispute over candidates, 'has sold his soul to Winston and the Dukes.' Yet they were always on friendly terms, and the Prof was a regular visitor to Elsfield, dropping in at the end of an afternoon's drive round the county to retail the gossip he had picked up at Blenheim or the Birkenheads'. And by passing on some remarks of Buchan's about Churchill he helped to keep open the gap between them.

More congenial and less controversial was the work Buchan did for the Oxford Exploration Club. This had been launched in 1927, mainly with the object of organising an expedition to Greenland; it was the idea of Max Nicholson (later Director-General of the Nature Conservancy) that Buchan should be President. At the inaugural meeting the chief speaker was the Himalayan traveller Dr Tom Longstaff, who led this first Greenland expedition; his subject was 'Blanks on the Map.' Buchan, introducing him, spoke about some of the blanks that intrigued *him*; and Dr Longstaff had quickly to think up an entirely new set for his talk. A President may have a purely decorative function in an undergraduate society, but Buchan also put in some hard work. For the 1932 Sarawak expedition, which was organised in England by Tom Harrisson (with whom Johnnie had gone to St Kilda the summer before), Buchan raised much of the money, and interested the Rajah in the project. When the expedition came back in an aura of disapproval, Harrisson having been 'tactless' with the administration, Buchan spoke up in defence of his tremendous drive and energy. Other Exploration Club expeditions which he helped in various ways were J. R. Baker's to the New Hebrides in 1933, Wilfred Thesiger's to Abyssinia in 1933, Edward Shackleton's to Ellesmere Land in 1934. 'He was first-class to us', is the opinion of Dr Charles Elton, then Secretary of the Club: 'he did not interfere, but when help was needed, gave it at once.' He could go straight to the essentials of a problem, and deal with it firmly and quickly. The Exploration Club counted itself an efficient club, and appreciated his efficiency. And Dr Elton had been impressed by Buchan's unassuming self-confidence: 'No man who was nervous about his reputation would give his name to a club and then tell them to get on without fussing.'

Summing up his miscellaneous activities, Buchan's secretary Mrs Killick said that 'he never grudged time on things he liked, and never wasted time on things that had no appeal.' And Buchan gave gladly of his time to such projects as these Oxford expeditions, because they were just what he would have liked to do himself, but now knew he could not. One of his cherished pipe-dreams before the War had been an expedition to Everest. His interest in the Himalaya was part of his general interest in mountaineering; it came also from his devotion to his brother Willie, who had trekked in Sikkim, and seen Jannu, Pandim, Kabru and, eighty miles off, 'a unique view of Everest, humped between a broad-backed snow mass and a range of white, serrated peaks.' Willie had planned to write a book on Tibet with his friend Cecil Rawling, a soldier who had been on the Younghusband mission to Lhasa in 1904 and explored the sources of the Brahmaputra. He introduced Rawling to his brother in 1909, and after Willie's death in 1912 Buchan continued to see much of Rawling, who was planning an expedition to Everest in two successive years: in the first they would reconnoitre a possible route, in the second they would attempt the climb. Rawling had been dazzled by the mountain's size and splendour when he had seen it from Tibet, and he thought the northern side looked possible. Buchan eagerly joined in the planning ('Rawling thinks the Everest expedition has a good chance of being sanctioned by the India Office,' he wrote to his mother in February 1914) and had hopes of joining in the climb the second year, combining the trip with business for Nelson in India. Others involved in the scheme were Dr A. M. Kellas and Major J. B. Noel. The outbreak of war put an end to the plan; Rawling was killed in 1917, and by the end of the war Buchan was no longer fit to go on any big expedition. The fascination with Everest remained, and with exploration generally, and showed itself in his writings—*The Last Secrets* (1923) has chapters on Everest and on the Gorges of the Brahmaputra—and in the help which he gave to expeditions and explorers. If this door had closed for him, he would do all he could to open it for younger men.

When the Everest project was revived after the War Buchan helped the 1921 reconnaissance expedition with arrangements for publishing despatches and photographs. He kept in touch with a number of Himalayan travellers: Reginald Farrer, who had worked with him in the Ministry of Information, Colonel F. M. Bailey, Captain O'Connor and Lord Cawdor, who wrote Buchan a long account of his exploration with Captain Kingdon Ward of the Tsangpo and Salween rivers in 1923.

In 1933 Buchan was asked to help with the project for flying over Everest. The situation was delicate, for neither of the two organisers was a flying man, the venture was being largely financed by the erratic and formidable Lady Houston, and permission had to be obtained from the Governments of India and Nepal. Buchan smoothed out a number of difficulties with tact, and arranged for Wing-Commander Fellowes to be put in charge of all flying, which made things easier for the pilots. One of them, Lord Clydesdale (later the Duke of Hamilton), remembers how, as a young M.P. who also held a commission in the R.A.F.V.R., he was asked by Buchan in the House if he would like to fly over Everest: he had never thought of such a thing, but assented with pleasure. He also remembers a visit with Buchan to Lady Houston, who rather startled them by receiving them in bed.

There was a last manifestation of this interest of Buchan's in Everest when, in response to a request from Anthony Asquith for a film scenario, he sketched out a thriller whose climax was a flight over the mountain. (The typescript, now in the library at Queen's University, is not dated, but 1933 seems probable.) The plot turns on a pact between the Chinese Government and Bolshevik Russia: the three 'good' characters (American, Englishman, English girl) escape from China with vital documents in a light aeroplane, fly over the Himalaya and drop down to safety on the lawn of the Palace of Katmandu.

Buchan's wish to help people was by no means confined to adventurous young men. When any of his wide range of acquaintance struck difficulties in writing, whether books of history, travel or memoirs, Buchan would be asked for help and advice, which he seems never to have refused: his library is full of books inscribed by authors with thanks for 'unfailing kindness' or 'generous and never-failing assistance.' 'He had the most happy gift of not giving perfunctory advice, like so many people, but of bending the whole weight of his mind and experience to help a friend.' Buchan said these words of James Bryce, but they are as true of himself. 'You are the man of all the world for backing your friends,' wrote G. M. Trevelyan on one occasion, 'and that is one of the many reasons we all love you.' But it was not only his famous friends whom he backed. If he took trouble to help T. E. Lawrence return to the R.A.F. and to help Robert Graves secure a professorship in Cairo, he also took trouble to help a young woman who had an inadequate schooling to go up to Oxford, and a young Italian, who preferred England to Fascist Italy, to find work cataloguing the North papers in the Bodleian. He helped any number of people to find their first jobs. He put himself about for people: when his old Glasgow friend John Edgar had a nervous breakdown and was miserable in the hospital to which he was first sent, Buchan arranged for him to come to the Warneford near Oxford. There he visited him every Friday, bringing him books and taking him for drives, though it meant cutting down the precious writing-hours of the Elsfield week-end.

'I often long for peace like yours,' Buchan wrote in 1931 to his other old friend Charlie Dick in Shetland, 'but that does not seem to be my fate, so I can only attempt to cultivate a certain peace and seclusion of the mind.' It did seem to be his choice, if not his fate, to be involved in a fantastic variety of activities, and his special pride to be able to deal, deftly and cheerfully, with them all. 'Rigidly punctual' was the first thought about Buchan that came to the mind of Bruce Richmond, former Editor of *The Times Literary Supplement*; 'if a thing was promised for a date, it came on that date.' Unpunctuality was a fault that Buchan found most irritating

in others. 'He was so quick in all his ways,' said a former colleague
at Nelson's; 'in his mind and in his step—almost a trot.' Mrs
Killick found him 'entirely purposeful:' he dealt briskly with business visitors, there was no time wasted in gossip or trivial talk, all
was to the point—and he did not suffer fools gladly. He could write
or dictate at any time. 'He directed his energies always towards the
right point,' noted Hugh Walpole. 'He wasted no moment, although he could relax and was delightful when he did. A *very* good
friend to me.' He saved energy by never repining: in this the very
opposite of his mother, who was for ever brooding 'If only,' 'I
should have,' 'Why didn't we?'. Buchan scolded her for indulging
in 'the Masterton perquisite, REMORSE'; if *he* did not do what
he had hoped to do in one direction, he cut his losses and looked
elsewhere.

Arnold Bennett entered in his Journal for 7 March 1928:

John Buchan, invited for tea at 4.30, arrived at 4.27. He is a thoroughly
organised man. He had a Committee Meeting for 5.30. And at 5.15 he
simply got up and left.

F. S. Oliver in 1932 wrote to Susan:

John always shames me. He has dire diseases and at times much suffering;
but he always looks as well fed, as spruce and smiling as a robust ploughman on a Sunday morning.

And the verdict of Dr Plesch (a Hungarian refugee doctor to whom
Buchan was introduced by his mother-in-law), who gave him treatment in 1935, was that

There are two kinds of horses, short-tailed and long-tailed. The short-
tailed are the most difficult to make plump, because they are specially
annoyed by flies and are therefore active and restless. You are a short-tailed
horse.

'John Buchan, looking as ever alive and alert as a fox-terrier,'
was Bishop Hensley Henson's impression after a meeting in 1934.
'Fox-terrier' is apt, with its suggestion of the compact, the neat,
the purposeful, though Buchan had none of the aggressive manner
which small men, like terriers, often cultivate. 'So cheerfully trig
and keen a figure' was another description. (Photographs, Johnnie
Buchan thought, were misleading, for they 'gave him a look of
frozen gloom, a travesty of his good-humoured self.') Buchan never
put on any weight—his ulcer saw to that; he dressed well, buying
good clothes from an expensive tailor and then taking good care of
them; and whether in tweed jacket and grey flannels at Elsfield, in

dark suit and spats in London, in the kilt for dinner at a Highland
lodge, or striding over Border hills with a shepherd's crook, he
wore his clothes almost as regimentals, very trim, very spruce.

Catherine Carswell, the biographer of Burns, friend and biographer of D. H. Lawrence, wrote a description of a meeting with
Buchan in these years which is so vivid that I must quote it at
length. Her husband Donald Carswell had written a book on Walter
Scott and his circle, which Buchan used for his own life of Scott:

I received my first letter from him in 1930. I had written a Life of
Robert Burns, and he sent me a page or two of the most genial encouragement.

At this time we were in lower water than usual. My husband, however,
had high hopes of a useful, permanent appointment for which he had
applied. He seemed in all ways eligible and had good backing. John
Buchan, among others, had given his name in recommendation; but, at a
late moment, a change in procedure ruled out the appointment of a barrister. It was one of those mishaps that are not less discouraging for being
nobody's fault, and it is mentioned here chiefly to indicate the nature and
extent of the acquaintance. In 1932, when *Sir Walter Scott* appeared, it
was my husband's turn to write a letter of congratulation spiced with
difference; this brought a friendly, polemical riposte. Some weeks passed.
A further letter arrived. John Buchan wished, he said, to express his lasting
appreciation of my husband's book on Scott (he had adopted some of its
findings for his own) and his disappointment over the failure of the application. He hoped we should be as happy in accepting as he in sending us a
present of forty pounds.

We were surprised, even taken aback. I was even more surprised—after
a considerable lapse of time—to have a letter addressed to myself; my
second letter, coming more than two years after the first and without explanatory circumstances. He asked me to lunch with him a few days hence.

So brief were his terms that the note read less like an invitation than a
polite summons from one duellist to another. I could not help wondering
if I was to be arraigned for some unconscious trespass. As no other guest,
not even my husband, was mentioned, the meeting was to be without
seconds. I was to be in the lounge of a small restaurant in Jermyn Street
promptly at one o'clock. My host would be coming from the House of
Commons with little time to spare.

I arrived a couple of minutes before time. But he was before me—in both
senses. There he sat under the clock in the lounge on a sort of sofa covered
with red velvet. Rather, he was disposed there in a posture of the most
admirable relaxation, his head leaning against the high back of the seat, his
eyes closed.

I had sometimes wondered how he managed to get through his many and
varied undertakings. How did he compass it all? He had, as I then but
vaguely knew, suffered from illness. He looked a frail being here before
me, unconscious as yet of my presence. I found, however, at least part

answer to my question. He is always the first, I reflected, at any rendezvous. He uses the extra minutes to rest every nerve and muscle. At this moment his mind is emptied of everything except the brief opportunity for repose or meditation.

The picture I had carried away from his public appearance was of a man spare, even meagre; precise, even prim; compressed in manner and movement. His speech, somewhat clipped and—to a critical Scottish ear—synthetic, had confirmed this impression. A cautious correctness had seemed in him to be personified. Here, at close quarters and in a light at once more intimate and more exposed, he gained immeasurably. His face was revealed as 'fine-drawn'—to use one of his own favourite terms of description—in lines of energy and fatigue, sensibility and asceticism, recklessness and reserve: fastidious lines composing a delicate harmony of contradictions which lost very much with distance. The scar from an accident in childhood drew attention to the strikingly noble contours of his head. The long, queer nose, questing and sagacious as a terrier's, was in odd contrast with the lean, scholarly cheeks and with the mouth narrowed as by concentration or the hint of pain subdued. A peculiar countenance, subtle, in no respect trivial.

From time to time I had heard it suggested that this man was something of a careerist; worthy, of course, and admirable, but with something of what the term might imply of distaste. Those who made the suggestion—usually fellow-Scots of less luxurious attainment than his—had not the smallest personal acquaintance with him. It was perhaps natural that they should see in him the typical, never wholly sympathetic hero of the 'success story.' Such a verdict has little weight, but it was not for me wholly contradicted by his public appearances. Add to this that his tastes in men and books had seemed to be as contrary to mine as were his politics. True, he had shown us both courtesy and signal kindness. But unbiassed judgment does not always accompany proper gratitude in the uneasy commerce between wealthy success and needy obscurity. If poor as against rich people have some disadvantages, their liberalities are less liable to misunderstanding. In that moment, however, I was divested of all prejudice. Here he was, a man of my own generation and country, all unknowing under my regard. I had been interested; I became disposed to friendliness without reservations. At the same time I was also conscious to an acute degree that we should presently be talking together—of what?

The clock struck one. His eyes opened and saw me. He sprang up smiling, without a hint of lassitude, to make me welcome. On the instant he was the perfect host, with no apparent thought outside the existence of his guest whom he immediately set at ease.

We sat down on opposite sides of a table for two reserved for us by the farthest wall of the restaurant and, with smooth, unwasteful gestures, he ordered our meal.

His next remark astonished me.

'Is it to be business or pleasure first?' he asked, looking across at me with an expression of extreme, if also purposeful, kindliness.

Now it's coming, I told myself. 'I thought,' said I, 'that I'd take this chance of asking your advice about my son, John. He's about fourteen

now, and he's bent on getting to one of the Universities if he can do it by
scholarship, as, of course, he'll have to do.'

Then came the greatest surprise of all.

'It's to talk about John that I've asked you to come today,' he said.
'I have a great favour to ask of you and from what I guess of you, you'll
perhaps find it difficult to grant. I want you to let me be a kind of godfather
to John. I've thought a good deal about the most useful and pleasant thing
a man like myself can do with his experience, and it has seemed to me that
few things can be better than to give a hand to the younger ones who may
most need it.'

I had no reply ready. He filled the gap by speaking about my husband's
books and mine. He expressed regret that these should, as he correctly
surmised, have brought 'small pecuniary reward.' 'I have quite a number
of adopted godchildren,' he said, 'and I find great satisfaction in the
relationship. What I want you to understand and, if you can, accept, is
just this. If John at any time should need a pair of boots, or help or
advice of any kind, you'll write and tell me so that I'll know what to do.
If you can bring yourself to agree, you can't think how it will please
me. First, of course, he and I must get to know each other. Has he ever
had tea on the Terrace? May I write and ask him to come there one day
soon?'

So far as I am able after the lapse of time I have given his exact words.
In particular I remember the boots, which raised in my agitated mind the
vision of seeing my son off to college in a brand new pair. I knew that I
should never ask John Buchan for boots. But the suggestion made his
offer both clear and homely. I say I have tried to give his exact words. I
cannot hope to convey the friendly simplicity and the sincere, gentle energy
with which he spoke them. He did everything to make it seem that I, not
he, was the donor. He made it not merely impossible to refuse but easy and
natural to accept.

A few weeks afterwards the Carswells were able to give him a
present beyond price. They had discovered a French translation of
Macchiavelli, *Discours de l'estat de paix et de guerre*, printed in
Paris in 1548, which had belonged to Montrose and had his signature on the title-page. 'Your wonderful present has simply left me
gasping,' wrote Buchan. 'I have never had a gift which I valued
more. And I am most deeply touched by the kindness of both of
you. You are really mensefu'—only a Scots word expresses what is
chiefly a Scots virtue!'*

The godfatherly duty was not discharged only by cheques and
teas on the Terrace. When John Carswell got into hot water in a
trial trip for an Oxford scholarship—an affair of brashness and
iconoclasm in his essay paper—Buchan interceded with the head of

---

* '*Mensefullie*—in a mannerly way, with propriety'—*Jamieson's Scottish Dictionary*.

the college and asked him not to hold it against the boy when he came up for the examination again the following year.

Mrs Carswell touched upon one of the charges most often brought against Buchan. Careerism—a trait that Scots are particularly quick to spot in each other, and which may be the term which an envious person uses to describe another's success—implies, in distinction to honourable ambition, a wish to succeed and to get to the top at all costs.

Buchan had always been full of ambition. His upbringing had stressed the need, and indeed the virtue, of 'getting on.' He had set himself targets and had hated not to reach them. From his student days he had planned to go into Parliament; and once there he would —like most M.P.s—have liked office. His uncertain health had sharpened his pride in accomplishing anything he set out to do; he would not let his ulcer get the better of him. The light had played strongly on him as a young man; both his contemporaries and his seniors had looked to him to do brilliantly. 'Everything he put his hand to prospered,' Alec MacCallum Scott had written of him at Glasgow University, and his success at Oxford, his position with Milner, his marriage to Susan Grosvenor, his popularity as a novelist, his reputation as a historian, had all borne out this estimate. There was an aura of success about him that there was not, exactly, about his slightly older friend L. S. Amery—who too had had to make his own way, and in one direction had gone much further, in becoming a Cabinet Minister. And always hovering over Buchan's career was his devoted admiring family in Scotland, who felt that there were no limits at all to what John could do.

Yet Buchan's ambition had not just been a matter of attaining a great position, wielding great power—though he liked to be the familiar and confidant of those who did have power. It was rather a matter of stretching himself and using his abilities to the full. He wanted to be a Minister because he really did think he could run a Department very well. Indeed, he may have failed as a politician just because he tried to stretch all his abilities and talents and did not, in the American phrase, 'bunch his hits.' He certainly had not the single-mindedness, or the ruthlessness, of the true careerist, who would never have wasted his time helping with the affairs of undergraduates or obscure old friends, or writing books for good causes but no particular renown or profit (like the history of *The Kirk in Scotland*, which Buchan undertook to mark the

Union of Churches in 1929), let alone helping other people write their books. If there was a certain ill-will towards Buchan because he was 'too successful,' that was not the light in which he saw himself. His daughter remembers having dinner alone with him at Elsfield and for once he was out of spirits: 'Things have never gone right for me. I've been a failure.'

The other charge commonly brought against Buchan is snobbery. It was touched on in a sketch of him in *The Feet of the Young Men*, published in 1928. ('Janitor' was the pseudonym for two authors— J. G. Lockhart and Mary Lyttelton.)

There are few men in England with so wide a circle, not of acquaintances, but of friends, as John Buchan. In fact, friendship with him is a hobby. He must know everybody, be on the best of terms with everybody, call everybody by his or her Christian name. He may have only met you twice, he may not get your Christian name quite right; but whether you are a gillie or a duchess or an American traveller, you are Donald or Dorothy or Hiram and his very good friend. This is not snobbery, as I have heard suggested; for while the snob might enjoy calling a duke 'Fred,' he would scarcely derive equal pleasure from addressing the duke's third footman as 'Bill.'

Moreover, to do John Buchan justice, neither Fred the duke nor Bill the footman will be anything but gratified by his familiar address. For he has the great man's art of persuading you, whoever you may be, that you are the very person of all others whose society he wants. He is delightful company; he can talk well on almost any subject under the sun; he has a fund of entertaining stories, of which the best are those he tells in his own Lowland Doric; and he is particularly nice and helpful if you are young and quite unimportant. . . .

He aspires, perhaps a little self-consciously, to be all things to all men. Down in Oxfordshire he is a plain, bluff country gentleman, with a couple of hunters in his stable* and a knowing eye for the state of the crops. When he is taking the chair at a University dinner, he is almost an undergraduate among undergraduates, overflowing with wit and good fellowship. He will roar as well as any lion at a literary gathering, and talk simple good sense at a public meeting.

Buchan, there is no doubt, enjoyed knowing people who were famous and people with ancient titles; like the butler in *Castle Gay*, 'for ancient families with chequered pasts he had a romantic reverence.' A good deal of his pleasure in these sprang from his ever-active imagination—a trait he had observed in Ramsay MacDonald but seemed unconscious of in himself. 'You have no idea of the bores we had to put up with,' said one of his sons, 'because their ancestors had fought at Crecy.' Buchan had a romantic belief

* In fact, an elderly ex-hunter and a pony.

—it was the theme of *The Path of the King*—that where once there has been greatness, something of it will stay in the blood, and one day the spark will again be fanned into a flame. And so, behind the plain or spotty face of an Oxford undergraduate, or the smooth countenance of a young Tory M.P., he would see the features—handsome in their delineation by Lely or Raeburn—of some famous ancestor, and wonder whether it was in the present generation that the greatness would again appear.

Dearly as he liked the idea of the noble family, the historic house, the glittering reception, with the reality he very quickly got bored. He enjoyed having the entrée to Londonderry House or Devonshire House, but tended to slip away early from the actual parties. The heroes of his tales often make an appearance at the Duchess's ball or the political hostess's dinner-table, but they can never endure much 'society,' and their real life is played out in more uncouth surroundings. Buchan too liked to be in society—in short spells: with his exacting programme of work, his carefully plotted time, mere sociability could quickly become irksome. Week-end parties in great houses were, by the twenties, no attraction: he was far happier at Elsfield.

If the true snob collects fine friends at the expense of the unimportant, Buchan was not a snob: he was much too interested in people: 'interested, appreciative, receptive,' as Walter Elliot said:

He liked to know your name, even your nickname, whether he got it right or not.* He would stand and face you and discuss endlessly—wedge-nosed, his head forward and to one side, his lips parted, eager to speak, eager to listen. I do not remember that he ever broke off a conversation.

'He possessed all the qualities which make clever young Scots attractive,' Hensley Henson considered,

and he was wholly free from the faults which make clever young Englishmen not infrequently repugnant. Perhaps of these last the silent assumption of an unconfessed but indisputable and almost mystic superiority is due to the public schools in which young Englishmen of the upper class are mostly educated.

Buchan expected to like people and went forward to meet them. He would say he had no use for a certain type—'the Bohemian,' 'the rootless intellectual'—but, faced with one of these creatures, in two minutes he would be finding something to like in him.

* It always amused the late John Strachey, who was very fond of him, that Buchan persistently called him 'Jack,' the only person ever to do so.

Buchan's name-dropping, his fondness for the famous and titled, his liking to be in the know about politicians, explorers or wild birds, were there for all to see. They amused his friends, but a further circle of acquaintances was irritated or antagonised, and stories of them got about. What this further circle did not know was the continual giving of time and money and of the energy that buoys others up. Buchan took over the education of a boy whose father had been killed in the war; he helped a number of adopted godsons like John Carswell. 'I want to look after your rates and mortgage,' he said to one man, not very well known to him, who was having difficulty in re-establishing himself after the war. And all the time only his wife and his nearest friends realised the extent and the frequency of his bodily pain. He might boast about knowing a duke or two, or recognising a lesser redpoll, but he never took any credit for his stoicism when his ulcer was giving him hell. Applicable to Buchan himself is a passage which he quoted, in an essay written in 1908, from the eighteenth-century Lady Louisa Stuart. She distinguishes between true and false vanity:

When people are vain of some trifle not part of their *essence*, it is a foible, an excrescence, a weak side; you may laugh at it, silly people triumph over it, as bringing them down to their own level, but are mistaken, for it does not touch the character. Queen Elizabeth, who had more of these foibles than anybody, was vain of her beauty, of her feminine accomplishments, etc., but the solid *stuff* of her character stood quite apart. She was not vain of her talents for business or government. Sir Robert Walpole, a great, coarse, vulgar man, was vain of his gallantry among the ladies, and was laughed at accordingly; he had no vanity, no pretensions, about managing the House of Commons and guiding the State for twenty years.

So Buchan's friends would smile at his foibles without feeling that these affected the solid stuff of his character. 'He was so transparent and ingenuous about it,' said one about Buchan's liking for the famous; and of his knowingness Henry Newbolt wrote (after a drive with the Buchans to Salisbury in 1927):

J.B. in the evening asked if the Cathedral (which he thought finer than Winchester *and* larger!!!)—if it was Perpendicular in style. I restrained myself from saying 'Very nearly—the spire is only two feet out.' After all why should a Scot know—and this one knows nearly everything else.

They were amused at the frequency with which 'intimate friend' and 'a very old friend' tripped from his lips about people whom he had met half a dozen times, at the way all his geese were swans. But they did not think these foibles of much importance when set beside his solid virtues. It was not a careerist of whom Robert Graves writes: 'It is impossible to do justice to John Buchan's warmth, modesty, generosity.' It was not a snob whom Bishop Hensley Henson considered as 'of all my contemporaries, the most brilliant, the most modest, and the most lovable.'

Part of Buchan's charm for his friends was indeed the mixture in him of opposites. He was so vain about small things, so humble about his real merits; so sanguine in the daily business of life, yet so drawn to a seventeenth-century melancholy; so broadminded and large-hearted, and yet so pledged to orthodoxy; so mature in his actions, so boyish in his enthusiasms; at once the romantic and the realist with, as Catherine Carswell observed, 'a recreative interplay between them.'

Scots at home keep a sharp eye on Scots abroad. In public they will notch up the successes—a Permanent Under-Secretary, a Governor of Bengal, a foreign decoration, an honorary doctorate— but in private they will look out for signs of pride, of putting on airs, of the slackening of old ties. 'We do not rate highly the Scotsman who has succeeded in becoming an Englishman' was James Bridie's view, 'unless his Rugby is exceptionally good. We are too apt to search him closely for signs of affectation, and in Scotland alien affectations are treated very harshly indeed.' Many an eminent Scot in England has felt himself under this scrutiny from his friends and contemporaries at home; sometimes it acts as a bracing reminder of the Scottish way of life, plain, strenuous and democratic; at others it may reflect a grudging and suspicious attitude, which, in turn, may be the expression of a national uneasiness that, to do certain kinds of work, Scotsmen have to leave their own country.

Buchan, as Mrs Carswell implied, was the target for a good deal of Scottish criticism. It was not his romantic imagination that bothered fellow-Scots—this is a national trait—nor his liking to be in the know. What did arouse misgivings was the way in which, with his Oxfordshire manor-house, his boys at Eton, and his high London contacts, he seemed to be fitting far too snugly into the traditional life of the English upper classes. When his autobiography was published after his death there was one sentence which read startlingly north of the Border: 'I never went to school in the conventional sense, for a boarding school was beyond the narrow means of my family.' This from a Hutchesonian and first President of the Former Pupils' Club! In going to the local grammar-school

Buchan had enjoyed exactly the conventional education of almost every minister's son, lawyer's son, doctor's son, professor's son, in the Scotland of his day: it was the boarding school that would have been unconventional. It was understandable that Buchan should send his sons to Eton,* for he was living in England and that was the conventional education for his wife's family; it was fantastic that he should almost seem to believe that, because he had not himself been there, he had not gone to school 'in the conventional sense.' One should not make too much of an unfortunate sentence which Buchan himself might have changed before publication had he lived, but it illustrates something in him which both amused and irritated other Scots. He met his many commitments by a strict portioning of his time, which sometimes made him appear curt to less well-organised friends, who felt they no longer counted for so much; he was too brisk, with too little leisure for the rather un-purposeful chat and reminiscence on which old friendships thrive. They would retaliate with jokes about 'John calling all the dukes by the wrong Christian names.' But of the Scots I have met who did not like Buchan none had known him well.

Buchan's ties with his country were far more than a matter of family and sentiment. It was not only on Burns Night or St Andrew's Day that he kept up his Scottishness, nor on his stalking or fishing holidays. 'There are many different Scotlands,' he wrote in one of his *Graphic* articles (20 September 1930), 'but the shooting-lodge, Highland-gathering world is not one of them. It has no relation to anything in the country that matters.' In the Scotland that matters Buchan was actively involved. His work in representing the Scottish Universities brought him back to the Scotland from which he had started: the Scotland of teachers and doctors, professors and ministers, of men and women who had been to local academies and high schools, who had sat on hard benches at eight-o'clock classes. He had been active in the negotiations to transform the Advocates' Library in Edinburgh into the National Library of Scotland, and after this had been made possible through the generosity of Sir Alexander Grant, he became one of the Library's first trustees. He had solidly established himself as a Scottish writer and

---

* Buchan once admitted to another Scot in Canada that he now regretted having sent his boys to Eton 'instead of some decent Scots school like Ayr Academy;' which would indeed have been an unconventional choice for a man living in Oxfordshire.

literary man, with *The Northern Muse*, his biographies of Montrose
and Scott, his historical novel *Witch Wood*, as well as the many
thrillers which abounded, as Hugh MacDiarmid put it, 'in loving
and delightful studies of Scottish landscape and shrewd analyses
and subtle aperçus of Scottish character.'

When Buchan was a young man 'Scottish writing' had been
identified with the Kailyard School, whose mawkish parochialism
he had firmly repudiated: about the only modern Scottish writer
whom the young Buchan had admired was George Douglas Brown
of *The House with the Green Shutters*. But after the war there were
new voices, and a literary climate with which he was in sympathy
and which, through *The Northern Muse*, he had a hand in establishing. For in an article on Buchan the leader of this new movement,
Hugh MacDiarmid, said that *The Northern Muse* stood

in relation to Scots poetry as Palgrave's *Golden Treasury* to English, and is
in every respect worthy to sit cheek-by-jowl with the latter: a labour of
love, equipped with a delightful apparatus of notes which shows what a
fine, and so far as Scots letters are concerned hitherto quite unequalled,
critic (conservative albeit rather than creative) other, and less necessitous,
branches of literature have so largely denied us in this Admirable Crichton:
a definitive book, supplying a long-felt want in a fashion that seems likely
to give such an impetus to Scottish poetry that it will stand as a landmark
in our literary history not far from the beginning of what seems destined
to be known as the period of our National Renascence. It was, indeed,
compiled in the renaissance spirit—literary merit being the criterion of
selection. It was not too rigorously applied, perhaps, but Buchan thus
quietly, but decisively, aligned himself with the younger men who were
clamouring for the erection of literary standards in Scotland comparable
to those obtaining elsewhere. It will probably be unique among his works
in its effect.

Buchan, introducing MacDiarmid's *Sangschaw* (1925), wrote that
the poet

has set himself a task which is at once reactionary and revolutionary. He
would treat Scots as a living language and apply it to matters which have
been foreign to it since the sixteenth century.

Such a broadening of scope was congenial to the man who before
the war had tried to make the *Scottish Review* a paper concerned
with issues far beyond Scotland.

Half-jokingly MacDiarmid referred to Buchan in his article as
'Dean of the Faculty of Contemporary Scottish Letters.' Certainly
Buchan took seriously his duty as an older writer to read and help
his juniors. 'He had a way of writing to any author who drew his

attention as a Scot,' wrote Catherine Carswell, 'and he possessed the art of conveying acceptable praise, together with lively difference of opinion, on one side of a small sheet of notepaper.' Three books which he particularly praised were her own *Burns* (1930), her husband's *Sir Walter: A Four Part Study in Biography* (1930) and Edwin Muir's *John Knox* (1929), all of which ran into trouble in Scotland for speaking too frankly about national heroes. 'It was very generous of you to write so warmly,' wrote Muir; 'no one seems to have given me credit for acknowledging his greatness but yourself.' And Carswell, who had sent Buchan his typescript for comment, wrote:

> I can't tell you what pleasure your letter has given me. It was like the shadow of a great rock in a weary land (How we all get back to the pulpit!) Scott represents many months of toil when my heart often failed. Some of it I felt was good, but I could get no view of the ensemble. That was why I sent it to you and I awaited your verdict with some anxiety.

Writers can be prickly; Scottish writers can be especially prickly, but—whatever their reservations about some of his productions— most of his Scottish contemporaries and juniors seem to have liked Buchan well: dedicating their books to him (as Hugh MacDiarmid dedicated his *Annals of the Five Senses* in 1923) or sending inscribed copies, as Edwin Muir did his *Six Poems* (1932), 'in gratitude and admiration.' After dealing firmly with Buchan's novels, and with the admirers of his novels, MacDiarmid concluded his article on Buchan with 'The man himself, with this great tale of work to his credit, is utterly unspoiled.' Yet from many writers came, in one form or another, the wish that Buchan would respect his talent better: would stop trying to 'reach that wider public that demands that a writer shall amuse as well as enthral,' and concentrate on 'the smaller one which matters infinitely more;' would, at the risk of shedding some of his present popularity, put the whole of himself into a work of mature imagination. 'His fiction,' said MacDiarmid, placing him 'in the respectable but unexciting company of James Grant, William Black and George Macdonald,'

well deserves its vogue; would that many whose popularity is greater wrote half so well. But that is saying little! And very moderately-sized in the British scale, his work as a novelist disappears entirely in the light of European assessment.

Both MacDiarmid and Neil Munro felt that Buchan would best realise his potentialities if he came back to Scotland. MacDiarmid's attitude, indeed, resembled that of the Clydeside M.P.s: disapproving certain things in Buchan, yet unable not to be fond.

In 1932 Buchan published his second Scottish biography. Nobody since Lockhart had written a full-scale life of Scott; it was time for another. The centenary of Scott's death, Buchan said,

is my excuse for the re-cutting of some of the lines of Lockhart's imperishable memorial, and for an attempt at a valuation of the man and his work after the lapse of a hundred years. It is a book which I was bound one day or another to write, for I have had the fortune to be born and bred under the shadow of that great tradition.

No less than Montrose, Scott stood for an ideal of Scotland. In him also were reconciled the two strains in her history; the aristocratic and Cavalier, the Covenanting and democratic. He too knew what Presbyterianism could be at its best; he too had shunned the harsher ways of Calvinism. He had looked at Jacobite and Covenanter, Highlander and Lowlander—at the Laird of Redgauntlet and Balfour of Burleigh, Fergus MacIvor and Davie Deans—with 'detached fairness' and 'a moderate central mind.' In the values implicit in his books, in his temper as revealed in his *Journal*, he had taught his countrymen a lesson much in season:

The old fires of Calvinism had burned too murkily, the light of the *Aufklärung* had been too thin and cold, but in Scott was a spirit which could both illumine and comfort his world. He gave it a code of ethics robuster because more rational, and he pointed the road to a humaner faith.

He was

the greatest, because the most representative, of Scotsmen, since in his mind and character he sums up more fully than any other the idiomatic qualities of his countrymen and translates them into a universal tongue.

With Burns he was Scotland's 'great liberator and reconciler.'

So once again, as with Montrose, Buchan was writing with his whole heart, and perhaps with a better understanding, for the similarities between himself and his subject were so much greater. Buchan would have liked to do what Montrose did; he had in fact done much that Scott did. Likenesses abound. Both were children of the Borders, with a sheepfarming grandfather, brought up to hear ballads and range the hills. Both were trained in the law, whose 'complexity and exactness formed a valuable corrective to a riotous imagination;' had a prodigious memory, a tireless industry, great power of concentration, and wrote with happiness and ease. Both were fortunate young men, in marriage and income and reputation. Both had an appetite for hard exercise, and both for years endured regular bouts of bodily pain. (Into such a phrase as 'that testing-period of middle life when a man has to make terms with his body' went Buchan's knowledge of himself as well as of Scott.) Each had an 'inner world of dream and memory,' though Buchan perhaps took warning from Scott not to let that world invade the world of facts. Each had 'an old-fashioned reverence' for women, but on the whole preferred the society of men. Each had a vast acquaintance, but a small inner circle of friends; found it easy to get on well with political opponents; was good at helping lame dogs and, when it came to ministers of religion, detested unction and 'those who are at ease in Zion.' And each had the same feeling for the past of Scotland.

In addition to the likenesses that came from birth and nurture, were those cultivated by Buchan, as any young writer models himself on the author he admires. Buchan's spring tours in Galloway and the Borders in his student days deliberately echoed Scott's annual 'raids' into Liddesdale as a young lawyer. In compiling *The Northern Muse* he was helping to preserve his country's own tradition in the same field as the compiler of *The Minstrelsy of the Scottish Border*. In writing his early stories his conscious model had been Stevenson, but it was Scott's example that he followed in the scope of his historical novels, in the idea of the various interlocking groups of characters. Above all it was from Scott that he took his rôle as a writer. Something has already been said of this in the chapter on 'The Story-Teller;' here we can just note how Buchan followed Scott in thinking 'the making of books not enough to fill the life of an active man,' in hungering 'always for action, for a completer life than could be lived only in the mind,' in discouraging talk about his books, particularly in his own home. He followed Scott too in his attitude to the rewards of literature. These were, says Buchan in words which I could well be using of him,

so utterly incommensurate with the pains that his attitude was always a little apologetic, as of one to whom the gods had given too generous gifts.

In some ways it was a harder job to write Scott's life than to write Montrose's. There Buchan was telling in full a story hitherto familiar only in its outline; here he is re-telling a story almost too well known. Admirably does he keep in view all the strands in

Scott's life—literary, domestic, professional, financial—and he intersperses his criticism of the books without breaking the narrative flow. Again he puts his man fully into his context. His section on Border society, G. M. Trevelyan told him,

is as good a piece of history as Scott or Macaulay ever wrote. The very thing you have been living all your life to be able to write.

Firmly too Buchan places Scott's financial crash in the context of contemporary credit and publishing practices. For his analysis of Scott's business arrangements he owed a good deal to Donald Carswell's *Sir Walter*,* and in threading his way through the tangle of Scott's dealings with Ballantyne and Constable, Buchan was much helped by his own experience as an author-publisher.

In dealing with Scott's character Buchan shows—to quote his own words on another biographer—'the discriminating affection which enables him to read deep into the heart of the man.' He is clear-eyed about Scott's faults, such as his unreasoning opposition to Parliamentary Reform, his extravagance, his secrecy over money, his unkindness to Constable at the time of the crash. After discussing Scott's romanticism, his love of action and impatience at the limitations of a professional literary life, Buchan points out that

Such a man . . . will run two risks. His world of fancy and thought, since he refuses to parade it, may become a secret domain which, owing to its very seclusion from outer realities, may insensibly colour his whole attitude to life. Again, his robust insistence upon the value of common standards may induce a vein of worldliness, a false approbation of things as they are.

Buchan's frankness served his purpose well. G. M. Trevelyan, writing of Scott's battle to pay his creditors, put it thus:

The fact is that Scott rose to a moral level few 'men of genius' have touched . . . And this is all the more significant in that he was no *saint*— you have pointed out all the faults he had, good man—he was fashioned like unto us and therefore his rising to the height at the *crisis* makes him the greater example to us all. And that he was cruel to poor old Constable even at the moment of his greatest heroism makes the tale the more humanly credible.

'Discriminating affection' is also the mood in which Buchan looks at Scott's writing. Here he knew there was hard work to be done.

* Perhaps he might have acknowledged it more fully; there are only two footnote references to Carswell in Buchan's book.

This wide popular acceptance as a classic has had a paralysing effect on the critical study of Scott. He has been too much taken for granted, as if he were a statue in a public place. He has had detractors such as Borrow and idolators such as Ruskin, but he has been praised and blamed in a spirit of rhetoric rather than of science.

Buchan's criticism of the novels has a simple virtue which today we may too easily take for granted. He discusses the book on the table before him—its structure, its tone, its characters, its language—and does not use it as an occasion for fine writing of his own. His close study produces some sharp observations. He is one of the first to note how important, in *Waverley*, is the slow building-up of the hero's character in the first six chapters:

> The fullness with which the hero is realised and expounded provides the reader with a basis of judgment, a standpoint from which to view the whimsicalities and the heroics of the other characters.

He is shrewd about the ending of *The Heart of Midlothian*:

> There is no defence to be made for the death of Sir George Staunton at the hands of his own son. There was a story there of the Greek tragedy type, but it demanded a different kind of telling; as it stands, the reader is not awed by dramatic justice but staggered by inconsequent melodrama. Yet, apart from this blemish, I feel that the conception of the Roseneath chapters is right. Scott was always social historian as well as novelist, and he wanted to show Scottish life passing into a mellower phase in which old unhappy things were forgotten.

He explains why the lyrics scattered through the novels contain Scott's best poetry:

> His inspiration here came from the vernacular songs and ballads, and was the chief boon which his work on the *Minstrelsy* gave him. It put tunes in his head far subtler than the conventional things which he officially admired; and these tunes remained, singing themselves to him at work and play, so that, when in the novels he needed a snatch of verse, they rushed upon him unbidden, and flowed from his pen as easily as dialogue.

In talking of *The Bride of Lammermoor* he emphasises how:

> From a tale conceived in the highest mood of romance Scott seems to set himself to strip off all that is conventionally romantic. The old women are consumed with hatred of rank and youth and beauty, and Mortsheugh has no pity for the decline of a family which had forgotten his class.

It was a fresh tone of voice for a writer on Scott, and it had an effect on readers who had dismisssed the Waverley Novels with the 'tushery' of their youth.

As a historical novelist Buchan himself has talent where Scott has genius. 'If I could ever hope to write anything as good as Scott I'd be happy,' he told Michael Adeane, 'but I know I never would.' Yet having chosen the same road, Buchan could the better appreciate the qualities which had taken Scott so much further. His own practice is behind his recognition (apropos of Scott *not* putting the Armada into *Kenilworth*) of 'the necessity of the historical romancer keeping off the main roads,' his comment (on *Guy Mannering*) that:

The strange and the romantic are made to flower from the normal, and thereby their effect is heightened, while the normal is portrayed with a sober geniality which makes it in itself romantic,

and his defence of Scott's lapses of style (when 'his sentences can trip up each other's heels, and he can weaken his effects by an idle superabundance of words'):

The truth is that any man, whose business it is to portray life in action and who is caught up in the white heat of his task, is certain at times to take the first phrase that comes into his head, and jar the ear and the taste of a fastidious reader.

Buchan's *Scott* is, to my mind, his best biography. In *Montrose*, as T. E. Lawrence told him, he had 'put a very great man on a pedestal.' In *Sir Walter Scott* he took a very great man down from his pedestal and gave him fresh life.

In March 1932, the month in which *Sir Walter Scott* was published, Buchan told his wife that 'I have begun to collect Cromwell books from the London Library, for I must tackle that subject seriously.' By January 1934 this longest of his biographies was finished. Even with Buchan's exceptional powers of fast reading, concentration and memory, it was an astonishing feat. (Sir Keith Feiling thinks that the book shows the marks of speed, and a greater borrowing from other men's writings than *Montrose*.) Buchan regarded *Cromwell* as his biggest undertaking, even though it was a work of re-interpretation rather than of original research. It sold satisfactorily on both sides of the Atlantic and, more important to Buchan, was very well reviewed. Reviews of his thrillers did not matter to him—he had established his own reputation in that line which no review could change. But reviews of his biographies did matter, for, till the 1928 *Montrose*, he had no general reputation as a historian or biographer. Now the notices of *Cromwell* confirmed the

verdict on *Montrose* and *Scott*, and the holiday entertainer was seen
to be also, as G. M. Trevelyan told him,

one of the few really effective historical writers of our time . . . I fear professional historians so seldom get it across to people, though Herbert
Fisher does. And the non-professional historians so often have bees in
their bonnets, like Wells and Belloc. So I am exceedingly grateful to you
and Churchill and G. M. Young for writing sense about history that gets
read.

Once again Buchan sets his hero in his context. He himself was
very proud of his first chapter, on the state of England before the
Civil War, and rightly so, for it is a splendid recreation of the look
and feel of a past age, no less than of its actions and thoughts. In
this kind of historical reconstruction, where the physical circumstances of the lives of men are the groundwork of the historical
events, Buchan excels; but he is also successful when focusing on
one dramatic scene. In *Cromwell* Charles is sent to the scaffold as
strikingly as Montrose was to the gallows. Once more, as in
Montrose, Buchan's eye for country and his sense of weather add
much to the clearness and vigour of his battle-pieces. In all his
historical work, fact or fiction, landscape is never a picturesque
decoration; it is a fact moulding a man's temperament—as the
environment of the fens 'with their infinite spaces of water and sky'
moulded Cromwell's—and the kind of action possible to him.

In *Cromwell* are good examples of Buchan's liking for the might-
have-beens of history (suppose that Montrose, not Hamilton, had
been at the head of the invading Scottish army in 1648), for the
strange encounter and the symbolic incident (the gale blowing down
the standard raised by the King at Nottingham in 1642) and for the
odd detail (Bradshaw the regicide's shot-proof hat). These likings
of Buchan's account for much of the colour of his biographies and
their interest for the general reader; again, they were not romantic
decoration, but a central part of his thinking about the past. He
firmly believed that chance played a greater part in human affairs
than historians usually allowed, and one of his criticisms of intellectuals, in war and in politics, was that they did not 'allow for the unforeseen accident.' In dealing with Serajevo in his *History of the
Great War* he quoted Burke's sentence that 'a common soldier, a
child, a girl at the door of an inn, have changed the face of fortune
and almost of Nature,' and his Rede Lecture at Cambridge in 1929
was a discussion of *The Causal and the Casual in History*.

Cromwell was attractive to Buchan for many of the same reasons

as Montrose. Both were 'Puritan aristocrats,' a type to which
Buchan warmed as he never did to the Charles James Fox type (one
of his reasons for coolness towards Churchill). Like Montrose,
Cromwell too was a man who stood at a point of change, whose
inclinations were all for tolerance and moderation, whose convictions were arrived at slowly then acted on wholeheartedly, who
showed genius in the field and vision as a statesman—Buchan
dwells on Cromwell's colonising achievements, and his dreams of
Empire. He was another 'iron dreamer;' and if Montrose stood for
an ideal of Scotland, Cromwell

in his good and ill, his frailty and his strength, [was] typical in almost every
quality of his own English people, but with these qualities so magnified as
to become epic and universal.

Above all Buchan was fascinated by 'this iron man of action whose
consuming purpose was at all times the making of his soul.' He
charts Cromwell's spiritual life as carefully as his military campaigns,
noting his spells of dryness and heart-searching as well as his
moments of serenity and assurance. Buchan could enter with particular sympathy into this side of Cromwell. His spiritual experiences, his visions, his wrestlings in prayer, and 'the language of
Zion' in which he talked of them, were things familiar to Buchan
from his boyhood; in just such terms his father might have described the spiritual condition of some member of his congregation.
It is with a summary of his religious, not his political, creed that
Buchan ends his account of Cromwell's life:

His creed was the Christian fundamentals—a belief in God, and in His
revelation through the Scriptures, in man's fall, in Christ's death and
atonement for sin, in a new life on earth made possible by grace, in the
resurrection of the dead and the life everlasting—coloured by the Calvinist
interpretation . . .
His theology was simple, like all theologies of a crisis [Buchan had been
reading Karl Barth]. He accepted the Calvinist's unbending fatalism,
which instead of making its votaries apathetic moved them to a girded
energy . . . He never assented to the view that intellectual error was a sin
to be implacably punished in this world and the next. The foundation was
a personal experience, a revelation which he might have described in
Luther's words: 'I do not know it and I do not understand it, but, sound-
ing from above and ringing in my ears, I hear what is beyond the thought
of man' . . .
The majesty and transcendence of God is the rock of his faith.

In these passages Buchan may have come as near as he ever allowed
himself, in print, to affirm the creed he too lived by.

Talking to a Canadian audience in 1936 Buchan explained that he had

always tried to have one or two subjects on hand on which I worked, and which engaged a different part of oneself from that which was employed in earning one's bread . . . I found it a great relief to be able to turn from day-to-day practical affairs to a world in which there was no 'turbid mixture of contemporaneousness,' and where the only aim was the pursuit of truth.

Montrose, Scott, Cromwell maintained a balance in himself. On one side was the public figure, with the committees and engagements, the speeches in Parliament and articles in the Press; on the other a man who in the effort to understand other men and other times came better to know himself.

In 1933 Buchan appeared in Scotland in a new rôle, as Lord High Commissioner to the General Assembly of the Church of Scotland —a Parliament of ministers and laymen which meets for ten days in Edinburgh in May. He had been an elder of St. Columba's for over twenty years; with George Adam Smith he had written *The Kirk in Scotland* to mark the union of the Established and United Free Churches in 1929; and now he was invited by Ramsay Mac-Donald to discharge the most conspicuous function that a layman can undertake for the Church. The High Commissioner is, for the duration of the Assembly, the representative of the Crown. He goes in pomp and state. He lives in the Palace of Holyroodhouse, and above his head flies the lion rampant, the royal standard of Scotland. He has a military guard of honour which turns out each time he leaves or returns to the Palace. He is presented with the keys of the city by the Lord Provost; he is given a twenty-one-gun salute from the Castle when he drives to the opening of the Assembly, and a silver mace is borne before him. He is called 'Your Grace;' he has a retinue of Purse-bearer and aides, and his wife is attended by ladies-in-waiting and maids of honour.

Stevenson described this pomp in the passage on Holyrood in his *Edinburgh: Picturesque Notes*.

For fifty weeks together, it is no more than a show for tourists and a museum of old furniture; but on the fifty-first, behold the palace re-awakened and mimicking its past.

The Lord Commissioner, a kind of stage sovereign, sits among stage courtiers; a coach and six and clattering escort come and go before the gate; at night, the windows are lighted up, and its near neighbours, the workmen, may dance in their own houses to the palace music. And in this the palace is typical. There is a spark among the embers; from time to time the old volcano smokes. Edinburgh has but partly abdicated, and still wears, in parody, her metropolitan trappings.

Since Stevenson wrote this in 1878, Holyrood has often been a real court, with the Sovereign in residence; but the only person who holds state in it regularly every year is the High Commissioner. So his residence there during the Assembly is not merely an ecclesiastical occasion, but a Scottish occasion; it ministers to the sense of national identity. For once Scots are assembled in their capital to deal with matters with which the English have nothing to do; and the presence of the sovereign's representative underlines the dignity and significance of the event.

The appointment as High Commissioner is for one Assembly only, though many Commissioners have served more than once. In the early days of the Assembly a commoner had often been appointed, but since the seventeenth century it had always been a Scottish peer until 1924, when Ramsay MacDonald appointed James Brown, the Scottish miners' leader and M.P. for South Ayrshire. Buchan was the third commoner—and the first son of the manse—to hold the office in modern times.

The Kirk is firm about keeping its independence from secular authority, so the High Commissioner has no function in its deliberations, which are presided over by the Moderator. He is not a member of Assembly; his duty is simply to address it at the opening and close of its proceedings. He is also expected to attend various services in St Giles Cathedral; to visit and speak to church societies and committees, hospitals, and good works of every sort; and to entertain at Holyrood hundreds of Scots—members of Assembly, provosts, professors, judges, doctors and trade-unionists.

To discharge this hospitality the Commissioner is given an allowance, which seldom meets the cost of all that he is expected to do. Holyrood used to be notoriously ill-equipped: the High Commissioner might have to supplement the stock of linen and silver himself. When first approached by Ramsay MacDonald about the Commissionership, Buchan had hesitated a good deal on account of these domestic reasons. 'I made it clear that I would only take it in the last resort,' he wrote to Susan in March 1933, 'since I meant to make my terms.' These terms, which referred to the amount of entertaining he felt he could afford, were accepted; and early in April the appointment was made public.

Buchan was familiar with Assembly doings, for he had attended the Reunion Assembly in 1929 as an elder representing St Columba's, and in 1930 he had been the guest of James Brown at Holyrood. Now, soon after his appointment, he went up to Edinburgh to survey the scene and make the arrangements for inhabiting Holyrood with the help of the experienced and invaluable Purse-bearer Captain E. D. Stevenson. On May 22 he went into residence in this Palace which has a sense of history which neither Buckingham Palace nor Balmoral can convey. 'The real authentic place,' as Lord Crawford put it in a letter to Buchan,

the actual seat and environment of things that happened—things that happened in this very room, or that passage, with the ruined Chapel as evidence of our violences. In its way the place is more genuine than Glamis itself, for at Holyrood long neglect has preserved all the coarse second-rate plenishings of our impoverished Scotland.

The following day, in the uniform of a Deputy Lieutenant (of Peeblesshire and Oxfordshire), he held a Levee at the Palace for members of Assembly, the Senators of the College of Justice and other dignitaries; drove in an open carriage to service at St Giles Cathedral, then on to the Assembly Hall. All the way were tartans, plumes, heralds' tabards, military uniforms and civic robes. Buchan enjoyed it greatly, but made it plain in his address that the King's representative had not effaced the son of the manse: 'I come to you today with a full heart, for I am one of yourselves, and I have in my bones the tradition of Scottish Presbyterianism.'

The Church to whose Assembly he was commissioned had been formed by the union of the Established Church of Scotland and the United Free Church—itself the result of the previous union of Free Church and United Presbyterians. The Wee Frees—the minority who had refused to unite on that occasion—still held their Assembly in Edinburgh at the same time as the Church of Scotland. The Buchans had originally been Free Church; and so, after the opening of the main Assembly with all ceremony, Buchan went across to visit the Free Church Assembly in its rather bleak and half-empty hall— 'a gathering which might have been a persecuted remnant,' Violet Markham recalled, 'mostly ageing men and women with here and there a child who looked on wide-eyed at this sudden influx of pomp and colour.' It was the first time that they had been visited by a High Commissioner.

In the next few days Buchan addressed the Women's Guild and the Colonial Churches Committee, opened the Edinburgh Castle war museum and spoke at the Royal Infirmary Thanksgiving Service.

He visited schools and boys' clubs and nurses' homes, smallholdings and centres for the unemployed. He had dozens of people to lunch and dinner, hundreds to a garden-party and an evening reception. All went with a swing, and the Buchans were judged to have carried themselves with all the dignity that the position demanded. 'The whole thing has a sort of fairy-tale touch about it,' wrote Mrs Grosvenor to her other daughter:

When I see people being led up to Susie and curtseying nervously to her, and when I have to curtsey myself I feel as if I must wake up and find it a dream . . . I must say I am very proud of John and Susie. They both do it with much dignity and simplicity.

One of Buchan's strengths was that he knew much more about the Kirk than many High Commissioners: to ministers he could talk of parish matters with the familiarity of one brought up in a manse, to divinity professors he could talk of Karl Barth with a reader's enthusiasm.

If it was a time of form and ceremony, it was also something of a family party. Buchan's chaplain was his old familiar Charlie Dick, who came down from his manse in Shetland; Susan's two ladies-in-waiting were Anna Buchan and Lady Kinross—who as Car Johnston-Douglas had danced reels barefoot with John by the Cherwell after a Commem ball. Alice and her friends were the maids of honour, and would end a day of formalities by playing Murder with the A.D.C.s in Queen Mary's apartments, or slipping out to the pictures in the Canongate. Johnnie came briefly from Oxford with his friend Roberto Weiss. Billy and Alastair were allowed a week-end from Eton and disorganised the plumbing of Prince Albert's elaborate bathroom in the royal suite. Old friends came to stay for a night or two—among them G. M. Trevelyan, who particularly remembered the moment when Buchan left the High Commissioner's throne and came on to the floor of the Assembly to take his seat as an elder of St. Columba's. Above all it was a gala time for old Mrs Buchan who (like Mrs Grosvenor) stayed all the time. She had always dearly loved an Assembly. When she had been very ill in London in the spring of 1911 Sir Almroth Wright had told her son that 'she is very anxious to be present at some assembly in May, but she isn't fit to go to a dance.' And in 1932 Buchan told his wife that 'Mother writes from Edinburgh—as usual she is not finding the Assembly quite up to her expectations.'

For her it was a triumph, if not exactly the one she had hoped for in John's youth, when she had looked to see her son some day occupying the Moderator's chair and conducting the business of the Assembly, not observing it from the High Commissioner's throne. Now she could see her paragon publicly acclaimed, at the centre of grand and ceremonious occasions, sitting in the King's place, his family and friends standing up when he entered a room and calling him 'Your Grace.' She relished it all, but she saw no particular reason why his mother too should defer. One of the A.D.C.s remembers her as 'very naughty—she didn't do any of the ceremonious things towards her son that she was meant to.' She was an indefatigable attender at the Assembly debates and assumed that they would be as fascinating to everyone else at Holyrood; one day she suggested that Mrs Killick would like to go—'I shouldn't think she would for a moment,' said her son firmly. The occasion gave her a splendid chance to exercise her considerable powers of deflating, that particularly Scottish trait. So as she sat in the Commissioner's special gallery, plying her knitting-needles while her son addressed the Assembly in his rather nasal voice, 'I should have had his adenoids out as a child,' she would whisper in an aside. But her lifelong knowledge of church affairs and her wide acquaintance among church people were of enormous value to him; when it was all over he gave her a book into which he had pasted cuttings and photographs, and inscribed it 'To my dearest Mother, this record of what was as much her show as mine.'

The Lord High Commissioner and his entourage left Edinburgh with ceremony, seen off with a flourish by the Lord Provost into a first-class carriage to London. But it was the Buchan family and friends who had a hilarious tea in the refreshment room at Paddington and continued the journey to Oxford third class, with Buchan relishing the contrast. He had been a stickler for protocol at Holyrood, but he could switch his formality on and off as readily as he could his writing. One happy consequence of the High Commissionership was the engagement of Alice Buchan to Captain Brian Fairfax-Lucy, one of the A.D.C.s: they were married at St Columba's that same summer.

Scots, perhaps because they respond so readily to anything in the way of historical tradition, are correspondingly ready, when the occasion is over, to mock their own sentiment and be caustic about the person in whom, for a moment, history has been embodied. So among his friends and acquaintances there were some good-natured jokes at Buchan's elevation to quasi-royal status, but it was generally held that he had discharged his duties well. 'I am very pleased by

the way your gracious graces comported yourselves at Holyrood,'
wrote Fred Oliver from Edgerston: 'I have heard a good deal about
your doings there from various very different sources and everyone
seems to agree that Their Majesties have never, in recent years,
been so well represented.' So it was no surprise in Scotland when
Buchan was appointed High Commissioner again for the 1934
Assembly. Again there was a certain financial anxiety: after talking
to the Prime Minister Buchan reported that 'I gathered from him
that he rather thought that we should have smaller dinner-parties
this year, lest we create a precedent which makes Edinburgh people
think that they are entitled by right to dine at the Palace.' All went
much as before. To Alastair, who did not come up this year, Buchan
wrote:

Yesterday was gorgeous weather, and our escort of Scots Greys in full
dress was magnificent. The whole thing went very well, and my opening speech at the Assembly was, I think, fairly good. It is a heavy life, for
I have a terrible lot of speaking to do, and I find an hour's bowing at the
levee a pretty wearying job.

One of the maids of honour of that year remembers the feeling of
shyness and apprehension with which she arrived at the Palace,
knowing none of the other members of the suite. On her second
morning, as the party moved into the breakfast-room after prayers,
Buchan invited her to sit next to him and talked to her about her
approaching wedding and her future home. To be singled out from
a roomful of distinguished guests, and to have her host showing
knowledgeable interest in her doings, sent her morale soaring.
Buchan insisted on her fiancé being invited to Holyrood for the
week-end, a gesture for which she has always been grateful.
Another memory she has is of the last night when, with the Assembly
over, the pomp suddenly extinguished—there was no guard of
honour as they returned from the closing meeting—the suite were
invited to ask their friends to a party.

It was the greatest fun, and a completely relaxed atmosphere. Ian Whyte,
who was then the Music Director of the BBC in Scotland, improvised on
the piano musical sketches of some of the people present. We all immediately recognised as a 'portrait' of J.B. a sort of vaguely Scottish tune with
a thread of the Old Hundredth solemnly running through it. *He* applauded
it with enthusiasm—like everyone else, but looked round in wide-eyed
innocence, quite puzzled as to whom it could represent (very unconvin-
cingly, I thought!). His expression of modest surprise when it was explained amused me so much that I've remembered it ever since.

'So you've been to Hollywood,' said a puzzled country neighbour to Susan when the Buchans returned to Elsfield.

Later in 1934 Buchan had another ceremonial duty: to deliver the dedicatory address at the opening of the new Library presented by Mr Harkness of the Pilgrim Trust to Columbia University in New York, now generally known as the Butler Library. He enjoyed this second trip to America: the vast audience at Columbia, the honorary degree conferred on him as 'man of letters, statesman, public servant,' the Pilgrims dinner in his honour, the visit to the British Embassy at Washington. He met Roosevelt, though the man in Washington who most impressed him was Henry Wallace, then Secretary for Agriculture. In New York, at the instigation of Alice Duer Miller and Alexander Woollcott, he visited the blind and crippled playwright Edward Sheldon, who was a devoted Buchan fan, and discovered that this shrouded and recumbent figure, who for years had been confined to his bed, was the most delightful of talkers. A new friendship was made as they talked about Scotland and Scottish writers, and the need for Britain and the United States to stick close together; after this visit Buchan wrote to Sheldon that 'you have given me a new view of human courage.'

The liveliest part of the trip was, in spite of winter storms, the voyage back in the *Berengaria*. Several other writers were on board. Hugh Walpole, with an attack of arthritis, had to keep to his bed, but the Buchans, the J. B. Priestleys and Beverley Nichols spent much time in his cabin. 'Do you realise,' said Walpole one day, 'that if this ship goes down tonight four of Britain's best-selling writers will be lost, and that all the non-best-selling writers will probably have a party to celebrate the event?'

Two influential people had taken a special interest in the Edinburgh High Commissionership. Mackenzie King, who had received a long description of her visit from Violet Markham, asked her to send him some of the official photographs showing the Buchans among their 'court'. Stanley Baldwin had watched Buchan closely in the Assembly, and noted how his face was 'fine-drawn, sensitive to every emotion, full of pride in his own country and his own people, and happy that the lot had fallen to him to be the King's representative in his own home.' Baldwin had for some time been certain that Buchan's future in public affairs did not lie in Parliament; and one of his reasons for turning down suggestions that

Buchan should be given a Ministry was that, as he put it to a colleague, he was 'saving him for Canada,' and it would have been a waste of time making him a Minister and fitting him into the governmental jigsaw. Now he had seen for himself that Buchan could carry out the formal duties of such a post with dignity, efficiency, and good sense. In 1932 such a possibility had come up. On May 31 Buchan wrote to Susan:

Now here is something important which I want you and Alice to talk over before I come back on Friday. They are going to separate Burma from India, and make it a separate Dominion under a Governor-General, and, since the Burmese are a reasonable and docile people, they believe that if self-government succeeds there, it will be a model for India. I was sent for last night, and they asked me to be the first Governor-General. I have been whistling 'Mandalay' while shaving for some weeks, and that seems to have been an omen. What do you think about the old 'Moulmein Pagoda'? This would not be like Canada, a quasi-royal affair, but a piece of solid and difficult work. There is no hurry about a decision, for I have only been sounded, but I wish you would turn it over in your mind. Are we too old for a final frisk?

But Burma had not been separated.

In the ten years since 1925, when Buchan had been first mentioned as a possible Governor-General of Canada, he had become very much of a public figure. Speeches and chairmanships, work in Parliament and education, had built up a picture of 'a sixty-year-old smiling public man' to stand beside the picture of the romantic story-teller. He had won public honours: LL.D. from St Andrews in 1930, D.C.L. from Oxford in 1934 (along with Archbishop Temple, Sir Edwin Lutyens, Sir Maurice Hankey and Geoffrey Dawson). 'Yesterday was one long day of ceremonial,' he wrote to Alastair,

when I masqueraded in a scarlet gown and a blue velvet biretta, and received a great deal of cheek from the Public Orator in Latin, and in English from the Dean of Christ Church in the evening.

He had been made a Companion of Honour. And now he had the Holyrood experience. So it was no great surprise that the question of Canada should come up again. At a dinner in London in 1934 Buchan sat next to Dr Cody, the President of the University of Toronto, who told him that 'everybody in Canada was hoping that I would succeed Bessborough as Governor-General. Not for me!' But by the following March, when a firm offer was made from Buckingham Palace, he was not so sure.

The Governor-General is appointed by the Crown; before the

Imperial Conference of 1930 the Ministers whose advice was sought were the British Prime Minister and Secretary for the Dominions, though there would, of course, be informal consultations with the Dominion Prime Minister. (When Buchan's name was suggested in 1925, it was the British ministers Amery and Devonshire whose interest Violet Markham tried to enlist.) But at the Imperial Conference of 1930 it was resolved that the King should act solely on the advice of his Ministers in the Dominion concerned. In the spring of 1935 the Conservative R. B. Bennett was Prime Minister of Canada; but when the question of a successor to Lord Bessborough came up, an election was in the offing, and Mackenzie King, who was confident of winning it—and who indeed felt that after losing several by-elections the Bennett Government had no longer any right to exist—said that he could not concur in any nomination made by Bennett, and the selection should wait till *he* was Prime Minister. The King did not consider it could be left so late, and Bessborough was anxious to go; so Bennett and Mackenzie King were induced to consult together. When Bennett suggested Buchan, Mackenzie King, who had told Violet Markham a few months before that 'he was *determined*' that Buchan should be the next Governor-General, had no difficulty in concurring. So Bennett was able to submit Buchan's name as an agreed nomination.

'Let me put the Canadian problem in writing,' Buchan told his wife; and proceeded to list the pros and cons. Among them were:

AGAINST   Too easy a job for a comparatively young man.
              A week further away from Mother.
              A country and a people without much glamour.
FOR   A very easy life for J.B.
              The possibility of doing good work—closer contact with Washington—the fact that I have been paid the enormous honour of being asked by both Bennett and M.K.
              Only five days from England, so that the boys could come out for all their holidays.
              The right to return when we wanted, so that we could be in England when Johnnie was there. We could also bring him out to Canada and give him a hunting trip.
              Apart from special clothes and uniforms, we could do it on our salary, and the rest of my income would mount up.

An immediate peerage might revive Mother. All the same, my heart is in my boots. I hate having to make these decisions.

After a few days deliberation, when both Baldwin and MacDonald urged him to go, he agreed. His family in Scotland were overjoyed: 'I am sure the King is fortunate to get you,' wrote his mother. His wife was not so delighted. Susan had thrown herself into the doings of Elsfield, of the Oxfordshire Women's Institutes, of the Oxford settlement at Risca in South Wales. She liked to work in a small group, where real contacts are possible; she never cared for crowds. To have her husband represent the King was one thing in Edinburgh, and for ten days only; it would be quite another on the other side of the Atlantic, and for five years. Also—for in 1935 only adventurers flew the North Atlantic—they would be a week away from the children in England, and a week further away from Johnnie, now in the Colonial Service in Uganda. She had renewed reason to be anxious about her husband's health: he was horribly thin, and had been suffering more than his usual pain. But it was his great chance, and she would not stand in his way; and Canada would give them more time to be together.

The appointment was well received in Canada, but one tricky question at once came up. Almost every leader-writer in the Dominion approved the innovation of choosing a commoner for Governor-General. Mackenzie King let it be known through Miss Markham that he would prefer Buchan to follow Bryce's example: to discharge his transatlantic mission as a commoner, and then return to a peerage. Surveying the scene from the United States, *Time* magazine reported that 'Britain hoped George V would make his man a peer before John Buchan goes to Canada in the early autumn; Canadians fervently prayed he would not.' The King however was firm that his representative in the Dominion should be a peer; nor did Buchan demur. Men often protest that they are accepting honours only for their wife's or mother's sake. Buchan frankly enjoyed having a title (once it was clear that his House of Commons career was over); it was a symbol of success in his public life, the counterpart of a First in Greats in his Oxford life. But when, in the letter quoted above, he said he would be glad to have a peerage for his mother's sake, it was no mere form of words. Ever since the first war Mrs Buchan had been nagging him on the subject; as every Honours List came out she would convey her disappointment that 'your work had not been acknowledged as I hoped it would be,' or tell him of some Border worthy who had been knighted—so why not John? The New Year of 1935 produced this routine complaint—'I am bitterly disappointed that your name is not in the Honours List'—and on first hearing of the Canadian appointment Mrs Buchan was worried because John had not mentioned a peerage: 'but surely the King cannot go back on that for this appointment . . . I must say I would like to live to see you a Peer. I wonder at myself being so vain.' 'You well deserve this honour as you have been a hard worker,' wrote his uncle John Masterton from the farm at Bamflat.

Mackenzie King accepted the accomplished fact but rather rubbed it into Buchan, in a letter of 14 July, that nothing would have been lost, and much gained, if His Majesty had at this juncture been represented by a commoner—in such appointments more recognition should be given 'to worth and character, and less to place, position, power and privilege'—and proceeded, in a characteristically lengthy epistle, to read Buchan a little lecture on the current social revolution, taking as his text Violet Markham's recently published book about her grandfather, *Paxton and the Bachelor Duke.*

What title was he to take? He could not be Lord Buchan, for there was one already; someone facetiously suggested Lord Greenmantle, and someone else pointed out that one of the Heralds was already Greenmantle Pursuivant. In the end Buchan took the name of the village on the upper waters of Tweed, in the country where he had been happy as a boy; and added to it the name of his Oxfordshire home. Canadians, who had thought they were being sent John Buchan, had to accept in his place Lord Tweedsmuir of Elsfield.

On 28 March Buchan wrote to Susan from London:

My leaving the House yesterday afternoon was a terribly melancholy affair. At three o'clock, when the official announcement came from the Palace, I ceased automatically to be a member. I went in at ten minutes to three, and took my old seat behind Baldwin. The Speaker smiled at me and he and I kept our eyes on the clock. At one minute to three I got up, shook hands with Baldwin and Ramsay, bowed to the Speaker, and walked out. The debate suddenly stopped, and Members standing behind the Bar grasped my hand. I could not have spoken without breaking down.

Buchan's last Parliamentary duty was to draft the address of the House of Commons to King George V on his Silver Jubilee, which was read to their Majesties by the Speaker in Westminster Hall on 9 May.

Congratulations poured in on Governor-Generalship and peerage. 'I am beginning to wonder where you will end your romantic career,' wrote that other romantic, Cosmo Lang, now Archbishop of Canterbury. Weizmann cabled 'affectionate regards' from Palestine. Violet Markham jubilated because 'for once the Government has done the right thing.' Robert Cecil considered Buchan just the man to study the problem of what was to replace 'the old conception of an Empire more or less dependent on the mother country.' Colleagues from South African days were particularly pleased. 'I congratulate you and Canada. It will be a new experience for them to get a change from the conventional run of aristocratic fainéants,' wrote Patrick Duncan from Cape Town (himself to become the first home-grown Governor-General of South Africa). To Lionel Hichens the news was 'really glorious.' Recalling all the problems which the Kindergarten had tackled with so much light-hearted enthusiasm, he was sure Buchan would be 'one of our great proconsuls and carry on nobly the Milner tradition.' 'I wish you all luck in your imperial job,' wrote Harold Nicolson. 'It is a fine task and you will do it magnificently. I envy you your chances of public service. I seem to have muddled all my own, and literature, while one is still active, is not enough.' A bizarre note was struck by Ezra Pound—'Thank god for one Brit. peer who didn't BUY it or get it by DIRT''; and belated good wishes arrived from Peter Fleming in Kashgar—explaining, with a touch of Sandy Arbuthnot, that on emerging from Tartary he had read the news in a three-months-old *Times* picked up at the British Consulate.

There was indeed some apprehension that this would mean the end of Hannay, Leithen and their friends; and great regret at Buchan's going so far away, and at the ending of useful associations. 'We shall miss you very much in the House,' wrote C. R. Attlee, 'for although you spoke seldom, your influence was pervading and you will leave a gap which will not be easy to fill in the scanty ranks of those who are to a large extent above the battle.' 'Almost every cause with which I have been connected,' wrote Professor Namier, 'had you for one of its leaders.'

But many of his friends were delighted with the appointment just because he would have to cut loose from a multitude of causes and activities. They had worried because he had seemed to be taking on far too much, to have a finger in too many pies. When they read of his being a prior in a pageant, or adjudicating at the Oxford verse-speaking contests, or acting as one of the jury for the Peace Propaganda Film, or opening an exhibition of Peter Scott's paintings, or becoming one of the original governors of Gordonstoun, or addressing a literary society run by an old friend, or attending the jubilee of a Glasgow minister, or appearing at yet another speech-day or Unionist fête—they felt that, for all his formidable powers of organisation, he was spreading himself too thin. Captain Liddell Hart greatly admired his *Montrose*, Keith Feiling his *Cromwell*; both were convinced that these would have been even better books, 'absolutely first-class,' if Buchan had been able to give more time to them. To such friends, jealous that he should give of his best, the Governor-Generalship seemed ideal: his public activities would be canalised and he would have far more free time for his best writing.

Certainly Buchan's last months before going to Canada were a whirl of activities and sociabilities. There was his staff to collect. There were long talks with the Canadian High Commissioner. There was a visit to Windsor. There was the unwinding from all the organisations in which he had been actively involved, and he did not want to leave loose ends. (On giving up the chairmanship of the School Age Council, for instance, he fired a parting shot in *The Times* at the Government for their dilatoriness in raising the school-leaving age.) There were lunches and dinners in his honour given by the Canada Club, the Royal Empire Society and other public bodies. Representatives of the Governor-General's Households since 1872 entertained him at the Ritz. Brasenose gave a dinner which was said to be the largest in the history of the college; in the chair was Sir Richard Lodge, who had spoken up for Buchan at Brasenose forty years before, and Buchan was particularly pleased by the number of people who remembered his brother Willie. There was a dinner to celebrate the première of Hitchcock's film of *The Thirty-Nine Steps* (which proceeded to break all box-office records at its first showing in New York). The Scottish M.P.s entertained him at the Scottish Office: and though the Clydesiders were not there, for the I.L.P. had principles about not attending public junketings, Jimmy Maxton put his good wishes on paper:

Dear John,

I usually pride myself on not observing the conventional congratulations, but I feel I must just send you a line on your Canadian appointment.

I wish you a very happy and useful time for yourself and Canada. Don't let them stop you writing a book or two.

Yours for the cause
JAS MAXTON

In April Buchan was elected an Honorary Bencher of the Middle Temple. In June he was given the freedom of Edinburgh, and afterwards put in a few days on Tweeddale, taking part (as Warden of

Neidpath) in the Beltane celebrations at Peebles, and going the rounds of the family:

Walter and I took a bus to the head of Tweed, and then walked back through my barony to the Crook, where we had an excellent tea. The upper Tweed was looking very wild and lovely. I saw two redshanks—very rare birds here; I think they must have come up from Otmoor to have a look at Tweedsmuir for John's sake! Today we are going up to Broughton and Bamflat.

Leaving home was a protracted business. First the Canadian Premier asked Buchan to come immediately after the General Election on 14 October; then, when he was about to sail on the 18th, he was asked by Bennett to postpone his departure for a week. 'He meant to receive me,' Buchan explained to his mother,

if he had had a big following, or if there had been a sort of stalemate as an election result. But now that he has been beaten to a frazzle it would look ridiculous for him to continue, and Mackenzie King wants to get his whole Cabinet assembled and bring them all down to meet me. . . . It is not much fun, this prolongation of the misery of farewells.

There was a last meeting with Baldwin, now Prime Minister, who 'said he had no words to say what I had been to him in the last eight years.'

Finally on 25 October the Buchans sailed from Liverpool to the supreme opportunity of John's life. Before making for the open sea the *Duchess of Richmond* sailed up the Clyde past the Tail of the Bank, and gave him a last sight of the place from which he had started. 'We had great expectations for you,' his mother had written not long before, on his birthday, 'but they have been all far exceeded.'

CHAPTER THIRTEEN

GOVERNOR-GENERAL
1935-37

'There have been many failures among those sent abroad to represent the British Crown, due largely to the narrowly circumscribed area from which they are chosen; but that does not derogate from the tremendous importance of the office or belittle the success of the rare few who have succeeded.'

John Buchan: *Lord Minto* (1924)

On 2 November the *Duchess of Richmond* sailed into Quebec, with a flaming red sunset behind the dark line of the Citadel and the old town, and every ship in the harbour hooting its welcome. The Tweedsmuirs landed at Wolfe's Cove, from which the British climbed up to the Heights of Abraham in 1759. They were received by the Chief Justice of Canada, Sir Lyman Duff (who had been Administrator since the departure of Lord Bessborough in September), and by the Prime Minister and members of the Cabinet. By torchlight they went up the Rock and along the cobbled streets in a horse-drawn carriage, with cavalry escort. Red-coated soldiers were drawn up in the Old Square for Tweedsmuir to review.

At the Legislative Building the new Governor-General was sworn in by the Senior Puisne Judge (Mr Justice Rinfret) and there was a salute of guns. The Prime Minister spoke, and made it plain that it was John Buchan they were welcoming rather than the new Lord:

It is as John Buchan, the commoner chosen to represent His Majesty in other spheres, that you will find the warmest welcome and an abiding place in the hearts of Canadians. In your aristocracy of mind and wealth of imagination you are the familiar friend of thousands of Canadian homes.*

Tweedsmuir replied, in English and in French. There were other

* For all Mackenzie King's words, almost everyone whom I talked to in Canada, including people who had known him before he became Governor-General, spoke of 'Tweedsmuir'; so I have used this name in my Canadian chapters, except where I discuss his books, which continued to be published over the name of John Buchan.

speeches—and longer. The Mayor of Quebec, winding up, said,
'This is the first time we have had a professional poet as Governor-
General!' There were five hundred hands to shake, 'and when we
got to the sanctuary of our train I was pretty well all out. My uniform
is very heavy.'

Then followed a day of holiday, with the Governor-General's
train in a siding fifteen miles from Quebec. Tweedsmuir drove
forty miles down the St Lawrence with his Comptroller, Colonel
Eric Mackenzie, to see the snow-geese which assemble there on
their way from the Arctic to the Carolina keys—ten thousand in the
air at once wheeling in orderly formations 'in a sort of aerial
quadrille'—and to meet some French-Canadian bird-enthusiasts.
On 4 November they went on to Ottawa, where there were Cameron
Highlanders to review, and another welcome from Prime Minister
and Cabinet. There was another drive in an open carriage with
outriders and cavalry escort, through crowded streets, with now and
then a cry of 'Good luck, John,' to Government House. For three
days the Tweedsmuirs had lived in public, and they were glad to
reach the house which for the next five years was to be their home.

Rideau Hall, on the farther side of the Rideau River from Ottawa, was built for himself in the 1830s by Mackay, the mason
responsible for the stonework of the Rideau Canal. It was taken
over as Government House in the 1860s. It is a handsome house
with a classical facade and architrave—one would guess late eighteenth century if it were in England or Scotland—though in 1872
it struck the Dufferins, who expected to find a splendid vice-regal
palace, as 'a two-storied villa with a small garden at one side.' The
first impression of the Tweedsmuirs' Elsfield butler, 'It is something after the Windsor style,' was an overstatement in the other
direction. Tweedsmuir himself found it 'like a very big, comfortable
English country-house.' The gardens on the far side might be small
by the side of Windsor or Blenheim, but they were quiet and
sunny; and there was pleasant walking in the wooded park, which
was full of squirrels and chipmunks. Indoors the Tweedsmuirs
found everything immensely improved since they had stayed there
in 1924 with Lord Byng. This was largely the work of Lady Willingdon, who had taken great trouble about refurnishing the house,
though her taste had run rather monotonously to mauve. A Chinese
room, whose furniture and *objets d'art* she had collected, had been
her special concern. The upkeep was now the responsibility of the
Department of Public Works. The chief drawback was the complete

absence of a view: after Elsfield it felt shut in, and only from the upper windows could they catch a glimpse of the Ottawa River. In this respect the Tweedsmuirs envied the British High Commissioner, whose house, high above the river, looked upstream to the city and across to Gatineau Point. The private quarters were delightful: 'In my library I have all the family photographs around me, and in our little private breakfast-room I shall have prayers with Alastair and Susie,' Tweedsmuir told his mother (Alastair had come with his parents, for a year between school and Oxford). The rooms where they would entertain officially were light, well proportioned, and not overpoweringly large, and hung on these walls were portraits of Tweedsmuir's predecessors: Lord Willingdon in full-dress civil uniform with white breeches and white silk hose, the Duke of Connaught and Lord Minto as soldiers, Lord Aberdeen in Doctor's scarlet robes, Lord Grey—'gone native' as a Canadian put it to me—in a fur hat.

Tweedsmuir was the thirty-fifth British Governor-General: what exactly was his job? And how did it compare with the job which his predecessors had crossed the Atlantic to discharge? In his life of Lord Minto, he described how

A Governor-General in an autonomous Dominion walks inevitably on a razor-edge. His powers are like those of a constitutional monarch, brittle if too heavily pressed, a shadow if tactlessly advertised, substantial only when exercised discreetly in the background.

He went on to quote the words of Sir Wilfrid Laurier, who was Prime Minister in the time of Minto, Lansdowne and Grey:

The Canadian Governor-General long ago ceased to determine policy, but he is by no means, or need not be, the mere figurehead the public imagine. He has the privilege of advising his advisers and, if he is a man of sense and experience, his advice is often taken. Much of his time may be consumed in laying corner-stones and listening to boring addresses, but corner-stones must be laid, and people like a touch of colour and ceremony in life.

'Let not Ambition mock their useful toil' had been Tweedsmuir's comment on those Governor-General's duties.

From the British North American Act of 1867 to the Imperial Conference of 1926 the Governor-General had represented both the Crown and the British Government. After 1926 he represented only the Crown. He was no longer an agent of the British Government: he had an undivided responsibility to Canada. Nor was he now the channel of communication between the two Governments: there was no scope for writing State papers. Communications between Governments now went through various channels, one of which was the High Commissioner for the United Kingdom, whose functions were comparable to an Ambassador's; the Governor-General communicated direct with the King. Like the King, he was entitled to be kept fully informed of everything that took place, to be 'shown the telegrams,' and his rights were those of the sovereign as described by Bagehot: 'the right to be consulted, the right to encourage, the right to warn.' Like the King's, his constitutional duties were to open Parliament, read the speech from the Throne, grant dissolutions, receive a Prime Minister's resignation, summon a party leader to form a Government, give his assent to legislation. His ceremonial duties were to lay all those corner-stones or their equivalent, to hold levees and drawing-rooms, and to entertain in a style befitting the head of a state.

Several of Tweedsmuir's friends, in congratulating him on his appointment, had commented on the Governor-Generalship being in a phase of transition—'a rather critical' phase, said W. H. Clark, who had been the first British High Commissioner in Canada and now held the same office in South Africa. The former Prime Minister of Canada, Sir Robert Borden (who had given Buchan his *Canadian Constitutional Studies* to read on his voyage home in 1924), assured him that 'the ideal Governor-General is one thoroughly accustomed to, and versed in, the conventions and ethics of constitutional usage.' And Mackenzie King, in a letter written on 19 July, 1935, before Tweedsmuir arrived, put the position as he saw it:

While it is true, and now clearly recognised, that the Governor-General is an appointee of the King, and in no way the appointee of the British Government, the Governor-General of Canada is, nevertheless, as much the appointee of a Government today as he has been at any time since the office was created, the only difference being that it is the Government of Canada, and not the Government of Great Britain, which is responsible. In other words, the appointment of The King's representative to the Dominions is as much a matter of the respective Dominions Governments as the appointment, say, of Dominion ministers to foreign countries. The old maxim, 'The King can do no wrong' still holds, if the prerogative of the appointment of Governor-General, like all else, is exercisable upon the advice of ministers. He must accept the responsibility of their advice, and neither the Sovereign, nor the Ministry, can escape responsibility—the one of accepting, and the other of tendering, advice.

I have not the least doubt that your appointment will be one of those historic milestones which help to mark by pleasant, rather than painful, transition, the path of a new order.

So it was not a proconsulship Tweedsmuir had taken on, such as had been his goal when, after serving with Milner in South Africa, he had hoped to serve under Cromer in Egypt. But neither was it a colourful sinecure. At the first announcement it struck at least one of his friends as too ornamental a job for a man of John Buchan's capacities. 'A high office, to which I grudge you immensely,' had been T. E. Lawrence's words in his last letter, 'You are too good to become a figure.' That was certainly not how Tweedsmuir himself saw it. He had always been ambitious, not just to reach a certain position, but to stretch himself, to use all his talents. Much as he enjoyed a certain amount of ceremonial, he would not have been content with a job that was mainly a matter of stepping on a red carpet and going in first to dinner. 'Canada is a biggish job,' he told Donald Carswell, 'but I never could resist the challenge of an adventure.'

The challenge and the adventure were in what he could make of the job beyond the constitutional and ceremonial requirements. As to one point he was quite clear: the Statute of Westminster had given a new meaning to Dominion status, and his Governor-Generalship must reflect, and help to define, the new status, in ways that he would have to work out as he went along. He was quick to realise one advantage: 'the new position of the Governor-General, who represents the King only, has the advantage that Canada regards him as their own man and is very frank and confidential with him.'

His predecessors had all had their particular 'lines.' Lord Byng, who had commanded the Canadians in France, had special links with ex-Service men; Lord Willingdon was sociable and sporting; Lord Bessborough was enthusiastic about amateur drama and successfully revived the Dominion Drama Festival. To Tweedsmuir his friend Byng offered a sympathetic model, and he wrote in 1926:

His simplicity, his utter freedom from pro-consular frills, his humanity, friendliness and humour, were soon realised from the Atlantic to the Pacific, for he travelled much more than the ordinary Governor-General, and he made a practice of mixing freely with every class.

Very helpful to Tweedsmuir in thinking out his approach was a frank account of Canada, the Canadians, and the Governor-General's job, written confidentially for him by Alan Lascelles, Secretary to Lord Bessborough from 1931 to 1935. On the matter of representing the King Lascelles wrote:

The most difficult thing about it is to know when it ends—to know when

the Viceroy should become the Man . . . Any man of education and imagination who is used to public life can adequately play the King on ceremonial occasions, or in official relationships; to win the sympathy and
affection of a very diverse, self-conscious, and politically restless people is
more difficult.

He pointed out how different qualities were appreciated in different
parts of Canada. In Quebec they liked a Governor-General with a
sense of tradition and a sympathetic interest in French culture and
the Church of Rome; in British Columbia they were happy with an
English gentleman and sportsman; while in the Prairies the ideal
was 'a regular fellow with no frills' and some understanding of
agriculture. There was some sensible advice about clothes, and a
warning that towards the end of each winter, what with all the cold
out-of-doors and the heat indoors, 'a tendency to mild melancholia'
was apt to manifest itself. This was 'purely seasonal, and no notice
should be taken of it.' Two of Lascelles's suggestions—that in
entertaining the Governor-General should cast his net widely, and
that occasionally in his travels he should get off the beaten track
and into the wilds—were very much to Tweedsmuir's taste.

Tweedsmuir was certainly coming to his job with a solid stock of
assets. In a country where the tone of public life has been largely
set by Scots, it was an advantage to be a Scot, a Presbyterian and a
son of the manse. He had made his way by his own efforts: for
once, as a proconsular friend put it, there was 'some damned merit'
about the appointment. He had experience of administration, of
politics, of business, of journalism. He was known to have a great
liking for and interest in the United States: and, as a Canadian
explained to me, if a Briton is anti-American, then Canadians
(themselves keen critics of America) are at once suspicious; they
know they are like Americans in many ways, and feel that the anti-
American Briton will, behind their backs, be anti-Canadian too.
Tweedsmuir was known as a popular novelist, though not so well
as in the United States. On Lord Bessborough's farewell tour in the
Prairies, one of his A.D.C.s found a good deal of ignorance as to
who 'this Colonel Buchan' was: nor did mention of his books help.
But when the A.D.C. remarked 'He's the brother of O. Douglas,'
that rang a bell. Anna's books had great popularity, and her brother
was delighted to hear of their relative fame.

These assets were in Tweedsmuir's public record: others were
soon to be apparent. He arrived with a determination to get on with
his Prime Minister, and a fair knowledge of Mackenzie King,

gathered over twelve years. Moreover he was a historian, with a curiosity about the forces that had made Canada, and the forces that were moving Canada now. ('There are some,' the ancient historian Hugh Last wrote to him, 'to whom historians as Governors seem even more suitable than philosophers as kings.') His Scottishness meant, not just that he had common ground with all the Scots Canadians, but that he was quite free from the peculiar English assumption (commoner then than now) that English ways and customs are the norm, and that nearly all variations on them are for the worse. Never did Tweedsmuir feel inclined to say: 'Why isn't this as it is in Britain?' His question would be 'What is this, and how does it work?' His training at the Bar, his work with Milner, and his leader-writing at the *Spectator*, had made him quick at getting up a subject, at pumping information from people. His love of expertise, of being in the know, had a new field in which to deploy. He had what Amery described as 'an endless affectionate curiosity about his fellow-men of all classes and ages'—particularly about the young—and a store of experiences which made it possible to find some point of contact with nearly everyone he met. A Governor-General is expected to make a show of interest in—to take examples from only one official tour—pedigree bulls, milk-condensing plants, centenarians, dinosaur remains, juniper-root carvings, Indian dances, and veterans of bygone wars and historic occasions (Tweedsmuir met one who had taken part in the 1867 Confederation ceremonies). Tweedsmuir really was interested in most of these, and had no need to whip up a spurious enthusiasm.

He also had a characteristic which could be an asset: a passionate interest in politics. But in a country fresh from a General Election and still in the trough of economic depression, at a time of crisis overseas with the German and Italian dictators challenging democratic government and embarking on foreign conquest (Mussolini invaded Abyssinia just about the time Tweedsmuir sailed for Canada), it could also, in a Governor-General, be a liability.

One of Tweedsmuir's assets was quickly manifest. Soon after his arrival he made a number of speeches at Montreal and Toronto, where he attended the Winter Fair. At McGill and the University of Toronto, quoting Plato, St Augustine, Blake and Jefferson, he was the intellectual. At the Canadian Club, where his audience included business men to whom the depression was an ever-present fact, he spoke as a historian, about the clever men who at various times had prophesied disaster and been wrong. 'I purposely spoke rather seriously,' he told one correspondent, 'for it is a grave time for Canada and the world, and I remember in 1924 how Lloyd George and Robert Horne offended the Canadian audiences by jocosity, which they interpreted as "talking down" to them.' But on a more informal occasion—the dinner of the York Club during the Winter Fair—he was short, witty and gay. Here was a Governor-General who, talking out of his own experience, his own reading, his own reflection, had plenty to say, was able to say it in ways appropriate to his various audiences, and could do it all himself. He used no notes, and no one ever had to write his speeches for him. Tweedsmuir learnt two lessons from his early speeches: to keep clear of 'persiflage and irony: everything one says is taken at the foot of the letter;' and to provide reporters with a typescript even if he did not need it himself. Grattan O'Leary of the *Ottawa Journal* warned him that few Canadian journalists knew shorthand, and a hand-out was the only way to ensure accuracy.

Here too was a Governor-General who was formal when necessary, but approachable, not in the least a stuffed shirt; a frail man, with a direct and sensitive approach, who did not look like an august person: who, though less Scottish in voice than they had expected, certainly did not at all fit into the Canadian stereotype of what an English Governor-General was like. There was no aura of a grand ancestry and a storied family, no clanking chains or rattling sabres; a gentle, intelligent man. 'A complete change,' one Canadian put it, 'from nonentities as to the manner born.'

After the visits to Montreal and Toronto there was a quiet Christmas in Ottawa, and on New Year's Day 1936 Tweedsmuir held the traditional levee in the Parliament Buildings for the men of Ottawa, 'a relic of the old days when the French Governor received all the population of the little settlements.' The Conference of Provincial Prime Ministers gave him some useful first impressions,

for they are very varied in type, and they have all behind them a good deal of solid practical experience in other walks of life than politics.

The most interesting to Tweedsmuir—who had been given a correspondence course in Major Douglas's theories by Ezra Pound*—

* Though as far as I can discover the two never met, Pound started a correspondence with Tweedsmuir in 1934. A letter from Rapallo of 18 March 1934 begins:

Jock Ritchie has spent the morning telling me that you are very great pot indeed (Ld. High Admiral of the Free Kirk (or the other one), etc.) and that you are much too conservative etc. etc. to commit yourself. [*continued opposite*] was Aberhart, the new Premier of Alberta, who had been returned by a great majority on a Social Credit policy.

He is entirely different from what I expected—not a lean, fiery-eyed fanatic, but the real sheep in wolf's clothing; a bland old gentleman in considerable confusion of mind.

They talked of Major Douglas, and when Tweedsmuir said that he had never been able to get Douglas to answer any of his questions, Aberhart agreed, adding 'Do you think the fellow has got something up his sleeve?'*

Early in the New Year Mackenzie King, feeling rather overwhelmed by his duties as both Prime Minister and Secretary of State for External Affairs, asked Tweedsmuir to help him arrange his work better. Drawing on his experience of Ramsay MacDonald's problems, Tweedsmuir willingly drew up a memorandum suggesting various procedures which would lighten the load.

The big formal functions of the Governor-General's year were due in February, but though Tweedsmuir opened Parliament as arranged, the State Banquet and Drawing-room were cancelled because of King George V's death at the end of January. The period of official mourning gave him an excellent chance to make the acquaintance of politicians and others in Ottawa, in a fairly informal way. Three mornings a week, following a custom instituted by Lord Grey, he went down to his room in the East Block on Parliament Hill,† where any Senator or M.P. could come and talk to him. 'I fancy that they are more confidential and frank with me than they are with their own leaders,' he reported to Baldwin, 'for my office is now blessedly free of any ordinary political colouring.' Every evening at Rideau Hall, after tea, he would talk to journalists and 'young men of every type.'

'NEVERTHELESS, things are sufficiently tangled to make it nearly a duty for honest men to try to find out what, if anything, they are agreed on/for example I wd like to draw you as to WHICH of Doug's premises you grant.'

After Tweedsmuir's appointment to Canada, and after the Alberta election which brought the Social Credit party to power, Pound wrote on 1 September 1935: 'I trust the Alberta Elections have renewed your faith in humanity.'

* In 1937 Mr Aberhart, whose usual dress was a tail-coat, bowler hat and elastic-sided boots, asked Tweedsmuir what he ought to wear at the Coronation. 'Whatever you wear, Mr Aberhart, will be a social credit to Alberta' was Tweedsmuir's reply.

† The fact that the Governor-General had an 'office' in Parliament was a relic of Colonial days. During the 1939–45 war additional offices were built at Government House and the secretarial staff moved up from the East Block: a constitutional move as well as a practical convenience.

On the whole I am greatly impressed by the young men here. Most of them are thinking seriously about the problems of Canada's future. The slump of business is turning the mind of many of the best towards the public service.

Here are some of his impressions after these early contacts:

Canada has some very difficult problems before her, but they are, I believe, temporary and terminable. She has enormous assets which, if well managed, are ample to tide her through.

The public spirit seems to me in the highest degree wholesome. There is nobody in Canada now who casts sheep's eyes at the United States. Indeed, the troubles south of the border have made Canadians rather condescending now to their neighbours.

The so-called isolationists are really quite a reasonable people. They want Canada kept out of foreign entanglements and are very jealous of any commitment in Old World affairs. At the same time they realise that Canada's position under the new theory of Empire means either that sooner or later she must take a larger share in Imperial defence, or that there must come a lessening of the need for defensive measures owing to some international arrangements. That is why they are very keen, most of them, about the League of Nations: indeed I have never met more rational defenders of the League than I have found here.

Determined as he was to get a sure feel of Canadian politics, Tweedsmuir had no illusions about the narrow range of a Governor-General's power to influence them. Many of the Government's actions indeed he heard of for the first time in the newspapers. But he saw that there were many possible areas for a Governor-General's influence outside politics, and he waited his chance to explore them.

The moratorium after the King's death gave the Tweedsmuirs a chance to settle into life at Rideau Hall much more peacefully than they had expected, though the Edwardian scale of the mourning—no outside sociabilities, everyone in black, writing-paper with thick black edges—induced gloom and claustrophobia in most of the household. Some of the staff were new to Canada. Shuldham Redfern, the Secretary, had come from the Sudan Political Service; he had been Governor of Kassala Province. The Assistant Secretary, Mr Pereira, had been on the staff since the days of Lord Grey, and could always produce the right precedent. Colonel Eric Mackenzie, the Comptroller (responsible for the running of Government House), and Michael Adeane, one of the three British A.D.C.s, had been with Lord Bessborough; and the Canadian A.D.C., Colonel

Willis O'Connor, had served since his original appointment by
Lord Byng. Susan Tweedsmuir's lady-in-waiting was her daughter's friend Beatrice Spencer-Smith. Mrs Killick had come with
them as Tweedsmuir's private secretary, and from Elsfield came
their chauffeur Amos Webb and their butler James Cast.

Tweedsmuir's working day at Rideau Hall began with his official
paper-work. 'I could never give him enough work,' said Shuldham
Redfern. He would go through his papers briskly, make quick
decisions on which invitations to accept, what speeches to make,
then leave the details to Redfern. He had to sign piles of documents
about comparatively trivial affairs—land-grants to individuals in
Nova Scotia, for instance—and he would just sign steadily on, never
looking at the text above. He economised time and energy. When
he agreed to give a speech, or accept an honorary degree, even if
the occasion were some months ahead he would dictate the speech
for it the same day to Mrs Killick. Copies would be filed, in due
course circulated to the Press, and though Tweedsmuir was seldom
seen to look at the typescript again, and spoke without notes, 'it
came out practically the same.' Once a month he wrote a long letter
to the King, with news of his doings and his impressions of Canada.
When he had disposed of the day's chores, he would turn at once
to the biography of Augustus, on which he had started work soon
after his arrival in Canada. His staff were at first surprised—as
visitors at Elsfield had been—by his ability to stand interruption:
switching off his attention from the work in hand, dealing with the
new matter, and then switching back again.

In the afternoons he would take exercise according to the season.
When the ground was open he would walk—with Susan and Alastair
or one of the A.D.C.s—in the grounds of Rideau Hall, or round
Rockcliffe Park, or drive out to the Gatineau Hills and walk there:
'It is wonderful to look a hundred miles north and know that there
is nothing between you and the North Pole.' When the snow came he
took to ski-ing; King George V's last message to him was that this
was no sport for a middle-aged man. Between tea and dinner he
had his informal interviews, and after dinner he read.

When official entertaining began again, the Tweedsmuirs made
a point of giving informal luncheon-parties, where they could get
to know people better, and talk to them more directly than at the
formal dinners where the guests had to be chosen mainly because
they were Ambassadors, civil servants, Senators, M.P.s. Such a
party, stiff with protocol, could be a bit of an ordeal for hosts as

well as guests. The luncheons were altogether more relaxed, and real contact could be made. One point the Tweedsmuirs made very clear was that any kind of 'society' life in Ottawa must do without them. As one Canadian put it, 'they cut down the social glitter.' It was no use ambitious matrons angling for invitations to Government House, or trying to lure the Tweedsmuirs into any kind of fashionable gathering. They would go formally to the Ottawa receptions which were in the line of duty, they would go informally to see their own friends, but they would not go near the large social crushes. In making his plans for 1936 Tweedsmuir was determined to be out of Ottawa in November and December, 'when there is nothing to do except to give tea-parties.' Seeing the Prairies would be 'much more useful work for me than making speeches to the genteel in Eastern Canada.'

It was clear that only a part, and perhaps a lesser part, of his job lay in Ottawa. 'We lead a very comfortable, not to say cosseted life,' he told Stair Gillon, 'but I think I shall be happier when I go on tour and feel that I am really getting my teeth into the country.'

In January 1936, just before the King's death, he made a short trip to the gold-mines in Northern Ontario, which had been such a financial resource to Canada during the depression. 'Gold,' he told the Institute of Mining a few weeks later, 'is a fairly obvious thing when you find it in the shape of dust or nuggets, but when you extract it from rock that looks like nothing so much as a bit of frozen haggis, then you work a marvel and a miracle.' In March the Tweedsmuirs spent a week in the Eastern Townships of Quebec: country originally settled by United Empire Loyalists after the American Revolution, but now almost entirely French, a region of small industrial towns and mixed family farms which had not greatly felt the depression. In spite of having to make thirty-two speeches in English and seventeen in French, Tweedsmuir enjoyed himself immensely.

I found myself at one moment driving in state in a sledge, accompanied by an old bishop in a tall fur hat, and at another rigged up in full miner's costume in the bowels of the earth among Nova Scotia mine captains [at the asbestos mines at Thetford]. I dined with an eminent lumber magnate, and was given Coca-Cola to drink, while lunching at one convent we had cocktails and an excellent dry champagne! The total impression was of immense warmth and friendliness. Most of the places had never seen a Governor-General before.

He was struck by the good manners he found everywhere, by the rootedness of the French farmers, who would never sell their land—'*pas à vendre: c'est pour ma famille*'—and by the aspect of the Catholic Church 'in a place where it is dominant.' He thought some of the criticisms he had heard of it were justified: it was out of touch with the newer forces in national life, it had been rather spoilt in the past by successive Governments in Quebec, 'and allowed to do many things which should be in secular hands.' But at the same time he felt

that there is tremendous value in an institution which has so great a hold upon the affections of its people, which holds firm to spiritual standards, even though they be sometimes narrow, and which has in its bones a sense of historical continuity.

Two Protestant institutions also struck him as very good: Bishop's University and Bishop's College School at Lennoxville, 'a curious enclave of old-fashioned Anglican civilisation, with as stalwart a tradition behind them as the Catholic schools.'

Early in May there was a week in the rich farming district of Western Ontario, 'with stalwart little cities full of memories of the 1812 war;' at Queenston Tweedsmuir was interested to see the ruins of William Lyon Mackenzie's printing-office, and reported the fact to his grandson Mackenzie King. Ten days after the end of this tour he was off again to Hamilton—'a model of how a city can be industrial and yet beautiful'—London, Stratford and Kitchener. In June the Tweedsmuirs extended their knowledge of French Canada. First, while the household was being moved from Ottawa to Quebec, they stayed at Murray Bay on the St Lawrence. They talked to the *habitants* in the hill-farms and stony fields, took tea with the local *seigneuresse* in a house built in 1765, attended a *veillée* in the village of St Agnes and were drawn up the hill in a four-seater carriage with horses 'almost smothered in lilac, which was tied to their backs, ears and tails.'

With Johnnie, who was convalescing in Canada after being invalided home from Uganda with amoebic dysentery, Tweedsmuir had a few days' fishing on the Lac des Truites. Then followed two months in Quebec, meeting the politicians and officials of the Province and the leaders of the Church. Tweedsmuir found Cardinal Villeneuve 'a very wise man;' having been Bishop of Saskatchewan, he knew British as well as French Canada, and was less provincial in his outlook than many of the Quebec politicians.

The Governor-General's residence at Quebec is in the Citadel,

converted by the Dufferins out of the officers' quarters of the
fortress originally built to Vauban's design. So the walls were six
feet thick, the ceilings barrel-vaulted, and on one side was the
barrack square shaded by willow trees. The Tweedsmuirs loved it—
'this delightful house . . . pleasantest abode in Canada'—and the
outlook from the Bastion terrace was superb. Four hundred feet
sheer below them was the St Lawrence with its shipping, and down-
stream they could see blue hills, rather like the Sound of Mull.
Indeed in Quebec Tweedsmuir often felt as if he were in an old
French town that had miraculously been put down in the West
Highlands. He was soon at home at Laval University, where he used
to drop into the library to check the references for his *Augustus*:
the Rector, Monsignor Camille Roy, became a real friend. French-
Canadian intellectuals liked the idea of an intellectual Governor-
General: '*On lit Proust à Rideau Hall*' was one appreciative
comment on the new regime.

It was a particularly happy first visit to the Citadel, for, as well
as Johnnie and Alastair, they had with them Mrs Buchan and Anna
and, following them, Mrs Grosvenor. The Buchans had come out in
April, as soon as the St Lawrence was free from ice, and Anna had
been delighted to find that

John seems absolutely in his element, enjoying everything he has to do and,
except now and again, not at all overburdened with work. I do think this
is just the job for him.

Mrs Buchan, now in her eightieth year, was indefatigable: noting
and appraising the state and ceremony, keeping a wary eye on the
Cardinal and other Papists, nipping off to visit a hospital and returning in high spirits because she had seen a man with a broken neck.
One of the A.D.C.s noted that the Governor-General was 'quite
frightened' of her and what she might say; while she, as at Holyrood, kept her independence. 'Did you and Anna curtsey?' she was
asked on her return to Scotland. 'Oh they all curtseyed,' she
answered, 'but I just gave John a kindly nod.' 'There is nothing of
her,' wrote her son, 'but her spirit is unflagging.' Walter joined them
in July, and Charlie Dick too left his Shetland manse to visit them in
Quebec. He was appointed to preach—'by vice-regal command'—
at St Andrews Church, where Tweedsmuir was an elder.

On 31 July came a five-star visitor: Franklin Roosevelt. The visit
had been suggested soon after Tweedsmuir's arrival in Canada, and

was originally planned to take place in Ottawa in June; owing to Congress adjourning late, it was put off till August. Tweedsmuir was glad of the change to Quebec: he felt this emphasised that it was not entirely a state visit, but partly a personal one, that Franklin Roosevelt and John Buchan were already good friends, with a number of common interests, public and private.

It was the first time an American President had officially visited Canada, and the Stars and Stripes floated over the Citadel beside the Union Jack. Roosevelt, who had been yachting off Nova Scotia, landed at Wolfe's Cove on a glorious day and drove through the town to the Citadel. The only flaw on a delightful occasion was that Canadians felt there were far too many security men about—the Grande Allée was thick with them—and that the Mounties could have been trusted to give adequate protection. There was a State lunch, for Canadian Ministers to meet the President, and after lunch Roosevelt, Tweedsmuir and Mackenzie King had a long talk while, at Tweedsmuir's suggestion, Canadian journalists were entertaining their American colleagues. Susan noticed that her husband and the President 'talked to each other like old friends, wasting no time in the preliminaries of acquaintanceship.'

Mackenzie King, who had been staying at the Citadel throughout, was wildly enthusiastic: he told Tweedsmuir that it must have been 'one of the happiest days in the President's life,' and considered that 'the visit will do the present world much more good than any meeting of the Assembly of the League of Nations.'

Soon after the Roosevelt visit Tweedsmuir set out on his first long trip across the Continent, travelling in—to quote one of his successors, Vincent Massey—'the two venerable but homelike railway cars that were called, in a grandiose and inaccurate phrase, "the Governor-General's train"' and were attached to trains on the regular schedule. They went by the Northern Prairies to Vancouver, then returned east through the Southern Prairies, which had been hardest hit by the recent droughts. When planning his tours soon after his arrival Tweedsmuir had considered this one to be the most important, 'for the Prairie Provinces have been having a terrible time, and there is the largest proportion of non-British blood among the people.' He also hoped

to cut loose from my special train and, with one A.D.C., to go touring the back parts, taking my own sleeping valise with me and picking up a lodging where I can. . . . There is not much I can do, but I can at any rate show that the King's representative is deeply interested in them. Half of the trouble of the Prairie Provinces is that they feel cut off from the rest of the world.

The tour proper started at Winnipeg in the second week of August. G. V. Ferguson, later editor-in-chief of the *Montreal Star*, then senior editor of the *Winnipeg Free Press* under J. W. Dafoe, remembers being asked to visit Tweedsmuir

one morning about 11 a.m. on his private car in the C.P.R. station. He asked me if I'd like a drink. I asked for a Scotch and soda. This was brought and the waiter at the same time brought in a tray on which stood a can of baking soda, a glass and a jug of water. Tweedsmuir mixed himself a stiff bicarbonate of soda while I had my Scotch and a most convivial time was had.

At Regina there was 'a splendid out-of-doors reception to which women came carrying their children, and men in their shirt-sleeves —the kind of thing that I like.' At Carlton, near Saskatoon, Tweedsmuir attended an Indian celebration and was made a Chief of the tribe. Warned that the Indians would be dressed up to the nines, the Governor-General's party reluctantly donned top-hats and tail-coats and proceeded by car along a very dusty road. The result, Shuldham Redfern remembers, was that 'though we left Saskatoon looking like undertakers, we reached the reservation looking like flour-millers.' However, Tweedsmuir was delighted to be given the same name—Teller of Tales—in Indian as Stevenson had been given when the Samoans called him Tusitala. (Just before leaving Quebec he had been made a Chief of the Hurons, as 'The Scribe.')

The Rockies welcomed them with real Scottish weather, rain and mist; in British Columbia there was yachting up the coast, and fishing for salmon and steel-head trout as well as the receptions, inspections, garden-parties, and the celebrations for the Jubilee of Vancouver. 'They are extraordinarily kind people here,' Tweedsmuir wrote to his mother, 'with something which Eastern Canada has not got—a kind of mirthfulness and sense of adventure. No wonder, for this is an incredibly beautiful city.'

Calgary was the first stop on the return journey. Tweedsmuir was fascinated by this land-locked town—named after a place in Mull where a grey house stands above the Atlantic—which had grown up in the space of a lifetime and was still full of old-timers who had seen the wilderness recede. From there he went to Lethbridge, in the irrigated ranching country near the Montana border, where the dead flat Prairies run up against a sudden wall of mountain and the streams are clear. He visited one ranch with a marvellous garden carved out of the wild, and he addressed a meeting of white-robed Mormons in a Mormon temple.

The irrigation work . . . is largely in the hands of Mormons, who were brought up from Utah as experts—very hard-working and decent citizens, but with a most incredible religious creed. I insisted on being instructed in it, and I never heard such a farrago of nonsense.

From Medicine Hat he drove 135 miles to the bad country on the Saskatchewan border, to visit an old Hutcheson friend Alec Fraser, who was farming at Alsask. It was one of the worst of the drought areas, where the cattle were pitiably thin, and they were facing their seventh year without a crop. Where once the wheat grew nearly as high as a man, all was now khaki-coloured and withered. The car plunged through drifts of sand, sand silted up by the side of the road, everywhere lay the skeletons of giant thistles. Tweedsmuir stayed at the inn at Alsask, but had his meals with Alec Fraser and his wife, who seemed brave beyond words in the face of their crushing difficulties.

At Swift Current Tweedsmuir saw the Government Experimental Farms, and the work they were doing on the drought problems: strip-fallowing to prevent soil-drifting, the use of a disk-plough to preserve the humus, and the construction of dams, which made Tweedsmuir think of South Africa, 'in every way a much drier country than the Prairies. But every Boer farmer has his dam and his few acres of irrigated land, which see him through the dry period.'

From Moose Jaw he went to Estevan on the North Dakota border:

A most gallant little town in the midst of a desolate area. We travelled through miles of drifting sand. There is a certain amount of coal mining in the neighbourhood—a poor quality of lignite, and it is mined by funny little gopher holes in the sides of the valley. Many of the miners are from Lancashire and very good fellows. We made a circuit of some little mining villages, and were very well received. Yesterday we reached Brandon, which is a green oasis after the desert.

I read the lessons in church this morning, and heard a very good sermon from a minister born in Perth.

Then he returned to Winnipeg, and went north to address the Ukrainian settlement at Fraserwood—the mounted guard gay in the riotously coloured costumes of their native country—and the Icelandic at Gimli. To both he emphasised that 'the strongest nations are those that are made up of different racial elements,' and he begged them, in becoming good Canadians, not to forgo their own culture and traditions—'our Canadian culture cannot be a

copy of any one old thing—it must be a new thing created by the
contributions of all the elements that make up the nation.' The
tour ended in the bush country north of Prince Albert, to which
many of the farmers from the drought areas had migrated. Most of
them were educated men, but hard hit by their losses, with few
household goods and hardly any books. So the idea was born of
small circulating libraries in the lonelier parts of the Prairies. At
Wakesiu Tweedsmuir stayed in a cottage which Mackenzie King
had lent him, 'and where Grey Owl is joining me for a few days
prowling in the woods.' In the end the prowling was done near
Grey Owl's cabin, which the party reached by plane. Tweedsmuir
liked Grey Owl, not because he passed as an Indian but because he
wrote well and had a remarkable knowledge of wild life. They were
shown a beaver dam, and trees sawn through by beavers to fall in
the most convenient direction, and were promised the sight of
beavers coming to feed at 6 p.m. The pilot demurred: they ought
to be off by 5.30 to make a safe landing by daylight. Tweedsmuir
begged for an extension till 6.10 and lo, the beavers obliged, and
made their entry on the stroke of six. A great success.

Tweedsmuir had not been as unconventional as he had planned:
an attack of gastritis in June had ruled out his idea of touring the
back parts with an A.D.C. and 'picking up a lodging where I can.'
But he had travelled with the minimum of fuss. In his predecessors'
day protocol had been observed in the open spaces as in Rideau
Hall. A Canadian I met has a memory of coming back from the
West Coast on a train to which the Governor-General's coach was
attached, and stopping at a one-horse station in the bush somewhere
east of Lake Superior. On the platform was the one inhabitant, in
check shirt, jeans and high boots, when suddenly out of the Governor-General's car stepped the whole suite in evening dress, His
Excellency in claret-coloured dinner-jacket, the ladies with long
skirts and bare shoulders—as strange a sight, to the man in jeans,
as if they had stepped out of a flying saucer. The Tweedsmuirs did
nothing like this. They dressed up—as for the visit to the Indians at
Carlton—if the people they were meeting expected them to dress
up and it would have been discourteous not to; but they saw no
point in keeping up the standards of the capital when on tour. As
far as possible Tweedsmuir cut down the purely ceremonial side:
'We'll take the red carpets with us,' he told one friend, 'because
that's what people like. Then step out, leave them all behind, and
talk to people.'

There is an account of a visit to a small prairie town, which,
although it relates to 1938, I shall put here, for it gives the feel of
those occasions when Tweedsmuir, with the red carpet left behind,
stepped out and talked to people. The account was written by
George R. Spence of Regina, Director of the Prairie Farm Rehabilitation Administration, who accompanied Tweedsmuir to Val-Marie
a little Saskatchewan town close to the United States border
which had been badly hit by the drought. Spence's instructions
from the Governor-General's secretary 'were explicit and to the
point. There were to be no formal receptions, no speech-making—
all nonsense of the kind was strictly taboo.' But the inhabitants of
Val-Marie were bent on putting on a show for the first Governor-
General to come to town. With only a week to do it in, they cleaned
up the place out of all recognition. Mounds of rubbish were
dumped in the river. Smelly outside privies were ruthlessly bull-
dozed. The cows that roamed in Main Street were tethered and the
hens banished indoors. There was an orgy of painting: 'It took all
of three coats of white lead to completely blot out the black letters
SLIM'S BARBER SHOP AND POOL ROOM which adorned the front of
the Town Hall.' But as there was only enough paint for the fronts
of the houses, ropes marked off a route which would allow no view
of the unpainted backs. Schools up to a hundred miles away were
alerted. A set of bagpipes was unearthed, and enough oddments of
Highland dress to clothe the piper.

When the Governor-General arrived, he was taken off to see the
dam under construction by the P.F.R.A. and to lunch in the crew's
mess-tent. A separate place had been provided for him to wash,
but he insisted on washing with the men, and taking his turn in the
line-up. There was a tremendous spread on a table laid with brand-
new white oilcloth, and grace was said for the first time in the
camp. Barely was the soup finished when word came that 'the
crowd up town have been standing for hours and are now hollerin'
their heads off for the Governor!' As the party walked to Tweedsmuir Park—an old field given a new name—the piper struck up:
his name was Olson and he came from Minnesota, but the drum-
mer was a Cameron from Inverness. It was splendid: 'drought and
relief, even death and taxes, were forgotten in the ecstasy of that
enchanting moment.' Then a brass band played 'God Save the
King' and 'O Canada.' Mr Spence read his speech of welcome into
the microphone, and every word bounced back at him from the
milk-cans and tin pails strung up on horizontal poles to make a

public address system. On the field was everyone in Val-Marie, and many who had come long journeys by horseback, waggon or car, to share the occasion. One elderly Scots couple travelled over a hundred miles in an old and battered car 'to get a good look at John Buchan,' and he talked to them of the Border home they had left forty years before. It was a shot in the arm for Val-Marie: 'the Governor-General had chosen of his own accord to travel thousands of miles across the country to see conditions for himself and make their problem his problems too.'

On such visits Tweedsmuir really could talk to the farmers and agricultural experts and construction-crews and not just make encouraging noises. Though the farms of the prairies were very different from those of the Borders—or the Transvaal—he had a basic knowledge to which he could add the new knowledge he was picking up all the time. He knew what farming was about. So he talked with these drought-ridden men about yields and prices, fertilisers and irrigation, labour and machinery. Many were Scots and he talked to them of the places they, or their forebears, had come from: and several had particular links with him. One had been baptized by his father at Pathhead, one had been under-keeper at Ardwall, one had been taught by his Aunt Jane in Sunday-School, and several had been at Hutchesons' ('Tell Walter the number of Hutchie bugs I have come across here is extraordinary'). One old lady at Winnipeg had made his mother's wedding-dress when she was a girl at Peebles. Indeed, his aides noted, Canada seemed to be full of people from Peebles. A second cousin, Robert Brown from Haddington, was discovered to be farming in the Bayton district by Lake Manitoba.

'The Prairies have completely gone to my head,' Tweedsmuir told his mother-in-law; 'their immense spaces, wonderful colours and wonderful people.' 'I am really intoxicated by the Prairies,' he wrote to Alastair:

The immense landscape gives one the same feeling as the sea, and the effects of light and shadow are amazingly beautiful. The Prairie sunset is like nothing in the world.

And to his wife:

When the harvests are anything like good the country is marvellous—miles and miles of golden stubble running into the sunset. . . . The beauty of the Prairies has never been sufficiently recognised.

Of the courage and resilience of the people he could not say enough. In Alberta he noticed 'something tonic in the air, not only physically but spiritually, for it has the feeling of a Borderland,' and admired the vigorous optimism of the people. In the drought areas they were facing the future 'with such fortitude.' 'The whole tour has been a wonderful refreshment to me, and I feel that I have got among a younger and stronger race.'

At the end of the tour Tweedsmuir drew up some 'Notes on the Agricultural Condition of the Prairies,' in which he made two main points: that the cause of the crop failure was less the drought than the nature of the soil; and that high profits from wheat in the good years had made the prairie-farmer 'careless of the interests of the soil . . . more a miner than a farmer:' and that, thanks to the far-sighted and practical work of the government experimental farms, these problems were remediable, with reasonable care, in a comparatively short time.

Of all this, he was convinced, Eastern Canada knew far too little and he was increasingly struck by the gulf between Eastern Canada and the Prairie Provinces. 'So few Easterners know anything about them, and the great distances give the communities small chance of contact with the outer world.' He returned to Ottawa with his head full of this problem of lack of communication among the different parts of Canada.

On this, as on all his tours, Tweedsmuir was expected to make speech after speech. Everything the Governor-General says is, strictly speaking, put into his mouth by a responsible Minister. This was a constitutional nicety which it was impossible to observe, because Canadians are insatiable for the spoken word and like their Governor-General to be constantly uttering, and because speeches prepared by the Canadian Government for John Buchan would have been quite out of character and of little interest. Yet ultimately a Minister was answerable for any remark of the Governor-General that might be called in question. So long, therefore, as Tweedsmuir confined himself to what he called 'Governor-Generalities' he was on safe ground. But the minute he strayed on to the contro-versial ground of the Government's responsibilities—and any such excursion would almost certainly be reported out of context, and appear even more controversial than it was—he was asking for trouble. And trouble came with a speech which Tweedsmuir delivered on 3 September at Calgary.

He was addressing the Alberta Military Institute, a group of service people and their friends who met occasionally for lunch and a speech. To this specialised audience he spoke of defence, saying that the breakdown of the League of Nations had compelled every democracy, however unwillingly, to give some attention to defence questions and that Canada could be no exception:

> No country today is safe from danger. No country can be isolated. Canada has to think out a policy of defence and take steps to implement it.

On 4 September the speech was front-page news from Halifax to Vancouver, with the sentences quoted above high-lighted and made the subject of editorial comment. Tweedsmuir knew well, from his work on Minto, that defence has often been a flashpoint in the relations of Britain and Canada: but this view expressed in Calgary never struck him as controversial. Uttered in 1936—after the remilitarisation of the Rhineland and the Italian campaign in Abyssinia, in a year when commercial aeroplanes had begun to fly the North Atlantic—these sentences seemed almost a platitude. But to neither the Premier nor his Canadian critics were they a platitude. In Mackenzie King's view Tweedsmuir was trespassing on a particularly sensitive area. As a Gladstonian Liberal Mackenzie King had a horror of the sheer irrationality of war, a reluctance to face the likelihood of a second world war, and a resentment (expressed later, when Great Britain gave her guarantee to Poland in 1939) 'that a country which has all it can do to run itself should be called upon to save, periodically, a continent which cannot run itself.' In this view he had the solid backing of the French Canadians (on whom he depended politically) who saw the most tentative move towards rearmament as the fatal first step on the slippery slope to war; as did the leaders of the Co-operative Commonwealth Federation which, though numerically small, was an articulate and influential political party. And to all those Canadians who had emerged from the economic blizzard with an obsession about a balanced budget rearmament was an economic bogy.

So when Tweedsmuir appeared to be telling Canada that it did not have a defence policy, Mackenzie King quite properly blew up. In a stiff letter (4 September) he told Tweedsmuir that the speech would certainly be construed as an attempt on the part of H.M. representative to influence Canadian defence policy. He personally acquitted the Governor-General of any 'imperialist intent,' but, while displaying an almost Pecksniffian concern about the attacks that would certainly be made on Tweedsmuir for meddling in

Canadian politics, he reminded him sharply that he must not be drawn into controversy. He may already have taken some alarm when Tweedsmuir reported, just before his Calgary visit, an address which he had given to the Canadian Club at Vancouver on the present status of the Empire. 'I tried to emphasise the necessity of Canadians thinking out for themselves a foreign policy, since in the world of today no geographical position gives security' (31 August 1936). Again perhaps a platitude to Tweedsmuir; again a sensitive area for Mackenzie King. In the outcome many of the attacks provoked by the Calgary speech were directed not at the supposedly indiscreet Governor-General but at the inactive Government. On defence, said the *Toronto Globe*, drawing unfavourable comparisons with Australia, 'public opinion remains leaderless. The Government has held aloof in studied silence ... Surely the Prime Minister, his Minister of National Defence and his Cabinet have carried aloofness and silence too far.'

On 8 September Tweedsmuir replied to Mackenzie King's letter with an apology for not having realised that these sentences, quoted out of context, might be misconstrued, and assured him 'I thought that I was helping to hold up the hands of your Government.' Mackenzie King, again acquitting Tweedsmuir of improper designs—'Were it not that I know so well just what your own thought and intention were in what was said, I should be much concerned' —again impressed on him (8 September) that 'the last of all troubles I wish to encounter is one which directly or indirectly concerns His Majesty's representative in Canada. At all costs, this must not arise during your term of office.'

Five months later, after a debate on defence in Parliament, Tweedsmuir diplomatically congratulated Mackenzie King on 'a really fine and final statement, not only of Canada's own policy, but of the true meaning of Imperial Defence' (20 February 1937). Mackenzie King replied the next day:

I was immensely pleased at the way in which the party stood behind me to a man. It was not easy for many of them even to appear to be supporting increased expenditure on defence, and it has required a lot of persuasion in caucuses of the party, and by personal interviews, to bring them all into line, but the effort quite clearly has been well worth while and I feel we have jumped the one big hurdle of the session.

If at Calgary Tweedsmuir had unwittingly stuck his neck out too far, he would draw back: he had come to Canada with full awareness of his constitutional position, and determined not to fall out with his Prime Minister. The first year had revealed one minor matter on which they differed: the question of recommending for honours, in which the Governor-General acts as post-office between the Dominion Government and Buckingham Palace. The Liberal Party had abolished titles, but these had been reintroduced by Bennett's Conservative Government. Tweedsmuir, who would have enjoyed exercising initiative in this direction, felt that honours were an important bond with the Crown, and a recognition of public work: not to be associated with snobbery, but with service to the State.

Mackenzie King was entirely loyal to the Crown, and sentimental as well as loyal; but about titles and honours he was hard-headed. Like most Canadians, he had no particular objection to the system in Britain, but resented any attempt to import an English social structure to Canada. Titles could be politically dangerous, especially in the depression: and if you cut out the Lords and Sirs, then there is not much place for minor orders. Tweedsmuir, though he accepted the decision, did not like it, and occasionally returned to the question. When, one Christmas, Tweedsmuir sent his Prime Minister a signed photograph of himself in plain clothes, and not in the full rig of a Governor-General, Mackenzie King thanked him 'for your photograph *as a man before all else,*' and assured him that 'both you and I will live to see many trappings disappear.'* But for all his genuine wish to see an end to privilege and class-barriers, Mackenzie King found it much more difficult to make contact with people than the titled and title-liking Tweedsmuir. The Calgary intervention on the delicate ground of defence showed a difference of outlook in a more important field, but Tweedsmuir was no more anxious for constitutional friction than Mackenzie King, and thereafter kept off defence questions in his speeches.

On one major issue they were in entire agreement: America. Mackenzie King may have slightly inclined to the idea of Canada being a bridge between the United States and United Kingdom—an idea which flatters Canada's sense of importance, her wish for a distinctive rôle to play—whereas Tweedsmuir preferred direct dealings between each pair of partners in the trio. But on the paramount

---

* In *What's Past is Prologue* (1964), p. 504, Vincent Massey notes that Mackenzie King 'after years of effort to eliminate honours from Canadian life . . . was prepared to accept the Order of Merit from the late King and the highest decoration of a number of Allied powers at the end of the Second World War.'

importance of close relations between Britain, Canada and United States, they were of one mind.

Back in Ottawa for the fall of 1936, Tweedsmuir furthered his acquaintance with other Canadian politicians, and reported his encounters to Susan, who was spending the autumn in England ('This is a dull house without you!'). He found 'Mitch' Hepburn, the Premier of Ontario, 'an extraordinarily attractive fellow, with a wonderful power of lucid statement and a merry twinkle in his eye,' and had a good first impression of Duplessis, the new Premier of Quebec—'He has a strong jaw and a mirthful eye'—though later he thought that there was a 'strong spice of the bandit' in him. Dunning, the Minister of Finance, struck him as 'a really able and courageous man . . . extraordinarily interesting and very optimistic. I like his merry eye.' (To Grattan O'Leary Tweedsmuir observed that 'Dunning can never forget that he arrived in this country steerage, and so he likes to go and put his feet up on the desk of the President of the C.P.R.'; O'Leary considered this very shrewd.) Ian Mackenzie, the Minister of National Defence, who came from Assynt in Sutherland and was a graduate of Edinburgh, and Tom Crerar the Minister of Mines and Resources, came to dine quietly with him; there is no mention of their mirthful or merry eyes.

One of his visits this autumn was to the Neurological Institute at Montreal. Dr Wilder Penfield, the Director, noticed how fascinated Tweedsmuir was

by the operating room and the operative photographs placed there. He had many questions to ask and he described the fracture of the skull which he himself had received at the age of four. He told of how he lay seven days unconscious and of the trepannation that saved his life. He lingered in the operating room and inquired how we would go about such a procedure nowadays.

At the end of November Tweedsmuir was back in the Prairies, this time to stay in the provincial capitals and see something of the administrative end of the Prairies problem. It was mild bright weather, no snow or frost—'after Ottawa it is like coming into summer again'—and when he flew over Edmonton he saw the Rockies quite clearly about 200 miles away. At Regina

I visited the community halls of the Germans, Poles, Hungarians, Rumanians, Ukrainians White and Red, and the Jews, and spoke in each. The police didn't want me to go to the Red Ukrainians on the ground that they were dangerous Communists; so of course I insisted on going, and was received deliriously in a hall smothered with Union Jacks.

He thought it most important to keep in touch with those 'new Canadians' and make them feel part of the community and less vulnerable to foreign agitators, a genuine danger at a time when Hitler was demanding the loyalty of all Germans abroad to Nazi Germany.

At Winnipeg he received an honorary degree and attended the St Andrew's Night Dinner, 'a display of Caledonian enthusiasm which I have never seen equalled at home.' Here indeed, no less than on the farms and ranches of the southern Prairies, he was among Scots: they ran everything in the West. Social experiment was still lively in the Prairie Provinces, and the main stream of social and political thinking was familiar to Tweedsmuir, for one of the main influences on the Farm Movement was the Independent Labour Party. Ideas and ideals which had been forged in the shipyards and engineering shops of the Clyde were here being applied to the problems of producing and marketing wheat. The secretary of the Saskatchewan Wheat Pool, George Robertson, was an old I.L.P. man from Dumfries; Robert Gardiner, one of the United Farmers members of the Ottawa Parliament, was another Scot who had learnt his politics at home. Talking to them was for Tweedsmuir a continuation of his talks with Kirkwood, Maxton and Tom Johnston. Businessmen in Toronto might mutter 'Red' about these Prairie Radicals; Tweedsmuir could recognise them as something reassuringly home-grown. It was a Scot, too, Major Douglas of Fearnan in Perthshire, who had inspired the Social Credit movement which Mr Aberhart's party was trying to adapt for the salvation of debt-ridden Alberta. Tweedsmuir had little patience with the provincial Government in its notion that 'finance can be run on the lines of a religious revival,' but he could see why Social Credit appealed, 'for it is a natural resort of the moderate and conservative mind when in desperation.'

On this tour Tweedsmuir's A.D.C. was Willis O'Connor, who assured Susan that:

It was the nicest trip I have been on since the time of Lord Byng, I think. His Excellency gets down so close to the people. He is so frightfully interested in everything that happens, and is a perfect delight to look after. We haven't had an enthusiastic Governor-General like this for many a day.

There was a solid gain too: during the Prairie tour Tweedsmuir put on four pounds in weight.

. . .

Throughout the autumn there had been a sad preoccupation: the private life of King Edward VIII. Tweedsmuir was not a man who ever much enjoyed gossip about people's private lives (gossip about jobs was another matter) and he particularly disliked it when it concerned the private life of his sovereign. Divorce was a subject that in any case he found distasteful; it would never have been discussed in the Buchan manse. But he could not pass off as irresponsible rumours the reports which came to him from old friends like Violet Markham and Lord Crawford about the King's infatuation with Mrs Simpson. And in October he was reluctantly brought right into the affair.

So far, out of a combined respect for the King's private life and for the laws of libel, the British Press had kept silent on the subject. But it was splashed all over a section of the American Press, and articles, with a modicum of fact carrying a lurid superstructure of rumour and speculation, had been published in papers with a big Canadian readership. So Canadians as a whole were more aware of the situation than Britons in the other Dominions—or, indeed, than most Britons in the United Kingdom.

On 15 October Major Alexander Hardinge, the King's Private Secretary, wrote confidentially to Tweedsmuir asking if there were any marked reaction in Canada to articles in *Time* and other American magazines, and any evidence of damage to the prestige of the monarch. To this 'most difficult question' Tweedsmuir replied on 27 October, pointing out that although he had done his best to collect opinions through his staff, it was not a matter which he, as the King's representative, could broach directly with anyone in Canada. His impression was that Canadians, though at first incredulous and indignant about the American articles, had reluctantly come to believe them; and he considered there were three elements which strongly affected their reaction. First, their complex feelings about the United States, which made them particularly resentful when Americans rather gloatingly wrote scandal about *their* King. Second—in this reminding Tweedsmuir of the Scotland of his youth—they had retained far more of the Victorian tradition in conduct than any other part of the Empire: in private life, if at times pedantically and pharisaically, they set great store by the Victorian decencies. Finally there was the King's personal popularity among Canadians—a point also stressed by Mackenzie King when he saw King Edward in England that October—which might not stand the strain of what was felt to be unkingly behaviour.

Tweedsmuir, who had done something to build up this popularity by references to the King being 'a Canadian farmer' (on the strength of his ranch near Calgary), concluded that the situation was most anxious and disquieting.

This letter to Hardinge was shown to the King, and to the British Prime Minister. Baldwin had also written to Tweedsmuir on the matter, for he too needed to know more of the reaction in Canada to the American articles, about which he had spoken plainly to the King. Answering Baldwin on 9 November, Tweedsmuir again underlined the points he had made to Hardinge:

> Canada is the most Puritanical part of the Empire and cherishes very much the Victorian standards in private life . . .
>
> She has a special affection of loyalty for the King, whom she regards as one of her own citizens. This is strongly felt particularly by the younger people, who are by no means straitlaced; and they are alarmed at anything which may take the gilt off their idol.
>
> Canada's pride has been deeply wounded by the tattle in the American press, which she feels an intolerable impertinence. She is very friendly to America, but she has always at the back of her head an honest chauvinism.

Surely, he felt, if the King could only be brought to realise how much he, and the monarchy, meant to Canadians, he would discontinue a course of action which would reluctantly line them up against him. The only man to make the King see this was Baldwin; 'the Archbishop should be kept out of it.' Tweedsmuir ended by emphasising again 'this deep and serious feeling in Canada in the matter.'

Mrs Simpson's divorce from her husband at the end of October —which left her free to marry the King after the decree absolute six months later—set off the final stage of the crisis. Throughout November Tweedsmuir was kept in touch with the latest developments. Susan, who was specially bidden to lunch at Chequers so that Baldwin could talk to her privately, emphasised the French-Canadian attitude to divorce. Several of Tweedsmuir's regular correspondents were concerned about Lord Beaverbrook's assuming the rôle of interpreter of Canadian opinion, particularly as his enthusiasm for the King struck them as a by-product of his vendetta against Baldwin. Churchill too was suspected of fishing in troubled waters. 'The line he is taking,' wrote L. S. Amery on 7 December,

> is that a ruthless and dictatorial Government, wishing for a thoroughly tame monarch, have suddenly put the King into an impossible choice between his inclinations and his Throne and are prepared to 'bump him off' without giving him any time to look round and reflect on the situation. With a public that knows nothing about the weeks of coming and going

since the King first sprung this business on his Ministers, and still less of the more sordid sides of the story, and who can be persuaded that a band of old fogies are trying to stop a simple love affair, on the grounds that Mrs Simpson has been twice married before, the danger of his succeeding in getting up a really formidable agitation is a real one.

As events moved to their climax in December, Tweedsmuir was in daily contact with Baldwin and Mackenzie King, who kept coming in agitatedly, 'like a wet hen.' But he thought that the Canadian Prime Minister handled the affair well, and praised his 'wisdom' to Violet Markham, who told him in return that Mackenzie King had come in for some sharp comment in Britain on the score that 'just when the attitude of the Dominions was of first-class importance in clarifying the issue here . . . Canada, *apparently*, said nothing and appeared to be sitting on the fence'. When news of the Abdication came through, there was much constitutional business to be done, and Tweedsmuir had to sign the Order in Council on behalf of Canada. He comforted himself with the reflection that the whole affair had revealed 'an entirely new mechanism in the Empire,' and had shown how modern communications could in a few hours bring about what was in effect a Round Table Conference of Prime Ministers; but he was 'desperately sad about the whole business. I cannot bear to think of that poor little man with no purpose left in life except a shoddy kind of amusement.'

Some of his correspondents were bitter about the King; most, like himself, were sympathetic and sorry, reserving their anger for those false friends who had misled him about British public opinion, had fawned and flattered him, only to fade away as his troubles grew. They were the subject of Osbert Sitwell's 'National Rat-Week.' This satire, 'a fine passionate thing . . . almost with the swing of the Scottish Bards,' had, Lord Crawford told Tweedsmuir, given special pleasure to Baldwin: 'He read it to me on Friday at Chequers—this is one of his week-end relaxations and the best entertainment he can give his guests.' There was a sympathetic word from Stair Gillon in Scotland. 'I did not like the Canterbury homily,' he wrote (the Archbishop had boldly criticised the King and his friends in a broadcast *after* the Abdication):

I preferred my good old minister who thanked for the many good qualities and actions and prayed for his future, and then switched right on to the new Monarch.

Switching into the new reign, Tweedsmuir prepared for the customary ceremonial occasions which had been curtailed the year before on account of King George's death. With Susan back from England to help him, he opened Parliament, held a State Banquet and Drawing-room (where he was pleased to note the number of French-Canadian girls who dropped their curtseys to Their Excellencies). 'I am more than ever convinced,' he told the new King George in February,

that 'locomobility' is one of my chief duties here. Canadians know uncommonly little about their own country, and the result is that each part is apt to feel isolated from the rest, especially those areas which have been having a bad time.

His first trip in 1937, though, was outside the borders of Canada. At the end of March the Tweedsmuirs were the guests in Washington of President Roosevelt, who, since their last meeting, had won a massive victory in the 1936 Presidential election.

At the White House Tweedsmuir was given Lincoln's study for his sitting-room: 'from its windows he used to look across the Potomac to where the guns were grumbling in Virginia.' He was invited to share the President's press conference. 'They treated me very kindly, and we simply gossiped, after I had explained I had no authority to say anything about politics.' He reviewed troops and the midshipmen at Annapolis. He laid wreaths on the Cenotaph in the Arlington National Cemetery and, after sailing down the Potomac in the presidential yacht, on Washington's grave at Mount Vernon. Attended by the British Ambassador and the Canadian Minister in Washington, and by the United States Minister to Canada, he visited Congress. He had been told that he need not make any speeches, but in the Senate Vice-President Garner, and in the House of Representatives Speaker Rayburn, announced that 'His Excellency will now address you' and he had to do his best.

Between the ceremonies and the junketings came the real business of the visit: long and confidential talks with the President and the Secretary of State, Cordell Hull, on international questions. When Roosevelt was asked what he and Tweedsmuir had been discussing he replied 'We'd just been thinking aloud.' President and Governor-General, he said, tended to 'soliloquise' when they were together, and each could pitch his soliloquy upon a note that could be heard by the other. Tweedsmuir found Cordell Hull

a very remarkable man. There is a quiet patience and tenacity about him

which make him a very real force in his country's policy. He is without
any kind of vanity or rhetoric, but he has an uncommon stock of practical
wisdom.

He thought that the President

stands by himself. His vitality oxygenates all his surroundings, and
his kindliness diffuses a pleasant warmth about him wherever he goes. His
reception out of doors was unbelievable. He is a real leader of the people.
What impressed me most was his extraordinary mental activity. I have
never met a mind more fecund in ideas. And these ideas are not mere
generalities, for he has an astonishing gift of worming his way into a subject.
His thought is not only spacious, but close-textured.

To the King he had written the previous November, after the
Presidential election:

He is one of the most remarkable men of our time, for I do not think he
has any equal on the globe at the moment as a mass-persuader. His talents
in this respect seem to me far greater than those of Hitler or Mussolini, for
he never condescends to melodrama, and has not the argument of physical
force in the background. His weapon is simply his personality with its
uncanny vitality and force.

On Dominion Day that year Roosevelt broadcast a message to
Canada, to which Tweedsmuir responded. Gleefully reporting the
exchange to Mackenzie King in Britain, he said 'It was as if the
King were to broadcast to the United States on Thanksgiving Day.'
'I think my most important job is in connection with the United
States,' he told Stair Gillon later in the year. 'I think I really have
the confidence of that Government; at any rate they do me the
honour to talk very frankly to me.' And the following summer
Roosevelt told Arthur Murray, a mutual friend who was staying at
the White House, that 'Tweedsmuir is the best Governor-General
that Canada has ever had.'

In June 1937 there was a tour of the Maritimes, postponed from
the previous July when Tweedsmuir had to go into hospital in
Montreal for a thorough examination. At Halifax he sailed in a
destroyer round the harbour. At Fredericton he had an afternoon's
fishing on the Hartt's Island pool in the St John River, where he
impressed the guides by his skill in casting, while Susan visited a
Women's Institute Convention and was 'placed under a gilt canopy,
which was flanked on either side by two very good portraits of
George III and Queen Charlotte.' At Saint John they visited the
dockyard, saw the museum with its Chinese collection and had a

trip up the river to 'a marvellous camp owned by Donald Strathcona, which he has put at our disposal.' At Campbellton, New Brunswick, a five hundredweight coping-stone fell from the top of the railway station, crushing an express truck a few seconds after Tweedsmuir had moved from the spot—an episode reminiscent of Edward Leithen in *The Power-House* miraculously escaping the machinations of his enemies in the streets of London. The Tweedsmuirs relished the strong sea air—'so delicious after Ottawa. I felt as if I were back on the coast of Fife'—the marvellous lilac, the fish which tasted of fish 'rather than like wet cottonwool,' the soft voices, the Georgian atmosphere, people 'more British than in Britain.'

In October Tweedsmuir was back in the Maritimes, to visit Prince Edward Island and Cape Breton Island: a round of speeches, dinners, openings of schools, visits to farms, and presents of apples and oysters. Of Prince Edward Island he wrote:

It is the old Canada of half a century ago. There is no great wealth and no great poverty, and there is no distinction between town and country. The whole place is really a village community. A pleasanter or a quainter society could scarcely be imagined. The atmosphere is like that of Cranford. At the party which the Lieutenant-Governor gave for me local talent performed with recitations and songs—songs and recitations which were new about 1850. It is a secure and happy little community, desperately British in spirit, and I felt during my visit as if I had suddenly been transplanted to a Scottish parish.

From Charlottetown on Prince Edward he flew to Annapolis, Nova Scotia—'an exquisite little place, full of eighteenth-century houses, in a valley of orchards'—where he was made a Grand Master of Champlain's Order, and smoked a pipe of peace with the Mic-mac Indians. There was a very bumpy flight to Sydney on Cape Breton, 'a big industrial city in a countryside like Scotland.' Tweedsmuir found Cape Breton 'more Highland than the Highlands.' On Sunday he read the lessons in kirk; on another occasion he was welcomed by six pipers, 'all MacDonalds in faded tartans—long, lean men from the mines whom one could easily picture leading a raid through the Lochaber passes.' He was constantly addressed in Gaelic (about a quarter of the population of the Maritimes spoke it). 'I wish to goodness I knew some Gaelic,' he told Stair Gillon:

I can only look sheepish. The worst of it is I have got a bogus reputation, for at first, when I received letters of welcome in Gaelic, with the help of Ian Mackenzie, my Minister of Defence, I answered in Gaelic. 'Oh what a tangled web we weave when first we practise to deceive!'

The over-riding impression was that 'they are very loyal to Britain, and very loyal to their own Province but not so loyal to Canada as a whole.'

His reading on this tour was Gilbert Murray's *Aeschylus*. 'Alas!' he told Murray,

while my Latin scholarship is still good, I find that my Greek vocabulary becomes increasingly imperfect, and I can only read the Greek texts where I have marked a good many of the words (except, of course, Homer).

The tour which gave Tweedsmuir most satisfaction, and caused most stir in Canada, was his journey to the Arctic in the summer of 1937. 'Thank goodness! On July 3 I leave top hats behind me and depart for the Wild West. "Tweedsmuir's on and awa'" as the ballad says.' The trip thus announced to Stair Gillon, to wild North as well as to wild West, had been one of Tweedsmuir's strongest wishes ever since he came to Canada. Three months after his arrival he told Gillon of his intention

to go to the Arctic, down the Mackenzie River, coming back by air . . . This vast country has enormously whetted my appetite for travel, and the people who live and work in these outland places are the salt of the earth.

He had long been interested in the opening-up of Canada: Jacques Cartier,* Mackenzie, Simpson, were heroes to him. In his two years in the Dominion he had established links with explorers of his own day: with Edward Shackleton, continuing the work in Ellesmere Land begun by the Oxford expedition of 1934; with Bradford Washburn—'how extraordinarily good this type of young American is!'—pioneering in the Mount St Elias range in Alaska; with Major McKern of the R.C.M.P. who sailed the North-west Passage. (The help and encouragement which he gave to a number of expeditions were recognised by his being made, in January 1940, a Patron of Exploration by the Explorers Club of New York.)

Tweedsmuir was fired to this northern journey by more than a love of exploration or a personal wish for adventure. He was going to the North because the North was all-important to Canada, and most Canadians knew nothing about it. To Baldwin he had written a year before that 'mining is Canada's chief asset at present . . . I think I may be able to do some good work in awakening Canada to

---

* 'One of the most attractive figures in exploration' he called Cartier in a review in the *Spectator* (of S. E. Dawson's *The St Lawrence Basin and the Borderlands*) as far back as 15 July 1905.

the real meaning of its possessions in the northern wilds.' Magnificent work had been done by miners and mining engineers, by agriculturalists and the men who flew small aircraft up to the Arctic shore, to push the habitable frontier further North. Little of this had been publicised—especially when compared with the parallel Russian development in Northern Siberia, which was the subject of books and films and general national pride. By the 1930s most Canadians were urban-minded, not pioneers; facing southward from their coast-to-coast corridor, backs turned on the North. Tweedsmuir's journey was a challenge to Canadians to use their imagination: to discard the conventional picture of a cold and barren North, to look at Canada as a land stretching from the American border to the Arctic Ocean, with its northern sector a treasure-house of minerals and not unfriendly to life.

The North could also, Tweedsmuir believed, be used to counterbalance Canadian provincialism. 'It makes a link with all Canada,' he told Mackenzie King shortly before starting his tour, 'for the North is a common interest.' Among some notes which he made for Mackenzie King's speeches in Britain that summer of 1937 was one about Canada's East and West belonging to 'slightly different economic worlds':

Now the North, which is common to both East and West, is a natural bridge to unite the two divisions. I look to the North as one of the great unifying factors in the future of the Dominion.

The Governor-General was going North as traveller, showman, interpreter and unifier.

His journey was to be on the lines he had sketched a year before to Stair Gillon: he would sail down the Mackenzie River to the Arctic shore, then fly over the Barrens and back to Edmonton. It was not the first visit of a Governor-General to the North; Lord and Lady Minto had visited the Yukon in 1900 (and been presented by the miners of Dawson City with a gold basket filled with nuggets). But it was the first time a Governor-General had gone to the Arctic. Fifteen years earlier the proposed trip would have taken two years; now five thousand miles would be covered in a month.

Before the northern tour began there was a brief return visit to the Prairies to see how the badly hit areas were faring this year. The drought area had moved north since the previous summer; though Manitoba had good rains, Saskatchewan was a 'melancholy spectacle.' The Tweedsmuirs stopped at Drumheller to see the mines, were fascinated by the 'tiny hills shaped like beehives or small pyramids with the tops sliced off, cactuses growing everywhere and wonderful roots of petrified trees.' They were in Calgary for the Stampede, and again went out to visit the Alec Frasers at Alsask. Susan found it a tragic place, but the spirit of the people was like that of the South Wales unemployed with whom she had worked at Risca—beyond praise.

At Edmonton on 20 July the main journey began. The first lap was by train, the 'Muskeg special' that switchbacked through fire-weed, yarrow and golden-rod to Waterways on the Clearwater. Waterways was the railhead for the North, base depot for the Hudson's Bay Company's Stores, and the starting-point both for water-borne traffic and for the planes carrying mail, goods and passengers to the mines, fur-posts, trading settlements and missions. Here Susan saw her husband aboard the barge which took the party out to join the Hudson's Bay steamer at the junction of the Clearwater and the muddy Athabasca, then she went back to Edmonton and on to British Columbia. It was a fortunate separation for Tweedsmuir's biographer: on his letters to his wife, written on paper headed 'Down North' with a map of the river route in the margin, and on a memorandum prepared when the tour was over, the following account is based. 'I am glad to say that John is very well,' Susan Tweedsmuir told her mother after she had seen the party sail into the sunset, 'and I think the peaceful three weeks will do him a world of good, as he won't get any letters, and will live a regular life.'

On the *Athabasca River*, a stern-wheeler of the type common on Nile and Mississippi, were Tweedsmuir, his secretary Shuldham Redfern and Mrs Redfern, and one A.D.C., Lieutenant Gordon Rivers-Smith, R.N. Fellow-passengers included Dr George Mac-donald, a minister from Edmonton—'the first Canadian I have met who is passionately keen on the whole of Canada'—and Dr Thomas Wood the composer, who contributed two articles on the tour to *The Times*. He had come to Canada to write a book about the country, and stayed at Government House; Tweedsmuir took a great liking to him and invited him along for the trip. There were also Colonel Reid and Mr Bonnycastle of the Hudson's Bay Company, Inspector Martin of the R.C.M.P., and Guy Rhoades representing the Canadian Press. Mr Bonnycastle had been rather apprehensive about travelling with a Governor-General, but fears about formality were dispelled the minute Tweedsmuir stepped on board, 'a most natural, friendly and charming person.' Soon after they started, a plane with pontoons landed on the river and delivered a last passenger, a photographer from the new magazine *Life*. This was the enterprising Margaret Bourke-White, who dropped from the skies with a mass of gear; packed among her flashbulbs were ten chrysalises of the mourning cloak butterfly, whose life-cycle she was recording. Startled at first by her trousers and tartan shirt, Tweedsmuir was soon admiring her professional zeal, holding the reflectors as she took pictures of the emerging butterflies, and describing her as 'the best photographer in the U.S.A.' She liked him too: 'From the very start there was a kind of affectionate friendship between His Excellency and myself.'

The steamer trip was as restful as Susan had hoped. 'The last two days have been purely idyllic,' Tweedsmuir wrote to her on 23 July,

cool bright weather, no flies, and slipping down broad rivers among great woods. I simply sat in the bows and basked and dreamed—a perfect rest . . .

We pushed two barges in front of us and I sat in the prow of the first— the most peaceful form of voyaging I have ever discovered. It was rather like sailing down an immense Cherwell . . .

We are really getting into the North, for the nights are short, and the sunsets are beyond belief . . . The Hudson's Bay people are taking the most wonderful care of our comfort. It is great fun talking to the old folk of the North. . . .

I have started on my *Augustus* index.

Miss Bourke-White has described this index-making:

A long narrow table had been contrived for him with a couple of planks, and there he sat with the fluttering little white paper markers of his index all over the place. Our cargo almost swallowed him up. His spare form was all but lost in the midst of the pig crates, the cage of chickens, the tractor, the assortment of agricultural implements which surrounded him. Several times I tiptoed up and photographed his expressive back, but I never interrupted him while he was working.

She found him 'a wiry, astute man of few words,' and one of her photographs shows a game of bridge in progress in the smoking-room, with interested bystanders looking over the players' shoulders, while in a corner Tweedsmuir plays solitaire.

After Fort Chipewyan—from which Mackenzie started on his

two journeys to the Arctic and the Pacific, and Sir John Franklin
on his journeys to the Polar Sea—they entered the Slave River. At
Fort Fitzgerald a car took them over the sixteen-mile portage round
the rapids, and at Fort Smith, the capital of the North-West Territories, they joined another stern-wheeler, the *Distributor*, for the
1300 miles to the Arctic shore. Here they saw 'good crops of wheat,
oats and potatoes, and some superb gardens of delphiniums fifteen
feet high.'

The Forts—which originally were fortified to protect traders
against Indians and commercial rivals—are Hudson's Bay posts.
They are painted red and white, over each flies the Company's
red flag, and above the entrance to the compounds is the legend
'Incorporated 2nd May 1670.' When Sir George Simpson, Gover-
nor-in-Chief of the Company, journeyed through his empire in the
1820s and 1830s, he arrived at the Forts with dash and style. 'The
little Emperor' would sweep up with his cavalcade of canoes man-
ned by scarlet-shirted Iroquois, and step ashore preceded by his
kilted piper. Tweedsmuir, slipping down the gangway from the
Distributor in his tweed jacket and flannel trousers, arrived with less
drama. But the scarlet-coated Mounties—not to speak of Miss
Bourke-White's tartan shirt—gave colour to the scene, and the
welcome at each Fort was enthusiastic, when Company's factors,
priests, missionaries, nuns, trappers and Indians, turned out to
greet the Governor-General.

After Fort Smith the next call was at the fur-post at Fort Resolution, where 'the Slave enters Great Slave Lake as the Oxus enters
the Aral Sea, through many reedy channels, and "matted rushy
isles;"' then they crossed the western end of the lake, lucky to
find it dead calm, and at Fort Providence they were on the Mackenzie River proper.

It is perfect weather, as warm as an English June, and there are only about
three hours of dark. We slip gently down rivers three quarters of a mile
wide, and stop at little posts where I receive deputations of Indians and
Grey Nuns . . .

It is impossible to describe the country, for it is built on a scale outside
that of humanity. Great Slave Lake, for example, could comfortably hold
Scotland and Wales. In spite of the heat there is an exhilarating freedom
and purity in the air. It is the essential romance of Nature with man left out.
At the same time the country is curiously busy. We are always passing
Indians and aeroplanes often swoop over us. I simply must bring you here,
for it can be like nothing else in the world—a sort of West Highlands on a
colossal scale. . .

At Fort Providence . . . I was deeply impressed by the French Mission, which has seventy Indian children, who gave us an entertainment. The Fathers had beautiful faces. One had been badly wounded at Verdun in the French army.

The Indians here were the Hares, a tribe ravaged by tuberculosis, a consequence of under-nourishment following some bad seasons of hunting and trapping. The French fathers were Oblates. About the Catholic missions generally Tweedsmuir felt that

a brotherhood is the right mechanism for such work, and the Oblate priests and lay brothers are the kind of people suited for a wild country: strong, purposeful, capable of turning their hand to any job, and with their hearts in their work.

He was ready to think well of anyone who lived in the North, but he was surprised at the quality of one group, the half-breeds, who seemed

of a far higher type than the ordinary *métis* . . . upstanding, straight-forward folk, who look you frankly in the face and have excellent manners. Most of them are the offspring of the old Hudson's Bay employees brought from Scotland and the Orkney Islands, and most of them have Scots names, a few Irish, and very few English. When an old Hudson's Bay factor was asked the reason for this scarcity of English names he replied that the Indians had to draw the line somewhere!

At Fort Simpson, 'the most elaborate of the river stations,' where the Liard flows in from the mountains and muddies the waters of the Mackenzie,

I had my usual pow-wow with the Indians . . . and they presented me with a wonderful map of the Mackenzie embroidered on moose-skin. Maggie was a rampant photographer. She had the whole settlement fetching and carrying for her.

Now the Mackenzie Mountains came close to the left bank of the river, and Tweedsmuir—as Leithen was to do in *Sick Heart River* —with his eye 'picked out ways of ascent by their ridges and gullies.' But when they reached Fort Norman the sight of Bear Rock, rearing up 1300 feet from the water's edge where the Bear River joins the Mackenzie, was too much for him. 'The face had never been climbed,' he told Stair Gillon, his old partner on Ben Nevis and the hills of Galloway,

so I set out to do it. The rock was rotten and slanting the wrong way, but I took it cautiously and had no difficulties except at the very top, where there is an overhang. I managed to drag up an Indian so that he could give me a back, and wriggled my way up. The only trouble was that the hang-over I jumped for came away with me, and I had an uncomfortable bit of sprawling to do. This seems to have got into the newspapers and been ridiculously exaggerated.

Mr Bonnycastle, the Hudson's Bay officer, had gone up by the easy route at the back of the Rock, where it was wooded and far less steep; he arrived at the top just in time 'to find the Governor-General crawling flat on his stomach over the crest.' Dr Macdonald and Lieutenant Rivers-Smith, who had also attempted the climb, stuck within about a hundred feet of the top, just below the hardest part; there they stayed till a couple of Indians climbed up behind them with ropes, and helped them down. Tweedsmuir's account to Amery, who, though a year or two older, had just announced *his* climbing success on the Dachstein—'a really vertical rock face of some 3000 feet'—ended:

I am glad to say that the rest of my staff, including an inspector of police, got stuck on the lower rocks and had to be rescued by ropes!

Everybody, including the Governor-General, had torn their trousers.

Susan, reading of this exploit in the papers, wired to Shuldham Redfern 'This tomfoolery must stop.' But he had already reported to her that 'His Ex. is in tremendous form and a weighing machine at Fort Simpson disclosed a gain of, I think, 5 lbs.'

Fort Norman, where the first plane to reach the Canadian Arctic landed in 1921, was one of the busiest of the posts: boats and planes went east up the Bear River with supplies for the mining-camps which had recently sprung up on the shores of the Great Bear Lake. Here Tweedsmuir visited a coal-seam on the river-bank which had been burning since Mackenzie passed a hundred and fifty years before. Then they proceeded down the river, now the colour of milky coffee and three miles wide, through the Ramparts, past Fort Good Hope, 'where the Catholic missions are doing fine work in agricultural experiments,' and across the Arctic Circle to Arctic Red River and Fort McPherson on the Peel.

It was near here that Fitzgerald's mounted patrol perished in the snow in their attempt to cross the divide to the Yukon. Their bodies are buried in the churchyard. Here I met one Firth, an Orcadian of eighty-seven, who had been a Hudson's Bay employee and had come out seventy years ago!

Mr Firth had always refused to give credit to Catholics in the Company's store, with the result that Fort McPherson was the only place on the river without a Catholic mission.

Tweedsmuir had expected the last stretch of the valley to be 'a

gaunt waste, to the charms of which I am always predisposed:'
something cold, hard and bleak, but also keen and tonic. But he
found that here

the North is altogether beyond the human scale and it has no cleanness
and simplicity. I expected bleak moors and cold ice-gray waters. Instead
I found a kind of coarse lushness—immense rivers pouring billions of
dirty gallons to the ocean, too much coarse vegetation, an infinity of mud,
and everywhere a superfluity of obscene insect life. The impression was
not of a Nature beautiful and austere, though cold and hard, but of a
Nature as coarsely exuberant as a tropical forest.

The delta of the Mackenzie struck him as

the most sinister place I have ever seen. I saw it under mist and cold
winds, but a bright sun would make no difference to it. It is one vast
quagmire—muskeg on a colossal scale. Three main channels pierce it, and
between them there is an infinity of what look like carefully engineered
canals of a mathematical regularity. Between the canals are oily mud-holes
and lawn-like stretches of an unwholesome green, into which whole armies
could disappear. God help the man who gets lost in it! I understand that
even the Eskimos have difficulty in picking their way through it. It reminded
me of nothing so much as the no-man's-land between the trenches in the
War—but a colossal no-man's-land created in some campaign of demons—
pitted and pocked with shell-holes from some infernal artillery. Looking
down on it from the air at first glance one might be looking at suburban
Surrey—broad tarmac highways, lines of newly planted fir trees, and
behind them the smooth lawns of some suburban householder. It is only
at the second look that one realises that the highways are channels of yellow
mud and that the green lawns are bottomless swamps.

Mackenzie in 1789 had brought his boats down one of the main
channels through this delta to the open sea, there to gaze in disappointment at the tideless ocean and the whales at play, the end of
all his hopes that the long river flowed to the Pacific. Journey's
end for the *Distributor* was Aklavik, which is on the delta but eighty
miles south of the Arctic Ocean: a town only twelve years old in
1937; the centre for the fur-posts along the Arctic shore and offshore
islands. There Tweedsmuir opened a new hospital and gave a
party on board the *Distributor* to all the inhabitants. He admired the
dedicated priests, doctors and nurses who worked there but not the
place itself, with oil-drums littering the beach and a pestilence of
mosquitoes:

Aklavik seems to me a complete mistake. A settlement should be at the
head of a delta or on the seashore, and not in the middle . . . There is no
fall and therefore no proper sanitation, and the foreshore is foul. It is only
the long antiseptic winters which prevent epidemics.

It was a relief, on the day after arrival, to fly to Tukta-Yaktuk, the northernmost settlement on the mainland and depot for supplies for the middle Arctic, for it was sited on 'an open clean shore. . . . It might have been a Scots moor, for in the foot or two of peat which covers the ice there were blaeberries, crowberries and cranberries.' The Arctic coast was a place of 'clear half-lights and halftones' and after the nauseous delta it gave 'a wonderful feeling of space and peace.' Flying low over Richards Island they saw the vast herd of reindeer which had been brought from Alaska after a five years' trek to encourage the Eskimos to be herdsmen as well as hunters, then returned over the delta in fog to make a difficult landing at Aklavik.

The return trip to Edmonton was by a single-engined Fairchild plane of the Royal Canadian Air Force, with floats. On the first stage rain and mist compelled them to follow again the course of the river up to Fort Norman, where they were grounded for a day. Mrs Skinner, wife of the Hudson's Bay factor, cheerfully found room in her house for Tweedsmuir, the Redferns, Lieutenant Rivers-Smith and—from another plane—a brace of Bishops, Roman Catholic and Anglican; but she was startled next morning to find the Governor-General shaving in her kitchen sink, to save her carrying up hot water. After 'a rather bold take-off from a very stormy river' they flew to Great Bear Lake to see the pitchblende mine, the only one in the world to compare with those of the Congo.

That night we put up at the Eldorado mine with Harry Snyder and a delightful company. I had a hut to myself perched high on a rocky knoll, with a blazing fire to keep me company. The following morning I spent going over the mine, which is the chief radium producer in the world. In the afternoon we flew far into the Barren Lands to a river called the Camsell, where I got my first Arctic grayling. I fished in the Great Bear Lake in the evening, but could do nothing with the lake trout. The following day, the weather being quite perfect, we flew north to the upper waters of the Coppermine and then down that river to Coronation Gulf. The weather was so fine that we flew right over the ocean to the edge of the pack ice—an experience I never thought would be mine.

At Coronation Gulf they met an Eskimo family who had sailed from distant Victoria Land in their own neat and well-found schooners; merry, competent people with a talent for mechanics and for making themselves snug. Eskimos generally seemed far more able than Indians to 'take what is best in white civilisation and leave out what is bad.'

In the afternoon we flew far into the Barrens and fished in a lake where no one, I am sure, has ever cast a fly before. I had hopes of a chance of a Barrens grizzly, but the only thing we saw was caribou, which we stalked, and Gordon [Rivers-Smith] got a good bull. We had a wonderful luncheon off steaks cooked in the open, and got back late in what was almost bright daylight.

Great Bear Lake, with its blue waters and rocky shores like the West Highlands, had restored the sense of 'the clean, antiseptic North':

But I think the most wonderful impression I had was flying over the Barrens on a cloudy day. The cloud shadows on these infinite plains, in constant motion, made a beautiful fantastic world. It was all out of scale with humanity; but it is a good thing now and then if you manage to realise that the world was not created on your own scale. It sharpens the adventure of living.

William Buchan, reflecting on his father's enthusiasm for flying, thought that 'he always liked to be *above* things, to have a wide sweep, not to be too near human complexities'.

From their next stop, Fort Rae on the Great Slave Lake, there was another flight into the Barrens, 'from above, a delicate lace-work of lakes and streams criss-crossed by ridges of bald rock and banks of gravel,' to Gordon's Lake in the Yellowknife area, where gold had just been discovered. Then they rejoined their outward track at Fort Smith, and followed the river-route back to Waterways with a final 'dry hop' to Edmonton, which they reached on 8 August. They had been 2000 miles by steamer and well over 3000 by air.

At Edmonton were Susan and Alastair, and the reunited family took the train westward to finish the summer with a tour of Tweedsmuir Park in British Columbia, an area of 5000 square miles east of the Coast Range, which had been lately established by the provincial Government as a reserve. It is a high table-land, studded with lakes, and rising to mountains nine thousand feet high—the dazzling Rainbows, the glacier-streaked Thunder Mountain, the craggy Whitesails—while far to the South loom the stupendous spires of Mount Waddington. 'The Rockies seem to me an ugly and muddled range,' wrote Tweedsmuir to Stair Gillon, 'but the Coast range is as exactly architected as the Alps.' There they spent ten days camping and trekking. They followed the trail by which the Indians from the Bella Coola valley used to travel to their summer hunting-grounds by Ootsa Lake; they swam their horses across the Ootsa River, and the animals' heads emerging from the cold and

angry waters 'were like bodiless steeds from the Parthenon frieze.'
They saw grizzlies and caught rainbow trout and salmon; they sat
round camp-fires and talked to air-pilots, ranchers, miners, mountaineers, foresters and British Columbia policemen. Susan, who
two years ago at Elsfield had never dreamed that she would ever
wear trousers or fly, found herself in an aeroplane flying in bad
weather through the passes of the Coast Range to Bella Coola. As
on her honeymoon in the Dolomites, she was a victim of vertigo,
while her unperturbed husband played his favourite game of looking
for a secret sanctuary, in the tangle of hills below. This time he
found a perfect one: a cup in the hills, 'with a lake, a half-moon of
wild meadow and behind it another half-moon of forest.'

Mackenzie, on his journey to the Pacific, had crossed the southern
corner of the present Tweedsmuir Park. The Tweedsmuirs, on their
way from Bella Coola towards the sea, saw the rock on which he
painted 'Alex Mackenzie from Canada by Land 22 July 1793.' 'In
six weeks,' wrote Tweedsmuir after his return to Ottawa, 'I was
able to cover, under most comfortable conditions, both of Mackenzie's famous journeys.'

Tweedsmuir summed up his impressions of the tour in the
memorandum which he made for the Prime Minister and for the
Hudson's Bay Company. Air transport was, he thought, of first
importance: not only within the North, but because the North
would be in the line of future services between Europe and the Far
East. Agriculture could be greatly extended: with the double ration
of sunlight, with the production of new strains, the cultivation line
could be steadily pushed North. There were great possibilities in
the Hay River Valley and, for ranching, in the foothills of the
Upper Liard. Tourism of a strenuous kind could be organised:
Canada was already a playground for North America, and on the
eastern slopes of the Rockies north of the Peace River the rich
American with pioneer longings could hunt, fish, and live the
simple life. As for the people of the North, 'I cannot imagine a
more pleasant or wholesome society.'

There is an immense friendliness in the North. It is a true democracy, for
there are no distinctions of classes. The trapper is on the same social level
as the Hudson's Bay post-master, or the police sergeant. Everybody is
known by his Christian name, and they are all ready to help each other.
A man will take enormous pains to get a neighbour out of a difficulty, even
though he may not be a particular friend of his. In the face of a harsh
Nature human beings seem to have acquired a keener sense of responsibility towards each other.

Summing up his impressions, he wrote:

The vision I have of the future of the North is of a large number of smallish industrial centres, in close touch with civilisation by radio and the air.

('It is curious,' he wrote on the trip, 'how the latest mechanical inventions, like the radio and the aeroplane, are used here not to complicate but to simplify life.')

The winter climate on the whole is much milder than in the Prairies. Such centres would have all the decent appurtenances of civilisation in the shape of frequent mails, a properly varied food supply, and medical attention. Heavy plant and ores would go in and out by water, but the main form of transport would be the air . . . But this future depends upon a chain of hypotheses, the most important being the cheapening of air transport, which in turn depends largely upon the development of local oil fields. The North is not an easy problem for Canada, but it offers a wonderful chance. She has already a fine performance to her credit—just as fine as the much-vaunted Russian development of northern Siberia—and though there is still much to do she starts with two great advantages; the assets are there, and she can produce the right kind of men to develop them.

Tweedsmuir's foray into the North was well reported: that had been part of his intention, though he did not want the spotlight on the Governor-General, but on the places he visited and on the ease of his travelling. Canadians now read in their newspapers of the North as a place of activity, power and potential wealth, where life could certainly be hard, but not hopeless. The Governor-General had gone there, using the normal transport of the North, had been perfectly comfortable and had positively enjoyed himself—the reports made plain that this was not just a tour in the way of duty, but an enterprise enthusiastically undertaken. They heard too that the tour had been well reported in Britain and the United States: he had made a part of Canada highly interesting to the world outside, and he had helped to redress a balance. 'Canada gets plenty of publicity,' he told one correspondent, 'for her failures and disasters, like Mr Aberhart and the drought, and her freaks, like the Quintuplets, but very little for her successes and her assets.' By his interest in the pioneers he had injected a sense of the past into territories which had appeared to be a blank in history, as for so long they had been a blank on the map: it was as if Alexander Mackenzie from Stornoway and George Simpson from Loch Broom had carried the long memories of the Highlands to humanise the West and North of Canada.

Encouraging others to use their imagination about the North,
Tweedsmuir found in it nourishment for his own. This 'country
and people without much glamour,' as he had called them when
debating the pros and cons of his appointment to Canada, had
taken a firm hold of him. The North gave him a vision of a true
community, where in a difficult environment men worked together
in a real brotherhood. It fired his old exploring dreams. Harry
Snyder, of the Eldorado Mine, had asked him to fly over to the
western side of the Mackenzie: there had been no time for this,
but the talk of this country into which Snyder had once dropped
from the air struck a deep response. After the tour Tweedsmuir
wrote:

There are three geographical mysteries in Canada. One is the Rivière
de l'Enfer, far up in the Laurentides, which I hope to visit some day.
Another is the strange tongue of forest land which runs north far up into
the Barrens on the Thelon river. This has been more or less explored now
since John Hornby and young Christian perished there. The third is the
South Nahanni, which comes down from the mountains on the north bank
of the Liard. It used to be a kind of no-man's-land over which the Yukon
and the Mackenzie Indians fought. It is believed to be full of mineral
wealth, but it is extraordinarily difficult to explore, for a boat is impossible
since there is a fall of over three hundred feet high. In the last twenty years
nine white men have gone into the valley and have not returned. Harry
Snyder is exploring it by plane and has established a camp far up it,
where he has shot some wonderful specimens of mountain fauna, and discovered glaciers and snow-fields and peaks as big as anything in the Rockies.
There may be some real geographical secret there waiting to be discovered.

There stayed in his mind too the memory of that cup in the hills,
seen from the air as they flew over the Coast Range to Bella Coola:
a half-moon of wild meadow in a half-moon of forest.

CHAPTER FOURTEEN

CANADIAN

'I am a passionate Canadian in my love for the country and the people.'
John Buchan: Letter to friends in Britain, January 1937

More than ever, the trip to the North strengthened Tweedsmuir's resolution to make Canadians prouder of Canada—of all Canada. On all his journeys he had reacted with much more than the routine interest which it is the Governor-General's job to show. His imaginative sympathy had been touched again and again. He had warmed to the traditionalism of Quebec and its jealous guarding of a French culture, to the Highland pride and loyalty of the Maritimes, to the social adventurousness of the Prairies, to the heroic living of the North. He savoured the Victorian atmosphere of Prince Edward Island, the Englishness of British Columbia, and thought a country lucky to have such diverse cultures, so many loyalties. These should be a matter of pride to all, and so help to bring the provinces together, not push them apart.

It was not an easy task. Canada, when he arrived, struck him as having a nationalist spirit but not much sense of being a nation. The depression had generated a malaise and sense of isolation; the mood was inward-looking, not expansionist. (In those years there was actually emigration from Canada to Britain.) There was little agreement as to the general direction of the nation's development. Loyalty to the principle of the Commonwealth was not in question —without the Commonwealth Canada might have been absorbed by the United States. But loyalty to Canada was not much in evidence. 'The Fathers of Confederation,' Tweedsmuir said in a Dominion Day broadcast, 'gave Canada union. They could not give her unity'. Provincialism was rampant:

Each Province tends to regard itself as a separate unit and to look at a policy on the narrowest grounds, without any consideration of Canada as a whole. They are all perfectly loyal to the Empire but by no means so loyal to the Dominion.

Quebec was the major problem here, but this was not only the doing of French Canadians:

A great deal of blame attaches, I think, to the English population. There is a truculent Orange element in Ontario, and in Montreal, where the whole business world is run by the English, who are only a quarter of the population, there has been in the past a good deal of arrogance and unfriendliness . . . It is not easy to get any kind of imaginative outlook from the ordinary hard-faced business man.

Having written to one correspondent of 'the desperate amount of provincial jealousy,' he went on:

It is odd how difficult it is on this side of the Atlantic to harmonise provincial with national rights. America fought her Civil War on the subject.

'We must handle the problem delicately,' he told Amery, apropos constitutional reform (4 February 1937),

for there is a great deal of provincialism in Canada. They are much more loyal to the Empire than to the Dominion. We have some excellent people here to deal with constitutional problems—men like our Federal Chief Justice [Sir Lyman Duff], and the new Chief Justice of Ontario, Rowell, and Dafoe of Winnipeg. Until we get our constitution revised it is impossible to have any nation-wide social policy, or to get the provincial finances straight.

'Our biggest problem here,' he told Baldwin (24 March 1936),

is the way everybody thinks in compartments. This will go on, I fear, until Canada gets some national leader who will really touch its imagination, and that can only be a gift of the gods.

To the King he wrote (16 March 1939):

The crying need for Canada is for some national leader who would really guide the thought and touch the imagination of the whole country. In recent history Canada has had two such leaders—Sir John Macdonald, who was mainly responsible for Canadian Federation, and Sir Wilfrid Laurier, who first preached the gospel of Dominion Nationalism, not only for Canada, but for the whole Empire. Since then there has been no man with the same appeal, and the lack of such a figure explains the incomplete integration of the country and the danger of provincial sentiment being stronger than national . . . But great personalities are the gift of Providence, they cannot be manufactured.

In the meantime, while Canada waited for such a leader, Tweedsmuir would try to give a push in the right direction: to give her more sense of her different cultures, more interest in her history, more pride in her heroes, more confidence in her maturity.

There was one method he was sure would not work: to beat the big imperial drum. On 3 March 1937 he wrote to the King:

The word 'imperialism' has become generally unpopular here, for it is identified in most minds with large vague obligations to the world at large which do not touch Canada's real interests . . . The truth is, I think, that we no longer need the old rhetoric about the Empire.

But there was another line he could use, which was part of his own fabric: Scotland. Again and again in his speeches to gatherings of Scots in Canada he made the point that Scotland represented the successful fusion of two races, Highland and Lowland, which had 'different economic interests, different social traditions, different religious creeds.' 'This is a fact which we too often forget, and it is one of the miracles of history.' (A point which he did not make openly was that one of the people who had most helped to create a general Scottish sentiment, which could be shared by High-lander and Lowlander, was a writer: Walter Scott.) Tweedsmuir emphasised how natural it was to the Scot to hold multiple loyalties —to Highlands or Borders, Edinburgh or Glasgow—within the loyalty to Scotland; to Scotland within the loyalty to Britain. 'A man can never have too many loyalties,' he told an audience on Prince Edward Island. He would like to see a dual patriotism come as easily to the English Canadian of Vancouver or the French Canadian of Quebec as it did to the Scot.

After the Northern tour, which completed his survey of the country, he was ready for plainer speaking. Six weeks after his return he had to speak at the anniversary dinner of the Canadian Institute of International Affairs in Montreal (on 12 October 1937) and he took for his subject 'Canada's Outlook on the World.' With memories of the storm raised by his words at Calgary the year before, he was careful to cover himself by sending an advance copy of his speech to the Prime Minister for approval (given immediately) and by prefacing it with prudent disclaimers:

A Governor-General, I need hardly remind you, has to walk warily. In the domestic affairs of the country where he represents the King, he can have no views on policy except those of his ministers. And even on international questions he is in a position of some delicacy, for today inter-national problems have the unhappy knack of also becoming domestic problems.

But he felt, he told his audience, that he could safely consider the impact of democracy upon international affairs. Foreign questions used to be of remote and academic interest to the ordinary British citizen, and could be left to a handful of experts, but now

the problems affect us all too vitally in our private interests. The foreign policy of a democracy must be the cumulative views of individual citizens, and if these views are to be sound they must in turn be the consequence of a widely diffused knowledge.

Sound, straightforward stuff, such as he used to expound to the electors of Peebles, or to the Conservative Central Office when he emphasised the needs of an educated democracy. But they were immediately followed by words which startled his audience and rang across Canada:

From this duty no country is exempt. Certainly not Canada. She is a sovereign nation and cannot take her attitude to the world docilely from Britain, or from the United States, or from anybody else. A Canadian's first loyalty is not to the British Commonwealth of Nations, but to Canada and to Canada's King.

This led on to the point that

If the Commonwealth, in a crisis, is to speak with one voice it will be only because the component parts have thought out for themselves their own special problems, and made their contribution to the discussion, so that a true common factor of policy can be reached. A sovereign people must, as part of its sovereign duty, take up its own attitude to world problems.

And Tweedsmuir rounded off the argument with a plea that this attitude should be based on the exact knowledge of foreign affairs which it was the Institute's object to provide.

It was not the argument as a whole which was discussed right across the Dominion and commented on in every newspaper—nor perhaps did Tweedsmuir mean it to be. It was the one sentence, about a Canadian's first loyalty being to Canada.* The reaction was strong and varied. Full-blooded Imperialists were outraged at what they took to be a weakening of loyalty to the Commonwealth. Constitutionalists smelt interference in domestic politics, and a

* Mr Robert Grant Irving has drawn my attention to a comparable statement in a speech delivered by Lord Dufferin to the Toronto Club on 2 September 1871 (the text is given in William Leggo's *History of the Administration of the Earl of Dufferin*, Montreal, 1878): 'Words cannot express what pride I feel as an Englishman in the loyalty of Canada to England. Nevertheless, I should be the first to deplore this feeling if it rendered Canada disloyal to herself, if it either dwarfed or smothered Canadian patriotism, or generated a sickly spirit of dependence. Such, however, is far from being the case.' The speech was widely hailed in the press, and applauded by the Colonial Office.

Conservative ex-Minister raised the matter in Parliament. The Prime Minister, in his reply, did not admit that he had read and passed the speech. No one was a firmer believer in the sovereignty of Canada than Mackenzie King, but however much he acted on this belief it was not his way to proclaim it with a trumpet from the battlements as Tweedsmuir, with some relish, had done. The editors of *Le Devoir*, then the most articulate and uncompromising spokesman of Quebec 'nationalism,' were delighted. They were convinced that French Canada was the only part of the country which really believed in Canadian autonomy and independence, that all English-speaking Canadians were colonials who believed in Britain's imperial mission and would always accept the British lead in all matters of foreign policy. Tweedsmuir's statement hit them between the eyes, and for some years the key sentences of his speech were carried in what journalists call a 'lug' at the top left corner of the front page, at first in French and then in both languages. The speech certainly persuaded a few Quebecois that there were Canadians who thought, more or less, in the same autonomous vein as they did. To Canadians in general it was a startling pronouncement of something which they then realised was true. The Statute of Westminster had assured the Dominions of their status as independent, equal and autonomous powers, but the idea of this independence and equality had not seeped through into popular imagination. Tweedsmuir gave the idea body and force. He lifted it above the level of squabbles over the price of wheat or co-operation in air-defence—matters which had produced some friction between the Governments of equal and independent Britain and Canada. Canada was to be felt as not just independent *from* Britain or anyone else, but as independent and free to be Canada in the fullest sense.

Since the Statute of Westminster, many Canadians in public life had wondered if anybody could successfully carry out the office of Governor-General now that it had become so much more difficult in its new and almost indefinable stage. The job had not lost its meaning, but the meaning had now largely to be created by the individual who held it. Tweedsmuir had been two years in the country when he made his 'Canadian's first loyalty' speech, and his particular interpretation of the rôle of Governor-General was beginning to emerge. Canadians saw a man who was on terms of easy and confidential friendship with the President of the United States, who liked to be up and about and seeing for himself, who enjoyed going to small places with little fuss, and who showed enterprise and courage in his travels (the trip to the North had sent his stock up greatly, Dr Thomas Wood told Tweedsmuir's friends in London). A man who could speak his mind plainly, and with wit, who, except for the Calgary speech, had not transgressed constitutional bounds but had struck notes not usually heard from Governor-Generals—or indeed from any successful and established persons—as on the occasion when he told an audience of students at Toronto:

Do not take your creed secondhand from anyone, but shape it for yourselves. . . . I would far rather have a young man talk the uttermost nonsense, provided it is his own, than repeat like a gramophone the sagacities of other people. He may be foolish, but it is better to be foolish than to be dead.

They saw a man who could focus his attention sharply on one subject, but was interested in a dozen, who plied them with questions about their jobs and interests, who listened to their answers as if they mattered to him, who wrote romantic novels but had an insatiable appetite for facts. After half an hour's talk with him, said one Canadian, you felt as if your brains had been raked over in the most polite but penetrating manner. Tweedsmuir was a Briton who did not measure them by English yardsticks—perhaps because he was a Scot; who indeed seemed rather to enjoy emphasising anything that kept the Englishman in his place. They never felt that he was representing the British Raj, treating Canada as his satrapy, as some of his predecessors had done. He was putting roots down in Canada—his eldest son was working for the Hudson's Bay Company; he often seemed to be thinking and feeling as a Canadian; he said 'Our' and not 'Your.' They saw a Governor-General who operated across the whole country, and not just in an island round Government House, who worked hard at his job, who performed his ceremonial duties with style and efficiency but seemed happiest when talking to farmers in the Prairies or young men with strong views on politics at Rideau Hall.

Canadians, especially in Ottawa, observed that the range of visitors to Government House went far beyond the usual run of official guests and personal friends. Tweedsmuir clearly had a liking for explorers, writers, journalists, painters, Labour leaders, anybody who was articulate and had ideas. It caused something of a sensation in Ottawa when Henry Wise Wood, the agrarian leader from Calgary, was invited for a week-end. Wood, an American Populist who had come north to Alberta and become the outstanding figure in the agrarian movement, was now in his seventies, a picturesque and militant character. Ottawa was mildly startled too by the Governor-General's interest in the young men of the Canadian Co-operative Federation. He would be seen in a corner absorbed in conversation with David Lewis, the National Secretary of the C.C.F. (and later its Chairman)—conversation ranging, Mr Lewis remembers, far beyond social and political matters into 'all aspects of Canadian life about which I knew anything.' Another young C.C.F. man, Graham Spry, the Ontario secretary of the party who at that period led rather a double life, moving between the unemployed and the Top People of Ottawa, recalls his surprise when told by Willis O'Connor at a Country Club dance that Tweedsmuir wanted a word with him. 'I've been reading your papers,' said Tweedsmuir without any preliminaries. 'You people aren't hitting hard enough. You should be more radical.' He then read Spry a lecture on how essential it was in a democracy to have a brisk conflict of ideas through parties. 'The conflict educates people. Also it's the way you get a better policy.' Spry, who was convinced that Tweedsmuir really had studied the weekly *New Commonwealth* and the monthly *Canadian Forum*, was always surprised by his familiarity, indeed sympathetic involvement, with 'those minority movements run by a small group of highbrows,' like the League for Social Reconstruction, a Fabian-style body which produced the symposium *Social Planning for Canada*.

A few of Tweedsmuir's overseas friends who visited Government House felt slightly oppressed by the formality, the doors flying open as His Excellency appeared, the rigid punctuality. Americans who had been delighted to have such a very unstuffed-shirt British friend were rather put off by the protocol which now encircled him, and thought that state was being kept up too much among friends. But these younger Canadian visitors, arriving perhaps a little apprehensively to lunch or dine, found the atmosphere refreshingly informal, with their host giving them his full attention and 'never looking past you,' as one young woman remembered, 'to someone more important.'

From Tweedsmuir's own point of view the job was going well. There were, of course, drawbacks. He was often irritated by the irregular flow of the official papers which he was entitled to see: the supply would dry up, then there would be a spate of documents and telegrams, many of them of no great interest. He wished Canadians were not such gluttons for speeches: 'About speaking Canada has no bowels of compassion;' 'Canada is leading me into unbridled garrulity, but there is no way out of it.' The better he spoke, the more likely he was to be broadcast and fully reported, and the less he could repeat himself. It was a strain to be on view throughout a day which (to take an example from October 1937) began with opening a Gate of Remembrance, went on with an official lunch, a Graduation ceremony, the opening of a University Hall, and ended with a couple of addresses to a society and a hospital. It was an effort to be always giving out: 'The first duty of a Governor-General is to have plenty of small talk, and to be able to make a party go,' he wrote after the visit of a tongue-tied peer with aspirations to a Governor-Generalship. He wished that some of the functions he had to attend were not quite so long. There was a Jewish service at the Holy Blossom Temple in Toronto which lasted three hours. As sermon succeeded sermon Shuldham Redfern became more and more worried: His Excellency would be very late for lunch, his careful regime upset, Redfern would get a rocket for letting him in for this. All Tweedsmuir said on coming out was 'Now I know why it took them forty years to cross the wilderness.' And though Tweedsmuir did enjoy ceremonial more than one fellow-Scot thought he should (a professor, who found something odd about 'a very able middle-class Scot clad in the panoply of semi-royalty and so obviously enjoying it'), after the first flush of novelty even that palled. The most ardent historical imagination could not disguise the fact that the opening of Parliament, with the Speech from the Throne, always long, to be read in English and then all over again in French,* was a gruelling performance; and that State banquets could be deadly dull.

Natural instincts of hospitality and friendliness might have to be curbed. Except for informal parties with their staff, the Tweedsmuirs could lunch and dine out only at ministerial and ambassadorial level. They would have liked to see much more of one very congenial ambassador and his wife than protocol allowed. Of a dinner with the Japanese Minister in 1938 Tweedsmuir wrote that 'it is always a delicate business dining with people you like but of whose country you disapprove.' Personal convenience might have to be forgone: the more convenient sailing from New York in an American boat passed over for the less convenient date from Quebec

* Now, more mercifully, alternate paragraphs are in English and French.

in a C.P.R. boat. All this bore more hardly, perhaps, upon Susan, who hated always being on show, never able to go out alone. She found the tours, so stimulating to her husband, very tiring: 'She finds it an effort to be constantly switching off and talking to different kinds of people, whereas I do not mind it.' But she developed a great flair for extempore speaking. Faced with a young man proffering a microphone and begging for 'a message to the women of Western Canada' or 'a few words to the women of America,' she would respond with grace and verve. She was happiest, though, with the work which she created for herself, with the Prairie Libraries—in two years she collected over 40,000 volumes—and with the writing of local histories by the Women's Institutes. Compiled from photographs, letters and personal memories, these were invaluable records of rapidly changing communities. She found Government House life good for work, and wrote a novel based on her experiences with the South Wales unemployed, *The Scent of Water*, and a volume of impressions, *Carnets Canadiens*.

There was a personal worry about money. When Tweedsmuir went to Canada, the Governor-General had to provide, out of his salary of 50,000 dollars, his own cars, all the presents he was expected to hand out (cuff-links, photographs in silver frames—'Their Excellencies' combinations' they were termed if it was a double portrait) as well as the salary of some of his personal staff and the running expenses of Government House. To start off, Tweedsmuir had to borrow a large sum from his Scottish friend Sir Alexander Grant (the benefactor of the National Library) which he hoped to repay out of his salary, and did; but a careful eye had always to be kept on the budget if the Tweedsmuirs were to live at the expected standard yet not be out of pocket at the end (Mr Vincent Massey, who became Governor-General in 1952, found it 'quite impossible to meet the expenses of the post from the money provided'). With no new novels appearing after 1936, Tweedsmuir's literary earnings dropped from £7000 in 1937 to £3000 in 1938 and £1500 in 1939.

One restriction which he found particularly irksome came from his being John Buchan as well as Governor-General. From the time he arrived in Canada, invitations had poured in from universities in the United States—in 1936 there were twenty-seven—offering honorary degrees and inviting him to lecture. He would have liked to accept, for his books were popular with many young Americans, and the lecture-fees would have been useful. But as the King's representative he could not visit the States for any public purpose except with the full paraphernalia of a Governor-General, a suite, guards of honour and all. More than once he tried to get permission to modify the general rule as far as universities were concerned, so that he could go 'without the trappings of officialdom.' 'John Buchan is desperately keen to be allowed to lecture in the States,' Baldwin told Tom Jones in May 1936; 'I don't think we ought to let him.' Most Canadians who knew of the matter thought this a perfectly reasonable limitation. In 1938 he was allowed to accept degrees from Yale and Harvard, and at the latter he gave the Commencement Address; otherwise he never delivered a formal lecture in the States.

Before coming to Canada he had raised the question of his writing with King George V, and asked whether it would be in order for him to publish anything during his term of office. He was told he could publish anything he pleased, provided it was not on current controversial politics. Tweedsmuir himself did not intend to publish any fiction while Governor-General, except for the already-written *Island of Sheep* which came out in 1936, and during his first two years he was content to work only on his *Augustus*. But after his tour in the North in 1937 he wrote a couple of articles for the *Sunday Times* which Mackenzie King thought splendid, and wished to distribute to schoolchildren all over Canada. These articles brought an unexpected rebuke from Buckingham Palace; if one Governor-General started singing the praises of part of his Dominions, then he was being a publicity agent for that Dominion, which was not a dignified rôle for His Majesty's personal representative to play. It might even lead to other Governor-Generals, less gifted in the literary line, feeling they ought to follow suit. Tweedsmuir was also chided for standing, late in 1937, for the Chancellorship of Edinburgh University, on the grounds that it would have been undignified had he been defeated. In fact he had comfortably beaten Lord Lothian by 4802 votes to 2582, though when he accepted the nomination he had not expected a contest. And there was a word about using the utmost discretion in public speeches.

A year after Tweedsmuir's arrival in Canada there was an article in the Toronto *Globe and Mail* by J. V. McAree on 'Serving the King in Exile,' in which, with the traditional type of English Governor-General in mind, he described his lonely state, 'deprived of the sports, the society, the entertainments, the intellectual nourishment in which he has been born and bred.' Indeed many an

English nobleman, representing his Sovereign in a Dominion, has regarded his term in distant parts as so many years out of his real life at home: as a duty, and if sometimes a painful one, *noblesse oblige*.

Tweedsmuir did not regard it in the least like this. He was hardly even homesick: 'One may be a little homesick for Oxfordshire here,' he told Stair Gillon, 'but not for Scotland, for Canada is simply Scotland on an extended scale.' Nor did he particularly mind not being 'at the heart of things' as he had been in the war and in his years in Parliament. 'I feel,' he told Baldwin,

rather like a Scots laird at the end of the eighteenth century, who cultivated his estate in the wilds of Sutherland, while Pitt and Fox and Burke were hard at it in the House of Commons and the Revolution was blazing away in France.

He kept himself well posted with news of London and exchanged long letters with Amery, Baldwin, Neville Chamberlain, Violet Markham and Lord Crawford, who was an excellent retailer of behind-the-scenes political activity. Any visiting journalist or M.P. would be taken off to the library and eagerly interrogated: 'How's Ll.G. and Max? What is Winston up to?' He often asked Grattan O'Leary of the *Ottawa Journal*, or John Stevenson, Ottawa correspondent of the London *Times*, to come over to Rideau Hall between tea and dinner to hear what they thought of the latest news from Europe. He liked being up to date. When he was in Winnipeg, at the beginning of the Abdication crisis, he asked for G. V. Ferguson of the *Winnipeg Free Press* to come up and talk to him after a state luncheon. Ferguson demurred, for he had talked an hour with the Governor-General the day before, and knew there must be many who would now like the same opportunity. But Tweedsmuir sent an A.D.C. back to say he really did want to see him,

so over I went, and I have always laughed at the eagerness with which he sat me down, leaned over and asked, 'What's the latest?' in the eager voice of a schoolboy. I had of course read the latest despatches and, indeed, when I left him, went to the phone and gave his A.D.C. even later details. He was quite engaging.

Government House, if not at the heart of things, was certainly, as a Canadian put it to me, 'a high-class inn at a busy cross-roads.'[*]

* According to an article in *Maclean's Magazine* (15 July 1939) between November 1935 and mid-1939 the following were entertained at Rideau Hall: 2100 to lunch or dinner, 2700 to tea, 3150 to dances, and there were 400 house-guests.

The Crown Prince of Japan and his wife came to stay on their way to the Coronation in London. ('The Princess had never heard the pipes before, and my six pipers going round the table greatly excited her.') Lord Lothian and Colonel Arthur Murray came after visiting Roosevelt. From Washington too came Cordell Hull and the Victor Mallets from the British Embassy. From New York came Alice Duer Miller, Alexander Woollcott and the financier Jules Bache ('who, like all his kind, can think of nothing except the misdeeds of the President'). Other American visitors were Ruth Draper, Ferris Greenslet and the Roger Merrimans. A young German diplomat, whom Tweedsmuir had known as a Rhodes scholar at Oxford, stayed on his way to the Far East: Adam von Trott, who was to be executed in 1944 for his part in the Generals' plot against Hitler. Another German visitor was Dr Brüning, the former Chancellor. Among the British friends whom they had to stay, most of whom had crossed the Atlantic to give a lecture or attend a conference, were Stanley Baldwin, the Hugh Wyndhams, Violet Markham, Harold Macmillan, the Duff Coopers, Carola Oman, Lord Kemsley, Grace Hadow, Mrs Arthur Grenfell. The annual Drama Festival brought some appreciated guests in the adjudicators, who included Michel St Denis and Harley Granville-Barker. 'What a good time you gave us,' wrote the latter,

but something better than that. For I felt myself made a temporary member of your happy and able official family—Under-Secretary for the Drama or the like—and very proud to be!

Friends in Canada were bidden for week-ends. Early in 1938 Tweedsmuir entertained the Sandwells from Toronto—B. K. Sandwell was editor of *Saturday Night* and Tweedsmuir admired his writing—and the new American President of McGill, Lewis Douglas (later Ambassador in London), 'about the most interesting man on this continent.' One of the Tweedsmuirs' private visits which they remembered with particular pleasure was a winter week-end with the Jack McConnells (the owner of the *Montreal Star*) in the Laurentians: 'a wonderful place, built by Norwegians on the Norwegian model, high up among wooded hills' which they reached by sleigh. 'It was exceedingly nice,' wrote Susan to her mother,

jingling along through the snowy countryside with the sleigh bells almost playing a tune. The air was quite beautiful. The mountains roll away in every direction and have enormous toad-shaped boulders standing at intervals—the remains left by some glacial upheaval. The silver birches looked like filigree against the sky, and suddenly you come on a patch of orange dogwood in this utterly colourless landscape, which is most lovely.

The life was good for Buchan's writing. (I revert to 'Buchan' when I talk of his books, as he himself did on their title-pages.) During his spells in Ottawa, still better in the peace of the Citadel at Quebec, while other people saw to the practical organisation of his days, he could have long quiet stretches such as he had not known for years. In Ottawa he made good use of the charming octagonal library in Parliament Buildings; at Quebec there was the library of Laval University hard by the Citadel.

He started work on *Augustus* almost as soon as he arrived in Canada. The difficulties in writing on such a subject at such a distance from Europe were mitigated by the help of two friends: Hugh Last, the Professor of Ancient History at Oxford, and Roberto Weiss, who summarised articles, looked out for new material in foreign journals, and checked references. When the book was published in October 1937 Professor Last told Buchan that

it puts us so-called experts as much in your debt for its demonstration of the way in which Augustus should be treated as it does the larger public for what is by far the best general interpretation of its subject.

Augustus was welcomed both by historians and the general reader; and though Buchan was unlucky in publishing his book so shortly before Ronald Syme's *The Roman Revolution* (1939), which caused so much re-thinking about the man and the period, the book still holds its own as a scholarly popularisation.

Mussolini, Lord Crawford told Buchan early in 1936, had appeared at a reception for ambassadors dressed up in an Augustan toga; and after *Augustus* was published Buchan wrote to Baldwin 'I wish to goodness his mantle *had* descended upon the present ridiculous Dictator of Italy'. Certainly one of his interests in writing his book during the heyday of Hitler and Mussolini was the chance which it gave him of discussing dictatorship and power. 'The convulsions of our time,' he said in his preface,

may give an insight into the problems of the early Roman empire which was perhaps unattainable by scholars who lived in easier days.

At the end of the book he underlined the similarities between the two ages:

Once again the crust of civilisation has worn thin, and beneath can be heard the muttering of primeval fires. Once again many accepted principles of government have been overthrown, and the world has become a laboratory where immature and feverish minds experiment with unknown forces. Once again problems cannot be comfortably limited, for science has brought the nations into an uneasy bondage to each other. In the actual business of administration there is no question of today which Augustus had not to face and answer.

And in his final sentence he deplores 'the craving of great peoples to enslave themselves and to exult hysterically in their bonds.' (On its first translation into Italian certain passages in *Augustus* which were held to reflect unfavourably on dictatorship were omitted. Roberto Weiss helped with a second, uncensored, Italian translation in 1960.) 'I hope it may interest you,' wrote Buchan to Roosevelt with a copy of the book, 'for many of his problems are your own.' He was startled, however, when his American publishers, in an advertisement, pressed the similarity in a direction which he had not intended:

The Governor-General of Canada tells how a Republic became a Dictatorship. Americans, has this no message for you?

A number of readers in the United States were very ready to assume that, in discussing one-man rule, Buchan had their President in mind;* Roosevelt himself, who read it on a fishing-trip, did not refer to any such likeness.

The book 'brilliantly flatters the reader's ignorance of the period,' Buchan's daughter told him; and once more he revelled in painting a broad and lively canvas for the reader with scanty background knowledge. There is a masterly tour of the Empire, such as a contemporary traveller might have made; the Roman poor are in the picture as well as the poets and the consuls; there is the same sense of the life being lived by people whose names have long been forgotten that we have in the background of his *Cromwell*. And for Augustus there is the same intuitive sympathy that Buchan gave to Oliver.

Near the end of the book there is a comparison between Julius Caesar and Augustus. To Buchan the appeal of Julius was in his having, like Montrose, 'the mind of a dreamer joined to the temperament of a soldier.' The appeal of Augustus was more

---

* 'The suggestion in the *Times* that you have broken a lance in favour of one-man rule struck me as absurd,' wrote Edward Sheldon from New York after reading the reviews of *Augustus*. He went on to tell Buchan how two years earlier he had been invited to collaborate in a play whose 'ostensible subject was to be Augustus, but the real subject was none other than Franklin D. Roosevelt and the whole thing an exposure of the New Deal'—a suggestion which Sheldon did not take up.

down-to-earth: 'He was a builder whose concern was with things, not fancies.' 'The more I study him,' Buchan told Amery,

the more I feel that he was probably the greatest practical genius in statesmanship that the world has seen. He was the Scotsman *in excelsis*, not rich in ideas, but immensely good at giving practical effect to those of other men.

Above all, to *this* Scot who had watched the statesmen of his own day at work in a world shattered by one war and threatened with another, Augustus was worthy of the highest praise because 'he saved the world from disintegration.'

After *Augustus* was finished, Buchan embarked on a pleasant stretch of reading, or rather re-reading: Thoreau, Boswell, Dickens and Thackeray. ('How good he is! But I wish he would not fondle his characters.') But he could not long be happy without a book to write. 'Having no *Augustus* this winter,' he told Anna at the beginning of 1938,

I am trying to write a Canadian *Puck of Pook's Hill*. You see Canadian history is obligatory for the schools, but the books are perfectly deadly, and there is really nothing to engage the imagination of a child, and yet there are few more romantic stories in the world.

So in *The Long Traverse* (published in 1941; in Canada and the United States it is called *Lake of Gold*) he gave a Canadian boy the living sense of people of the past that Kipling had given his Dan and Una. Puck's rôle is taken by an Indian through whose magic Donald has visions of the Norsemen, the *voyageurs*, the Highland explorers, the fur-traders and the Eskimos.

The Governor-Generalship gave Tweedsmuir the chance, which he had enjoyed in South Africa, and in France during the war, of being physically active in the course of his duties. His knowledge of South Africa had come to him from his long rides on the veld and in the Wood Bush as much as from his office-work in Johannesburg and Pretoria; his knowledge of Canada too was something that came to him physically, as he bumped over the dusty prairie road to Alsask, sailed down the yellow waters of the Mackenzie or flew over the Barrens. If, like Dick Hannay in *The Island of Sheep*, he had begun to think that 'I was old and stale and that all my youth had gone,' the trip down North, particularly the climb up Bear Rock, had proved that he was still fit for adventure, 'not too old for a final frisk.' The long winter did not depress him as it did Susan—like all Buchans, it was heat that he dreaded—though he admitted that the monotonous snowy landscape could become rather trying. He skated regularly on the rink in the grounds of Rideau Hall. He made a brave shot at ski-ing, but he had started too late—'I dare not risk too much, for, being very lean, I might be rather brittle, and I cannot afford to break bones'—and in his third winter he gave it up. To Amery, a lifelong skier, he wrote regretfully that

it is not my sport. I am not good enough at it to get proper exercise, and spend too much of my time standing on my head in snowdrifts! I find that snow-shoeing gives me much more what I want.

But even after he had renounced it for himself he liked going up to Camp Fortune at a week-end and talking to the skiers, delighted that this excellent sport, then available only to a small minority in Britain, should be so popular in Canada, so truly democratic. In the spring he tramped on the Gatineau Hills: 'The woods are scented like honey with young leaves,' he wrote one May, 'and the flowers are beginning to appear. Canada before the flies arrive is a perfect Garden of Eden!' Absence of flies too made early summer the best season for enjoying Canada's rivers and lakes. In a letter to Alastair from Quebec in June 1937 he described a day on the Metis:

Using my big rod, I managed to cover most of the pools in the Metis from the bank, rather to the astonishment of the natives. I proved the value of trying different patterns of flies, for I got most of my fish after going over the same water with three or four different flies. They use a smallish pattern out here—about the size one would use for the Helmsdale. I did not try the greased line, for it was not needed. I fished with fairly fine tackle, and I have never had better fights than with these Canadian salmon, for they were fresh from the sea.

All this activity, he was convinced, was good for him: 'whenever I am on tour I am well,' he told Susan. His friends were not so sure. 'I have rejoiced at the good things I have heard about you,' wrote Baldwin in October 1937:

I knew you'd do the job as well as it could be done—but aren't you doing too much? You've got to last for all our sakes and don't work yourself out in middle life.

Tweedsmuir himself came to admit that the Arctic tour, though he felt splendid at the time, had perhaps been rather much for a man of his age, 'and the unconscious fatigue went straight to my digestion.' In 1936 he had been given a thorough overhaul at Montreal ('one of the best clinics in the world') by Dr Jonathan Meakins ('one of the greatest doctors on the American Continent'), who gave him a clean bill for heart, lungs, circulation and blood-pressure, and prescribed a regime for his gastritis. The standby of his diet was poached eggs and oysters: this led to some difficulty at formal parties at Government House, where protocol decrees that when His Excellency has finished, everyone else's plate is swept away. It is difficult to spin out a poached egg or half-a-dozen oysters: Tweedsmuir would let fragments congeal on his plate to give his guests a chance to deal with their better-filled dishes. He kept on assuring his family at home that 'there is nothing dangerous about my ailments, which are just like a bad toothache,' and talked of 'discomfort,' not illness. But in spite of recurring hopes that the trouble would be cleared up, he had to face the fact that it would always be with him. 'My innards are not good but they can be borne,' he told Stair Gillon early in 1938; 'but after all each of us has to live his life on the terms on which it is given to him.'

Canada was giving Tweedsmuir more than physical refreshment. Though he himself was in a more exalted position, it was easier than in his English years to live in tune with the values of his upbringing. Here were no young men of romantic lineage, no glamour of Londonderry House. Men were judged by what they did and by what they, and not their ancestors, were. When strangers meet, in the world Tweedsmuir frequented in England, the questions they ask—concerning school, college, regiment, family—often seem to be sighting-shots, aimed at placing each other in the intricate and overlapping hierarchies of the English social system. Between Canadians such questions are asked rather with the aim of establishing links between two human beings in a country of vast spaces and small population, where mutual help is not a virtue but a necessity. Down North and in the Prairies, on the frontiers of civilisation, Tweedsmuir had found a moral simplicity and force that were deeply refreshing. He was seeing for himself the truth of the words which he had written nearly forty years before in the *Spectator*:

Canada is essentially a country of the larger air, where men can still face the old primeval forces of Nature and be braced into vigour, and withal so beautiful that it can readily inspire that romantic patriotism which is one of the most priceless assets of a people.

Canada was giving him back some of the 'morning hopefulness' that he had known in South Africa. His Scottish friends were per-

haps readier than his London ones to appreciate the glory as well
as the duty of Canada. Stair Gillon wrote from Edinburgh that
'your old friends love to think of you in that great place in that great
country and to go on reminding you at intervals that we believe in
you and your work and wish you well in it.' Amery, who was in
Canada in 1936, found him 'supremely happy in his work as
Governor-General.'

After two years Tweedsmuir felt involved in Canada. He would
give his family in Scotland and his mother-in-law in London news
of rainfall and soil-drifting, grain-crops and dam-building, as if
these could not fail to be of interest to all. He grew to feel that, as
well as fostering a sense of loyalty to Canada, he had another prime
task: 'to get more quality into Canadian life and a wider outlook':

> The Canadians are a great people, with every human good quality; but
> having had to struggle pretty hard for a livelihood, they have been apt to
> miss some of the essentials of civilisation. In scientific and technical work
> they are quite admirable, but in what might be called 'the humanities'
> they are a little backward . . . The influence of the Churches, both Roman
> and Protestant, is apt to run on narrow and conventional lines, when the
> problems are not narrow and conventional.

When, one St Andrew's Day in Ottawa, he drew attention to some
of the faults in the Scottish character—'We are inclined to accept
the second- or the third-rate and praise it unduly merely because it
is our own'—he may also have had Canadians in mind.

To do such work was profoundly satisfying, and he would not
think of cutting it short. 'The papers, here and in the States,' he
told Sir Alan Lascelles early in 1938,

> have been full of idiotic rumours that I am going to be transferred to
> Washington. There has been this much in them that the President and
> Cordell Hull keep on saying they want me. But only His Majesty and the
> Canadian Government can move me, and the Canadian Government cer-
> tainly won't agree. I am determined not to desert Mrs Micawber, for my
> work here is only beginning.

Neither drawback nor asset, but simply to be counted as part of
the job, was Tweedsmuir's relationship with Mackenzie King. At
the official level Governor-General and Prime Minister had no
great difficulty in getting on. But Mackenzie King had originally
envisaged himself and Tweedsmuir as 'getting on' at a far more
personal level. Here was a Governor-General of his own choosing
and of his own age; like himself a Scot and a Presbyterian; like himself (for Mackenzie King was proud of the books he had written

and of his writer friends) a literary man. They had often met before they became officially connected, and Tweedsmuir had introduced him to far more people in Britain than he would have known on his own account.

When Tweedsmuir arrived in Canada, so Violet Markham told him, all Mackenzie King's sentiments and emotions

were keyed up to the highest point about you. His second house at Kingsmere [in the Gatineau Hills] was enlarged and beautified and rooms added for the express purpose of occupation by yourself. He dreamt of long walks and talks with you in the woods and among those distressing ruins.

Mackenzie King had re-erected stones from a demolished house in the form of a ruin on a hill and kept on adding to it—now a portico from the Bank of Montreal, now a Tudor gateway from an Ottawa mansion, even a block from the Palace of Westminster. 'Seen from a distance,' he told Tweedsmuir in a letter of 19 July 1935,

the semi-circular shaped window, which is some twenty feet high and sixteen feet in diameter, with five larger apertures separated by hand-carved stone pillars, has the appearance of a Greek temple. The door, as it is reconstructed, is not unlike a small battlemented tower. I think and speak of it as my 'abbey ruin,' and to more minds than my own it has brought thoughts of Melrose, and even of the Parthenon! In the construction of this ruin, over the stones of which the ivy has already begun to climb, you were constantly in my thoughts. I am looking forward with childish delight to showing it to you when you come. It is not the Old World, but it is as nearly like some bit of it as anything I have been able to make and have in store for you.

Later in the same letter he wrote:

I shall have you at my side as a counsellor and friend and shall be holding toward yourself a similar position.

He would have not only the perfect Governor-General, but the perfect friend.

Tweedsmuir, with every wish to discharge the first rôle, could not fulfil the second. He admired Mackenzie King as a politician of almost unparalleled dexterity: he was prepared to give him all the sympathy and support for which a lonely Prime Minister may have to look beyond his political colleagues. But he could not bring himself wholeheartedly to *like* Mackenzie King, and still less to give him the mystical-intellectual companionship he craved.

The surface similarities—both Scots, both Presbyterian—masked deep differences. Mackenzie King was a bachelor with a cult of his mother: there were photographs of her on almost every table in Laurier House, his Ottawa home, and in the place of honour, on an easel lit from below as a sort of shrine, an oil-painting of her in the same attitude as Whistler's mother. (Mrs King is reading a book, which can be discerned as Morley's *Life of Gladstone*, open at the chapter, 'The Prime Minister.') 'That mausoleum of horrors Laurier House,' declared Violet Markham, 'is like wife and child to him.' He was a strict Calvinist, with his beliefs unmodified from childhood, accepting predestination—and shocked that Tweedsmuir did not—and convinced that he was to be saved, and to be great. Convinced too that his interests *must* also be the country's interests, the world's; and that his friendship with Tweedsmuir was fore-ordained. (In one letter he spoke of 'the Providence that has made our friendship and companionship a part of His will.')

'Rex's mind,' noted Miss Markham (Rex was the name he liked an inner few to use), 'was uninhibited by either metaphysics or philosophy,' and he managed also to be a spiritualist. He greatly admired the works of J. M. Barrie, to which Tweedsmuir was anti-pathetic. Immensely tough and crafty in his political life, in his private relations he was a great sentimentalist. He never put himself out for his friends, or allowed them to make demands upon him, but he longed to be loved. And he had to be first.

Tweedsmuir found the spiritualism, the general softness, dis-tasteful. Mackenzie King, weeping buckets over being misunder-stood, embarrassed him. Mackenzie King's style—in talk, speeches and letters—recalled the unctuousness of that type of Scottish Liberal against which he had reacted so strongly in his youth. Happy in his family life, firm in his religious beliefs, with plenty of work on hand, he had not the least wish to spend long intimate evenings with his Prime Minister: John and Rex mulling over life and religion as if they were a couple of undergraduates.

Both men were absorbed by politics; but here also their interests were of a different kind. Tweedsmuir's was the historian's, full of curiosity, concerned with ideas, and rather detached. Mackenzie King's was the working politician's, concerned with compromises and majorities, with securing and retaining power, the interest of a man committed to the belief that the country cannot do without him.

So although there were few, and in the main unimportant, causes of dissension in their official relations, though there was a general cordiality in their social contacts, there was an undercurrent of uneasiness and resentment on Mackenzie King's part—on one occasion he even asked for an appointment, so that they could discuss the unsatisfactory nature of their personal relationship. A great stickler for protocol, he addressed Tweedsmuir as 'Your Excellency,' yet was disappointed when Tweedsmuir answered with 'Prime Minister' instead of 'Rex.' He was sad because the Tweedsmuirs, though they often went out to Kingsmere for the day, never stayed in his guest-house there. He was jealous of Tweedsmuir's greater social ease and of the number of people who far preferred the company of the Governor-General, who wanted them to speak about themselves, to that of the Prime Minister, with his endless talk about his mother and his old rebel grandfather. He was sensitive about not ranking No. 1 in Canada: after visiting Tweedsmuir's successor in 1940, he confided to his diary with true feeling if imperfect syntax that

> It is an absurdity for a Prime Minister of a country to have second place in the public eye to any one in official position not belonging to one's own country and in fact appointed by the Government of the country itself.

He was sensitive too about any fame which came to the Governor-General through his also being John Buchan—and perhaps about the legends which circulated about him. ('One is that I speak perfect French—notoriously untrue; another is that I can beat any Canadian, however young, at walking, which may have been once true, but alas! not now.') He was distinctly put out by the different treatment they were given by the Press. The Prime Minister's speeches, long and cliché-ridden, were reported very briefly; the Governor-General's, short and lively, were usually reported in full, not only in the local press, but all over the Dominion.*

So again and again offence would be taken. Mackenzie King, peppering his letter with 'Excellency,' would declare that both their personal friendship and official relationship had been threatened; Tweedsmuir would briskly explain, or say he never meant what Mackenzie King had thought he meant; and Mackenzie King, now writing 'My dear Friend,' and signing himself 'Rex,' would make it up, protesting renewed friendship and admiration, and the tiff

* On the menu of a Press Gallery dinner to Tweedsmuir at Ottawa on 22 April 1939 was printed a ditty 'His Excellency,' to be sung to the tune of 'The Laird of Cockpen':

> O the Laird o' the Tweed, he's wee but he's great,
> He's travelled through life at a glorious rate . . .
> His speeches are short, and he speaks 'em with ease
> (O Laird, teach the art tae our local M.P.s).

would be over—if 'tiff' can be used of a situation where one party is excessively quick to take offence, and the other doggedly bent on not giving it.

Tweedsmuir would seek occasion to congratulate or praise Mackenzie King—on a performance in Parliament ('I do not think your words about our relations with the United States could be bettered'), on his voice when broadcasting, on his appointments to non-political offices ('You have a real conscience in these matters, like Asquith'). He would gladly, when requested, help with speeches, which Mackenzie King found heavy weather: 'I fear they are very gewgaw and trite,' he wrote when priming Mackenzie King with notes before he departed for the Coronation in 1937, 'but I know how barren one begins to feel when one has many speeches to make on the same topic.' When Mackenzie King was downhearted ('I have been so dreadfully pressed . . . and am so frightfully fatigued') Tweedsmuir would beg him to relax, to take life a bit more easily. He would dedicate *Augustus* to him. He would even, at a pinch, find a word of praise for the ruins. Praise, congratulation, encouragement, help, concern, would be warmly, even gushingly, received ('I have just read over the "collection of notes" and they have given me new heart and hope'); but there would be no guarantee that the warmth would not be suddenly turned off, that a cold blast would not unpredictably blow through their relations, that 'Your devoted friend, Rex' would not once again be 'Yours very sincerely, W. L. Mackenzie King.'

Yet this undercurrent remained an undercurrent—from Tweedsmuir's point of view it was just one of the conditions of the job—and did not much affect the general stability of the relations between Governor-General and Prime Minister. Nor could this relation any longer count as a major factor in the Canadian political scene (Bruce Hutchison's study of Mackenzie King, *The Incredible Canadian*, barely mentions Tweedsmuir at all). And whatever his private irritations Tweedsmuir kept them strictly to himself. With one or two close friends in Canada, with his political correspondents in Britain, he would discuss other Ministers: never his Prime Minister. And he had never the slightest doubt that Mackenzie King was one of the ablest politicians Canada had ever produced, and the only man who could give the country a stable Government in those difficult years. And when Mackenzie King came to sum up their relationship, to Amery, 'Nothing could have been happier than our official relations,' he said; 'we never had a real difference of view on anything.'

CHAPTER FIFTEEN

STOIC

1938–40

'There comes a time to everyone when the world narrows for him to a strait alley, with Death at the end of it.'

John Buchan: *Salute to Adventurers*

The year 1937 ended sadly for Tweedsmuir, with his mother's death. On 20 December, when the news reached him, he wrote to Anna:

I have been spending the afternoon in bed and thinking of the long road Mother and I travelled together. I think my furthest back clear memory of her is in a green velvet dress, rather plump, at Walter's christening. Thirty years ago we never thought we would have her so long with us, and what a blessing she has been! I begin to realise how much I will miss her, for I always thought about everything 'What will Mother think of that?'

Clear in his mind's eye was the picture of her at the foot of the staircase in the Citadel when they said goodbye in Quebec in 1936, and in his head ran a ditty which Mr Buchan used to sing:

> My auld mither deed
> In the year auchty-nine
> And I've never had peace
> In the warld sinsyne.

As the condolences showered in, Tweedsmuir reflected what a funny fate it was for the minister's wife of the John Knox Church in the Gorbals 'to have called forth expressions of sympathy from the King, the President of the U.S.A., Catholic Cardinals and Anglican Archbishops!' He felt bitterly not being able to go to the funeral in Peebles, but his four children were there, and he was pleased to hear that the Canadian Prime Minister had been represented by Colonel Georges Vanier (who was himself to become Governor-General of Canada), 'one of the nicest people in the world and a most gallant soldier.'

He was concerned about his sister as she adjusted her life:

I do hope you will be firm about giving yourself leisure. . . . You are a professional woman and your hours of work must be respected. You ought to let no one come into the house any day before tea-time. Otherwise you will simply turn into a temperance hotel.

And concerned too about his Masterton uncles up at the Bamflat—'I cannot get these two poor old men out of my head'—and the long lost Uncle Tom in Australia. His thoughts continually went back to his childhood, and he told Anna that when he came over in the summer to be installed as Chancellor of Edinburgh University, they must have a day in Pathhead 'going over our old haunts.'

He now wrote regularly to Anna, as he had done to his mother, telling her about the opening of Parliament, the LL.D. at Laval University (which pleased him particularly, for he was the first Governor-General to be honoured there since Dufferin), the visitors to Government House, the books he was reading. He cheered her up about the situation in Europe. In a letter written on 14 March 1938, just after Hitler had taken over Austria, he wrote:

I do not myself quite see what there is to fuss about. Austria will be much more comfortable, economically, under Germany's wing. That should have been done long ago in the Versailles Treaty. The chief trouble will be if there is any real threat to Czechoslovakia; but there again, I think, the frontier should be rectified. Surely the Versailles arrangement was the most half-witted thing ever perpetrated! We are beginning to realise now how strongly Balfour and Milner fought against it, and how wholly it was the creation of France—to her own detriment.

Some of his correspondents in London took a rather different view. 'Suddenly,' wrote L. S. Amery to Tweedsmuir,

we all realised that we were in the presence of a Power which might not hesitate to strike at us, regardless of any pledge, if the moment seemed favourable.

And Lord Crawford described how, all at once, it had become impossible to forecast the future, how everywhere was 'a sense of impending tragedy.'

But Tweedsmuir continued to think that nothing very terrible had happened. What he could not understand, as he surveyed the European scene, was the resignation of Anthony Eden as Foreign Secretary three weeks before Hitler's march into Austria, the reason given being disagreement with Chamberlain over the timing of talks with Mussolini.

Tweedsmuir sent his good wishes to the new Foreign Secretary, Lord Halifax, begging him to make contact with Dr Weizmann, and commending to him the new American Ambassador in London, Joseph Kennedy: 'He is a man of great ability and a good deal of independence of character, and I hope he will get the proper sort of welcome.' And he wrote to Chamberlain on 26 March:

Like everybody else, I was completely puzzled by Anthony Eden's resignation, and now that I have read the recent despatches I am more puzzled than ever.

Chamberlain could have answered—but does not appear to—that Tweedsmuir himself had a hand in the events which led to the resignation. To follow this sequence we must go back to Roosevelt's visit to Quebec in August 1936, and to Tweedsmuir's visit to Washington in April 1937, and his long talks with Roosevelt and Cordell Hull. At Quebec there had been talk about the possibility of the United States intervening 'beneficially' in the affairs of Europe. Tweedsmuir told the King:

It was on this point that the President specially wanted to talk to me. If he is returned to power in November . . . he will make a great effort to do something towards the pacification of Europe. What form this may take is not yet clear, but it will be, I think, an invitation to the leaders of the great Powers to confer, before it is too late, not on any particular question, but on the need of doing something to save civilisation before it crashes.

This suggestion of a world conference to be called by the President was further discussed at Washington, and immediately on his return to Canada Tweedsmuir summarised their conclusions in a memorandum to the President.* He also gave the gist of the conversations in a private letter to Baldwin (8 April 1937), making it clear that his standing was that of an 'Amicus curiae (with no kind of status except as a private friend)'.

The important point was my private conversations on international questions, with the President, which was really the object of my visit. We began them last summer in Quebec, and have continued them by correspondence. My Prime Minister a month ago, on his visit to Washington, carried the matter further, and last week I had the privilege of several hours of private conversation. I have, of course, no official standing in this matter, and I am only reporting to you as to a private friend. But I think you ought to know what the President feels.

He has his country behind him as no President has ever had since Washington. He is quite clear that in the event of another world war

* Printed as Appendix B on pp. 473–5.

America could not stay out, and that her participation would probably mean something in the nature of a domestic revolution. He therefore feels that international peace is a bread-and-butter problem for his country, and no mere piece of idealism. His general idea is to make an appeal for a Conference to deal with the fundamental economic problems, which are behind all the unrest. He believes that now is the right moment, when so many things have happened to make the dictators pause and consider— the British defence programme; the fiasco of the German aeroplanes and the Italian troops in Spain; the strong stand taken by the Vatican; the advertisement to the world of the closer understanding of the Western democracies, and so forth. Any such Conference would, of course, merely take soundings and try to come to some agreement on general principles, which could be worked out in detail by special committees. He is not clear yet about the right peg on which to hang his appeal, or the right moment to make it, or the best place for the Conference to meet. But he is determined himself to be present—which I think would have a great moral effect—and he believes that he would have America whole-heartedly behind him.

I see many difficulties in the scheme, most of which I have put before him. But at the same time I feel that it does offer some kind of hope, and that it is very much in our interests to meet any proposals half-way. My Prime Minister, who sails on the 24th for England, is fully informed about the President's mind, and can give you further details. . . .

We have a chance now, which we have never had before, of coming to that real understanding with America on which I believe the future of the world depends.

Baldwin, deep in preparations for the Coronation and looking forward to his own retirement, apparently did not respond. When he did retire, Tweedsmuir lost no time in reiterating the main point of the Washington conversations to the new Prime Minister, Neville Chamberlain, in a letter on 29 May. The response (8 June) was luke-warm: Chamberlain, like many of his Cabinet colleagues, thought Roosevelt a bit of a demagogue and was dubious about the economics of the New Deal. In the past, he told Tweedsmuir, he had found the United States 'extremely unhelpful, and they have some-how become aware of my opinion about them.'

In June Tweedsmuir, in an address to the Canadian-American Conference at Kingston which was broadcast all over North Ameri-ca, expressed himself as strongly as he could on the subject of British-American relations.

I believe—I have always believed—that on a close understanding between the British Commonwealth and the Republic of the United States depends the peace and freedom of the world.

On 24 September Roosevelt wrote to Tweedsmuir from Wyoming:

I do not dare be away from Washington long because of the international

clouds. I am, as you know, an impatient soul and it is especially difficult
not 'to speak out loud in meeting.' I like to think that you also occasionally
suffer in silence in the presence of expert and wise counsellors!

Within a few days however (on 5 October) the President did 'speak
out loud' at Chicago about the breakdown of international law, with
the Germans, Italians and Japanese in mind, though he named no
names. He proposed a general boycott of all aggressors, 'a quarantine . . . to protect the health of the community against the spread of
the disease.'

Tweedsmuir wrote at once (8 October) in admiration of

your great speech in Chicago—the bravest and most important utterance
of any public man for many a day. If your country is strongly behind you
I believe that you have it in your power to save a rather precarious civilisation. God bless and prosper you!

The same day he wrote to Gilbert Murray:

I keep in very close touch with Roosevelt, and his recent speech at
Chicago was the culmination of a long conspiracy between us. (This must
be kept secret!) I think there is just a chance of America now coming back
into the fold and working along with the European democracies. I have
many domestic troubles here to face, but I feel that almost the most useful
work I can do is in connection with the U.S.A. I have Cordell Hull coming
up to stay with me in a fortnight for some serious talks.

Murray wrote back that this development 'may alter the whole
course of world history, though one does not dare to hope too much.'

Tweedsmuir reported his impression of the talks with Cordell
Hull to Chamberlain, who answered (on 19 November):

In recent speeches I have gone out of my way to encourage those sections
of American opinion that seem to have welcomed the President's Chicago
speech. I have done so because I wish to give the utmost possible support
to any tendency towards a closer understanding and a more complete
community of purpose between our two nations. Nevertheless I am very
conscious of the difficulties that have still to be overcome by the President
before it can be said that he has his people behind him. His Chicago speech
can be regarded, I think, as evidence that he recognises the need for the
education of public opinion; but I should doubt whether such education
can yet be said to have proceeded very far and it would seem likely that its
development must take time. No doubt the set-back in trade will continue
to occupy public attention in the States and to divert discussions from
external matters.

Chamberlain ended with what may have been meant as a warning:

I have written at length, if only for the purpose of showing my appreciation
of your letter to me. Needless to say, I realise how careful you have to be—

as Governor-General—not to lay yourself open to the charge (in Canada or elsewhere) that you are going outside your province and are seeking to influence 'politics.'

In January 1938 Roosevelt took action on the lines of the memorandum in which Tweedsmuir had summarised their talks in April 1937. He informed the British Government that he was proposing to summon the whole Diplomatic Corps in Washington to the White House, when he would speak of the horrors of modern war, the need for reduction of armaments, the keeping of treaties, and equal access to raw materials; and would then call for a world conference to deal with these questions. He was informing the British Government first, for only if he were assured of their whole-hearted support would he proceed with his plan.

Chamberlain, in spite of the letters from Tweedsmuir, seems to have been startled: he referred to the Roosevelt proposal as a 'bomb,' 'a bolt from the blue.' Though he acknowledged American good intentions, he was deeply sceptical of American readiness to follow up inspiring words with practical action. Also he considered that this proposal for a world conference would cut across his own plan for direct approaches to Mussolini and Hitler, and he was confident that *he* knew best how to deal with the Dictators. So without informing his Foreign Secretary, Eden, who was on holiday in the South of France, or any of his other Cabinet colleagues, he sent an answer which Sumner Welles (the Assistant Secretary of State) described as 'a douche of cold water.' Eden, outraged at not being consulted, and dismayed at this rebuff to the kind of American initiative which he had hoped and worked for, would have resigned then and there if the whole business had not been secret. The episode sharply exposed the difference between himself and Chamberlain; and Chamberlain's insistence on starting talks immediately with the Italian Government (news of which was leaked through the Italian Embassy in London) gave him the public occasion for the resignation which puzzled Tweedsmuir. Eden continued to believe that a comparable opportunity to avert war never occurred again— or was never created—after Chamberlain's douche of cold water.*

---

* Winston Churchill's comment in *The Gathering Storm* (1948), p. 199, was:

'No event could have been more likely to stave off, or even prevent, war than the arrival of the United States in the circle of European hates and fears. To Britain it was a matter almost of life and death. No one can measure in retrospect its effect upon the course of events in Austria and later at Munich. We must regard its rejection—for such it was—as the loss of the last frail chance to save the world from tyranny otherwise than by war. [*continued overleaf*]

In May 1938 Tweedsmuir made a short visit to the Prairies, whose plight had been so much on his mind. He had tried to persuade Roosevelt to cross the border on one of his western tours:

It would give them enormous pleasure, and the kind of 'buck-up' that they want. You see, they have the same problems as your own Middle West and they are full, too, of American settlers.

This spring there had been enough rain to make the black soil of Saskatchewan safe for crops, and he came back much more hopeful than in 1936:

I went all over the worst drought areas, which I have already seen twice before. This year things are very different. The pastures are as green as Oxfordshire, the wheat is springing, and the sloughs are full of water. It is impossible to overpraise the rehabilitation work of the Canadian Government, both in irrigation and dam-making, and in dealing with the drifting soil. The trouble is that they get no publicity for their successes here, for the rest of Canada knows nothing about what they are doing in the Prairies.

It was on this tour that he paid his visit to Val-Marie which was described in Chapter Thirteen.

Early in June there was a week among the lakes of Eastern Ontario, travelling mostly by boat. He described it to Susan, who had gone home to Elsfield in the spring:

I have never seen lovelier country or a pleasanter way of travelling than down that old canal. We passed several most flourishing little cities, and at every lock there were hordes of children, veterans, and Women's Institute representatives all clamouring for you. . . . That bit of Ontario is like nothing else in Canada. It is simply Oxfordshire or Warwickshire, only if possible greener and more flowery; and in Oxfordshire one does not see a bald-headed eagle sitting in its nest!

'That Mr Chamberlain, with his limited outlook and inexperience of the European scene, should have possessed the self-sufficiency to wave away the proffered hand stretched out across the Atlantic leaves one, even at this date, breathless with amazement.'

Lord Attlee, leader of the Opposition at the time of Roosevelt's proposal, gave his opinion in conversation with Francis Williams in 1959 (*A Prime Minister Remembers*, 1961, p. 17):

Williams: What about Roosevelt's proposal in January 1938 for a conference in Washington to try to ease international tension?

Attlee: Chamberlain never told us about that either. He turned it down out of hand on his own: an odd thing to do. Never even told his Foreign Secretary, Eden, I believe. There was no consultation at all, no information given to the Opposition that this had come forward. We knew nothing about it until it was all over.

Williams: What would you have done if you'd been in power?

Attlee: Accepted right away. America was the great uncertainty everywhere. If Hitler had realised that there was also America, and America was going to stand in, he would have thought twice about it, or his generals would.

Later in the month he went to the States to receive honorary degrees from Yale and Harvard. First there was a brief visit to New York with Johnnie, who was on his way home to see his family before going off to Baffin Land for a year, as under-post-manager for the Hudson's Bay Company at Cape Dorset. They lunched with the Morgans in Wall Street, 'where I think more millions of money must have been represented than anywhere else in the world,' and visited Edward Sheldon.

At Yale President Seymour addressed him as 'versatile as Richard Hannay, reliable as Mr Standfast,' and in his speech after receiving the degree Tweedsmuir refused to

talk the usual platitudes about how closely related the United States and the British Empire are, and what good friends they should be. I believe most profoundly in that friendship, but don't let's get self-conscious about it. . . . I think the best way for Americans and Britons to understand each other is not by analysing their feelings, but by doing things together.

He found Yale

a most wonderful place, and the new Gothic buildings are the finest modern architecture I have ever seen. What an impression of opulence and efficiency these American Universities give one!

At Harvard, where he stayed with the Merrimans, he received his degree along with Thomas Mann, Walt Disney and Serge Koussevitsky, and gave the Commencement Address in Harvard Yard, taking as his subject Henry Adams's description of himself as 'a conservative Christian anarchist.'

At the end of the month he sailed for Britain, his first visit for three years. He hoped not to be away for more than five or six weeks, 'for having got into the Canadian atmosphere I don't want to break the continuity.' He was delighted to be back at Elsfield, but it could be for only a few days. He had to be up in London for a thorough vetting by Lord Dawson of Penn, for some talks with the Prime Minister, Baldwin, Halifax, Hoare, Eden and others, and for some parties.

Last night the Londonderrys gave a dinner for us as Queen Mary wanted to talk to us. It was a regular Edwardian affair—gigantic tiaras and half a dozen Orders of the Garter—the Portlands, the Clarendons, the Crewes, the Duke of Alba etc.

On 20 July he was installed as Chancellor of Edinburgh University and, it now being his turn to confer degrees, was able to cap three old friends: Violet Markham, Walter Elliot and W. S. Morrison. In his address on 'The Interpreter's House,' discussing the rôle of the University and the prospects for its students, he drew on his experience of Canadian and American education as well as British, and ended up with a strong plea for more research in the social sciences.

He had planned to do all sorts of things in Scotland: to stay some time with Walter and Anna at Peebles, to revisit Pathhead, to walk with Stair Gillon on the Tweedsmuir hills. But there was to be none of that. Lord Dawson had been reassuring about his health, but insisted on his doing a cure and trying to put on some weight. 'You have always kept the figure of a schoolboy,' a friend put it, 'which is nice until the age of forty, but then becomes chilly.' So immediately after the Edinburgh ceremonies he went off to Sir Edmund Spriggs's clinic at Ruthin Castle in the Vale of Clwyd and stayed there till mid-September. 'You must not pity me,' he told Susan; 'I console myself with reflecting how many good men have had to endure a spell in jug.' And he ended another letter with 'Much, much love from Johannes Incarceratus, otherwise John the Binned.' He read—Sterne, Sydney Smith's letters, Canning's speeches, and two thrillers, A. E. W. Mason's *Königsmark* and Michael Innes's *Lament for a Maker*—and he rested, put on a stone in weight, and did no work except, at royal request, to draft a speech for King George VI to deliver at Clydebank when the Queen launched the *Queen Elizabeth*.

He came back to London in the last week of September, when the crisis over the Sudeten Germans in Czechoslovakia came to a head. Chamberlain flew three times to Germany to meet Hitler and finally at Munich signed the agreement which, on his return, he declared would mean 'peace in our time.'

Alastair Buchan has a memory of the night Chamberlain came back from Munich.

On the evening of September 30, 1938, I was dining with my father at my grandmother's house in Upper Grosvenor Street, for the chance of a last talk before he returned to Canada and I to Oxford. At about nine o'clock an impending transatlantic telephone call from Mackenzie King in Montreal was announced. King, so my father reported when the call was over, was in a state of high excitement about the Munich agreement and had called J.B. direct in order to ensure that his warmest congratulations to Chamberlain as the saviour of world peace, and his most emphatic expressions of Canadian solidarity and her support for the four-power agreement on Czechoslovakia, should be personally conveyed to the British Prime Minister with the greatest speed and authority.

Attempts to reach Downing Street on the telephone proved futile, so my father sat down and wrote a personal letter to Chamberlain giving the gist of Mackenzie King's flood of transatlantic eloquence, and asked me to take it to Number Ten. But the approaches to Downing Street were densely packed with a seething mob of people, made light-headed by relief from fear, and I could make no headway. Eventually I found a friendly police inspector to whom I explained my errand and who, with the help of several colleagues, forced a passage to the door. Since the letter bore no official superscription it was hard to get anyone inside to take it seriously until I encountered Lord Dunglass (now Sir Alec Douglas-Home) the Prime Minister's P.P.S., who fortunately recognised my father's handwriting.

For twenty-five years I have considered this a most eccentric way of conveying a fairly important message from one Commonwealth Government to another, namely using a head of State as an intermediary, until I recently read Mr Vincent Massey's memoirs, *What's Past is Prologue*. Here Mr Massey, who was Canadian High Commissioner in London from 1935 to 1946, recalls King's admonition that he was not to regard himself as a normal ambassador—perhaps because King considered him too Anglophil—and that King would deal directly with London on all important matters. Mr Massey recalls that he himself received a telephone call from King later that night—euphoria always encourages communication—the first time he had heard directly from his Prime Minister since the previous spring.

For all the reassuring words, it was in an atmosphere of crisis that Tweedsmuir sailed for Canada early in October. But he carried with him one heartening piece of news. King George VI and Queen Elizabeth had agreed to visit Canada the following year. Tweedsmuir had first raised the question as soon as King George had succeeded to the throne; Mackenzie King had followed it up when he was in London for the Coronation in May 1937; and now on this visit, Tweedsmuir told Anna, 'I pressed it with the persistence of a horse-leech. As soon as I got Neville on my side I knew it would be all right, for the King was most sympathetic.' So delighted was Tweedsmuir that he could not help telling his secret to a young Canadian M.P., Paul Martin (later Minister for External Affairs), who was crossing on the same boat. During a walk round the deck Tweedsmuir gave him the news, adding, rather to Mr Martin's embarrassment, that no other Canadian knew it yet, not even the Prime Minister.

The more Tweedsmuir thought about the Munich agreement, the more he thought Chamberlain was right. 'My own view, for what it is worth,' he wrote to B. K. Sandwell of the Toronto *Saturday Night* (26 November 1938), is that Chamberlain took the right course. The mistake he made was to represent the result as anything in the nature of a triumph, for it was merely a miserable acceptance of the lesser of two evils . . .

If, as Chamberlain believed, and I believe, war, though it would have ended Germany, might also end civilisation, the only plan was to avert it at almost any cost, in the belief that every month made it more unlikely.

To Lord Halifax he wrote on 5 November:

> I whole-heartedly agree with the policy of you and Neville, and I believe that by the grace of God it may be the beginning of a new era in Europe, when war may steadily go out of the picture.

In Tweedsmuir's support of appeasement there was nothing (as there was with certain Tories) of sympathy with Nazis or Fascists, nothing of admiration for the dictators. Indeed, he could hardly bring himself to take them seriously: 'This tom-fool Nazi rule,' he wrote to Amery, and 'a couple of lunatics' was his way of referring to Hitler and Mussolini. Dictatorship he saw as a consequence of (a favourite phrase) 'a failure of nerve.' But like many other Britons he did feel that Germany had been given a raw deal at Versailles, he distrusted France, and placed no hope in Russia. The war had given him his fill of Europe—he had been only three times on the Continent since—and a wish to keep out of its troubles. 'What an unholy mess things are in in the Old World!' he wrote to John Edgar shortly after Hitler's remilitarisation of the Rhineland, and later was worried that Anna should be so preoccupied with the politics of 'that distressing old Europe.' To Mackenzie King, attending the League Assembly at Geneva ('I felt sorry for you in the dust and discomfort of Europe'), he once wrote (29 September 1936):

> The Empire, if it remains detached, and keeps its head, can play a great part in pacification; but that part will be impossible if we are once dragged into the European dog-fight. What Europe is witnessing at present is not a conflict of genuine principles so much as the wrangling of ambitious mob-leaders, who have behind them nations who have lost their nerve. In this wrangling we have no real interest, except as peace-makers . . . Hammer into the British Cabinet's head that the most loyal people of Canada will refuse to return to the old eighteenth-century game in Europe. We have other things to think about.

Personalities played some part in forming his view: he trusted Neville Chamberlain, with whom he had fished for salmon in the Dee, and he distrusted Winston Churchill, the most eloquent of the anti-appeasers. Above all he had the absolute horror of war of a man who had seen friend after friend killed between 1914 and 1918. At a lunch to Norman Angell in 1930 he spoke of 'the waste of war, the ludicrous folly of war, the cruel squandering of splendid material.' In *The King's Grace* (1935) he wrote of some of the miseries and disorders that followed the first War:

> Little farms in Touraine, in the Scottish Highlands, in the Apennines, were untilled because there were no men; Armenia had lost half her people: the folk of North Syria were dying of famine; Indian villages and African tribes had been blotted out by plague; whole countries had ceased for the moment to exist, except as geographical terms. Such were but a few of the consequences of the kindling of war in a world grown too expert in destruction, a world where all nations were part one of another!

Every November in his Poppy Day broadcast he would underline the 'horror and futility,' the 'folly and barbarity' of war. He was shocked at so many people's short memories:

> The lesson of the four years' struggle seems to have been largely forgotten. People talk glibly of new wars, as if the thing were a natural incident of national policy.

He could not bring himself to believe that anyone could be so wicked or so mad as to start this hideous process again, that, another generation—to which his three sons belonged*—should be engulfed as his had been. And so, though many of his friends at home, like Amery, were critical of the policy of appeasement, Tweedsmuir remained firm in his support of Chamberlain, firm in his belief that anything was better than war.

In the uneasy winter after Munich much of Tweedsmuir's energies went into helping Hitler's victims. In November he wrote to Anna that

> I am trying to get Canada to take some 5000 Sudeten German Social Democrats who are skilled in the glass industry. We have all the raw materials here, and it would be a new industry for Canada.

Two months later he reported that Canada was taking in small groups from Central Europe with special techniques in glove-making, glass and pottery. He helped many individual refugees find work, among them some Austrian ski-experts: 'They will be very useful in developing the ski-resorts in the West.' And he was

---

* Three days before the Armistice in 1918 Stair Gillon ended a letter with 'Love to Susie and the newest recruit of the army of eternal peace [the recently born Alastair]. His triumphs will be football, the horse, the sérac and the skate and ski and the sea—not fatuous war.'

indignant that the British Government was not doing more to help Jews from Germany to get into Palestine.

Chief among his activities in this winter of 1938–9 were preparations for the Royal Visit in May. Tweedsmuir's aim was to show what the Statute of Westminster meant in practice. He wanted Canadians to see *their* King perform his royal duties, supported by Canadian ministers with no British minister in sight. It must be 'Canada's own show.' He also hoped that the visit would help the growth of national feeling. In his mind were thoughts of Walter Scott organising the visit of George IV to Edinburgh in 1822 so that Scotland should have a feeling of sharing the monarchy, and Highlanders and Lowlanders should have the chance of joining together on a major national occasion.

How to translate the Statute of Westminster into the actualities of a tour was a delicate affair. This was the first visit of a reigning monarch to a Dominion, and precedents were being made. A good deal of the work fell on Tweedsmuir and his staff, particularly on Shuldham Redfern; and the King's assistant private secretary, Alan Lascelles, came over for a fortnight in February to co-ordinate plans. First of all the main idea must be put across. 'How extraordinarily ignorant,' wrote Tweedsmuir to Lord Crawford,

even the well-informed at home are about the new status of the Dominions! I see that *The Times* assumes that a British Minister will accompany the King—which would be starkly impossible, for the King's only advisers in Canada are his Canadian Ministers.

(Sir Gerald Campbell, arriving as High Commissioner for the United Kingdom in 1939, found that he 'had mighty little idea of what it means to a Dominion to be independent of all control from the country it once called Mother.') Tweedsmuir felt strongly that 'I should keep as much in the background as possible, and let it be Canada's show. I cease to exist as Viceroy, and retain only a shadowy legal existence as Governor-General in council.'

So, after meeting the King and Queen at Quebec, and entertaining them in Ottawa, he proposed to disappear. But soon a snag was struck: the Prime Minister thought that, as the elected representative of the Canadian people, *he* should be the first to welcome the King and Queen, and he made a constitutional issue of it. Letters and telegrams passed between Ottawa and London, between Laurier House and Rideau Hall: perhaps Tweedsmuir could meet them on board ship, and Mackenzie King on dry land? In the end it was the Prime Minister who went to Quebec, while the Governor-General stayed in Ottawa.* There was some Canadian criticism on this point, and when Queen Elizabeth II visited Canada in 1959 it was the Governor-General who met her and handed over his responsibility as her representative. On this later visit, too, the Queen was accompanied across Canada by a succession of Ministers; in 1939 the Prime Minister insisted on being with the royal party all the way. 'Poor King and poor Rex,' wrote Violet Markham on hearing of the plans, 'tied up to each other for three weeks—they will bore each other to tears before the end of the time. I wonder who will weary first!'

One of Tweedsmuir's tasks during these weeks was to prepare drafts of the four main speeches which the King would deliver: at Quebec, at Ottawa, at Vancouver, and on departure from Halifax. Then, as the details of the tour were fixed, all over Canada the mayors of towns to be visited wrote to Government House for speeches to make to His Majesty: and protocol demanded that the King, though not speaking himself, had to hand over a written speech in return. So Rideau Hall became a speech-factory, with the Governor-General at work on the King's, Mr Pereira the Assistant Secretary on the mayors', while Shuldham Redfern in the office below composed the King's replies to the mayors. To one point Tweedsmuir gave special attention: that the journalists who accompanied the party on tour should be properly looked after and recognised.

Dark as the outlook in Europe might be, Tweedsmuir was firm in his view that the visit should take place in any circumstances short of war. But it was with great relief that he heard that the royal party were actually on the Atlantic. They were duly met by Mackenzie King at Quebec on 17 May; then it was the Tweedsmuirs' turn in Ottawa, where they stayed for three days at Government House. There was a drive through the town in an open state carriage, a state dinner in Rideau Hall, a ceremony in the Senate at which the King gave the royal assent to certain Parliamentary bills, the Trooping the Colour, a garden-party ('I never expected to see genteel Ottawa so carried out of itself'), a parliamentary dinner

* On 10 March 1940 Mackenzie King wrote to Amery that 'in the arrangements for the Royal Visit there were matters which must have been a little embarrassing to him [Tweedsmuir]. In seeking to go as far as he could in one direction meet the wishes of the Palace, he had to, and I had to go equally far in another direction, in trying to have the visit conform in all particulars with what I knew would be the wishes of the people, his tact and judgment in these matters were disclosed at their best' [*sic* throughout]. This letter is in the Amery Papers.

at the Château Laurier, and the unveiling of the war memorial. After this ceremony Tweedsmuir told his sister:

The Queen told me that she must go down among the troops, meaning the six or seven thousand veterans. I said it was worth risking it, and sure enough the King and Queen and Susie and I disappeared in that vast mob! —simply swallowed up. The police could not get near us. I was quite happy about it because the veterans kept admirable order. It was really extraordinarily touching; old Scotsmen weeping and talking about Angus. One old fellow said to me, 'Ay, man, if Hitler could see this!' It was a wonderful proof of what a people's king means.

Then the party were off to the West, and Tweedsmuir—rather glad to be going to bed early again after some late nights talking with the King—went off happily to fish on the Cascapedia with Tom Lamont, and to receive enthusiastic progress-reports from the Prime Minister. (His telegram from Victoria, B.C., opened with 'Words cannot begin to describe triumphal nature of royal tour to date it has surpassed all expectations.') Mackenzie King stuck close to his royal charges—at every station where their train drew up he would be out almost before it had stopped and running down the platform to greet the King and Queen as they descended from their coach—and as Canada's Minister for External Affairs he crossed the border with them when they visited the President at Washington. It was indeed 'Canada's show.'

Tweedsmuir came back into the picture at the very end of the tour, when the King and Queen were about to embark at Halifax. He joined the royal train at Truro, had a long talk with the King on his impressions of Canada, and was invested with the G.C.V.O. ('They had a great time trying to get the box open,' Susan told her family, 'and used first a penny and then a knife before they managed it.') The Queen, who diffused a great sense of enjoyment throughout, told Tweedsmuir that practically every Scot she met in Canada seemed to come from Glamis or Peebles, 'a compliment, I suppose, to you and me!' On 15 June, with their convoy of Canadian cruisers and destroyers, and seen off by all the yachts and fishing-boats in Halifax, they sailed for home: and Tweedsmuir delightedly reckoned the gains.

The tour had given a great impulse to the growth of Canadian national feeling, as against provincial. French Canadians had begun to talk of 'our' rather than 'your' King and Queen. It had demonstrated the new status of the Dominion; Lord Crawford wrote from London that

The visit has given Canada a status never quite conceded hitherto. Canada now stands out more distinct from the U.S.A., with her own personality clearly defined; but at the same time, more emphasis has been laid upon the neighbourliness of mutual understanding and tolerance, which I fancy must be the fact most impressive to Continental observers.

And it had broken down, if only for a time, a good deal of Canadian isolationism, particularly in Quebec.

Everyone was happy: the Governor-General, whose enthusiasm had inspired the whole affair; the Prime Minister, who had figured so often at his sovereign's side; and the King and Queen, who arrived home with a new self-confidence and assurance. 'I can tell you,' wrote the King in his letter of thanks to Tweedsmuir,

that our tour has done *me* untold good in every way. I was longing to see Canada, its people, its scenery, its possibilities, and I was not disappointed. I was thrilled by it all, and its climate has made me a new person. I have come back with a renewed vigour to all the problems which beset this Old World of ours. I feel that I have had a rest, despite the very arduous programme we undertook to do, as everyone in Canada made our visit such an enjoyable one. I cannot thank you enough for all the help you gave me with my speeches, which I am sure struck the right note, and I was able to carry it on in my Guildhall speech, which was a great ordeal. The Prime Minister, to whom I showed it, had very few alterations to suggest. I did so want to make people in these islands realise what they have done in their institutions.

In July the Tweedsmuirs were again in Quebec, where they were joined at the Citadel by Alastair, fresh from his final Schools at Oxford, and by Violet Markham, on her way to study unemployment in the United States. She also visited Mackenzie King, and told Tweedsmuir that 'he spoke of you in warmest terms as the best Governor-General he has ever worked with—that you have been perfect throughout.' After her came Anna and Walter Buchan from Peebles, and in August the family party travelled to Churchill on Hudson's Bay to meet the *Nascopie* which was bringing Johnnie back to civilisation after his year at the Company's post at Cape Dorset. 'I expected someone jungly and burly,' wrote his father, 'but found an elegant young man in a respectable flannel suit with an O.E. tie!' From Churchill—'the end of the earth—a flat moorland like a Hebridean island and the muddy shores and the grey waters of Hudson's Bay'—they went across to Jasper, so that Anna and Walter could see the Rockies. Then they visited the settlements which in the last twenty-five years had been established on the Peace and Smoky River valleys. Forest had been cleared and farms established on soil as good as the best of eastern Manitoba, and the fields were now golden with harvest against the bare green hills. At a latitude of 55 the summer was short, but the sun shone for so many hours that the vegetables were large, the flowers huge and brilliant. Tweedsmuir found it 'an extraordinary place—a sort of land beyond the North Wind, which the Elizabethan voyagers dreamed of.' It had been in his mind eight years earlier when in *The Gap in the Curtain* he had written of a British Prime Minister who dreams of a large-scale settlement on the Peace River for the unemployed. In reality few of the settlers were from Britain. Some had come from the drought areas of the Prairies, some from the United States, some recently from Europe. At Tupper Creek the Tweedsmuirs visited a settlement of anti-Nazi Sudeten-Germans, whose members included lawyers, doctors, craftsmen, a professor from Prague and a former member of the Reichstag.

So went the last days of peace, and the war which Tweedsmuir a year ago had thought to be averted broke out on the first day of September, when German troops moved across the Polish frontier. On 7 September Tweedsmuir opened Parliament without any ceremonial, and two days later signed Canada's declaration of war on Germany. ('I had staying in the house at the time,' he told Stair Gillon, 'Prince Felix, the son of the late Emperor of Austria. Could anyone twenty-five years ago have foretold such a combination of improbabilities?') This declaration came a week after Britain's, and Tweedsmuir was careful to explain to British friends the reason for the delay: Canada, as a sovereign nation, was not automatically involved in Britain's declaration; if the country came into the war, it must be as the result of a decision of the Canadian Parliament. 'My Prime Minister,' he told Violet Markham,

has succeeded very skilfully in aligning Canada alongside Britain with a minimum of disturbance. He, of course, is being criticised for not declaring himself roundly and clearly, but in my view his policy has been the right one.

Now that the war was here, there was some relief from tension, but no exhilaration. 'This is the third war I have been in,' Tweedsmuir wrote to Edward Harkness, 'and no one could hate the horrible thing more than I do.' 'This preposterous war,' he wrote to another friend, and to Anna:

I hate this war as I never hated the last. Then we were fighting with a barbarous and dangerous enemy, but at any rate he was adult. Now I feel that we are contending with diseased and vicious children.

'My old work is over,' he told Stair Gillon on 29 September:

It was, as you know, principally educative, travelling everywhere and trying to make the different parts of Canada understand each other . . . Now I shall have nothing to do except review troops, keep an eye on war charities to prevent waste (I am President of most of them), and hold the hands of Ministers. I may also be a little use in connection with the U.S.A.

He was impatient of this wartime rôle: he would have liked to write himself, as he had done in the 1914–18 war, to explain to Canadians and Americans the issues involved, and he followed with the closest concern the early days of the new Ministry of Information in London. The Minister was Hugh Macmillan, who had been his assistant in 1918, and Tweedsmuir lost no time in sending him advice, the fruits of his own hard experience: no direct propaganda to America, no gibes at transatlantic isolationism but a genuine effort to understand it, 'no attempt to varnish,' 'never deny a disaster.' 'Our news should follow the Reuter plan and be as objective as possible. That means, of course, that you will have a battle with the War Office and the Admiralty.' Tweedsmuir felt too that he could play a useful part in keeping the British Government in touch with American opinion. Though he considered it wiser to put off a visit to Roosevelt in his country house at Hyde Park, for a meeting at such time would have set off all sorts of rumours, at the end of October he was in New York for a medical examination and took the chance of seeing a number of influential Americans. He stayed with Tom Lamont of J. P. Morgan's, spent an evening with John D. Rockefeller and an afternoon with Edward Sheldon, lunched with the staff of the *New York Times* and talked to several other journalists. Lord Lothian, the new British Ambassador to the United States, came up from Washington to meet him. (On Lothian's appointment Tweedsmuir wrote: 'You are one of the few Englishmen who really know America, and above all you like the country, and there is no nation so sensitive to liking.')

There was an interpreter's rôle for him in Canada too, where at times the various British missions concerned with war supplies did not appear to have grasped what kind of a country Canada was. Her rôle in the war often seemed clearer to the planners in London than to Canadians themselves. Back in May 1938 Tweedsmuir had written to Susan:

I am having a difficult time in trying to mediate between the British Air Ministry and my Government. Canada is anxious to do all she can to help air production in Britain, but we must go cautiously, because certain things she is asked to do would really mean a commitment which would shackle the power of Parliament to decide, if a crisis came. People at home—at least some of them—do not seem to understand the real delicacy of the position of the self-governing Dominions, especially of Canada, who is so much out of the possible war area.

One of the Ministry's schemes was to establish British training-schools for pilots in Canada. In October 1939 a mission arrived to discuss the plan, and its leader at once called on Mackenzie King, who noted

the sort of railroading, taking for granted style . . . amazing how these people . . . from the Old Country . . . seem to think that all they have to do is to tell us what is to be done. No wonder they get the backs of people up on this side.

Tweedsmuir was several times called in to help deal with such displays of colonial attitudes and misunderstandings of the status of a self-governing Dominion. In December there was a final hitch about the air-training agreement, when the British service adviser, Air Chief Marshal Sir Robert Brooke-Popham (a former Governor of Kenya), made difficulties about Canadian air-crews being serviced by British ground-crews, for this would mean a Canadian might be commanding a much larger number of Englishmen. Mackenzie King wanted no further delay: he was determined to have the agreement signed before the announcement of the landing of the first Canadian troops in Britain. So, although he had always stressed that the Governor-General must keep entirely clear of affairs of state, he now made use of him to solve what should have been a purely administrative matter. He went off to Government House, where (I quote from Mackenzie King's diary)

The Governor was propped on his pillows looking pretty frail . . . I said to him I had come on the most important matter I had ever had occasion to speak to him of.

Tweedsmuir was in fact very ill. Once he realised how worked up Mackenzie King was, he agreed to talk to Brooke-Popham, and put his point so forcibly that he went off to sign the agreement with no further demur, looking, so Mackenzie King put it, 'as if he had been spanked.'* Tweedsmuir's A.D.C.s found him almost too mild a

---

* Sir Shuldham Redfern considers that the account of this episode in Mackenzie King's diary should be regarded with caution. He observed no signs of Sir Robert Brooke-Popham, on his arrival from Government House at the Prime Minister's office, looking 'as if he had been spanked.'

chief (most of them were used to service discipline) but he could be forthright enough when the issue was the status of Canada.

The cure at Ruthin Castle in the summer of 1938, when he had put on a stone in weight, had given Tweedsmuir high hopes that he had his duodenal trouble under control. In December of that year he told Violet Markham that 'I am less like an El Greco'—the comparison had been hers—'and more like a Rubens,' while Susan reassured Anna that 'John is marvellously well and enjoying life so much,' and at the opening of Parliament a few weeks later she noted that he was filling out his uniform. But by June 1939 he was saying sadly that 'I do everything I did at Ruthin and yet it doesn't seem to me to have the effect of Ruthin.' Ferris Greenslet, visiting the Tweedsmuirs that summer, thought that he kept going at a heavy cost in 'dogged nervous effort.' After his examination in New York in October the most Tweedsmuir hoped for was that the new regime would give him 'a little more comfort during the winter.' Dr Miller at the Rockefeller Medical Centre found that his blood-pressure was very low, pronounced the gastritis 'serious but not dangerous,' and ordered him to take one day a week in bed. All his life he had been a good sleeper, though he had never needed many hours in bed; now, however long he slept, he woke tired. His sight was getting worse, particularly in the eye under the scar, and he had bad headaches. Those round him hardly realised at the time how ill he was: 'I never heard him complain,' said David Walker, who joined his staff in 1938, 'about his discomfort or the slops he had to eat.' Pain did not make him peevish or self-centred. David Walker was struck by his 'gentle kindness. He was never arrogant nor clever at anyone else's expense.' Mrs Killick noticed that 'the older he got, the kinder he got': more considerate, more tolerant of other people's slowness.

The only hope of improvement Tweedsmuir could see was to go again to a clinic for a long spell. 'Two months at Ruthin did me a world of good,' he told Sir Alexander Hardinge, 'and four months would probably have cured me. Unless I am to drag my wing for the remainder of my life I really ought to take the matter in hand.'

This was a main factor in his decision to leave Canada at the end of his appointed term in September 1940. The Prime Minister and the Cabinet had asked if he would be willing to be nominated for a second term of five years; when he refused, they suggested 'the duration of the war, or in any case for an extra year.' But he was clear that he ought to go when his five years were up. His other main reason he put in a letter to Stair Gillon:

My habits as Governor-General are rather individual, and I do not want my idiosyncrasies turned into precedents which might embarrass my successor.

And with the change in his work owing to the war he felt that 'my principal task in Canada is now over.'

At one time he had hoped that he might follow his predecessors Dufferin, Minto and Willingdon, from Canada to India: he even spoke of this ambition in the summer of 1939 to David Walker, but by then it was only a wishful dream. After Canada it would probably be Elsfield, and books, and the life of a semi-invalid: 'dragging his wing.'

The end of a job is a time for stocktaking and looking back. Tweedsmuir had been purposefully looking back on his life, for all through 1939 he was at work on his autobiography. His reading in 1938 and 1939 had been mainly of memoirs and biographies: Boswell, Greville, Logan Pearsall Smith's *Unforgotten Years*, Siegfried Sassoon's *The Old Century*, Somerset Maugham's *The Summing-Up* ('a very honest confession of faith'). His own book, he told a correspondent,

is not an ordinary autobiography or any attempt to tell the unimportant story of my life; but rather an attempt to pick out certain high lights and expound the impressions made upon me at different stages—Oxford, the Bar, South Africa, Parliament etc. I have written about no personalities, except those who are dead . . . I have not touched in any way upon Canada.

Memory Hold-the-Door was to present his public face; the tone was to be calm and reflective.* But in 1939 he also started a novel.

* Two extracts from *Pilgrim's Way* (the title of *Memory Hold-the-Door* in the United States) were included in an article on the books President Kennedy liked, in the 'J.F.K. Memorial Issue' of *Look* (17 November 1964), with a commentary by Mrs John F. Kennedy: '*Pilgrim's Way*, the memoirs of John Buchan, Lord Tweedsmuir, he once said was his favourite book. He gave it to me before we were married. The part for which he cared most was a portrait of the brilliant Raymond Asquith . . . who was killed in action in World War I. The poignancy of men dying young always moved my husband—possibly because of his brother Joe dying in World War II. I think the first line ['He disliked emotion, not because he felt lightly but because he felt deeply'] could have been written of John F. Kennedy.

Other passages that drew him, and profoundly shaped his thinking, were Buchan's views on democracy and the profession of politics. For it was the way he himself saw politics. His book *Profiles in Courage* is about this—to make people think of politics as a noble profession again, as it was in Greece and in the early days of our Republic.'

'His Excellency is writing a very odd book,' Mrs Killick told Susan in the autumn of 1939, 'so unlike him, so introspective.' In *Sick Heart River* this writer, in general so reticent about himself, lets his guard down. He had always been a rock to so many—to his parents, to his brothers and sister, to his wife and his children— and a generator of energy and encouragement. To expose his own doubts, reveal his own disappointments, was a luxury he could not allow himself. But in a novel he could do it at one remove.

Sick Heart River is the tale of Sir Edward Leithen, under sentence of death. When his doctor tells him that he has advanced tuberculosis and about a year to live, he cannot face a slow decline, creeping into 'the bleak bag's end of life.' Opportunely his old friend Blenkiron turns up demanding help in tracing his niece's husband Paul Galliard, a French-Canadian who is a partner in a New York banking-house, and who has walked out of his home leaving a note that he is 'sick in mind.' Leithen takes on the job, which will give him 'activity for the mind and a final activity for the body,' and be an excuse for 'a defiant finish to his career.' He will go out with a bang.

His quest starts in New York, then takes him to a farmhouse in Quebec, by air across the Barrens to the Arctic shore, then to the country west of the Mackenzie. After a march across the mountains that takes Leithen to the limit of his strength, he and his companion, the half-breed Johnny Frizel, find Galliard. He is wandering in his mind and has been abandoned by his companion, Johnny's brother Lew, who has pressed on to the mysterious Sick Heart River, from which other travellers have not returned. Lew is needed if they are to get Galliard out alive; so off goes Leithen to the Sick Heart, a mighty volcanic rift, with green meadows, tall trees and a winding river in the valley-bottom—a pastoral sanctuary in the heart of high snow mountains. Leithen just manages to bring Lew out, then collapses. The need to look after Leithen brings Lew back to sanity; he had been crazed by his vision of the Sick Heart River, which he believed to be a paradise away from the world where he could save his soul. Now he sees it is a place of death, where no creature lives, and if he is to save his soul it must be done 'by a sane man, and not by a loony, and in a man's job.' Leithen too begins to look on his quest in a new light. He had undertaken it for his own ends. In setting out to find death in the wilds he had been as self-obsessed as Lew in seeking his salvation in the Sick Heart River. Now he begins to feel involved with life again, and is concerned with Galliard for his own sake, and not as the object of his quest.

Then there is a miracle. Tended by Lew and Johnny, Leithen gradually grows stronger in the antiseptic northern air, and the pain in his lungs is less. He begins to think of a return to England, a quiet old age among his friends. On the return march the party reach an encampment of Hare Indians; they too have been ravaged by tuberculosis and have fallen into despair, neither hunting nor keeping themselves warm, and Father Duplessis of the Oblate mission is at his wits' end. Leithen is at first unmoved by the plight of 'a few hundred degenerate Indians' at the end of the world: then news comes of the outbreak of war with Germany, and his daydreams of a quiet old age are blown away. He remembers the last war: 'waste, futile waste, and death, illimitable, futile death. Now the same devilment was unloosed again.' His job is at last clear: not to think about *his* death, but to fight against death, and save life. So he and Galliard and the Frizels join Father Duplessis in the fight to feed the Hares and give them back the will to live; and the fight gives Galliard back his nerve. The exertion undoes Leithen's new-found health, the lung-trouble revives, but Leithen is no longer centred on himself, and is content. As spring comes, and the Hares recover, he grows weaker and dies.

It is plain how much Buchan put into the novel of his experience in Canada and his feelings about Canada, particularly Quebec and the North. The Scottish-Indian half-breeds whom he had met on the Mackenzie, the tubercular Hares, the Oblate Fathers, the Eskimos on their well-found schooner in Coronation Gulf, all are here. The cup in the hills with a meadow of wild hay which he had seen from the air when flying over the Coast Range to Bella Coola becomes the setting for the Galliard farm in Quebec. The Sick Heart River is placed in the country beyond the South Nahanni which Buchan had longed to explore with Harry Snyder. He knew the Arctic only in summer, but he cross-examined Johnnie who had wintered at Cape Dorset, and it is his son's experience that lies behind such a passage as:

The cold was more intense than anything he had ever imagined. Under its stress trees cracked with a sound like machine-guns. The big morning fire made only a narrow circle of heat. If for a second he turned his face from it the air stung his eyelids as if with an infinity of harsh particles. To draw breath rasped the throat. The sky was milk-pale, the sun a mere ghostly disc, and it seemed to Leithen as if everything—sun, trees, mountains—were red rimmed. There was no shadow anywhere, no depth or softness. The world was hard, glassy, metallic; all of it except the fantasmal, cotton-wool skies.

Contrast between civilisation and the wilds had been part of his stock-in-trade as a novelist; here the wild is presented as harshly and realistically as he described the Mackenzie delta in the report of his 1937 tour.

Folks come down here thinking the North's a pretty lady, and find that she can be a cruel, bloody-minded old bitch.

Buchan has made Leithen much more like himself than on any of his earlier appearances. Leithen's body—lean and getting leaner, needing sleep and waking tired, active in spite of pain—is Buchan's. (This struck Mrs Killick strongly as she took down the book, often dictated by Buchan from his own manuscript as he lay in bed, turning uncomfortably because he had so little flesh to lie on.) Like Buchan, Leithen has a horror of 'dragging his wing.' His memories —of childhood on the Borders, of Oxford, of holidays on Exmoor and the Dolomites—are Buchan's. The writers whose words come to his mind are those who had meant much to Buchan in his youth, whom he had lately been re-reading: Whitman, Thoreau, Stevenson. (Echoing Weir of Hermiston, Leithen stoically climbs 'the bleak staircase of his duty'.) When Leithen remembers some 'bad verses' he had written long ago, it is a poem of Buchan's that he quotes. The old print which comes vividly to his mind's eye, *Die Toten-Insel*, hung in Buchan's dressing-room. His musings and meditations are cast in the phrases and cadences of Presbyterian worship: 'There was a purpose of pity and tenderness,' 'count his mercies,' 'in the article of death.' The creed he confesses smacks less of Eton and Oxford than of the manse in Queen Mary Drive.

This Leithen is more introspective than any of Buchan's heroes since Lewis Haystoun in *The Half-Hearted*. He scrutinises his motives, broods over his life, takes stock of his career. He has enjoyed his life, and has few regrets, though there have been disappointments. He sees himself as a successful man who worked hard for his success, but who has not quite reached the highest rung of his particular ladder—he has never been Prime Minister—and now finds that the world in which he succeeded has lost some of its solidity.

His castles had been tumbled down. Pleasant things they had been, even if made of paste-board; in his heart he had always known that they were paste-board.

(The successful man who discovers the inadequacy of success was the theme of Buchan's early story 'Fountainblue.') Brought back to life after the descent into the Sick Heart canyon, he has an overpowering sense of God's mercy, and it makes his ambitions and achievements look pretty small. (Galliard too has been very successful, but in pursuing his career in New York he has cut himself off from his Canadian roots. Success goes sour on him and he has to go back to Quebec and the far North, has to recognise the claims of his own country and people, before he can reintegrate himself.) Leithen finds peace of mind after he has given up his romantic notion about going off to die on a forlorn quest, and has settled down to the practical job of helping the Hare Indians. One of the steady themes in Buchan's novels from *Prester John* onwards was the band of brothers, brought together from very different backgrounds to fight the common enemy. At the end of *Sick Heart River* Leithen forms such a group, with Galliard, the Frizels, the chief of the Hares and Father Duplessis.* This time they are brought together not to smash a world conspiracy, nip a rising in the bud, turn the tide of battle or save an empire. They are here to fight disease, cold, hunger, the malevolence of Nature in the North: 'To war on Death —for Life; not men—for flags.'

I think it is clear that through Leithen Buchan was saying something about himself; I would offer this interpretation. He had been successful, but he had not reached the heights he had once aspired to: had not been a Milner or a Cromer, had not sat in the Cabinet. (He once observed to Michael Adeane that Scotland produced more very good second-class people than any other country, but very few of the first class.) He had enjoyed his years at the heart of affairs, but these no longer seemed so important. His mother's death had turned his thoughts back to his early years, to his father with his stern and simple creed—'Trifle with your earthly master, if you will, but trifle not with God'—and he measured his worldly success against the older Buchan's worldly failure. (Two of the possible titles which he jotted down for the novel were *Pride's Purge* and *The Winepress*.) And for all the hopes with which he might cheer others, he knew in his bones that physically he was going downhill, and could not much longer lead a fully active life. Death was at the end of the slope and

* On 17 January 1940 Buchan wrote to the Rev. George Macleod of the Iona Community: 'I believe that something of that sort is needed everywhere today to vitalise the Church. I was greatly struck, in my Arctic travels, with the work of the Oblates—a celibate missionary brotherhood, who can do everything from skinning a moose to building a boat, and who can minister both to the body and the soul.'

he wondered how he would meet it: *Timor Mortis Conturbat Me*. I am not suggesting that in writing of Leithen's death Buchan was consciously foreshadowing his own. To Violet Markham he spoke cheerfully in the summer of 1939 of killing off Leithen and the other familiar characters because they 'have been on hand too long and I am getting bored with them.' But death was on his mind.

But if there were some things to depress him in this backward look, there was also much to cheer. In Canada, in his sixties—a time of life which often stimulates personal doubts and dissatisfaction—he had rediscovered a sense of purpose. His job as Governor-General could not be as straightforwardly heroic as that of a priest or airman in the Arctic, or of a farmer in the drought-stricken prairies: men in whom there was little personal ambition, who went steadily on with the work in hand. But the sight of such men at their work, the knowledge that he had links with them and had been of some use to them, had given him a pride and pleasure in his job that he had not found in his years in Parliament. And the best way that he could face the prospect of his failing strength was to be like them, doggedly doing the work that lay nearest his hand, and keeping his pain to himself. For the first time this is a Buchan story with no sense of physical exhilaration.

There was one area of Buchan's life which could not appear in Leithen's balance-sheet. Buchan was in many ways Leithen; but he was also Leithen's creator. If he had been casting up his own balance-sheet, how would his writings have weighed? I doubt whether he would have made much to-do over them, or examined his books to see on which side of the account they should go. Not for him such a scrutiny as Stevenson's in his last year at Samoa, when he let his Calvinist conscience play over his achievement, to find out what use he had made of his gift:

My skill deserts me, such as it is, or was. It was a very little dose of inspiration, and a pretty little trick of style, long lost, improved by the most heroic industry . . . I cannot take myself seriously, as an artist; the limitations are so obvious. I did take myself seriously as a workman of old, but my practice has fallen off.

I must seem to you to blaze in a Birmingham prosperity and happiness, and to myself I seem a failure.

Buchan never revealed himself like this, and kept off the subject of his books as much as possible. He would occasionally talk about his histories and biographies, David Walker remembered, but 'if ladies at Sault Ste Marie brought up the subject of his fiction, he would become quite shy, didn't like to talk about it.' Any enthusiasm about his thrillers would be met by some deprecatory remark to the effect that only the young and simple-minded could like them. One night at Rideau Hall Susan found him for once absorbed in a novel, and noticed with astonishment that it was *Greenmantle*. 'It's rather good,' he said with a guilty start. These books were pure pleasure to invent, no trouble to write, and they made a lot of money; no doubt he felt that they could not therefore be counted for virtue. He was lucky to have had the story-teller's gift, and does not seem to have questioned whether he could have made more of it.

It was a quiet winter at Government House, there were fewer engagements, and ceremonial was cut down. Most of Tweedsmuir's speeches were made to troops, in the open air, often in sleet or snow. In November he flew to Camp Borden to see Alastair, in training with his tank regiment; Johnnie, in the Governor-General's Foot Guards, was among the first Canadian troops to land in Britain in December. In the New Year he went to Halifax to see a convoy before it sailed. 'I visited all the ships,' he told Anna,

both of the Royal and Canadian Navies, and went out to sea in a destroyer. I tramped in the snow around all the coast defences, and I had a long day with the Air Force . . . I had only one disappointment. I was going out with the Air escort to accompany the convoy for the first part of its journey, but the morning dawned with a howling snow blizzard, and it was impossible for aeroplanes to go up.

The most dramatic thing I did was to attend the conference of the old merchant skippers before the convoys sailed. You never saw such magnificent old fellows—engaged on one of the riskiest jobs on earth, and perfectly placid about it

At New Year there was a visit from the Pitney van Dusens of New York. He was a professor at Union Theological Seminary who had studied in Edinburgh—'the very best type of parson,' Tweedsmuir considered—and she was a Scot, an old friend of Anna Buchan's, who had spent her childhood summers near Broughton. So after dinner they settled down by the fire with *The Northern Muse*, Betty van Dusen and Tweedsmuir reading poems alternately; rather, she read from the book, but when it was his turn he barely needed to give it a glance. The poems were safe in his memory.

He was sad at the prospect of leaving Canada the following autumn: 'It will be a great wrench in many ways, for I have got my roots very deep down,' he wrote to Lord Lothian, and to Anna: 'Leaving Canada is going to be like pulling up mandrakes!' However, he was warmed and cheered by the appreciation shown when the news was made public. 'You know and love the country,' wrote a man in Toronto, 'and the country knows and loves you.' And from his old teacher Gilbert Murray came 'congratulation and admiration for the firmness and courage with which in the midst of bad health you have fulfilled your great office.'

On 25 January he opened Parliament, and granted the Prime Minister an immediate dissolution. 'The result,' he wrote to Anna, has been such a buzzing in political circles as to resemble nothing so much as a bee-skep which has been overturned. The election is on March 26.' (He ended this letter with 'How magnificent Winston was in his last speech!'*) At the beginning of February he went to Montreal for a couple of days:

I spent Friday morning with the Sulpician Brotherhood. I never saw more beautiful faces than those of the brothers. We went into the cathedral in state, and the organ actually played 'God Save the King' and 'Land of Hope and Glory'—a thing which must be almost unparalleled. Then we had the Forestry luncheon, at which I spoke, and in the afternoon Susie and I went over some Red Cross depots. We brought back with us for the night Father D'Arcy, who is head of the Jesuit College at Oxford, and an old friend of ours.

Father D'Arcy remembers this journey in 'the royal train' to Ottawa, and how as they talked they seemed to be back in Oxford. He had always been greatly drawn to Tweedsmuir: 'he made me feel that his friendship was given to me, and he was courteous and high-minded.'

During these days he was reading two books with enjoyment: Lionel Trilling's *Matthew Arnold* and Werner Jaeger's *Paideia, The Ideals of Greek Culture*, which had just arrived from Blackwell's: a stiff book, but to Alastair it seemed that his father was becoming more intellectual in his interests, less concerned with current events.

On 5 February Tweedsmuir told Anna that

I have finished my novel and my autobiography, and am almost at the end of my children's book about Canada. This will leave me with a clear field for farewells this summer.

---

* In his speech on the death of Winston Churchill in the House of Lords on 25 January 1965 Lord Longford, Leader of the House, quoted Buchan's words on the qualities of the great captains. Thus Buchan was able to make posthumous amends to Churchill, though in life he had found it difficult to do justice to him.

Take great care of yourself, and make Walter do the same. I am really putting on a little weight now.

His weight was eight stone, twelve pounds.

The next morning while shaving he had a cerebral thrombosis, fell, and struck the back of his head. A few hours later he briefly regained consciousness; then there was a secondary development of pressure, so an emergency trepanning of the skull was carried out at Government House on 9 February, which made it possible to transfer him to Montreal. In the operating room at the Neurological Institute, where four years earlier Tweedsmuir had described his fracture of the skull as a child, Dr Wilder Penfield and Dr William Cone performed two further operations to relieve pressure, and found that he had great recuperative powers. Hopes went up and down but he was never again conscious, and on 11 February 1940 he died.

'It is a horrible thing, the slow ebbing of vitality,' he wrote when his uncle Willie died in 1906; 'why should we pray to be delivered from sudden death?'

All over Canada flags were at half-mast, on private houses as well as on government buildings. J. W. Dafoe, the veteran editor of the *Winnipeg Free Press*, a moulder of nationalist thought and not naturally sympathetic to Governor-Generals, described the feeling in the country in a private letter to a friend in England:

Ordinarily, a certain proportion of grief for the death of eminent people is, so to speak, official, but I think there was a universal sense of bereavement in the death of Tweedsmuir . . .

I have known all the Governors-General we have had for the past fifty years, either in a journalistic sense or on personal grounds as well, and I think Tweedsmuir was the pick of the lot.

Tweedsmuir's body was brought back to Ottawa, to lie in state in Parliament Buildings, where for two days crowds filed past the coffin in the draped Senate Chamber. The funeral service was at St Andrew's Church, where he had been an elder, with Mackenzie King taking the most personal concern over the details. All official Ottawa was there. There was a nineteen-gun salute as the coffin, on a gun-carriage drawn by sailors, moved off towards the Union Station on its way to cremation in Montreal. To Grattan O'Leary it appeared that the crowds, waiting on this day of bitter cold in streets banked high with snow, were greater than on any occasion since the funeral of Sir Wilfrid Laurier, and that they were there in 'instinctive recognition that this was a great man.'

There were memorial services in London at Westminster Abbey, in Edinburgh at St Giles Cathedral, in Oxford at the University Church, and in Glasgow at the John Knox Church. And when his ashes had been brought home in a destroyer, they were buried in the churchyard at Elsfield. 'I don't think I remember anyone,' G. M. Trevelyan wrote to Susan, 'whose death evoked a more enviable outburst of sorrow, love and admiration.'

It had been on the whole a fortunate life. Into his sixty-four years he had packed more activity than most men could expect in twice that span. He had left a shelf of books to entertain and a shelf to add to knowledge. He had played a number of parts with competence and success; his final rôle had been the most rewarding, and he had spent himself in it. He had been most happy in his marriage and his friends. He had not allowed his pain to sour his life, and he had not feared death. He had kept to the end his capacity for delight and his sense of expectancy. His boy's dreams were still bright.

APPENDIX A

HENRY JAMES, JOHN BUCHAN AND BYRON'S LETTERS

The passage in *Memory Hold-the-Door* (p. 151) runs:

'An aunt of my wife's, who was the widow of Byron's grandson, asked Henry James and myself to examine her archives in order to reach some conclusion on the merits of the quarrel between Byron and his wife. She thought that those particular papers might be destroyed by some successor and she wanted a statement of their contents deposited in the British Museum. So, during a summer week-end, Henry James and I waded through masses of ancient indecency, and duly wrote an opinion. The thing nearly made me sick, but my colleague never turned a hair. His only words for some special vileness were "singular"—"most curious"—"Nauseating, perhaps, but how quite inexpressibly significant."'

The text of the 'opinion' runs:

'In writing his book *Astarte* the late Lord Lovelace quoted passages from Lord Byron's letters to Augusta Leigh and from a large mass of family correspondence. He was however debarred from quoting the important evidence contained in Byron's intimate and very copious letters to Lady Melbourne during the three years immediately preceding his marriage. He had been permitted by the owner (Lady Dorchester) to take careful copies of these letters: and these copies from the original MSS in Lord Lovelace's own handwriting we were permitted by Lady Lovelace to see in the autumn of 1909. We can bear witness that they afford most weighty corroborative evidence of the truth of the story told by Lord Lovelace. They also incidentally have the effect of completely pulling down the house of cards erected by Mr R. Edgcumbe in his *Byron the last phase*.

'Mr Edgcumbe's theory is that a "liaison" was formed in the summer of 1813 between Byron and his early love, Mrs Chaworth-Musters. Byron's own letters show, not only that he was otherwise occupied at the above date, but also that it was many months later that he received Mrs Chaworth-Musters's invitation to him to come and renew their old acquaintance. In January 1814 he sent Lady Melbourne Mrs Chaworth-Musters's letters to advise upon. He seems to have projected a visit to her, but in February 1814 he wrote that he had returned to London without having seen her. He writes of the lady with perfect respect and indifference; and at this very time he was answering Lady Melbourne's remonstrances and expressing contrition as to that connection of which he himself said that it had an element of the *terrible* which made all others loves seem insipid.'

Henry James, 7 April 1910
John Buchan, 4 April 1910

APPENDIX B

THE ROOSEVELT–TWEEDSMUIR TALKS

[The following is the text of the memorandum prepared by Tweedsmuir on 8 April 1937 after his visit to Washington. The original is in the Franklin D. Roosevelt Library, Hyde Park, N.Y., among the Roosevelt papers, President's Secretary's File]

Private

NOTE FOR THE PRESIDENT

A Propitious Moment

I. The moment seems appropriate for some attempt to break the vicious circle of fear among the nations of the world. Recent events have, I think, disposed all the European dictators to reflect upon the future. The huge defensive programme of Britain, which is rapidly nearing completion; the stand taken by the Vatican with regard to the German Catholic Church; the better position of the National Government in Spain, and the weakness which the war has revealed in the Italian fighting quality in Spain and in the German aeroplanes; the growing *rapprochement* between the great democracies of the United States, Britain and France—all point a moral which even the blindest cannot miss. A pause for reflection, and an attempt to obtain some settlement of the fundamental economic questions which are behind all the unrest, would do something to save the face of both Germany and Italy; and it is desirable to save their face, for the situation would be in no way bettered by an internal breakdown in either country.

The initiative can be taken only by the President of the U.S.A., for he alone is in a position of sufficient detachment and authority. For any such policy to succeed it is essential (a) that all the Powers should be brought into conference; (b) that the representatives at such a Conference should be the governing figures in each country.

The First Step

II. It is the first step which is the most difficult, as St Denis observed when he perambulated Paris with his head in his hand. There seem to me to be two possible lines of approach.

(a) The chief difficulty will lie in securing the presence of Germany, Italy and Japan. This might be arranged privately before the President issued his appeal to the world.

(b) The appeal might be made without such previous consultation, and, if the response from the rest of the world were prompt and enthusiastic, it is difficult to see how Germany, Italy and Japan could stand out.

Clearly the safer plan would be the first, and a confidential approach might be made to the three Governments at once through the ordinary diplomatic channels.

The Peg for an Appeal

III. If such a preliminary arrangement should be felt to be impossible, then it would be important for the President to find a peg on which to hang his appeal. The American representative on the Raw Materials Commission, at present sitting in Geneva, might declare that it would be desirable to extend the purpose of this Commission to cover all the main economic problems. The President could then use this as a text for his appeal. It might be possible, simultaneously, for the Imperial Conference in Britain, while in session, to raise the same question. This would give the President sufficient material for his first step.

Nature of Conference

IV. It would have to be made clear that the object of the Conference was not to come to any detailed agreement, but simply to take soundings of the different problems. There would be no question of binding any member beforehand to any policy. The aim would be to reach some understanding on broad principles, and then to have the details worked out by a number of expert committees, the terms of reference of such committees being laid down by the Conference.

Relation to League of Nations

V. It seems to me vital that such a Conference should not be in any way identified with what remains of the League of Nations. If it were, prejudice would at once be created in Germany, Italy and Japan. Also, since it is essential to have America whole-heartedly behind the President, it would never do to let the suggestion get abroad that America was being brought into the League by a side-wind.

Place of Meeting

VI. This consideration makes the place of meeting of extreme importance. Any suspicion of the League would be removed if the place chosen were in the Western hemisphere—on the mainland of America or in one of the islands. At the same time there are obvious advantages in having Geneva for the locality. The International Labour Bureau there has a trained staff and valuable data at its disposal. The new Palace of the League has never yet been used, and is not identified with the former work of the League. It might be a good gesture to use it for the first time for this Conference. Also Geneva would be a more convenient centre for most of the conferring Powers than any place in the Western hemisphere. But if Geneva were selected it must be on one condition—that the President of the United States attended himself in person. Unless the Conference has behind it all the time a great personality it will never achieve its purpose. I feel, also, that the visit to Europe of the President at such a time would have a very great moral effect upon European opinion.

Agenda of Conference

VII. The agenda of the Conference would have to be carefully framed. Political and defence questions in the ordinary sense would be wholly excluded, and the aim would be to deal only with those fundamental economic difficulties which are the real cause of world disquiet. I suggest the following as some of the items on such an agenda:

(a) The supply of raw materials.
(b) The different standards of living which make fair competition difficult.
(c) The narrow economic nationalism which is setting up needless barriers.
(d) The possibility of assistance being given, by loan and otherwise, to nations which are in difficulties over their foreign exchanges.
(e) The question of emigration.

I mention these few as examples of the questions which would have to be discussed.

Summary

VIII. My conclusions are that the best plan, if it is possible, would be to come to a preliminary arrangement for their presence at the Conference of Germany, Japan and Italy. Failing that, a peg for the President's appeal could be found in a declaration by the American representative at the Raw Materials Commission, and by some similar statement at the British Imperial Conference. The question of the best meeting-place depends upon whether it can be so arranged that Geneva would not rouse needless suspicion in America or in the three doubtful Powers. I feel that here America is the danger point, but that is a matter of which the President is the best judge. In any case it seems to me essential that the President must be present himself at the Conference, both for the sake of his personal influence and as an advertisement that America means serious business.

T. 8:IV:37.

LIST OF BOOKS BY JOHN BUCHAN

(The American title, where it differs from the British, is given in square
brackets)

1894 *Essays and Apothegms of Francis Lord Bacon* (edited with intro-
      duction)
1895 *Sir Quixote of the Moors*
1896 *Scholar Gipsies*
      Containing: 'Scholar Gipsies,' 'April in the Hills,' 'Milestones,'
      'May-Fly Fishing,' 'The Men of the Uplands,' 'Gentlemen of
      Leisure,' 'Sentimental Travelling,' 'Urban Greenery,' 'Nature
      and the Art of Words,' 'Afternoon,' 'Night on the Heather,' 'On
      Cademuir Hill,' 'An Individualist,' 'The Drove Road,' 'Nuces
      Relictae,' 'Ad Astra'
1898 *John Burnet of Barns*
      Brasenose College
1899 *Grey Weather*
      Containing: 'Ballad for Grey Weather,' 'Prester John,' 'At the
      Article of Death,' 'Politics and the May-fly,' 'A Reputation,' 'A
      Journey of Little Profit,' 'At the Rising of the Waters,' 'The
      Earlier Affection,' 'The Black Fishers,' 'Summer Weather,'
      'The Oasis in the Snow,' 'The Herd of Standlan,' 'Streams of
      Water in the South,' 'The Moor Song,' 'Comedy in the Full
      Moon'
      A Lost Lady of Old Years
1900 *The Half-Hearted*
1902 *The Watcher by the Threshold*
      Containing: 'No-Man's-Land,' 'The Far Islands,' 'The Watcher
      by the Threshold,' 'The Outgoing of the Tide,' 'Fountainblue'
1903 *The African Colony*
1905 *The Law Relating to the Taxation of Foreign Income*
1906 *A Lodge in the Wilderness*
1908 *Some Eighteenth Century Byways*
      Containing: 'Prince Charles Edward,' 'Lady Louisa Stuart,'
      'Mr Secretary Murray,' 'Lord Mansfield,' 'Charles II,' 'The
      Making of Modern Scotland,' 'Castlereagh,' 'A Comic Chester-
      field (the 11th Earl of Buchan),' 'A Scottish Lady of the Old
      School (Lady John Scott),' 'The Victorian Chancellors,' 'The
      First Lord Dudley,' 'Mr Balfour as a Man of Letters,' 'John

Bunyan,' 'Count Tolstoi and the Idealism of War,' 'The Heroic Age of Ireland,' 'Rabelais,' 'Theodor Mommsen,' 'The Apocalyptic Style'

1910   *Prester John* [*The Great Diamond Pipe*]

1912   *The Moon Endureth*
Containing: 'From the Pentlands, looking North and South,' 'The Company of the Marjolaine,' 'Avignon, 1759,' 'A Lucid Interval,' 'The Shorter Catechism (Revised Version),' 'The Lemnian,' 'Atta's Song,' 'Space,' 'Stocks and Stones,' 'Streams of Water in the South,' 'The Gipsy's Song to the Lady Cassilis,' 'The Grove of Ashtaroth,' 'Wood Magic,' 'The Riding of Ninemileburn,' 'Plain Folk,' 'The Kings of Orion,' 'Babylon,' 'The Green Glen,' 'The Wise Years,' 'The Rime of True Thomas'

1913   *The Marquis of Montrose*
Andrew Jameson, Lord Ardwall

1915–19   *Nelson's History of the War*

1915   *The Thirty-Nine Steps*
Salute to Adventurers

1916   *The Power-House*
Greenmantle

1917   *Poems, Scots and English*

1919   *Mr Standfast*
These for Remembrance
Memoirs of Tommy Nelson, Bron Lucas (Auberon Herbert), Cecil Rawling, Basil Blackwood, Jack Stuart-Wortley and Raymond Asquith
The Island of Sheep 'by Cadmus and Harmonia' (with Susan Buchan)

1920   *The History of the South African Forces in France*
Francis and Riversdale Grenfell

1921   *The Path of the King*

1921–22   *A History of the Great War*

1922   *Huntingtower*
A Book of Escapes and Hurried Journeys
Containing: 'The Flight to Varennes,' 'The Railway Raid in Georgia,' 'The Escape of King Charles after Worcester,' 'From Pretoria to the Sea,' 'The Escape of Prince Charles Edward,' 'Two African Journeys,' 'The Great Montrose,' 'The Flight of Lieutenants Parer and M'Intosh across the World,' 'Lord Nithsdale's Escape,' 'Sir Robert Carey's Ride to Edinburgh,' 'The Escape of Princess Clementina,' 'On the Roof of the World'

1923   *The Last Secrets*
Containing: 'Lhasa,' 'The Gorges of the Brahmaputra,' 'The North Pole,' 'The Mountains of the Moon,' 'The South Pole,' 'Mount McKinley,' 'The Holy Cities of Islam,' 'The Explorations of New Guinea,' 'Mount Everest'
Midwinter

1924   *The Three Hostages*
      Lord Minto
      The Northern Muse (compiled)

1925   *The History of the Royal Scots Fusiliers*
      John Macnab

1926   *The Dancing Floor*
      Homilies and Recreations
          Containing: 'Sir Walter Scott,' 'The Old and the New in Literature,' 'The Great Captains,' 'The Muse of History,' 'A Note on Edmund Burke,' 'Lord Balfour and English Thought,' 'Two Ordeals of Democracy,' 'Literature and Topography,' 'The Judicial Temperament,' 'Style and Journalism,' 'Scots Vernacular Poetry,' 'Morris and Rossetti,' 'Robert Burns,' 'Catullus,' 'The Literature of Tweeddale,' 'Thoughts on a Distant Prospect of Oxford'

1927   *Witch Wood*

1928   *The Runagates Club*
          Containing: 'The Green Wildebeeste,' 'The Frying-Pan and the Fire,' 'Dr Lartius,' 'The Wind in the Portico,' '"Divus" Johnston,' 'The Loathly Opposite,' 'Sing a Song of Sixpence,' 'Ship to Tarshish,' 'Skule Skerry,' 'Tendebant Manus,' 'The Last Crusade,' 'Fullcircle'
      Montrose

1929   *The Courts of the Morning*
      The Causal and the Casual in History (Rede Lecture)

1930   *The Kirk in Scotland* (with George Adam Smith)
      Castle Gay

1931   *The Blanket of the Dark*
      The Novel and the Fairy Tale

1932   *Sir Walter Scott*
      The Gap in the Curtain
      Julius Caesar
      The Magic Walking-Stick

1933   *The Massacre of Glencoe*
      A Prince of the Captivity

1934   *The Free Fishers*
      Gordon at Khartoum
      Oliver Cromwell

1935   *The King's Grace*
      The House of the Four Winds

1936   *The Island of Sheep* [*The Man from the Norlands*]

1937   *Augustus*

———

1940   *Memory Hold-the-Door* [*Pilgrim's Way*]
      Comments and Characters
      Canadian Occasions

1941   *Sick Heart River* [*Mountain Meadow*]
      The Long Traverse [*Lake of Gold*]

The next works which Buchan planned were a novel, *The Island Called Lone*, and a book about fishing of which he completed two chapters (printed at the end of *Memory Hold-the-Door*) with the pencilled title *Pilgrim's Rest*.

SOURCES AND REFERENCES

ACKNOWLEDGMENTS

For my principal acknowledgments, the reader is referred to pages 10 and 11. Most of the other people to whom I am indebted are named under the notes to each chapter.

In addition to these, I am indebted to the collectors of Buchan, who have put their books and knowledge at my disposal: Mr Walter J. Beinecke, whose collection is now at Yale University, Mr Lyman G. Bloomingdale of New York, and particularly Mr John Cavanagh of London, whose knowledge of the publishing history of Buchan's books has been of great help, and who added to his other kindnesses by reading the proofs.

There are a number of others whom I would like to thank for help given in a variety of directions, from spotting Buchan titles in second-hand book-shops to driving me round the Gorbals. They are:

Dr William Beattie and Mr W. Park of the National Library of Scotland
The Rev. George Buchanan-Smith
Professor Bruce Dickins
The late William A. Jackson, of the Houghton Library, Harvard University
Mr Geoffrey Rhodes
Professor David A. Robertson
Miss Felicia Taylor
Dr George A. Williams
Miss Marjorie G. Wynne, Rare Book Room, Yale University Library

SOURCES

1. Buchan's papers; notebooks, manuscripts, letters written or received by him, the volumes of cuttings which he kept from 1904, and other material, the bulk of which is now the property of Queen's University, Kingston, Ontario.

2. The memories of his family, friends and colleagues. His family—Susan Lady Tweedsmuir, the Hon. Mrs Brian Fairfax-Lucy, Lord Tweedsmuir, the Hon. William Buchan and the Hon. Alastair Buchan—supplied material for every chapter in the book. Mrs Hawley (formerly Mrs Killick), who was Buchan's personal secretary from 1906 till his death, contributed to every chapter from VII onwards; the late Violet Markham, the late G. M. Trevelyan and Captain Liddell Hart contributed to a number of

chapters. They are named on the first occasion only. The many others whom I consulted are named in the notes to each chapter.

3. Buchan's own published works. See list on page 476.

4. The following books about Buchan and his family:

ANNA BUCHAN (O. Douglas):
Unforgettable, Unforgotten (1945)
Farewell to Priorsford (1950). A book by and about Anna Buchan
Two of her novels, which are based on the Buchan family life:
The Setons (1917)
Eliza for Common (1928)
Privately printed memoirs:
John Buchan 1847–1911. With appendices by Rev. Charles Shaw, W. G. Livingstone and David Honeyman (1912)
W.H.B. 1880–1912 (William Buchan) (1913)
A.E.B. 1894–1917 (Alastair Buchan) (1917)

LORD TWEEDSMUIR (Johnnie Buchan):
Hudson's Bay Trader (1951)
Always a Countryman (1953)

SUSAN TWEEDSMUIR:
John Buchan by his Wife and Friends (1947). Includes contributions from Charles Dick, Roger Merriman, Violet Markham, Sir Roderick Jones, Lord Macmillan, Lord Baldwin, Walter Elliot, Catherine Carswell, A. L. Rowse, Janet Adam Smith, Leonard Brockington, Sir Shuldham Redfern, Alastair Buchan.
Carnets Canadiens (1938)
The Lilac and the Rose (1952)
A Winter Bouquet (1954)

VIOLET MARKHAM:
'A Man of Many Gifts' in *Friendship's Harvest* (1956)

S. A. GILLON:
Article on Buchan in *Dictionary of National Biography*, *1931–40*

ARTHUR C. TURNER:
Mr Buchan, Writer (1949)

ARCHIBALD HANNA:
John Buchan, a Bibliography (1953), which has been of great help throughout the writing of this book.

I have also been much helped by the bibliography which Mr John Cavanagh has compiled, and kindly allowed me to use.

5. The books etc. listed in the notes to each chapter.

NOTE ON REFERENCES

REFERENCES TO BOOKS:
Where the book is by Buchan or one of the family (see sections 3 and 4 above), I give the titles only, and I use these abbreviations:

M.H.D.=*Memory Hold-the-Door*
W.F.=*John Buchan by his Wife and Friends*
U.U.=*Unforgettable, Unforgotten*
A.A.C.=*Always a Countryman*

Where a book by Buchan, clearly identified in the text, is under discussion, I give no references, but I do where a book of his is quoted to illustrate some other point.

REFERENCES TO LETTERS:

For quotations from letters not in the Buchan Papers I give the source in the references.

For quotations from letters to or from Buchan in the Buchan Papers I have not given references where these concern his day-to-day activities. Where they have a further biographical or literary importance I have given the date and the name of the correspondent in the text.

In the references the numerals on the left refer to pages in the book. The italicised words which follow are the end of the sentence or phrase which is being annotated.

CHAPTER ONE: SON OF THE MANSE

CONVERSATIONS AND CORRESPONDENCE WITH:

Mr John Cavanagh, who showed me some notes in his possession, written by the late W. G. Russell, a master at Peebles High School, about John Buchan's mother as a girl

Mr John M. Hutchison, Rector of Hutchesons' Boys' Grammar School, Glasgow, and Mr Whyte, principal teacher of History, who compiled a note for me on Buchan's career at Hutchesons'

Mr Edward Laverock and Mr John Gibb of J. and W. Buchan, Writers, Peebles

Sir William Sinclair, who was at Hutchesons' with Alastair Buchan

Mrs H. P. van Dusen (Betty Bartholomew), a close friend of Anna Buchan

The Rev. Graham N. Warner, Secretary of the Church and Ministry Department of the Church of Scotland

REFERENCES:

13   *across the Border.*' David Cairns: *An Autobiography* (1950), p. 86
14   *headachy little boy.*' M.H.D., p. 81
15   *like a nightmare.* From a paragraph on Lewis Carroll in 'A Spectator's Notebook' by Auspex (Buchan), *Spectator* (13 February 1932)
15   *in the cabin.*' M.H.D., p. 20
16   *my bonny man.*' *Prester John*, chap. 1
17   *in the Promised Land.*' U.U., p. 24
17   *life's troubled way.* I saw a photographic copy of this hymn as printed for the Pathhead Free Church Sabbath School, in the collection of Mr John Cavanagh

18   *called only once a week.* An account of Tweedsmuir, when he came to
      it in 1894, by Dr W. S. Crockett, minister of the parish, the *Scots-
      man* (25 May 1935)

19   *a herd's cottage.* 'Pan,' the *Scottish Mountaineering Club Journal*
      (April 1939)

19   *silent and aware.* 'The Green Glen,' *The Moon Endureth*

20   *room to steer in.* 'The Men of the Uplands,' *Scholar Gipsies*

20   *far-wandering, shy.* U.U., p. 31

21   *country notes to town.* The garden is described in 'Urban Greenery,'
      Scholar Gipsies

21   *rich spiritual harvest.* Rev. Charles Shaw in *John Buchan 1847–1911*,
      p. 314

22   *wrath to come.* David Honeyman, *ibid.*, p. 324

22   *of God's elect.* Anna Buchan, *ibid.*, p. 11

22   *among the members.* Rev. Charles Shaw, *ibid.*, p. 315

22   *sales of work.* *Eliza for Common*, chap. 15

22   *a grocery establishment.* *The Setons*, chap. 5

23   *in the spring.* U.U., p. 20

25   *he was adamant.* U.U., p. 90

25   *trifle not with God!* *John Buchan 1847–1911*, p. 224

27   *an outstanding teacher, James Cadell.* Buchan wrote an appreciation
      of him in the *Hutchesonian* (December 1920)

CHAPTER TWO: GLASGOW STUDENT

CONVERSATIONS AND CORRESPONDENCE WITH:

Professor David Cairns, University of Aberdeen
Miss Katie Cameron (Mrs Arthur Kay)
Mr J. H. MacCallum Scott
Mr R. O. MacKenna, Librarian, and Mr George P. Richardson, Assistant
   Registrar, of the University of Glasgow
The late Neil Macmillan, who knew the Buchan family as a boy
Mr C. A. Oakley, University of Glasgow

UNPUBLISHED MATERIAL:

Buchan Papers:
   Letters to and from his family and friends
   Book of manuscript poems
   Commonplace book
   Lecture notebook on Moral Philosophy
   MS and TS of unfinished novel, *The Mountain*
Notebooks of the late Alexander MacCallum Scott, which I was allowed
   to see and quote from by courtesy of Mr J. H. MacCallum Scott.

BOOKS:

James Bridie: *One Way of Living* (1939)
David Cairns: *An Autobiography* (1950)

G. E. Davie: *The Democratic Intellect: Scotland and her Universities in the Nineteenth Century* (1961)

Fortuna Domus: Lectures given by Professors of Glasgow University on the history of their subjects (1952)

Glasgow University Magazine, 1892–95

Tom Jones: *Welsh Broth* (1951)

Liber Saecularis Glasguensium: The Book of the Jubilee (1901)

John Lochhead: *A Reach of the River*. Privately printed (1955)

J. D. Mackie: *The University of Glasgow 1451–1951* (1954)

Gilbert Murray: *An Unfinished Autobiography* (1960)

> Preface to *The Clearing House*: a selection from the writings of John Buchan (1946)

C. A. Oakley: *The Second City* (1946)

REFERENCES:

29   *Ben Nevis.* Bridie: *One Way of Living*, p. 110

30   *taught they would be.'* Murray: *An Unfinished Autobiography*, p. 98

31   *philosophy and literature.'* H. J. C. Grierson: *Problems of National Education* (1919), p. 317. I found the quotation in Davie's *The Democratic Intellect*, p. 102

31   *obviously a treasure.'* Preface to *The Clearing House*, p. vii

31   *of intelligent undergraduates.* J. A. K. Thomson: 'Gilbert Murray 1866–1957,' *Proceedings of the British Academy*, Vol. XLIII (1958), p. 248·

32   *and social reform.'* Murray: *An Unfinished Autobiography*, p. 97

32   *philosophy didn't matter.'* Professor C. A. Campbell in *Fortuna Domus*, p. 119

32   *quest for a faith.'* M.H.D., p. 37

32   *to be a philosopher.'* 'Some College Memories,' the *Student* (8 February 1928)

33   *Glasgow University Magazine.* Buchan's contributions were 'On Cademuir Hill' (19 December 1894), 'Robert Louis Stevenson' (9 January 1895), and a review of Walter Pater's *Greek Studies* (6 February 1895)

38   *by Cademuir Law.* 'The Fishers,' *Poems Scots and English*

40   *hole again at night.'* 'The Men of the Uplands,' *Scholar Gipsies*

40   *such a painful thing.'* Mr John Cavanagh has in his collection an 18-page booklet *A Violet Wreath*, 'In Memoriam Violet Katharine Stuart Buchan, 20 March 1888–16 June 1893'

41   *in his other papers.* Report of 'The Tweedsmuir Dinner,' in the *Brazen Nose* (November 1935)

43   *are not enemies.'* Professor C. A. Campbell in *Fortuna Domus*, p. 118

44   *unenterprising dullness.'* Speech at Glasgow University Club Dinner, 27 June 1924

CHAPTER THREE: OXFORD UNDERGRADUATE

CONVERSATIONS AND CORRESPONDENCE WITH:

The Hon. Mrs Raymond Asquith

The late Rt Hon. Harold Baker
The late B. C. Boulter
Lady Kinross and Mrs Olive Carruthers
Lord Salter
Mrs Jerrard Tickell (daughter of the late E. S. P. Haynes)

Mr Barry Nicholas, Vice-Principal, and Mr S. Smith, Library Clerk, Brasenose College
Mrs Richmond, Assistant Librarian, Balliol College
Mr R. Walters, Assistant Librarian, Union Society, Oxford
Mr J. D. Wells, City Librarian, Oxford

UNPUBLISHED MATERIAL:

Buchan Papers:
  Letters to and from his family and friends. The letters of Raymond
    Asquith are quoted by permission of the Hon. Mrs Raymond Asquith
  Lecture Notebooks: On Philosophy, October 1898 (also contains
    literary work), Miscellanea, Logic, The Ethics, The Constitution
    of Athens

Notebooks of the late Alexander MacCallum Scott
Minute-Books of the Oxford Union Society

BOOKS AND ARTICLES:

Balliol College Register 1832–1914 (1914)
Brasenose College Register, Vol. I (1910)
The *Brazen Nose* 'The Tweedsmuir Dinner' (November 1935) and 'In
  Memoriam, Lord Tweedsmuir' with note by Dr F. W. Bussell (June
  1940)
Edward Cadogan: *Before the Deluge* (1961). Has accounts of Raymond
  Asquith and Aubrey Herbert by a Balliol contemporary
G. B. Gundy: *Fifty-Five Years at Oxford* (1945)
The Book of the Horace Club 1898–1901 (n.d.)
The *Isis*, 1895–99
Compton Mackenzie: *Sinister Street* (1913–14)
Gilbert Murray: *An Unfinished Autobiography* (1960)
The *Oxford J.C.R.*, 1897–99
Oxford Times Centenary Supplement (7 September 1962)
Lord Salter: *Memoirs of a Public Servant* (1961)
Buchan and John Lane:
  J. Lewis May: *John Lane and the Nineties* (1936)
  Reginald Pound: *Arnold Bennett* (1952)

REFERENCES:

46 *of his ordered society.*' Salter: *Memoirs*, p. 27
47 *there are no girls.*' Compton Mackenzie: *Sinister Street*, Book III,
      chap. 16
48 *neither late nor soon. Glasgow Herald* (19 October 1895). The article
      was signed 'B' and was wrongly attributed, by some of their
      Glasgow friends, to H. N. Brailsford; there is a reference to
      Buchan's authorship in a letter to C. H. Dick, 22 October 1895

49   *to another country.*' J. G. Lockhart: *Cosmo Gordon Lang* (1949), p. 12

49   *enlightenment and philosophy.*' Murray: *An Unfinished Autobiography*, p. 87

49   *impossible to extract*. I found this anecdote in Arthur Machen's *Far-Off Things* (1922), p. 146

51   *classics were for himself.*' Salter: *Memoirs*, p. 28

56   *one who 'counts.' Journals of Arnold Bennett*, Vol. I (1932), p. 10

60   *gets to the top first.*' Mr Buchan, quoted in *W.H.B.*, p. 53

60   *makes a man take risks*. 'Some Scottish Characteristics,' Buchan's contribution to *The Scottish Tongue*, ed. W. Craigie (1924), p. 57

60   *and not the prize*. Speech at Domum Dinner at Winchester, 28 July 1930

62   *manager with a gun*. This anecdote comes from a letter on Aubrey Herbert by St J. L[ucas], *Spectator* (6 October 1923)

63   *of the University.*' Violet Markham: 'Sir Robert Morant,' *Friendship's Harvest* (1956), p. 170

66   *in his best days.*' This and the other quotations in this paragraph come from *Andrew Jameson, Lord Ardwall*, pp. 146, 117, 19

74   *beer all round. These for Remembrance*, p. 70

CHAPTER FOUR: BARRISTER AND JOURNALIST

CONVERSATIONS AND CORRESPONDENCE WITH:

The late Rt Hon. Harold Baker
Mr Douglas Blackwood
Mr Charles Monteith, All Souls
Mr C. A. Seaton, Librarian, the *Spectator*
Miss Doreen Smith, of the Bodley Head
Mrs Jerrard Tickell

UNPUBLISHED MATERIAL:

Buchan Papers:
     Letters to and from his family and friends. The letter from Cosmo Lang on page 77 is printed by permission of his literary executor, the Rev. Dr A. C. Don
     Book of manuscript poems
Letter-books of William Blackwood & Son in the National Library of Scotland.

BOOKS AND ARTICLES:

George Blake: *Barrie and the Kailyard School* (1951)
Joseph Conrad: *Letters to William Blackwood and David S. Meldrum* (ed. William Blackburn) (1959)
Peter Green: *Kenneth Grahame* (1959)
J. G. Lockhart: *Cosmo Gordon Lang* (1949)
J. Lewis May: *John Lane and the Nineties* (1936)
K. L. Mix: *A Study in Yellow* (1960)
The *Spectator*, 1899–1901

F. D. Tredrey: *The House of Blackwood* (1954)
The *Yellow Book*, Vols. VIII–XII (1896–97)

REFERENCES:

76 *turned away from him.*' Robert Speaight: *The Life of Hilaire Belloc* (1957), p. 95
86 *scholar and gipsy.* Annual Report of the Robert Louis Stevenson Club, 1929
87 *commented much later.* In an interview published in the *Book Window* (December 1927)
88 *loiters in the past.*' Preface to *The Poetry of Neil Munro* (1931)
93 *Salvation Army, renouncing all.* Sir Arthur Quiller-Couch: *Memories and Opinions* (1944), p. 74
96 *and smelt.*' Review in *Oxford J.C.R.* (7 June 1898)
102 *The Finest Story in the World.*' Conrad to Blackwood, 8 November 1899, *Letters to William Blackwood*, p. 72

CHAPTER FIVE: MILNER'S YOUNG MAN

CONVERSATIONS AND CORRESPONDENCE WITH:
The late H. E. Bell, Librarian, New College, Oxford
The late Lord Brand
Sir James Butler, biographer of Lord Lothian
Professor F. W. Gibson, Queen's University, Kingston, Ontario
The late Lord Leconfield (formerly the Hon. Hugh Wyndham)
The late Violet Markham (and subsequent chapters)
The late Lady Milner
Mr Dermot Morrah, the *Round Table*
Professor George Shepperson, University of Edinburgh

UNPUBLISHED MATERIAL:
Buchan Papers:
    Letters to and from his family and friends
    Three volumes of Proceedings of the Inter-Colonial Council of the Transvaal and Orange River Colony 1903, of which Buchan was Secretary
Violet Markham: 'Milner,' a 24-page typescript article written in the 1950's, mainly about Milner's career in South Africa, with quotations from Milner's letters to the author
Milner Papers at New College, Oxford

BOOKS:

L. S. Amery: *My Political Life*, Vol. I (1953)
            The Times History of the War in South Africa, Vol. VI (1909)
J. R. M. Butler: *Lord Lothian* (1960)
Lionel Curtis: *With Milner in South Africa* (1951)
Ruth Fry: *Emily Hobhouse* (1929)
W. K. Hancock: *Smuts*, Vol. I (1962)

Edgar Holt: *The Boer War* (1958)
Rayne Kruger: *Goodbye, Dolly Gray* (1959)
J. G. Lockhart and C. M. Woodhouse: *Rhodes* (1963)
A. C. Martin: *The Concentration Camps 1900–1902* (1958)
Milner Papers (ed. Cecil Headlam): *South Africa*, Vol. II 1899–1905 (1933)
H. W. Nevinson: *Changes and Chances* (1923)
Lionel Phillips: *Some Reminiscences* (1924)
George Shepperson and Thomas Price: *Independent African* (1958)
L. M. Thompson: *Unification of South Africa 1902–1910* (1960)
A. P. Thornton: *The Imperial Idea and its Enemies* (1959)
E. A. Walker: *History of Southern Africa* (1957)
Evelyn Wrench: *Alfred Lord Milner* (1958)

REFERENCES:

107   *work in them.* Sir Percy Fitzpatrick: *Lord Milner and His Work* (1925),
       p. 4. I found the quotation in A. M. Gollin's *Proconsul in Politics*
       (1964), p. 41

107   *who had written it.* Buchan's articles on South Africa were 'The
       "Edinburgh" on South Africa' (26 January 1901), 'Report on the
       Hospitals' Commission' (2 February 1901), 'The Debate on
       the Refugee Camps' (22 June 1901). Strachey was the author of
       'The Dead Set against Sir Alfred Milner' (9 March 1901)

109   *of heath and sky.* 'From the Pentlands, Looking North and South,'
       Poems Scots and English

111   *Winston S. Churchill.* Churchill to Milner, 17 March 1901. This
       manuscript letter, which is among the Milner Papers at New
       College, Oxford, is quoted by permission of the Chartwell Literary
       Trust and of New College

113   *new, raw, and fortuitous.'* *African Colony*, p. 311

114   *of settling principles.'* *Milner Papers*, Vol. II, p. 315

115   *to an adequate defence. Ibid.*, Vol. II, p. 229

115   *a sad fiasco.' Ibid.*, Vol. II, p. 230

116   *wounds or illness.* The figure for refugee deaths is from E. A. Walker's
       History of Southern Africa, p. 498; those for military casualties
       from the Report of the Royal Commission on the War, quoted in
       Evelyn Wrench's *Alfred Lord Milner*, p. 236

117   *dust and withered grass.'* Nevinson: *Changes and Chances*, p. 323

117   *commercial British one.'* Wrench: *Alfred Lord Milner*, p. 229

119   *as the essentials.* This article, 'The Reconstruction of South Africa—
       Land Settlement,' is signed 'Johnnesburg'; a second article in
       the *National Review* (January 1903) on 'Johannesburg' is signed
       'Pseudo-Africanus.' Both were later incorporated into *The African
       Colony*

122   *the average peasant.' African Colony*, p. 62

123   *till the end of time. Ibid.*, p. 67

123   *White and Black.'* Wrench: *Alfred Lord Milner*, p. 182

123   *fitness for civic rights.' Milner Papers*, Vol. II, p. 466

124   *centuries to climb.' Ibid.*, Vol. II, p. 467

124   *free societies are based. African Colony*, p. 289

124 *citizen's right to vote.'* Ibid., p. 336
125 *full of Jews.'* Nevinson: *Changes and Chances*, p. 319
127 *and falling softly. African Colony*, p. 81
128 *East and South. Ibid.*, p. 82
129 *perforce to leave it. Ibid.*, p. 103
129 *remote malarial tropics.'* Ibid., p. 134
129 *of a friendly universe.'* M.H.D., p. 120
131 *edge of a wilderness. African Colony*, p. 126
131 *of a boy's dream. Ibid.*, p. 122
132 *adjusting of problems.'* Ibid., p. 31
133 *a gigantic task.* Amery: *My Political Life*, Vol. I, p. 177
133 *the facts, however dismal.* The article (4 April 1905) is a composite
       work; Buchan in his cutting-book indicates where his contribution
       begins, at the paragraph 'Long before the conclusion of peace . . .'.
       Buchan also wrote of Milner in the *Quarterly Review* (July 1905):
       'Lord Milner and South Africa'
140 *Buchan's short stories.* 'The Grove of Ashtaroth' and 'The Kings of
       Orion' were collected in *The Moon Endureth* (1912), 'The Green
       Wildebeeste' first appeared in *The Runagates Club* (1928)
145 *John Chilembwe in Nyasaland.* The article, 'Some Lessons from the
       Chilembwe Rebellion' by C. G. Rawlinson, appeared in *Central
       Africa: A Monthly Record of the Universities Mission to Central
       Africa* (1917), p. 61. Professor Shepperson has also told me of
       another novel about the Ethiopianist African (though he con-
       siders it much inferior to Buchan's), *Bayete! or Hail to the King*,
       by G. Heaton Nicholls, a former High Commissioner for South
       Africa in the United Kingdom, written about 1912 or 1913,
       though not published until 1923

CHAPTER SIX: INSIDER

CONVERSATIONS AND CORRESPONDENCE WITH:
Professor F. W. Gibson
Mrs F. S. Oliver

UNPUBLISHED MATERIAL:

Buchan Papers:
  Letters to and from his family and friends. For permission to quote
  from letters by Violet Markham, St Loe Strachey and Virginia Woolf,
  I thank Miss Persis Tallents, the late John Strachey and Mr Leonard
  Woolf
  MS and TS of unfinished novel, *The Mountain*

Alpine Club: Papers relating to Buchan's candidature
Amery Papers
Cromer Papers (Public Record Office)
Violet Markham: 'Milner'

BOOKS AND ARTICLES:

L. S. Amery: *My Political Life*, Vol. I (1953)

A. M. Gollin: *Proconsul in Politics* (1964)
Christopher Hassall: *Edward Marsh* (1959)
Violet Markham: *Return Passage* (1953)
Dudley Sommer: *Haldane of Cloan* (1960)
The *Spectator*, 1903–07

REFERENCES:

146 *scarcely care for at all.*' Milner to Jowett, 2 February 1882, quoted in
      Geoffrey Faber's *Jowett* (1957), p. 362
149 *finish the conversation outside.*' *Lord Ardwall*, p. 66
150 *as much fighter as conciliator.*' '"Spectator" Memories,' the *Spectator*
      (3 November 1928)
152 *article in Blackwood's.*' 'Mountaineering of Today' (May 1905).
      Other articles by Buchan on mountaineering are 'The Vulgarisa-
      tion of the Alps' (*Spectator*, 19 August 1905), 'Rock-climbing in
      the British Isles' (*Spectator*, 26 May 1906), 'Spring in the Alps'
      (*Spectator*, 16 June 1906), 'In the Heart of the Coolins' (*Black-
      wood's*, June 1906), 'The Freemasonry of the Alps' (*Spectator*, 21
      December 1907), and 'The Alps' (*Scottish Review*, 25 July 1907,
      reprinted in *Comments and Characters*)
153 *the Union of South Africa.* Obituary of F. S. Oliver by Buchan, *The
      Times* (5 June 1934). Dougal Malcolm wrote the article on Oliver in
      the *D.N.B.* and there are passages on him in L. S. Amery's *My
      Political Life*, A. M. Gollin's *Proconsul in Politics* and Austen
      Chamberlain's *Politics from the Inside* (1937). Susan Tweedsmuir
      gives a vivid account of him in w.f.
154 *of the Action Française.* See, for instance, the letters quoted in
      Gollin's *Proconsul in Politics*, pp. 273 and 539.
155 *valued at the Court.*' James Pope-Hennessy: *Queen Mary* (1959), p. 359
156 *in the National Review.* 'The Judgment of Posterity,' *National
      Review* (February 1903)
156 *in all northern nations.*' 'The Government and South Africa,' *Quar-
      terly Review* (April 1906)
158 *in schools in England.*' Gollin, *Proconsul in Politics*, p. 69; in chapters
      III and IV there is a full account of the Chinese labour contro-
      versy and its long-term effects on British politics
158 *patronising and tactless.*' Margot Asquith: *Autobiography*, Vol. II
      (1922), p. 85
165 *gave away money so unsparingly.* Susan Tweedsmuir in *Farewell to
      Priorsford*, p. 45
166 *John and Pierre.*' w.f., p. 39

CHAPTER SEVEN:
PUBLISHER AND PARLIAMENTARY CANDIDATE

CONVERSATIONS AND CORRESPONDENCE WITH:
Mrs Hawley, formerly Mrs Killick (and subsequent chapters)
Sir Allen Lane

The Earl of Longford
Mr Dermot Morrah, the *Round Table*
Nelson's:
 The late Mr James Hartley, Dr H. P. Morrison, Mr L. Murby; the late
 Mr G. S. Dickson and Miss N. T. Yule, both of whom worked with
 Buchan in Edinburgh; Madame Paul Maze (formerly Mrs T. A. Nelson)
Byron Letters:
 Professor Leon Edel
 Miss Doris Langley Moore
 Miss Jenny Lewis, Department of Manuscripts, British Museum

UNPUBLISHED MATERIAL:
Buchan Papers:
 Letters to and from his family and friends. For permission to quote
 from a letter from T. A. Nelson, I thank Madame Paul Maze.

Amery Papers

BOOKS:

L. S. Amery: *My Political Life*, Vol. I (1953)
A. M. Gollin: *Proconsul in Politics* (1964)
W. Forbes Gray (ed.): *Comments and Characters* by John Buchan (1940).
 Mr Gray was Buchan's assistant on the *Scottish Review*, and describes
 his editorship in the Introduction to this selection of Buchan's con-
 tributions

Byron Letters:
 Lord Byron's Correspondence, ed. J. Murray (1922)
 Henry James: *Notebooks*, ed. F. O. Matthiessen and K. B. Murdock
 (1947)
 Lady Lovelace: *Ralph, Earl of Lovelace* (1920)

REFERENCES:

167 *too much for this hen.*' W.F., p. 48
169 *with ordinary humanity.*' M.H.D., p. 139
169 *sold in the same way.* 'The Philosophy of the Reprint,' *Scottish Review* (28 November 1907), reprinted in *Comments and Characters*,
 p. 241
170 *from the library.* Unpublished address, 'Literature and Life,' 1910
171 *well-known theologian.* Introduction to *Comments and Characters*,
 p. xiii
173 *in the casual bus.* W.F., p. 42
175 *Suicide Cottage.*' W.F., p. 65
175 *Byron and his wife.*' M.H.D., p. 151
176 *never turned a hair.*' M.H.D., p. 152
176 *mildly Rabelaisian turn.*' Ferris Greenslet: *Under the Bridge* (1943),
 p. 158
177 *in another world.*' M.H.D., p. 143
181 *of the pulpit (Mr Gladstone).* Lord Ardwall, p. 18
181 *emotions at high tension.*' 'The New Jesuitry,' *Blackwood's* (June
 1913). Other political articles which Buchan contributed to

CHAPTER EIGHT: PROPAGANDIST

CONVERSATIONS AND CORRESPONDENCE WITH:

The late Rt Hon. Harold Baker
The late Lord Beaverbrook
Captain B. H. Liddell Hart (and subsequent chapters)

UNPUBLISHED MATERIAL:

Buchan Papers:
   Letters to and from his family, friends and others
   Folder of 'G.H.Q. Intelligence Summaries'
   Folder of memoranda about the Department and Ministry of Informa-
   tion

Amery Papers

Correspondence between John Buchan and Walter Hines Page at the
   Houghton Library of Harvard University, whom I thank for permission to quote

BOOKS:

L. S. Amery: *My Political Life*, Vol. II (1953)

Lord Beaverbrook: *Politicians and the War 1914–16* (1928–32)
     Men and Power 1917–18 (1956)
A. M. Gollin: *Proconsul in Politics* (1964)
F. S. Oliver: *Ordeal by Battle* (1915)
    The Anvil of War. Letters between F. S. Oliver and his
      brother 1914–18 (1936)
Reginald Pound and Geoffrey Harmsworth: *Northcliffe* (1959)
Department and Ministry of Information:
 Sir Roderick Jones: *A Life in Reuter's* (1951)
 Lucy Masterman: *C. F. G. Masterman* (1939)
Other biographies and memoirs with references to the Department and
Ministry are:
 Arnold Bennett: *Journals*, Vol. II (1952)
 Ian Colvin: *Life of Lord Carson*, Vol. III (1936)
 Rupert Hart-Davis: *Hugh Walpole* (1952)
 F. A. Mackenzie: *Lord Beaverbrook* (1931)
 Lord Macmillan: *A Man of Law's Tale* (1952)
 M. Newbolt: *Later Life and Letters of Sir Henry Newbolt* (1942)
 Reginald Pound: *Arnold Bennett* (1952)
 Pelham Warner: *Long Innings* (1951)
 Lina Waterfield: *Castle in Italy* (1961)
War Artists:
 Anthony Bertram: *Paul Nash* (1955)
 Christopher Hassall: *Edward Marsh* (1959)
 Paul Nash: *Outline* (1949)
 Poet and Painter: Letters between Gordon Bottomley and Paul Nash (1953)
 H. W. Nevinson: *Last Changes, Last Chances* (1928)
 Sir William Rothenstein: *Men and Memories*, Vol. II (1932)

REFERENCES:

193 *as a duty.*' Preface to *The History of the Great War*, Vol. I, p. vii
194 *to you for consideration.* Buchan to Blackwood, 7 December 1914.
   The letter is printed on the dust-cover of Blackwood's 1958
   edition of *The Thirty-Nine Steps and the Power House*
197 *the holes they made.* Oxford Magazine (1 March 1923), quoted in
   H. A. L. Fisher's *James Bryce*, Vol. II (1927), p. 148
200 *yours very sincerely, Milner.* Milner to Lloyd George, 17 January
   1917. This letter is in the Lloyd George Papers, and was quoted by
   A. M. Gollin in *Proconsul in Politics*, p. 378
201 *with my own hands.*' Oliver: *Anvil of War*, p. 187
201 *story was faked.* Mrs Masterman treats fully of this episode in her
   C. F. G. Masterman, and there are references to it in the letters
   exchanged between Amery and Buchan on 22 and 23 May 1917, in
   the Amery Papers
201 *with half-truths.*' Oliver: *Ordeal by Battle*, p. 436
202 *a long way to go.*' Hassall: *Edward Marsh*, p. 414
202 *he deserves it.*' Nash: *Outline*, p. 207
203 *weaken his hands.* Unpublished speech at National Liberal Club,
   14 November 1917

203 *Buchan is attractive.' The Diary of Lord Bertie of Thame 1914–1918* (1924), Vol. II, p. 203

204 *two delightful people.* Waterfield: *Castle in Italy*, p. 170

204 *strange ideas on warfare!'* Duff Cooper: *Haig*, Vol. II (1936), p. 93

205 *your Intelligence Bureau.* Amery to Buchan, 3 July 1917, in Amery Papers, quoted by permission of the Rt Hon. Julian Amery

208 *vastness into stagnation.' The King's Grace*, p. 146

210 *yours very sincerely, John Buchan.'* Buchan to Page, 6 December 1917, in the Page Papers at the Houghton Library, Harvard University; the other letters quoted are from the same source

212 *can be concrete.'* Macmillan: *Man of Law's Tale*, p. 165

212 *Lowell Thomas found T. E. Lawrence.* I learned this from Brian Gardner's *Allenby* (1965), p. 204

214 *preposterous mutual suspicions.* Oliver: *Anvil of War*, p. 328

214 *hysteria and Bolshevism.* Bennett: *Journals*, Vol. II (1932), p. 241

214 *I was not surprised. Ibid.*, p. 242

215 *act of just mercy. The Times* (4 January 1919)

215 *or public policy. History of the Great War*, Vol. II, p. 19

216 *be called genius').* 'Mr Lloyd George's Future,' *Graphic* (2 April 1932)

217 *mools aside him.* 'Home Thoughts from Abroad,' *Poems Scots and English*

CHAPTER NINE: COUNTRY GENTLEMAN

CONVERSATIONS AND CORRESPONDENCE WITH:

The late Mr G. S. Dickson and Miss N. T. Yule, of Nelson's
Sir Keith Feiling
Mr Robert Graves
Professor A. W. Lawrence (whom I also thank for permission to quote from the letters of T. E. Lawrence)
Madame Paul Maze
The late G. M. Trevelyan (and subsequent chapters)
Dr C. V. Wedgwood
Rosebery:
    The Countess of Rosebery
    Mr Robert Rhodes James

UNPUBLISHED MATERIAL:

Buchan Papers:
    Letters to and from his family and others. For permission to quote from letters by G. M. Trevelyan, I thank Mrs J. H. Moorman
Rosebery Papers

BOOKS:

G. N. Clark: *The Manor of Elsfield* (1927)
M. Newbolt: *Later Life and Letters of Sir Henry Newbolt* (1942)

Reuter's
Sir Roderick Jones: *A Life in Reuter's* (1951)
Graham Storey: *Reuter's Century* (1951)

Lord Rosebery
John Buchan: 'Lord Rosebery,' from *Proceedings of the British Academy*,
Vol. XVI (1930), included in *Men and Deeds* (1935)
Robert Rhodes James: *Rosebery* (1963)

T. E. Lawrence
Letters of T. E. Lawrence, David Garnett (ed.) (1938)
Letters to T. E. Lawrence, A. W. Lawrence (ed.) (1962)

Canada and United States:
L. S. Amery: *My Political Life*, Vol. II (1953)
Ferris Greenslet: *Under the Bridge* (1943)
Blair Neatby: *William Lyon Mackenzie King*, Vol. II (1963)

REFERENCES:

220   *do you good.'* Newbolt: *Sir Henry Newbolt*, p. 269
222   *put down his roots.* Buchan wrote of his new countryside and its past
       in 'Thoughts on a Distant Prospect of Oxford,' *Blackwood's*
       (October 1923)—included in *Homilies and Recreations*—in the
       Preface to the Council for the Preservation of Rural England's
       survey of *The Thames Valley* (1929), and in 'The Oxford Country',
       Oxford (Summer 1934)
222   *older English world.'* Both quotations in this sentence come from
       Buchan's Introduction to *The Compleat Angler* (1901)
223   *came over him.* A.A.C., p. 19
223   *in the sycamore!* Envoy to Underwoods, Book I, *Collected Poems of
       R. L. Stevenson* (1950), p. 111. I heard about Buchan writing these
       lines in his copy of Quiller-Couch's *Studies in Literature* from Mr
       Francis Hardy, formerly Librarian of the Houses of Parliament,
       Ottawa, to whom Lady Tweedsmuir gave the book after her
       husband's death
225   *and courtesy itself.* A. L. Rowse in W.F., p. 175
226   *of physical origin.'* W.F., p. 165
227   *those who know you.'* Newbolt: *Sir Henry Newbolt*, p. 304
229   *at your disposal.'* Jones: *A Life in Reuter's*, p. 264
229   *historical parallels.'* *Army Quarterly* (January 1922)
230   *War Office documents.* Lloyd George: *War Memoirs*, Vol. III (1934),
       p. 1492
231   *to correct my views.* Buchan to Borden, 25 August 1932, in the Borden
       Papers, Public Archives of Canada
231   *to Lloyd George.'* *Canadian Historical Review* (March 1925)
232   *severely taken to task.* S. A. Gillon: *D.N.B.* 1931–40
232   *to avowed fiction.* *British Weekly* (12 February 1914)
233   *accurately set forth.* *Scottish Historical Review* (October 1913)
234   *we were born.* Edwin Muir: *Collected Poems* (1960), p. 97
235   *spirit of a crusader.'* Unpublished address at Stowe School, 10
       March 1929

236 *else of yours.* Lawrence to Buchan, 26 December 1928, in *Letters of T. E. Lawrence*, p. 626

237 *glass of champagne.*' Bishop Walpole, quoted in U.U., p. 159

238 *church of Uyeasound.* Susan Buchan contributed an account of this holiday to the *Spectator* (6 August 1927), 'Three Travellers to the Shetland Islands,' signed 'L'

238 *do its own work.* A.A.C., p. 64

239 *had no responsibilities.* A.A.C., p. 104

240 *as its centre.* 'Lord Rosebery,' *Scottish Review* (5 March 1908), reprinted in *Comments and Characters*, p. 297

240 *from the eighteenth century.*' 'Lord Rosebery,' *Proceedings of the British Academy*, Vol. XVI, p. 19, reprinted in *Men and Deeds*

240 *saw only its triviality.*' Review of Lord Crewe's *Lord Rosebery* (1931) in the *Observer* (15 November 1931)

241 *on the Borders.* Buchan to Rosebery, 19 July 1925. I am grateful to Mr Robert Rhodes James for telling me about this letter in the Rosebery Papers, and to the Countess of Rosebery for looking it out for me

241 *of his bondage.* M.H.D., p. 157

242 *of my youth.*' M.H.D., p. 218

242 *like a passion.* Review of *Revolt in the Desert* in the *Saturday Review of Literature* (19 March 1927)

242 *put yourself!*' Lawrence to Buchan, 19 May 1925, *Letters of T. E. Lawrence*, p. 475

242 *against Hoare's will.*' T. E. Lawrence: *Letters to His Biographers* (1963), Vol. II, p. 24

243 *very deepest thanks.* Lawrence to Buchan, 5 July 1925, *Letters of T. E. Lawrence*, p. 478

243 *will be great years.* Lawrence to Buchan, 20 June 1927. In this unpublished letter Lawrence corrects several misstatements about himself made in the Introduction to the American edition of *Revolt in the Desert*, which he had been told was Buchan's work. Buchan denied the rumour in a letter of 13 July 1927, which is published in *Letters to T. E. Lawrence*, p. 20

243 *not everyone's prescription.* Lawrence to Buchan, 26 December 1928, *Letters of T. E. Lawrence*, p. 626

243 *your real opinion.* Lawrence to Buchan, 20 December 1934, *Letters of T. E. Lawrence*, p. 836

244 *a new service.*' Buchan to Lawrence, *Letters to T. E. Lawrence*, p. 22

244 *on your opinion.*' Lawrence to Buchan, 1 April 1935, *Letters of T. E. Lawrence*, p. 862

245 *can think of.*' Buchan to Bradford, 27 August 1924. In the Houghton Library of Harvard University, whom I thank for permission to quote

245 *victory was assured.*' Address to the National Liberal Club, February 1916

245 *Monroe Doctrine in Practice.*' The articles appeared on 18 February and 28 January 1905. Other *Spectator* articles by Buchan on American topics were 'the Kinship of the English and American

Bars' (4 August 1900), 'American Experiments in Imperial Reconstruction' (27 February 1904), 'President Roosevelt's Opportunity' (3 December 1904), 'Mr Root and the Monroe Doctrine'
(31 December 1904), 'The United States and Cuba' (22 September 1906), 'Britain and the United States' (26 January 1907). For
the *Scottish Review* (reprinted in *Comments and Characters*) he
wrote 'The American Constitution and its Defects' (7 May 1908),
'The "Handy Man" of American Politics'—Mr Taft (12 November 1908)

247 *Fredericksburg to Washington.* Greenslet: *Under the Bridge*, p.
203

249 *antithesis of this type.* 'John Buchan,' *Ottawa Citizen* (8 November
1924)

CHAPTER TEN: STORY-TELLER

CONVERSATIONS AND CORRESPONDENCE WITH:

Colonel R. Macleod and Mr R. D. L. Kelly, editors of *The Ironside
Diaries 1937–40* (1962)
John Buchan's agents, Messrs A. P. Watt & Son, and his publishers,
Messrs Blackwood, Cassell, Doubleday, Hodder & Stoughton, Hough-
ton Mifflin, Nelson, Pan and Penguin, who took much trouble to obtain
for me the figures of his sales and royalties

UNPUBLISHED MATERIAL:

Buchan Papers:
Letters to and from his family and others

BOOKS AND ARTICLES:

Graham Greene: *The Lost Childhood* (1950)
C. M. Grieve (Hugh MacDiarmid): *Contemporary Studies* (1926), origin-
ally printed in the *Scottish Educational Journal* (19 June 1925)
Aubrey Herbert: *Mons, Anzac and Kut* (1919)
               Ben Kendim (1924)
Louis Pauwels and Jacques Bergier: *Le Matin des Magiciens* (1961)
John Raymond: *England's On the Anvil* (1958)
Richard Usborne: *Clubland Heroes* (1953)

Of all the articles on Buchan I have seen, I have found the following the
most informative and stimulating:

Jacques Bergier: 'Redécouverte du roman d'aventure anglais,' *Le Planète*
(October–November 1961)
Gertrude Himmelfarb: 'John Buchan. An Untimely Appreciation,'
Encounter (September 1960)
Walter Keir: 'Public Servant,' *Saltire Review* (Autumn 1956)
Times Literary Supplement: 'Out of the Ordinary' (25 February 1955)
and 'The Hunted and the Heather' (1 June 1956)
Philip Toynbee: 'John Buchan,' *Observer* (10 June 1956)

REFERENCES:

252 *when he read the passage.* Raymond Chandler to James Sandoe, 28 December 1949, in *Raymond Chandler Speaking*, ed. D. Gardiner and K. S. Walker (1962), p. 85

252 *like Trent's Last Case.'* E. C. Bentley: dedication ('To the Memory of John Buchan') to *Elephant's Work* (1950)

255 *revelling in life.'* St J. L[ucas] in a letter on Aubrey Herbert to the *Spectator* (6 October 1923). There are further accounts of Herbert in Edward Cadogan's *Before the Deluge* (1961) and Adrian Carton de Wiart's *Happy Odyssey* (1950)

256 *engrossed in tactics.* Herbert: *Ben Kendim*, p. 15

256 *made our plans quickly. Ibid.,* p. 51

258 *over the river.'* Lord Ardwall, p. 75

259 *résistance physique.* 'Redécouverte du roman d'aventure anglais,' *Planète* (October–November 1961)

261 *loss of identity.* 'A Spectator's Notebook,' by Auspex (Buchan), *Spectator* (13 February 1932)

263 *in Inverlochy Forest.* Captain Brander Dunbar, letter to the *Field* (17 November 1951)

265 *hills and promontories.* W.F., p. 54

273 *J. B. Priestley thought it.* Review in the *London Mercury* (November 1923)

276 *what I dreaded.* M.H.D., p. 135

277 *'tragically fated' Lovels.)* Buchan wrote a 'Spectator's Notebook' paragraph about them (19 March 1932)

280 *undeserving generation.* Lawrence to Edward Garnett, *Letters of T. E. Lawrence*, p. 772

282 *big names for themselves.'* Usborne: *Clubland Heroes*, p. 92

282 *not the termination.* Himmelfarb: *Encounter* (September 1960)

284 *and an ethical appeal.* Himmelfarb: *Ibid.*

285 *major influence on his novels.* Graham Greene, interviewed in *Books and Bookmen* (January 1963)

287 *and guilefully preserved.* J. M. Keynes: 'My Early Beliefs,' *Two Memoirs* (1949), p. 99

287 *protection of civilisation.'* Greene: *The Lost Childhood*, p. 105

287 *ou même du monde.* Bergier: *Candide* (24–31 juillet 1963)

288 *normal lives and identities.* Himmelfarb: *Encounter* (September 1960)

288 *la nausée, sinon plus.* Bergier: Preface to *Le Camp du Matin* (1963)

289 *and a wide horizon?'* *The Novel and the Fairy Tale*, English Association pamphlet 79 (1931)

290 *keenest personal enjoyment.'* 'Janitor': *The Feet of the Young Men* (1928), p. 148

290 *flesh and blood.'* M.H.D., p. 195

291 *an idle child.'* 'A Gossip on Romance,' *Memories and Portraits*

291 *and write David Balfours too.'* Stevenson to Will. H. Low, 15 January 1894, *Letters*, Vol. V (1924), p. 111

291 *drudgery of his art.* 'Nonconformity in Literature,' *Glasgow Herald* (2 November 1895)

298 *or slackening attention. Scotsman* (13 February 1940)

CHAPTER ELEVEN: MEMBER OF PARLIAMENT

CONVERSATIONS AND CORRESPONDENCE WITH:
Earl Attlee
Lord Boothby
The Earl of Crawford and Balcarres
Lord Davidson
Mr Tom Driberg
Sir Keith Feiling
The Duke of Hamilton
Sir Barnett Janner, President, Board of Deputies of British Jews
The Rt Hon. Tom Johnston
Mr David Marquand, biographer of Ramsay MacDonald
Mr Stanley Reed, the British Film Institute
Lord Reith

UNPUBLISHED MATERIAL:
Buchan Papers:
    Letters to and from his family and others

BOOKS:

L. S. Amery: *My Political Life*, Vol. II (1953)
C. R. Attlee: *As it Happened* (1954)
A. W. Baldwin: *My Father, The True Story* (1955)
Hugh Dalton: *The Fateful Years 1931–1945* (1957)
'Janitor' (Mary Lyttelton and J. G. Lockhart): *The Feet of the Young Men* (1928)
Tom Jones: *A Diary with Letters 1931–1950* (1954)
Emanuel Shinwell: *The Labour Story* (1963)
Beatrice Webb: *Diaries 1924–32* (1956)
G. M. Young: *Stanley Baldwin* (1952)

Clydesiders:
    Thomas Henderson: *The Scottish Socialists* (1931)
    Tom Johnston: *Memories* (1952)
    David Kirkwood: *My Life of Revolt* (1935)
    John H. McNair: *James Maxton* (1935)

British Film Institute:
    R. S. Lambert: *Ariel and all his Quality* (1940)

Pilgrim Trust:
    Tom Jones: *Welsh Broth* (1951)
    Lord Macmillan: *A Man of Law's Tale* (1952)

REFERENCES:

301   *most people have no idea.* 'The Two Nations,' *Oxford Fortnightly Review* (28 April 1921)
301   *sound of things breaking.*' *The King's Grace*, p. 183
301   *slow and difficult construction.*' Article summing up the decade, *Morning Post* (31 December 1929)

301 *who try to heal.*' *The King's Grace*, p. 280

302 *almost too far.* 'Conservatism and Progress,' *Spectator* (23 November 1929)

302 *misty horizons.*' Speech at a Glasgow University Dinner, 27 June 1924

302 *in which to be young.*' Shrewsbury School Speech Day, 23 June 1928

302 *entrenchment of vested interests.* 'Janitor': *The Feet of the Young Men*, p. 152

303 *which is in distress.* Broadcast on the Federated Welfare Services for the Canadian Broadcasting Corporation, October 1936

303 *forces of the Right.*' Young: *Stanley Baldwin*, p. 54

304 *they started it.*' *Ibid.*, p. 31

304 *of his responsibility.*' *Ibid.*, p. 207

304 *two ways at once.*' *Ibid.*, p. 55

304 *deserve to beat them.*' *Ibid.*, p. 74

305 *showered upon all of you.* *The Times* (16 May 1925)

307 *delightful to meet.* Ellen Wilkinson: 'Men in the Commons,' *Evening News* (8 May 1928)

308 *can bar the way?*' Hansard (6 July 1927), *208*, 1310–17

308 *to use them.*' *Daily News* (7 July 1927)

308 *Mr Buchan had risen.*' 'The Week in Parliament,' *Spectator* (16 July 1927)

308 *an oratorical domination.*' James Johnston: *Westminster Voices* (1928), p. 249

310 *back-bench Tories.* 'Personalities of the Session,' *Nation* (11 August 1928)

310 *but not in Parliament.* M.H.D., p. 224

312 *will be also the Best.* *Island of Sheep* (1919), p. 187

315 *Empire Free Trade.* *Nation* (1 February 1930)

316 *tremendously unlike*'). *Graphic* (10 May 1930)

317 *interpreted with facts.*' Speech on 30 April 1934, reported in *Jewish Chronicle* (4 May 1934)

319 *Scottish Tory M.P.s.*' *Forward* (3 March 1928)

321 *trust the people.*' Hansard (22 February 1933), *274*, 1845–51

322 *with no Jerusalem.*' Hansard (24 November 1932), *272*, 259–67

324 *to the public detriment.*' Violet Markham to Tom Jones, 29 June 1932, *A Diary with Letters*, p. 42

326 *he was completely unconscious.*' Buchan to Amery, 16 May 1936, in the Amery Papers

326 *subject-matter of politics.* Amery: *My Political Life*, Vol. I, p. 266

326 *master its moods.*' Lord Lothian's obituary of Buchan in the *American Oxonian* (April 1940)

327 *it was serious?*') Lawrence to Buchan, 21 March 1930, *Letters of T. E. Lawrence*, p. 685

328 *material treasures.*' Macmillan: *Man of Law's Tale*, p. 290

328 *bleak and hopeless.*' *Ibid.*, p. 291

328 *stroke or two.*' Jones: *Welsh Broth*, p. 27

328 *in public life.*' M.H.D., p. 237

328 *on my Prime Minister.*' Young: *Stanley Baldwin*, p. 167

329 *was very heavy.*' *Ibid.*, p. 186

329   *to their opponents.'* Johnston: *Memories*, p. 217
329   *lonely inward-looking soul.* M.H.D., p. 239
330   *toy sword and all the rest of it.'* Johnston: *Memories*, p. 217
332   *The Real War 1914–18.'* *Week-End Review* (24 May 1930)

CHAPTER TWELVE:
HISTORIAN AND HIGH COMMISSIONER

CONVERSATIONS AND CORRESPONDENCE WITH:
Lt-Col. F. M. Bailey
The late Sir Beverley Baxter
Mr John Carswell
Mrs Ian Clarke
Dr Charles Elton
Sir Keith Feiling
Mrs Mary Fernald
Mr Robert Graves
The Duke of Hamilton
Mr Alfred Hitchcock
Lord Kemsley
Lady Kinross
The late Sir Bruce Richmond
Dr C. V. Wedgwood
Professor Roberto Weiss

Appointment to Canada:
   Professor George Glazebrook, University of Toronto
   Professor Blair Neatby, University of British Columbia

UNPUBLISHED MATERIAL:
Buchan Papers:
   Letters to and from his family and others
   Folder with draft of two film scenarios

BOOKS:
'Janitor' (Mary Lyttelton and J. G. Lockhart): *The Feet of the Young Men* (1928)
Stewart Mechie: *The Office of Lord High Commissioner* (1957)

REFERENCES:
336   *and almost insulting.'* U.U., p. 181
336   *entered the front door.'* W.F., p. 157
336   *on the library shelves.'* W.F., p. 280
339   *white, serrated peaks.'* W. H. Buchan: 'A Journey in Sikkim,' *Blackwood's* (April 1912)
340   *on any big expedition.* There are references to Rawling's proposed Everest expedition in Buchan's obituary of him in the *Alpine Journal* (February 1918); in Major J. B. Noel's 'A Journey to Tashirek in Southern Tibet and the Eastern Approaches to Mt Everest' in the *Geographical Journal* (May 1919) and his *Through*

Tibet to Everest (1927); in Kenneth Mason's *Abode of Snow* (1955); and the *Alpine Journal* (May 1963, p. 155*n*, and May 1964, p. 143)

341   *to help a friend.*' Speech at the Bryce Dinner at Oxford, 29 May 1932

342   *a very good friend to me.*' Hugh Walpole in his diary on hearing of Buchan's death, quoted by permission of Walpole's literary executor, Mr Rupert Hart-Davis

342   *got up and left. Journals of Arnold Bennett*, Vol. III (1933), p. 258

342   *on a Sunday morning.* W.F., p. 156

342   *short-tailed horse.* W.F., p. 156*n*

342   *alert as a fox-terrier.*' H. Hensley Henson: *Retrospect of an Unimportant Life*, Vol. II (1943), p. 354

342   *his good-humoured self.*') A.A.C., p. 20

345   *natural to accept.* This description by Catherine Carswell has been slightly abridged, with the permission of Mr John Carswell, from her contribution to W.F., p. 150

347   *at a public meeting.* 'Janitor': *The Feet of the Young Men*, p. 141

348   *broke off a conversation.* Walter Elliot in W.F., p. 134

348   *are mostly educated.* H. Hensley Henson: *Retrospect*, Vol. III (1950), p. 81

349   *for twenty years. Some Eighteenth-Century Byways*, p. 44

349   *knows nearly everything else.* M. Newbolt: *Sir Henry Newbolt*, p. 351

350   *the most lovable.*' H. Hensley Henson: *Retrospect*, Vol. II, p. 354

350   *very harshly indeed.*' James Bridie: *One Way of Living*, p. 86

350   *narrow means of my family.*' M.H.D., p. 30

351   *in the country that matters.*' 'Paradox beyond the Tweed,' *Graphic* (20 September 1930)

352   *in its effect.* These and the previous quotations from Hugh MacDiarmid are from his chapter on Buchan in *Contemporary Scottish Studies* (1926), originally printed as an article in the *Scottish Educational Journal* (19 June 1925)

353   *small sheet of notepaper.*' W.F., p. 149

353   *of European assessment.* Hugh MacDiarmid: *Contemporary Scottish Studies*

356   *heart of the man.*' Review of Lord Crewe's *Lord Rosebery* in the *Observer* (15 November 1931)

359   *the unforeseen accident.*' 'The Folly of the Wise,' address to the Canadian Club, Montreal, November 1935, printed in *Canadian Occasions*, p. 172

359   *almost of Nature.*' Burke: *Letters on a Regicide Peace*, quoted in *History of the Great War*, Vol. I, p. 7

361   *pursuit of truth.* 'The Double Life,' the *McGill News* (Spring 1936), reprinted in *Canadian Occasions*, p. 172

363   *pomp and colour.*' Violet Markham: *Friendship's Harvest*, p. 123

364   *to go to a dance.*' U.U., p. 186

365   *her show as mine.*' U.U., p. 48

367   *of human courage.*' E. W. Barnes: *The High Room* (1957), p. 226

367   *to celebrate the event?*' W.F., p. 214

367   *in his own home.*' Stanley Baldwin in W.F., p. 146

CHAPTER THIRTEEN: GOVERNOR-GENERAL
CHAPTER FOURTEEN: CANADIAN
CHAPTER FIFTEEN: STOIC

As so many of the entries apply to all three of these chapters, I have grouped them together

CONVERSATIONS AND CORRESPONDENCE WITH:
Rt Hon. Sir Michael Adeane
Mr Leonard Brockington, Toronto
Mr Esmond Butler, Secretary to the Governor-General, Ottawa
Rev. M. C. D'Arcy, s.j.
Mr G. V. Ferguson, Editor-in-Chief, *Montreal Star*
Mr J. C. Furnas, Lebanon, New Jersey
Mr and Mrs Maurice Fyfe, Ottawa
Professor F. W. Gibson, Queen's University, Kingston, Ontario
Professor George Glazebrook, University of Toronto
Professor J. King Gordon, University of Alberta
Dr H. P. Gundy, Queen's University, Kingston, Ontario
The Dowager Lady Hardinge of Penshurst
Mr Francis Hardy, former Parliamentary Librarian, Ottawa
Mrs Isobel Henderson, Somerville College, Oxford
Mr Robert Grant Irving, Yale University, New Haven
Dr W. Kaye Lamb, Public Archives of Canada
Mr Thomas S. Lamont, New York
Mr David Lewis, Q.C., Toronto
Hon. James Macdonell, Toronto
Hon. Paul Martin, Minister for External Affairs, Ottawa
Rt Hon. Vincent Massey, Port Hope, Ontario
Mrs Roger Merriman, Cambridge, Mass.
Professor Blair Neatby, University of British Columbia
Mr Grattan O'Leary, President, *Ottawa Journal*
Mr Raleigh Parkin, Montreal
Commander F. J. D. Pemberton, Government House, Ottawa
Dr Wilder Penfield, Montreal Neurological Institute
Sir Shuldham Redfern
Mr Norman Robertson, Department of External Affairs, Ottawa
Dr George Spence, Regina, Saskatchewan
Mr Graham Spry, Agent-General for Saskatchewan, London
Mr and Mrs John Stevenson, Ottawa
Professor A. P. Thornton, University of Toronto
Dr and Mrs H. P. van Dusen, Princeton, N.J.
Mr David Walker, St Andrews, New Brunswick
Professor Roberto Weiss
Professor George Whalley, Queen's University, Kingston, Ontario
Sir John Wheeler-Bennett
Professor Robin Winks, Yale University, New Haven

Mr A. J. D. Woods, Historical Section, Cabinet Office
Mr R. Mackworth Young, Librarian, Windsor Castle

BOOKS AND ARTICLES:

Gerald Campbell: *Of True Experience* (1949)
J. W. Dafoe: *Laurier, A Study in Canadian Politics* (1922)
R. MacGregor Dawson: *William Lyon Mackenzie King*, Vol. I (1958)
Violet Markham: 'Mackenzie King,' in *Friendship's Harvest* (1958)
Vincent Massey: *What's Past is Prologue* (1964)
Blair Neatby: *William Lyon Mackenzie King*, Vol. II (1963)
J. W. Pickersgill (ed.): *The Mackenzie King Record 1939–44* (1960)
O. D. Skelton: *Life and Letters of Sir Wilfrid Laurier* (1922)
A. P. Thornton: *The Imperial Idea and its Enemies* (1959)
Frank H. Underhill: *In Search of Canadian Liberalism* (1960)
J. W. Wheeler-Bennett: *King George VI* (1958)

The Arctic:
 R. H. G. Bonnycastle: 'Lord Tweedsmuir's Trip down the Mackenzie
 River and Ascent of Bear Mountain,' in the *Canadian Alpine Journal*
 (1942–3)
 Margaret Bourke-White: *Portrait of Myself* (1963)
 Life Magazine: 'A 10,000-mile Tour of Canada's North-West with
 Lord Tweedsmuir' (25 October 1937), with photographs by Margaret
 Bourke-White
 Malcolm MacDonald: *Down North* (1943)
 Lady Tweedsmuir: 'Tweedsmuir Park. The Diary of a Pilgrimage,' in
 the *National Geographic Magazine* (April 1938)
 'Down North—Lord Tweedsmuir's Tour of Arctic Canada,' *Sunday
 Times* (5 and 12 December 1937)
 Dr Thomas Wood: 'Down North: Lord Tweedsmuir on Tour,' in *The
 Times* (12 and 13 October 1937)

Roosevelt–Tweedsmuir Memorandum:
 Earl of Avon: *The Eden Memoirs: Facing the Dictators* (1962)
 Winston Churchill: *The Gathering Storm* (1948)
 Keith Feiling: *Life of Neville Chamberlain* (1946)
 Samuel Hoare (Lord Templewood): *Nine Troubled Years* (1954)
 Memoirs of Cordell Hull, Vol. I (1948)
 The Roosevelt Letters, Vol. III (ed. Elliott Roosevelt and Joseph P. Lash)
 (1952)
 The Times Literary Supplement: 'Another Eden,' review of *The Eden
 Memoirs: Facing the Dictators* (23 November 1962). This is the only
 published reference I have found to the Roosevelt–Tweedsmuir
 Memorandum
 Sumner Welles: *The Time for Decision* (1944)
 Francis Williams: *A Prime Minister Remembers* (1961)

UNPUBLISHED MATERIAL:

Buchan Papers:
 Letters to Their Majesties King George V, King Edward VIII and
 King George VI, quoted by permission of Her Majesty the Queen

Letters to and from his family and others. For permission to quote from the letters by the late Earl of Crawford and Balcarres, L. S. Amery, Stanley Baldwin, Neville Chamberlain and Lord Hardinge of Penshurst, I thank the present Earl of Crawford and Balcarres, the Rt Hon. Julian Amery, Earl Baldwin of Bewdley, Mrs Neville Chamberlain and the Dowager Lady Hardinge of Penshurst

Memorandum prepared for Lord Tweedsmuir by Sir Alan Lascelles in 1935, quoted with his permission

Report by Mr George R. Spence, Regina, Saskatchewan, 'When the Governor-General Came to Val-Marie,' May 1938, quoted with Mr Spence's permission

Lord Tweedsmuir: Notes and Reports

> January 1936: no heading, 'I have now been two months here'
> March 1936: 'Notes on Tour of the Eastern Townships'
> September 1936: 'Notes on the Agricultural Conditions of the Prairies'
> January 1937: no heading, 'I have now been for the better part of a year and a half in Canada' (referred to as 'Midway Report')
> April 1937: 'Notes on the Washington Visit'
> September 1937: 'Down North'

Lord Tweedsmuir: Speeches and Addresses in Canada. Forty of these are collected in *Canadian Occasions* (1940)

Roosevelt Papers:

Memorandum prepared by Tweedsmuir for President Roosevelt, 8 April 1937, printed in Appendix A (p. 473) by permission of the National Archives and Records Service, Franklin D. Roosevelt Library, Hyde Park, New York. I acknowledge with thanks the help of Miss Elizabeth B. Drewry, Director

REFERENCES:

375   *Canadian homes. The Times* (4 November 1935)
376   *small garden at one side.*' Harold Nicolson: *Helen's Tower* (1937), p. 148
377   *discreetly in the background. Minto*, p. 121
377   *ceremony in life.* Skelton: *Life and Letters of Sir Wilfrid Laurier*, Vol. II, p. 86; quoted in Buchan's *Minto*, p. 122
378   *constitutional usage.*' Borden to Buchan, 29 March 1935, Borden Papers, Public Archives of Canada
379   *to become a figure.*' Lawrence to Buchan, 1 April 1935, *Letters of T. E. Lawrence*, p. 862
379   *every class.* 'English Tidings,' in *English Life* (October 1926)
381   *all classes and ages.*' Amery: *My Political Life*, Vol. I, p. 266
386   *a marvel and a miracle.*' Speech at the Canadian Institute of Mining and Metallurgy Dinner, Ottawa, 19 March 1936, *Canadian Occasions*, p. 203
388   *Proust à Rideau Hall.*' Introduction by Fernand Rinfret to Susan Tweedsmuir's *Carnets Canadiens* (1930)
389   *the Governor-General's train.*"' Massey: *What's Past is Prologue*, p. 473, quoted by permission of the Rt Hon. Vincent Massey and the Macmillan Company of Canada

391 *different racial elements.*' Speech at Fraserwood, Manitoba, 21 September 1936

392 *that make up the nation.*' Ibid.

396 *cannot run itself.*' Mackenzie King on the guarantee to Poland, quoted in Thornton's *The Imperial Idea and its Enemies*, p. 261

397 *silence too far.*' Toronto *Globe and Mail*, 5 October 1936

399 *procedure nowadays.* Dr Wilder Penfield's address at the Memorial Meeting for the Governor-General, Montreal Neurological Institute, 14 February 1940

404 *grumbling in Virginia.*' 'Notes on the Washington Visit'

404 *anything about politics.*' Ibid.

404 *thinking aloud.*' The Times (31 March 1937)

405 *practical wisdom.* 'Notes on the Washington Visit'

405 *but close-textured.* Ibid.

410 *and charming person.*' Bonnycastle: *Canadian Alpine Journal* (1942–43)

410 *His Excellency and myself.*' Bourke-White: *Portrait of Myself*, p. 158

410 *he was working. Ibid.*, p. 156

412 *hearts in their work.* Report 'Down North,' III

412 *draw the line somewhere!*' Ibid., III

413 *over the crest.*' Bonnycastle: *Canadian Alpine Journal* (1942–43)

413 *seventy years ago!* Report 'Down North,' I

414 *as a tropical forest. Ibid.*, II

414 *are bottomless swamps. Ibid.*, II

414 *which prevent epidemics. Ibid.*, I

415 *would be mine. Ibid.*, I

416 *almost bright daylight. Ibid.*, I

416 *adventure of living. Ibid.*, II

416 *banks of gravel.*' Sick Heart River, Part I, 13

417 *from the Parthenon frieze.*' W.F., p. 252

417 *half-moon of forest. Ibid.*, p. 254

417 *towards each other.* Report 'Down North,' III

418 *and the air. Ibid.*, IV

418 *to simplify life.*') Ibid., I

418 *to develop them. Ibid.*, IV

419 *waiting to be discovered. Ibid.*, I

421 *provincial finances straight.* Tweedsmuir to Amery, 4 February 1937, in the Amery Papers

422 *miracles of history.*' St Andrew's Day speech at Winnipeg, 1936, *Canadian Occasions*, p. 44

422 *too many loyalties.*' Speech at Charlottetown, Prince Edward Island, September 1937, *Canadian Occasions*, p. 32

422 *domestic problems* (and three following quotations). 'Canada's Outlook on the World,' speech to the Canadian Institute of International Affairs, 12 October 1937, *Canadian Occasions*, p. 79

425 *than to be dead.* 'The Fortress of the Personality,' University of Toronto, 27 November 1935, *Canadian Occasions*, p. 160

428 *from the money provided.*') Massey: *What's Past is Prologue*, p. 464

429 *ought to let him.*' Tom Jones: *A Diary with Letters*, p. 206

Sources and References 507

429 *they ought to follow suit.* There was a preamble to the first article in *The Sunday Times* (5 December 1937) making clear their unofficial character: 'A friend in this country has received those notes describing Lord Tweedsmuir's remarkable tour of Northern Canada last summer. They are a personal record which formed the basis of Lord Tweedsmuir's broadcast in Canada on the completion of his journey.'

429 *born and bred.' Toronto Globe and Mail* (16 December 1936)

430 *Winston up to?'* Beverley Baxter, the *Sunday Graphic* (11 February 1940)

434 *those of other men.* Tweedsmuir to Amery, 4 February 1937, in the Amery Papers

436 *assets of a people.* 'Canada,' *Spectator* (6 July 1901)

437 *his work as Governor-General.'* Amery: *My Political Life*, Vol. III, p. 208

437 *narrow and conventional.* 'Midway Report'

437 *because it is our own.'* St Andrew's Day speech in Ottawa, 1938, *Canadian Occasions*, p. 47

439 *metaphysics or philosophy.'* Markham: *Friendship's Harvest*, p. 162

440 *of the country itself.* Pickersgill: *Mackenzie King Record*, Vol. I (1939–44), p. 146, quoted by permission of the University of Toronto Press

441 *view on anything.'* Mackenzie King to Amery, 22 February 1940, in the Amery Papers

445 *freedom of the world.* Speech at the Canadian-American Conference, Kingston, Ontario, 17 June 1937. *Canadian Occasions*, p. 63

446 *spread of the disease.'* Quoted in Welles: *Time for Decision*, p. 62

447 *from the blue.'* Feiling: *Neville Chamberlain*, p. 336

447 *of cold water.'* Welles: *Time for Decision*, p. 66

449 *doing things together.* Speech at Yale University, 2 June 1938

453 *one of another.' The King's Grace*, p. 227

453 *of national policy.* Broadcast on Poppy Day, 1936, for Canadian Broadcasting Corporation

454 *once called Mother'*). Campbell: *Of True Experience*, p. 76

460 *on this side.* Pickersgill: *Mackenzie King Record*, p. 41

460 *to speak to him of. Ibid.*, p. 55

467 *getting bored with them.'* Markham: *Friendship's Harvest*, p. 129

467 *has fallen off.* Stevenson to Colvin, 6 October 1894, *Letters*, Vol. V (1924), p. 172

467 *I seem a failure.* Stevenson to Baxter, August 1893, *ibid.*, p. 69

470 *pick of the lot.* Dafoe to Viscount Greenwood, 29 March 1940, Dafoe Papers, Public Archives of Canada

Many of those cited above have since died or acquired titles, but I have left the names as they were in 1965.

1985   J. A. S.

INDEX